Comprehensive
Structured
COBOL

Comprehensive
Structured
COBOL

James Bradley
University of Calgary

Mitchell McGRAW-HILL

New York St. Louis San Francisco Auckland Bogotá Caracas
Hamburg Lisbon London Madrid Mexico Milan Montreal
New Delhi Oklahoma City Paris San Juan São Paulo
Singapore Sydney Tokyo Toronto Watsonville

Mitchell McGraw-Hill
55 Penny Lane
Watsonville, CA 95076

Comprehensive Structured COBOL

3 4 5 6 7 8 9 0   WEB WEB   9 5 4 3 2 1

ISBN 0-07-007078-4

This book was set in Syntax and Berkeley Old Style by TBH/Typecast. The editors were Karen M. Jackson and Raleigh S. Wilson; the designer was Randall Goodall, Seventh Street Studios; drawings were done by Joseph Maas, Advanced Presentations. Development and production management were provided by Cole and Associates. Webcrafters was the printer and binder.

Library of Congress Cataloging-in-Publication Data

Bradley, James, 1942-
    Comprehensive structured COBOL / James Bradley.
    p. cm.
    ISBN 0-07-007078-4
    1. COBOL (Computer program language) 2. Structured programming.
    1. Title.
    QA76.73.C25B73   1990   89-13743
    005.13'3--dc20   CIP

PREFACE

COBOL REMAINS A MOST important programming language, with more than 75 percent of business application programs still being written in COBOL. COBOL does not, however, stand still, but continues to develop in light of experience and advances in programming theory. COBOL 85 compilers are now commonplace on both mainframes and microcomputers. While this book teaches COBOL 85 (COBOL 85 facilities are clearly marked throughout the book), it also provides a complete presentation of COBOL 74.

The major theme of *Comprehensive Structured COBOL* is that learning COBOL and the ideas associated with it should be both challenging and interesting. *Comprehensive Structured COBOL* emphasizes understanding COBOL and programming concepts as the key to becoming a successful COBOL programmer. Thus, the amount of explanatory material in the text is greater than would normally be expected, and many examples are given to strengthen the concepts and techniques presented. The student is taught to understand, in a commonsense manner, the "why" of COBOL concepts and programming techniques.

Explanations and analogies used in the book have been verified for complete accuracy. Having been an instructor in computer programming for more than 15 years and having been involved in computer-related research and commercial programming for some 20 years, I have experienced the ideas inherent in COBOL 85 from many different viewpoints.

This book was written with the goal of making it easy to read and understand and with the hope that the ideas will leap off the page at you. I have been encouraged by reviewers who are of the opinion that this writing goal has been successfully met. However, *Comprehensive Structured COBOL* does not neglect detail. The book includes a level of COBOL detail that should make learning COBOL an achievable goal of every student.

In addition to the movement from COBOL 74 to COBOL 85, exciting as that is, another transition is taking place. Computer file processing, the original domain of COBOL applications programming, is moving to relational data base processing using COBOL with embedded SQL.

Every student of COBOL must learn the difference between file processing and relational data base processing and must develop the ability to write COBOL/SQL programs for processing relational data bases. Relational data base systems that can interface with COBOL are now commonly available, and systems for use with supermini computers and workstations can be purchased at a nominal cost. For example, at the University of Calgary, where the relational system ORACLE runs on supermini computers, workstations, and personal computers, the mainstream COBOL 85 course includes assignments on the use of COBOL with SQL for data base processing. That relational data base processing using COBOL with embedded SQL will become a strong component of COBOL courses in the 1990s seems clear, and *Comprehensive Structured COBOL* contains the necessary COBOL/SQL material.

Organization and presentation

The book is organized into three sections:

I. COBOL Foundations

The first section deals with the foundations of COBOL and presents the divisions of COBOL programs, as well as the use of IF-statements and looping with the PERFORM verb. The first chapter assumes that the student has no prior programming experience and explains computer processing and elementary data processing concepts, together with elementary COBOL programming concepts. The student with programming experience can begin either in Chapter 1 with COBOL programming concepts or with Chapter 2.

Chapters 2 through 4 explain the common considerations in writing the four divisions of a COBOL program. In addition, Chapter 4, which deals with the PROCEDURE DIVISION, details the use of the common COBOL verbs. Many program examples are used throughout these three chapters to illustrate the concepts and COBOL constructs presented.

The IF-statement and the new EVALUATE statement are given an entire chapter (Chapter 5), with particular attention paid to understanding conditions, both simple and compound, and to nested IF-statements. Chapter 6 is devoted to looping, including nested loops, using the PERFORM . . . UNTIL and PERFORM . . . TIMES verbs. Structured programming is used throughout the first section, and principles are explained gradually at appropriate points in the text.

II. COBOL Processing Methods

The second section is devoted to COBOL programming methods. I believe that the order chosen is the best one, although it could easily vary according to the wishes of the instructor or experiences of the students. The section begins with a chapter on printing simple reports, followed by a chapter on validation of input data. Then comes a chapter on the COBOL SORT verb as a preliminary to the next chapter, which presents the all-important topic of control-break processing for generating more complex reports. The final two chapters of the section cover programming techniques for single- and multiple-level arrays.

With the possible exception of the use of the Report Writer (in Chapter 20 in the third section), material presented in the first two sections is generally covered in many extensive one-semester introductory COBOL courses.

III. COBOL for File and Data Base Processing

The final section teaches file and data base processing using COBOL. Chapter 13 covers sequential file processing and file updating techniques in detail; Chapter 14 details indexed sequential files. VSAM is used in programming examples, although provision is made for the use of ISAM. Coverage of secondary key processing is also included. The elements of relative files are covered in Chapter 15. Students are taught the three different types of relative files, including hash files, that can be used. Coverage of the concept of hash files extends as far as chained progressive overflow for handling collisions. Full coverage of hash files with chained progressive overflow will be included in a forthcoming advanced COBOL book.

Relational data bases and SQL are covered in Chapters 16 and 17. Chapter 16 covers essential relational data base and SQL concepts, and Chapter 17 shows how COBOL and SQL together can be used to process a relation (or "file") in a relational data base.

Chapter 18 covers on-line processing using COBOL and CICS. Many instructors include CICS in a COBOL course because of its importance in business programming. The chapter material is sufficient for an explanation of the basic concepts involved and for some introductory COBOL/CICS programming. However, if you intend doing extensive CICS programming, you will need a supplementary CICS text.

Chapter 19 covers some remaining peripheral topics, including CALL and COPY statements, the USAGE clause, and STRING and UNSTRING statements. Chapter 20 covers the use of the COBOL Report Writer feature. The chapter includes basic Report Writer concepts and instructions for generating reports using programs that utilize this feature.

Supplementary material

An effective course is dependent on a team effort involving the instructor and students, as well as the teaching and learning materials they both share. The complexities of teaching COBOL to a varied student audience gives rise to the need for a truly useful instructional support package to assist the process. For this reason, I have spent considerable time talking to COBOL instructors about their course needs to determine what combination of teaching materials would be most useful. With these conversations as a backdrop, I have developed a comprehensive instructor's manual to accompany *Comprehensive Structured COBOL* that satisfies a broad cross-section of course needs.

Included for each chapter are

- a chapter guide
- topics for classroom discussion
- solutions to chapter questions
- solutions to chapter programming assignments
- complete examination materials containing true/false, multiple-choice, fill-in, and debugging questions, and questions requiring students to write COBOL program excerpts

Also in the instructor's manual is a complete set of overhead transparency masters with art from the text and both full programs and program excerpts.

To bring COBOL into the lab, there is an accompanying data disk in ASCII for convenient up- or downloading of files in either mainframe or micro environments. Utilizing this data disk enables students to learn while doing, without the drudgery of having to rekey the assignments in the text.

Acknowledgments

The author is grateful for the hard work of the following people who reviewed several versions of the manuscript and contributed many constructive comments: Eileen Bobman, Spring Garden College, Philadelphia; Lawrence E. Jeralds, Southern Illinois University, Carbondale; Dr. Mo Adam Mahmood, University of Texas, El Paso; Jeretta Horn Nord, Oklahoma State University, Stillwater; Karen Schnepf, Metro Community College, Omaha; Dr. S. Srinivasan, University of Louisville, Louisville; and Michael M. Werner, Wentworth Institute, Boston.

Dennis L. Varin, of Southern Oregon State University, Ashland, must be thanked for independently running and checking all the programs used in the text.

I would also like to warmly acknowledge my editors at Cole and Associates, Annette Gooch and Brete Harrison, and at McGraw-Hill, Karen Jackson and Raleigh Wilson, for their patience and commitment; the book designers, Seventeenth Street Studios, for a design that contributes significantly to the book as a learning tool; and my production editor at Cole, Lorna Cunkle, for her untiring efforts in bringing it to fruition. Developing a good book is a team effort; to those at Cole and McGraw-Hill who brought a successful team together, thank you.

Another essential aspect of this team effort is the continuing dialogue with adopters of a book, whose comments can be valuable in developing subsequent editions. For this reason, I'm always open to ideas and suggestions for improving the book. Please write to the author (Computer Science Department, University of Calgary, Calgary, Alberta, Canada T2N 1N4). Your contributions, if incorporated, will be acknowledged.

James Bradley
January, 1990

CONTENTS

/ COBOL FOUNDATIONS

2

The IDENTIFICATION and ENVIRONMENT divisions, 44

3
The COBOL data division, 68

COMPREHENSIVE STRUCTURED COBOL

4

The essentials of the PROCEDURE DIVISION, 112

5
Selection of alternatives with conditional statements, 166

6
Looped instruction sequences, 210

∥ COBOL PROCESSING METHODS

7
Printing reports, 244

8
Validation of input data, 290

9
Sorting and merging, 318

10
Control-break processing, 354

11
Single-level arrays, 398

12
MULTIPLE-LEVEL ARRAYS, 460

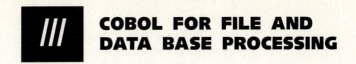

III COBOL FOR FILE AND DATA BASE PROCESSING

18
On-line processing with COBOL and CICS, 692

19
Useful COBOL facilities, 718

20
The Report Writer feature of COBOL, 734

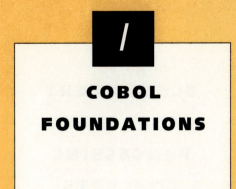

/

COBOL
FOUNDATIONS

ELEMENTARY COBOL DATA PROCESSING CONCEPTS

1.3 Diagrams can help you write correct programs
You can draw diagrams of programs
Flowcharts are used to display structure and logic
File navigation diagrams relate input and output records

1.4 Programs have to be tested thoroughly
You can play computer: desk checking
You must detect and correct errors
      Syntax errors
      Logical errors
      Run errors
Extensive testing of programs is often necessary
You can always improve a program

1.5 You have learned some COBOL instructions

*I*N THIS CHAPTER we investigate two basic ideas: business data processing by computer and using the COBOL language to write programs for specific data processing tasks. We begin with computer data processing concepts.

1.1 Business data processing puts data into a more useful form

*D*ATA PROCESSING consists of converting raw data to a more useful form. It can be carried out manually or by computer. In this book, we are concerned with computer data processing using programs of instructions written in COBOL.

A computer is simple in concept. In essence, it is an electronic calculator with a recording device attached. The calculator part of the computer is called the processor. The processor of a computer can add, divide, multiply, subtract, and do a few other simple things. The recording device is called the memory. The memory of a computer is somewhat like a collection of the kinds of data display panels used in calculators. In a computer, the memory holds the data for the processor to process. It also holds the program of instructions that guide the processor in processing the data. With business data processing, this program of instructions is usually initially written in an artificial language called "COBOL," for Common Business-Oriented Language.

Data for computer processing are stored on disk or tape

Suppose a company has three lines of raw business data to be processed, as follows:

PARTNUMB	UNIT-PRICE	QUANTITY
W1	20	10
W2	15	40
W3456	30	15

Each line of data describes a purchase by a customer. For example, one customer has purchased 10 parts of type W1 at $20 per part. Let's call the raw data the input data for the processing.

The company would like to compute the total of each purchase, which is quantity times unit price plus a commission of $10. The desired data resulting from the processing is therefore

PARTNUMB	UNIT-PRICE	QUANTITY	COST
W1	20	10	210
W2	15	40	610
W3456	30	15	460

Let's call the preceding the output data from the processing. After processing of the input data, the output data would probably be printed on paper by the computer's printer.

The input data nowadays would usually be stored on magnetic tape or magnetic disk, ready for computer processing. The processor cannot immediately process data on disk or tape, however. It can immediately process only data in the computer memory. Therefore it has to read each line of data from disk or tape into memory before processing it.

Tapes and disks have a magnetically recorded code for each letter or digit of the data stored there. A line of data stored on disk or tape can be read into memory for processing when the processor executes a READ instruction.

A collection of items of data on a tape or disk (or when printed out) is called a *computer file*. The following explains how data are stored in a file on tape or disk.

Data Recording Technology with Disks and Tapes

Figure 1.1a illustrates input data stored in a file on magnetic disk. On the surface of a disk there are many concentric tracks. Each character or digit is stored in sequence along a track of the disk. There is a magnetic code for each possible character. Running along the track are magnetization areas, called *bits*, with 8 bits (also called a *byte*) being used to code a character or digit. Some of these magnetization areas will be magnetized and some not. This determines a binary code, consisting of 1s and 0s. The computer interprets a magnetized bit as a 1, and an unmagnetized bit as a 0.

There is a unique binary code (of 8 bits, or a byte) for each character or digit of data stored along a disk track (Figure 1.1b). For example, the standard ASCII code for the digit "3" is 00110011 and the code for the character "A" is 01000001. (ASCII is an acronym for American Standard Code for Information Interchange.) Each ASCII-coded character on a disk track can be read and transferred to memory. Reading from a disk track occurs when the magnetization areas for each character pass a set of reading coils, or a *read head*, adjacent to the track.

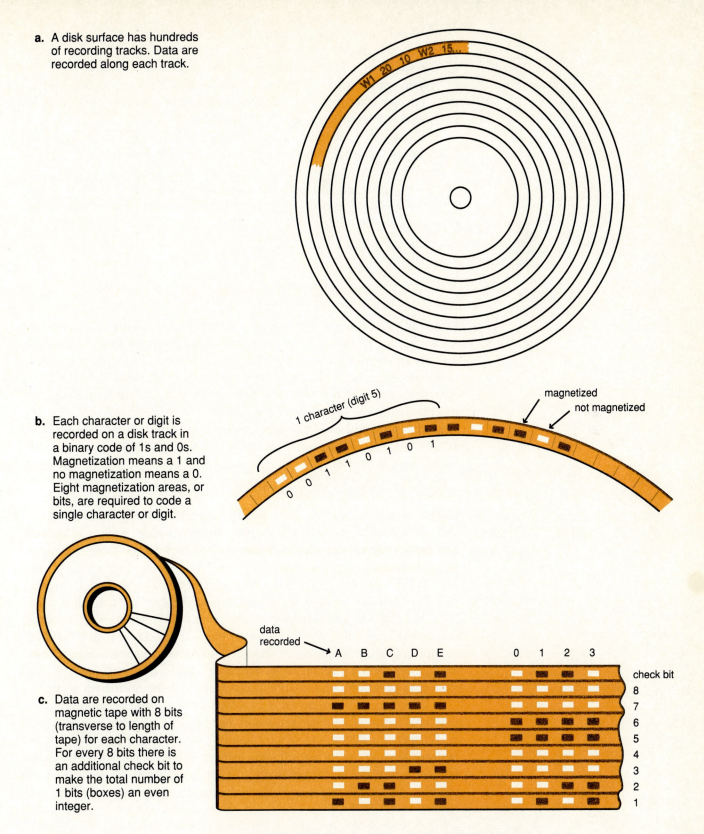

a. A disk surface has hundreds of recording tracks. Data are recorded along each track.

W1 20 10 W2 15...

b. Each character or digit is recorded on a disk track in a binary code of 1s and 0s. Magnetization means a 1 and no magnetization means a 0. Eight magnetization areas, or bits, are required to code a single character or digit.

1 character (digit 5)

magnetized

not magnetized

0 0 1 1 0 1 0 1

c. Data are recorded on magnetic tape with 8 bits (transverse to length of tape) for each character. For every 8 bits there is an additional check bit to make the total number of 1 bits (boxes) an even integer.

data recorded

A B C D E   0 1 2 3

check bit

8
7
6
5
4
3
2
1

Figure **1.1** *Recording data on magnetic disk and tape.*

As well as the ASCII code, which is used by all computers, a nonstandard code called EBCDIC (Extended Binary Coded Decimal Interchange Code) is commonly used with IBM mainframe computers.

Data are recorded on magnetic tape in a similar manner, with 8 bits per character recorded (plus an extra bit for error checking purposes), as illustrated in Figure 1.1c.

The simplest way to initially get data onto the disk tracks (or magnetic tape), ready for processing, is to enter the data at the keyboard of a computer terminal. As you enter the data, the processor of the computer will be executing a program of instructions (called an *editor*) that reads the data from the keyboard into its memory and then writes, or transfers, it to the disk or tape.

Both instructions and data can be recorded in computer memory

Before any data processing can be done, the program of necessary instructions must be recorded in the memory of the computer. Instructions are also recorded in a binary code that the processor can respond to. Such instructions are called *machine language instructions*. However, unlike the data storage codes for tape and disk, there are no standard codes for machine language instructions. For example, the binary code for an ADD instruction, to add two numbers, differs from one type of computer to another. A machine language instruction is typically 32 bits long, and might look like this:

10010100110101010011001010001010

Human beings rarely write machine language instructions, however. Instead they write their instructions in a quasi-English language and use a special computer program, called a *compiler*, to translate those instructions into machine language instructions.

When data are moved from disk or tape to computer memory, the same binary format is used as on the disk or tape. There are two differences, however. The first is that the recording method in memory is electrical rather than magnetic as it is on disk and tape. The second is that memory cannot hold data permanently; memory is a transient recording medium. Thus, when the computer is switched off the contents of memory are erased. In contrast, the contents of disk and tape are permanently stored.

The electrical method used to record data in memory is the same as that used for recording instructions in memory. The memory is made up of small electrical switches (called transistors), which can be either turned on (current flowing) or turned off (no current). When a switch is on, a 1 bit is recorded. When a switch is off, a 0 bit is recorded. These miniature switches are etched onto the surface of silicon chips.

Instructions for computer processing can be written in COBOL

There are a number of standard quasi-English languages for writing programs that are later converted into machine language. COBOL is one such standard language; other languages are Pascal, Fortran, BASIC, and PL/1. COBOL is the language most commonly used for business data processing.

Plain English language instructions to generate output data from input data (assumed to be on disk) could also be written. However, instructions for data processing rarely are written in plain English. But sometimes you just want to communicate the exact data processing method to other people, such as a programmer who will write the detailed COBOL program, or the reader of a book or article. In that case, it is common to write the instructions in a form close to English, but more concise, which is called *pseudocode*. Note that pseudocode instructions tend to very closely mirror the instructions of the intended computer language, such as COBOL.

Pseudocode instructions to process the input data given earlier might look like this:

```
OPEN the input data file, ready for use.
OPEN the (blank) output data file, ready to receive output
    data.
READ first line of PARTNUMB, UNIT-PRICE, QUANTITY data.
PERFORM UNTIL no lines left

    COMPUTE COST = QUANTITY * UNIT-PRICE + 10,
    WRITE next line of PARTNUMB, UNIT-PRICE,
        QUANTITY, COST data,
    READ next line of PARTNUMB, UNIT-PRICE, QUANTITY
        data,
END-PERFORM.
CLOSE input and output files.
```

There is informative detail here. Notice how the READ instructions are placed. They are placed this way because the number of lines of input data is not known in advance. Instructions will be executed in the order READ, PERFORM UNTIL, COMPUTE, WRITE, READ, PERFORM UNTIL, COMPUTE, WRITE, READ, PERFORM UNTIL, and so on. Only when the READ instruction tries to read beyond the end of the file of data does the processor become aware that there are no lines left. Thus READ must be executed before PERFORM UNTIL in time sequence. If the READ fails because there are no lines left, the execution of the subsequent PERFORM UNTIL will stop further execution of the group of instructions between PERFORM and END-PERFORM.

We will look at a simple COBOL program for data processing shortly.

There is a standard sequence for preparing and executing a COBOL program

To get the required machine language instructions for the processing into memory and have them executed, the programmer goes through a standard sequence of activities. You may already be familiar with this sequence. If not, you will become very familiar with it before long, if you are taking a COBOL course, because you will go through it many times. The sequence is as follows:

1. The programmer writes the instructions of the COBOL program on paper.
2. The programmer goes to a terminal of the computer and enters a command to start the execution of a special program of instructions called an *editor.* The editor is used for initially entering programs and data into memory and making any necessary corrections.
3. Once the editor is running, the programmer enters the COBOL program at the terminal, line by line. As this is going on, the processor, which is carrying out the instructions of the editor, reads each line of COBOL into a part of memory called an editor buffer. The programmer continues entering program data until all the COBOL lines have been entered.
4. The programmer can then enter commands that cause the editor to correct any errors made in entering the program. The programmer then asks the editor to store a permanent copy of this program on disk.
5. Next, the programmer enters a command to have the COBOL compiler translate the COBOL *source program* into a machine language version, called the *object program.* This object version will also be stored on a disk for use as required.
6. If the compiler indicates there are errors in coding in the program, the steps are repeated from 4; otherwise the programmer continues to 7.
7. Finally, the programmer can enter a command at the terminal to have the program loaded from disk into memory and executed.

As the object version of the program executes (without any further human intervention), each instruction gives the processor something to do. As each instruction is carried out, typically something happens to the data in locations in memory. For example, the READ instruction causes the first line of data items to be copied from the disk track into locations in the computer's memory (Figure 1.2a). Then the COMPUTE instruction causes the cost to be computed, using the unit price and quantity data items in memory locations; the processor also stores the computed cost in a memory location (Figure 1.2b). Then the WRITE instruction causes the line of data items in memory, plus the cost, to be copied onto a printer page (Figure 1.2c). The whole process is repeated for each of the line of input data. The result is the required output data printed out on paper.

A computer has memory, input and output devices, and a processor

You can get a better perspective on data and instructions by viewing the structure of a computer, as illustrated in Figure 1.3. There are one or more input devices (such as a disk drive, tape drive, or terminal keyboard), a memory (for data and program of instructions), one or more output devices (such as a printer, terminal display screen, tape drive, or disk drive), and a processor. The processor is often called the central processing unit or CPU.

The processor does something in response to each instruction in the program: it moves data from input device to memory, carries out arith-

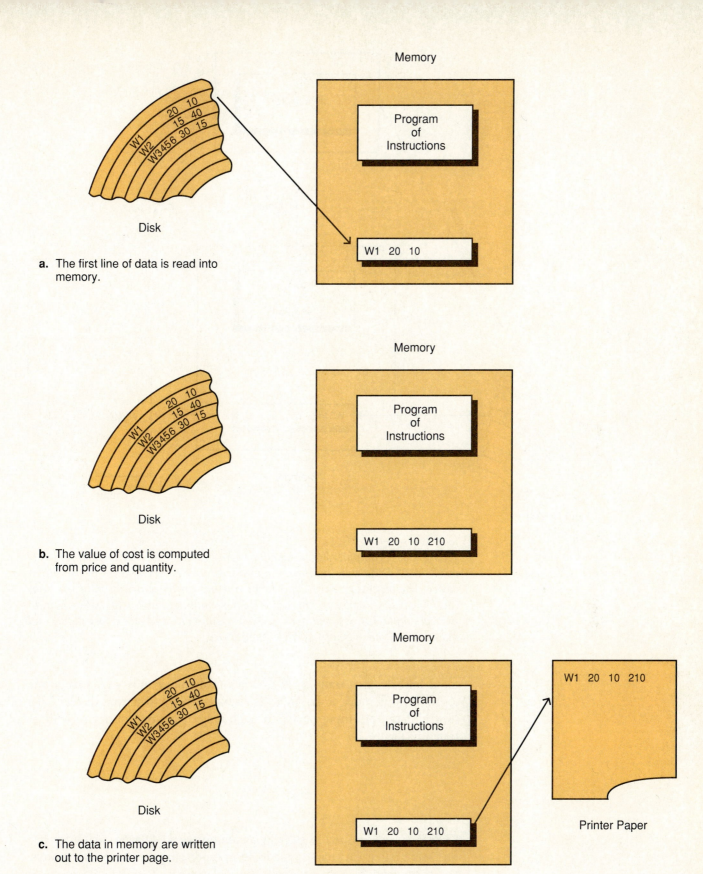

a. The first line of data is read into memory.

b. The value of cost is computed from price and quantity.

c. The data in memory are written out to the printer page.

Figure 1.2 *Essentials of data processing by computer.*

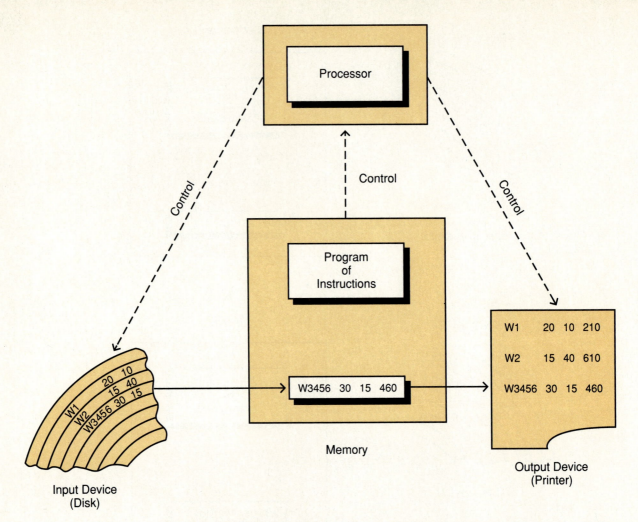

Figure 1.3 *A computer has a memory and a processor, as well as input and output devices. Data flow from the input device to memory and on to an output device. The processor carries out the instructions in the program of instructions (also located in memory). The processor, responding to instructions, moves data from the input device to memory, performs arithmetic and other operations, and moves data from memory to an output device.*

metic and other operations on the data in memory, moves data from one location in memory to another and from memory to output device. This flow of data from input device through memory to output device is illustrated in Figure 1.3.

COBOL goes back many years

COBOL was developed in 1959 by a committee of CODASYL (COnference on DAta SYstem Languages), made up of representatives from user groups, computer vendors, and academia. The goal was a user-friendly language for business data processing that would be standard; that is, a program written in the language would be executable on all computers with a suitable compiler. The new language was called COBOL and COBOL compilers became available in 1960. It has been a great success.

In the mid-1960s the *American National Standards Institute (ANSI)*, an organization that recommends standards in many areas of technology, became involved. There were many different versions of COBOL in use at the time, all based on the 1959 CODASYL proposal—the original aim of a standard language had not quite been realized. With the benefit of experience with COBOL in the 1960s, in 1968 ANSI recommended a new version of COBOL, called ANS COBOL 68. Vendors of computers accepted the recommendation and developed compilers consistent with the new standard. An improved ANS COBOL standard was released in 1974. COBOL 74, in turn, benefitted from experience with COBOL 68. A further revision took place in 1985. ANS COBOL 85 is used in this book. We can expect another upgrade before the year 2000.

1.2
A simple example illustrates COBOL program development

*I*N THIS BOOK you will be learning the rules for writing COBOL programs to process business data. There is a lot to learn. Not only must you learn how to put instructions together to form a program, you have to learn how to structure a program so that it does what it is supposed to and is easy for a human being to read and understand.

You need to structure COBOL programs carefully

COBOL programs are intended for use over many years, and it frequently happens that the business environment changes. For instance, perhaps sales tax has to be computed differently. This means that existing programs often have to be altered to reflect changed business conditions. If a program was not structured initially so it could be easily understood, it will be difficult to change it without introducing errors. Thus, modern COBOL programs must be carefully structured. The writing of such programs is called structured programming. Fortunately, it has also been found that it takes less time to develop a structured program than an unstructured one.

A pseudocode program is often written first

Recall that a disk is an input device that can store data in machine format. Let us suppose our input data is the data we had earlier, as follows:

[PARTNUMB]	[UNIT-PRICE]	[QUANTITY]
W1	20	10
W2	15	40
W3456	30	15

Each line of data describes a purchase order, and gives the quantity ordered of a given type of part and the price per part. Note that the names of the columns, for example, Unit-price, are not part of the input data and are not stored on the disk.

We want to generate the following output data:

[PARTNUMB]	[UNIT-PRICE]	[QUANTITY]	[COST]
W1	20	10	210
W2	15	40	610
W3456	30	15	460

Recall that the last column gives the cost of the order. There is a $10 commission on each sale, so that the cost of an order is

Unit-price × Quantity + 10

We shall base a COBOL program on the pseudocode program of instructions from the previous section:

```
OPEN the input data file, ready for use.
OPEN the (blank) output data file, ready to receive output
    data.
READ first line of PARTNUMB, UNIT-PRICE, QUANTITY data.
PERFORM UNTIL no lines left
     COMPUTE COST = QUANTITY * UNIT-PRICE +
         COMMISSION,
     WRITE next line of PARTNUMB, UNIT-PRICE,
         QUANTITY, COST data,
     READ next line of PARTNUMB, UNIT-PRICE, QUANTITY
         data,
END-PERFORM.
CLOSE input and output files.
```

You should work your way carefully through these instructions to confirm that they do generate the output data from the input data.

Data are stored as computer files

You recall that tables of data processed or generated by a program, such as those above, are called computer files, or just *files*, when recorded on magnetic disk or printed out.

You can look at a file as either a table with rows, or as a long sequence of data items recorded along disk tracks or tapes. The best way is to imagine a computer file as a sequence of rows of data; each row is called a *record* and the items of data within a record are called *fields*. This is illustrated in Figure 1.4. The input data file in Figure 1.4 thus has three records, each containing three fields.

Working storage is a part of memory

With computer processing of a file, the fields of input data must first be brought into memory for processing. After processing, they are transferred to the output file. This is illustrated in Figure 1.5. The important point is that fields are made available in memory one record at a time. A READ instruction makes one record from an input device available in memory.

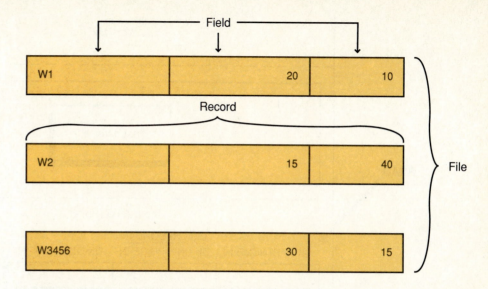

Figure 1.4 A computer file consists of records. A record can be represented on paper as a row in a table. Each record is made up of fields.

The place in memory where a record arrives from the device is called the *input area* or input buffer. A new record (for output) is typically constructed in another part of memory, called working storage, prior to being transferred to the output device. But before that transfer to the output device, the record is first moved to a third part of memory called an *output area* or output buffer.

In Figure 1.5 you see a new record being transferred (by a READ instruction) from an input device to the input area of memory. Then fields from this record in the input area are moved to a new record under construction in working storage; the field PR-COST-OUT in the new record is computed. When the new record in working storage is completed, it is first transferred to the output area (or buffer) and then to the output device; these two transfers are accomplished by means of a WRITE instruction.

To recapitulate, a READ command causes the processor to bring the next record in sequence from the input file to the input area. A WRITE command causes the processor to send a record formed in working storage to the output file via the output area.

You can now see more clearly the steps in processing the input file.

1. The first record is read into the input area.
2. The fields are copied into another record structure in working storage, which is what will be written out to the output file.
3. The cost field is computed for this second record structure.
4. Then this record is written to the output file via the output buffer.

This process repeats as long as there are unprocessed records remaining in the input file.

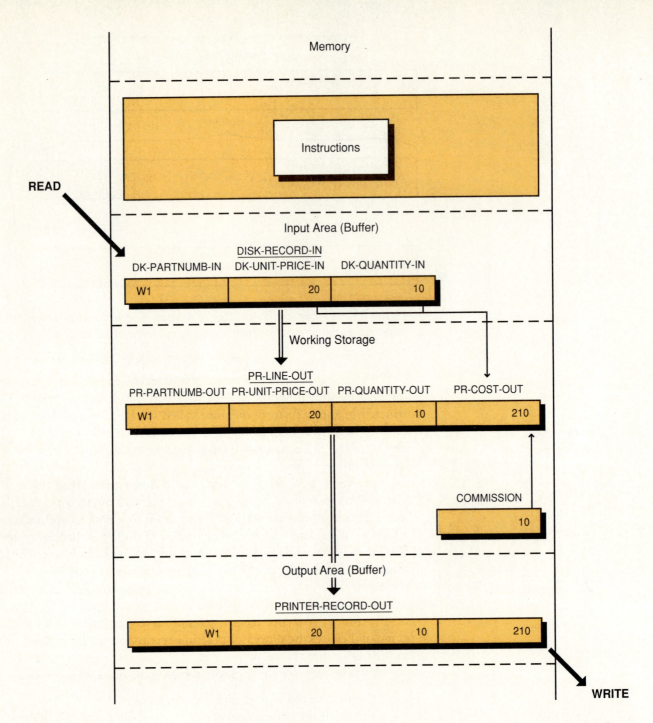

Figure 1.5 *The important parts of memory used by a program and its associated data, along with the named memory locations for holding data.*

A detailed pseudocode program helps

We can now write another pseudocode program that more closely reflects what goes on in the computer. Refer to Figure 1.5 as you read the following:

START
OPEN the input file.
OPEN the output file.

READ first input file record into RECORD-IN in input area.
PERFORM UNTIL no more input records
    MOVE PARTNUMB-IN value in RECORD-IN
        to PARTNUMB-OUT in LINE-OUT,
    MOVE UNIT-PRICE-IN value in RECORD-IN
        to UNIT-PRICE-OUT in LINE-OUT,
    MOVE QUANTITY-IN value in RECORD-IN
        to QUANTITY-OUT value in LINE-OUT,
    COMPUTE COST-OUT value in LINE-OUT as
        UNIT-PRICE-IN times QUANTITY-IN plus
        commission,
    WRITE LINE-OUT to output file via RECORD-OUT
    READ next input file record into RECORD-IN in input,
        area,
END PERFORM.
CLOSE input file.
CLOSE output file.
STOP.

With processing of a computer file, the file has to be opened. Opening an input file is necessary before a record can be taken from it by a READ instruction and placed in working storage. Opening an output file is necessary before a record can be placed in it by a WRITE instruction.

Most names in a program represent locations in memory

Notice the importance of names used in program instructions. As far as data are concerned, a name either refers to a file or to a location, or box, in memory that holds one or more items of data. Referring to Figure 1.5, let us be very exact about these names, as follows:

DISK-FILE-IN	name of input file
DISK-RECORD-IN	input area location for an input file record
DK-PARTNUMB-IN	location in DISK-RECORD-IN for a PARTNUMB value
DK-UNIT-PRICE-IN	location in DISK-RECORD-IN for a UNIT-PRICE value
DK-QUANTITY-IN	location in DISK-RECORD-IN for a QUANTITY value
PRINTER-FILE-OUT	name of output file
PRINTER-RECORD-OUT	output area location for an output file record
PR-LINE-OUT	working storage location for an output file record
PR-PARTNUMB-OUT	location in PR-LINE-OUT for a PARTNUMB value
PR-UNIT-PRICE-OUT	location in PR-LINE-OUT for a UNIT-PRICE value
PR-QUANTITY-OUT	location in PR-LINE-OUT for a QUANTITY value

PR-COST-OUT	location in PR-LINE-OUT for a COST value
COMMISSION	working storage location to hold the value 10
MORE-RECORDS	working storage location for special uses

Recall that three distinct parts of memory are used in the processing: the input buffer or input area for receiving an input record, the *working storage* for constructing a record to be output and holding other data, and the output buffer or output area for holding a record being output. When a record moves from input file to memory it is transferred to the input buffer. The output process is not symmetrical in practice, however. When a record is transferred from working storage to the output file, it moves via the output buffer, so that the record is first transferred to the output buffer, and then to the output file. This is illustrated in Figure 1.5.

Notice that we use abbreviated prefixes with the names of items of data, such as DK (for "disk") in DK-QUANTITY-IN or PR (for "printer") in PR-QUANTITY-OUT. You do not have to use such prefixes, but it is commom practice to do so. It has two benefits. First, it helps you keep track of the names in a program. Second, when you have the computer generate lists of the names used in a program to track errors, the names are usually sorted in alphabetical order, so that names with the same prefix appear together.

The core of a COBOL program contains instructions

Using the preceding names, here is the core of an actual COBOL program to process DISK-FILE-IN and generate PRINTER-FILE-OUT. It is based on the detailed pseudocode version given earlier.

```
PROCEDURE DIVISION.
100-MAIN-MODULE.
    OPEN INPUT DISK-FILE-IN.
    OPEN OUTPUT PRINTER-FILE-OUT.
    MOVE 'YES' TO MORE-RECORDS.
    READ DISK-FILE-IN
        AT END MOVE 'NO' TO MORE-RECORDS.
    PERFORM 200-PROCESS-RECORD
        UNTIL MORE-RECORDS = 'NO'.
    CLOSE DISK-FILE-IN.
    CLOSE PRINTER-FILE-OUT.
    STOP RUN.
200-PROCESS-RECORD.
    MOVE DK-PARTNUMB-IN TO PR-PARTNUMB-OUT.
    MOVE DK-UNIT-PRICE-IN TO PR-UNIT-PRICE-OUT.
    MOVE DK-QUANTITY-IN TO PR-QUANTITY-OUT.
    COMPUTE PR-COST-OUT = DK-UNIT-PRICE-IN
                        * DK-QUANTITY-IN + COMMISSION.
    WRITE PRINTER-RECORD-OUT FROM PR-LINE-OUT.
    READ DISK-FILE-IN
        AT END MOVE 'NO' TO MORE-RECORDS.
```

For this example, the names of the two files, the different locations (boxes) in working storage, and the locations for buffer records are shown in bold in the program core. You would not use bold type if you were entering the program for compilation, however. Remember also, these names are arbitrary; you could use any names you want.

The instructions are grouped into the two paragraphs called 100-MAIN-MODULE and 200-PROCESS-RECORD. The names of the two paragraphs are also arbitrary. It is normal to group instructions that have to be repeatedly executed (such as those for processing a single record) into a paragraph, such as 200-PROCESS-RECORD. Thus the instruction PERFORM 200-PROCESS-RECORD UNTIL causes repeated execution of the instructions within 200-PROCESS-RECORD.

Notice that we used a name COMMISSION. We have to arrange for the memory location called COMMISSION to hold the value 10. You will see how this is done presently.

All the other words are required parts of COBOL syntax.

Watch what happens as each instruction executes

Let us follow the execution of this program, that is, what happens as each instruction executes. This will enable you to understand exactly what the instructions do. (But keep in mind that the instructions the processor carries out will be coded as machine language instructions in memory.) Refer to Figure 1.6; a, b, and c show what is in memory following processing of each input record.

The high-level description of what happens is in the first paragraph of instructions, 100-MAIN-MODULE. First the files are opened. Then the value 'YES' is put into MORE-RECORDS using a MOVE instruction. (You will see why we need the memory location MORE-RECORDS shortly.) Then the first DISK-FILE-IN record is read (with READ) into the location DISK-RECORD-IN in the input area.

Next the instructions in the paragraph 200-PROCESS-RECORD are repeatedly carried out until there are no more records in DISK-FILE-IN. Each execution of 200-PROCESS-RECORD processes the latest record in DISK-RECORD-IN and ends with putting the next DISK-FILE-IN record in DISK-RECORD-IN. When there are no further repetitions of 200-PROCESS-RECORD, the file DISK-FILE-IN has been processed and PRINTER-FILE-OUT has received all the new records generated. The files are now closed (CLOSE instruction) and execution of instructions stops (STOP).

Let us look at what goes on during an execution of 200-PROCESS-RECORD. Just before execution of 200-PROCESS-RECORD is begun, the READ instruction will have placed the record for part W1 in DISK-RECORD-IN (Figure 1.6a). The three MOVE instructions move the contents of DISK-RECORD-IN to PR-LINE-OUT.

The COMPUTE instruction computes the cost of the parts and places it in PR-LINE-OUT as well. Notice the meaning of the COMPUTE instruction:

Take the contents of the memory location called DK-UNIT-PRICE-IN (or 20) and multiply them by the contents of the memory location called DK-QUANTITY-IN (or 10), then add

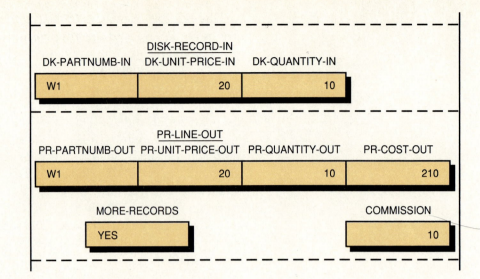

a. The input buffer and working storage after the first record has been processed.

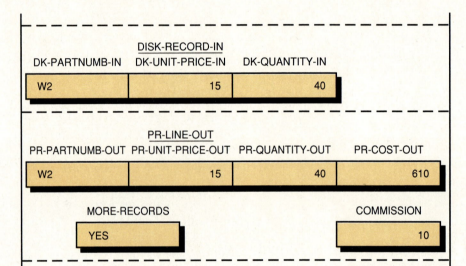

b. The input buffer and working storage after the second record has been processed.

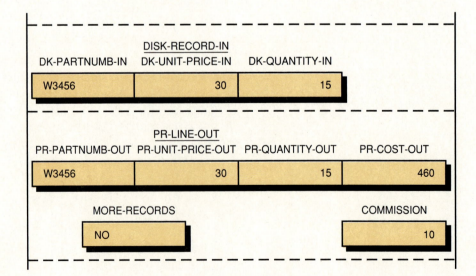

c. The input buffer and working storage after the third record has been processed.

Figure 1.6 *How memory is affected by processing of input records.*

the value in COMMISSION to the result and place the final result (210) in the memory location called PR-COST-OUT.

The following WRITE instruction writes PR-LINE-OUT, that is, copies the contents of PR-LINE-OUT, via the buffer record PRINTER-RECORD-OUT, to the output file PRINTER-FILE-OUT. The subsequent READ instruction in the 200-PROCESS-RECORD paragraph then reads the the next DISK-FILE-IN record, for part W2, into the location DISK-RECORD-IN in the input area.

Note that the output file PRINTER-FILE-OUT is not specified in the WRITE instruction, whereas the output buffer record is. In contrast, with the READ instruction, the input buffer record is not specified but the input file DISK-FILE-IN is.

In the top paragraph the PERFORM UNTIL instruction was given for the paragraph 200-PROCESS-RECORD, specifying that the paragraph be executed repeatedly until the contents of the memory location called MORE-RECORDS acquired the value 'NO'. Following the first execution of 200-PROCESS-RECORD (and the processing of the record for part W1), the memory location MORE-RECORDS still has the value 'YES' (see Figure 1.6a) and so 200-PROCESS-RECORD executes again. As a result, the second record, for part W2, is written to PRINTER-FILE-OUT (see Figure 1.6b). Then the final READ instruction brings the record for part W3456. Again 200-PROCESS-RECORD executes, and the WRITE moves the third record to PRINTER-FILE-OUT.

The READ instruction at the end of the paragraph is executed following output of the third record by the preceding WRITE. There are no more records, so a record is not placed in DISK-RECORD-IN this time; instead, the AT END clause of the READ instruction executes, and the value 'NO' is placed in MORE-RECORDS (see Figure 1.6c). No further execution of 200-PROCESS-RECORD can now occur, since the instructions of this paragraph are executed only until MORE-RECORDS acquires the value 'NO'.

Notice that this core COBOL excerpt will work no matter what values the input data have. Furthermore, we could have executed the program with 100 records in DISK-FILE-IN and it would still work. We could have used 100,000 records, for that matter, and it would still work.

Space must be specified for items of data

The preceding program instructions are just the core of the program. There are some peripheral but important things missing. Earlier the names of the files and memory locations used in the processing were listed; and then they were used in the instructions of the program. These names are somewhat like the list of the cast of characters in a movie, whereas the instructions are like the plot. A complete program consists of a list of both the names needed and the instructions.

There is an additional point about the names of memory locations. For each memory location named in the list, you must specify exactly how much space in memory will be used up, and what kind of data will be recorded in that location.

For the present, we can say that the data placed in a memory location

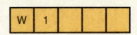

a. A named memory location, or "box," that can hold up to five character symbols. Notice that data are stored left to right, or left justified. Unused spaces hold blanks.

b. A named memory location, or "box," that can hold up to five digits. Data are stored from right to left. Unused spaces are assumed to hold zeros.

Figure 1.7 *Memory locations.*

will be either character data or numeric data. The space taken up is measured as the number of characters or digits required; a blank space also counts as a character. Character data contain letters and symbols on which arithmetic *cannot* be performed. Examples are 'YES', 'W2', 'SMITH', 'JAN. 2ND'. Thus if we needed a memory location called DK-PARTNUMB-IN to hold part identification numbers ranging from W0001 to W9999, that is, with length up to five characters, we could specify the name of the memory location and the type and amount of memory space needed as follows:

```
DK-PARTNUMB-IN        PICTURE X(05).
```

This defines a box (sometimes called a *bucket*) in memory that can hold up to five characters. The PICTURE clause uses X to signify character data (alphanumeric data); the number in parentheses (05) gives the maximum number of characters that are allowed in the box. Notice that the data are stored in this box left to right (see Figure 1.7a). Any unused spaces are filled with blanks. A blank is a valid character.

Numeric data contain numbers on which arithmetic *can* be performed. The simplest kind of numbers are integers, and the simplest kind of memory location for numbers has a space for every digit. Thus if we need a memory location called DK-QUANTITY-IN that will hold integers with values between 0 and 9999, we can specify it as follows:

```
DK-QUANTITY-IN PICTURE    9(04).
```

This defines a box in memory that will hold integers with four digits. Notice that integer data are stored right to left in a box; unused space on the left is assumed to hold zeros (see Figure 1.7b).

A complete COBOL program includes definitions

The complete COBOL program is shown in Figure 1.8. The exact layout on disk of the input records is shown later, in Figure 1.9a. What prints out when the program executes is shown in Figure 1.9d.

The exact layouts and specifications for the boxes, or locations, in memory that will hold the input data for the program are shown in Figures 1.9b and 1.9c. The layouts and specifications for the boxes to hold the data to be output are shown in Figures 1.9e and 1.9f. These specifications are incorporated into the program in Figure 1.8.

The program is written on a COBOL coding sheet. It does not have to be. Any sheet of paper would do, but the coding sheet reduces the chance of error.

COBOL programs have several divisions

All COBOL programs have four divisions. The first three give the title and list the names of the files and memory locations needed, that is, the "cast of characters." The last one, called the PROCEDURE DIVISION, gives the instructions to be carried out, that is, the "plot." In Figure 1.8 PROCEDURE DIVISION is the same as the core COBOL excerpt given earlier. A COBOL program thus has the following overall subdivisions:

IDENTIFICATION DIVISION
The name of the program must be listed. Optionally, documentation describing the program can be included. In commercial practice such documentation is always included.

ENVIRONMENT DIVISION
Essentially this contains a specification of the input or output device to be used with each file. In other words, it lists the physical input/output device environment.

DATA DIVISION
This has two major parts:
FILE SECTION Lists each file, and the accompanying input or output area record definition.
WORKING-STORAGE SECTION Lists each memory location that will hold a record structure and all other memory locations that will be used to hold data to be manipulated by program instructions.

PROCEDURE DIVISION
Gives the sequence of instructions used to process the data. The instructions can be grouped into paragraphs, headed by a paragraph name.

Record layouts and printer spacing charts are indispensible

The exact layouts of the input and output data shown in Figures 1.9a and 1.9d are reflected in the program data division specifications. Remember that memory space can be measured in characters or digits. The space taken up by a field of a record on a disk can also be measured in characters or digits. When a record is read from a disk to the input area, the exact number of characters, including blanks, will be moved to the input area, and this number must match the size of the input area record DISK-RECORD-IN.

Similarly, when a record is moved from working storage to the output

System		Sheet **1** of **2**
Program *Sample*		Date
Programmer J. BRADLEY		

Sequence		Cont.	A	B	COBOL Statement

```
00101    IDENTIFICATION DIVISION.
00102    PROGRAM-ID. SAMPLE.
00103
00104    ENVIRONMENT DIVISION.
00105    INPUT-OUTPUT SECTION.
00106    FILE-CONTROL. SELECT DISK-FILE-IN       ASSIGN TO UT-S-DISKIN.
00107             SELECT PRINTER-FILE-OUT    ASSIGN TO UR-S-SYSPRINT.
00108
00109    DATA DIVISION.
00110    FILE SECTION.
00111    FD  DISK-FILE-IN                    LABEL RECORDS ARE STANDARD.
00112    01  DISK-RECORD-IN.
00113        05  DK-PARTNUMB-IN     PIC  X(05).
00114        05  FILLER             PIC  X(02).
00115        05  DK-UNIT-PRICE-IN   PIC  9(04).
00116        05  FILLER             PIC  X(02).
00117        05  DK-QUANTITY-IN     PIC  9(04).
00118
00119    FD  PRINTER-FILE-OUT                LABEL RECORDS ARE OMITTED.
00120    01  PRINTER-RECORD-OUT     PIC X(133).
00121
00122    WORKING-STORAGE SECTION.
00123    01  WORK-AREAS.
00124        05  COMMISSION         PIC  9(02)      VALUE 10.
00125        05  MORE-RECORDS       PIC  X(03).
00126 *COMMENT.  MORE-RECORDS IS USED FOR LOOP-CONTROL.
00127
00128    01  PR-LINE-OUT.
00129        05  FILLER             PIC  X(01)      VALUE SPACES.
00130        05  PR-PARTNUMB-OUT    PIC  X(05).
00131        05  FILLER             PIC  X(02)      VALUE SPACES.
00132        05  PR-UNIT-PRICE-OUT  PIC  9(04).
00133        05  FILLER             PIC  X(02)      VALUE SPACES.
00134        05  PR-QUANTITY-OUT    PIC  9(04).
00135        05  FILLER             PIC  X(02)      VALUE SPACES.
00136        05  PR-COST-OUT        PIC  9(09).
00137        05  FILLER             PIC  X(104)     VALUE SPACES.
00138
00139    PROCEDURE DIVISION.
00140    100-MAIN-MAIN-MODULE.
00141        OPEN INPUT DISK-FILE-IN.
00142        OPEN OUTPUT PRINTER-FILE-OUT.
00143        MOVE 'YES' TO MORE-RECORDS.
00144        READ DISK-FILE-IN
00145             AT END MOVE 'NO' TO MORE-RECORDS.
00146        PERFORM 200-PROCESS-RECORD
00147             UNTIL MORE-RECORDS = 'NO'.
00148        CLOSE DISK-FILE-IN.
00149        CLOSE PRINTER-FILE-OUT.
00150        STOP RUN.
```

System											Sheet **2** of **2**
Program *Sample*											Date
Programmer J. BRADLEY											

Sequence (Page) 1 3 (Serial) 4 6	Cont. 7	A 8	B 12 16 20 24 28 32 36 40 44 48 52 56 60 64 68 72 COBOL Statement
00201			
00202			200-PROCESS-RECORD.
00203			MOVE DK-PARTNUMB-IN TO PR-PARTNUMB-OUT.
00204			MOVE DK-UNIT-PRICE-IN TO PR-UNIT-PRICE-OUT.
00205			MOVE DK-QUANTITY-IN TO PR-QUANTITY-OUT.
00206			COMPUTE PR-COST-OUT = DK-UNIT-PRICE-IN * DK-QUANTITY-IN +
01207			COMMISSION.
00208			WRITE PRINTER-RECORD-OUT FROM PR-LINE-OUT.
00209			READ DISK-FILE-IN
00210			AT END MOVE 'NO' TO MORE-RECORDS.

Figure 1.8 *A complete COBOL program, SAMPLE.*

```
---------1---------2---------3
W1      0020    0010
W2      0015    0040
W3456   0030    0015
```

Figure 1.9a *Records of the input file DISK-FILE-IN.*

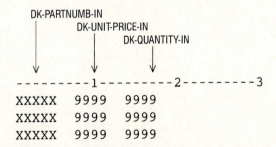

```
---------1---------2---------3
XXXXX   9999    9999
XXXXX   9999    9999
XXXXX   9999    9999
```

Figure 1.9b *Layout for the records of DISK-FILE-IN.*

```
01   DISK-RECORD-IN.
     05   DK-PARTNUMB-IN      PIC   X(05).
     05   FILLER             PIC   X(02).
     05   DK-UNIT-PRICE-IN    PIC   9(04).
     05   FILLER             PIC   X(02).
     05   DK-QUANTITY-IN      PIC   9(04).
```

Figure 1.9c *Structure of the input buffer record that receives a record from DISK-FILE-IN.*

```
----------1---------2---------3
W1        0020    0010    000000210
W2        0015    0040    000000610
W3456     0030    0015    000000460
```

Figure 1.9d *Records output to the printer as the file PRINTER-FILE-OUT.*

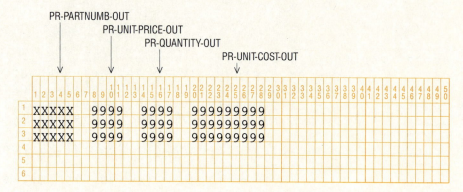

Figure 1.9e *Printer spacing chart for records output to the printer.*

```
01   PR-LINE-OUT.
     05   FILLER              PIC  X(01)      VALUE SPACES.
     05   PR-PARTNUMB-OUT     PIC  X(05).
     05   FILLER              PIC  X(02)      VALUE SPACES.
     05   PR-UNIT-PRICE-OUT   PIC  9(04).
     05   FILLER              PIC  X(02)      VALUE SPACES.
     05   PR-QUANTITY-OUT     PIC  9(04).
     05   FILLER              PIC  X(02)      VALUE SPACES.
     05   PR-COST-OUT         PIC  9(09).
     05   FILLER              PIC  X(104)     VALUE SPACES.
```

Figure 1.9f *Structure of the record output to the printer.*

area PRINTER-RECORD-OUT and from there to the printer page, an exact number of characters is moved, including blanks.

Thus the length of a record on the input file must match the length of the input area record. And lengths of records or lines on the printed page of output data must also match record lengths in working storage and the output area.

Looking closely at Figure 1.9a, you can see that an input record on disk has five fields: the first is five characters, the second is two space characters, the third is four digits, the fourth two space characters, and the fifth is four digits long, for a total length of 17 characters. Thus each input record is 17 characters long, including blanks. (Remember, a blank is a character.) In the program FILE SECTION we have specified the input area location DISK-RECORD-IN as being made up of five fields, as follows:

```
01  DISK-RECORD-IN.
       05 DK-PARTNUMB-IN      PIC X(05).
       05 FILLER              PIC X(02).
       05 DK-UNIT-PRICE-IN    PIC 9(04).
       05 FILLER              PIC X(02).
       05 DK-QUANTITY-IN      PIC 9(04).
```

This specification of DISK-RECORD-IN as level 01, and the fields DK-PARTNUMB-IN, DK-UNIT-PRICE-IN, and DK-QUANTITY-IN as level 05, means that these three fields are located within DISK-RECORD-IN in memory. Thus, in a COBOL program PROCEDURE DIVISION, for example, an instruction MOVE DISK-RECORD-IN means that the entire contents of DISK-RECORD-IN will be moved somewhere else in memory. In contrast, MOVE DK-QUANTITY-IN means that only the contents of the memory location DK-QUANTITY-IN will be moved somewhere else.

The name FILLER is a standard name used for a field that will never be otherwise referenced in any COBOL instruction. Thus you cannot write

```
MOVE FILLER TO . . .            error!
```

FILLER fields often have blanks placed in them; they are very convenient.

In the program in Figure 1.8, the instruction

```
READ DISK-FILE-IN . . .
```

causes the next record on disk, blanks and all, to be moved to input area location DISK-RECORD-IN.

The *record layout* in Figure 1.9b shows how the input records are composed in terms of characters and digits. It is strongly recommended that you construct a record layout for the records of the input file when you write a program. It is remarkably easy to mismatch the structure of a record of the input file to the input area record (such as DK-RECORD-IN) if you leave out the record layout. In this book record layouts are included with each program.

Looking at Figure 1.9d, you can see how the output data are to appear. The output is drawn up on a *printer spacing chart* (Figure 1.9e), so you can see the exact lengths involved. The data should be well spaced, so FILLER fields are used that will contain only blanks. There are blank printer spacing charts at the end of the book for you to use.

Printer spacing charts are indispensable with printer files. Typically there is fairly complex formatting of the lines to be printed. The only way to specify the output record structures correctly with printer files is to make up a printer spacing chart for the data.

The first field of a line to be printed is one blank character. The next field has five characters followed by filler of two, then a field of four digits followed by filler of two, then another field of four digits followed by filler of two. This is followed by the field PR-COST-OUT, which contains nine digits. Finally, in order to make up the length of 133, the length of the output buffer record PRINTER-RECORD-OUT, a field FILLER of 104 blank characters is added.

The total length of a line of output data is thus 133 characters, including blanks. Accordingly, the output area record PRINTER-RECORD-OUT has to be 133, and PR-LINE-OUT must be specified as

```
01  PR-LINE-OUT.
    05   FILLER              PIC  X(01)      VALUE SPACES.
    05   PR-PARTNUMB-OUT     PIC  X(05).
    05   FILLER              PIC  X(02)      VALUE SPACES.
    05   PR-UNIT-PRICE-OUT   PIC  9(04).
    05   FILLER              PIC  X(02)      VALUE SPACES.
    05   PR-QUANTITY-OUT     PIC  9(04).
    05   FILLER              PIC  X(02)      VALUE SPACES.
    05   PR-COST-OUT         PIC  9(09).
    05   FILLER              PIC  X(104)     VALUE SPACES.
```

The VALUE SPACES clauses ensure that blank characters are placed in the memory locations named FILLER.

The first blank character in PR-LINE-OUT is used by the printer for control purposes and is not printed. A printed line on a standard line printer normally has a length of 132 characters. With many computer installations it is no longer necessary to include the extra space at the beginning of a record being printed. Check with your installation. In this book the extra space is included as a reminder.

You can see now that the COBOL programmer must pay close attention to the lengths of records and fields in input and output records and must arrange for memory locations that will be able to match the lengths of records and fields. Record layouts and printer spacing charts are an invaluable tool for making sure that the specifications fit the shape of the data.

VALUE clauses are used to place initial values in memory locations

Notice the entry

```
05 COMMISSION        PIC 9(02)      VALUE 10.
```

at the end of the WORKING-STORAGE SECTION in Figure 1.8. Here the VALUE 10 clause causes the program to begin executing with the value 10 already in the memory location with the name COMMISSION. VALUE clauses are commonly used for placing such an initial value in a memory location, that is, for initializing a memory location. Earlier we used a VALUE SPACES clause to initialize a memory location with the name FILLER to blank characters. Miscellaneous working storage memory locations, such as MORE-RECORDS and COMMISSION are commonly grouped under a name like WS-WORK-AREAS. (WS denotes working storage.)

A and B margins must be observed with COBOL programs

There are a few other details to be aware of when writing a COBOL program for the first time. Look at the program on the coding sheet in Figure 1.8 again. Notice that there two margins, the A margin at column 8 and the B margin at column 12.

Division names, section names, and paragraph names must start at the A margin. So must level 01 specifications and the FD (file definition) specification in the file section of the data division.

Instructions in the PROCEDURE DIVISION begin at the B margin—or to the right of the B margin. The 05 level specifications also begin on the B margin (by convention, although with COBOL 85 they can begin on the A margin). There are always four spaces between the A and B margins.

There are seven spaces between the beginning of a line on the coding sheet and the A margin. Here there are five digits for the line number and two blank spaces. However, since COBOL programs can take up many pages, the first three spaces might be used for the page number and the next two or three for the line number. Page and line numbers were common when programs were initially entered onto punched cards—if you dropped the cards you could easily order them again. With terminals, such line and page numbers are usually not entered, but are printed with a printout or *listing* of the program.

If there is an asterisk in column 7 the compiler ignores the entire line; an asterisk is used to indicate that the line contains a comment that is not part of the program. A comment is inserted to explain something to the reader about the program, and thus make it more readable.

Here is a summary:

Columns 1-3
> Page numbers

Columns 4-6
> Line numbers (often multiples of 10; this permits insertion of a line without disturbing the sequence)

Column 7
> An asterisk (*) means a comment line
> A hyphen (-) means continuation of a literal value (see Chapter 3 for examples)

Column 8, A margin
> Division names, section names, and paragraph names
> Level 01 names
> Environment division specifications
> FD entries in data division

Column 12, B margin
> Names with level number greater than 01
> Instructions or instructions in PROCEDURE DIVISION

Some files have labels

There are some further details that may be troublesome for the beginner. Line 111 of figure 1.8, an FD (file definition) specification, states "LABEL RECORDS ARE STANDARD." Disk and tape files usually have a label that is inspected by the processor when the file is opened. Labels are usually standard, and are formed automatically by the computer system when the file is created.

On line 119 we have a further FD specification stating the "LABEL RECORDS ARE OMITTED." A printer file has no file label, and this must be stated.

You may need to change the SELECT statements

Note the two SELECT statements in the ENVIRONMENT DIVISION (lines 106 and 107 in Figure 1.8). If you try to run this program at your computer installation, in both statements you may have to change the last word. UR-S-SYSPRINT is commonly used with the standard printer unit in many IBM computer installations, but the convention differs from one computer type to another. Check with your instructor for the correct words to place after ASSIGN TO. There are more details in Chapter 2.

Names of memory locations are called identifiers

You may have wondered about the arbitrary names we used for memory locations that hold data, such as DK-QUANTITY-IN and MORE-RECORDS. In the source program the same name is used everywhere we want to refer to the contents of a specific location, or box, in memory. Almost any name will do, although there are some restrictions (see Chapter 3).

The compiler replaces a name such as DK-QUANTITY-IN with a specific address of a location in memory, such as A5000 (the memory address) when it constructs the machine language instructions corresponding to the source program. The COBOL programmer need never be concerned about memory addresses. These arbitrary memory location names thus are not used in the execution of the object program, that is, the machine language program. They are more for the convenience of the programmer, so the compiler will let you use any allowable name as long as you always use the same name for the same box or location in memory. Thus you can be confident that an arbitrarily chosen name like DK-QUANTITY-IN will actually refer to fixed piece of real estate in memory when the machine language version of the program executes.

In discussing COBOL programs, the fact that an arbitrary name such as DK-QUANTITY-IN actually refers to a small piece of memory is tacitly understood but rarely specified. Thus the term "memory location" is not much used. Instead, DK-QUANTITY-IN would be called a data name, or an *identifier*. Since the value in the memory location DK-QUANTITY-IN will vary as the program executes, another name for DK-QUANTITY-IN is variable.

To summarize, the terms data name, identifier, and variable all mean the same thing in discussions of COBOL programming. They refer to the name of a memory location, the contents of which can change following execution of an instruction by the processor. This book will mostly use the term "identifier," as it is the most common.

1.3
Diagrams can help you write correct programs

OVER THE YEARS, many diagrammatic techniques have been developed to ease visualization and communication of the logic and structure of programs and the processing carried out by them. These techniques will be used throughout the book and you will learn to use them as well.

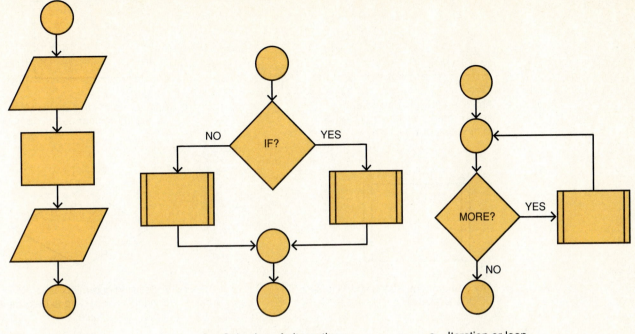

a. Straight sequence.　　　**b.** Selection of alternatives.　　　**c.** Iteration or loop.

Figure 1.10 *The three basic types of structure in programs. All programs are made up of combinations of these three structures.*

You can draw diagrams of programs

Using diagrams to display the logic of the steps behind a computer program has long been popular. The most commonly used type of diagram is the flowchart. A more recent but quite different type of diagram is the *file navigation diagram*. This is useful for displaying the file processing involved in a program. Let's look at flowcharts first.

Flowcharts are used to display structure and logic

In Figure 1.10 flowcharts are used to illustrate the three basic types of structure that can occur in a program. These are the straight sequence flowchart in Figure 1.10a, the selection of alternatives flowchart in Figure 1.10b, and the iteration or loop flowchart in Figure 1.10c. The meanings of the symbols used in flowcharts are shown in Figure 1.11.

In the straight sequence flowchart (Figure 1.10a), the instructions or groups of instructions corresponding to each box are carried out in the linear sequence shown in the diagram.

In the selection of alternatives flowchart (Figure 1.10b), one of two sets of instructions is carried out, depending on the condition depicted in the diamond. If the condition holds, that is, if 'YES', the condition is true, and the set of instructions to the right is carried out; otherwise the set on the left is carried out. You can also regard the diamond symbol as a decision symbol, where a decision on how to proceed is made.

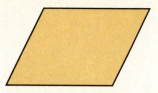

a. Any operation connected with moving data from an input device to memory, or vice versa.

b. Any operation on data in memory, excluding input or output operation.

c. Any group of operations coded in a COBOL paragraph.

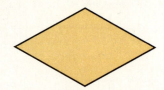

d. A decision operation, wherein a condition is checked to determine if it is true or false.

Figure 1.11 *Flowchart symbols.*

In the iteration (Figure 1.10c), if the decision is 'YES', for example, the set of instructions to the right executes and then the decision is made again. If still 'YES', the set of instructions executes again. If the decision is 'NO', the iteration stops.

The flowchart for the program in Figure 1.8 is shown in Figure 1.12. You can see that it contains all four of the structures in Figure 1.11. Actually, there are two flowcharts in Figure 1.12. Near the bottom of the flowchart to the left in Figure 1.12, there is an iteration in which paragraph 200-PROCESS-RECORD executes repeatedly. The contents of 200-PROCESS-RECORD are shown as the separate flowchart to the right.

File navigation diagrams relate input and output records

An example of the file navigation diagram for the program in Figure 1.8 is shown in Figure 1.13. The records of both DISK-FILE-IN and PRINTER-FILE-OUT are shown, and the sequence of circles shows the sequence in which the records are read or written. A solid circle indicates reading a record and an open circle indicates writing a record.

File navigation diagrams are simple and powerful, and usually show at a glance just what processing is going on.

1.4
Programs have to be tested thoroughly

IN BUSINESS, important data are processed by computers; it is clear that this data should be processed correctly. The only way to ensure that is to have correctly functioning programs. And the only way to ensure that a program functions correctly is to test it thoroughly before it goes into use.

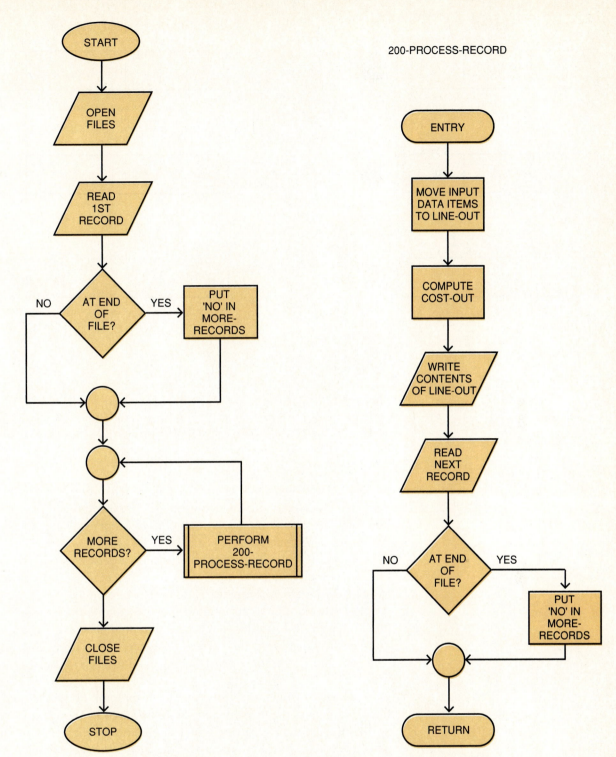

Figure 1.12 *The flowchart for the program in Figure 1.8.*

You can play computer: desk checking

One way to find out if a program does what it is supposed to is to enter it into the computer, have it compiled (translated to machine language), and run it (having first arranged for the file with the input data to be available

Input File   Output Printer File

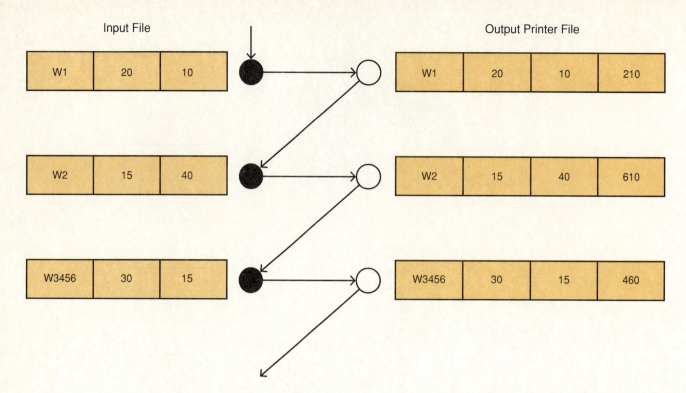

Figure 1.13 *An example of a file navigation diagram for the processing in the program in Figure 1.8. A solid circle means a record has been read, an open circle that a record has been written. The arrows give the sequence of READs and WRITEs.*

on disk). This is the "try it and see" approach. Unfortunately, programs rarely work correctly the first time, unless they are very simple. Obviously, however, you should aim for writing correct programs, so you have only a few errors, at worst.

A good way to eliminate errors is to do a desk check of the program first. This usually uncovers most of the errors, so there is very little work left to do when the program is actually tried on the computer. The person doing the desk check simply imagines being the computer processor: using a piece of paper for locations in memory that hold data, obeying the instructions in the program in the correct sequence, and making changes to the data contained in the paper memory locations according to the instructions.

For each memory location there is one column of a table; going down the column gives the sequence of values acquired by the memory location as the instructions are carried out. The column on the extreme left of the table gives the sequence numbers of the instructions executed.

An example of desk checking the program in Figure 1.8 is shown in Figure 1.14. The first instruction executed is a MOVE, which places 'YES' in MORE-RECORDS. Other memory locations have nothing assigned to them, as yet.

Then a READ executes, which transfers the first record to DISK-RECORD-IN. The value in MORE-RECORDS is unchanged and this is recorded. Other memory locations still have nothing assigned to them.

The MOVE instructions in 200-PROCESS-RECORD transfer the contents of DISK-RECORD-IN to PR-LINE-OUT. Then the COMPUTE instruc-

		DISK-RECORD-IN			PR-LINE-OUT			
Step	MORE-RECORDS	DK-PARTNUMB-IN	DK-UNIT-PRICE-IN	DK-QUANTITY-IN	PR-PARTNUMB-OUT	PR-UNIT-PRICE-OUT	PR-QUANTITY-OUT	PR-COST-OUT
143	YES							
144	YES	W1	20	10				
146	YES	W1	20	10				
203–205	YES	W1	20	10	W1	20	10	210
206	YES	W1	20	10	W1	20	10	210
207	YES	W1	20	10	W1	20	10	210
208	YES	W2	15	40	W1	20	10	210
146	YES	W2	15	40	W1	20	10	210
203–205	YES	W2	15	40	W2	15	40	610
206	YES	W2	15	40	W2	15	40	610
207	YES	W2	15	40	W2	15	40	610
208	YES	W3456	30	15	W2	15	40	610
146	YES	W3456	30	15	W2	15	40	610
203–205	YES	W3456	30	15	W3456	30	15	460
206	YES	W3456	30	15	W3456	30	15	460
207	YES	W3456	30	15	W3456	30	15	460
208	NO	W3456	30	15	W3456	30	15	460

Figure 1.14 *A desk check of the execution of the program in Figure 1.8. The numbers in the Step column at left refer to line numbers in the program.*

tion places a value in PR-COST-OUT, so that formation of PR-LINE-OUT is completed. But notice that after the MOVE instruction has been completed, DISK-RECORD-IN still retains its original values. Thus a MOVE instruction really *copies* the contents of one memory location and transfers them to another memory location.

Next a WRITE copies the contents of PR-LINE-OUT to the output file. But note, at the end of execution of the WRITE instruction, the contents of PR-LINE-OUT are unchanged. All that has happened is that a copy of the contents has been transferred to PRINTER-RECORD-OUT. You can make a note of this transfer by circling the contents of PR-LINE-OUT in the file navigation diagram.

Then a READ executes and the next record fills DISK-RECORD-IN. Then there is another sequence of MOVEs followed by a WRITE and another READ.

At the end, the last READ causes the value of MORE-RECORDS to shift to 'YES', stopping the iteration of 200-PROCESS-RECORD.

Desk checking a program can be fun. It is also a very practical thing to learn to do, and you are encouraged to become expert at it, at least when you are just beginning. It enables you to gain confidence quickly, since desk checking helps you understand just what is going on in the memory of a computer as a program executes. You can then understand clearly that all that is involved is the carrying out of simple instructions in a well-defined sequence.

You must detect and correct errors

Three different kinds of error are commonly encountered when developing a new program.

- Syntax errors
- Logical errors
- Run errors

Syntax Errors

Syntax errors are simply mistakes or inconsistencies in the use of the COBOL language. For example, misspelling an identifier one place in the program, but not in another, would be a simple syntax error. Leaving out the word COMPUTE or the = in a COMPUTE statement would also be an error in syntax.

You can detect some syntax errors yourself by carefully reading the program before submitting it to the compiler for translation. If it contains syntax errors when it is submitted to the compiler, the compiler will not be able to translate the program into machine language. Instead, it will list the errors on the terminal screen by program line number.

Thus you can consider the compiler as a tool for getting syntax errors out of programs, as well as a translation tool. The list of errors generated by the compiler should be taken positively. You simply use the list (and the system editor) to make corrections to the source program, and then reissue the compile command. There will probably still be errors, but probably fewer than before. So you go back to the text editor and make more corrections. Then you attempt to compile again. Perhaps this time the source program will be translated successfully, giving you the machine language version of your source program. However, you should still aim to write COBOL programs so carefully and neatly that the chance of a syntax or compiler error is very low.

Logical Errors

To have a program executed, you normally enter a program execution command from a terminal keyboard. This command varies from one computer system to another.

As the program executes, if all goes well, its instructions will simply read the input data from the input file (or files), and generate the output data. However, even if the program has successfully compiled and executes without stopping abnormally, it can give you wrong results. That means there are logical errors in your program.

If you have a logical error in your program, it may execute, but will generate the wrong output. Logical errors can range all the way from trivially simple to very complex. For example, in the program earlier the cost had to be computed as Unit-price x Quantity + 10. Suppose the programmer thought the commission was rebated to the customer, instead of being charged; so instead of writing

```
COMPUTE COST = UNIT-PRICE * QUANTITY + COMMISSION.
```

the programmer wrote

```
COMPUTE COST = UNIT-PRICE * QUANTITY - COMMISSION.
```

The program will compile (if there are no other errors). It will also execute. But the resulting costs computed will be wrong.

Logical errors are detected by comparing output with expected output. They are corrected by tracing the instructions that gave the incorrect output and correcting them.

Run Errors

A run error will cause a program to stop execution abruptly—before it has properly finished. A very common cause of a run error is attempted division by zero. For example, suppose we have the following instructions within a COBOL program:

```
MOVE QUANTITY-IN TO QUANTITY.
COMPUTE UNIT-PRICE = COST / QUANTITY.
```

There will not be a problem with these instructions as long as the value in QUANTITY-IN is never 0. But if one day the program is executed and the value 0 is read into QUANTITY-IN, then the processor will not be able to carry out the COMPUTE UNIT-PRICE statement because the result would be infinity. A variable or identifier cannot store the value infinity.

The compiler will not object to the preceding instructions, since it cannot be designed to anticipate what data a user will feed to the program as input data. It is only during an execution of the program where QUAN-TITY acquires the value 0 that things go wrong. The program will execute as far as the COMPUTE command and then abruptly stop when the run error occurs. At the point where it stops, the computer system will usually print a message on the terminal screen outlining why the program execution abnormally ended, or "abended."

Run errors are detected by the abnormal ending of the program. They are corrected by altering the logic of the program to take care of the contingency that gave rise to the error in the first place.

Extensive testing of programs is often necessary

A program can contain a logical error or a potential run error that will show up only when a specific but rare combination of input data is processed. Thus a program might normally run correctly but one time in a hundred will give a totally wrong result or cause an abnormal ending.

Such hidden flaws or "bugs" are not acceptable. Normally, before a program goes into everyday commercial use, it must be extensively tested to see if it contains any such errors. The testing consists of running the program many times. Each execution uses a different selection of input data. You check the output for correctness with each test run and, of course, record and investigate any abnormal endings.

You can always improve a program

Notice the COMPUTE instruction

```
COMPUTE PR-COST-OUT = DK-UNIT-PRICE-IN
     * DK-QUANTITY-IN + COMMISSION.
```

in the program in Figure 1.8. It would be better practice to replace it with the COMPUTE and MOVE instructions

```
COMPUTE COMPUTED-COST = DK-UNIT-PRICE-IN
     * DK-QUANTITY-IN + COMMISSION.
MOVE COMPUTED-COST TO PR-COST-OUT.
```

where COMPUTED-COST is an additional identifier, defined in the WORKING-STORAGE SECTION as

```
WORKING-STORAGE SECTION.
...
    05 COMPUTED-COST     PIC 9(09).
```

Both versions are correct. However, the new version is considered to be better practice. In the new version an additional identifier, COMPUTED-COST, is used to do the calculations and receive an intermediate result, and then the intermediate result is moved to the identifier PR-COST-OUT, which is to be output. There is not much possibility of error with this procedure.

On the other hand, if you use an identifier, the contents of which will be printed, for calculations, there is a possibility of subtle errors. Thus the version in Figure 1.8, although correct in this case, is not as good because you are doing calculations with the identifier PR-COST-OUT, which has contents that are to be printed, and possibly automatically edited, as will be explained in Chapters 2, 3, and 4.

1.5
You have learned some COBOL instructions

OU HAVE ENCOUNTERED the following COBOL instructions or statements in this overview chapter. The following examples will help you become more familiar with them.

OPEN statement examples

```
OPEN INPUT FILE-A.
```

Records can now be read from FILE-A.

```
OPEN OUTPUT FILE-B.
```

Records can now be written into FILE-B.

CLOSE statement example

```
CLOSE FILE-A.
```

Records cannot be read from, or written into, FILE-A until the file is opened again. If a file is open for writing out records (OUTPUT), to then read records from it you must CLOSE it first, and then OPEN it for INPUT.

READ statement example

```
READ FILE-A
    AT END . . .
```

The next record in the file is placed in the input area record. If the READ attempts to read beyond the end of the file, that is, the last record plus one, no record is read and the statement following AT END is executed.

WRITE statement examples

```
WRITE PRINTER-RECORD-OUT FROM PR-LINE-OUT.
```

The record in PR-LINE-OUT in working storage is copied into the output area record and also written to the output file.

MOVE statement examples

```
MOVE DK-PARTNUMB-IN TO PR-PARTNUMB-OUT.
MOVE 25 TO PR-UNIT-PRICE-OUT.
MOVE 'W13' TO PR-PARTNUMB-OUT.
```

MOVE copies the contents of an identifier into another identifier, or moves a numeric value (such as 25) into a numeric identifier or an alphnumeric value (such as 'W13') into an alphanumeric identifier.

COMPUTE statement examples

```
MOVE 4 TO Y.
MOVE 7 TO Z.
MOVE 15 TO W.
MOVE 5 TO V.
COMPUTE P = Y * Z + 3.          P gets 31.
COMPUTE P = W / V + Y.          P gets 7.
COMPUTE P = (5 + W) / V.        P gets 4.
COMPUTE P = 5 + W / V.          P gets 8.
```

Note that you must have a space before and after *, /, +, and - arithmetic operators. Instead of COMPUTE statements, when an arithmetic operation is a simple addition, subtraction, multiplication, or division, the statements ADD, SUBTRACT, MULTIPLY, and DIVIDE are more commonly used. These statements are considered to be easier to read. You will learn about them in Chapter 4.

Summary

1. Business data processing by computer consists of transferring raw data from input disk or tape file to memory, processing that data in memory, and then transferring the processed data from memory to an output file. The output file can also be a tape or disk file, but is often a printer file, that is, a printed report.

2. Data are permanently recorded magnetically on disk or tape. Each character of data is recorded in a unique 8-bit code. A bit is recorded magnetically and is interpreted as a 1 or a 0. A standard recording code, called the ASCII code, is used. The same code is used for characters stored in memory. Storage in memory is temporary. An electrical recording mode is used for bits in memory. With IBM computers an additional code called EBCDIC can be used for storing characters.

3. The program of instructions used to carry out business data processing is commonly written in an artificial language called COBOL. The processor of a computer carries out the instructions. The instructions are stored in memory and the processor carries them out sequentially, one-by-one. Instructions written in COBOL must first be translated into machine language instructions by a special program called a compiler before they can be stored in memory and executed by the processor.

4. A COBOL program has four parts or divisions. The first part, the IDENTIFICATION DIVISION, names the program. The second and third parts, ENVIRONMENT and DATA DIVISION, list the files and the memory locations to be used in the processing. The last part, the PROCEDURE DIVISION, lists the sequence of instructions.

5. A memory location can hold either character or numeric data, but

not both. Each memory location is given an arbitrary name; its size, in characters of memory space, must be specified in the DATA DIVISION. A memory location is usually called an identifier.

6. Flowcharts and other diagrams communicate the logic of a program. A program can contain syntax errors, logical errors, and run errors, which should be eliminated by extensive testing before the program goes into routine use. Record layouts and printer spacing charts are used to plan the size of identifiers needed with input and output data.

Key Terms

bits	object program	printer spacing chart
byte	files	identifier
machine language	record	file navigation
instructions	fields	diagram
compiler	input area	syntax errors
pseudocode	output area	logical errors
source program	working storage	run errors
editor	record layout	

Concept Review Questions

1. In computer processing, what are input data?
2. In computer processing, what are output data?
3. What is the nature of data recording on (a) disk, (b) tape?
4. Explain the difference between data recorded permanently on disk and data recorded temporarily in memory.
5. Where are instructions recorded during execution of a program?
6. What instruction causes data in memory to be printed on printer paper?
7. What instruction causes data in an input file to be transferred to memory?
8. What is machine language?
9. List the versions of COBOL that have been used up to the present.
10. Why should COBOL programs be structured?
11. What is pseudocode?
12. What does a COBOL compiler do?
13. Can any COBOL compiler be used with any computer? Explain.
14. Explain the difference between an object and source program.
15. What is the input buffer or input area of memory?
16. What is the output buffer or output area of memory?
17. What is the working storage area of memory?
18. Where does a READ instruction normally deliver a record taken from an input file?
19. What is a COBOL paragraph?
20. What is a record layout? What is a printer spacing chart?
21. List the three types of structures found in programs.
22. Point out an iteration in the program in Figure 1.8.
23. What is a desk check of a program?
24. What is a COBOL syntax error?
25. What is a COBOL logical error?

26. What is a COBOL run error?
27. How is a program entered into a computer ready for compilation?

COBOL Language Questions

1. What are the divisions of a COBOL program? Explain briefly the function of each division.
2. What are A and B margins?
3. What is the common use of column 7 in a COBOL coding sheet?
4. Why should you take care with SELECT entries at a new computer installation?
5. What is an FD entry?
6. Give the PIC specification for an output area record that will be used with a printer.
7. If an input file CUSTOMER has a corresponding input area record defined as

```
01   CUSTOMER-RECORD-IN.
     05 CUST-NAME-IN      PIC X(20).
     05 FILLER            PIC X(05).
     05 CUST-ASSETS       PIC 9(06).
```

   a. What is the length, in characters, of a record of CUSTOMER?
   b. How much space is taken up by numeric data?
   c. How much space is taken up in a CUSTOMER record by non-numeric data?
8. Explain briefly the entries
   a. LABEL RECORDS ARE STANDARD.
   b. LABEL RECORDS ARE OMITTED.
9. What is a VALUE clause used for?
10. If a file IN-FILE is to be opened for reading, give the full OPEN statement.
11. If a file PRINTER-FILE is to be opened for writing, give the full OPEN statement.
12. What is the function of the AT END clause with a READ statement?
13. Write a MOVE statement to place the value 'NO' in the identifier NOT-FOUND.
14. If the output buffer record identifier is PR-RECORD-OUT for a printer file, and a line to be printed is in the identifier DETAIL-LINE, give a WRITE statement to print the line.
15. What is the largest number that can be held in an identifier X defined as

```
01 X   PIC 9(05).
```

16. If you have

```
01 V       PIC 9(06).
01 X       PIC 9(03)    VALUE 5.
01 Y       PIC 9(03)    VALUE 10.
01 Z       PIC 9(03)    VALUE 25.
01 W       PIC 9(05)    VALUE 3.
```

   a. What is in the identifier V after execution of the following instruction?

```
COMPUTE V = Y + Z / X.
```

b. What is the value of the identifier V following execution of this instruction?

```
COMPUTE V = (Y + X) / W
```

c. What is the value of the identifier V after execution of the following instruction?

```
COMPUTE V = Y * X + W
```

d. What is the value of the identifier V following execution of this instruction?

```
COMPUTE V = Y * (W + Z)
```

17. What does the STOP RUN instruction do?
18. Explain the operation of the instruction

```
PERFORM 200-MR-PARAGRAPH UNTIL MORE-RECORDS = 'NO'.
```

Programming Assignments

1. **Entering and running a simple program**

To run a program you have to enter it, save it on a disk, and have it compiled and then executed. You use the editor on your computer to enter the program and save it.

The details of these steps vary from one computer to another. (You will need information from your instructor here.) Once learned, these steps are always the same, whether the program is short and simple or long and complicated.

To go through the exercise for the first time it is best to use a program as simple as possible. Here is a very short and simple one for printing the message "HELLO, COBOL USER" on the printer:

```
IDENTIFICATION DIVISION.
PROGRAM-ID. SIMPLE.
ENVIRONMENT DIVISION.
INPUT-OUTPUT SECTION.
FILE-CONTROL.
    SELECT PRINTER-FILE-OUT        ASSIGN TO UR-S-SYSPRINT.
DATA DIVISION.
FILE SECTION.
FD  PRINTER-FILE-OUT              LABEL RECORDS ARE OMITTED.
01  PRINTER-RECORD-OUT   PIC X(133).
WORKING-STORAGE SECTION.
01  PR-LINE-OUT.
    05   FILLER          PIC  X(01)  VALUE SPACE.
    05   PR-MESSAGE       PIC  X(17)  VALUE 'HELLO, COBOL USER'.
    05   FILLER           PIC  X(115) VALUE SPACES.
PROCEDURE DIVISION.
100-ONLY-MODULE.
    OPEN OUTPUT PRINTER-FILE-OUT.
    WRITE PRINTER-RECORD-OUT FROM PR-LINE-OUT.
    CLOSE PRINTER-FILE-OUT.
    STOP RUN.
```

There are two practical points to note:

a. The ASSIGN TO clause requirements for the SELECT statement vary from one computer system to another. You may have to change UR-S-SYSPRINT to PRINTER or to something else. Check with your installation.

b. With some systems, particularly IBM systems, a program must be accompanied by commands to the operating system, called Job Control Language (JCL) commands. Check with your instructor or installation for correct JCL, if needed. Note also that with COBOL 74 you need a CONFIGURATION SECTION. See Chapter 2 of this book.

2. **Entering an input file and running a program to process it**

a. Use the editor to enter the three records of the file DISK-FILE-IN in Figure 1.9a, and store these records on disk. Take care that you space the data exactly as in Figure 1.9a.

b. Enter the program in Figure 1.8, making any necessary changes and additions to fit with conventions at your installation; then run it.

c. When you have the program executing correctly, introduce minor errors in the source program, such as changing OUTPUT to INPUT, leaving out periods, forgetting AT END clauses, and so on. Compile the source program again, and observe the list of error messages produced by the compiler.

3. **Entering a new input file and altering and running an existing program**

a. Make up a new version of the input file, called DISK-FILE-IN. This version should have no blanks between fields, as shown here. The input data are

```
---------1---------2---------3
W1    00200010
W2    00150040
W345600300015
```

The record layout is

```
---------1---------2---------3
XXXXX99999999
XXXXX99999999
XXXXX99999999
```

b. Rewrite the program in Figure 1.8 to process this input file and give the same output as before. You have to

  ▪ Change the input file name.
  ▪ Alter the FD specifications for the input file.

4. **Writing your own program**

In this exercise you will write a program that is similar in structure and function to the one in Figure 1.8.

   The input data are

```
---------1---------2---------3---------4
BROWN, J.P.                  04599   00650
GREEN, F.M                   00870   00180
SHOSTAKOVITCH, T.G.          84867   02174
```

The record layout is

```
---------1---------2---------3---------4
XXXXXXXXXXXXXXXXXXXX   99999   99999
XXXXXXXXXXXXXXXXXXXX   99999   99999
XXXXXXXXXXXXXXXXXXXX   99999   99999
```

An input record gives a bank customer's name, followed by the amount in a savings account, followed by the amount in a checking account.

The output data to be printed are

```
---------1---------2---------3---------4---------5---------6
BROWN, J.P.                  04599      00650      005247
GREEN, F.M                   00870      00180      001048
SHOSTAKOVITCH, T.G.          84867      02174      087039
```

The printer spacing chart is

An output record gives a bank customer's name, followed by the amount in a savings account, followed by the amount in a checking account, followed by a total of the amounts in the two accounts, less a monthly banking charge of $2.00.

a. Enter the input data and store on disk as the input file.
b. Draw a flowchart for the processing.
c. Develop and run a COBOL program to process the input file and generate the output file on a printer. Remember not to do calculations with an identifier that will be printed.

5. **Entering a new input file and altering and running an existing program**
Repeat Assignment 4, using a version of the input file without blanks between the fields. The input data are thus

```
---------1---------2---------3---------4
BROWN, J.P.         0459900650
GREEN, F.M          0087000180
SHOSTAKOVITCH, T.G. 8486702174
```

The record layout is

```
---------1---------2---------3---------4
XXXXXXXXXXXXXXXXXXXX9999999999
XXXXXXXXXXXXXXXXXXXX9999999999
XXXXXXXXXXXXXXXXXXXX9999999999
```

THE IDENTIFICATION AND ENVIRONMENT DIVISIONS

You cannot use identifiers with edit symbols in arithmetic operations
An output file usually has headers
Make spacing charts for input and output data
A program that processes one record after another in a simple loop
You need AFTER ADVANCING with every WRITE
You can use ADD, SUBTRACT, MULTIPLY and DIVIDE statements

*I*N THIS CHAPTER and the next two chapters we will look at the main features of the four divisions of a COBOL program. The first two divisions, the IDENTIFICATION and ENVIRONMENT divisions, are the shortest and simplest. They will be examined in this chapter.

It is best to illustrate major features of COBOL using a complete program so you can retain an overall perspective. To this end, the program from the previous chapter is used, with some modifications. You recall that the program processed a file of input records on disk, called DISK-FILE-IN, to generate a printer file, or report, called PRINTER-FILE-OUT. The contents of DISK-FILE-IN are shown in Figure 2.1a.

Each record describes the purchase of a quantity of parts of a given type with a certain unit price. The output file is shown in Figure 2.1b. In the output, the total cost of the parts, which is computed in the program, has been added to each input record.

The program is shown in Figure 2.1c. It has a longer IDENTIFICATION DIVISION than before; this will be explained presently. It also computes the cost of parts to be printed somewhat differently.

```
---------1---------2---------3
W1      0020   0010
W2      0015   0040
W3456   0030   0015
```

Figure 2.1a *Input disk file (DISK-FILE-IN).*

```
---------1---------2---------3
W1      0020   0010   000000210
W2      0015   0040   000000610
W3456   0030   0015   000000460
```

Figure 2.1b *Records output to the printer (PRINTER-FILE-OUT).*

```
      IDENTIFICATION DIVISION.
      PROGRAM-ID. SAMPLE1.
      AUTHOR. J. BRADLEY.
      INSTALLATION. DATA CENTER,
                    NORTH WEST BRANCH.
      DATE-WRITTEN. 20 DECEMBER 1988.
                    REVISED 5 APRIL 1989.
      DATE-COMPILED.
      SECURITY. FOR INSTRUCTIONAL USE
              NO SECURITY CODE APPLIES.
      ENVIRONMENT DIVISION.
      INPUT-OUTPUT SECTION.
      FILE-CONTROL.
                      SELECT DISK-FILE-IN           ASSIGN TO UT-S-DISKIN.
                      SELECT PRINTER-FILE-OUT       ASSIGN TO UR-S-SYSPRINT.
      DATA DIVISION.
      FILE SECTION.
      FD   DISK-FILE-IN                    LABEL RECORDS ARE STANDARD.
      01   DISK-RECORD-IN.
           05  DK-PARTNUMB-IN     PIC   X(05).
           05  FILLER            PIC   X(02).
           05  DK-UNIT-PRICE-IN   PIC   9(04).
           05  FILLER            PIC   X(02).
           05  DK-QUANTITY-IN     PIC   9(04).
      FD   PRINTER-FILE-OUT                LABEL RECORDS ARE OMITTED.
      01   PRINTER-RECORD-OUT    PIC X(133).
      WORKING-STORAGE SECTION.
      01 WS-WORK-AREAS.
           05  MORE-RECORDS       PIC   X(03).
      *  COMMENT: USE MORE-RECORDS FOR LOOP CONTROL.
           05  COMMISSION         PIC   9(02)      VALUE 10.
           05  WS-COMPUTED-COST   PIC   9(09).
      *  COMMENT: USE WS-COMPUTED-COST TO AVOID CALCULATIONS WITH
      *           AN IDENTIFIER FROM WHICH DATA WILL BE PRINTED.
      01   PR-LINE-OUT.
           05  FILLER             PIC   X(01)      VALUE SPACES.
           05  PR-PARTNUMB-OUT    PIC   X(05).
           05  FILLER             PIC   X(02)      VALUE SPACES.
           05  PR-UNIT-PRICE-OUT  PIC   9(04).
           05  FILLER             PIC   X(02)      VALUE SPACES.
           05  PR-QUANTITY-OUT    PIC   9(04).
           05  FILLER             PIC   X(02)      VALUE SPACES.
           05  PR-COST-OUT        PIC   9(09).
           05  FILLER             PIC   X(104)     VALUE SPACES.
      PROCEDURE DIVISION.
      100-MAIN-MODULE.
         OPEN INPUT DISK-FILE-IN.
         OPEN OUTPUT PRINTER-FILE-OUT.
         MOVE 'YES' TO MORE-RECORDS.
         READ DISK-FILE-IN
                    AT END MOVE 'NO' TO MORE-RECORDS.
```

```
       PERFORM 200-PROCESS-RECORD
                UNTIL MORE-RECORDS = 'NO'.
       CLOSE DISK-FILE-IN.
       CLOSE PRINTER-FILE-OUT.
       STOP RUN.
   200-PROCESS-RECORD.
       MOVE DK-PARTNUMB-IN TO PR-PARTNUMB-OUT.
       MOVE DK-UNIT-PRICE-IN TO PR-UNIT-PRICE-OUT.
       MOVE DK-QUANTITY-IN TO PR-QUANTITY-OUT.
       COMPUTE WS-COMPUTED-COST = DK-UNIT-PRICE-IN * DK-QUANTITY-IN
                                         + COMMISSION.

       MOVE WS-COMPUTED-COST TO PR-COST-OUT.
       WRITE PRINTER-RECORD-OUT FROM PR-LINE-OUT.
       READ DISK-FILE-IN
       AT END MOVE 'NO' TO MORE-RECORDS.
```

Figure 2.1c COBOL program SAMPLE1 with an extended IDENTIFICATION DIVISION.

2.1
The IDENTIFICATION DIVISION identifies a program

T H E I D E N T I F I C A T I O N D I V I S I O N is a necessary but somewhat trivial part of a COBOL program.

The basic syntax for the IDENTIFICATION DIVISION is brief

The minimum specification for the IDENTIFICATION DIVISION is given in this language syntax box:

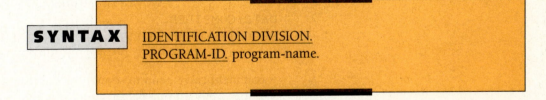

SYNTAX IDENTIFICATION DIVISION.
PROGRAM-ID. program-name.

What is underlined must be used. Uppercase words are COBOL reserved names. What is given in lowercase must be replaced by an arbitrary program name, such as SAMPLE. A program name must have only letters and digits, and should not exceed eight characters.

Thus, the syntax

```
IDENTIFICATION DIVISION.
PROGRAM-ID. SAMPLE1.
```

used in the preceding program is a valid syntax for the IDENTIFICATION DIVISION.

A more elaborate IDENTIFICATION DIVISION can also be specified. The possible syntax is specified here:

SYNTAX

```
IDENTIFICATION DIVISION.
PROGRAM-ID. program-name.
[AUTHOR. [comment] ]
[INSTALLATION. [comment] ]
[DATE-WRITTEN. [comment] ]
[DATE-COMPILED. [comment] ]
[SECURITY. [comment] ]
```

In this syntax specification, anything within brackets can be omitted. If it is included, anything underlined must be used.

Thus, either of the following would be acceptable:

Example 1: Using author and dates

```
IDENTIFICATION DIVISION.
PROGRAM-ID. SAMPLE.
AUTHOR. PETER PETERSON.
DATE-WRITTEN.
DATE-COMPILED. 5, JANUARY, 1990.
```

Example 2: Adding more information

```
IDENTIFICATION DIVISION.
PROGRAM-ID. SAMPLE.
AUTHOR. PETER PETERSON.
INSTALLATION. DATA CENTER,
              DENVER SOUTH.
DATE-WRITTEN.  20 DECEMBER, 1989.
               REVISED 5 JUNE, 1991.
DATE-COMPILED.
SECURITY. FOR THE EYES OF FINANCIAL PERSONNEL.
          SECURITY CODE SD325 APPLIES.
```

A comment can extend to several lines, as the second example shows. However, the comment must always appear within area B on a line, that is, after column 12. There is just such an extended IDENTIFICATION DIVISION in the program in Figure 2.1c.

2.2
The ENVIRONMENT DIVISION links files to hardware

N COBOL 74 the ENVIRONMENT DIVISION had two sections: a CONFIGURATION SECTION and an INPUT-OUTPUT SECTION. Since COBOL 85 has gained acceptance, the CONFIGURATION SECTION has become obsolete and is rarely used. This book uses only the INPUT-

OUTPUT SECTION. The section links the file names you use in a program to physical files on hardware devices. Note that a minimum CONFIGURATION SECTION is required with COBOL 74.

Essential ENVIRONMENT DIVISION coding involves the SELECT statement

The coding for the ENVIRONMENT DIVISION from the program in Figure 2.1c on page 46 is typical.

```
ENVIRONMENT DIVISION.
INPUT-OUTPUT SECTION.
FILE-CONTROL.   SELECT ACCOUNT-IN  ASSIGN TO UT-S-DISKIN.
                SELECT ACCOUNT-OUT  ASSIGN TO UR-S-SYSPRINT.
```

The SELECT statement can be written on several lines, but must be within area B on each line. There has to be a SELECT statement for each file used in the program.

If a CONFIGURATION SECTION is included, as required with COBOL 74, the ENVIRONMENT DIVISION could be

```
ENVIRONMENT DIVISION.
CONFIGURATION SECTION.
SOURCE COMPUTER.   IBM-370.
OBJECT COMPUTER.   IBM-370.
INPUT-OUTPUT SECTION.
FILE CONTROL.   SELECT ACCOUNT-IN  ASSIGN TO UT-S-DISKIN.
                SELECT ACCOUNT-OUT  ASSIGN TO UR-S-SYSPRINT.
```

You simply place the name of the computer used after SOURCE COMPUTER and after OBJECT-COMPUTER. A standard word will be used at your installation for the name of the computer, such as IBM-370.

The SELECT statement has a simple syntax

Here is the syntax for the SELECT statement:

SYNTAX   SELECT file-name
              ASSIGN TO implementor-name

The same rules used for identifiers are used for file names:

- Use up to 30 characters, of which one must be a letter.
- Use any combination of letters, digits, and hyphens.
- Use no embedded blanks.

The file name is used within the PROCEDURE DIVISION with READ statements. Thus we can have the statement

```
READ ACCOUNT-IN INTO . . .
```

where ACCOUNT-IN is a file name specified with a SELECT statement.

The purpose of the SELECT statement is to link the file name, as used in the program, with the name or reference used by the operating system for the physically existing file.

Let us take a very simple example of this. Suppose that you have a physical file on disk that can be referred to using the name UT-S-ACCOUNT4. You might then code the following:

```
ENVIRONMENT DIVISION.
...
        SELECT ACCOUNT-IN
               ASSIGN TO UT-S-ACCOUNT4.
...
PROCEDURE DIVISION.
    ...
        READ ACCOUNT-IN INTO . . .
```

The file name ACCOUNT-IN is used only in the program. The SELECT statement tells the compiler and the operating system that the physically existing file referred to by UT-S-ACCOUNT4 is to be used wherever the name ACCOUNT-IN is encountered.

You could rewrite the program with a different file name, such as CUSTOMER-IN. Provided you linked the new file name to the same physical file UT-S-ACCOUNT4 using the SELECT statement, the program would perform exactly the same. Thus you could have

```
ENVIRONMENT DIVISION.
...
        SELECT CUSTOMER-IN
               ASSIGN TO UT-S-ACCOUNT4.
...
PROCEDURE DIVISION.
    ...
        READ CUSTOMER-IN INTO . . .
```

without materially affecting the program.

This is only in theory, however. In practice, the details of how to fill in the implementor name depend on the computer you are using. Sometimes the implementor name (see the preceding syntax box) should be replaced by the physical file name, and sometimes it should be replaced by something closely resembling the physical file name. The exact method of specifying the implementor name will be available to you through your computer installation or instructor.

There are several types of physical files

You can have the following kinds of physical files:

Disk
Data are recorded in bit format using magnetization. A record can have any length, but lengths between 20 and 500 characters are typical. Can be used for input or output.

Tape
Data are recorded in bit format using magnetization. A record can have any length. Typical lengths range from 20 to 500 characters. Can be an input or output file.

Printer
Data are printed on paper. Each record has a fixed length equal to the length of a line on the page. This is often 132 characters long. Can only be an output file.

Video screen display output file
Data are displayed on screen. Each record has a fixed length equal to the length of a line on the screen. The length of a record depends on the terminal.

Terminal keyboard input file
Data are entered using keys. Each record is stored in bit format in the keyboard register and has a fixed length that depends on the terminal.

Punch card input file
Data are coded on punch cards in a special code. The file is used for input. Each record is 80 characters long. This type of file was once common, but is now almost obsolete.

SELECT implementor names depend on the computer system

With many computers, the following implementor names are used in the SELECT statement for the physical files:

Disk file	DISK
Printer file	SYSOUT or SYSPRINT
Card file	SYSIN, SYSRDR, or SYSIPT
Terminal output file	SYS$OUT
Terminal input file	SYS$IN

If any of these are specified, the system assumes that a standard input or output device (out of many possible ones) is being used. The computer installation personnel will have decided what the standard device is. For example, the installation may have 10 disk drives, and one of them is allocated as the standard. However, the standard terminal will be the one from which the program is executed.

IBM has two common operating system families for mainframe computers, the IBM DOS systems and the IBM OS systems (which include OS/MVS). The methods used to specify implementor names with these systems follow. Use these sections for reference.

IBM DOS Systems

Here are some examples of DOS implementor names:

SYS006-UT-3400-S
SYS005-UR-2501-S
SYS007-DA-3380-D

An implementor name is made up of the following elements:

[symbolic-unit]-[device-class]-[device-make]-[file-organization]

Symbolic-unit This refers to a system number used by the operating system to identify a specific device. For example, SYS005 is often a printer. A symbolic unit is made up of SYS followed by three digits.

Device-class For device class, you use DA (direct access), UT (utility), or UR (unit record). Disks are direct-access devices. Tapes are utility devices. Printers, card readers, and terminals are unit record devices.

DA	Disks
UT	Tapes, sequential disk files
UR	Card readers, printers, terminals

Device-make This designates the make or model of a device type. There are many different makes of disk. For example, there are the IBM 3330, IBM 3350, and the IBM 3380. If the IBM 3380 was being used, you would use 3380 for device-make.

File-organization Files can be organized in different ways. Two common ways are *sequential* (S) and *direct access* (D). With sequential files, records must be accessed in the sequence in which they are recorded, one after another. In a tape file the organization is always sequential. Direct-access file records can be accessed in any sequence. We will look at direct-access files much later in the book. A file on disk can be either sequential or direct-access. The elementary files used in most of this book are sequential. Printer, card, and terminal files are always sequential.

IBM OS Systems

Examples of OS system implementor names are

UR-S-SYSPRINT
UR-S-SYSIN
UT-3340-S-CUSTOMER

```
UT-3380-S-MASTER
UT-S-CUSTOMER
UT-S-MASTER
```

Such a name is made up of

[device-class]-[device-make]-[file-organization]-[external-name]

where device-make can be omitted.

Device-class   For device-class, you use DA (direct access), UT (utility), or UR (unit record).

DA   Disks
UT   Tapes, sequential disk files
UR   Card readers, printers, terminals

Device-make   This designates the make or model of a device type; for example, IBM disk drive 3350 or 3380. Device-make can be omitted.

File-organization   With sequential files use S. With direct-access files, commonly no symbol is used.

External-name   This is an arbitrary name (with a maximum of eight characters) that refers to a physical file on the device. The name also directly refers to an operating system statement that will follow the program when the program is submitted for execution. This statement is called a DD statement (dataset definition statement); it defines the physical file and specifies file properties. A DD statement is part of an operating system command language called IBM Job Control Language, or JCL. Normally systems programmers prepare involved DD statements.

A DD statement is not part of a COBOL program but is placed after the program when it is submitted to the operating system. As an example, the SELECT clause and DD statement at the end of the program could be

```
IDENTIFICATION DIVISION.
...
ENVIRONMENT DIVISION.
...
    SELECT CUSTOMER-IN
        ASSIGN TO UT-S-CUST04.
...
DATA DIVISION.
...
PROCEDURE DIVISION.
....
[end of COBOL program]
...
//CUST04    DD    DATASETNAME=CUST04,UNIT=3350,VOL=SER=007...
```

A DD statement begins with //. Here CUST04 is the name of the physical file recorded on a disk pack with the serial number 007. The disk pack will be mounted on an IBM 3350 disk drive.

Remember, however, that implementor names for physical files are dependent on the computer type and the installation. Consequently, all this book can do is give you an idea of what to expect. In practice, you must find out how to write implementor names from your instructor or your installation manual.

You can still make common errors with SELECT

The following is wrong:

```
ENVIRONMENT DIVISION.
INPUT-OUTPUT SECTION.
FILE-CONTROL.
SELECT CUSTOMER-IN
              ASSIGN TO UT-S-ACCOUNT4.    error!
```

The SELECT must begin the B area.
The following is also wrong:

```
ENVIRONMENT DIVISION.
INPUT-OUTPUT SECTION.
FILE-CONTROL.
        SELECT CUSTOMER-IN
              ASSIGN TO UT-S-ACCOUNT4    error!
        SELECT REPORT-OUT
              ASSIGN TO UR-S-SYSPRINT.
```

A period is needed after each SELECT statement.

2.3
A program development example

*I*N THIS SECTION a program is developed to print data from a disk input file, AIRCRAFT-IN, about aircraft belonging to an airline. The input file gives the year an aircraft was built. The program computes the age of each aircraft in 1990 and prints the age in the output file. The output file also has headers. The input data are in Figure 2.2. The output data are shown later, in Figure 2.3. The program is at the end of the chapter, in Figure 2.4.

Input files do not have spaces between fields

The input data are shown in Figure 2.2a. Notice there are no spaces between the fields of the input file; it is shown as the characters are recorded on disk, which makes this file hard to read. A more readable version is shown in Figure 2.2d, where spaces have been inserted between the fields for readability.

These spaces are not needed on tape and disk. They waste space, especially with large files. In commerce, a file can have tens of thousands, or hundreds of thousands, of records. In addition, depending on how data are entered, eliminating spaces can save many keystrokes.

The disadvantage is that files recorded without these spaces can be

```
--------1---------2---------3--------4
AB12AIRBUS-300198710655
B001BOEING-747197711542
B003BOEING-707197107777
B014BOEING-747198210856
B015BOEING-767198809689
D901DC-9      197515724
D101DC-10     198007938
```

Figure 2.2a Input records of the file AIRCRAFT-IN.

```
--------1---------2- --------3---------4
XXXXXXXXXXXXXX9999999V99
XXXXXXXXXXXXXX9999999V99
```

Figure 2.2b Record layout for the input file.

```
01   AIRCRAFT-RECORD-IN.
     05 AC-AIRCRAFT-ID-IN    PIC X(04).
     05 AC-MAKE-IN           PIC X(10).
     05 AC-YEAR-BUILT-IN     PIC 9(04).
     05 AC-HOURLY-COST-IN    PIC 9(03)V99.
```

Figure 2.2c Specification of matching input area (buffer area) identifier AIRCRAFT-RECORD-IN used to receive records from the input file.

```
AB12     AIRBUS-300    1987    10655
B001     BOEING-747    1977    11542
B003     BOEING-707    1971    07777
B014     BOEING-747    1982    10856
B015     BOEING-767    1988    09689
D901     DC-9          1975    15724
D101     DC-10         1980    07938
```

Figure 2.2d A version of the input file with spaces inserted to make it easier for humans to read.

difficult for humans to read. But then, if you think about it, no human being can read the characters on a tape or disk. They are recorded in a magnetic code that we cannot sense. So it actually makes no difference to us, for purposes of readability, whether there are spaces between the fields on disk or not. If we want to see the records in a disk file, we get a program to read them and then either print them out or display them on a screen. And in that case, the program can easily insert spaces between the fields printed to permit ease of readability. This is exactly what the program in Figure 2.4 does in printing the output data in Figure 2.3a.

The input file has four fields

The fields of the input file are:

Field 1   Aircraft identification code
Field 2   Aircraft type
Field 3   Year aircraft was built
Field 4   Average hourly maintenance costs, in dollars (three digits) and cents

Decimal points are not stored on disk or tape

Notice the last field of the input file. There is a five-digit field, but there is no period to show that the last two digits are fractional, denoting cents. It is normal not to store decimal points on tape and disk, since they would waste space.

In addition, identifiers used for computation in memory do not use a character space to store the decimal point. A decimal point marker, which takes up only 1 bit of memory space, is denoted in a PICTURE clause by V. This marker is stored in memory instead. Thus, the last field of an input record will take up five digits, and these five digits will be read into the identifier AC-HOURLY-COST-IN, defined as

```
05 AC-HOURLY-COST-IN    PIC  9(03)V99.
```

It follows that the five-digit field on disk exactly matches the five-digit memory location called AC-HOURLY-COST-IN. But in addition, because of the marker stored after the third digit in the version in memory, the processor knows where the decimal point is supposed to be. *The decimal point simply does not occupy a character space — only a single bit taken from another character that does not use that bit.*

Decimal point markers do not print

The decimal point marker, denoted by V, is said to be an implicit decimal point. It will not print. After reading the first record into the input area identifier AIRCRAFT-RECORD-IN (see Figure 2.3c), if you printed the contents of AC-HOURLY-COST-IN, you would see

10655, *not* 106.55

To print a decimal point you must use a decimal point edit symbol in the PICTURE of the identifier to be printed.

Edit symbols are often printed

For each line of the body of the report in Figure 2.3a there is a corresponding record in the input file. Each such line is called a *detail line*. A detail line is normally contructed in a working storage identifier before printing. In

```
--------1---------2---------3---------4--------5
AGE OF FLEET IN 1990


ID          TYPE             AGE    MAINTENANCE


AB12        AIRBUS-300       03     $106.55
B001        BOEING-747       13     $115.42
B003        BOEING-707       19     $ 77.77
B014        BOEING-747       08     $108.56
B015        BOEING-767       02     $ 96.89
D901        DC-9             15     $157.24
D101        DC-10            10     $ 79.38
```

Figure 2.3a Output data generated by the program in Figure 2.4 in
an output file REPORT-OUT.

Figure 2.3b Printer spacing chart for the ouput file REPORT-OUT.

```
01   DETAIL-LINE-OUT.
     05   FILLER              PIC X(01)      VALUE SPACES.
     05   DL-AIRCRAFT-ID-OUT  PIC X(04).
     05   FILLER              PIC X(05)      VALUE SPACES.
     05   DL-MAKE-OUT         PIC X(10).
     05   FILLER              PIC X(05)      VALUE SPACES.
     05   DL-AGE-OUT          PIC 9(02).
     05   FILLER              PIC X(05)      VALUE SPACES.
     05   DL-HOURLY-COST-OUT  PIC $Z99.99.
     05   FILLER              PIC X(94)      VALUE SPACES.
```

Figure 2.3c Structure of the identifier DETAIL-LINE-OUT from which a line
of the body of the report (a detail line) is printed.

this case, the identifier is usually called DETAIL-LINE-OUT. It contains
elementary identifiers, with values that will be printed. Here is the PIC-
TURE clause for DL-HOURLY-COST-OUT:

```
     05   DL-HOURLY-COST-OUT   PIC $Z99.99.
```

The $ sign is an *edit symbol*. It signifies that a character space in memory
will contain the $ character, which will be printed if the identifier contents
are printed.

The letter Z is another common edit symbol. It means that a leading zero will be recorded in memory as a space, instead of 0. If you print the contents of identifier X, defined with PIC 9(04), where X contains 42, you get 0042. If X is defined with PIC ZZZ9, however, and you print the contents of X, the leading zeros are suppressed and you get 42.

Another edit symbol is the period (.). Where used, it means a period is recorded in memory as a character and will be printed if the identifier contents are printed.

The symbol 9 means that a digit, 0, 1, 2, 3, 4, 5, 6, 7, 8, or 9, will be recorded. Understand that if the identifier K is defined with PIC 9(04), for example, and K contains zero, the contents of K will be 0000. Then if we print the contents of K, what will be printed is also 0000. Similarly if K contains 2, what is recorded in memory is 0002, and 0002 will be printed if the contents of K are printed.

From these considerations you can see that the preceding identifier, DL-HOURLY-COST-OUT containing edit symbols, takes up 1 + 1 + 2 + 1 + 2, or 7 character spaces in memory.

Edit symbols are used for printing characters associated with numeric quantities that are not used in computation. Thus they are used to edit, or "dress up", a numeric quantity before printing.

Suppose you have the MOVE statement

```
MOVE AC-HOURLY-COST-IN TO DL-HOURLY-COST-OUT.
```

If AC-HOURLY-COST-IN contains 08427, then DL-HOURLY-COST-OUT will contain $ 84.27 after the MOVE has been carried out. (Note that 08427 denotes 084.27 stored in memory with a decimal point marker.) The following shows some other results of the MOVE:

AC-HOURLY-COST-IN	DL-HOURLY-COST-OUT
00677	$ 6.77
12367	$123.67
04000	$ 40.00

The contents of DL-HOURLY-COST-OUT will be printed exactly as stored.

Another edit symbol is the comma (,). Thus, if you have

```
05   DL-QUANTITY-OUT      PIC ZZ9,999.
```

and you move the value 005678 to DL-QUANTITY-OUT, it will hold the value bb5,678, and that is what will print. Note that if you have

```
05   DL-QUANTITY-OUT      PIC ZZZ,Z99.
```

and move 000047 to DL-QUANTITY-OUT, instead of a comma a blank character will be stored. Thus, you get bbbb47 in memory, and that is what will print.

You cannot use identifiers with edit symbols in arithmetic operations

Suppose that X is numeric, defined with PIC 9(05)V99. The following is very wrong:

```
COMPUTE X = DL-HOURLY-COST-OUT + 1.          error!
```

DL-HOURLY-COST-OUT may be a numeric identifier, but it contains edit symbols, and so it cannot be used in arithmetic operations. However, you can MOVE a numeric value into an identifier containing edit symbols, and you can print its contents. It is also legal for an identifier containing edit symbols to receive the result of an arithmetic operation, but, as will be discussed shortly, this is poor practice.

An output file usually has headers

The output file in Figure 2.3a has both a report header and a set of column headers and there is a blank line after the report header line and after the column headers line.

```
AGE OF FLEET IN 1990                    ← report header
                                        ← blank line
ID      TYPE       AGE    MAINTENANCE ← column headers
                                        ← blank line
```

These have to be printed before the detail lines are printed. The instructions to do this are as follows:

```
WRITE REPORT-RECORD-OUT FROM REPORT-HEADER
      AFTER ADVANCING 1 LINE.
WRITE REPORT-RECORD-OUT FROM COLUMN-HEADER
      AFTER ADVANCING 2 LINES.
MOVE SPACES TO REPORT-RECORD-OUT.
WRITE REPORT-RECORD-OUT
      AFTER ADVANCING 1 LINE.
```

Here REPORT-RECORD-OUT is the output area (output buffer) identifier for the output file.

The working storage identifier REPORT-HEADER contains the report header AGE OF FLEET IN 1990:

```
01  REPORT-HEADER
    05  FILLER        PIC X(01)      VALUE SPACES.
    05  TITLE         PIC X(20)      VALUE 'AGE OF FLEET IN 1990'.
    05  FILLER        PIC X(112)     VALUE SPACES.
```

The value 'AGE OF FLEET IN 1990' is placed in the identifier TITLE using a VALUE clause. The value in TITLE never changes and never needs to be referenced in the program. So instead of TITLE you could use FILLER, as in

```
01  REPORT-HEADER.
    05  FILLER        PIC X(01)      VALUE SPACES.
    05  FILLER        PIC X(20)      VALUE 'AGE OF FLEET IN 1990'.
    05  FILLER        PIC X(112)     VALUE SPACES.
```

There is no difference, but FILLER is probably best.

The first WRITE statement causes the contents of REPORT-OUT to be moved to the output buffer identifier REPORT-RECORD-OUT and then printed.

```
WRITE REPORT-RECORD-OUT FROM REPORT-HEADER
      AFTER ADVANCING 1 LINE.
```

Notice that both REPORT-HEADER and REPORT-RECORD-OUT have matching lengths of 133 characters.

The AFTER ADVANCING 1 LINE clause means that the printer is instructed to advance one line and then print.

Next the column headers are printed. These remain in the identifier COLUMN-HEADER during execution of the program.

```
01   COLUMN-HEADER.
     05   FILLER           PIC X(01)      VALUE SPACES.
     05   FILLER           PIC X(09)      VALUE 'ID'.
     05   FILLER           PIC X(15)      VALUE 'TYPE'.
     05   FILLER           PIC X(07)      VALUE 'AGE'.
     05   FILLER           PIC X(11)      VALUE 'MAINTENANCE'.
     05   FILLER           PIC X(90)      VALUE SPACES.
```

Each column header is placed in a FILLER memory location by means of a VALUE clause.

The WRITE statement to print the column headers is

```
WRITE REPORT-RECORD-OUT FROM COLUMN-HEADER
          AFTER ADVANCING 2 LINES.
```

At the end of the previous WRITE the printer is positioned at the line just written (not the next blank line). AFTER ADVANCING 2 LINES causes it to advance two lines and print. This means that it leaves a single blank line between the report header and the column headers.

Finally, you need another blank line after the column headers. You get this by placing blanks in the output buffer identifier and printing it.

```
MOVE SPACES TO REPORT-RECORD-OUT.
WRITE REPORT-RECORD-OUT
          AFTER ADVANCING 1 LINE.
```

Make spacing charts for input and output data

With every program, remember to use a record layout for the input file and a printer spacing chart for the output file. If you do not, you are certain to make mistakes.

A program that processes one record after another in a simple loop

The program in Figure 2.4 is similar in structure to the program about the sale of parts in Figure 2.1, except for the headers output before the detail lines.

Once the headers have been printed, when an input record is read into the input buffer it is used to construct the detail line in DETAIL-LINE-OUT. This continues until the last input record has been processed. An attempt to read beyond the end of the file causes the AT END clause to be executed and the value 'NO' to be placed in MORE-RECORDS. This means that the paragraph 200-PROCESS-RECORD is not executed any further, the files are closed, and program execution stops.

Notice that this was used to print a detail line:

```
WRITE REPORT-RECORD-OUT FROM DETAIL-LINE-OUT
                AFTER ADVANCING 1 LINE.
```

Whereas, in the earlier program, only this was used:

```
WRITE REPORT-RECORD-OUT FROM DETAIL-LINE-OUT.
```

This would be wrong in the program in Figure 2.4, because the AFTER ADVANCING clause was used to print the headers. There is a rule here: If you use AFTER ADVANCING with one WRITE statement you must use it with all WRITE statements.

You can use ADD, SUBTRACT, MULTIPLY, and DIVIDE STATEMENTS

Notice that this was used in Figure 2.4:

```
SUBTRACT AC-YEAR-BUILT-IN FROM CURRENT-YEAR GIVING WS-AGE.
```

This is exactly equivalent to

```
COMPUTE WS-AGE = CURRENT-YEAR - AC-YEAR-BUILT-IN.
```

The following are also equivalent:

```
ADD A TO B GIVING C.
COMPUTE C = A + B.

MULTIPLY A BY B GIVING C.
COMPUTE C = A * B.

DIVIDE A INTO B GIVING C.
COMPUTE C = B / A.
```

RULES   **Interpreting syntax formats**

- A word in capitals is a COBOL reserved word.
- An underlined word is required to be in any statement or option specified.
- A lowercase word represents a user-defined word, such as an identifier or file name.
- One of the clauses within braces { } is required.
- A clause within brackets [] is optional.
- Ellipses (. . .) mean that the preceding entry or name may be repeated as often as required.
- Any punctuation included in the format is required.

```
      IDENTIFICATION DIVISION.
      PROGRAM-ID. SAMPLE2.
      AUTHOR. EIDOR EWING.
      INSTALLATION. AIR AMERICA HQ,
                    MIAMI.
      DATE-WRITTEN. 20 JANUARY, 1990.
                    REVISED 5 FEBRUARY, 1990.
      SECURITY. FOR THE EYES OF MAINTENANCE PERSONNEL.
              SECURITY CODE SD325 APPLIES.
    * SAMPLE2 - WILL GENERATE THE AGE OF AIRCRAFT IN THE FLEET IN 1990
      ENVIRONMENT DIVISION.
      INPUT-OUTPUT SECTION.
      FILE-CONTROL. SELECT AIRCRAFT-IN         ASSIGN TO UT-S-AIR90.
                    SELECT REPORT-OUT          ASSIGN TO UR-S-SYSPRINT.
      DATA DIVISION.
      FILE SECTION.
      FD  AIRCRAFT-IN                          LABEL RECORDS ARE STANDARD.
      01  AIRCRAFT-RECORD-IN.
          05 AC-AIRCRAFT-ID-IN    PIC X(04).
          05 AC-MAKE-IN           PIC X(10).
          05 AC-YEAR-BUILT-IN     PIC 9(04).
          05 AC-HOURLY-COST-IN    PIC 9(03)V99.
      FD  REPORT-OUT                           LABEL RECORDS ARE OMITTED.
      01  REPORT-RECORD-OUT       PIC X(133).
      WORKING-STORAGE SECTION.
      01  WS-WORK-AREAS.
          05 MORE-RECORDS         PIC X(03).
          05 CURRENT-YEAR         PIC 9(04)     VALUE 1990.
          05 WS-AGE               PIC 9(02).
      01  REPORT-HEADER.
          05 FILLER               PIC X(01)     VALUE SPACES.
          05 TITLE                PIC X(20)     VALUE 'AGE OF FLEET IN 1990'.
          05 FILLER               PIC X(112)    VALUE SPACES.
      01  COLUMN-HEADER.
          05 FILLER               PIC X(01)     VALUE SPACES.
          05 FILLER               PIC X(09)     VALUE 'ID'.
          05 FILLER               PIC X(15)     VALUE 'TYPE'.
          05 FILLER               PIC X(07)     VALUE 'AGE'.
          05 FILLER               PIC X(11)     VALUE 'MAINTENANCE'.
          05 FILLER               PIC X(90)     VALUE SPACES.
      01  DETAIL-LINE-OUT.
          05 FILLER               PIC X(01)     VALUE SPACES.
          05 DL-AIRCRAFT-ID-OUT   PIC X(04).
          05 FILLER               PIC X(05)     VALUE SPACES.
          05 DL-MAKE-OUT          PIC X(10).
          05 FILLER               PIC X(05)     VALUE SPACES.
          05 DL-AGE-OUT           PIC 9(02).
          05 FILLER               PIC X(05)     VALUE SPACES.
          05 DL-HOURLY-COST-OUT   PIC $Z99.99.
          05 FILLER               PIC X(94)     VALUE SPACES.
```

```
 PROCEDURE DIVISION.
 100-MAIN-MODULE.
* COMMENT:  CONTROLS OVERALL PROCESSING.
     OPEN INPUT AIRCRAFT-IN.
     OPEN OUTPUT REPORT-OUT.
     WRITE REPORT-RECORD-OUT FROM REPORT-HEADER
             AFTER ADVANCING 1 LINE.
     WRITE REPORT-RECORD-OUT FROM COLUMN-HEADER
             AFTER ADVANCING 2 LINES.
     MOVE SPACES TO REPORT-RECORD-OUT.
     WRITE REPORT-RECORD-OUT
             AFTER ADVANCING 1 LINE.
     MOVE 'YES' TO MORE-RECORDS.
     READ AIRCRAFT-IN
             AT END MOVE 'NO' TO MORE-RECORDS.
     PERFORM 200-PROCESS-RECORD
             UNTIL MORE-RECORDS = 'NO'.
     CLOSE AIRCRAFT-IN.
     CLOSE REPORT-OUT.
     STOP RUN.
 200-PROCESS-RECORD.
* PROCESSES A SINGLE INPUT RECORD.
     MOVE AC-AIRCRAFT-ID-IN TO DL-AIRCRAFT-ID-OUT.
     MOVE AC-MAKE-IN TO DL-MAKE-OUT.
     SUBTRACT AC-YEAR-BUILT-IN FROM CURRENT-YEAR GIVING WS-AGE.
     MOVE WS-AGE TO DL-AGE-OUT.
     MOVE AC-HOURLY-COST-IN TO DL-HOURLY-COST-OUT.
     WRITE REPORT-RECORD-OUT FROM DETAIL-LINE-OUT AFTER ADVANCING 1 LINE.
     READ AIRCRAFT-IN
             AT END MOVE 'NO' TO MORE-RECORDS.
```

Figure 2.4 *SAMPLE2, a program that processes the input file in Figure 2.2 to generate the output file in Figure 2.3.*

Summary

1. In the IDENTIFICATION DIVISION the name of the program is specified. It must not exceed eight characters. In addition, optional clauses that have the effect of comments may be included for documentation purposes.
2. In the ENVIRONMENT DIVISION each of the file names used in the program is linked to a physical file by means of a SELECT statement. The details of specifying the physical file name depend on the computer system being used.
3. When the output file is a printer file, different kinds of records can be output to the same file. For example, one kind of record can be a report header, another a set of column headers, and another a detail line. Each type of record is constructed in a working storage group identifier, and output via the same output area (output buffer) identifier using a WRITE statement. The AFTER ADVANCING clause is used with WRITE statements and printer files for skipping lines.

Key Terms

sequential access   detail line   edit symbol
direct access

Concept Review Questions

1. What does the SELECT statement do?
2. Explain the difference between a file name, as used in a COBOL program, and the physical file name, as known to the operating system.
3. Why are spaces not stored between fields in tape and disk files?
4. Why are periods not stored in numeric fields in tape and disk files?
5. Explain the concept of an implicit decimal point used with an identifier.
6. What is an edit symbol?
7. Why does an implicit decimal point not print?
8. Where should identifiers with edit symbols be used? Where should they not be used?
9. How is a header printed?
10. Explain how the output area (output buffer) identifier is involved in printing both headers and detail lines.
11. Explain how AFTER ADVANCING works.

COBOL Language Questions

1. What is wrong with

```
IDENTIFICATION DIVISION.
PROGRAM-ID. SAMPLEPROGRAM.
```

2. What is wrong with

```
IDENTIFICATION DIVISION.
PROGRAM ID. SAMPLE2.
```

3. What is wrong with

```
ENVIRONMENT DIVISION.
INPUT-OUTPUT SECTION.
FILE-CONTROL.  SELECT CUSTOMER-IN ASSIGN TO UT-S-CUST23.
SELECT ACCOUNT-OUT ASSIGN TO UR-S-PRINTER.
```

Fix it.

4. What is wrong with

```
ENVIRONMENT DIVISION.
INPUT-OUTPUT SECTION.
FILE-CONTROL.  SELECT CUSTOMER-IN ASSIGN TO UT-S-CUST23,
               SELECT ACCOUNT-OUT ASSIGN TO UR-S-PRINTER.
```

5. What is wrong with

```
ENVIRONMENT DIVISION.
INPUT-OUTPUT SECTION.
FILE-CONTROL.  SELECT CUSTOMER-IN ASSIGN TO DISKCUST.
...
READ DISKCUST
         AT END . . .
```

Fix it.

6. How many characters does a record of a printer file have?

7. If you have

```
WORKING STORAGE SECTION.
01 X                    PIC 9(03)V99        VALUE 16.42.
01 DETAIL-LINE-OUT.
   01 FILLER            PIC X               VALUE SPACE.
   01 DL-Y              PIC $ZZ9.99.
   01 FILLER            PIC X(125)          VALUE SPACES.
...
MOVE X TO DL-Y.
WRITE REPORT-RECORD-OUT FROM DETAIL-LINE-OUT.
```

what is printed?

8. Given

```
01 DETAIL-LINE-OUT.
   01 FILLER     PIC X                  VALUE SPACE.
   01 AMOUNT     PIC $ZZ999.99.
   01 FILLER     PIC X                  VALUE SPACE.
   01 COMMISSION PIC $Z9.99.
   01 FILLER     PIC ?
```

complete the FILLER entry.

9. If you have

```
01 DETAIL-LINE-OUT.
    01 FILLER          PIC X              VALUE SPACE.
    01 DL-Y            PIC 999V99         VALUE 15.47.
    01 FILLER          PIC X(127)         VALUE SPACES.
...
```

What is printed following this?

```
WRITE REPORT-RECORD-OUT FROM DETAIL-LINE-OUT.
```

10. Fix the following:

```
01 X                   PIC 9(03)V99       VALUE 16.42.
01 Y                   PIC 9(07)V9(05).
01 DETAIL-LINE-OUT.
    01 FILLER          PIC X              VALUE SPACE.
    01 DL-Y            PIC $ZZ9.99.
    01 FILLER          PIC X(126)         VALUE SPACES.
...
MOVE X TO DL-Y.
COMPUTE Y = DL-Y * DL-Y.
```

Programming Assignments

1. **Modification of an existing program to include editing of output fields and printing of headers**

   Modify the program in Figure 2.1. The input file is changed to

   ```
   W1        0020    0010
   W2        2015    0040
   W3456     0730    4000
   ```

   The output file is altered to include headings, suppress leading zeros, and include a dollar sign in the last field.

   ```
   --------1--------2--------3--------4--------5--------6
                    SALES REPORT


   PART-NUMBER   UNIT-PRICE   QUANTITY        TOTAL-COST

   W1                20          10         $      210
   W2              2015          40         $    80610
   W3456            730        4000         $   292010
   ```

   The printer spacing chart is

1	SALES REPORT			
2				
3	PART-NUMBER	UNIT-PRICE	QUANTITY	TOTAL-COST
4				
5	XXXXX	ZZZ9	ZZZ9	$ZZZZZZZZ9
6	XXXXX	ZZZ9	ZZZ9	$ZZZZZZZZ9
7	XXXXX	ZZZ9	ZZZ9	$ZZZZZZZZ9
8				

a. Enter the new input file.

b. Write and run the program.

2. A program to generate a report on the value of ships' cargoes

The input data are

```
---------1---------2---------3---------4---------5
BLUENOSE        240000OIL       2025
BALOCHSIDE      150500ORE       7550
DALSOHN         064400WHEAT     0480
```

The record layout for the input file is

```
---------1---------2---------3- ---------4---------5
XXXXXXXXXXXXXXX999999XXXXXXX99V99
XXXXXXXXXXXXXXX999999XXXXXXX99V99
XXXXXXXXXXXXXXX999999XXXXXXX99V99
```

The output file is

```
---------1---------2---------3---------4---------5---------6---------7
            SHIPPING REPORT

SHIP            CARGO   UNITS           UNIT            CARGO
NAME                                    PRICE           VALUE

BLUENOSE        OIL     240,000         20.25           $ 4,860,000.00
BALOCHSIDE      ORE     150,500         25.50           $ 3,837,750.00
DALSOHN         WHEAT    64,450         04.81           $   310,004.50
```

The printer spacing chart is

	1234567890	11111111112 0123456789	222222222 23456789	33 01	33333 23456	333 789	44 01	44444 23456	444 789	55 01	55555 23456	555 789	66 01	66666 23456	666 789	7 0
1		SHIPPING REPORT														
2																
3	SHIP	CARGO	UNITS				UNIT				CARGO					
4	NAME						PRICE				VALUE					
5																
6	XXXXXXXXXXXXXXX	XXXXXXXX	ZZZ,Z99				Z9.99				$ZZ,ZZZ,ZZ9.99					
7	XXXXXXXXXXXXXXX	XXXXXXXX	ZZZ,Z99				Z9.99				$ZZ,ZZZ,ZZ9.99					
8	XXXXXXXXXXXXXXX	XXXXXXXX	ZZZ,Z99				Z9.99				$ZZ,ZZZ,ZZ9.99					
9																

The value of the cargo is simply the number of units times the unit price.

a. Draw a flowchart for the processing.

b. Write a program for the processing.

3

THE COBOL
DATA DIVISION

OBJECTIVES

- To learn how to define and use group identifiers for receiving and constructing records.
- To learn to edit output data using edit identifiers.
- To learn to write COBOL programs with extensive DATA DIVISION specifications.

Literals are limited in size
Large alphanumeric literals can span several lines
Avoid extensive use of literals with MOVE and arithmetic statements
You can also initialize with figurative constants
You can also use INITIALIZE for initialization
FILLER specifications are commonly used for specifying fields in output records
A FILLER field can contain characters other than blanks
Edited identifiers are used to print numeric quantities including non-numeric symbols
An edited identifier cannot be used for arithmetic operations
Edit items take up space in memory
Edited identifiers are versatile
There are two ways to specify plus and minus signs
    Use of S with numeric identifiers
    Use of an explicit sign in a numeric identifier
    Use of + or - edit symbols to print a sign

3.3 A program development example
You can display the input file so it can be understood
Processing complies with some simple business rules
The output data is a printer report on the state of each account
The data in input records are highly condensed
The calculations involve simple interest
Auxiliary identifiers are needed for calculations
The calculations are repeated for each input record
Use ROUNDED to have a computed result rounded off
Intermediate results require sufficient decimal places
Specify complex headers one item at a time using FILLER fields

THE COBOL DATA DIVISION

THIS CHAPTER PRESENTS the essentials of writing the DATA DIVISION of COBOL programs. In the DATA DIVISION there can be up to four sections, although only two are commonly needed: the FILE SECTION and the WORKING-STORAGE SECTION. These are covered in this chapter. In the FILE SECTION, you closely specify properties of the files involved, as well as the identifiers for records located in the input and output areas of memory. In contrast, in the WORKING-STORAGE SECTION, you specify identifiers for data located in the working storage part of memory.

First, the rules involved in writing these two sections are illustrated with a version of the program SAMPLE2, developed in Chapter 2. The new version of the program, called SAMPLE3, has the normal, short IDENTIFICATION DIVISION used in the remainder of this book. At the end of the chapter a more extensive program is developed.

The input data for SAMPLE3 are in Figure 3.1a, the output data are in Figure 3.1b and the program is in Figure 3.1c. Recall that the program reads records, each describing an aircraft, including the year it was built, and outputs each record with a new field giving the age of the aircraft in 1990.

3.1
You specify file details and buffer record identifiers in the FILE SECTION

THE FILE SECTION FROM the program in Figure 3.1c specifies the input file AIRCRAFT-IN and its associated input area record identifier AIRCRAFT-RECORD-IN. It also specifies the output (printer) file REPORT-OUT and its associated output area record identifier REPORT-RECORD-OUT.

```
DATA DIVISION.
FILE SECTION.
FD  AIRCRAFT-IN         LABEL RECORDS ARE STANDARD.
01  AIRCRAFT-RECORD-IN.
     05 AC-AIRCRAFT-ID-IN              PIC X(04).
     05 AC-MAKE-IN                     PIC X(10).
     05 AC-YEAR-BUILT-IN               PIC 9(04).
     05 AC-HOURLY-COST-IN              PIC 9(03)V9(02).
FD  REPORT-OUT         LABEL RECORDS ARE OMITTED.
01  REPORT-RECORD-OUT             PIC X(133).
```

This is an example of a simple FILE SECTION. There are two types of entry. First you define a file using an FD (file definition) entry and specify the file labels involved. Next you define the input (or output) area record identifier to be used with the file. Another term for an input or output area record is *buffer record*.

The term input or output area record, or buffer record, is useful for distinguishing between a record defined in the FILE SECTION (such as AIRCRAFT-RECORD-IN) and a record defined in the WORKING-STORAGE SECTION (such as DETAIL-LINE-OUT, in Figure 3.1c). In reality, a buffer record is the contents of an identifier located within a buffer in memory. For each file used with a program, there is an input buffer if the file is an input file, and an output buffer if the file is an output file. The latest record read is always to be found in the input buffer record identifier, and a record being written is always moved to the output buffer record identifier before transfer to the output device.

```
          ---------1---------2---------3---------4
          <--><--------><--><--->
          AB12AIRBUS-300198710655
          B001BOEING-747197711542
          B003BOEING-707197107777
          B014BOEING-747198210856
          B015BOEING-767198809689
          D901DC-9       197515724
          D101DC-10      198007938
```

Figure 3.1a *Input data to SAMPLE3 program in Figure 3.1c*

```
          AGE OF FLEET IN 1990

          ID        TYPE           AGE     MAINTENANCE

          AB12      AIRBUS-300     03      $106.55
          B001      BOEING-747     13      $115.42
          B003      BOEING-707     19      $ 77.77
          B014      BOEING-747     08      $108.56
          B015      BOEING-767     02      $ 96.89
          D901      DC-9           15      $157.24
          D101      DC-10          10      $ 79.38
```

Figure 3.1b *Output data generated by SAMPLE3 program.*

```cobol
        IDENTIFICATION DIVISION.
        PROGRAM-ID. SAMPLE3.
      * SAMPLE3 - WILL GENERATE THE AGE OF AIRCRAFT IN THE FLEET IN 1990
        ENVIRONMENT DIVISION.
        INPUT-OUTPUT SECTION.
        FILE-CONTROL.
                    SELECT AIRCRAFT-IN     ASSIGN TO UT-S-AIR90.
                    SELECT REPORT-OUT      ASSIGN TO UR-S-SYSPRINT.
        DATA DIVISION.
        FILE SECTION.
        FD  AIRCRAFT-IN                     LABEL RECORDS ARE STANDARD.
        01  AIRCRAFT-RECORD-IN.
            05 AC-AIRCRAFT-ID-IN   PIC X(04).
            05 AC-MAKE-IN          PIC X(10).
            05 AC-YEAR-BUILT-IN    PIC 9(04).
            05 AC-HOURLY-COST-IN   PIC 999V99.
        FD  REPORT-OUT                       LABEL RECORDS ARE OMITTED.
        01  REPORT-RECORD-OUT      PIC X(133).
        WORKING-STORAGE SECTION.
        01 WS-WORK-AREAS.
            05   MORE-RECORDS       PIC X(03).
            05   CURRENT-YEAR       PIC 9(04)       VALUE 1990.
            05   WS-AGE             PIC 9(02).
        01  REPORT-HEADER.
            05   FILLER             PIC X(01)       VALUE SPACES.
            05   TITLE              PIC X(20)       VALUE 'AGE OF FLEET IN 1990'.
            05   FILLER             PIC X(112)      VALUE SPACES.
        01  COLUMN-HEADER.
            05   FILLER             PIC X(01)       VALUE SPACES.
            05   FILLER             PIC X(09)       VALUE 'ID'.
            05   FILLER             PIC X(15)       VALUE 'TYPE'.
            05   FILLER             PIC X(07)       VALUE 'AGE'.
            05   FILLER             PIC X(11)       VALUE 'MAINTENANCE'.
            05   FILLER             PIC X(90)       VALUE SPACES.
        01  DETAIL-LINE-OUT.
            05   FILLER             PIC X(01)       VALUE SPACES.
            05   DL-AIRCRAFT-ID-OUT PIC X(04).
            05   FILLER             PIC X(05)       VALUE SPACES.
            05   DL-MAKE-OUT        PIC X(10).
            05   FILLER             PIC X(05)       VALUE SPACES.
            05   DL-AGE-OUT         PIC 9(02).
            05   FILLER             PIC X(05)       VALUE SPACES.
            05   DL-HOURLY-COST-OUT PIC $Z99.99.
            05   FILLER             PIC X(94)       VALUE SPACES.
        PROCEDURE DIVISION.
        100-MAIN-MODULE.
      * COMMENT:  CONTROLS OVERALL PROCESSING.
            OPEN INPUT AIRCRAFT-IN.
            OPEN OUTPUT REPORT-OUT.
            WRITE REPORT-RECORD-OUT FROM REPORT-HEADER
                    AFTER ADVANCING 1 LINE.
```

```
        WRITE REPORT-RECORD-OUT FROM COLUMN-HEADER
                AFTER ADVANCING 2 LINES.
        MOVE SPACES TO REPORT-RECORD-OUT.
        WRITE REPORT-RECORD-OUT
                AFTER ADVANCING 1 LINE.
        MOVE 'YES' TO MORE-RECORDS.
        READ AIRCRAFT-IN
            AT END MOVE 'NO' TO MORE-RECORDS.
        PERFORM 200-PROCESS-RECORD UNTIL MORE-RECORDS = 'NO'.
        CLOSE AIRCRAFT-IN.
        CLOSE REPORT-OUT.
        STOP RUN.
  200-PROCESS-RECORD.
* PROCESSES A SINGLE INPUT RECORD.
        MOVE AC-AIRCRAFT-ID-IN TO DL-AIRCRAFT-ID-OUT.
        MOVE AC-MAKE-IN TO DL-MAKE-OUT.
        SUBTRACT AC-YEAR-BUILT-IN FROM CURRENT-YEAR GIVING WS-AGE.
        MOVE WS-AGE TO DL-AGE-OUT.
        MOVE AC-HOURLY-COST-IN TO DL-HOURLY-COST-OUT.
        WRITE REPORT-RECORD-OUT FROM DETAIL-LINE-OUT
        READ AIRCRAFT-IN
            AT END MOVE 'NO' TO MORE-RECORDS.
```

Figure 3.1c SAMPLE3 program.

If you are still having trouble with the concept of input and output buffers (input and output areas), imagine that memory is like a factory floor. The input buffer corresponds to an unloading bay for trucks bringing parts to the factory from a warehouse (the input file). The output buffer corresponds to the loading bay for loading finished products into trucks that transfer them to permanent storage in a finished products warehouse (output file). Goods that are partially completed (work in progress) are on the factory floor (working storage). This is illustrated in Figure 3.2.

The FD entry has a file label entry

In its simplest form the FD entry looks like this:

SYNTAX

$$\underline{\text{FD}}\text{ file-name }\underline{\text{LABEL RECORDS}}\text{ ARE }\begin{Bmatrix}\underline{\text{STANDARD}}\\\underline{\text{OMITTED}}\end{Bmatrix}$$

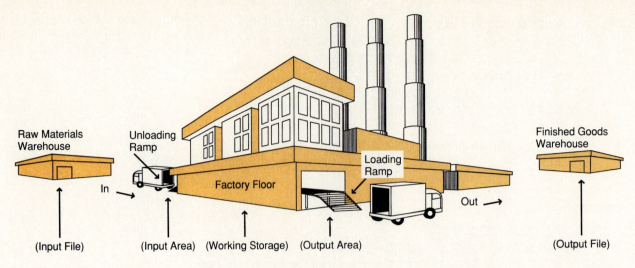

Raw Materials
Warehouse

Unloading
Ramp

Finished Goods
Warehouse

In →

Factory Floor

Loading
Ramp

Out →

(Input File)   (Input Area) (Working Storage) (Output Area)   (Output File)

Figure 3.2 *Data processing is analogous to manufacturing.*

The braces indicate a choice. Thus you can have

```
FD AIRCRAFT-IN   LABEL RECORDS ARE STANDARD.
```

or

```
FD AIRCRAFT-IN   LABEL RECORDS ARE OMITTED.
```

Actually, since COBOL 85 was introduced, if the choice is STANDARD the entire LABEL RECORDS clause can be omitted. However, practice has been to include the clause at all times, since it is wise to consider the question of file labels. Note the following:

- Tape files almost always have labels. Disk files always have labels.
- Printer, punch card, and terminal files never have labels.

The following sections explain what a file label is and how a file gets one.

What are file labels?

A label is a special record with a standard format that contains information about the file. For example, a label may contain information about how much data are in the file. Typically file labels are 80 characters long. They are of no concern to the programmer, except that the COBOL programmer has to know whether the file has one. Typically a file with labels will have a header label record at the beginning of the file and a trailer label record at the end of the file.

You can create a file with a label

When a new file is created by means of a COBOL program and WRITE commands, the file will be created with labels if LABEL RECORDS ARE STAN-

DARD has been coded in the FD statement for that file. Otherwise it will not get labels. It is normal practice to create tape and disk files with labels via programs.

The file labels you specify vary

In practice, to specify a file label in a COBOL program, you do the following in the FD statement:

- When creating a new disk or tape file, use STANDARD.
- When reading an old disk or tape file originally created with labels, use STANDARD.
- When reading a disk file created with an editor, use STANDARD.
- When reading a terminal input file or a card input file, use OMITTED.
- When creating a file to be displayed on a printer or terminal screen, use OMITTED.

If you use STANDARD when a tape or disk file is being created, instructions that are part of the overall computer system (the operating system) will create the header and trailer labels. If you use STANDARD when a file with labels is being read, instructions from the operating system will check both the header and trailer labels for possible errors. Labels thus serve a useful purpose.

There are other useful FD entries

In addition to the LABEL records clause, some additional optional entries are possible. The two most important are given in the more complete FD syntax box here:

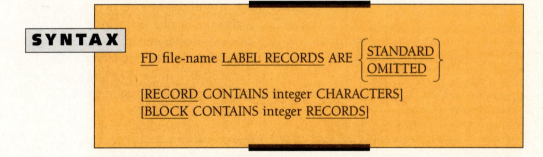

SYNTAX

FD file-name LABEL RECORDS ARE { STANDARD / OMITTED }

[RECORD CONTAINS integer CHARACTERS]
[BLOCK CONTAINS integer RECORDS]

The RECORD CONTAINS clause specifies the space taken up by a record of the file. The space is measured as the number of characters or bytes taken up by a record in memory.

The BLOCK CONTAINS clause gives the number of records that form a *block* in the device storage medium. A block of records is transmitted between buffer and storage during input and output of records with disks and tape. A block typically contains between 10 and 250 records. Records are said to be blocked on disk and tape. Records transmitted to printers and terminals, or transmitted from a card reader, are *not* blocked.

Blocks of records increase efficiency

Only disk and tape files can have records stored in blocks. Blocking allows records to be stored with less space and allows for faster movement of records between memory and device. Systems analysts normally decide how many records will form a block (the *blocking factor*) when a file is to be created.

The BLOCK CONTAINS statement is optional since system programmers can also specify the block size in special operating system commands (part of Job Control Language with IBM systems) that are not part of COBOL. However, if you want records on a new tape or disk file to be blocked, you may insert the BLOCK CONTAINS clause. Thus, for a new disk file AIRCRAFT-MASTER to be created by the program, you might code

```
FD AIRCRAFT-MASTER   LABEL RECORDS ARE STANDARD
                     RECORD CONTAINS 23 CHARACTERS
                     BLOCK CONTAINS 260 RECORDS.
```

As a practical matter, an efficient size for a block is usually about 6000 characters. Block size is the blocking factor times record length. Thus, AIRCRAFT-MASTER, has a block size of 23 × 260, or 5980 characters.

The Block Concept

Figure 3.3 shows records on tape blocked with a blocking factor of four. Within a block there is no unused space; thus, one record continues into the next. Between blocks there is a very large empty space or an interblock gap, often equivalent to 960 blank characters (sometimes more). When the tape is not being read it is stopped and the read/write head mechanism is over the interblock gap. When the next block is read, the tape moves quickly until the head is over the next gap. Thus the gaps between the blocks give the head a place to "park" between readings of blocks.

If a block is small compared with the interblock gap size, or if records are not blocked at all (blocking factor unity or one record per block), the amount of space taken up by interblock gaps becomes very large relative to the space taken up by the actual records. That would mean that the space

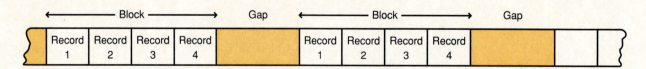

Figure 3.3 *Blocked records on tape. Each block is made up of records (the blocking factor). A large gap separates the blocks. When the tape is stopped, the read/write head is parked adjacent to the gap. Records on disk are also blocked. With disk and tape records are always blocked, although the blocking factor can be unity.*

on the tape is very poorly utilized. Similar, but more complex, blocks are used with disks. Remember that only disk and tape records can be blocked.

Buffer record identifiers can be elementary or group

In the simplest case, the input or output area record definition is as follows:

01 record-name   PICTURE-clause.

Thus, the FILE SECTION entry for the output file REPORT-OUT in Figure 3.1c is

```
FILE SECTION.
. . . .
FD   REPORT-OUT                    LABEL RECORDS ARE OMITTED.
01   REPORT-RECORD-OUT       PIC X(133).
```

Recall how data are moved in that program (shown in Figure 3.4). A record moves from the file AIRCRAFT-IN to the input area record AIRCRAFT-RECORD-IN. Then data are placed in the working storage record DETAIL-LINE-OUT, which is moved via the output area record REPORT-RECORD-OUT to the output device. With such processing there is no need to specify the individual fields of the output area record REPORT-RECORD-OUT, since no instruction in the PROCEDURE DIVISION ever refers to them.

In contrast, the input record in AIRCRAFT-RECORD-IN has fields that either must be moved individually to DETAIL-LINE-OUT or must be used in computations. This means that instructions in the PROCEDURE DIVI-SION refer to the individual fields of AIRCRAFT-RECORD-IN, so these fields must be specified in the definition of the input area record AIRCRAFT-RECORD-IN. Thus, the FILE SECTION specification for the file AIRCRAFT-IN must include field definitions.

```
DATA DIVISION.
FILE SECTION.
FD   AIRCRAFT-IN                   LABEL RECORDS ARE STANDARD.
01   AIRCRAFT-RECORD-IN.
       05 AC-AIRCRAFT-ID-IN        PIC X(04).
       05 AC-MAKE-IN               PIC X(10).
       05 AC-YEAR-BUILT-IN         PIC 9(04).
       05 AC-HOURLY-COST-IN        PIC 9(03)V99.
```

The name AIRCRAFT-RECORD-IN in the program in Figure 3.1c names a location in that part of memory called the input area (or input buffer). The name AC-MAKE-IN names a location of memory within the location called AIRCRAFT-RECORD-IN. The names of locations in memory are called data items or identifiers. In this book we use the term identifier.

Because AIRCRAFT-RECORD-IN names a location that contains other named locations, it is called a *group identifier*. AC-MAKE-IN is called an *elementary identifier*, since it is a location in memory that does not contain any other named locations.

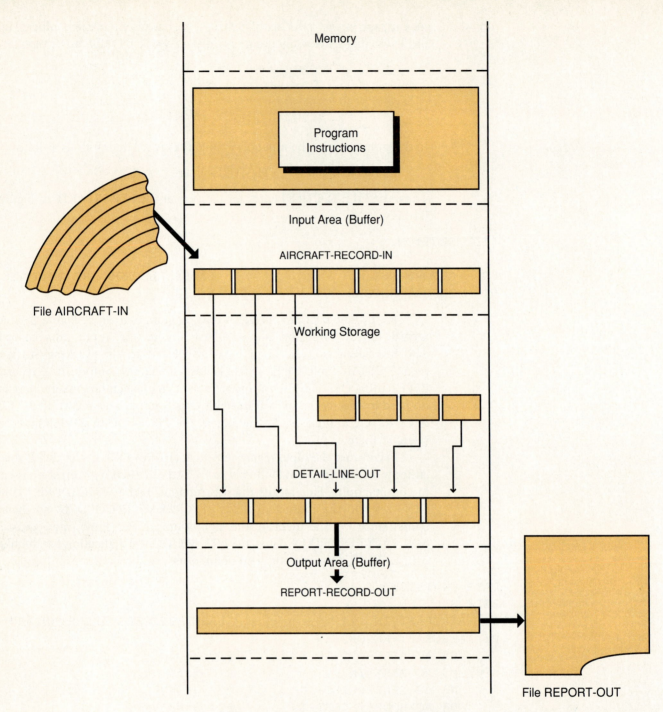

Figure 3.4 *Data move from input file to input area (input buffer), to working storage, and then, via the output area (output buffer), to the output file (compare with Figure 3.2).*

Identifiers with contents that will be printed should be 133 characters

In the program in Figure 3.1c the identifier REPORT-RECORD-OUT is used to hold an output buffer record that will be transmitted to the printer. Consequently, it is specified with PIC X(133).

An output buffer record that will be printed should be specified with PIC X(133), when a standard line printer is used, to match the printer's line length. A standard line printer prints lines exactly 132 characters in length. However, usually a line of 133 characters should be transmitted to the printer, with a blank in the first space for printer control purposes. The system places one of a special group of control characters in the first space. This character tells the printer to skip one, two, or more lines. The control character is not printed.

Note that with some computer installations, the extra blank character for printer control does not have to be specified. In such cases you use PIC X(132).

Identifiers are used with both buffer record and working-storage locations

Identifiers, both group and elementary, are used for naming the locations of records in both the buffers and working-storage parts of memory. In the program in Figure 3.1c, AIRCRAFT-RECORD-IN is an example of a group identifier that names a location for a record in the input area of memory; DETAIL-LINE-OUT names a location that holds a record in the working-storage part of memory.

The rules for specifying identifiers are the same for buffers and working storage

The rules for specifying identifiers are the same whether you are defining an identifier in the FILE SECTION (for a record in an input or output area) or in the WORKING-STORAGE SECTION (for records and other items of data located in working storage). The rules concern

- Names for identifiers
- Specification of level numbers for elementary and group identifiers
- PICTURE clauses for elementary identifiers

When naming identifiers consider both rules and style conventions

As you have seen, an identifier identifies or denotes a location in memory that can hold data. The programmer defines identifiers in the FILE SECTION or WORKING-STORAGE SECTION of a program, to suit the data being processed. An arbitrary name is created by the programmer for each identifier used.

There are rules for naming identifiers. A name cannot be completely arbitrary. The following simple rule can be used:

Identifier name composition   An identifier name can be up to 30 characters long, can contain letters, digits, and hyphens, must not contain any blanks, and must have at least one alphabetic character.

The complete set of rules is shown here:

RULES	**Naming Identifiers**

- A name may have up to 30 characters.
- A character may be a letter, digit, or hyphen. Blank characters (embedded blanks) are not permitted.
- The first and last characters must not be hyphens.
- One of the characters must be alphabetic.
- The name must not form a COBOL reserved word, such as WRITE, MOVE, LINE-COUNTER, and so on. Appendix 2 contains a list of reserved words.

The following are thus valid identifier names:

TAX   YEAR-91
CUSTOMER-RECEIPT   1990-TAXABLE-INCOME
AIRCRAFT-DATA-IN   A600
AIRCRAFT-100

The following are invalid identifier names:

NAME	PROBLEM
CUSTOMER NAME	Embedded blank
4689	No alphabetic character
AIRCRAFT#	# is not a letter
PREMIUM%	% is not a letter
LINE-COUNTER	COBOL reserved word

In addition to the COBOL syntax rules, the following style conventions are commonly observed:

- Each identifier used with an incoming record should end with "-IN," for example, AIRCRAFT-RECORD-IN, AC-MAKE-IN.
- Each identifier used with an outgoing record should end with "-OUT," for example, REPORT-RECORD-OUT, DETAIL-LINE-OUT, DL-MAKE-OUT.

Every identifier must be defined with a level number

Each identifier specified in the DATA DIVISION must be preceded by a level number. If the identifier is not part of a group identifier, the level number 01 should be used. For example, the program in Figure 3.1c had

```
01    REPORT-RECORD-OUT              PIC X(133).
```
(from FILE SECTION)

An elementary identifier within a group identifier has a level number greater than 01.

```
01    AIRCRAFT-RECORD-IN.
      05 AC-AIRCRAFT-ID-IN           PIC X(04).
      05 AC-MAKE-IN                  PIC X(10).
      05 AC-YEAR-BUILT-IN            PIC 9(04).
      05 AC-HOURLY-COST-IN           PIC 9(03)V99.
```

Notice that there is no PICTURE clause with the group identifier AIRCRAFT-RECORD-IN. However, all elementary identifiers, no matter what the level numbers, must have a PICTURE clause.

All identifiers at the same level must have the same level number. Thus, the following would be wrong:

```
01  AIRCRAFT-RECORD-IN.
    05 AC-AIRCRAFT-ID-IN           PIC X(04).
    10 AC-MAKE-IN                  PIC X(10).         error!
    05 AC-YEAR-BUILT-IN            PIC 9(04).
    15 AC-HOURLY-COST-IN           PIC 9(03)V99.      error!
```

You can collect identifiers into subsidiary group identifiers

You can have group identifiers within group identifiers. Thus, a group identifier can contain elementary identifiers plus subsidiary group identifiers, which in turn contain elementary group identifiers. For example, you could take the specification for AIRCRAFT-RECORD-IN from the program in Figure 3.1c

```
01    AIRCRAFT-RECORD-IN.
      05 AC-AIRCRAFT-ID-IN           PIC X(04).
      05 AC-MAKE-IN                  PIC X(10).
      05 AC-YEAR-BUILT-IN            PIC 9(04).
      05 AC-HOURLY-COST-IN           PIC 9(03)V99.
```

and change it to

```
01    AIRCRAFT-RECORD-IN.
      05 AC-AIRCRAFT-ID-IN           PIC X(04).
      05 AC-MAKE-IN                  PIC X(10).
      05 AC-TECHNICAL-DATA-IN.
         10 AC-YEAR-BUILT-IN         PIC 9(04).
         10 AC-HOURLY-COST-IN        PIC 9(03)V99.
```

Here AC-TECHNICAL-DATA-IN is a subsidiary group identifier. It can be an advantage to combine identifiers into subsidiary group identifiers if the identifiers have to be moved as a group (a *group MOVE*). Thus, if you have

```
      ...
      05 AC-TECHNICAL-DATA-IN.
         10 AC-YEAR-BUILT-IN         PIC 9(04).
         10 AC-HOURLY-COST-IN        PIC 9(03)V99.
```

```
01 WS-REFERENCE-DATA.
    05 WS-YEAR-BUILT                          PIC 9(04).
    05 WS-HOURLY-COST                          PIC 9(03)V99.
```

you can have a group MOVE with:

```
MOVE AC-TECHNICAL-DATA-IN TO WS-REFERENCE-DATA.
```

This MOVE would cause the contents of all the identifiers making up AC-TECHNICAL-DATA-IN to be moved to the identifiers in WS-REFERENCE-DATA. This group MOVE is equivalent to

```
MOVE AC-YEAR-BUILT-IN TO WS-YEAR-BUILT.
MOVE AC-HOURLY-COST-IN TO WS-HOURLY-COST.
```

For the group MOVE to take place without error, WS-REFERENCE-DATA should be a group identifier with exactly the same structure as AC-TECHNICAL-DATA-IN, except for the names of the identifiers.

In carrying out such a group MOVE, the identifiers within the group identifiers are ignored, and the contents of AC-TECHNICAL-DATA-IN would simply be moved character by character (from left to right) to WS-REFERENCE-DATA. This is the basic characteristic of a group MOVE, and should be remembered.

Use level numbers 01, 05, 10, 15 . . .

It is conventional to use level numbers 01, 05, 10, 15, and so on, for the levels within a group identifier. This makes it simple to insert levels between those used originally, should it later become necessary. Level numbers 01, 02, 03, 04, and so on, are allowable, but if you use these numbers, a later insertion could make it necessary to change most of the other level numbers in the group. Level numbers up to level 49 may be used with COBOL 85.

You can collect 01 elementary identifiers into a group identifier

It is common practice to group 01-level working storage identifiers under a single group identifier, for ease of reference. For example, instead of the following

```
01 INTEREST-ON-PRINCIPAL      PIC 9(06)V9(05).
01 INTEREST-ON-DEPOSIT        PIC 9(06)V9(05).
01 TOTAL-INTEREST             PIC 9(06)V9(05).
01 NEW-PRINCIPAL-COMPUTED     PIC 9(07)V9(02).
01 WS-PRINCIPAL-IN            PIC 9(07)V9(05).
01 WS-DEPOSIT-IN              PIC 9(07)V9(05).
01 MORE-RECORDS               PIC X(02)        VALUE 'YES'.
```

which could have been used in the program in Figure 3.8, you should code:

```
01 WS-WORK-AREAS.
    05 INTEREST-ON-PRINCIPAL    PIC 9(06)V9(05).
    05 INTEREST-ON-DEPOSIT      PIC 9(06)V9(05).
    05 TOTAL-INTEREST           PIC 9(06)V9(05).
    05 NEW-PRINCIPAL-COMPUTED   PIC 9(07)V9(02).
    05 WS-PRINCIPAL-IN          PIC 9(07)V9(05).
    05 WS-DEPOSIT-IN            PIC 9(07)V9(05).
    05 MORE-RECORDS             PIC X(02)        VALUE 'YES'.
```

PICTURE specifications give the size and data type of a memory location

Every identifier names a location in memory, which will have a specific size measured in characters or bytes. The PICTURE clause specifies how large the memory location named by an identifier will be. It also specifies the type of data the memory location can hold. An identifier is specified as naming a memory location capable of holding only one of three distinct types of data:

- **Alphabetic data** These data consist of only letters of the alphabet or blanks. An identifier capable of holding six letters would be specified with PICTURE A(06). PIC A(n) is rarely used, however. Alphabetic identifiers cannot be used in arithmetic operations.
- **Alphanumeric data** These data can be made up of characters of any type, including letters of the alphabet, punctuation symbols, digits, or blanks. An identifier capable of holding six characters would be specified with a PICTURE X(06). Alphanumeric identifiers cannot be used in arithmetic operations.
- **Numeric data** If a named memory location can hold only data consisting of digits (and possibly an implied decimal point), it may be specified with a PICTURE clause that specifies a 9 for each digit, for example, 9999 or 9(04) for a four-digit integer. The specification character V is used for an implied decimal point, for example, 9999V99 or 9(04)V9(02) for a memory location that can hold a number up to 9999.99. However, more complex PICTURE specifications for identifiers for numeric data are often needed.

Alphabetic types are almost never specified in PICTURE clauses since alphanumeric types can be used instead. This book uses only alphanumeric and numeric types of data with identifiers.

Alphanumeric identifiers cannot be used for arithmetic operations

Some examples of alphanumeric identifier specifications from the program in Figure 3.1c are

```
01   AIRCRAFT-RECORD-IN.
     05 AC-AIRCRAFT-ID-IN        PIC X(04).
     05 AC-MAKE-IN               PIC X(10).
     ...
...
01   REPORT-RECORD-OUT          PIC X(42).
```

(from FILE SECTION)

```
...
01   DETAIL-LINE-OUT.
     05   FILLER                 PIC X(01) VALUE SPACES.
     05   DL-AIRCRAFT-ID-OUT     PIC X(04).
     05   FILLER                 PIC X(05) VALUE SPACES.
     05   DL-MAKE-OUT            PIC X(10).
     05   FILLER                 PIC X(05) VALUE SPACES.
     ...
```

(from WORKING-STORAGE SECTION)

In these identifier specifications, X(*n*) denotes *n* alphanumeric characters, that is, characters that can be digits, letters, punctuation symbols, or blanks. Thus the specification PIC X(12) could be for an identifier that would hold the date '02 JULY 1990'.

You cannot carry out arithmetic operations on the contents of any identifier specified with PIC X(*n*), at least directly. (There is, however, an indirect way of doing it, in rare circumstances, with the REDEFINES option.) Thus, if you were to write the following COBOL sentence in a program

```
COMPUTE AC-MAKE-IN = 1990 - AC-YEAR-BUILT-IN.
```

the compiler will notice that you are employing an alphanumeric identifier (AC-MAKE-IN) in an arithmetic operation and reject the program.

Data are left justified in alphanumeric identifiers

A value placed in an ordinary alphanumeric identifier always sits at the left side, with unused space to the right occupied by blanks. Alphanumeric data are thus said to be stored *left justified*. This has two practical effects.

First, when you print the value, the blanks appear on the right. Thus, if CUSTOMER-NAME holds the value 'MARY SMITH', when you print a record containing CUSTOMER-NAME, it appears as

```
MARY SMITH
```

with 15 blanks (not printed) to the right. It does not appear as

```
                MARY SMITH
```

with the 15 blanks on the left.

Second, if you put a name that is too long into CUSTOMER-NAME, it goes in left to right and thus is truncated on the right. Suppose CUSTOMER-NAME was assigned "President Dwight Eisenhower," as in

```
MOVE 'PRESIDENT DWIGHT EISENHOWER' TO CUSTOMER-NAME.
```

Then when you print a record containing CUSTOMER-NAME you would get

```
PRESIDENT DWIGHT EISENHOW
```

with truncation on the right, and not

```
ESIDENT DWIGHT EISENHOWER
```

with truncation on the left.

Simple numeric specifications are used for identifiers participating in arithmetic operations

Numeric data identifiers can be specified in a number of different ways. A common way is to use a memory byte (a character space) for each digit, but with no character space for a decimal point. Instead a marker occupying zero bytes is used for the decimal point. This method of specifying numeric identifiers is used with identifiers that will be used in arithmetic operations.

- PIC 9(n) means n digits to the left of the decimal point are allowed.
- PIC 9(n)V9(m) specifies n digits to the left of the decimal point and m digits to the right of the decimal point. The V means a decimal point, but no character space is stored for it. The V specifies an implicit decimal point, for which only a marker is recorded in memory. This marker (denoted by V) occupies no character space. The marker V must be used if the identifier will be used in arithmetic operations.
- PIC V9(m) means m digits right of the decimal point.

The maximum number of digits allowed is 18.

The following gives examples of what specification would be required for identifiers to hold the following numbers:

15678	PIC 9(05)	or	PIC 99999
0015678	PIC 9(07)	or	PIC 9999999
8	PIC 9(01)	or	PIC 9
678.23	PIC 9(03)V9(02)	or	PIC 9(03)V99
0.23	PIC 9V9(02)	or	PIC 9V99
0.0023	PIC 9V9(04)	or	PIC 9V9999
.00234	PIC V9(05)	or	PIC V99999

STYLE HINT It is recommended that you use parentheses to specify the number of digits, as in 9(07). This allows easy alignment of the specification on the decimal point, whether implicit or absent. Such neat alignment makes it easier to spot errors and add up the number of characters in a group identifier.

Within the group identifier AIRCRAFT-RECORD-IN in the program in Figure 3.1c, there are two numeric identifiers that could be used in computations

```
01   AIRCRAFT-RECORD-IN.
     ...
     ...
     05 AC-YEAR-BUILT-IN              PIC 9(04).
     05 AC-HOURLY-COST-IN             PIC 9(03)V99.
```

3.2
The WORKING-STORAGE SECTION has definitions of elementary and group identifiers

THE WORKING-STORAGE SECTION of the DATA DIVISION has essentially only one kind of entry, namely the specification of identifiers, either elementary or group. These identifiers are used with "work in progress." (See Figure 3.4 again.) In contrast, the identifiers that name the locations in the input and output areas that will receive and transmit incoming and outgoing records, respectively, are specified in the FILE SECTION of the DATA DIVISION. All other identifiers are specified in the WORKING-STORAGE SECTION.

In the program in Figure 3.1c we had the WORKING-STORAGE SECTION entries as shown here:

```
DATA DIVISION.
...
WORKING-STORAGE SECTION.
01 WS-WORK-AREAS.
     05   MORE-RECORDS        PIC X(03).
     05   CURRENT-YEAR        PIC 9(04)        VALUE 1990.
     05   WS-AGE              PIC 9(02).
01 REPORT-HEADER.
     05   FILLER              PIC X(01)        VALUE SPACES.
     05   TITLE               PIC X(20)        VALUE 'AGE OF FLEET IN 1990'.
     05   FILLER              PIC X(112)       VALUE SPACES.
01 COLUMN-HEADER.
     05   FILLER              PIC X(01)        VALUE SPACES.
     05   FILLER              PIC X(09)        VALUE 'ID'.
     05   FILLER              PIC X(15)        VALUE 'TYPE'.
     05   FILLER              PIC X(07)        VALUE 'AGE'.
     05   FILLER              PIC X(11)        VALUE 'MAINTENANCE'.
     05   FILLER              PIC X(90)        VALUE SPACES.
01 DETAIL-LINE-OUT.
     05   FILLER              PIC X(01)        VALUE SPACES.
     05 DL-AIRCRAFT-ID-OUT    PIC X(04).
     05   FILLER              PIC X(05)        VALUE SPACES.
     05 DL-MAKE-OUT           PIC X(10).
     05   FILLER              PIC X(05)        VALUE SPACES.
     05 DL-AGE-OUT            PIC 9(02).
     05   FILLER              PIC X(05)        VALUE SPACES.
     05 DL-HOURLY-COST-OUT    PIC $Z99.99.
     05   FILLER              PIC X(94)        VALUE SPACES.
```

The rules for identifier names, level numbers, and PICTURE clauses given earlier for identifiers specified in the FILE SECTION also apply to identifiers specified in the WORKING-STORAGE SECTION. Some additional specifications are common with working-storage identifiers.

- VALUE clauses are used to initialize the values in identifiers.
- FILLER specifications are used, mostly to provide blank fields in output records.
- Edit identifiers are used for printing numeric data.

A VALUE clause initializes the value in an identifier

A VALUE clause is used to place a value in an identifier before any instructions from the PROCEDURE DIVISION are carried out. A VALUE clause is said to initialize an identifier.

A VALUE clause consists of the word VALUE followed by either a literal numeric value or a literal alphanumeric value enclosed in quotation marks (usually single but double at some installations). Some examples involving initialization with alphanumeric values, from the program in Figure 3.1c, are as follows:

```
01   REPORT-HEADER.
     05   FILLER              PIC X(01)      VALUE SPACES.
     05   TITLE               PIC X(20)      VALUE 'AGE OF FLEET IN 1990'.
     05   FILLER              PIC X(112)     VALUE SPACES.
01   COLUMN-HEADER.
     05   FILLER              PIC X(01)      VALUE SPACES.
     05   FILLER              PIC X(09)      VALUE 'ID'.
     05   FILLER              PIC X(15)      VALUE 'TYPE'.
     05   FILLER              PIC X(07)      VALUE 'AGE'.
     05   FILLER              PIC X(11)      VALUE 'MAINTENANCE'.
     05   FILLER              PIC X(90)      VALUE SPACES.
```

An example of initialization with a numeric value is

```
05   CURRENT-YEAR            PIC 9(04) VALUE 1990.
```

Literals are simply values

The alphanumeric and numeric values used in VALUE clauses are known as *literals*. (With other programming languages literals are called program constants.) Thus 'AGE OF FLEET IN 1990' is an alphanumeric literal, whereas 1990 is a numeric literal.

Literals can also be used in the PROCEDURE DIVISION with MOVE statements. An example from the program in Figure 3.1c is

```
MOVE 'YES' TO MORE-RECORDS.
```

Here 'YES' is an alphanumeric literal. Instead of using a VALUE clause to place an initial value in an identifier, a MOVE statement can be used instead. Thus

```
        05  CURRENT-YEAR    PIC 9(04)     VALUE 1990.
```

could have been written instead of

```
        05  CURRENT-YEAR    PIC 9(04).
     PROCEDURE DIVISION.
     100-MAIN-MODULE.
         MOVE 1990 TO CURRENT-YEAR.
```

Generally, if the value in an identifier remains constant throughout the execution of a program, such as the value in CURRENT-YEAR, it is common practice to initialize the identifier by means of a VALUE clause. Use of literals within the PROCEDURE DIVISION should be kept to a minimum.

Alphanumeric literals must be enclosed in quotes (usually single, but sometimes double). Some examples of literals are

ALPHANUMERIC LITERALS	NUMERIC LITERALS
'SMITH'	47
'JOAN P. SMITH'	-37
'8TH MARCH, 1987'	0045
'8/03/1987'	57.23
'XYZ COMPANY, INC.'	-47.678

A numeric literal may not contain a comma or a $, and must end with a digit. The following are invalid numeric literals:

2,562.76	error! Contains comma
$356.33	error! Contains $
45.35-	error! Minus sign at right
78.	error! Ends in decimal point

Literals are limited in size

The maximum length of a numeric literal is 18 digits. The maximum length of an alphanumeric literal is 160 characters.

Large alphanumeric literals can span several lines

When a literal is so large that it continues on to the next line, a continuation hyphen (-) must be placed in column 7 (the column before the A margin). Some examples are

```
 Cont. A    B                          COBOL Statement
 7    8    12   16   20   24   28   32   36   40   44   48   52   56   60   64   68   72
    01  DOCUMENT-TITLE      PIC X(100) VALUE       'A REPORT ON THE FAC
 -      'TORS INFLUENCING PURCHASE OF CONSUMER DURABLES'.

        MOVE 'TOTAL ANNUAL REVENUE FROM COMPUTER CONTROLLED MACHINE T
 -      'OOLS IN THE PLASTICS INDUSTRY' TO HEADER2-OUT.
```

These examples observe the following rules:

- Quotes are only at the beginning and end of the literal and in the B area at the beginning of the continuation text.
- Write to column 72 before going to the next line.
- Place a hyphen (-) in column 7 of the next line.
- Recommence writing the literal in column 13 or later, that is, anywhere in area B after the initial quote.

There is an additional section on literals in Chapter 4, in connection with the use of the MOVE statement.

Avoid extensive use of literals with MOVE and arithmetic statements

Literals are constant values. However convenient, it is bad practice to use a literal value in the PROCEDURE DIVISION of a program, if (a) there is a possibility that the value will have to be changed in the future, or (b) the same literal has to be used in many different places.

Instead of using a literal in the PROCEDURE DIVISION, with such statements as MOVE and COMPUTE, use a VALUE clause to place the literal in an identifier, and use that identifier in the PROCEDURE DIVISION. Thus, instead of

```
COMPUTE INTEREST = PRINCIPAL * 0.08.
...
MOVE 0.08 TO DL-INTEREST-RATE-OUT.
```

you should code

```
01 WS-INTEREST-RATE      PIC  9(02)V99       VALUE 0.08.
...
        COMPUTE INTEREST = PRINCIPAL * WS-INTEREST-RATE.
...
        MOVE WS-INTEREST-RATE TO DL-INTEREST-RATE-OUT.
```

You can also initialize with figurative constants

Suppose you want to initialize the numeric identifier TOTAL to zero. You could write

```
01 TOTAL     PIC 9(04) VALUE 0.
```

Or, alternatively, you could code

```
01 TOTAL     PIC 9(04) VALUE ZEROS.
```

Similarly, if you wanted to initialize the alphanumeric identifier ADDRESS with blanks you could write

```
01 ADDRESS     PIC X(20) VALUE '                    '.
```

However, it is more convenient to specify

```
01 ADDRESS      PIC X(20) VALUE SPACES.
```

ZEROS and SPACES are *figurative constants*. Figurative constants can also be used in the PROCEDURE DIVISION with the MOVE statement

```
MOVE SPACES TO ADDRESS-OUT.
MOVE ZEROS TO TOTAL2.
```

You can also use INITIALIZE for initialization

Suppose you have the working-storage identifier GROUPA

```
01 GROUPA.
    05 GA-ALPHA1     PIC X(10).
    05 GA-ALPHA2     PIC X(15).
    05 GA-NUMBER1    PIC 9(04).
    05 GA-NUMBER2    PIC 9(06).
```

You can set the alphanumeric identifiers to blank values and numeric identifiers to zero values simply by placing

```
INITIALIZE GROUPA.
```

in the PROCEDURE DIVISION. This statement is useful in cases in which you need to reinitialize a group identifier after it has been used to hold non-blank and non-zero values (this is a COBOL 85 feature).

FILLER specifications are commonly used for specifying fields in output records

In the specification of the group identifier DETAIL-LINE-OUT, a FILLER specification is used to specify space between the identifiers DL-AIRCRAFT-ID-OUT, DL-MAKE-OUT, DL-AGE-OUT, and DL-COST-OUT in the working-storage part of memory. The exact amount of space is specified by a PIC X(*n*) clause, where *n* is the number of characters of space. The VALUE SPACES clause specifies that blanks are to be inserted into the FILLER space. A VALUE SPACES clause must be used with a FILLER specification if the contents of the group identifier are to be printed, as shown here:

```
01  DETAIL-LINE-OUT.
    05  FILLER              PIC X(01)      VALUE SPACES.
    05  DL-AIRCRAFT-ID-OUT  PIC X(04).
    05  FILLER              PIC X(05)      VALUE SPACES.
    05  DL-MAKE-OUT         PIC X(10).
    05  FILLER              PIC X(05)      VALUE SPACES.
    05  DL-AGE-OUT          PIC 9(02).
    05  FILLER              PIC X(05)      VALUE SPACES.
    05  DL-HOURLY-COST-OUT  PIC $Z99.99.
    05  FILLER              PIC X(94)      VALUE SPACES.
```

Note that the word FILLER can be omitted (in COBOL 85), as follows:

```
01   DETAIL-LINE-OUT.
     05                        PIC X(01)      VALUE SPACES.
     05   DL-AIRCRAFT-ID-OUT   PIC X(04).
     05                        PIC X(05)      VALUE SPACES.
     05   DL-MAKE-OUT          PIC X(10).
     05                        PIC X(05)      VALUE SPACES.
     05   DL-AGE-OUT           PIC 9(02).
     05                        PIC X(05)      VALUE SPACES.
     05   DL-HOURLY-COST-OUT   PIC $Z99.99.
     05                        PIC X(94)      VALUE SPACES.
```

Remember that FILLER is not an identifier and may not be used in any instructions in the PROCEDURE DIVISION. The following is not allowed:

```
MOVE FILLER TO UNKNOWN-PERSON.          error!
```

Occasionally, FILLER specifications are used with an input area identifier (specified in the FILE SECTION), if there are spaces between the record fields in the input file, for example:

```
DATA DIVISION.
FILE SECTION.
FD   AIRCRAFT-IN          LABEL RECORDS ARE STANDARD.
01   AIRCRAFT-RECORD-IN.
     05   AC-AIRCRAFT-ID-IN   PIC X(04).
     05   FILLER              PIC X(08).
     05   AC-MAKE-IN          PIC X(10).
     05   FILLER              PIC X(08).
     05   AC-YEAR-BUILT-IN    PIC 9(04).
     05   FILLER              PIC X(08).
     05   AC-HOURLY-COST-IN   PIC 999V99.
```

You could use this specification if the records on the input tape file were formatted according to this:

```
---------1---------2---------3---------4---------5
AB12      AIRBUS-300      1987         10655
B001      BOEING-747      1977         11542
B003      BOEING-707      1971         07777
. . .
```

A VALUE SPACES clause is not used since the blank spaces will be placed in AIRCRAFT-RECORD-IN when the record is read from the tape, blank spaces and all.

A FILLER field can contain characters other than blanks

FILLER fields can contain data other than blanks. For example, referring to the program in Figure 3.1c, we could have specified:

```
01   REPORT-TITLE
     05  FILLER      PIC X(01)      VALUE SPACES.
     05  TITLE       PIC X(20)      VALUE 'AGE OF FLEET IN 1990'.
     05  FILLER      PIC X(112)     VALUE SPACES.

              as

01   REPORT-TITLE
     05  FILLER      PIC X(01)      VALUE SPACES.
     05  FILLER      PIC X(20)      VALUE 'AGE OF FLEET IN 1990'.
     05  FILLER      PIC X(112)     VALUE SPACES.
```

The TITLE field is not referred to in the PROCEDURE DIVISION instructions. So the name FILLER is adequate for the field. Such FILLER fields are common in group identifiers with contents that are report or column headings.

Edited identifiers are used to print numeric quantities including non-numeric symbols

Edited identifiers are a special class of numeric identifiers. They are usually found in a group identifier, such as DETAIL-LINE-OUT in the program in Figure 3.1c, that is to be printed. The identifier DL-HOURLY-COST-OUT is the only edited identifier used in that program.

```
01   DETAIL-LINE-OUT.
     ...
     05  DL-HOURLY-COST-OUT      PIC $Z99.99.
```

DL-HOURLY-COST-OUT could have been given the same PICTURE clause as AC-HOURLY-COST-IN, namely 999V99, in which case, DL-HOURLY-COST-OUT would have been a normal numeric identifier. The following contrasts the printed results:

Printed Values of DL-HOURLY-COST-OUT

$Z99.99 USED	999V99 USED
$106.55	10655
$115.42	11542
$ 77.77	07777
$108.56	10856
$ 96.87	09687
$157.24	15724
$ 79.38	07938

If you print a normal numeric identifier, you get only digits. Even the internal marker in memory for the decimal point is not printed. If you want a decimal point printed, you must place a decimal point in the PICTURE specification between the correct digits. A decimal point is an *edit symbol*.

The inclusion of one or more edit symbols in a PICTURE specification makes the identifier involved an edited identifier. Another common edited symbol is the $. Where it is included, a dollar sign is printed.

Another common edit symbol is the Z symbol, called the leading zero suppression symbol. It has the same effect as a 9, except that the leading zero(s) is not printed. When an edited identifier is viewed as a field in a record, it is often called an *edited field*.

Another common edit item is the comma. Thus, if you wanted to print quantities ranging between $1,000.00 and $99,999.99, you could use PICTURE $Z9,999.99. There are other edit items as well; these are described in Chapter 7.

An edited identifier cannot be used for arithmetic operations

An edited identifier is used only for numeric quantities that are to be printed, never for arithmetic operations. However, you can assign or move a value to an edited identifier, using the MOVE command, for example:

```
      05   SALARY-OUT          PIC $ZZ9,999.99.
...
      PROCEDURE DIVISION.
...
          MOVE 35678.86 TO SALARY-OUT.
```

If the value in SALARY-OUT was printed, you would get $ 35,678.86.

Edit items take up space in memory

The dollar sign and decimal point are edit items, and each occupies a character space in memory. Thus the identifier DL-HOURLY-COST-OUT, specified as

```
      05   DL-HOURLY-COST-OUT     PIC $Z99.99.
```

takes up 1 + 3 + 1 + 2, or 7 characters of space. You should check that the length of DETAIL-LINE-OUT in memory must be 1 + 4 + 5 + 10 + 5 + 2 + 5 + 7 + 94, or 133 characters.

Edited identifiers are versatile

There is a great deal to know about edited identifiers in COBOL. This section concentrates on simple edit identifiers that use the dollar sign, decimal point, leading zero suppression, and the comma. The following gives some examples of what would be printed for different identifiers with different numeric contents.

PICTURE	SPACE OCCUPIED	NUMERIC CONTENT	AS PRINTED
1. 9(04).99	7	0043.77	0043.77
2. 9(04)V99	6	0043.77	004377
3. $9(03)	4	240	$240
4. $9(03)	4	75	$075
5. $9(03).99	7	570.88	$570.88
6. $9(3).99	7	6.70	$006.70
7. $99,999.99	10	14567.89	$14,567.89
8. ZZ99.99	7	0007.87	07.87
9. $ZZ,999.99	10	04678.43	$ 4,678.43
10. $ZZ,ZZ9.99	10	00000.67	$ 0.67

In example 1, you see that the number held is much smaller than capacity. When printed the leading zeros are printed too.

In example 2, the edit item for the decimal point has not been included, so when the value is printed no decimal point is included.

In example 4, the leading zero appears preceded by the dollar sign. The same thing happens in example 6.

In example 7, a comma is printed. In example 9 there is a comma and suppression of a leading zero.

There are two ways to specify plus and minus signs

There are two ways of specifying plus and minus signs with numeric identifiers. One way is for numeric quantities used with arithmetic operations and involves the S symbol. The other way is with numeric quantities to be printed, that is, edit identifiers, and involves the + and - edit symbols.

Use of S with Numeric Identifiers

Suppose that you are dealing with a numeric identifier used in arithmetic operations, such as NEW-PRINCIPAL-COMPUTED. You could specify it as

```
01   NEW-PRINCIPAL-COMPUTED          PIC 9(08)V99.
```

This specification is fine as long as the value is positive. However, no provision has been made for the possibility that the value could be negative. To do that, you simply place an S at the beginning of the PICTURE specification

```
01   NEW-PRINCIPAL-COMPUTED          PIC S9(08)V99.
```

This identifier still takes up 10 characters or bytes of space in memory. No space is used for either the decimal point or the sign. Instead a marker is used for each.

The identifier NEW-PRINCIPAL-COMPUTED can be used for computations. It should not be printed, however. Recall that each digit is allocated a byte in memory, which is made up of 8 bits. To store the sign, one of the bits for the right-most digit is usually altered, so that only a sign marker is stored.

Suppose we place a negative number in the identifier NEW-PRINCIPAL-COMPUTED,

```
MOVE -82.75 TO NEW-PRINCIPAL-COMPUTED.
```

and then try to print the value in this identifier, using a WRITE statement. The correct value will not print. The decimal point does not print, as explained earlier, because it is not allocated a space in memory. (With printing, the contents of the identifier in memory are simply copied, space by space.) The sign does not print either because it is not allocated a space in memory.

Use of an Explicit Sign in a Numeric Identifier

Sometimes you need an explicit sign, which occupies a character space, in an identifier used for arithmetic purposes. The most common case arises when there are signs in input records. For example, suppose you have input records such as:

```
1 SMITH      -47 82
2 THOMPSON   -04 62
3 XXXXXXXXXS99V99
4
```

with record layout information as shown. A record could contain information about a customer and a negative balance of an account. In that case the sign is explicitly stored on disk or tape, and will be transferred to the input area when a record is read. The fields of the input area must match the input record character by character, and so you would code

```
01 ACCOUNT-IN.
   05 AC-CUSTOMER-IN    PIC  X(09).
   05 AC-BALANCE-IN     PIC S9(02)V99 SIGN LEADING SEPARATE.
```

The identifier ACCOUNT-IN would be 14 characters long, as an input record is. AC-BALANCE-IN would be 5 characters long, with the first character being occupied by the sign. If you have to use this value in extensive computations, it would be best to move it to another version with only the sign marker, and use that version in computations, as shown here:

```
01 WS-BALANCE         PIC S9(02)99.
...
MOVE AC-BALANCE-IN TO WS-BALANCE.
```

Use of + or - Edit Symbols to Print a Sign

To have a sign (and the decimal point) printed correctly, the value must be in a properly constructed edited identifier. To have the sign printed normally, whether plus or minus, you must place a + at beginning of the PIC specification, for example:

```
01  INTEREST        PIC  +9(3).99.
```

If you have this in the PROCEDURE DIVISION

```
MOVE 78.87 TO INTEREST.
```

and then have the value of INTEREST printed, you get +078.87 printed. If you used

```
MOVE -23.4 TO INTEREST.
```

and have the value of INTEREST printed, you get -023.40 printed.

If you want the sign printed only if it is negative, a - should be placed at the beginning of the PIC specification

```
01  INTEREST          PIC  -9(3).99.
```

Here, if INTEREST has the value 078.87, then 078.87 is printed. But if it has the value -23.4, then -023.40 is printed.

Note that the space taken up in memory by an identifier with PICTURE +9(3).99 or -9(3).99 is seven characters. Both the sign and the decimal point are allocated a space.

RULES Signs

Computational numeric identifiers Use the symbol S, as in PIC S9(8)V99. S does not occupy a character or byte of space in memory; it is stored as a sign marker by altering a bit of the byte for the right-most digit. The sign does not print and the right-most digit may print incorrectly.

Explicit sign with input data Use S and SIGN LEADING SEPARATE, as in PIC S9(02)V99 SIGN LEADING SEPARATE.

Edited identifiers, for use in printing If both + and - signs are to print, use the + symbol, as in PIC +9(3)V99. The sign occupies a single character space in memory.

If only - signs should print, use the - symbol, as in PIC -9(3)V99. The sign occupies a single character space in memory.

PICTURE specifications should be neatly aligned, as this enables errors to be spotted more easily. Do not use PIC X(4), for example; use PIC X(04) instead, as shown here:

```
01  AIRCRAFT-RECORD-IN.
       05 AC-AIRCRAFT-ID-IN        PIC X(04).
       05 AC-MAKE-IN               PIC X(10).
       05 AC-YEAR-BUILT-IN         PIC 9(04).
       05 AC-HOURLY-COST-IN        PIC 9(03)V99.
       05 AC-RUNNING-COST-IN       PIC 9(05)V99.
       05 AC-FUEL-RESERVE          PIC 9(03)V9.
```

Align on the implied decimal point as well. In the case of edit identifiers, align on the actual decimal point. VALUE clauses should also be aligned along the vertical. Many installations have quite strict style recommendations along these lines.

3.3
A program development example

IN THIS EXAMPLE, each record of a disk input file, ACCOUNT-IN, at a savings bank describes the state of a retirement savings account belonging to a customer. The processing generates a report, REPORT-OUT, showing interest earned for each customer during the preceding month.

You can display the input file so it can be understood

Some records of the input file are displayed in Figure 3.5. In this display, the data are in a clear format for ease of understanding; not in the format in which they are actually stored on disk.

CUSTOMER NAME	OLD PRINCIPAL	DEPOSIT	DAYS DEPOSITED	PRINCIPAL INTEREST RATE	DEPOSIT INTEREST RATE
M. Smith	100,000.00	500.00	20	08.00	06.00
P.F. Cole	5,000.00	100.00	10	09.00	07.00
L. Yee	2,500.00	150.00	05	08.50	06.00

Figure 3.5 *Input records for financial data.*

A record contains the principal in the account at the beginning of a month (Old Principal), the amount deposited (Deposit) during the month, the number of days since the deposit was made (Days Deposited), the annual interest rate applicable to the old principal (Principal Interest Rate) and the annual interest rate applicable to the deposit (Deposit Interest Rate).

Processing complies with some simple business rules

Some simple rules apply to an account.

- It is a retirement account. No withdrawals are allowed.
- Only one deposit is allowed per month.
- Interest is computed as follows at the end of each month:
  a. The interest for one month is computed for the old principal.
  b. Interest is computed for the deposit for the number of days since the deposit was made.
- The interest rates applicable vary from one customer to another, depending on the choice of investment medium. Different interest rates are used with the deposit and the old principal.

Each month, a program called SAMPLE4 at the bank generates a report that shows the new principal for each account and the interest earned. The new principal is computed by adding the deposit and the interest earned to the old principal.

The output data is a printer report on the state of each account

The initial lines of the monthly report generated from the data in Figure 3.5 are shown in Figure 3.6a. The layout of the fields of the group identifier DETAIL-LINE-OUT, from which each detail line was printed, is shown in Figure 3.6b. Details of the WORKING-STORAGE SECTION specification of DETAIL-LINE-OUT are shown in Figure 3.6c.

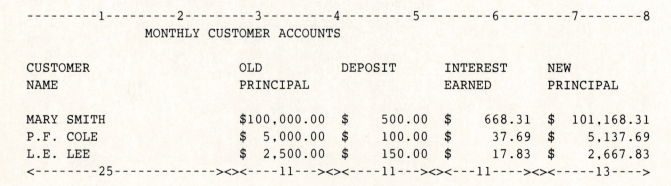

```
---------1---------2---------3---------4---------5---------6---------7-------8
                  MONTHLY CUSTOMER ACCOUNTS


CUSTOMER                   OLD         DEPOSIT        INTEREST      NEW
NAME                       PRINCIPAL                  EARNED        PRINCIPAL


MARY SMITH                 $100,000.00  $    500.00   $    668.31   $   101,168.31
P.F. COLE                  $  5,000.00  $    100.00   $     37.69   $     5,137.69
L.E. LEE                   $  2,500.00  $    150.00   $     17.83   $     2,667.83
<--------25------------><><----11---><><----11---><><---11----><><-----13---->
```

Figure 3.6a *Format of the printer file REPORT-OUT.*

COMPREHENSIVE STRUCTURED COBOL

```
          1         1 1 1 1 1 1 1 1 1 1 2 2 2 2 2 2 2 2 2 2 3 3 3 3 3 3 3 3 3 3 4 4 4 4 4 4 4 4 4 4 5 5 5 5 5 5 5 5 5 5 6 6 6 6 6 6 6 6 6 6 7 7 7 7 7 7 7 7 7 8 0
  1 2 3 4 5 6 7 8 9 0 1 2 3 4 5 6 7 8 9 0 1 2 3 4 5 6 7 8 9 0 1 2 3 4 5 6 7 8 9 0 1 2 3 4 5 6 7 8 9 0 1 2 3 4 5 6 7 8 9 0 1 2 3 4 5 6 7 8 9 0 1 2 3 4 5 6 7 8 9 0
 1           MONTHLY CUSTOMER ACCOUNTS
 2
 3 CUSTOMER                      OLD             DEPOSIT          INTEREST        NEW
 4 NAME                          PRINCIPAL                        EARNED          PRINCIPAL
 5
 6 XXXXXXXXXXXXXXXXXXXXXXXXX     $ZZZ,ZZ9.99     $ZZZ,ZZZ.ZZ      $ZZZ,ZZ9.99     $Z,ZZZ,ZZ9.99
 7 XXXXXXXXXXXXXXXXXXXXXXXXX     $ZZZ,ZZ9.99     $ZZZ,ZZZ.ZZ      $ZZZ,ZZ9.99     $Z,ZZZ,ZZ9.99
 8 XXXXXXXXXXXXXXXXXXXXXXXXX     $ZZZ,ZZ9.99     $ZZZ,ZZZ.ZZ      $ZZZ,ZZ9.99     $Z,ZZZ,ZZ9.99
 9 XXXXXXXXXXXXXXXXXXXXXXXXX     $ZZZ,ZZ9.99     $ZZZ,ZZZ.ZZ      $ZZZ,ZZ9.99     $Z,ZZZ,ZZ9.99
10 <--------25-------------><><----11---><><-----11--><><---11----><><-----13---->
11
12
```

Figure 3.6b *Printer spacing chart for lines of REPORT-OUT.*

```
01    DETAIL-LINE-OUT.
      05 FILLER                          PIC X(01)         VALUE SPACES.
      05 DL-CUSTOMER-NAME-OUT             PIC X(25).
      05 FILLER                          PIC X(02)         VALUE SPACES.
      05 DL-OLD-PRINCIPAL-OUT             PIC $ZZZ,ZZ9.99.
      05 FILLER                          PIC X(02)         VALUE SPACES.
      05 DL-DEPOSIT-OUT                   PIC $ZZZ,ZZ9.99.
      05 FILLER                          PIC X(02)         VALUE SPACES.
      05 DL-INTEREST-OUT                  PIC $ZZZ,ZZ9.99.
      05 FILLER                          PIC X(02)         VALUE SPACES.
      05 DL-NEW-PRINCIPAL-OUT             PIC $Z,ZZZ,ZZ9.99.
      05 FILLER                          PIC X(53)         VALUE SPACES.
```

Figure 3.6c *Details of the group identifier DETAIL-LINE-OUT.*

The data in input records are highly condensed

The exact format of the input data as stored on the disk is shown in Figure 3.7a. There are no spaces stored between the numeric fields, nor are there any commas or decimal points stored. This is common practice with data stored on tape and disk, in order to conserve space. However, when data are displayed on paper in that format, they are hard to read. Compare Figure 3.7a with Figure 3.5. The length of each input field is listed in Figure 3.7b, along with the names of the fields in the input area identifier ACCOUNT-RECORD-IN, which receives an input record. Details of the FILE-SECTION specification of ACCOUNT-RECORD-IN are given in Figure 3.7c.

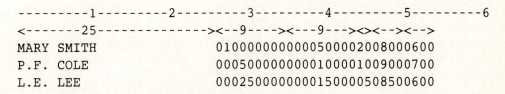

```
---------1---------2---------3---------4---------5---------6
<-------25-------------><--9----><---9---><><--><><-->
MARY SMITH              0100000000000500002008000600
P.F. COLE               0005000000000100001009000700
L.E. LEE                0002500000000150000508500600
```

Figure 3.7a *Format of the records in the input file ACCOUNT-IN.*

```
---------1---------2---------3---------4---------5---------6
XXXXXXXXXXXXXXXXXXXXXXXXX999999999999999999999999999
<-------25--------------><--9----><---9---><><--><-->
```

Figure 3.7b *Record layout for an input record.*

```
01   ACCOUNT-RECORD-IN.
     05   AR-CUSTOMER-NAME-IN            PIC X(25).
     05   AR-PRINCIPAL-IN                PIC 9(07)V9(02).
     05   AR-DEPOSIT-IN                  PIC 9(07)V9(02).
     05   AR-DEPOSIT-DAYS-IN             PIC 9(02).
     05   AR-PRINCIPAL-RATE-IN           PIC 9(02)V9(02).
     05   AR-DEPOSIT-RATE-IN             PIC 9(02)V9(02).
```

Figure 3.7c *Details of matching ACCOUNT-RECORD-IN.*

The calculations involve simple interest

The calculations carried out in the program are the same for each record. They are tedious for humans, but typical of the kind of things computers are used for. Consider the calculation for the first record for Mary Smith:

Old principal:	$100,000.00
Interest for one month at an annual rate of 8%: (100,000 * 8.00 / 100) / 12, which is:	$ 666.666
Deposit:	$ 500.00
Interest for 20 days at an annual rate of 6%: (500 * 6.00 / 100) (20 / 365), which is:	$ 1.6438
Total Interest:	$ 668.3098
Total Interest rounded to nearest cent:	$ 668.31
New principal: (old principal + deposit + total interest):	$101,168.31

Auxiliary identifiers are needed for the calculations

In carrying out the computation of the total interest and the new principal, the following additional variables are needed.

INTEREST-ON-PRINCIPAL	holds interest on the principal
INTEREST-ON-DEPOSIT	holds interest on the deposit

COMPREHENSIVE STRUCTURED COBOL

```
TOTAL-INTEREST              total interest earned
NEW-PRINCIPAL-COMPUTED      sum of old principal,
                               deposit, and total
                               interest earned
WS-PRINCIPAL-IN             holds old principal, to
                               five decimal places
WS-DEPOSIT-IN               holds deposit, to five
                               decimal places
```

These can be specified as

```
05    INTEREST-ON-PRINCIPAL        PIC 9(06)V9(05).
05    INTEREST-ON-DEPOSIT          PIC 9(06)V9(05).
05    TOTAL-INTEREST               PIC 9(06)V9(02).
05    NEW-PRINCIPAL-COMPUTED       PIC 9(07)V9(02).
05    WS-PRINCIPAL-IN              PIC 9(07)V9(05).
05    WS-DEPOSIT-IN                PIC 9(07)V9(05).
```

Notice that an implicit decimal point specification V has been used for all of these since they will be used in arithmetic computations.

Notice also that five digits to the right of the decimal point have been allowed for all three interest identifiers. This permits accuracy in the interest calculations.

Suppose that interest on the principal is $15.159 and interest on the deposit is $5.1587. Then the total interest will be $20.3177. When you add this to the new principal and round off to the nearest cent, you will be adding $20.32. If only two decimal places in the interest fields were allowed, you would lose significant figures, and the total would be only $20.30. The customer might not be credited with two cents of interest as a result.

Notice also that WS-PRINCIPAL-IN and WS-DEPOSIT-IN are used with five decimal places. This is to avoid possible error in calculations, as will be explained.

Computer mythology has it that there was once a programmer for a large bank who wrote COBOL programs that added the significant figures beyond the second for all customer accounts to the balance of his own account. This amounted to about a half cent per account per month. The bank had over 10 million accounts, so that each month, about $50,000 belonging to the bank's customers was credited to the programmer's account. The story continues that the programmer's fraud was discovered when he closed the account in preparation for fleeing the country with the proceeds, but forgot to correct the COBOL program. The program ended abnormally when it could not credit the significant figures to the closed account. This alerted other programmers, who traced the fraud.

The calculations are repeated for each input record

In the processing, the following operations must be performed:

1. Read the input record.
2. PERFORM the following steps, repeatedly, until no records are left:
   a. Compute the interest on the principal.
   b. Compute the interest on the deposit.
   c. Add all interest plus the deposit to the principal to get the new principal.
   d. Transfer all necessary fields to the output record.
   e. Print the output record.
   f. Read the next input record, and note if none available.

When a record is read, the interest is computed from the input data, and then the new principal is computed. The output record is formed in DETAIL-LINE-OUT and the record is written out to the printer, that is, it is printed. Then the next record is read and the same steps performed.

The complete program is shown in Figure 3.8. Refer to Figure 3.7c and Figure 3.6c for the relevance of the specifications of the input area record ACCOUNT-RECORD-IN and the working-storage record DETAIL-LINE-OUT.

Use ROUNDED to have a computed result rounded off

Suppose you have

```
01 W       PIC 9(02)V9(02).
01 X       PIC 9(02)V9(03).
01 Y       PIC 9(02)V9(03).
    MOVE 42.678 TO X.
    MOVE 10.111 TO Y.
    COMPUTE W = X + Y.
```

W will get the value 52.78, coming from the result 52.789. The last decimal place is truncated. If you want the rounded value 52.79, you simply write

```
COMPUTE W ROUNDED = X + Y.
```

Intermediate results require sufficient decimal places

Note that, in order to have an intermediate result (that is, the value of X + Y) that can hold up to three decimal places, prior to assignment to W, either X or Y, or both, should be defined with three digits after the implicit decimal point, for example, PIC 9(02)V9(03). This also holds for multiplication, division, and subtraction operations.

For this reason, WS-PRINCIPAL-IN and WS-DEPOSIT-IN were used with five decimal places in the computations in Figure 3.8, instead of AR-PRINCIPAL-IN and AR-DEPOSIT-IN, with only two decimal places.

```
        IDENTIFICATION DIVISION.
        PROGRAM-ID. SAMPLE4.
        **************************************************************************
        *   THIS PROGRAM COMPUTES THE INTEREST ON AN OLD PRINCIPAL AND ON A      *
        *   DEPOSIT, ADDS THE INTEREST AND DEPOSIT TO THE OLD PRINCIPAL, AND      *
        *   GENERATES THE NEW PRINCIPAL.                                          *
        **************************************************************************
        ENVIRONMENT DIVISION.
        INPUT-OUTPUT SECTION.
        FILE-CONTROL.     SELECT ACCOUNT-IN       ASSIGN TO UT-S-ACCNT50.
                          SELECT REPORT-OUT       ASSIGN TO UR-S-SYSPRINT.
        DATA DIVISION.
        FILE SECTION.
        FD   ACCOUNT-IN                          LABEL RECORDS ARE STANDARD.
        01   ACCOUNT-RECORD-IN.
             05   AR-CUSTOMER-NAME-IN       PIC X(25).
             05   AR-PRINCIPAL-IN           PIC 9(07)V9(02).
             05   AR-DEPOSIT-IN             PIC 9(07)V9(02).
             05   AR-DEPOSIT-DAYS-IN        PIC 9(02).
             05   AR-PRINCIPAL-RATE-IN      PIC 9(02)V9(02).
             05   AR-DEPOSIT-RATE-IN        PIC 9(02)V9(02).
        FD   REPORT-OUT                         LABEL RECORDS ARE OMITTED.
        01   REPORT-RECORD-OUT            PIC X(133).
        WORKING-STORAGE SECTION.
        01 WS-WORK-AREAS.
             05   INTEREST-ON-PRINCIPAL    PIC 9(06)V9(05).
             05   INTEREST-ON-DEPOSIT      PIC 9(06)V9(05).
             05   TOTAL-INTEREST           PIC 9(06)V9(02).
             05   NEW-PRINCIPAL-COMPUTED   PIC 9(07)V9(02).
             05   WS-PRINCIPAL-IN          PIC 9(07)V9(05).
             05   WS-DEPOSIT-IN            PIC 9(07)V9(05)
             05   MORE-RECORDS             PIC X(02)            VALUE 'YES'.
        01   HEADER.
             05   FILLER                   PIC X(15)            VALUE SPACES.
             05   FILLER                   PIC X(26)            VALUE
                                                 'MONTHLY CUSTOMER ACCOUNTS'.
             05   FILLER                   PIC X(92)            VALUE SPACES.
        01   COLUMN-HEADER1.
             05   FILLER                   PIC X(01)            VALUE SPACES.
             05   FILLER                   PIC X(08)            VALUE 'CUSTOMER'.
             05   FILLER                   PIC X(19)            VALUE SPACES.
             05   FILLER                   PIC X(03)            VALUE 'OLD'.
             05   FILLER                   PIC X(10)            VALUE SPACES.
             05   FILLER                   PIC X(07)            VALUE 'DEPOSIT'.
             05   FILLER                   PIC X(06)            VALUE SPACES.
             05   FILLER                   PIC X(08)            VALUE 'INTEREST'.
             05   FILLER                   PIC X(05)            VALUE SPACES.
             05   FILLER                   PIC X(03)            VALUE 'NEW'.
             05   FILLER                   PIC X(63)            VALUE 'SPACES'.
```

```
01   COLUMN-HEADER2.
     05   FILLER                     PIC X(01)        VALUE SPACES.
     05   FILLER                     PIC X(04)        VALUE 'NAME'.
     05   FILLER                     PIC X(23)        VALUE SPACES.
     05   FILLER                     PIC X(09)        VALUE 'PRINCIPAL'.
     05   FILLER                     PIC X(17)        VALUE SPACES.
     05   FILLER                     PIC X(06)        VALUE 'EARNED'.
     05   FILLER                     PIC X(07)        VALUE SPACES.
     05   FILLER                     PIC X(09)        VALUE 'PRINCIPAL'.
     05   FILLER                     PIC X(57)        VALUE 'SPACES'.
01   DETAIL-LINE-OUT.
     05 FILLER                       PIC X(01)        VALUE SPACES.
     05 DL-CUSTOMER-NAME-OUT         PIC X(25).
     05 FILLER                       PIC X(02)        VALUE SPACES.
     05 DL-OLD-PRINCIPAL-OUT         PIC $ZZZ,ZZ9.99.
     05 FILLER                       PIC X(02)        VALUE SPACES.
     05 DL-DEPOSIT-OUT               PIC $ZZZ,ZZ9.99.
     05 FILLER                       PIC X(02)        VALUE SPACES.
     05 DL-INTEREST-OUT              PIC $ZZZ,ZZ9.99.
     05 FILLER                       PIC X(02)        VALUE SPACES.
     05 DL-NEW-PRINCIPAL-OUT         PIC $Z,ZZZ,ZZ9.99.
     05 FILLER                       PIC X(53)        VALUE SPACES.
 PROCEDURE DIVISION.
 100-MAIN-MODULE.
************************************************************************
*   100-MAIN-MODULE:  DIRECTS PROGRAM LOGIC.                          *
************************************************************************
     OPEN INPUT ACCOUNT-IN
          OUTPUT REPORT-OUT.
     WRITE REPORT-RECORD-OUT FROM HEADER
                   AFTER ADVANCING 1 LINE.
     WRITE REPORT-RECORD-OUT FROM COLUMN-HEADER1
                   AFTER ADVANCING 2 LINES.
     WRITE REPORT-RECORD-OUT FROM COLUMN-HEADER2
                   AFTER ADVANCING 1 LINE.
     MOVE SPACES TO REPORT-RECORD-OUT.
     WRITE REPORT-RECORD-OUT
                   AFTER ADVANCING 1 LINE.
     READ ACCOUNT-IN
                 AT END MOVE 'NO' TO MORE-RECORDS.
     PERFORM 200-PROCESS-RECORD UNTIL MORE-RECORDS = 'NO'.
     CLOSE ACCOUNT-IN
           REPORT-OUT.
     STOP RUN.
 200-PROCESS-RECORD.
************************************************************************
*   200-PROCESS-RECORD:  PERFORMED FROM 100-MAIN-MODULE.  PROCESSES   *
*   LATEST INPUT RECORD BY COMPUTING INTEREST ON PRINCIPAL, INTEREST ON *
*   DEPOSIT, AND THUS TOTAL INTEREST.  ADDS TOTAL INTEREST AND DEPOSIT *
*   TO OLD PRINCIPAL TO GIVE THE NEW PRINCIPAL. OUTPUTS DETAIL LINE.   *
*   READS NEXT INPUT RECORD.                                          *
************************************************************************
```

```
        MOVE AR-PRINCIPAL-IN TO WS-PRINCIPAL-IN.
        COMPUTE INTEREST-ON-PRINCIPAL
              = (WS-PRINCIPAL-IN * AR-PRINCIPAL-RATE-IN / 100) / 12.
        MOVE AR-DEPOSIT-IN TO WS-DEPOSIT-IN.
        COMPUTE INTEREST-ON-DEPOSIT
              = ((WS-DEPOSIT-IN * AR-DEPOSIT-RATE-IN / 100)
                   * AR-DEPOSIT-DAYS-IN) / 365.
        COMPUTE TOTAL-INTEREST ROUNDED
              = INTEREST-ON-PRINCIPAL + INTEREST-ON-DEPOSIT.
        COMPUTE NEW-PRINCIPAL-COMPUTED
              = AR-PRINCIPAL-IN + AR-DEPOSIT-IN + TOTAL-INTEREST.
        MOVE    AR-CUSTOMER-NAME-IN      TO       DL-CUSTOMER-NAME-OUT.
        MOVE    AR-PRINCIPAL-IN          TO       DL-OLD-PRINCIPAL-OUT.
        MOVE    AR-DEPOSIT-IN            TO       DL-DEPOSIT-OUT.
        MOVE    TOTAL-INTEREST           TO       DL-INTEREST-OUT.
        MOVE    NEW-PRINCIPAL-COMPUTED   TO       DL-NEW-PRINCIPAL-OUT.
        WRITE REPORT-RECORD-OUT FROM DETAIL-LINE-OUT
                    AFTER ADVANCING 1 LINE.
        READ ACCOUNT-IN
                  AT END MOVE 'NO' TO MORE-RECORDS.
```

Figure 3.8 *The SAMPLE4 program, which computes interest and principal.*

Specify complex headers one item at a time using FILLER fields

Notice that the records for the headers are constructed by using FILLER fields. For example, the group identifier COLUMN-HEADER1, which will be used to print the first line of column headers, is made up of FILLER fields that contain either blanks or an item of data that will be printed as a column header. In theory, the entire header line could be placed in quotes after a single VALUE clause. However, this is regarded as poor practice unless the header is short and simple, as in the program in Figure 3.1c. If the header is long, with many blank spaces, you have to break it and continue on the next line, as was explained earlier in the section on literals, for example:

It is hard to know exactly where the break should occur. Since it is easy to get this wrong, you should avoid it and specify complex headers in small pieces.

It is also considered good practice to complete the header record with a FILLER field that brings the entire line up to 133 characters.

Summary

1. The DATA DIVISION consists of the FILE SECTION and WORKING-STORAGE SECTION.

2. In the FILE SECTION, for each file to be manipulated, you specify if the file has a label, and optionally, how the records of the file are, or will be, blocked. For each file, you also specify an input or output area identifier (or buffer record). This identifier can be either a group or elementary identifier and is defined using the same rules as for identifiers defined in the WORKING-STORAGE SECTION. However, the length in bytes of an input or output area identifier must match the length of the record being transmitted between file and buffer.

3. In the WORKING-STORAGE SECTION, each group and elementary identifier needed for auxiliary manipulation is specified. A group identifier may consist of elementary and further subgroup identifiers, which in turn may consist of elementary and subgroup identifiers, and so on.

4. A VALUE clause is used to place an initial value in an identifier. A literal is a constant value, as opposed to the name of an identifier. The + and - edit symbols are used for printing signs. The S symbol is used to denote a sign marker with numeric identifiers. No space is recorded for an S symbol, unless SIGN LEADING SEPARATE is also specified with the PICTURE clause.

Key Terms

buffer record	elementary identifier	figurative constant
block	group MOVE	edit symbol
blocking factor	left justified	edited field
group identifier	literal	

Concept Review Questions

1. Explain what a LABEL RECORD is and what it is used for.
2. What is a file label?
3. List the kinds of files that can have labels and those that cannot.
4. How does a file get a label?
5. Distinguish header and trailer labels.
6. How big should the input area record be for printer files?
7. In what section do you specify a file label?
8. In what section do you specify an input area (input buffer) identifier?
9. Distinguish group and elementary identifiers.
10. How many levels can you have with a group identifier?
11. What are blocked records?
12. What is the blocking factor?
13. If record size is 120 characters and the blocking factor is 50, what is the block size?
14. What kinds of records cannot be blocked?
15. How do you get the records in a file to become blocked, if they are not?
16. List the three kinds of data fields you can have in a record.
17. Explain the concept of a literal.
18. How many kinds of literal can you have?
19. What is a group MOVE?
20. What is the most important characteristic of a group MOVE?
21. Explain how a character value is assigned or moved to an alphanumeric identifier.
22. Explain left and right justification.
23. How do you place initial values in identifiers before a program is executed?
24. Explain what an edit symbol is.
25. What is an edit identifier?
26. Where are edit identifiers used?
27. Explain why you would not expect to find edit identifiers in a group identifier used as the input buffer record.
28. Explain the concept of an implicit decimal point.
29. What is a sign marker?
30. If you printed an identifer with a sign marker in it, what would happen?
31. What is a figurative constant? Give two examples.

COBOL Language Questions

1. What is wrong with the following?

```
01 A.
   05  B    PIC X(04).
   10  C    PIC 9(03).
```

2. Pick out the valid identifiers:

LINE-COUNTER	A-500-
CUSTOMER-NAME-	ACCOUNT#-IN
ACCOUNT-TOTAL	400-10
%-RAISE	SUMMARY-DATA-OUT

3. Pick out the invalid literals.

```
'DENVER'                  'DENVER, COLORADO'
'10,354'                  57.56
$97.82                    87.
'5,794.00+'               -67.8
```

4. What is wrong with the following?

```
COMPUTE TAX-PAYABLE = GROSS * 0.18.
...
MOVE 0.18 TO DL-TAX-RATE-OUT.
```

Fix it.

5. Suppose you have defined:

```
05  TEMPERATURE    PIC S9(03)  VALUE -12.
```

What would happen if you printed the contents of TEMPERATURE?

6. How much space (in characters) would be taken up in memory by identifiers defined with the following PICTURE clauses?

```
PIC X(04)              PIC 9(03).99
PIC S9(04)             PIC -999.99
PIC 9(04)V99           PIC ZZ,Z99.99
PIC $999.99            PIC SZZ,Z99.99
PIC +999               PIC S99V99
```

7. What is wrong with the following?

```
01   A.
     05 B   PIC 9(03).
     05 C   PIC X(02).
01   H.
     05 J       PIC X(02).
     05 K.
        10 M PIC  X(02).
        10 N PIC  0(03).
...
     MOVE A TO K.
```

8. In each of the following, what would appear if X were printed?
```
a.  01  X    PIC $ZZ,ZZ9.99        VALUE  52.35.
b.  01  X    PIC 999.99            VALUE  0.45.
c.  01  X    PIC ZZ9.99            VALUE  10.65.
d.  01  X    PIC 99V99             VALUE  47.45.
e.  01  X    PIC +99.99            VALUE  2.84.
f.  01  X    PIC +ZZ,Z99           VALUE  -4567.
g.  01  X    PIC -999.99           VALUE  89.72.
```

9. If you have

```
01 A.
   05  B   PIC X(04).
   05  C   PIC 9(03).
   ...
```

INITIALIZE A.

what values will B and C acquire?

10. What is wrong with the following?

```
01  A    PIC X(04)  VALUE ZEROS.
01  B    PIC 9(02)  VALUE SPACES.
```

Fix it.

11. What value will Z acquire in

```
a.  01 X    PIC 99V999      VALUE 11.235.
    01 Y    PIC 99          VALUE 5.
    01 Z    PIC 99V99.
        COMPUTE  Z = X / Y.
b.  01 X    PIC 99V999      VALUE 11.235.
    01 Y    PIC 99          VALUE 5.
    01 Z    PIC 99V99.
        COMPUTE  Z ROUNDED = X / Y.
```

Programming Assignments

1. **A program to handle signs in both the input and output data**
The input data are

```
---------1---------2---------3---------4
01/09+0067894
03/09-0004742
04/09+0045600
06/09-0127600
09/09+0267876
```

with this record layout:

```
---------1- --------2---------3---------4
XXXXXS99999V99
XXXXXS99999V99
XXXXXS99999V99
XXXXXS99999V99
XXXXXS99999V99
```

The output report is

```
---------1---------2---------3---------4
             MONTHLY TRANSACTIONS

DATE        TRANSACTION       BALANCE

01/09          00000.00     +   678.94
03/09         -00047.42     +   631.52
04/09         +00456.00     +1,087.52
06/09         -01276.00     -   188.48
09/09         +02678.76     +2,490.28
```

A record of the input file has two fields, and gives details of transactions on an account at a bank. The first field gives the date of the transaction, and the second the value of a deposit (+) or a withdrawal (-). The second field of the first record is the balance from the previous month (but can be regarded as an initial deposit for the month).

In the processing you must generate the account balance after each transaction, as shown in the report.

a. Make up a printer spacing chart for the output.
b. Enter the input file using your editor.
c. Make up a flowchart for the processing.
d. Develop and run the program. Note that you must use an identifier defined with SIGN LEADING SEPARATE in the input area group identifier in order to read the input records.

2. **A program to carry out interest computations**
The input data are

```
---------1---------2---------3---------4
1402151075
0956781125
```

with this record layout:

```
-------- -1---------2---------3---------4
99999999V99
99999999V99
99999999V99
```

The output data are

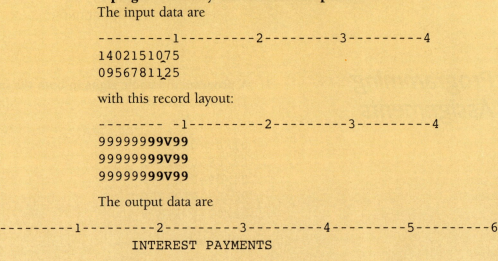

```
---------1---------2---------3---------4---------5---------6
                    INTEREST PAYMENTS


PRINCIPAL    ANNUAL INTEREST     MONTHLY       ANNUAL
             RATE                INTEREST      INTEREST

140215       10.75               1256.09       15073.08
095678       11.25                896.98       19763.76
135400        9.75               1100.12        1321.44
```

The first field of an input record gives the principal invested at a financial institution. The second field gives the fixed annual interest rate.

The processing consists of generating a report giving monthly and annual interest payments for each investment. Monthly interest is first computed and then rounded off. The monthly rounded figure is used to compute the annual interest payment.

a. Draw up a spacing chart for the output data.
b. Make up a flowchart for the processing.
c. Develop and run the program.

3. **A program that uses group identifiers with three levels of structure.**

The input data file has these records

```
---------1---------2---------3---------4
ACKRON            P345BOLT    0075100014/06
BETACORP          P689COG     1200020017/06
GRUMANN           P018FAN     0975007518/07
---------1---------2---------3---------4
```

with this record layout:

```
---------1---------2-------- -3---------4
XXXXXXXXXXXXXX XXXXXXXXXXX99V999999XXXXX
XXXXXXXXXXXXXX XXXXXXXXXXX99V999999XXXXX
XXXXXXXXXXXXXX XXXXXXXXXXX99V999999XXXXX
---------1---------2-------- -3---------4
```

The input fields are

> Customer name
> Part sold
>> Part identification number
>> Part type
>> Unit cost
> Transaction data
>> Quantity
>> Date

The output data are

```
---------1---------2---------3---------4---------5---------6---------7
                    SALES REPORT
```

CUSTOMER	PART SOLD * PART-ID#	TYPE	UNIT COST	TRANSACTION DATA * * * * * * * * * * * * * * QUANTITY	DATE	TOTAL COST
ACKRON	P345	BOLT	$ 0.75	1000	14/06	$ 750.00
BETACORP	P689	COG	$12.00	200	17/06	$ 2,400.00
GRUMANN	P018	FAN	$ 9.75	75	18/07	$ 731.25

In the processing, the input data are output as shown, with an additional value for the total cost (quantity times unit cost) of the goods purchased.

a. Make up a printer spacing chart for the output.
b. Make up group identifiers, containing three levels, for both input and detail line records.
c. Make up a flowchart for the processing.
d. Write and run the program.

THE ESSENTIALS OF THE PROCEDURE DIVISION

A group MOVE, with group identifiers, is alphanumeric
A table is useful for checking if a MOVE is allowed
Recall numeric identifiers with the SIGN LEADING SEPARATE attribute
Avoid ambiguous identifiers
A multiple ("shotgun") MOVE is allowed
There is a special MOVE called MOVE CORRESPONDING
You can use ACCEPT and DISPLAY for input and output of small amounts
     of data

4.3 COMPUTE is mainly used with more complex computations
The COMPUTE verb is powerful and flexible
          Exponentiation operator
Avoid the need to use ON SIZE ERROR
Avoid complex COMPUTE expressions
Use parentheses with COMPUTE expressions
Use ROUNDED to have a result rounded
Subtle truncation errors are possible with arithmetic operations

**4.4 ADD, SUBTRACT, MULTIPLY, and DIVIDE are used with simple
     computations**
          ADD . . . TO verb
          ADD . . . GIVING verb
          ADD . . . TO . . . GIVING verb
          SUBTRACT . . . FROM verb
          SUBTRACT . . . FROM . . . GIVING verb
          MULTIPLY . . . BY verb
          MULTIPLY . . . BY . . . GIVING verb
          DIVIDE . . . INTO GIVING verb
          DIVIDE . . . BY . . . GIVING verb
          REMAINDER options
          ROUNDED option
          ON SIZE error option
          Avoiding size errors
It is better not to use edit identifiers in the GIVING clause
You can use individual scope terminators with arithmetic verbs
It is poor practice to use more than one identifier after GIVING
COMPUTE and the other arithmetic verbs are used in different situations
          Reminder on how to read syntax formats

*T*HIS CHAPTER BEGINS by examining how you structure the PRO-
CEDURE DIVISION of a COBOL program. It then looks at the more
common instructions or statements that you use in the PROCE-
DURE DIVISION. The PROCEDURE DIVISION is where you write the statements that cause the processor to process the data in memory and to have
data transmitted between storage devices and memory. Non-computational
instructions are examined first, that is, instructions that do not cause an
arithmetic operation to be carried out. Then computational instructions are
dealt with.

The ideas discussed in this chapter are illustrated using a version of
the program for processing retirement accounts developed in Chapter 3.
Recall that for this program, each record in the input file ACCOUNT-IN
describes the state of a customer's retirement account. The processing
generates an end-of-month report (called REPORT-OUT) on the status of
each account, by computing interest earned for the month (interest on the
old principal plus interest on any deposit made during the month), and the
new principal (old principal plus interest earned plus deposit). The program, now called SAMPLE5, is shown with some minor reorganization in
Figure 4.1.

4.1
The PROCEDURE DIVISION is structured in paragraphs

*T*HE PROCEDURE DIVISION CONTAINS instructions that
cause something to happen to the contents of the identifiers specified in the DATA DIVISION. Instructions are usually grouped into
paragraphs, and the paragraphs are sometimes grouped into *sections*.

```
               MARY SMITH                    0100000000000500002008000600
               P.F. COLE                     0005000000000100001009000700
               L.E. LEE                      0002500000000150000508500600
```

Figure 4.1a *Format of the records in the input file ACCOUNT-IN.*

```
         MONTHLY CUSTOMER ACCOUNTS

CUSTOMER                   OLD           DEPOSIT        INTEREST      NEW
NAME                       PRINCIPAL                    EARNED        PRINCIPAL


MARY SMITH                 $100,000.00   $    500.00    $    668.31   $  100,508.31
P.F. COLE                  $  5,000.00   $    100.00    $     37.69   $    5,137.69
L.E. LEE                   $  2,500.00   $    150.00    $     17.83   $    2,667.83
<--------25------------><><----11---><><----11---><><---11----><><-----13---->
```

Figure 4.1b *Format of the printer file REPORT-OUT.*

```
IDENTIFICATION DIVISION.
PROGRAM-ID. SAMPLE5.
*********************************************************************************
*   THIS PROGRAM COMPUTES THE INTEREST ON AN OLD PRINCIPAL AND ON A          *
*   DEPOSIT, ADDS THE INTEREST AND DEPOSIT TO THE OLD PRINCIPAL, AND         *
*   GENERATES THE NEW PRINCIPAL. THE VERSION HERE IS MORE STRUCTURED         *
*   THAN SAMPLE4 IN CHAPTER 3.                                              *
*********************************************************************************
ENVIRONMENT DIVISION.
INPUT-OUTPUT SECTION.
FILE-CONTROL.    SELECT ACCOUNT-IN        ASSIGN TO UT-S-ACCNT.
                 SELECT REPORT-OUT        ASSIGN TO UR-S-SYSPRINT.
DATA DIVISION.
FILE SECTION.
FD   ACCOUNT-IN                           LABEL RECORDS ARE STANDARD.
01   ACCOUNT-RECORD-IN.
     05   AR-CUSTOMER-NAME-IN        PIC X(25).
     05   AR-PRINCIPAL-IN            PIC 9(07)V9(02).
     05   AR-DEPOSIT-IN              PIC 9(07)V9(02).
     05   AR-DEPOSIT-DAYS-IN         PIC 9(02).
     05   AR-PRINCIPAL-RATE-IN       PIC 9(02)V9(02).
     05   AR-DEPOSIT-RATE-IN         PIC 9(02)V9(02).
FD   REPORT-OUT                           LABEL RECORDS ARE OMITTED.
01   REPORT-RECORD-OUT              PIC X(133).
WORKING-STORAGE SECTION.
01   WS-WORK-AREAS.
     05   INTEREST-ON-PRINCIPAL     PIC 9(06)V9(05).
     05   INTEREST-ON-DEPOSIT       PIC 9(06)V9(05).
     05   TOTAL-INTEREST            PIC 9(06)V9(09).
     05   NEW-PRINCIPAL-COMPUTED    PIC 9(07)V9(02).
     05   WS-PRINCIPAL-IN           PIC 9(07)V9(05).
     05   WS-DEPOSIT-IN             PIC 9(07)V9(05).
     05   MORE-RECORDS              PIC X(03)        VALUE 'YES'.
```

```
01   HEADER.
     05  FILLER                           PIC X(15)           VALUE SPACES.
     05  FILLER                           PIC X(26)           VALUE
                                                         'MONTHLY CUSTOMER ACCOUNTS'.
     05  FILLER                           PIC X(92)           VALUE SPACES.
01   COLUMN-HEADER1.
     05  FILLER                           PIC X(01)           VALUE SPACES.
     05  FILLER                           PIC X(08)           VALUE 'CUSTOMER'.
     05  FILLER                           PIC X(19)           VALUE SPACES.
     05  FILLER                           PIC X(03)           VALUE 'OLD'.
     05  FILLER                           PIC X(10)           VALUE SPACES.
     05  FILLER                           PIC X(07)           VALUE 'DEPOSIT'.
     05  FILLER                           PIC X(06)           VALUE SPACES.
     05  FILLER                           PIC X(08)           VALUE 'INTEREST'.
     05  FILLER                           PIC X(05)           VALUE SPACES.
     05  FILLER                           PIC X(03)           VALUE 'NEW'.
     05  FILLER                           PIC X(63)           VALUE SPACES.
01   COLUMN-HEADER2.
     05  FILLER                           PIC X(01)           VALUE SPACES.
     05  FILLER                           PIC X(04)           VALUE 'NAME'.
     05  FILLER                           PIC X(23)           VALUE SPACES.
     05  FILLER                           PIC X(09)           VALUE 'PRINCIPAL'.
     05  FILLER                           PIC X(17)           VALUE SPACES.
     05  FILLER                           PIC X(06)           VALUE 'EARNED'.
     05  FILLER                           PIC X(07)           VALUE SPACES.
     05  FILLER                           PIC X(09)           VALUE 'PRINCIPAL'.
     05  FILLER                           PIC X(57)           VALUE SPACES.
01   DETAIL-LINE-OUT.
     05 FILLER                            PIC X(01)           VALUE SPACES.
     05 DL-CUSTOMER-NAME-OUT              PIC X(25).
     05 FILLER                            PIC X(02)           VALUE SPACES
     05 DL-OLD-PRINCIPAL-OUT              PIC $ZZZ,ZZ9.9(02).
     05 FILLER                            PIC X(02)           VALUE SPACES.
     05 DL-DEPOSIT-OUT                    PIC $ZZZ,ZZ9.9(02).
     05 FILLER                            PIC X(02)           VALUE SPACES.
     05 DL-INTEREST-OUT                   PIC $ZZZ,ZZ9.9(02).
     05 FILLER                            PIC X(02)           VALUE SPACES.
     05 DL-NEW-PRINCIPAL-OUT              PIC $Z,ZZZ,ZZ9.9(02).
     05 FILLER                            PIC X(53)           VALUE SPACES.
 PROCEDURE DIVISION.
 100-MAIN-MODULE.
 ************************************************************************
 *  100-MAIN-MODULE:  DIRECTS PROGRAM LOGIC.                           *
 ************************************************************************
     OPEN INPUT ACCOUNT-IN
          OUTPUT REPORT-OUT.
     PERFORM 300-WRITE-HEADERS.
     READ ACCOUNT-IN
                 AT END MOVE 'NO' TO MORE-RECORDS.
     PERFORM 200-PROCESS-RECORD
               UNTIL MORE-RECORDS = 'NO'.
```

```
        CLOSE ACCOUNT-IN
              REPORT-OUT.
        STOP RUN.
  200-PROCESS-RECORD.
*****************************************************************************
*   200-PROCESS-RECORD:  PERFORMED FROM 100-MAIN-MODULE. PROCESSES          *
*  LATEST INPUT RECORD BY COMPUTING INTEREST ON PRINCIPAL, INTEREST ON      *
*  DEPOSIT, AND THUS TOTAL INTEREST. ADDS TOTAL INTEREST AND DEPOSIT        *
*  TO OLD PRINCIPAL TO GIVE THE NEW PRINCIPAL. OUTPUTS DETAIL LINE.         *
*  READS NEXT INPUT RECORD.                                                 *
*****************************************************************************
        MOVE AR-PRINCIPAL-IN TO WS-PRINCIPAL-IN.
        COMPUTE INTEREST-ON-PRINCIPAL
            = (WS-PRINCIPAL-IN * AR-PRINCIPAL-RATE-IN / 100) / 12.
        MOVE AR-DEPOSIT-IN TO WS-DEPOSIT-IN.
        COMPUTE INTEREST-ON-DEPOSIT
            = ((WS-DEPOSIT-IN * AR-DEPOSIT-RATE-IN / 100)
                  * AR-DEPOSIT-DAYS-IN) / 365.
        COMPUTE TOTAL-INTEREST ROUNDED
            = INTEREST-ON-PRINCIPAL + INTEREST-ON-DEPOSIT.
        COMPUTE NEW-PRINCIPAL-COMPUTED
            = AR-PRINCIPAL-IN + AR-DEPOSIT-IN + TOTAL-INTEREST.
        MOVE      AR-CUSTOMER-NAME-IN     TO      DL-CUSTOMER-NAME-OUT.
        MOVE      AR-PRINCIPAL-IN         TO      DL-OLD-PRINCIPAL-OUT.
        MOVE      AR-DEPOSIT-IN           TO      DL-DEPOSIT-OUT.
        MOVE      TOTAL-INTEREST          TO      DL-INTEREST-OUT.
        MOVE      NEW-PRINCIPAL-COMPUTED  TO      DL-NEW-PRINCIPAL-OUT.
        WRITE REPORT-RECORD-OUT FROM DETAIL-LINE-OUT
                        AFTER ADVANCING 1 LINE.
        READ ACCOUNT-IN
                    AT END MOVE 'NO' TO MORE-RECORDS.
        300-WRITE-HEADERS.
*****************************************************************************
*   300-WRITE-HEADERS:  PERFORMED FROM 100-MAIN-MODULE. PRINTS REPORT       *
*  AND COLUMN HEADERS FOR REPORT-OUT.                                       *
*****************************************************************************
        WRITE REPORT-RECORD-OUT FROM HEADER
                        AFTER ADVANCING 1 LINE.
        WRITE REPORT-RECORD-OUT FROM COLUMN-HEADER1
                        AFTER ADVANCING 2 LINES.
        WRITE REPORT-RECORD-OUT FROM COLUMN-HEADER2
                        AFTER ADVANCING 1 LINE.
        MOVE SPACES TO REPORT-RECORD-OUT.
        WRITE REPORT-RECORD-OUT
                        AFTER ADVANCING 1 LINE.
```

Figure 4.1c The SAMPLE5 program.

An instruction is called a statement

An instruction in COBOL is usually called a *statement*. A group of statements can be joined together to form a COBOL *sentence*. A sentence is terminated by a period. Statements may be separated by a separator. A separator is a comma or a blank. However, the convention is to begin a new statement on a new line and omit the comma. For example, each of the following lines holds a statement. The collection of statements forms a sentence.

```
            ┌ MOVE A TO T  ◄──── statement
sentence  ─┤  MOVE B TO W
            └ WRITE G FROM P.
```

Several statements can be on the same line. But again, it is considered good programming style to begin each new statement on a different line and leave out the commas. If an error occurs on a line with many statements, it may be difficult to know which statement is incorrect, if all you know is the line number of the offending statement.

A statement or a sentence must begin in area B of a line, that is, in column 12 or more of the COBOL coding sheet.

Distinguish imperative and conditional statements

Most statements in COBOL are imperative statements. An *imperative statement* simply carries out one or more specified operations, without taking any conditions into consideration. OPEN, READ, MOVE, COMPUTE, WRITE, and CLOSE are common imperative statements, often called elementary imperative statements.

A sequence of elementary imperative statements is also an imperative statement, provided the statements are separated only by separators (blanks or comma). A sequence of imperative statements is sometimes called a composite imperative statement.

The following are examples of imperative statements:

Elementary imperative statement example

```
MOVE A TO B
```

Composite imperative statement example

```
MOVE 'NOT FOUND' TO REPORT-RECORD-OUT
WRITE REPORT-RECORD-OUT
MOVE 'YES' TO SEARCH-COMPLETED
```

Note that a period is placed at the end of an elementary or composite imperative statement only if it is the end of a sentence.

In contrast, a *conditional statement* will test for the validity of one or more conditions before an operation is carried out. Common conditional statements are the IF- and EVALUATE statements, which are covered in Chapter 5. An imperative statement *cannot* be a conditional statement.

Always use paragraphs

The sentences of the PROCEDURE DIVISION may be grouped into paragraphs. Paragraph names are arbitrary and the same rules as for identifiers are used to make up these names. Paragraph names must begin on the A margin. Thus in the program in Figure 4.1c, the PROCEDURE DIVISION is structured as:

```
PROCEDURE DIVISION.
100-MAIN-MODULE.
    ...
200-PROCESS-RECORD.
    ...
300-WRITE-HEADERS.
    ...
```

A program structured in paragraphs that carry out a well-defined and distinct function is much easier to understand, especially if instructive paragraph names are used. The operations performed within a paragraph should naturally group together. For example, the processing on a record can be often specified in a single paragraph.

A major advantage of paragraphing is that it promotes readability of the program. You can see what is going on in the procedure just by scanning through the paragraph names. Use paragraphs in all your programs.

Paragraphs are structured hierarchically

With most COBOL programs, except for very simple ones, a hierarchical paragraph structure is used. The procedure in Figure 4.1c is one of the simplest hierarchical structures possible. The structure is hierarchical because there is one paragraph, 100-MAIN-MODULE, that determines execution of 300-WRITE-HEADERS and 200-PROCESS-RECORD. Thus the essentials of this pyramid of control are as shown here:

```
100-MAIN-MODULE.
    ...
    PERFORM 300-WRITE-HEADERS.
    ...
    PERFORM 200-PROCESS-RECORD UNTIL ...
    ...
200-PROCESS-RECORD.
    ...
300-WRITE-HEADERS.
```

This is also illustrated in Figure 4.2.

Most programs have an initial, or overall control, paragraph with a name like 100-MAIN-MODULE. In this paragraph in simple programs, the files are usually opened, any headers used are written out, the first record is read, the processing paragraphs executed, and the files closed.

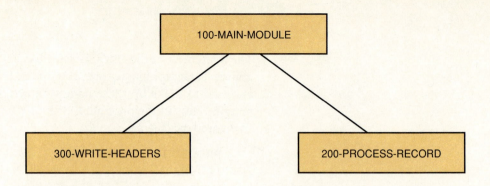

Figure 4.2 *Simple hierarchy diagram for the program in Figure 4.1c.*

A boxed comment should be used with each paragraph

Notice that in the program in Figure 4.1c an explanatory box comment has been inserted at the beginning of each paragraph. This is standard practice. The comment should state the paragraph name that calls up or performs the paragraph. This is useful in a very large program; without it you could waste a lot of time scanning the program for the PERFORM statement that calls up the paragraph. In addition, the comment should explain what the paragraph does.

Hierarchical structure is the essence of structured programming

The hierarchical structure has many advantages and is preferable for the following reasons.

- You can find out what goes on in the program merely by reading the first paragraph, and thus obtain an overview of the processing.
- You can select any single lower-level paragraph for more detailed study and be sure of how the details fit into the overall picture.
- If the paragraphs have been structured carefully, they will be independent of one another. The idea is to have only one type of operation carried out within a paragraph, so that you can make all changes to that operation in one place. For example, if you had to change the method of computing interest, only the 200-PROCESS-RECORD paragraph would need to be changed in Figure 4.1c.

In a nutshell, hierarchical structuring of the PROCEDURE DIVISION results in neat and tidy programs that can be easily changed. This may not appear so important when writing COBOL programs in a college course. However, in business, COBOL programs have a long life and often need modification for changing business conditions. It is probably true that more than half of the COBOL programming occurring on any day involves making changes to existing programs. Thus, hierarchical structuring is very

COMPREHENSIVE STRUCTURED COBOL

important, and henceforth all programs in this book will have such a structure. Hierarchical structuring is the essence of structured programming.

The paragraph 200-PROCESS-RECORD in the program in Figure 4.1c processes an input record. However, within the processing of a record, there are several subfunctions. Interest and new principal are computed and an output line prepared. You could structure the PROCEDURE DIVISION in an even deeper hierarchy, if you placed each of these subfunctions in a paragraph, as shown in Figure 4.3.

```
PROCEDURE DIVISION.
100-MAIN-MODULE.
*******************************************************************
*   100-MAIN-MODULE:  CONTROLS OPENING AND CLOSING OF FILES AND   *
*   DIRECTION OF PROGRAM LOGIC.                                   *
*******************************************************************
     OPEN INPUT ACCOUNT-IN
          OUTPUT REPORT-OUT.
     PERFORM 300-WRITE-HEADERS.
     READ ACCOUNT-IN
                 AT END MOVE 'NO' TO MORE-RECORDS.
     PERFORM 200-PROCESS-RECORD UNTIL MORE-RECORDS = 'NO'.
     CLOSE ACCOUNT-IN
           REPORT-OUT.
     STOP RUN.
 200-PROCESS-RECORD.
*******************************************************************
*   200-PROCESS-RECORD:  PERFORMED FROM 100-MAIN-MODULE. PROCESSES  *
*   LATEST ACCOUNT-IN RECORD. COMPUTES INTEREST AND NEW PRINCIPAL AND  *
*   PRINTS REPORT LINE.                                           *
*******************************************************************
     PERFORM 400-COMPUTE-INTEREST.
     PERFORM 500-COMPUTE-NEW-PRINCIPAL.
     PERFORM 600-PREPARE-DETAIL-LINE.
     WRITE REPORT-RECORD-OUT FROM DETAIL-LINE-OUT
                 AFTER ADVANCING 1 LINE.
     READ ACCOUNT-IN
                 AT END MOVE 'NO' TO MORE-RECORDS.
 300-WRITE-HEADERS.
*******************************************************************
*   300-WRITE-HEADER:  PERFORMED FROM 100-MAIN-MODULE.  PRINTS REPORT  *
*   AND COLUMN HEADERS FOR REPORT-OUT.                            *
*******************************************************************
     WRITE REPORT-RECORD-OUT FROM HEADER
                 AFTER ADVANCING 1 LINE.
     WRITE REPORT-RECORD-OUT FROM COLUMN-HEADER1
                 AFTER ADVANCING 2 LINES.
     WRITE REPORT-RECORD-OUT FROM COLUMN-HEADER2
                 AFTER ADVANCING 1 LINE.
     MOVE SPACES TO REPORT-RECORD-OUT.
     WRITE REPORT-RECORD-OUT
                 AFTER ADVANCING 1 LINE.
```

```
 400-COMPUTE-INTEREST.
************************************************************************
*   400-COMPUTE-INTEREST:   PERFORMED FROM 200-PROCESS-RECORD. COMPUTES   *
*   INTEREST ON PRINCIPAL, INTEREST ON THE DEPOSIT, AND SUMS THEM.        *
************************************************************************
     MOVE AR-PRINCIPAL-IN TO WS-PRINCIPAL-IN.
     COMPUTE INTEREST-ON-PRINCIPAL
         = (WS-PRINCIPAL-IN * AR-PRINCIPAL-RATE-IN / 100) / 12.
     MOVE AR-DEPOSIT-IN TO WS-DEPOSIT-IN.
     COMPUTE INTEREST-ON-DEPOSIT
         = ((WS-DEPOSIT-IN * AR-DEPOSIT-RATE-IN / 100)
                * AR-DEPOSIT-DAYS-IN) / 365.
     COMPUTE TOTAL-INTEREST ROUNDED
         = INTEREST-ON-PRINCIPAL + INTEREST-ON-DEPOSIT.
 500-COMPUTE-NEW-PRINCIPAL.
************************************************************************
*   500-COMPUTE-NEW-PRINCIPAL:   PERFORMED FROM 200-PROCESS-RECORD.       *
*   COMPUTES NEW PRINCIPAL AT END OF MONTH, OLD PRINCIPAL AT BEGINNING    *
*   OF MONTH, AND INTEREST EARNED DURING MONTH.                          *
************************************************************************
     COMPUTE NEW-PRINCIPAL-COMPUTED
         = AR-PRINCIPAL-IN + AR-DEPOSIT-IN + TOTAL-INTEREST.
 600-PREPARE-DETAIL-LINE.
************************************************************************
*   600-PREPARE-DETAIL-LINE:   PERFORMED FROM 200-PROCESS-RECORD. USES    *
*   FIELDS FROM ACCOUNT-IN-RECORD AND COMPUTED FIELDS TO CONSTRUCT A      *
*   DETAIL LINE OF THE REPORT, PRIOR TO PRINTING.                        *
************************************************************************
     MOVE    AR-CUSTOMER-NAME-IN      TO      DL-CUSTOMER-NAME-OUT.
     MOVE    AR-PRINCIPAL-IN          TO      DL-OLD-PRINCIPAL-OUT.
     MOVE    AR-DEPOSIT-IN            TO      DL-DEPOSIT-OUT.
     MOVE    TOTAL-INTEREST           TO      DL-INTEREST-OUT.
     MOVE    NEW-PRINCIPAL-COMPUTED   TO      DL-NEW-PRINCIPAL-OUT.
```

Figure 4.3 PROCEDURE DIVISION *showing hierarchical structure.*

If you examine the PROCEDURE DIVISION in Figure 4.3, you can easily get a clear idea of how the procedure functions simply by reading the paragraph names and comments. The hierarchical structure of the procedure can also be displayed by a diagram, as shown in Figure 4.4.

The PERFORM statement is crucial for writing structured programs

The key to writing hierarchically structured programs is the PERFORM statement. The full syntax and semantics for PERFORM are quite involved; you will learn more about them in Chapter 6. For now let us use the simplest version. (You will see the PERFORM . . . UNTIL statement later).

The simple PERFORM statement has the syntax shown in the box.

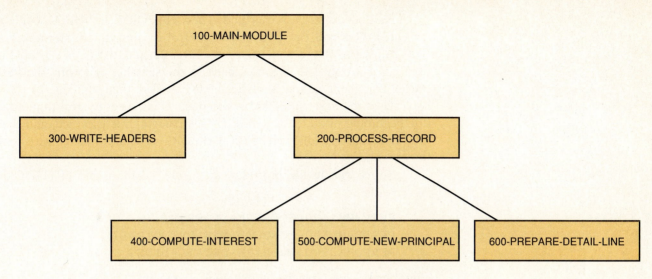

Figure 4.4 *A deeper hierarchy diagram.*

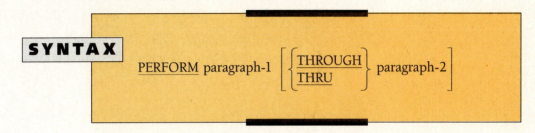

SYNTAX

$$\text{PERFORM paragraph-1} \left[\begin{Bmatrix} \text{THROUGH} \\ \text{THRU} \end{Bmatrix}\right. \text{paragraph-2}\Bigg]$$

Some examples of the simple PERFORM statement are

```
PERFORM 200-MODULE
PERFORM 600-EDIT THROUGH 900-TRANSFER.
PERFORM 500-TAX-DETAIL THRU 800-FINAL-TAX.
```

To fully understand what happens when a PERFORM statement is executed, consider the following:

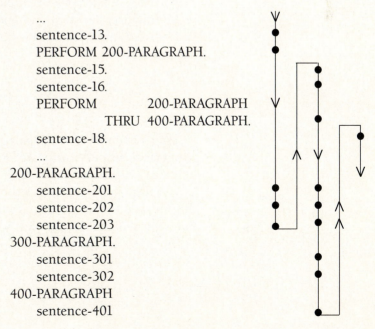

```
    ...
    sentence-13.
    PERFORM 200-PARAGRAPH.
    sentence-15.
    sentence-16.
    PERFORM          200-PARAGRAPH
                THRU  400-PARAGRAPH.
    sentence-18.
    ...
200-PARAGRAPH.
    sentence-201
    sentence-202
    sentence-203
300-PARAGRAPH.
    sentence-301
    sentence-302
400-PARAGRAPH
    sentence-401
```

First sentence-13 is executed. Then PERFORM 200-PARAGRAPH is executed. This will cause execution control to jump to the beginning of 200-PARAGRAPH and then sentences 201, 202, and 203 to be executed in that order. Control then jumps back to the sentence following the PER-FORM statement, so that sentence-15 is executed, then sentence-16.

Then the next PERFORM is executed. This causes control to jump to the beginning of 200-PARAGRAPH. This paragraph is executed, and then 300-PARAGRAPH, followed by 400-PARAGRAPH. Control then reverts back to sentence-18.

Notice that in the procedure in Figure 4.3 the group of PERFORM statements

```
PERFORM 400-COMPUTE-INTEREST.
PERFORM 500-COMPUTE-NEW-PRINCIPAL.
PERFORM 600-PREPARE-DETAIL-LINE.
```

could have been replaced by the single statement

```
PERFORM 400-COMPUTE-INTEREST
        THRU 600-PREPARE-DETAIL-LINE.
```

However, the separate PERFORM statements are considered to be better programming style. The use of the THRU option is not recommended.

Numbering paragraphs helps you to find them

It is common practice to prefix each paragraph name with a number, typically the series 100, 200, 300, and so on. The paragraphs are numbered in the order written. Thus 100 is prefixed to the first paragraph, 200 to the next, and so on.

Numbering becomes important when the program is large. Suppose you are reading a 30-page program and you encounter the statement 'PER-FORM 600-COMPUTE-TAX.' If paragraphs are numbered consecutively, it will be much easier for you to find that paragraph. This numbering system will be used in the rest of this book.

Paragraphs can be grouped into sections

In long programs, related paragraphs are often grouped into sections. (Remember, section names are arbitrary and use the same naming rules as identifiers.) A section name for a new section begins on the A-margin.

If there are sections in a program, conventionally, paragraphs within the first section should be prefixed with an 'A,' those within the second section with a 'B,' and so on. Thus you could have

```
PROCEDURE DIVISION.
A-SECTION SECTION.
A100-PARAGRAPH.
    ...
    MOVE . . .
    ...
A200-PARAGRAPH.
    ...
    WRITE . . .
    ...
B-SECTION SECTION.
B100-PARAGRAPH.
    ...
    READ . . .
    ...
B200-PARAGRAPH.
    ...
    READ . . .
    ...
```

PERFORM . . . UNTIL is used with repeated and conditional paragraph execution

Much business data processing involves applying the same set of instructions to a succession of records. The set of instructions or statements thus has to be executed repeatedly until there are no records left. The PERFORM . . . UNTIL statement is probably the most commonly used statement for repeated, or looped, execution of a paragraph.

Syntax for the PERFORM . . . UNTIL Statement

The syntax for PERFORM . . . UNTIL is

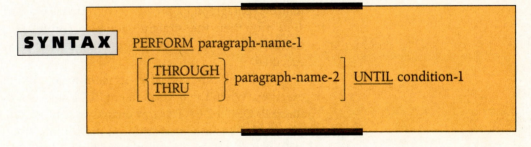

SYNTAX
PERFORM paragraph-name-1
$\left[\left\{ \begin{matrix} \underline{THROUGH} \\ \underline{THRU} \end{matrix} \right\} \text{paragraph-name-2} \right]$ $\underline{UNTIL}$ condition-1

Some valid statements are

```
PERFORM 300-ERROR-PARAGRAPH
        UNTIL MORE-DIGITS = 'NO'.
PERFORM 600-RECORD-PROCESSING
        UNTIL MORE-RECORDS = 'NO'.
```

```
PERFORM 200-READ-ROUTINE-1 THRU 600-READ-ROUTINE-4
          UNTIL EMPLOYEE-CODE = 'E2345'.
PERFORM 300-PARAGRAPH
          UNTIL X > 4
```

Be aware of how the condition affects the PERFORM . . . UNTIL statement

What follows UNTIL is a *condition*. When a condition is evaluated it is found to be either true or false.

The most common type of PERFORM . . . UNTIL statement involves a single paragraph of instructions, such as this:

```
PERFORM P2 UNTIL condition-1.
```

This statement will typically appear in a program in one paragraph, and P2 will be the name of some other paragraph. Thus, it typically appears as follows:

P1.
   ...
   statement-5.
   statement-6.
   PERFORM P2 UNTIL condition-1.
   statement-8.
   statement-9.
   ...
P2.
   statement-100.
   statement-101.
   statement-102.

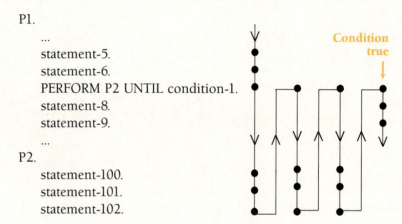

In paragraph P1 there is straight sequence of instructions. Statement-5 is executed, followed by statement-6, followed by the PERFORM . . . UNTIL statement. When the PERFORM P2 UNTIL is executed, execution control jumps to paragraph P2 provided condition-1 evaluates to false. If condition-1 is true, then the straight sequence continues, that is, statement-8 is executed, followed by statement-9, and so on; paragraph P2 would not be executed.

If condition-1 is false, execution of PERFORM causes P2 to be executed. When the last statement of P2 has been executed, condition-1 in the PERFORM P2 UNTIL is evaluated once more. If it evaluates to false, then paragraph P2 is executed again. At the end of executing P2 again, following execution of the last statement of paragraph P2, condition-1 will again be evaluated. If it is false, P2 is executed yet again, and so on.

Sooner or later, if condition-1 has been constructed properly, at the end of P2 execution condition-1 will evaluate to true. When this happens, execution control reverts back to the statement following the PERFORM, and repeated execution of P2 ends. Thus statement-8 is executed, followed by statement-9, and so on.

The logic connected with execution of this PERFORM P2 UNTIL statement is also illustrated in Figure 4.5.

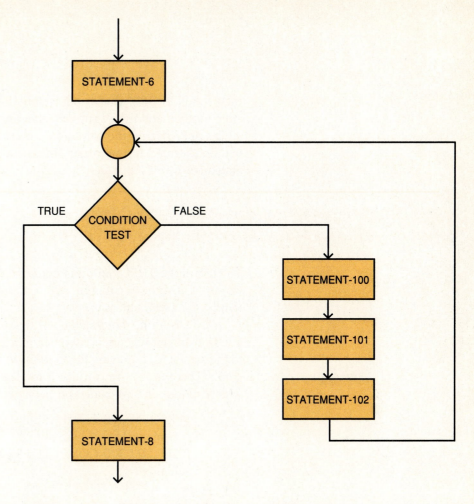

Figure 4.5 *Flowchart for a PERFORM . . . UNTIL statement.*

The important thing to remember about this PERFORM statement is that the condition-1 is evaluated before each execution of P2. If condition-1 is false, P2 is executed. If it is true, the statement following PERFORM is executed.

THRU allows looped execution of several paragraphs

If the THRU or THROUGH option is used, the only difference is that instead of a single paragraph being executed repeatedly, a group of pararaphs, written one after another in the program, is executed repeatedly. Thus if you have

P2.
    ...
    PERFORM P3 THROUGH P5 UNTIL condition-1.
    statement-6
    ...
P3.
    ...

P4.

    ...

P5.

    ...

then the PERFORM causes paragraphs P3, P4, and P5 to be executed one after another, and then again one after another, and so on. Before each execution of P3 begins, the condition-1 is evaluated. If it is false, P3, P4, and P5 will be executed in that order. If it is true, execution control will revert to Statement-6 in P1.

THRU is sometimes used with a paragraph containing only EXIT

The use of the THRU option is not common and is probably best avoided. However, at some installations it is commonly used with a paragraph containing the EXIT statement.

EXIT is a one-word statement that causes no operation to be carried out on data. But when it is used in a paragraph, it causes control to go back to the statement following the PERFORM statement that executed the paragraph. This means you can use it to clearly mark the end of a paragraph, with a special end-of-paragraph paragraph.

```
PERFORM 200-COMPUTE-INTEREST THRU 200-EXIT.
statement-4.
PERFORM 300-COMPUTE-PRINCIPAL THRU 400-EXIT.
statement-6.
200-COMPUTE-INTEREST.
    statement-21.
    statement-22.
    statement-23.
200-EXIT.
    EXIT.
300-COMPUTE-PRINCIPAL.
    statement-31.
    statement-32.
300-EXIT.
    EXIT.
```

This structure is useful if you sometimes want to stop processing a normal paragraph before the end, as in:

```
PERFORM 200-COMPUTE-INTEREST THRU 200-EXIT.
statement-4.

...
200-COMPUTE-INTEREST.
    IF (condition) GO TO 200-EXIT.
    statement-22.
    statement-23.
200-EXIT.
    EXIT.
```

Here an IF-statement (see Chapter 6) is used to cause a jump in execution control. At the beginning of paragraph 200-COMPUTE-INTEREST, if the condition is true, control jumps over the rest of 200-COMPUTE-INTEREST to the EXIT statement, which then causes control to revert back to Statement-4. The GO TO verb is used to jump, in a case like this. GO TO should be used rarely, if at all. Its arbitrary use can wreak havoc with the structure of a program.

4.2
The common non-computational COBOL verbs are MOVE, READ, WRITE, PERFORM, OPEN, and CLOSE

A COBOL INSTRUCTION normally begins with a verb in the form of an imperative or command. Thus, MOVE, READ, WRITE, PERFORM, OPEN, CLOSE, and so on are common COBOL verbs, although they are often referred to as commands. These verbs are also non-computational—no arithmetic operations are carried out when they are used.

For any verb, there is normally a variety of statement types that can be constructed, that is, several different syntax formats or constructions are possible. To be able to use a verb, you must know the syntax formats, understand the use of each one, and comprehend its semantics.

This overview takes the more usual syntax formats for the common non-computational verbs and discusses the semantics. The computational verbs COMPUTE, ADD, SUBTRACT, MULTIPLY, and DIVIDE are the computational COBOL verbs and are covered later in the chapter.

Later in the book, as appropriate, you will be given a fuller treatment of syntax formats and associated semantics.

The OPEN verb opens files

The following syntax applies to OPEN:

```
          ┌ INPUT    file-name-1 ... ┐
OPEN      │                          │
          └ OUTPUT   file-name-2 ... ┘
```

Note that the ellipses (. . .) mean that you can include further entries of the same type, as required.

The following are valid OPEN statements:

```
OPEN INPUT ACCOUNT-IN.

OPEN INPUT ACCOUNT-IN TRANSACTIONS-IN.

OPEN OUTPUT REPORT-OUT.

OPEN INPUT ACCOUNT-IN
     OUTPUT B-REPORT-OUT.
```

It is best to place each file on a separate line. That way, if there is a problem in opening the file, the system will display a line number pinpointing where the error occurred in the program. If each file is on a separate line, there will be no doubt as to which file caused the error.

The semantics of the OPEN statement are as follows:

- A file can be read when it is opened with INPUT.
- A file can be written when it is opened with OUTPUT.
- OPEN INPUT prepares a file for reading.
- OPEN OUTPUT prepares a file for writing.

The CLOSE verb closes files

It is standard practice to close a file after use. With most operating systems, however, the system will close the files automatically when the program stops executing if you omit the CLOSE statement. Nevertheless, this is poor practice, since there are operating systems in which peculiar things can happen if you do not close your files within the program.

The syntax for the CLOSE verb is

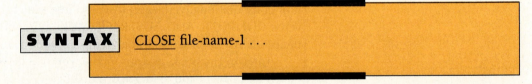

SYNTAX   CLOSE file-name-1 . . .

Valid CLOSE statements are

```
CLOSE ACCOUNT-IN.

CLOSE ACCOUNT-IN
      REPORT-OUT.
```

The semantics of the CLOSE statement are as follows:

- When a file previously opened for INPUT has been closed, it can no longer be read.
- When a file previously opened for OUTPUT has been closed, it can no longer be written.
- If you want to read a file currently open for OUTPUT, you close it first and then open it for INPUT.

Thus you could not have the following:

```
OPEN OUTPUT NEW-MASTER.
. . .
WRITE . . .
. . .
READ NEW-MASTER . . .                    error!
```

You would have to code:

```
OPEN OUTPUT NEW-MASTER.
...
WRITE . . .
...
CLOSE NEW-MASTER.

OPEN INPUT NEW-MASTER.
...
READ NEW-MASTER . . .
...
CLOSE NEW-MASTER.
```

The READ verb makes the next input record available for processing

The syntax for READ is shown here:

SYNTAX

READ file-name RECORD [INTO identifier]
                    AT END imperative-statement
[END-READ]

The following are valid READ statements:

```
READ ACCOUNT-IN
        AT END MOVE 'NO' TO MORE-RECORDS.

READ ACCOUNT-IN INTO AC-RECORD-IN
        AT END PERFORM END-OF-FILE-PROCESSING.

READ ACCOUNT-IN INTO AC-RECORD-IN
    AT END MOVE 'NO FIRST RECORD' TO REPORT-RECORD-OUT
            WRITE REPORT-RECORD-OUT
            STOP RUN
END-READ.
```

Note that the identifier following INTO (such as AC-RECORD-IN) must be specified in the WORKING-STORAGE SECTION of the DATA DIVISION.

The last example has a composite imperative statement following AT END. Instead of a collection of statements following AT END, it is common to use PERFORM with a paragraph, for example:

```
READ ACCOUNT-IN
        AT END PERFORM 500-NO-FIRST-RECORD.
...
```

```
500-NO-FIRST-RECORD.
    MOVE 'NO FIRST RECORD' TO REPORT-
        RECORD-OUT.
    WRITE REPORT-RECORD-OUT.
    STOP RUN.
```

The semantics for READ are

- If the INTO clause is omitted, the next record is read into
  the input buffer record identifier for the file specified in the
  FILE SECTION of the DATA DIVISION.
- If the INTO clause is included, the next record is read into
  a. The input area record for the file specified in the FILE
     SECTION of the DATA DIVISION, and
  b. Into the working-storage record structure specified after
     INTO.
- When the last record has been read and the next READ execution attempts to read a nonexistent record, then the AT
  END statements are executed.

Suppose you have a file ACCOUNT-IN, a buffer record structure
ACCOUNT-RECORD-IN, and a working-storage structure WS-RECORD-IN.
Then the statement

```
READ ACCOUNT-IN INTO WS-RECORD-IN.
```

is exactly equivalent to

```
READ ACCOUNT-IN.
MOVE ACCOUNT-RECORD-IN TO WS-RECORD-IN.
```

In either case, the result is that the next record becomes available in both
ACCOUNT-RECORD-IN and WS-RECORD-IN.

The INTO clause is quite commonly used. However, with reading of
sequential files it is common practice to read an input record only as far as
the input buffer (or input area), and not into working storage as well, as this
saves some processing time. But if using INTO makes your program clearer,
use it. Computers are getting to be very fast, so the extra processing time is
probably negligible.

The optional END-READ (in COBOL 85) is the *scope terminator* for the
READ statement and clearly signifies the end of the statement. It is useful
with READ statements within IF-statements. (See Chapter 5 for an example
of where it is needed.)

The WRITE statement sends records to output

The WRITE statement has quite extensive syntax and semantics. Most of
the syntax is for specifying new pages, new lines, and so on, when writing
records to a printer. The basic syntax is

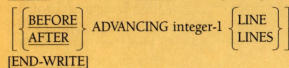

WRITE buffer-record [FROM working-storage identifier]

$$\left[\begin{matrix} \underline{BEFORE} \\ \underline{AFTER} \end{matrix} \right\} \text{ADVANCING integer-1} \left\{ \begin{matrix} \underline{LINE} \\ \underline{LINES} \end{matrix} \right\}$$

[END-WRITE]

These are valid WRITE statements:

```
WRITE REPORT-RECORD-OUT.

WRITE REPORT-RECORD-OUT FROM WS-LINE-OUT.

WRITE REPORT-RECORD-OUT FROM WS-LINE-OUT
      BEFORE ADVANCING 1 LINE

END-WRITE.

WRITE REPORT-RECORD-OUT FROM WS-LINE-OUT
      AFTER ADVANCING 2 LINES.
```

In this example, REPORT-RECORD-OUT is an output buffer (output area) identifier that would have to be specified in the FILE SECTION of the DATA DIVISION. The identifier WS-LINE-OUT would have to be specified in the working-storage section. If this had been specified:

```
FILE SECTION.
FD  REPORT-FILE     LABEL RECORDS ARE OMITTED.
01  REPORT-RECORD-OUT.
    05 . . .
```

then the preceding WRITE statements would all cause a record to be written to the file REPORT-FILE. But, notice that the name of the file does *not* appear in any of the WRITE statements. The compiler assumes that the record must go to the file REPORT-FILE because the output buffer record REPORT-RECORD-OUT specified in the WRITE statement belongs to the file REPORT-FILE.

In passing, notice that

```
WRITE REPORT-RECORD-OUT FROM WS-LINE-OUT.
```

is exactly equivalent to

```
MOVE WS-LINE-OUT TO REPORT-RECORD-OUT.
WRITE REPORT-RECORD-OUT.
```

The most commonly used form of the WRITE statement is

```
WRITE buffer-record
      FROM working-storage-identifier.
```

The BEFORE and AFTER clauses are used for skipping lines when the output record is being transferred to a printer or display screen. If you use WRITE . . . BEFORE ADVANCING 2 LINES, the record will first be printed and then the printer will leave one blank line. If you use WRITE . . . AFTER

ADVANCING 4 LINES, the printer will first leave three blank lines and then print the output record.

WRITE ... AFTER ADVANCING is the most commonly used form, since it is the most natural. Do *not* mix WRITE ... AFTER and WRITE ... BEFORE statements in a single program. (For the explanation, see Chapter 7.) Also, if you use WRITE ... AFTER with a printer file, all WRITE statements directing output to that file must be WRITE ... AFTER. Note that single spacing is achieved by using repeated executions of WRITE ... AFTER ADVANCING 1 LINE.

END-WRITE (in COBOL 85) is the optional scope terminator for the WRITE statement and simply signifies the end of the statement.

Literals can be used with many statements

Suppose you have the following MOVE statements:

```
MOVE 'MARY' TO FIRST-NAME.
MOVE 'STEVANOVITCH' TO LAST-NAME.
MOVE 3800.4 TO SALARY.
MOVE 500007.783 TO INTEREST.
```

As a result of executing the first statement, the identifier FIRST-NAME is assigned the value 'MARY'. As a result of executing the third statement, the identifier SALARY is assigned the value 3800.4.

The quantities 'MARY' and 'STEVANOVITCH' used in the first two examples are alphanumeric literals. The quantities 3800.4 and 500007.783 used in the remaining examples are numeric literals.

A literal in a statement is a quantity with a value that is spelled out in the statement. However, if the literal is alphanumeric, it must be enclosed in single quotes. (Some systems permit either single or double quotes, and some require double quotes, for instance, "MARY".) Thus literals are simply program constants, either numeric or alphanumeric.

> **RULES** **Forming Literals**
>
> **Alphanumeric literals** The maximum length for alphanumeric literals is 160 characters. Any characters are allowed, except quotation marks and apostrophes, since the literals must be enclosed in single quotes (some systems permit or require double quotes).
>
> **Numeric literals** The maximum length for numeric literals is 18 digits. A decimal point may be used, but it must not be the last character. A sign (+ or -) also may be used, but it must apppear first.

Literals are used most commonly with the VALUE clause, for placing an initial value in an identifier, as introduced in Chapter 3.

Avoid literals in the PROCEDURE DIVISION

You can use literals in many statements. They are not uncommon with MOVE and the arithmetic statements. However, literals should be kept to a minimum in the PROCEDURE DIVISION. It is best to use an identifier, initialized to the literal value by a VALUE clause, instead of the literal itself. This is particularly true if the same literal is used more than once in a program, or if it is a value that may be changed at some time in the future.

Thus,

```
COMPUTE TAX-PAYABLE = (GROSS * 18.5) / 100
```

should be replaced with

```
01   CURRENT-TAX-RATE    PIC 9(02)V99 VALUE 0.185.
...
     COMPUTE TAX-PAYABLE = GROSS * CURRENT-TAX-RATE.
```

The figurative constants SPACES and ZEROS are useful

Instead of using the alphanumeric literal ' ' (blank), you can use a figurative constant called SPACES, which is also a COBOL-reserved word. The statement

```
MOVE SPACES TO FIRST-NAME.
```

places blanks in the identifier FIRST-NAME.

Likewise, instead of using the literal 0, or 0.0, you can use the figurative constant ZEROS (or ZEROES or ZERO). The statement

```
MOVE ZERO TO SALARY.
```

will place the value 0 or 0.0 (depending on the picture) in the identifier SALARY.

There is more to the MOVE statement than you might think

At first glance, the MOVE statement is trivially simple. But in reality there are many aspects and much to know about it. This overview covers only the basics. The essential syntax for MOVE is

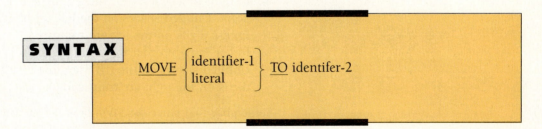

SYNTAX

$$\text{MOVE} \begin{Bmatrix} \text{identifier-1} \\ \text{literal} \end{Bmatrix} \underline{\text{TO}} \text{ identifer-2}$$

Suppose you have the following elementary identifiers specified in working storage:

```
01 WS-WORK-AREAS.
    05  FIRST-NAME        PIC X(08).
    05  LAST-NAME         PIC X(08).
    05  SALARY            PIC 9(05)V99.
    05  NET-WORTH         PIC S9(06).
    05  WAGE              PIC 9(05)V99.
01 ...
    05  WAGE-OUT          PIC $ZZ,Z99.99.
```

these identifiers are used here with examples of valid MOVE statements.

Example 1:   An alphanumeric MOVE to FIRST-NAME, PIC X(08)

```
MOVE 'MARY' TO FIRST-NAME.
```

The contents of FIRST-NAME become

```
MARYbbbbb
```

The value is inserted into the identifier from left to right, or left justified. Blank characters (each denoted by a "b") are placed in unused character spaces to the right.

Example 2:   An alphanumeric MOVE to LAST-NAME, PIC X(08)

```
MOVE 'STEVANOVITCH' TO LAST-NAME.
```

The contents of LAST-NAME become

```
STEVANOV
```

The excess characters on the right are truncated.

Example 3: A numeric MOVE to SALARY, PIC 9(05)V9(2)

```
MOVE 3800.4 TO SALARY.
```

The contents of salary become

```
0380040
```

Notice that zeros are inserted on both the right and left. The following rules apply: The number is aligned on the implicit decimal point, and digits are inserted

a. In right to left order for integer digits left of the decimal point. Unfilled spaces on the left are filled with zeros. Excess digits on the left are truncated.

b. In left to right order for digits right of the decimal point. Unfilled spaces on the right are filled with zeros. Excess digits on the right are truncated.

Remember that since 9(05)V9(2) is the picture for SALARY, no decimal point is stored.

Example 4: A numeric MOVE to SALARY, PIC 9(05)V9(2)

```
MOVE 500007.783 TO SALARY.
```

The contents of SALARY become

0000778

Here there is truncation on both right and left.

Example 5: A numeric MOVE to SALARY, PIC 9(05)V9(2)

```
MOVE -56.78 TO SALARY.
```

The contents of SALARY become

0005678

The minus sign is completely lost. If you now executed

```
COMPUTE X = SALARY + 100.
```

X would get the value 156.78, so that SALARY has a positive value for arithmetic purposes, which would be wrong.

Example 6: A numeric MOVE to NET-WORTH, PIC S9(06)

```
MOVE 7897 TO NET-WORTH.
```

The contents of NET-WORTH become

007897̟

A plus sign is assumed to be marked (by means of a 1-bit marker) within the last digit (7). The sign does not occupy a character space. It is conventional in textbooks to indicate this with the sign above the last digit.

Example 7: A numeric MOVE to NET-WORTH, PIC S9(06)

```
MOVE -56.42 TO NET-WORTH.
```

The contents of NET-WORTH become

000056̄

The fractional part is truncated, and the sign is stored with a 1-bit marker within the last digit (6). The sign does not occupy a character space. This is shown with a minus sign above the last digit.

Example 8: MOVEs with figurative constants

```
MOVE SPACES TO FIRST-NAME.
MOVE ZEROS TO SALARY.
```

The contents of FIRST-NAME become

b b b b b b b

The contents of SALARY become

0000000

As we saw in the previous section, SPACES and ZEROS are called figurative constants. SPACES has the value blanks and ZEROS the value zero. (ZEROS can be written ZERO, ZEROS, or ZEROES.)

Example 9: A MOVE between FIRST-NAME, PIC X(08) and LAST-NAME, PIC X(08)

```
MOVE 'JOHN' TO FIRST-NAME.
MOVE FIRST-NAME TO LAST-NAME.
```

LAST-NAME gets the value

```
JOHNbbbbb
```

Example 10: A MOVE between SALARY, PIC 9(05)V99, and WAGEs, PIC 9(05)V9(02)

```
MOVE 47.456 TO SALARY.
MOVE SALARY TO WAGES.
```

WAGE gets the value

```
0004745
```

The alignment is on the implicit decimal point.

Example 11: MOVEs to the edit identifier WAGE-OUT, PIC $ZZ,Z99.99

```
MOVE 26.42 TO WAGE-OUT.
```

WAGE-OUT gets the value

```
$    26.42.
```

```
MOVE 7,247.8 TO WAGE-OUT.          error!   7,247.8 not a literal
MOVE 7247.8 TO WAGE-OUT.
```

WAGE-OUT gets the value

```
$ 7,247.80
```

Note that the decimal point and dollar sign are given spaces in WAGE-OUT because WAGE-OUT was defined as an edit identifier. Alignment takes place on the stored decimal point, in exactly the same way as with the implicit decimal point marker V.

Example 12: A MOVE between SALARY, PIC 9(05)V9(02) and the edit identifier WAGE-OUT, PIC $ZZ,Z99.99

```
MOVE 57567.9 TO SALARY.
MOVE SALARY TO WAGE-OUT.
```

WAGE-OUT gets the value

```
$57,567.90
```

A group MOVE, with group identifiers, is alphanumeric

If a group identifier is used as the sending identifier in a MOVE statement, the contents of the entire group identifier are moved. In such a MOVE, the entire contents are treated as a composite alphanumeric quantity, even if the group identifier contains numeric identifiers. This composite alphanumeric quantity, the contents of the group identifier, is placed left justified in the receiving identifier. Thus, the receiving identifier has data assigned to it as if it were receiving an alphanumeric literal – even though the data are actually a composite of the identifiers comprising the sending group identifier.

To get the MOVE to work properly, the sending group identifier should have a structure exactly like the receiving group identifier. However, if the structures do not match, the MOVE will still be carried out, sometimes with disastrous results, as the following examples show.

Example 1: Correct group MOVE with matching structures

Consider the following:

```
01 A.
     05 B    PIC 9(02) VALUE 24.
     05 C    PIC X(03) VALUE 'YES'.
01 Q.
     05 R    PIC 9(02)
     05 S    PIC X(03).
...
MOVE A TO Q.
```

A has the value 24YES. Q gets the value 24YES, with R getting 24 and S getting 'YES'. This is a correct group MOVE.

Example 2: Incorrect group MOVE with mismatching group identifiers

```
01 A.
     05 B    PIC 9(02) VALUE 24.
     05 C    PIC X(03) VALUE 'YES'.
01 V.
     05 X    PIC 9(03).
     05 W    PIC X(02).
...
MOVE A TO V.                          error!
```

A has the composite alphanumeric value '24YES'. So V gets '24YES' left justified. But this means that the numeric identifier X gets 24Y, which is wrong, and W gets the value 'ES', also wrong. The MOVE is correct, but the way the receiving identifiers are arranged results in error. No error message will follow execution of this MOVE statement, and the program will continue execution. However, if you later try to use the numeric identifier X, containing 24Y, in an arithmetic statement, the program will stop and an error message will be displayed by the operating system.

Example 3: Some interesting group MOVEs

```
a. 01 A.
       05 B    PIC 9(02) VALUE 24.
       05 C    PIC X(03) VALUE 'YES'.
   01 TARGET   PIC X(07).
   MOVE A TO TARGET.
```

TARGET gets '24YESbb' ("b" represents a blank).

b. `MOVE ZEROS TO A.`

A gets '00000'. Thus, B gets 00, C gets '000'.

`MOVE SPACES TO A.`

A gets '   '. Thus C gets '   ', B gets ' '. B cannot be used in arithmetic statements.

c. `MOVE '24YES' TO A.`

B gets 24 and C gets 'YES'.

`MOVE 24555 TO A.`

B gets 24 and C gets '555'.

Note that you can literally MOVE anything, whether numeric or alphanumeric, to a group identifier. It is up to the programmer to ensure that the result makes sense.

A table is useful for checking if a MOVE is allowed

The following table is a handy way to check if a particular MOVE is allowed:

SENDING FIELD	RECEIVING FIELD		
	NUMERIC IDENTIFIER	ALPHANUMERIC IDENTIFIER	GROUP IDENTIFIER
Numeric identifier	yes	no	yes
Alphanumeric identifier	no	yes	yes
Group identifier	no	yes	yes
Numeric literal	yes	no	yes
Alphanumeric literal	no	yes	yes
Zeros	yes	yes	yes
Spaces	no	yes	yes

Notice that a group identifier will receive anything.

Recall numeric identifiers with the SIGN LEADING SEPARATE attribute

Suppose you have an input buffer record identifier

```
01  TM-RECORD-IN.
    05 TM-CITY-IN              PIC  X(10).
    05 TM-LOW-TEMP-IN          PIC  S9(02).
```

where the record will receive data giving a TM-CITY-IN name and its over-night low temperature.

There can be a problem with how the sign is stored on the input medium. Suppose the input record is being read from a disk file. In that case, it would need to have been previously written onto the disk file when the file was originally created. Thus, if the record to be read has the field values 'NEW YORK' and -16, the record on disk should have been stored as

NEWbYORKbb16
            ‾

with the minus sign stored as a 1-bit sign marker within the last digit. When this record is read from the disk into TM-RECORD-IN by a READ statement, the data are transferred as in a group MOVE. It is therefore transmitted to TM-RECORD-IN one character at a time, from left to right. The last digit of the record, altered by a sign marker, goes into the last character space of TM-RECORD-IN, as it should. There is no problem with this way of reading negative fields into signed numeric identifiers.

But now suppose the record is to be entered from punch cards or from a terminal. In that case, you might enter at the keyboard

NEWbYORKbb-16

This record is one character longer than TM-RECORD-IN, because you have entered the sign as a separate character. A READ on this record will transfer it from the keyboard, character by character, as in a group MOVE. The result is the identifier TM-LOW-TEMP-IN will get the value -1, which is an error. Furthermore, since the record transmitted is too long for TM-RECORD-IN, in many cases the program will terminate abnormally.

The solution to the difficulty is to define TM-LOW-TEMP-IN with the attribute SIGN LEADING SEPARATE in the FILE SECTION of the DATA DIVISION

```
FD   TERMINAL-FILE-IN    LABEL RECORDS ARE OMITTED.
01   TM-RECORD-IN.
     05 TM-CITY-IN             PIC  X(10).
     05 TM-LOW-TEMP-IN         PIC S9(02) SIGN LEADING SEPARATE.
```

This means TM-LOW-TEMP-IN now occupies three character spaces of memory space, with the first character space being used for the sign. In other words, the sign gets a space, instead of the usual 1-bit sign marker in the last digit. However, the identifier is still a numeric identifier, and not an edit identifier, and can be used in computations.

If the record NEWbYORKbb-16 is now read from the keyboard into TM-RECORD-IN, TM-LOW-TEMP-IN will get the value -16, which is correct.

If you wanted to store the records read from the terminal as a disk file, you have the option of converting the TM-LOW-TEMP-IN field value to the more compact two-digit field (with the sign stored as a 1-bit marker in the last digit). You could do this as follows:

```
FD   TERMINAL-FILE-IN    LABEL RECORDS ARE OMITTED.
01   TM-RECORD-IN.
     05 TM-CITY-IN             PIC  X(10).
     05 TM-LOW-TEMP-IN         PIC S9(02) SIGN LEADING SEPARATE.
FD   DISK-FILE-OUT       LABEL RECORDS ARE STANDARD.
01   DK-RECORD-OUT.
     05 DK-CITY-OUT            PIC  X(10).
     05 DK-LOW-TEMP-OUT        PIC S9(02).
...
READ TERMINAL-FILE-IN
            AT END . . .
MOVE TM-CITY-IN TO DK-CITY-OUT.
MOVE TM-LOW-TEMP-IN TO DK-LOW-TEMP-OUT.
WRITE DK-RECORD-OUT.
```

Thus if a record read from the keyboard is

NEWbYORKbb-16

the record written to the disk is

NEWbYORKbb16

Notice that in the preceding excerpt you could not use the group MOVE.

```
MOVE TM-RECORD-IN TO DK-RECORD-OUT.        error!
```

The two group identifiers do not have matching structures. Indeed, the receiving field is one character space longer than the sending field.

Avoid ambiguous identifiers

It is possible to have the same elementary identifier name in two quite different group identifiers.

```
01 ID-1.
   05 TAX          PIC 9(03).
   05 INCOME       PIC X(05).
01 ID-2.
   05 PERSON       PIC X(15).
   05 TAX          PIC 9(03).
```

If you write

```
MOVE 867 TO TAX.
```

there is ambiguity, since there are two quite different TAX fields. You have to qualify the identifier name, as in the following:

```
MOVE 867 TO TAX IN ID-1.
MOVE TAX IN ID-1 TO TAX IN ID-2.
```

You should avoid defining the same identifier name within different group identifiers. It is not considered good practice to need to qualify elementary identifier names. Thus, in one group identifier you might use D1-TAX, in another D2-TAX, in a third WS-TAX, and so on.

A multiple ('shotgun') MOVE is allowed

Notice that you can *also* move a literal or the contents of an identifier to multiple identifiers.

```
MOVE 'YES' TO VOTE-1, VOTE-3, VOTE-9, VOTE-12.
```

There is a special MOVE called MOVE CORRESPONDING

The MOVE CORRESPONDING verb does not have a good reputation and is probably best avoided. Good programs are clear and concise, and extensive

use of MOVE CORRESPONDING tends to "muddy the waters."
Suppose you have

```
01  A1.
    05  AX                  PIC 9(03).
    05  AY                  PIC X(04)
    05  AZ.
        10      AZ-P        PIC 9(05).
        10      AZ-Q        PIC X(08).
    05  AW                  PIC X(15).
01  A87.
    05  AZ-P                PIC 9(05).
    05  AQQ.
        10      AZ-Q        PIC X(08)
        10      AQ-R        PIC X(01)
        10      AX          PIC 9(03)
...
    MOVE CORRESPONDING A1 TO A87.
```

You can see that the group identifiers A1 and A87 do not match, so that a conventional MOVE would lead to nonsense. But what happens here is that data are moved between those identifiers with the same names, and *only* those identifiers. Thus, the MOVE is equivalent to:

```
MOVE AX        IN A1    TO    AX      IN A87.
MOVE AZ-P      IN A1    TO    AZ-P    IN A87.
MOVE AZ-Q      IN A1    TO    AZ-Q    IN A87.
```

The MOVE CORRESPONDING is not recommended because it is generally poor practice to have identifiers with the same names in different group identifiers. Avoid it.

You can use ACCEPT and DISPLAY for input and output of small amounts of data

Sometimes it is desirable to output a brief message or the value of a few identifiers on the screen of the system terminal. In that case, the DISPLAY verb is useful. For example, if you have

```
01 NAME       PIC X(8)        VALUE 'SMITH'.
...
DISPLAY NAME, 'VERY GOOD'.
```

the following will appear on the screen of the terminal:

```
SMITH     VERY GOOD
```

The list of identifiers or literals following DISPLAY are output.

To read a single literal input from a terminal into an identifier, you can use the ACCEPT verb. Suppose you have the identifier ANY-MORE, and are expecting a user or operator to enter a value 'YES' or 'NO' at the system terminal. You could code

```
01 ANY-MORE       PIC  X(03).
...
```

```
DISPLAY 'RESPOND YES OR NO.'.
ACCEPT ANY-MORE.
```

On the terminal screen, you would see

RESPOND YES OR NO.   **printed by DISPLAY statement**
YES   **entered at keyboard by user**

When the program executes DISPLAY, the message is printed. Then the program waits until the RETURN key on the terminal has been pressed. Then the first three characters (or fewer, if there are not three) entered before RETURN was pressed are transferred to the identifier ANY-MORE.

ACCEPT and DISPLAY are suitable for very small amounts of data. For large amounts, as with files, READ and WRITE should be used. DISPLAY is often used in debugging programs. For details see the end of Chapter 10.

4.3
COMPUTE is mainly used with more complex computations

THE COMPUTATIONAL VERBS are COMPUTE, ADD, SUBTRACT, MULTIPLY, and DIVIDE; they are used to perform arithmetic operations on the contents of numeric identifiers. The COMPUTE verb is studied in this section.

COMPUTE is used where calculations are relatively complex. With simple arithmetic, the ADD, SUBTRACT, MULTIPLY, and DIVIDE statements are more common and easier to read.

The COMPUTE verb is powerful and flexible

The syntax for the COMPUTE verb is

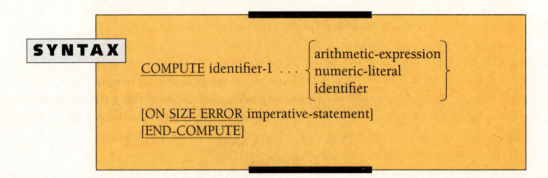

SYNTAX

COMPUTE identifier-1 ... { arithmetic-expression
                            numeric-literal
                            identifier }

[ON SIZE ERROR imperative-statement]
[END-COMPUTE]

The following are some valid COMPUTE statements:

```
COMPUTE NEW-PRINCIPAL = OLD-PRINCIPAL + INTEREST + DEPOSIT.
COMPUTE INTEREST = OLD-PRINCIPAL * (1 + RATE) / 100.
COMPUTE X = (A + B) / (A - B).
COMPUTE NEW-PRINCIPAL  =
        OLD-PRINCIPAL + INTEREST + DEPOSIT.
COMPUTE INTEREST = INTEREST-1 + INTEREST-2
        ON SIZE ERROR PERFORM 600-ERROR-PARAGRAPH.
```

```
COMPUTE COST = QUANTITY * UNIT-PRICE
              ON SIZE ERROR PERFORM 200-ERROR
                            PERFORM 300-RECOVERY
END-COMPUTE.
COMPUTE TOT1, TOTAL = 13 + 17 + 16 + 4.
```
(both TOT1 and TOTAL get the value 50.)

Note that it is poor practice to compute into two or more identifiers. The last COMPUTE statement above should be replaced with

```
COMPUTE TOT1  = 13 + 17 + 16 + 4.
MOVE TOT1 TO TOTAL.
```

When a COMPUTE statement is executed, the expression on the right of the equal sign is evaluated and the result placed in the identifier on the left of the equal sign. Thus, if you have

```
MOVE 100 TO GROSS.
MOVE 1.1 TO BONUS-RATE.
MOVE 20 TO AWARD.
MOVE 40 TO TAX.
COMPUTE NET = (GROSS + AWARD) * BONUS-RATE - TAX.
```

The value placed in NET is (100 + 20) * 1.1 - 40, or 132 - 40, or 92.

Note that the arithmetic operators + (addition), - (subtraction), * (multiplication), and / (division) must be preceded and followed by at least one space. The following is wrong:

```
COMPUTE TAX = INCOME*RATE.              error!
```

END-COMPUTE is the scope terminator (in COBOL 85) for the COMPUTE statement. It is useful for pointing out exactly where a COMPUTE statement ends, and for avoiding ambiguity in IF-statements, see Chapter 5.

Exponentiation Operator

There is a further arithmetic operator, **, for exponentiation. Thus, the following two statements are equivalent:

```
COMPUTE BOX-VOLUME = BOX-SIDE * BOX-SIDE * BOX-SIDE.
COMPUTE BOX-VOLUME = BOX-SIDE ** 3.
```

Conversely, you can get the cube root, for example, as follows:

```
COMPUTE BOX-SIDE = BOX-VOLUME ** (1 / 3)
```

Note that the ** operator requires a space on either side.

Avoid the need to use ON SIZE ERROR

You use ON SIZE ERROR if there is a chance that the result will overflow the identifier on the left. For example, suppose you have

```
WORKING-STORAGE SECTION.
...
01 TAX        PIC 999V99.
...
PROCEDURE DIVISION.
...
    COMPUTE TAX = 900.34 + 200.10
        ON SIZE ERROR PERFORM 500-OVERFLOW-ERROR.
```

Execution of the COMPUTE statement would result in 1100.44, which would be assigned to TAX. However, this value would be too large for TAX and would overflow on the left. This would cause the ON SIZE ERROR clause to be executed.

Note that if a size error does occur, the arithmetic operation specified in the statement is not performed. Only the imperative statement in ON SIZE ERROR clause is carried out. If no SIZE ERROR clause has been coded, the program will probably continue to execute with the loss of significant digits on the left.

Size or overflow errors are best avoided. You do this by making sure that the identifier left of the equal sign is large enough to hold any value that could possibly be assigned without overflowing on the left.

Avoid complex COMPUTE expressions

With the COMPUTE verb you can have a complex expression to the right of the equal sign. However, it is best not to allow such expressions to become too complex. Instead use a series of simpler expressions. For example,

```
COMPUTE A = (B * D - F) / ((G - C) * (E + P / D)).
```

could be replaced by

```
COMPUTE E1 = B * D - F.
COMPUTE E2 = (G - C) * ((E + P / D)).
COMPUTE A = E1 / E2.
```

In addition, where a COMPUTE expression involves a single addition, subtraction, multiplication, or division, it is common practice to use the corresponding ADD, SUBTRACT, MULTIPLY, or DIVIDE verb, since statements using these verbs are considered to be more readable and less mathematical. You could thus replace the preceding sequence of simple COMPUTE statements with

```
COMPUTE E1 = B * D - F.
SUBTRACT C FROM G GIVING E2.
COMPUTE E3 = E + P / D.
MULTIPLY E2 BY E3 GIVING E4.
DIVIDE E4 INTO E1 GIVING A.
```

The ADD, SUBTRACT, MULTIPLY, and DIVIDE verbs will be examined shortly.

With some computers, the operation

```
01 W  PIC 9  VALUE 8.
01 Y  PIC 9  VALUE 3.
01 Z  PIC 9  VALUE 4.
...
     COMPUTE X = W * (Y / Z).
```

will cause X to receive the result 0, instead of 6, as you would expect. The problem is that the intermediate result of Y / Z yields 0.75, but the machine allocates a memory location equivalent to a PIC 9 identifier to hold this intermediate result, so that the .75 is truncated, to give zero. When the intermediate result is multiplied by W the result is still zero.

The difficulty would not occur if you used either

```
01 Y  PIC 9V99  VALUE 3.
```

or

```
01 Z  PIC 9V99  VALUE 4.
```

or both.

If you have

```
01 Y  PIC rVf.
01 Z  PIC sVg.
```

then the intermediate memory location that holds the intermediate result of

Y op Z

where op is an arithmetic operation, is assumed to have been defined with

PIC pVd

where

d is the larger of f and g, and
p is 1 plus the larger of r and s.

This rule holds for many types of computers, particularly IBM computers. So make sure you specify enough digits right of the implicit decimal point for identifiers used in multiplication, division, and exponentiation operations. Otherwise, intermediate results may be truncated on the right, which can give rise to perplexing final results.

The program in Figure 4.1 could have fallen into this trap, where interest needed to be computed to at least three decimal places in order to round to the last cent.

```
200-PROCESS-RECORD.
    MOVE AR-PRINCIPAL-IN TO WS-PRINCIPAL-IN.
    COMPUTE INTEREST-ON-PRINCIPAL
        = (WS-PRINCIPAL-IN * AR-PRINCIPAL-RATE-IN / 100) / 12.
    MOVE AR-DEPOSIT-IN TO WS-DEPOSIT-IN.
    COMPUTE INTEREST-ON-DEPOSIT
        = ((WS-DEPOSIT-IN * AR-DEPOSIT-RATE-IN / 100)
            * AR-DEPOSIT-DAYS-IN) / 365.
```

```
COMPUTE TOTAL-INTEREST ROUNDED
       = INTEREST-ON-PRINCIPAL + INTEREST-ON-DEPOSIT.
COMPUTE NEW-PRINCIPAL-COMPUTED
       = AR-PRINCIPAL-IN + AR-DEPOSIT-IN + TOTAL-INTEREST.
MOVE    AR-CUSTOMER-NAME-IN     TO        DL-CUSTOMER-NAME-OUT.
MOVE    AR-PRINCIPAL-IN         TO        DL-OLD-PRINCIPAL-OUT.
MOVE    AR-DEPOSIT-IN           TO        DL-DEPOSIT-OUT.
MOVE    TOTAL-INTEREST          TO        DL-INTEREST-OUT.
MOVE    NEW-PRINCIPAL-COMPUTED TO         DL-NEW-PRINCIPAL-OUT.
WRITE REPORT-RECORD-OUT FROM DETAIL-LINE-OUT
              AFTER ADVANCING 1 LINE.
READ ACCOUNT-IN
          AT END MOVE 'NO' TO MORE-RECORDS.
```

Here the intermediate identifiers WS-PRINCIPAL-IN and WS-DEPOSIT-IN were used, each with PIC 9(07)V9(05) definitions, that is, five digits after the implicit decimal point, to ensure the correct degree of precision. If only

```
COMPUTE INTEREST-ON-PRINCIPAL
    = (AR-PRINCIPAL-IN * AR-PRINCIPAL-RATE-IN / 100) / 12.
COMPUTE INTEREST-ON-DEPOSIT
    = ((AR-DEPOSIT-IN * AR-DEPOSIT-RATE-IN / 100)* AR-DEPOSIT-DAYS-IN) / 365.
```

had been used, with many computers there would not be right precision, and all intermediate calculations would be truncated at the second decimal place. None of the quantities used in the expressions to the right of the equal sign are defined with more than two decimal places after the decimal point.

4.4

ADD, SUBTRACT, MULTIPLY, and DIVIDE are used with simple computations

IN COMMERCIAL PROGRAMS usually arithmetic operations are quite simple, involving simple addition, subtraction, multiplication, and division. As a result, in most commercial COBOL programs the COMPUTE verb is not used; the ADD, SUBTRACT, MULTIPLY, and DIVIDE are instead. It is reasonable to use COMPUTE only when more complex calculations, such as interest calculations, are involved, and use ADD, SUBTRACT, MULTIPLY, and DIVIDE for simple computations.

The following sections briefly summarize the syntax and semantics for the ADD, SUBTRACT, MULTIPLY, and DIVIDE verbs. Each example is followed by the COMPUTE equivalent.

ADD . . . TO Verb

The syntax is

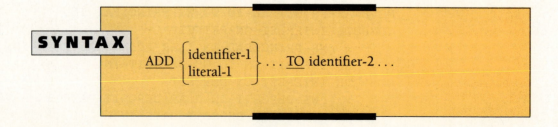

SYNTAX

$$\text{ADD} \begin{Bmatrix} \text{identifier-1} \\ \text{literal-1} \end{Bmatrix} \dots \underline{\text{TO}} \text{ identifier-2} \dots$$

Some examples, each followed by a corresponding COMPUTE, are

```
ADD INTEREST TO PRINCIPAL.
COMPUTE PRINCIPAL = INTEREST + PRINCIPAL.

ADD INTEREST, DEPOSIT TO PRINCIPAL.
COMPUTE PRINCIPAL = INTEREST + DEPOSIT + PRINCIPAL.
ADD 12, 15, 17, TAX TO TOT1.
COMPUTE TOT1 = 12 + 15 + 17 + TAX + TOT1.

ADD INTEREST, DEPOSIT TO PRINCIPAL, ACCOUNT-TOTAL.
COMPUTE PRINCIPAL = INTEREST + DEPOSIT + PRINCIPAL.
COMPUTE ACCOUNT-TOTAL = INTEREST + DEPOSIT + ACCOUNT-TOTAL.
```

Surprisingly, you have to take care with ADD . . . TO. There is a common beginner error: Suppose you have identifiers X, Y, and Z, where none of the identifiers has yet had a value assigned. Now suppose you have the following:

```
MOVE 10 TO X.
MOVE 3 TO Y.
ADD X, Y TO Z.          error!
```

This is incorrect because you are adding X, Y, and Z and placing the result in Z, but Z has no value. The ADD statement is equivalent to

```
COMPUTE Z = X + Y + Z.
```

All three identifiers must have a value. Thus the preceding sequence should be replaced with

```
MOVE 10 TO X.
MOVE 3 TO Y.
MOVE ZEROS TO Z.
ADD X, Y TO Z.
```

ADD . . . GIVING Verb

The syntax is

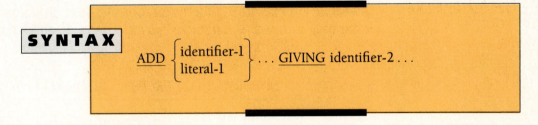

$$\text{SYNTAX} \qquad \underline{\text{ADD}} \left\{ \begin{array}{l} \text{identifier-1} \\ \text{literal-1} \end{array} \right\} \dots \underline{\text{GIVING}} \text{ identifier-2} \dots$$

Some examples are

```
ADD INTEREST, OLD-PRINCIPAL GIVING NEW-PRINCIPAL.
COMPUTE NEW-PRINCIPAL = INTEREST + OLD-PRINCIPAL.

ADD INTEREST, DEPOSIT, OLD-PRINCIPAL GIVING NEW-PRINCIPAL.
COMPUTE NEW-PRINCIPAL = INTEREST + DEPOSIT + OLD-PRINCIPAL.

ADD 12, 13, INTEREST GIVING TOTAL.
COMPUTE TOTAL = 12 + 13 + INTEREST.
```

ADD . . . TO . . . GIVING Verb

The syntax is

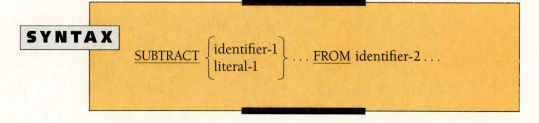

Some examples are

```
ADD INTEREST TO OLD-PRINCIPAL GIVING NEW-PRINCIPAL.
COMPUTE NEW-PRINCIPAL = INTEREST + OLD-PRINCIPAL.

ADD 12, INTEREST, 1000 GIVING NEW-PRINCIPAL.
COMPUTE NEW-PRINCIPAL = INTEREST + 12 + 1000.
```

SUBTRACT . . . FROM Verb

The syntax is

SYNTAX

$$\underline{\text{SUBTRACT}} \left\{ \begin{array}{l} \text{identifier-1} \\ \text{literal-1} \end{array} \right\} \dots \underline{\text{FROM}} \text{ identifier-2} \dots$$

Some examples are

```
SUBTRACT TAX FROM INCOME.
COMPUTE INCOME = INCOME - TAX.

SUBTRACT TAX, 100, PENSION-CONTRIBUTION FROM INCOME.
COMPUTE INCOME = INCOME - TAX - 100 - PENSION-CONTRIBUTION.
```

SUBTRACT . . . FROM . . . GIVING Verb

The syntax is

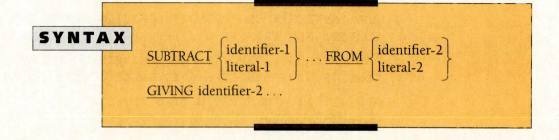

Some examples are

```
SUBTRACT TAX FROM INCOME GIVING NET-INCOME.
COMPUTE NET-INCOME = INCOME - TAX.

SUBTRACT TAX, 100, PENSION-COST FROM INCOME GIVING NET-INCOME.
COMPUTE NET-INCOME = INCOME - TAX - 100 - PENSION-COST.
```

MULTIPLY . . . BY Verb

The syntax is

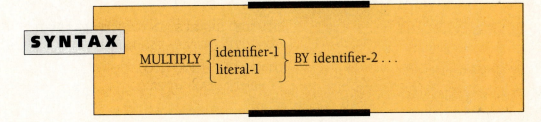

Some examples are

```
MULTIPLY RATE BY PRINCIPAL.
COMPUTE PRINCIPAL = PRINCIPAL * RATE.

MULTIPLY 4 BY TAX.
COMPUTE TAX = TAX * 4.
```

Study the MULTIPLY . . . BY verb carefully. Note that the result goes in the identifier(s) specified at the end.

MULTIPLY . . . BY . . . GIVING Verb

The syntax is

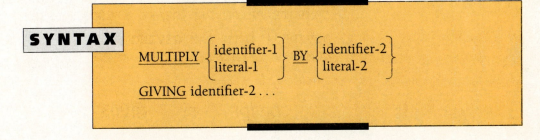

Some examples are

```
MULTIPLY PRINCIPAL BY RATE GIVING INTEREST.
COMPUTE INTEREST = PRINCIPAL * RATE.

MULTIPLY COST BY 1.15 GIVING FINAL-COST.
COMPUTE FINAL-COST = COST * 1.15.
```

DIVIDE . . . INTO GIVING Verb

The syntax is

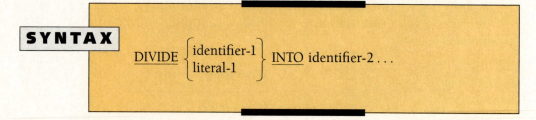

Some examples are

```
DIVIDE SHARES INTO TOTAL-ISSUE.
COMPUTE TOTAL-ISSUE = TOTAL-ISSUE / SHARES.

DIVIDE 4 INTO TAX.
COMPUTE TAX = TAX / 4.
```

DIVIDE . . . INTO . . . GIVING Verb

The syntax is

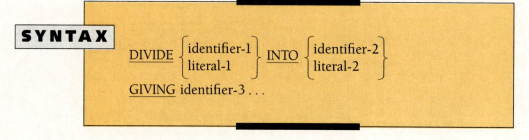

Some examples are

```
DIVIDE SHARES INTO TOTAL-ISSUE GIVING PRICE-PER-SHARE.
COMPUTE PRICE-PER-SHARE = TOTAL-ISSUE / SHARES.

DIVIDE 4 INTO TAX GIVING PAYMENT-1.
COMPUTE PAYMENT-1 = TAX / 4.
```

DIVIDE . . . BY . . . GIVING Verb

The syntax is

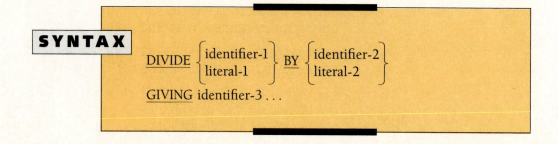

Some examples are

```
DIVIDE TOTAL-ISSUE BY SHARES GIVING PRICE-PER-SHARE.
COMPUTE PRICE-PER-SHARE = TOTAL-ISSUE / SHARES.

DIVIDE TAX BY 4 GIVING PAYMENT-1.
COMPUTE PAYMENT-1 = TAX / 4.

DIVIDE 108796 BY 2987 GIVING EARNINGS-PER-SHARE.
COMPUTE EARNINGS-PER-SHARE = 108796 / 2987.
```

REMAINDER Option

In DIVIDE statements with the GIVING clause, you can use a REMAINDER clause to have a remainder resulting from the division placed in a separate identifier. Some examples of the REMAINDER option are

```
DIVIDE 5 INTO 13 GIVING Q REMAINDER R.
(No COMPUTE equivalent; Q gets 2 and R gets 3.)

DIVIDE 13 BY 5 GIVING Q REMAINDER R.
(No COMPUTE equivalent; Q gets 2 and R gets 3.)
```

When the REMAINDER clause is used, only one identifier can be used in the GIVING clause. The REMAINDER clause is optional.

ROUNDED Option

The identifier that receives the result is called the receiving identifier. If you want a result rounded off, place ROUNDED after the receiving identifier with a value that is to be rounded. Here are some examples:

```
ADD A TO B ROUNDED.
ADD A TO B GIVING C ROUNDED.

SUBTRACT A FROM B ROUNDED.
SUBTRACT A, B, C FROM D GIVING E ROUNDED.

MULTIPLY A BY B ROUNDED.
MULTIPLY A BY B GIVING C ROUNDED.

DIVIDE A INTO B ROUNDED.
DIVIDE A INTO B GIVING C ROUNDED.
```

Note the following exception: With DIVIDE . . . REMAINDER, if you want the remainder rounded, ROUNDED goes in front of REMAINDER.

```
DIVIDE A BY B GIVING Q
              ROUNDED REMAINDER R.
```

Thus,

```
DIVIDE 13.1 BY 1.9 GIVING Q
              ROUNDED REMAINDER R.
```

Here Q gets 6 (no rounding is ever needed) and R gets 1.7 rounded off, that is, 2. Assume that R is PIC 9(01).

ON SIZE Error Option

As with the COMPUTE statement, the clause

ON SIZE ERROR imperative-statement

can be added to any of the arithmetic verbs. Thus, you can have

```
ADD TAX TO PAYMENT
        ON SIZE ERROR MOVE 100 TO ERROR-FACTOR
                        PERFORM 600-RECOVERY-ROUTINE.
MULTIPLY COST BY RATE GIVING TOTAL-COST
        ON SIZE ERROR PERFORM 200-ERROR-ROUTINE.
```

The imperative-statement is executed if any of the receiving identifiers overflow, that is, if the result is too large for the identifier, and significant digits on the left are truncated.

Avoiding Size Errors

The old adage that an ounce of prevention is worth a pound of cure applies to size errors. Avoid them by making sure that the receiving identifier will be large enough to hold the largest conceivable result without overflowing.

For example, if adding two numbers, as follows:

picture	999	999
value	890	889

the result 1769 clearly needs an identifier with a picture 9999.

As another example, if multiplying two numbers

picture	999	99
value	890	98

the result, 87220, clearly needs an identifier with a picture 99999.

It is better not to use edit identifiers in the GIVING clause

You can use edit identifiers in the GIVING clause with all of the arithmetic verbs. The identifier in the GIVING clause merely receives the result of the computation and does not otherwise participate in the computation; the identifier can thus be an edit identifier. However, using edit identifiers in this way is not considered good practice. All other identifiers must be non-edit numeric identifiers.

You can use individual scope terminators with arithmetic verbs

The scope terminators (in COBOL 85) for the arithmetic verbs are

```
END-ADD
END-SUBTRACT
END-MULTIPLY
END-DIVIDE
```

These are useful for unambiguously marking the end of the arithmetic statement. For example

```
ADD A TO B GIVING C
     ON SIZE ERROR PERFORM 600-RECOVER
                   PERFORM 700-ERROR-MESSAGE
END-ADD.

MULTIPLY PRINCIPAL BY RATE GIVING INTEREST.
     ON SIZE ERROR PERFORM 800-INTEREST-CHECK
                   PERFORM 700-ERROR-MESSAGE
END-MULTIPLY.
```

The scope terminators are particularly useful with IF-statements (see Chapter 5).

It is poor practice to use more than one identifier after GIVING

The following is a legal COBOL statement:

```
ADD REBATE TO GROSS-INCOME GIVING TOTAL-1, TOTAL-2.
```

However, this is poor practice. Instead use

```
ADD REBATE TO GROSS-INCOME GIVING TOTAL-1.
MOVE TOTAL-1 TO TOTAL-2.
```

This applies to GIVING with SUBTRACT, MULTIPLY, and DIVIDE verbs as well.

COMPUTE and other arithmetic verbs are used in different situations

COMPUTE is normally used only where the computation is complex and cannot easily be expressed without it. A common example is the case of interest calculations. In the program in Figure 4.1c, the COMPUTE verb was used four times. The first two times were with interest calculations, but the third and fourth times were for addition calculations. These addition statements using COMPUTE are probably better replaced with ADD statements, as they are easier to read. Thus, the paragraph 200-PROCESS-RECORD could be rewritten as follows:

```
200-PROCESS-RECORD.
    MOVE AR-PRINCIPAL-IN TO WS-PRINCIPAL-IN.
    COMPUTE INTEREST-ON-PRINCIPAL
        = (WS-PRINCIPAL-IN * AR-PRINCIPAL-RATE-IN / 100) / 12.
    MOVE AR-DEPOSIT-IN TO WS-DEPOSIT-IN.
    COMPUTE INTEREST-ON-DEPOSIT
            = ((WS-DEPOSIT-IN * AR-DEPOSIT-RATE-IN / 100)
                * AR-DEPOSIT-DAYS-IN) / 365.
    ADD INTEREST-ON-PRINCIPAL, INTEREST-ON-DEPOSIT
            GIVING TOTAL-INTEREST ROUNDED.
    ADD AR-PRINCIPAL-IN, AR-DEPOSIT-IN, TOTAL-INTEREST
            GIVING NEW-PRINCIPAL-COMPUTED.
    MOVE    AR-CUSTOMER-NAME-IN     TO      DL-CUSTOMER-NAME-OUT.
    MOVE    AR-PRINCIPAL-IN         TO      DL-OLD-PRINCIPAL-OUT.
    MOVE    AR-DEPOSIT-IN           TO      DL-DEPOSIT-OUT.
    MOVE    TOTAL-INTEREST          TO      DL-INTEREST-OUT.
    MOVE    NEW-PRINCIPAL-COMPUTED TO       DL-NEW-PRINCIPAL-OUT.
    WRITE REPORT-RECORD-OUT FROM DETAIL-LINE-OUT.
    READ ACCOUNT-IN
            AT END MOVE 'NO' TO MORE-RECORDS.
```

Reminder on How to Read Syntax Formats

Throughout the book you will encounter syntax format specifications for the various components of the COBOL language. The rules for interpreting these syntax specifications are summarized here.

RULES **Interpreting Syntax Formats**

- A word in capital letters is a COBOL reserved word.
- An underlined word is a required word in any statement or option specified.
- A lowercase word represents a user-defined word, such as an identifier or file name.
- One of the clauses within braces { } is required.
- A clause within brackets [ ] is optional.
- Ellipses (. . .) mean that the preceding entry or name may be repeated as often as required.
- Any punctuation included in the format is required.
- Note carefully the distinction between imperative-statement-1 and statement-1. The word "statement" means the statement, whether conditional or imperative, is allowed. The word imperative-statement means that no conditional statement is allowed. An imperative statement can be a group of non-conditional statements.

Summary

1. The PROCEDURE DIVISION normally consists of consecutively numbered paragraphs, each made up of statements that correspond to instructions. The PERFORM statement within a paragraph is used to execute another paragraph and then continue execution with the statement following that PERFORM statement. A PERFORM . . . UNTIL statement is used for repeated execution of a paragraph.
2. Statements begin with a COBOL verb. The common non-computational verbs are READ–to bring a record into either the input area or working storage, WRITE–for sending a record out of either the output area or working storage, and MOVE–to move data from one identifier (location) in working storage to another.
3. The computational verbs are COMPUTE and ADD, SUBTRACT, MULTIPLY, and DIVIDE. COMPUTE is used with more complex computations, such as interest computations, whereas the others are used with simple arithmetic operations.

Key Terms

paragraph	sentence	condition
sections	imperative statement	scope terminator
statement	conditional statement	

Concept Review Questions

1. Explain the concepts of
   a. a COBOL statement
   b. a COBOL sentence
2. Explain what an imperative statement is.
3. How many MOVE statements can make up an imperative statement?
4. What is a conditional statement?
5. Distinguish between composite and elementary imperative statements.
6. Why are paragraphs numbered in order of occurrence?
7. What is a boxed comment?
8. Explain how paragraphs can be used to give the PROCEDURE DIVISION a hierarchical structure.
9. Explain when the condition in a PERFORM . . . UNTIL statement is evaluated.
10. If you want to write records into a file and then read records from the same file within a single program, what must you do?
11. Explain the function of the READ . . . INTO statement.
12. Explain how a group MOVE works.
13. Why do you sometimes need SIGN LEADING SEPARATE?
14. Explain the idea behind MOVE CORRESPONDING. Why should you avoid it?

15. Why should literals be avoided in the PROCEDURE DIVISION?
16. Where are ACCEPT and DISPLAY used?
17. List sources of arithmetic error when using the COMPUTE verb.
18. What is the benefit of using parentheses in COMPUTE statements?
19. How does the ROUNDED option work?
20. What is a size error?
21. What is a scope terminator?
22. When should you avoid the COMPUTE statement?

COBOL Language Questions

1. How many times is paragraph 200-P executed?

```
        MOVE 1 TO CNT.
        PERFORM 200-P UNTIL CNT = 3.
200-P.
        ADD 1 TO CNT.
```

2. Rewrite the code in question 1, removing literals from the PROCEDURE DIVISION.

3. What is wrong with the following?

```
OPEN INPUT XFILE.
...
READ XFILE
        AT END MOVE 'NO' TO MORE-RECORDS.
...
WRITE XFILE-RECORD-OUT.
...
CLOSE XFILE.
```

Fix it.

4. What is wrong with the following?

```
READ ZFILE
    AT END MOVE 'NO' TO MORE-RECORDS
            IF RECORD-FOUND = 'YES'
                PERFORM 600-FOUND
            MOVE 'NO' TO RECORD-FOUND
END-READ.
```

5. Is anything wrong with the following?

```
READ ZFILE
    AT END DISPLAY 'NO FIRST RECORD'
            DISPLAY 'PROGRAM STOPPED'
            STOP RUN.
```

6. Rewrite the following without the INTO clause.

```
FD  ZFILE                           LABEL RECORDS STANDARD.
01  ZFILE-RECORD-IN  PIC X(50).
...
WORKING-STORAGE SECTION.
01 WS-ZFILE-RECORD.
...
      READ ZFILE INTO WS-ZFILE-RECORD,
                      AT END MOVE 'NO' TO MORE-RECORDS.
```

7. What kind of line spacing is generated by repeated execution of this statement:

```
WRITE REPORT-RECORD-OUT
             AFTER 1 LINE.
```

8. What is wrong with the following?

```
ADD 16,456.89 TO TOTAL-EARNED.
```

9. If you have

```
01 X   PIC S99.
...
MOVE -16 TO X.
```

what is the value within X?

10. If you have

```
01 X   PIC 9(03)V99.
...
MOVE 1547.987 TO X.
```

what is the value within X?

11. If you have

```
01 X   PIC 9(03)V99.
...
MOVE 7.9 TO X.
```

what is the value within X?

12. If you have

```
01  W   PIC   9(03)V999     VALUE   12.
01  Y   PIC   9(03)         VALUE   15.
01  Z   PIC   9(02)V99      VALUE   4.
01  T   PIC   9(02)         VALUE   8.
01  R   PIC   9(02)         VALUE   1.28.
01  X   PIC   9(04)V9.
```

What is the value placed in X by each of the following independent statements?

```
a.  COMPUTE X =  Y / Z + W.
b.  COMPUTE X = (Y + W) / Y - Z.
c.  COMPUTE X ROUNDED = Y / T + W.
d.  COMPUTE X ROUNDED = W / Y / Z.
```

```
   e. DIVIDE Y BY T GIVING X ROUNDED.
   f. MULTIPLY Y BY R GIVING X.
   g. MULTIPLY Y BY R GIVING X ROUNDED.
```

Which of these statements contain a certain logical error?

13. Improve the following:

```
COMPUTE TAX, PAYMENT = INCOME * RATE.
```

Programming Assignments

1. **A financial program involving a complex calculation**
   An annuity is an investment with a certain initial value. The owner receives a constant annual payment, made up of interest and principal, for a fixed number of years. Since the owner is receiving principal payments from the investment, at the end of the fixed number of years the annuity is worth nothing. In the following, each record of input data gives the annual payment from an annuity, the number of years in the future this fixed payment will last, and the annual interest rate used in computing the payment. In the output report, this input data is output again, plus the current value of the annuity. To compute the value of the annuity, use the formula

   $$P[(1/r) - 1/(r(1 + r)^t)]$$

   The symbols in the formula are

   P   Annual payment
   r   Annual interest rate divided by 100
   t   Number of years for which payment will be made

   The input data are:

```
---------1---------2---------3
5800151075
0800200980
4755121125
```

   with the record layout

```
-------- -1---------2---------3
99999999V99
99999999V99
99999999V99
```

   The output data are

```
---------1---------2---------3---------4---------5---------6
              ANNUITY INFORMATION REPORT
```

ANNUAL PAYMENT	YEARS PAID	ANNUAL RATE OF INTEREST	ANNUITY VALUE
$5800	15	10.75	$42,289.06
$ 800	20	9.80	...
$4755	12	11.25	...

a. Make up a printer spacing chart.
b. Draw a flowchart for the processing needed.
c. Write and run the program. The annuity value should be rounded to the last cent. Remember to use identifiers to hold intermediate values that have enough digits right of the implicit decimal point.

2. **A program to compute earnings data for corporations**

In this exercise, each record of the input file has information about annual revenue for a publicly traded corporation. For each input record, a report detail line has to be generated in which profits and certain profit ratios are included.

The input data are

```
---------1---------2---------3
ABD058456897095420000000012.25
IVM116378632112005500000025.75
HBX077895437085004000000006.30
RCB157893267092525000000019.50
```

The input record layout is

```
---------1---- -----2------ ---3
XXX99999999999V99999999999999V99
XXX99999999999V99999999999999V99
...
```

The fields of a record of the input file, from left to right, are

- The symbol used for the company on a major stock exchange
- The total annual revenue in dollars
- The profit margin for the company
- The total shares that have been issued for the company
- The latest price of a share

The output data are

```
---------1---------2---------3---------4---------5---------6---------7---------8
                       ANNUAL CORPORATION PROFIT REPORT
```

STOCK	TOTAL REVENUE	PROFIT MARGIN (%)	TOTAL SHARES	SHARE PRICE	EARNINGS	EARNING PER SHARE	P/E RATIO
ABD	$ 58,456,897	9.54	20,000,000	$12.25	$ 5,576,788	$00.28	43.93
IVM	$116,378,632	11.20	5,500,000	$25.75	$13,034,407	$02.37	10.87
...							

To compute the earnings for the company, use revenue times profit margin divided by 100.

To compute earnings per share, divide earnings by the number of shares.

To compute the P/E (price/earnings) ratio, divide the price by the earnings per share. Do not use a rounded value for the earnings per share in this calculation.

All results output should be rounded off.

a. Draw up a printer spacing chart for the output.
b. Draw a flowchart for the processing.
c. Develop and run the program.

3. **A program to compute the cost of expensive foreign automobiles**
The input data are

```
---------1---------2---------3
AUDI     0842500960000504,00
BMW      1043681276206035,0
MERCEDES230135241901234,25
```

with the record layout

```
---------1---------2--- ------3
XXXXXXXX99999999999999V99
XXXXXXXX99999999999999V99
XXXXXXXX999999999999999 99
```

The fields of the input file, in order of appearance are

- Make of car
- Base price of car in deutsche marks
- Cost of optional extras in deutsche marks
- Cost of freight in U.S. dollars

The output data are

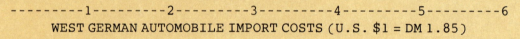

```
---------1---------2---------3---------4---------5---------6
        WEST GERMAN AUTOMOBILE IMPORT COSTS (U.S. $1 = DM 1.85)
```

AUTO	BASE PRICE (DM)	OPTIONS (DM)	FREIGHT (U.S.$)	TAX (7%)	TOTAL COST (U.S.$)
AUDI	84,250	9,600	$ 504.00	$ 3,586.36	$ 54,820
BMW	104,368	12,762	$ 603.50	$ 4,474.19	$ 68,391
...					

Tax is computed on the total value of the car (base price plus options plus freight), expressed in U.S. dollars. Base price and options are in West German marks (1 dollar = 1.85 DM).

a. Draw up a printer spacing chart for the output data.
b. Construct a flowchart for the processing.
c. Write and run the program. All computed values output should be rounded.

4. **A program to compute the profit or loss on apartment buildings**
The input data are

```
---------1---------2---------3
B15204250935001242550918654 2
B192539511376024253311254 535
B31343841474563872150856 3087
B41155100856801489620957 8400
```

with the record layout

```
---------1--------  -2------  ---3
XXX99999999999999999V99999999V99
XXX99999999999999999V99999999V99
. . .
```

The fields of the input file are, in order of appearance

- The apartment building identification number
- The number of rental units in the building
- The monthly rent per unit
- The annual revenue received from the building
- The annual cost of heating the building
- The interest payments made on a mortgage on the building

The output data are

```
---------1---------2---------3---------4---------5---------6---------7---------8
```

REVENUE STATEMENT 1990
SUNNYSIDE APARTMENTS INC.

APT. BDG.	UNITS	RENTAL RATE MONTHLY	ANNUAL REVENUE	ANNUAL HEATING COST	ANNUAL INTEREST COST	OCCUPANCY RATE (%)	GROSS PROFIT(+) LOSS (-)
B15	20	425	$ 93,500	$1,242.55	$ 91,865.42	91.67	$ 392.03+
B19	25	395	$113,760	$2,425.33	$112,545.35	96.00	$ 1,210.68-

. . .

In the output file, the occupancy rate is computed from the annual revenue as a percentage of the theoretically possible annual revenue from rents, that is, number of units times monthly rental times 12. The gross profit is the revenue less heating cost less interest payments.

a. Draw up a printer spacing chart for the output file.
b. Make a flowchart for the processing.
c. Write and run the program.

5

SELECTION OF ALTERNATIVES WITH CONDITIONAL STATEMENTS

OBJECTIVES

- To learn the use of the IF-statement.
- To understand simple and compound conditions.
- To learn to use condition tables.
- To learn the use of the EVALUATE statement.

OUTLINE

CHAPTER 4 MENTIONED that COBOL statements could be classified as either imperative or conditional. The previous chapters concentrated on imperative statements; this chapter will examine the conditional statements IF and EVALUATE.

In Chapter 1 you saw that instructions in a program form three basic types of structures: the straight sequence, the selection of alternatives, and the loop, illustrated in Figure 5.1. This chapter deals with the selection of alternatives structure. The conditional statements IF and EVALUATE are used to create selection of alternatives structures.

The IF-statement is used to choose between execution of two groups of instructions, whereas the EVALUATE statement can be used to choose among any number of alternatives (see Figure 5.2). As you will see, it is also possible to combine IF-statements to do without an EVALUATE statement.

Currently, the IF-statement is the one commonly used. The EVALUATE statement first became available in COBOL 85. It is expected to become increasingly common.

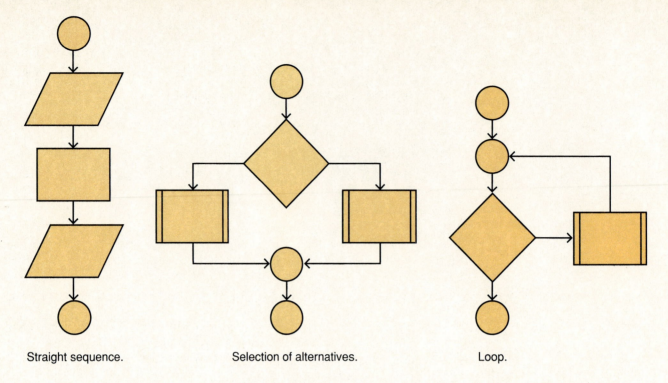

| Straight sequence. | Selection of alternatives. | Loop. |

Figure 5.1 *The basic structures found in programs. An IF-statement is used to program the selection between (two) alternatives.*

5.1
The IF-statement selects between alternatives

T HE IF-STATEMENT is one of the most powerful in computer languages. All computer languages have an IF-statement, all very similar in syntax and semantics. The IF-statement permits one of two groups of instructions to be executed; the group selected for execution depends on the result of evaluating a condition. Consider the following example:

```
DATA DIVISION.
FILE SECTION.
FD TOTAL-FILE-IN      LABEL RECORDS STANDARD.
01 TOTAL-RECORD-IN.
       05 TOTAL-1     PIC 9(03).
       05 FILLER      PIC X(02).
       05 TOTAL-2     PIC 9(04).
...
PROCEDURE DIVISION.
...
READ TOTAL-FILE-IN, AT END . . .
IF TOTAL-1 > TOTAL-2 THEN
       statement-10
       statement-11
       statement-12
ELSE
       statement-70
       statement-71
END-IF.
statement-300.
```

COMPREHENSIVE STRUCTURED COBOL

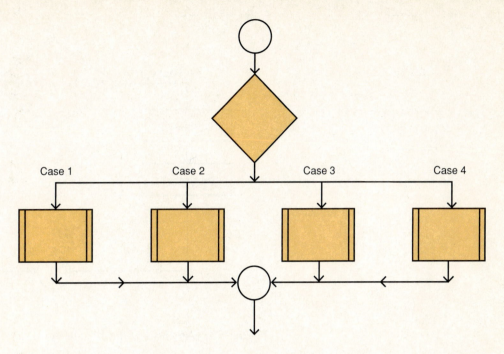

Figure *5.2* *Selection among several alternative structures. This can be programmed using the EVALUATE verb. The structure is commonly called a CASE structure, since in each case of execution, only one alternative (CASE 1, CASE 2, CASE 3, or CASE 4, in the above structure) is chosen.*

Suppose that the record being read has the data

    015   0006

which are assumed to mean that TOTAL-1 acquires the value 15, and TOTAL-2 acquires 6. The condition

    TOTAL-1 > TOTAL-2

will evaluate as true, so that the THEN statements (statement-10, statement-11, and statement-12) are executed. The ELSE statements (statement-70 and statement-71) are not executed. After statement-12 is executed, statement-300 will be executed.

In contrast, suppose that the record read has the data

    578   6890

In that case the condition TOTAL-1 > TOTAL-2 will evaluate to false. This means that the ELSE statements are executed, and not the THEN statements. When statement-71 has been executed, the next statement executed is statement-300.

These points are illustrated in the flowchart in Figure 5.3.

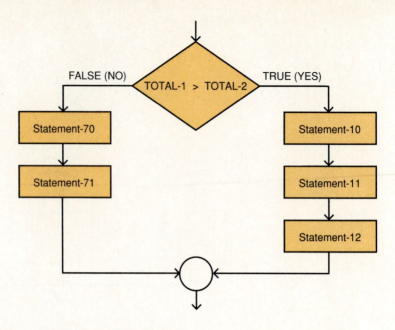

Figure 5.3 *Logic behind the IF-statement.*

Learn the IF-statement syntax thoroughly

The syntax for the IF-statement is

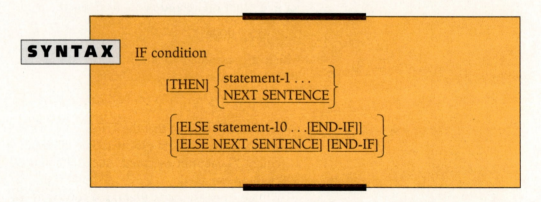

SYNTAX IF condition

$$\text{[THEN]} \begin{Bmatrix} \text{statement-1} \ldots \\ \text{NEXT SENTENCE} \end{Bmatrix}$$

$$\begin{Bmatrix} \text{[ELSE statement-10} \ldots \text{[END-IF]]} \\ \text{[ELSE NEXT SENTENCE] [END-IF]} \end{Bmatrix}$$

Some examples of correct IF-statements follow.

```
a.  IF TAX >= 1000 THEN
            ADD SUM TO TAX-CREDIT
            SUBTRACT TAX-CREDIT FROM TAX-PAYABLE
        ELSE
            ADD TAX-CREDIT TO CREDIT-TOTAL
            PERFORM 400-TAX
            MOVE SPACES TO DETAIL-LINE
        END-IF.

b.  IF TAX >= 1000
            ADD SUM TO TAX-CREDIT
            SUBTRACT TAX-CREDIT FROM TAX-PAYABLE
        ELSE
            ADD TAX-CREDIT TO CREDIT-TOTAL.
```

The THEN and END-IF may be omitted. (THEN is allowed only with COBOL 85.) THEN is often omitted. END-IF is the scope terminator for the IF-statement and clearly marks the end of the statement. (Note that some compilers use ENDIF, instead of END-IF. Check yours.)

END-IF was introduced with COBOL 85, so experience with it is limited. However, convention apppears to be in favor of including END-IF if the IF-statement contains an ELSE, or is nested within another IF-statement. As you will see, great care should be taken with ending an IF-statement if it is nested within another IF-statement. The only period that is allowed must come at the end of the enclosing, or outer, IF-statement. Here are some further examples:

```
c.  IF QUANTITY-IN = TOTAL-SHIPPED
            COMPUTE COMMISSION = RATE *
                                QUANTITY-IN + 100
            WRITE BUFFER-RECORD-OUT.
```

```
d.  IF QUANTITY-IN = TOTAL-SHIPPED
            NEXT SENTENCE
        ELSE
            COMPUTE COMMISSION = RATE *
                                QUANTITY-IN + 100
            WRITE BUFFER-RECORD-OUT
        END-IF.
```

```
e.  IF TAX >= 1000
            ADD SUM TO TAX-CREDIT
            SUBTRACT TAX-CREDIT FROM TAX-PAYABLE
        ELSE
            NEXT SENTENCE
        END-IF.
```

Notice the THEN and ELSE statements are indented and placed on separate lines. This is not required, but it is standard practice. Indentation makes the logic behind an IF-statement easier to understand. For example, the following is allowed, but is not very clear:

```
IF QUANTITY-IN = TOTAL-SHIPPED NEXT
SENTENCE ELSE COMPUTE COMMISSION = RATE *
QUANTITY-IN + 10 WRITE  BUFFER-RECORD-OUT END-IF.
```

Use indentation and separate lines when writing IF-statements.

```
f.  IF REBATE = TOTAL-PAID
            MOVE QUANTITY TO QUANTITY-OUT
            IF A < B
                    MOVE 100 TO SUM
                ELSE
                    ADD 1 TO TOTAL
            END-IF
        ELSE
            MOVE 0 TO QUANTITY-OUT
        END-IF.
```

Any statement, whether imperative or conditional, can be used following THEN or ELSE. In the preceding example, another IF-statement (shown in boldface) is used in the THEN group of statements. Such an IF-statement within an IF-statement is referred to as a nested IF-statement.

Notice that the END-IF of the nested IF-statement clearly indicates where the nested IF ends. You cannot use a period to show where a nested IF ends, unless it is the end of the entire IF-statement. It was for this purpose that END-IF was introduced with COBOL 85.

The following is incorrect:

```
IF A = B THEN
          MOVE 100 TO REBATE
          NEXT SENTENCE                    error!
     ELSE SUBTRACT A FROM NET-PROFIT
     END-IF.
```

Where NEXT SENTENCE is used, it must be the only statement following either THEN or ELSE.

Learn the exact semantics for the IF-statement

As you have seen, if a condition evaluates to true, the THEN statements are executed. If it evaluates to false, the ELSE statements are executed. Control then continues with the statement following the IF-statement.

NEXT SENTENCE can be used instead of a group of THEN or ELSE statements. NEXT SENTENCE is really a dummy statement; when it is executed, nothing happens and control goes to the statement following the IF-statement.

Where the ELSE clause is omitted, if the condition is true, the THEN statements are executed, otherwise they are not. Control then goes to the statement following the IF-statement.

IF-statements are useful for handling various possibilities

The end of the previous chapter had an example of a program that processed a file of retirement accounts. The processing consisted of

1. Computing the interest on the old principal
2. Computing the interest on the deposit
3. Adding the old principal, the deposit, the interest on the deposit, and the interest on the old principal to form the new principal

The computations were straightforward. But, let us now assume some conditions are associated with these computations. Suppose that

1. If the old principal exceeds $10,000, 0.5 percentage point is added to the interest rate used with the old principal.
2. If the total interest at the end of the month exceeds $100, an interest bonus of $5 is added; otherwise a service charge of $2 is deducted.

3. If the number of days the deposit has been in the institution exceeds 25, the rate of interest applicable to the old principal is used, but not including the increase of 0.5 percentage point where condition 1 is also satisfied.

These conditions can be handled by the following IF-statements:

```
1.  IF PRINCIPAL-IN > 10000
                ADD 0.5 TO WS-PRINCIPAL-RATE.
2.  IF TOTAL-INTEREST > 100
                ADD 5 TO TOTAL-INTEREST
            ELSE SUBTRACT 2 FROM TOTAL-INTEREST
        END-IF.
3.  IF DEPOSIT-DAYS-IN > 25
                MOVE PRINCIPAL-RATE-IN TO
                WS-DEPOSIT-RATE
            ELSE MOVE DEPOSIT-RATE-IN TO
                WS-DEPOSIT-RATE
        END-IF.
```

A program using IF-statements

The program for processing with the conditions in the last section is shown in Figure 5.4.

```
        IDENTIFICATION DIVISION.
        PROGRAM-ID. SAMPLE6.
        ***********************************************************************
        *   THIS PROGRAM COMPUTES THE INTEREST ON AN OLD PRINCIPAL AND ON A    *
        *   DEPOSIT, ADDS THE INTEREST AND DEPOSIT TO THE OLD PRINCIPAL, AND   *
        *   GENERATES THE NEW PRINCIPAL. IN THIS VERSION THERE ARE CONDITIONS  *
        *   ASSOCIATED WITH THE CALCULATIONS.                                  *
        ***********************************************************************
        ENVIRONMENT DIVISION.
        INPUT-OUTPUT SECTION.
        FILE-CONTROL.    SELECT ACCOUNT-IN        ASSIGN TO UT-S-ACCNT50.
                         SELECT REPORT-OUT        ASSIGN TO UR-S-SYSPRINT.
        DATA DIVISION.
        FILE-SECTION.
        FD  ACCOUNT-IN                            LABEL RECORDS ARE STANDARD.
        01  ACCOUNT-RECORD-IN.
            05  AR-CUSTOMER-NAME-IN        PIC X(25).
            05  AR-PRINCIPAL-IN            PIC 9(07)V9(02).
            05  AR-DEPOSIT-IN              PIC 9(07)V9(02).
            05  AR-DEPOSIT-DAYS-IN         PIC 9(02).
            05  AR-PRINCIPAL-RATE-IN       PIC 9(02)V9(02).
            05  AR-DEPOSIT-RATE-IN         PIC 9(02)V9(02).
        FD  REPORT-OUT                            LABEL RECORDS ARE OMITTED.
        01  REPORT-RECORD-OUT              PIC X(133).
```

```
WORKING-STORAGE SECTION.
01 WS-WORK-AREAS.
    05   INTEREST-ON-PRINCIPAL      PIC 9(06)V9(05).
    05   INTEREST-ON-DEPOSIT        PIC 9(06)V9(05).
    05   TOTAL-INTEREST             PIC 9(06)V9(05).
    05   NEW-PRINCIPAL-COMPUTED     PIC 9(07)V9(02).
    05   MORE-RECORDS               PIC X(03)          VALUE 'YES'.
    05   WS-PRINCIPAL-RATE          PIC 9(02)V9(05).
    05   WS-DEPOSIT-RATE            PIC 9(02)V9(05).
01 HEADER.
    05   FILLER                     PIC X(15)          VALUE SPACES.
    05   FILLER                     PIC X(26)          VALUE
                                        'MONTHLY CUSTOMER ACCOUNTS'.
    05   FILLER                     PIC X(92)          VALUE SPACES.
01 COLUMN-HEADER1.
    05   FILLER                     PIC X(01)          VALUE SPACES.
    05   FILLER                     PIC X(08)          VALUE 'CUSTOMER'.
    05   FILLER                     PIC X(19)          VALUE SPACES.
    05   FILLER                     PIC X(03)          VALUE 'OLD'.
    05   FILLER                     PIC X(10)          VALUE SPACES.
    05   FILLER                     PIC X(07)          VALUE 'DEPOSIT'.
    05   FILLER                     PIC X(06)          VALUE SPACES.
    05   FILLER                     PIC X(08)          VALUE 'INTEREST'.
    05   FILLER                     PIC X(05)          VALUE SPACES.
    05   FILLER                     PIC X(03)          VALUE 'NEW'.
    05   FILLER                     PIC X(63)          VALUE SPACES.
01 COLUMN-HEADER2.
    05   FILLER                     PIC X(01)          VALUE SPACES.
    05   FILLER                     PIC X(04)          VALUE 'NAME'.
    05   FILLER                     PIC X(23)          VALUE SPACES.
    05   FILLER                     PIC X(09)          VALUE 'PRINCIPAL'.
    05   FILLER                     PIC X(17)          VALUE SPACES.
    05   FILLER                     PIC X(06)          VALUE 'EARNED'.
    05   FILLER                     PIC X(07)          VALUE SPACES.
    05   FILLER                     PIC X(09)          VALUE 'PRINCIPAL'.
    05   FILLER                     PIC X(57)          VALUE SPACES.
01 DETAIL-LINE-OUT.
    05 FILLER                       PIC X(01)          VALUE SPACES.
    05 DL-CUSTOMER-NAME-OUT         PIC X(25).
    05 FILLER                       PIC X(02)          VALUE SPACES.
    05 DL-OLD-PRINCIPAL-OUT         PIC $ZZZ,ZZ9.9(02).
    05 FILLER                       PIC X(02)          VALUE SPACES.
    05 DL-DEPOSIT-OUT               PIC $ZZZ,ZZ9.9(02).
    05 FILLER                       PIC X(02)          VALUE SPACES.
    05 DL-INTEREST-OUT              PIC $ZZZ,ZZ9.9(02).
    05 FILLER                       PIC X(02)          VALUE SPACES.
    05 DL-NEW-PRINCIPAL-OUT         PIC $Z,ZZZ,ZZ9.9(02).
    05 FILLER                       PIC X(53)          VALUE SPACES.
```

```
PROCEDURE DIVISION.
100-MAIN-MODULE.
****************************************************************************
*   100-MAIN-MODULE:  CONTROLS OPENING AND CLOSING OF FILES AND           *
*   DIRECTION OF PROGRAM LOGIC.                                           *
****************************************************************************
     OPEN INPUT ACCOUNT-IN
          OUTPUT REPORT-OUT.
     PERFORM 300-WRITE-HEADERS.
     READ ACCOUNT-IN
                 AT END MOVE 'NO' TO MORE-RECORDS.
     PERFORM 200-PROCESS-RECORD
              UNTIL MORE-RECORDS = 'NO'.
     CLOSE ACCOUNT-IN
           REPORT-OUT.
   STOP RUN.
 200-PROCESS-RECORD.
****************************************************************************
*   200-PROCESS-RECORD:  PERFORMED FROM 100-MAIN-MODULE. PROCESSES        *
*   LATEST ACCOUNT-IN RECORD. COMPUTES INTEREST AND NEW PRINCIPAL AND      *
*   PRINTS REPORT LINE.                                                    *
****************************************************************************
     MOVE AR-PRINCIPAL-RATE-IN TO WS-PRINCIPAL-RATE
     IF AR-PRINCIPAL-IN > 10000
              ADD 0.5 TO WS-PRINCIPAL-RATE.
     COMPUTE INTEREST-ON-PRINCIPAL
          = (AR-PRINCIPAL-IN * WS-PRINCIPAL-RATE / 100) / 12.
     IF AR-DEPOSIT-DAYS-IN > 25
              MOVE AR-PRINCIPAL-RATE-IN TO WS-DEPOSIT-RATE
          ELSE
              MOVE AR-DEPOSIT-RATE-IN TO WS-DEPOSIT-RATE
     END-IF.
     COMPUTE INTEREST-ON-DEPOSIT
          = ((AR-DEPOSIT-IN * WS-DEPOSIT-RATE / 100)
               * AR-DEPOSIT-DAYS-IN) / 365.
     ADD INTEREST-ON-PRINCIPAL, INTEREST-ON-DEPOSIT
                 GIVING TOTAL-INTEREST ROUNDED.
     IF TOTAL-INTEREST > 100
              ADD 5 TO TOTAL-INTEREST
          ELSE SUBTRACT 2 FROM TOTAL-INTEREST
     END-IF.
     ADD AR-PRINCIPAL-IN, AR-DEPOSIT-IN, TOTAL-INTEREST
                 GIVING NEW-PRINCIPAL-COMPUTED.
     MOVE   AR-CUSTOMER-NAME-IN      TO    DL-CUSTOMER-NAME-OUT.
     MOVE   AR-PRINCIPAL-IN          TO    DL-OLD-PRINCIPAL-OUT.
     MOVE   AR-DEPOSIT-IN            TO    DL-DEPOSIT-OUT.
     MOVE   TOTAL-INTEREST           TO    DL-INTEREST-OUT.
     MOVE   NEW-PRINCIPAL-COMPUTED TO    DL-NEW-PRINCIPAL-OUT.
     WRITE REPORT-RECORD-OUT FROM DETAIL-LINE-OUT
                    AFTER ADVANCING 1 LINE.
     READ ACCOUNT-IN
              AT END MOVE 'NO' TO MORE-RECORDS.
```

```
 300-WRITE-HEADERS.
 **************************************************************************
 *  300-WRITE-HEADERS:  PERFORMED FROM 100-MAIN-MODULE. PRINTS REPORT    *
 *  AND COLUMN HEADERS FOR REPORT-OUT.                                   *
 **************************************************************************
     WRITE REPORT-RECORD-OUT FROM HEADER
                 AFTER ADVANCING 1 LINE.
     WRITE REPORT-RECORD-OUT FROM COLUMN-HEADER1
                 AFTER ADVANCING 2 LINES.
     WRITE REPORT-RECORD-OUT FROM COLUMN-HEADER2
                 AFTER ADVANCING 1 LINE.
     MOVE SPACES TO REPORT-RECORD-OUT.
     WRITE REPORT-RECORD-OUT
                 AFTER ADVANCING 1 LINE.
```

Figure 5.4 *The SAMPLE6 program, which uses IF-statements.*

Recall that the auxiliary identifiers WS-PRINCIPAL-RATE and WS-DEPOSIT-RATE are used for calculations because they allow five digits to the right of the decimal point. In this case there is a further reason for using these additional identifiers. The program makes changes to the interest rate values originally placed in the input area identifiers AR-PRINCIPAL-RATE-IN and AR-DEPOSIT-RATE-IN by a READ statement. It is not good practice to assign new values to input area identifiers. It is better to transfer the values in the input area to working storage identifiers first, such as WS-PRINCIPAL-RATE and WS-DEPOSIT-RATE, and then make necessary changes.

Pseudocode IF-statements are useful in planning programs

As you have seen, pseudocode is often used for the initial version of a program, before detailed COBOL code is written. IF-statements are also used in pseudocode to show the flow of control, that is, which of two groups of instructions will be carried out when there is a choice between alternatives. The following is acceptable pseudocode for the IF-statement:

```
IF condition
THEN
        actions
ELSE
        actions
END-IF
```

For example, you might write the following pseudocode:

```
IF rebate exceeds $1000
THEN
        compute interest owing
        add interest to rebate
ELSE
        deduct $2 penalty from rebate
END-IF.
```

5.2
You must understand conditions thoroughly

CONDITIONS ARE CENTRAL to the IF-statement. They are also central to the PERFORM ... UNTIL statement, which is used with loops. There is a lot to know about conditions, and you cannot be skilled in programming without a thorough grasp of conditions and logic. A condition can be either simple or compound. These two types are examined in detail in the following sections.

A simple condition compares two quantities

A simple condition compares two quantities, either of which can be a literal or the contents of an identifier. One quantity can be either equal, not equal, greater than or equal to, less than or equal to, greater than, or less than, the other quantity. Some examples of simple conditions are

```
EMPLOYEE-NUMBER = 'EMP89'
1990-EARNINGS < 1989-EARNINGS
QUANTITY > 100
SALARY >= INTEREST-INCOME
TAX IS NOT EQUAL TO AMOUNT-PAID
```

A simple condition is formed using the following syntax:

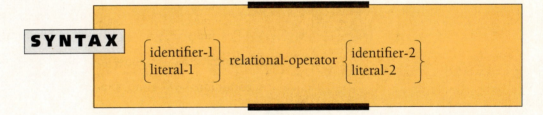

The relational operators can be written symbolically or using words as Table 5.1 shows.

Table 5.1 *Relational operators.*

OPERATOR	MEANING	WORDS
[NOT] =	[not] equal	IS [NOT] EQUAL TO
[NOT] >	[not] greater than	IS [NOT] GREATER THAN
[NOT] <	[not] less than	IS [NOT] LESS THAN
>=	greater than or equal to	IS GREATER THAN OR EQUAL TO
<=	less than or equal to	IS LESS THAN OR EQUAL TO

A simple condition will be either true or false. For example, suppose that TAX has the value 10 and AMOUNT-PAID has the value 5. The following conditions would be evaluated as shown:

TAX = AMOUNT-PAID	false
TAX = 10	true
AMOUNT-PAID IS GREATER THAN TAX	false

Compound conditions are more complex

Compound conditions are formed by connecting simple conditions with the logical connectives AND, OR, and NOT. Some examples are

```
X > Y  AND  P = 6
NOT (TAX = AMOUNT-PAID)
T < Q  OR  X > Y
```

Like a simple condition, a compound condition evaluates to true or false. However, it can be tricky to decide how a compound condition evaluates. The following rules should help:

RULES   **Evaluating Compound Conditions**

The AND connective   Suppose you have

condition-1 AND condition-2

This compound condition will be true only if *both* condition-1 and condition-2 are true. This can be expressed as shown in the following truth table:

Truth Table for AND

CONDITION-1	CONDITION-2	RESULT
true	true	true
false	true	false
true	false	false
false	false	false

The OR connective   Suppose you have the compound condition

condition-1 OR condition-2

This will evaluate to true only if either one or both of condition-1 and condition-2 are true. This can also be expressed as follows:

Truth Table for OR

CONDITION-1	CONDITION-2	RESULT
true	true	true
true	false	true
false	true	true
false	false	false

The NOT connective   Suppose you have the condition

NOT condition-1

This will have the value true only if condition-1 has the value false. The truth table for this is simply

Truth Table for NOT

CONDITION-1	RESULT
true	false
false	true

The use of NOT, or negation, requires care. Because there are no difficulties with NOT when only a simple condition is involved, beginners are often led to assume that the same is true when compound conditions are involved. This is not so, and negated compound conditions should be approached with caution. Examples 2 and 3 illustrate this.

Example 1

If you have the expression

```
NOT (TAX = 50)
```

it is the same thing as

```
TAX NOT = 50
```

which is the same as

```
TAX IS NOT EQUAL TO 50.
```

Example 2

Consider the compound condition

```
NOT (A = 'RICH' AND A = 'FAMOUS')
```

This is *not* equivalent to

```
NOT (A = 'RICH') AND NOT (A = 'FAMOUS')   error!
```

Rather it is equivalent to

```
NOT (A = 'RICH') OR NOT (A = 'FAMOUS')
```

This is one of two famous rules of logic called De Morgan's Rules. You can see that it is valid using some condition examples and the truth tables in the last section.

Example 3

The other De Morgan rule that is useful says that

```
NOT (A = 'RICH' OR A = 'FAMOUS')
```

is equivalent to:

```
NOT (A = 'RICH') AND NOT (A = 'FAMOUS')
```

For reference, De Morgan's Rules for negation of compound conditions are summarized in the box.

RULES   **De Morgan's Rules**

1. NOT (cond-1 AND cond-2)
   is NOT (cond-1) OR NOT (cond-2)
2. NOT (cond-1 OR cond-2)
   is NOT (cond-1) AND NOT (cond-2)

Order of Evaluation of Compound Conditions

You have to be careful with a compound condition involving three or more simple conditions. For example, consider

```
X > Y   AND A = B   OR P <= Q
```

The conditions are evaluated in pairs from left to right, with AND conditions being evaluated first. Thus

```
X > Y AND A = B OR P <= Q
```

is evaluated as

```
(X > Y AND A = B) OR (P <= Q)
```

If you do not want left to right evaluation, with AND given priority, you must use parentheses. If, instead of the preceding evaluation, the expression should be evaluated as

```
(X > Y) AND (A = B OR P <= Q)
```

it needs to be written with parentheses. The rules for evaluating a compound condition, also called a logical expression, are given here:

RULES   **Evaluating Logical Expressions**

Order of parenthetical expressions   The expression in the innermost parentheses is evaluated first.

Order within parentheses   Within a parenthesis or within an expression without parenthesis

- Each NOT condition is evaluated first.
- AND conditions are evaluated next, from left to right order.
- Then OR conditions are evaluated, in left to right order.

Using these rules, you can see that

cond-1 OR cond-2 AND cond-3 OR cond-4 AND cond-5

will be evaluated as

(cond-1 OR (cond-2 AND cond-3)) OR (cond-4 AND cond-5)

In practice, it is best to ignore these rules and *always* use parentheses in any compound condition with more than two simple conditions.

Collating Sequences: ASCII and EBCDIC

When comparing alphanumeric values, the collating sequence of the computer determines their relative sizes. For example,

```
'ABC' < 'AXYZ'
```

is true with all computers. However,

```
'46AB' < 'PQ74'
```

would be true with computers using ASCII code for storing characters and false with computers using the EBCDIC code (see Chapter 1 for a review of coding standards for data.) The EBCDIC sequence is used with IBM mainframes. ASCII is used with many mainframes and almost all micro- and minicomputers.

The codes give rise to two different *collating sequences*, that is, the ascending sort order for the characters. You should determine which collating sequence is used in your computer. The two collating sequences are given in Table 5.2.

Table 5.2 *Collating sequences.*

	EBCDIC (IBM MAINFRAMES)	ASCII
(Low)	blank	blank
	special characters	special characters
	a	0
	.	.
	.	.
	.	.
	z	9
	A	A
	.	.
	.	.
	.	.
	Z	Z
	0	a
	.	.
	.	.
	.	.
(High)	9	z

When comparing values, characters are compared from left to right, and the issue is decided by the first pair of corresponding characters that differ. If one value is shorter than the other, the short one is considered to be padded with blanks on the right. Thus, with ASCII both the following evaluate to true:

```
'ABC56' > 'ABC42'

'ABC' < 'ABC43'
```

There are some special conditions you must know about

In addition to the standard types of simple and compound conditions described above, COBOL allows for some special conditions. There are sign conditions and class conditions. Also, you can use somthing called a *condition name* in a condition. These will be examined in turn.

Sign conditions can be handy

Suppose you have a numeric identifier A, specified with a sign, as follows:

```
01   A            PIC   S9(03).
```

Because of the S in the picture clause, the value of A can be either positive or negative. Had the S been omitted, the value of A could only be positive, even if a negative value were moved to it. (Remember that, as you saw in Chapters 3 and 4, the use of S means that only a marker for the sign is stored, and not a character space.)

These are valid conditions:

```
A IS POSITIVE
A IS NEGATIVE
A IS ZERO
```

Depending on the value in A, they will evaluate to either true or false. Thus you could have the following COBOL code

```
MOVE -10 TO A.
IF A IS POSITIVE
        MOVE 1 TO B
    ELSE MOVE 25 TO B.
```

Here the ELSE statement would be carried out and B would get the value 25.

Class conditions are useful for validating input data

If A is any identifier, the following are valid class condition expressions:

A IS NUMERIC
This condition will be true if A contains a numeric quantity, including zero.

A IS ALPHABETIC
This condition will be true if A contains only alphabetic quantities, that is, any of A-Z, a-z, or a space. This condition is rarely used; names often contain hyphens (Smith-Barney), and even digits (3M Company).

A IS ALPHABETIC-UPPER
This condition will be true if A contains only uppercase alphabetic characters.

A IS ALPHABETIC-LOWER
This condition will be true if A contains only lowercase alphabetic characters.

Thus, suppose you have

```
01  GI.
    05  A         PIC X(04).
    05  B         PIC 9(02)V9(02).
    05  C         PIC X(03).
```

```
      MOVE 'JOHN1011000' TO GI.
      IF A IS NOT NUMERIC
              MOVE A TO NAME-OUT
         ELSE MOVE SPACES TO A
      END-IF.
      IF B IS NUMERIC
              ADD 20 TO B
         ELSE MOVE ZEROS TO B
      END-IF.                              B gets 30.11
```

Class conditions are normally used for validating input data. It can happen that a data entry operator will mistakenly enter numeric data for non-numeric or vice versa. Thus, when a record is read by a READ statement, it is possible that a numeric field such as B will receive non-numeric data. (Remember that a READ transfers data alphanumerically, as in a group MOVE, character by character, left justified, without regard to the nature of the characters, whether numeric or alphabetic.)

Condition names permit flexibility

Suppose an input record has a field MARITAL-STATUS, specified in the WORKING-STORAGE SECTION as

```
      05   MARITAL-STATUS        PIC X.
```

which can have any of the values

'M'   for married
'D'   for divorced
'S'   for single

In the program, different actions might be needed depending on the value of MARITAL-STATUS. So, using conventional conditions, you could code

```
      IF MARITAL-STATUS = 'M'
              PERFORM 200-MARRIED-ROUTINE.
      IF MARITAL-STATUS = 'D'
              PERFORM 300-DIVORCED-ROUTINE.
      IF MARITAL-STATUS = 'S'
              PERFORM 400-SINGLE-ROUTINE.
```

However, instead of writing out the conditions explicitly, you could use condition names for these conditions, as follows:

CONDITION	EQUIVALENT CONDITION NAME
MARITAL-STATUS = 'M'	MARRIED
MARITAL-STATUS = 'D'	DIVORCED
MARITAL-STATUS = 'S'	SINGLE

Condition names must be declared in the WORKING-STORAGE SECTION, with an 88 level number. Thus the identifier MARITAL-STATUS could be declared as follows, along with its associated condition names:

```
05    MARITAL-STATUS         PIC  X.
      88   MARRIED                         VALUE 'M'.
      88   DIVORCED                        VALUE 'D'.
      88   SINGLE                          VALUE 'S'.
```

In the PROCEDURE DIVISION these condition names would enable you to replace the preceding IF-statements with

```
IF MARRIED
      PERFORM 200-MARRIED-ROUTINE.
IF DIVORCED
      PERFORM 300-DIVORCED-ROUTINE.
IF SINGLE
      PERFORM 400-SINGLE-ROUTINE.
```

Thus, the words MARRIED, DIVORCED, and SINGLE are actually conditions, and will evaluate to true or false depending on the value in the identifier MARITAL-STATUS.

Alternatively you could have

```
05    MARITAL-STATUS         PIC  X.
      88   MARRIED                         VALUE 'M'.
      88   UNMARRIED                       VALUE 'D', 'S'.
      ...
   IF MARRIED
      PERFORM 200-MARRIED-ROUTINE.
   IF UNMARRIED
      PERFORM 600-UNMARRIED-ROUTINE.
```

The 600-UNMARRIED-ROUTINE will be carried out if the value read into MARITAL-STATUS is either 'D' or 'S'.

==Condition names are normally used to make the logic of conditions easier to read and understand, without requiring extra keying of input data.==

5.3
Nested IF-statements are used for multiple alternatives

C OMPLEX LOGIC can sometimes be handled with compound conditions and simple IF-statements, but often it is easier to use nested IF-statements.

Learn the semantics of nested IF-statements

When constructing *nested IF-statements,* remember the following rules:

- Indentation should be used to clarify the meaning of the statement.
- A nested ELSE belongs with the nearest preceding THEN and IF.
- You cannot use a period to terminate an IF-statement within

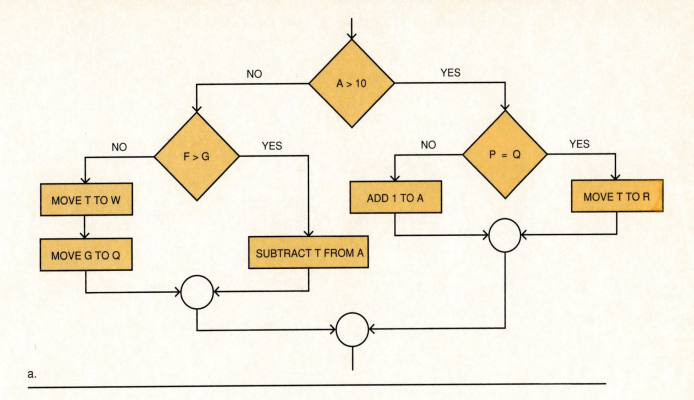

a.

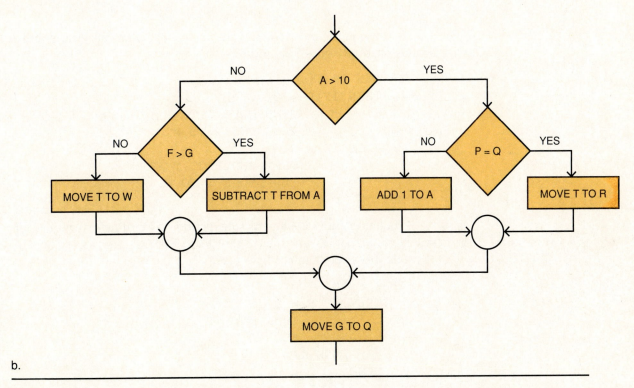

b.

Figure 5.5 *Flowcharts for similar but quite different nested IF-statements.*

an IF-statement. Instead use END-IF. A period can be used only to terminate the outer IF-statement.

- Use THEN and ELSE statements with every IF-statement. But remember that you cannot use THEN with COBOL 74.

Some examples should clarify these points.

Example 1

An error was made in constructing the following:

```
IF A > 10
    THEN IF P = Q
                THEN MOVE T TO R
                ELSE ADD 1 TO A
    ELSE IF F > G
                THEN SUBTRACT T FROM A
                ELSE MOVE T TO W
MOVE G TO Q.
```

This will be interpreted as follows (also as shown in the flowchart in Figure 5.5a):

```
IF A > 10
    THEN IF P = Q
                THEN MOVE T TO R
                ELSE ADD 1 TO A
    ELSE IF F > G
                SUBTRACT T FROM A
                ELSE MOVE T TO W
                    MOVE G TO Q.
```

Because of the indentation, you can see that what was clearly meant, as illustrated in Figure 5.5b, was:

```
IF A > 10
    THEN IF P = Q
                THEN MOVE T TO R
                ELSE ADD 1 TO A
    ELSE IF F > G
                THEN SUBTRACT T FROM A
                ELSE MOVE T TO W.
MOVE G TO Q.
```

The problem was the missing period to terminate the outer IF-statement. It is for reasons such as this that END-IF is useful as a terminator. Thus, the better code might have been

```
IF A > 10
    THEN IF P = Q
                THEN MOVE T TO R
                ELSE ADD 1 TO A
            END-IF
        ELSE
            IF F > G
                THEN SUBTRACT T FROM A
                ELSE MOVE T TO W
            END-IF
END-IF.
MOVE G TO Q.
```

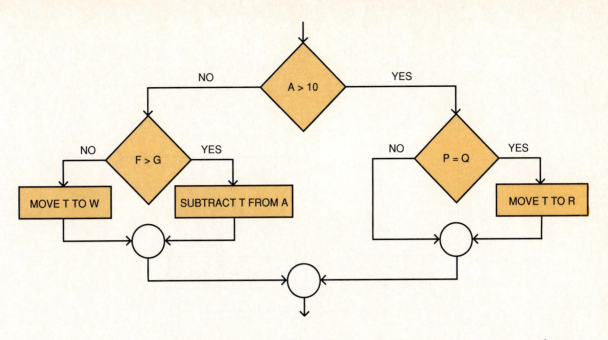

Figure 5.6 *Flowchart illustrating another IF-statement. Compare with Figure 5.7.*

With this, even if the period following END-IF had been omitted, no error of meaning would have occurred.

Example 2

Suppose you need to code the logic in Figure 5.6 and you use the following nested IF-statement:

```
IF  A > 10
    THEN IF P = Q
              THEN MOVE T TO R
         ELSE IF F > G
              THEN SUBTRACT T FROM A
              ELSE MOVE T TO W.
```

The two inner IF-statements, taken alone, are correct, but the entire statement will not be evaluated according to the logic in Figure 5.6. Instead, it will be evaluated as in Figure 5.7, and according to

```
IF  A > 10
    THEN IF P = Q
              THEN MOVE T TO R
              ELSE IF F > G
                     THEN SUBTRACT T FROM A
                     ELSE MOVE T TO W.
                   END-IF
         END-IF
END-IF.
```

To have it evaluated as intended in Figure 5.6, it should have been coded as either

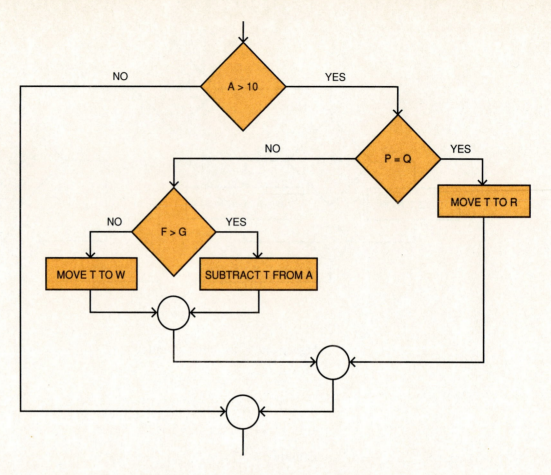

Figure 5.7 *Flowchart coding the logic of Figure 5.6.*

```
IF A > 10
    THEN IF P = Q
                THEN MOVE T TO R
            END-IF
    ELSE IF F > G
                THEN SUBTRACT T FROM A
                ELSE MOVE T TO W
            END-IF
END-IF.
```
or
```
IF A > 10
    THEN IF P = Q
                THEN MOVE T TO R
                ELSE NEXT SENTENCE
            END-IF
    ELSE IF F > G
                THEN SUBTRACT T FROM A
                ELSE MOVE T TO W
            END-IF
END-IF.
```

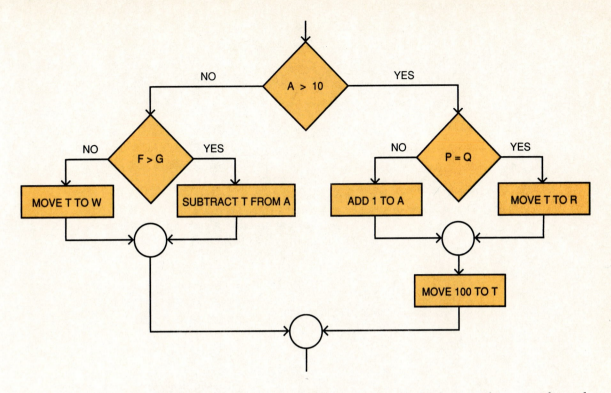

Figure 5.8 *Another flowchart illustrating the care that must be exercised in coding the logic of a nested IF-statement.*

It is generally clearest to use a THEN and an ELSE with each IF, even if this means inserting the occasional NEXT SENTENCE. END-IF should also be used to clarify intent. Leaving out END-IFs is comparable to leaving out parentheses in complex COMPUTE statements. The statement you construct can normally be executed, but unless you take great care it may not be what you want.

Example 3

Suppose that you have to code the logic in the flowchart in Figure 5.8. The obvious nested IF-statement for this logic is

```
IF A > 10
    THEN IF P = Q
            THEN MOVE T TO R
            ELSE ADD 1 TO A
        MOVE 100 TO T                    error!
    ELSE IF F > G
            THEN SUBTRACT T FROM A
            ELSE MOVE T TO W.
```

This is wrong. The statement will be evaluated as

```
IF A > 10
    THEN IF P = Q
                THEN MOVE T TO R
                ELSE ADD 1 TO A
                    MOVE 100 TO T
            END-IF
    ELSE IF F > G
                THEN SUBTRACT T FROM A
                ELSE MOVE T TO W
            END-IF
END-IF.
```

The only way to code it correctly, available in COBOL 85, is to insert an END-IF at the end of the first inner IF-statement.

```
IF A > 10
    THEN IF P = Q
                THEN MOVE T TO R
                ELSE ADD 1 TO A
            END-IF
            MOVE 100 TO T
    ELSE IF F > G
                THEN SUBTRACT T FROM A
                ELSE MOVE T TO W.
```

Prior to COBOL 85 the END-IF was not available, only the period. But a period could not be inserted because this terminated the entire nested IF-statement. With COBOL 74, the solution often involved contrivances that are now best relegated to history.

A decision table should be used with every nested IF-statement

Nested IF-statements are used with complex conditions. But no matter how complex the nested IF-statement is, the following always holds:

For a given set of true conditions, a specific set of instructions must be carried out.

For example, consider this IF-statement

```
IF A > B
    THEN IF C = D
                THEN PERFORM 300-ROUTINE
                ELSE PERFORM 400-ROUTINE
            END-IF
    ELSE IF P < Q
                THEN PERFORM 500-ROUTINE
                ELSE PERFORM 600-ROUTINE
            END-IF
END-IF.
```

This expression can be explained in terms of an action/condition table, such as that shown here, also commonly called a *condition table*:

REQUIRED TRUE CONDITIONS		ACTION
A > B	AND C = D	PERFORM 300-ROUTINE
A > B	AND NOT (C = D)	PERFORM 400-ROUTINE
A <= B	AND P < Q	PERFORM 500-ROUTINE
A >= B	AND P >= Q	PERFORM 600-ROUTINE

In the table, each course of action is listed along with the conditions that must hold for it. Such tables are often prepared for the programmer by a systems analyst expert in the business area for which a program is being written.

An advantage of the condition table is that it allows the analyst to make sure there is a listed course of action for every possible condition. For example, the following table is incomplete:

REQUIRED TRUE CONDITIONS		ACTION
A < B	AND F > G	PERFORM 300-ROUTINE
A < B	AND F <= G	PERFORM 400-ROUTINE
A = B	AND P < Q	PERFORM 500-ROUTINE
A = B	AND P >= Q	PERFORM 600-ROUTINE

There is no action specified for four distinct cases that involve A > B. A nested IF-statement should not be constructed without a condition table that covers all possibilities. If the omitted actions all involved no action at all, the condition table could be rewritten as follows:

REQUIRED TRUE CONDITIONS		ACTION
A < B	AND F > G	PERFORM 300-ROUTINE
A < B	AND F <= G	PERFORM 400-ROUTINE
A = B	AND P < Q	PERFORM 500-ROUTINE
A = B	AND P >= Q	PERFORM 600-ROUTINE
A > B	AND anything	no action

One IF-statement for this table would be

```
IF A < B
      THEN IF F > G
                 THEN PERFORM 300-ROUTINE
                 ELSE PERFORM 400-ROUTINE
            END-IF
      ELSE IF A = B
                 THEN IF P < Q
                            THEN PERFORM 500-ROUTINE
                            ELSE PERFORM 600-ROUTINE
                       END-IF
                 ELSE NEXT SENTENCE
            END-IF
END-IF.
```

Other equivalent IF-statements could also be constructed.

```
PROCEDURE DIVISION.
 100-MAIN-MODULE.
 ***************************************************************
 *  100-MAIN-MODULE:  CONTROLS OPENING AND CLOSING OF FILES, AND    *
 *  DIRECTION OF PROGRAM LOGIC.                                     *
 ***************************************************************
      OPEN INPUT ACCOUNT-IN
           OUTPUT REPORT-OUT.
      PERFORM 300-WRITE-HEADERS.
      READ ACCOUNT-IN
                   AT END MOVE 'NO' TO MORE-RECORDS.
      PERFORM 200-PROCESS-RECORD
                   UNTIL MORE-RECORDS = 'NO'.
      CLOSE ACCOUNT-IN
            REPORT-OUT.
      STOP RUN.
      200-PROCESS-RECORD.
 ***************************************************************
 *  200-PROCESS-RECORD:  PERFORMED FROM 100-MAIN-MODULE. PROCESSES  *
 *  LATEST ACCOUNT-IN RECORD. COMPUTES INTEREST AND NEW PRINCIPAL AND *
 *  PRINTS REPORT LINE.                                             *
 ***************************************************************
      COMPUTE INTEREST-ON-PRINCIPAL
          = (AR-PRINCIPAL-IN * AR-PRINCIPAL-RATE-IN / 100) / 12.
```

A program example using nested IFs

You have seen several examples involving processing of customers' retirement account data at a financial institution. Each record of the input file gives data about the state of an account. The processing generated an end-of-month report, showing the latest updated data for each account.

The processing involved computing the interest earned during the period, and adding the interest plus any deposit to the old principal to obtain the new principal.

Recall that to get the interest earned you had to compute both the interest on the old principal and the interest on the deposit. But suppose that the interest computed for the deposit depends on the following decision table:

DEPOSIT DAYS	DEPOSIT	ACTION
<= 10	<= 100	Pay zero interest (use zero interest rate)
<= 10	>100	Use deposit rate for interest rate
>10	<= 1000	Earns exactly $5 interest only
>10	>1000	Use deposit rate + 1 for interest

The procedure for generating the output record is given in Figure 5.9. The identifiers used are the same as those in the earlier version of this program, shown in Figure 5.4.

```
        IF AR-DEPOSIT-DAYS-IN <= 10
            THEN IF AR-DEPOSIT-IN <= 100
                    THEN MOVE 0 TO INTEREST-ON-DEPOSIT
                    ELSE COMPUTE INTEREST-ON-DEPOSIT
                        = ((AR-DEPOSIT-IN * AR-DEPOSIT-RATE-IN / 100)
                            * AR-DEPOSIT-DAYS-IN) / 365.
                END-IF
            ELSE IF AR-DEPOSIT-IN <= 1000
                    THEN MOVE 5 TO INTEREST-ON-DEPOSIT
                    ELSE COMPUTE INTEREST-ON-DEPOSIT
                        = ((AR-DEPOSIT-IN * (AR-DEPOSIT-RATE-IN + 1) / 100)
                            * AR-DEPOSIT-DAYS-IN) / 365.
                END-IF
        END-IF.
        ADD INTEREST-ON-DEPOSIT, INTEREST-ON-PRINCIPAL
                        GIVING TOTAL-INTEREST ROUNDED.
        ADD AR-PRINCIPAL-IN, AR-DEPOSIT-IN, TOTAL-INTEREST
                            GIVING NEW-PRINCIPAL-COMPUTED.
        MOVE    AR-CUSTOMER-NAME-IN     TO      DL-CUSTOMER-NAME-OUT.
        MOVE    AR-PRINCIPAL-IN         TO      DL-OLD-PRINCIPAL-OUT.
        MOVE    AR-DEPOSIT-IN           TO      DL-DEPOSIT-OUT.
        MOVE    TOTAL-INTEREST          TO      DL-INTEREST-OUT.
        MOVE    NEW-PRINCIPAL-COMPUTED  TO      DL-NEW-PRINCIPAL-OUT.
        WRITE REPORT-RECORD-OUT FROM DETAIL-LINE-OUT
                        AFTER ADVANCING 1 LINE.
        READ ACCOUNT-IN
                    AT END MOVE 'NO' TO MORE-RECORDS.
300-WRITE-HEADERS.
...
```

Figure 5.9 SAMPLE6 program with nested IFs.

The nested IF-statement in 200-PROCESS-RECORD that implements
the decision table could be replaced by four separate IF-statements, as
follows:

```
IF AR-DEPOSIT-DAYS-IN <= 10 AND AR-DEPOSIT-IN <= 100
    THEN MOVE 0 TO INTEREST-ON-DEPOSIT.

IF AR-DEPOSIT-DAYS-IN <= 10 AND AR-DEPOSIT-IN > 100
    THEN COMPUTE INTEREST-ON-DEPOSIT
        = ((AR-DEPOSIT-IN * AR-DEPOSIT-RATE-IN / 100)
                * AR-DEPOSIT-DAYS-IN) / 365.

IF AR-DEPOSIT-DAYS-IN > 10 AND AR-DEPOSIT-IN <= 1000
    THEN MOVE 5 TO INTEREST-ON-DEPOSIT.

IF AR-DEPOSIT-DAYS-IN > 10 AND AR-DEPOSIT-IN > 1000
    THEN COMPUTE INTEREST-ON-DEPOSIT
        = ((AR-DEPOSIT-IN * (AR-DEPOSIT-RATE-IN + 1) / 100)
                * AR-DEPOSIT-DAYS-IN) / 365.
```

You can use either of these methods of implementing the decision table. Many people believe separate IF-statements for each action in a complex condition table is clearer.

Other scope terminators are sometimes needed within an IF-statement

Recall that verbs, such as READ, COMPUTE, ADD, have scope terminators in COBOL 85. These scope terminators can sometimes be necessary when the verbs in question are used within IF-statements. For example, a subtle logical error can occur when you place a READ . . . AT END . . . statement without END-READ within an IF-statement. Consider the IF-statement

```
IF A > B
        READ INFILE
              AT END MOVE C TO D
        MOVE X TO Y
     END-IF.
```

The intended meaning is clear. If the condition is true, the READ should be executed, followed by the MOVE X TO Y statement. But that will not happen. Instead, when the condition is true only the READ is executed. The MOVE X TO Y is executed only when AT END is executed, that is, only when the end of the file has been reached, and not, as intended, with each READ.

The problem is that the compiler will assume the MOVE statement is part of the AT END clause. The solution is to use the END-READ option.

```
IF A > B
     THEN
           READ INFILE
                 AT END MOVE C TO D
           END-READ
           MOVE X TO Y
     END-IF
```

Similarly, this IF-statement with its obvious intended meaning will not execute as intended.

```
IF A > B
     ADD INTEREST TO PRINCIPAL GIVING NEW-PRINCIPAL
        ON SIZE ERROR MOVE C TO D
     MOVE X TO Y
  END-IF.
```

The MOVE X TO Y statement will be executed only if there is a size error, and not just when the condition A>B is true. To avoid this, the statement should have been written as

```
IF A > B
     ADD INTEREST TO PRINCIPAL GIVING NEW-PRINCIPAL
        ON SIZE ERROR MOVE C TO D
     END-ADD
     MOVE X TO Y
  END-IF.
```

The scope terminators, END-IF, END-READ, END-ADD, and so on, are available only in COBOL 85.

5.4
The EVALUATE statement can be used with multiple alternatives

A S STATED EARLIER, there are three basic constructs in programs: the straight sequence, the selection of alternatives, and the loop. The IF-statement is used when the selection is between two alternatives. When the selection is among more than two alternatives, a nested IF-statement can be used, as you have seen. However, if the selection is among many alternatives, and a simple condition involving an integer value can be devised for each alternative, you can use a special form of the selection of alternatives structure called the CASE structure.

For example, suppose you have the following decision table:

IDENTIFIER VALUE	ACTION
1	statement-1
2	statement-2
3	statement-3
4	statement-4
5	statement-5
<1 or >5	statement-6

The logic of this can be handled by a CASE structure. In pseudocode you could write the logic as

```
CASE identifier
      WHEN 1 carry out statement-1
      WHEN 2 carry out statement-2
      WHEN 3 carry out statement-3
      WHEN 4 carry out statement-4
      WHEN 5 carry out statement-5
      WHEN OTHER carry out statement-6
```

The logic of a structure like this is also illustrated by the flowchart in Figure 5.10.

It should be clear that the preceding pseudocode CASE sentence is equivalent to the following set of pseudocode IF-statements:

```
IF identifier = 1
      THEN carry out statement-1
END-IF.

IF identifier = 2
      THEN carry out statement-2
END-IF.
...

IF identifier = 5
      THEN carry out statement-5
END-IF.

IF identifier > 5 or identifier < 1
      THEN carry out statement-6
END-IF.
```

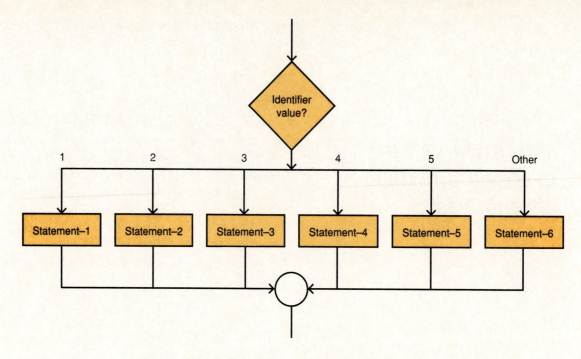

Figure 5.10 *A CASE structure. Which alternative is chosen depends on the value of an identifier.*

The CASE structure is clearer and thus recommended. The CASE structure was first implemented in COBOL with the 1985 standard. So check to see if your compiler allows for it. The word CASE is not used in COBOL. The COBOL verb used is EVALUATE.

The EVALUATE verb has two formats

There are two distinct formats for the EVALUATE verb. The first, and most important format, is shown in the box. The other appears later.

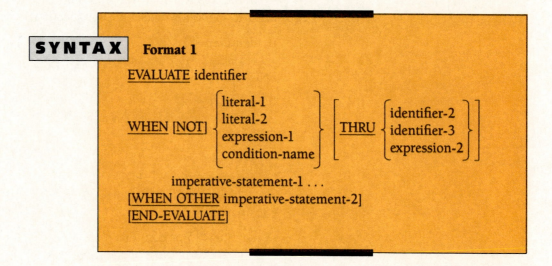

Some examples of correct format 1 EVALUATE statements are

```
EVALUATE SCORE
    WHEN 5      PERFORM 200-P2
    WHEN 6      PERFORM 300-P3
    WHEN 7      PERFORM 400-P4
    WHEN OTHER PERFORM 500-ERROR.

EVALUATE SCORE
    WHEN 5      PERFORM 200-P2
    WHEN NOT 5 PERFORM 300-P3.

EVALUATE SCORE
    WHEN X      PERFORM 200-P2
    WHEN Y      PERFORM 300-P3
    WHEN Z      PERFORM 400-P4
    WHEN OTHER PERFORM 500-ERROR.
```

Here X, Y, and Z are identifiers. When SCORE = X, paragraph 200-P2 is executed, when SCORE = Y, paragraph 300-P3 is carried out, and so on.

```
EVALUATE SERVICE
    WHEN 'EXCELLENT' PERFORM 200-P-A
    WHEN 'GOOD'      PERFORM 300-P-B
    WHEN 'POOR'      PERFORM 400-P-C
    WHEN OTHER       PERFORM 500-ERROR
END-EVALUATE.

EVALUATE SERVICE
    WHEN EXCELLENT PERFORM 200-P-A
    WHEN GOOD      PERFORM 300-P-B          declare conditional!
    WHEN POOR      PERFORM 400-P-C
    WHEN OTHER     PERFORM 500-ERROR
END-EVALUATE.
```

These last two examples are not the same. In the first case SERVICE is an ordinary alphanumeric identifier, and 'EXCELLENT', 'GOOD' and 'POOR' are simple values of SERVICE. In the second case SERVICE is an alphanumeric identifier declared along with condition names, perhaps as follows:

```
05   SERVICE          PIC X.
     88   EXCELLENT    VALUE 'A'.
     88   GOOD         VALUE 'B'.
     88   POOR         VALUE 'C'.
```

Thus, in the first case paragraph 400-P-C is executed if SERVICE has the value 'POOR'. In the second case, paragraph 400-P-C is executed if SERVICE has the value 'C'.

```
EVALUATE SCORE
    WHEN 5 THRU 8    PERFORM 200-P2
    WHEN 9 THRU 15   PERFORM 300-P3
    WHEN 16 THRU 50  PERFORM 400-P4
    WHEN OTHER       PERFORM 500-ERROR.
```

Paragraph 200-P2 is executed if SCORE $>=$ 5 AND SCORE $<=$ 8, that is, if SCORE lies between 5 and 8, and so on.

```
EVALUATE SCORE
    WHEN A THRU B    PERFORM 200-P2
    WHEN P THRU Q    PERFORM 300-P3
    WHEN X THRU Y    PERFORM 400-P4
    WHEN OTHER       PERFORM 500-ERROR.
```

Here A, B, P, Q, X, and Y are identifiers. They should be numeric if SCORE is numeric, and alphanumeric if SCORE is alphanumeric. Paragraph 200-P2 is executed if SCORE > = A AND SCORE < = B, that is, if the value of SCORE lies between the values of A and B, and so on.

```
EVALUATE SCORE
    WHEN A + B          PERFORM 200-P2
    WHEN (A + B) * D    PERFORM 300-P3
    WHEN A - B          PERFORM 400-P4
    WHEN OTHER          PERFORM 500-ERROR.
```

Paragraph 300-P3 is executed if the value resulting from computing (A + B) * D equals the value in SCORE. Where arithmetic expressions are used after WHEN, the values involved should all be integers.

```
EVALUATE SCORE
    WHEN A + B THRU B + C          PERFORM 200-P2
    WHEN P * Q THRU T * (R + S)    PERFORM 300-P3
    WHEN X THRU Y                  PERFORM 400-P4
    WHEN OTHER                     PERFORM 500-ERROR.
```

A, B, C, P, Q, T, R, and S are identifiers. The values in the expressions (A + B), (B + C), and so on are computed. If A + B = 6 and B + C = 10, then paragraph 200-P2 will be executed if SCORE has a value between 6 and 10, and so on.

The following is allowed:

```
EVALUATE GRADE
    WHEN 10
            MOVE 'YES' TO TOP-GRADE
            PERFORM 300-GRADE-PARAGRAPH
    WHEN 9
            MOVE 'NO' TO TOP-GRADE
            MOVE GRADE TO GRADE-OUR
            PERFORM 400-GRADE-PARAGRAPH
END-EVALUATE.
```

In a WHEN clause, only an imperative statement is allowed, but this can be a composite imperative statement, consisting of a sequence of elementary imperative statements. The following is not allowed:

```
EVALUATE GRADE
    WHEN 10
            MOVE 'YES' TO TOP-GRADE
            PERFORM 300-GRADE-PARAGRAPH
            IF STUDENT-AGE < 19 PERFORM 200-SPECIAL-AWARD    error!
    WHEN 9
            MOVE 'NO' TO TOP-GRADE
            MOVE GRADE TO GRADE-OUR
            PERFORM 400-GRADE-PARAGRAPH
```

```
      WHEN OTHER
             PERFORM 500-ERROR
   END-EVALUATE.
```

There cannot be a conditional statement following WHEN.
The following is incorrect:

```
EVALUATE SCORE
    WHEN < 5    PERFORM 200-P2
    WHEN > 5    PERFORM 300-P3          error!
    WHEN 5      PERFORM 400-P4.
```

The equal operator is implied for the value that follows WHEN, so that, if the value is numeric, it must be an integer.
The following is allowed:

```
EVALUATE SCORE
    WHEN 5 PERFORM 200-P2
    WHEN 6 PERFORM 300-P3
    WHEN 7 PERFORM 400-P4
    WHEN OTHER
             MOVE 'YES' TO ALL-TESTED
             PERFORM 200-ERROR
    END-EVALUATE.
```

A composite imperative statement may follow OTHER. But note that an IF-statement following OTHER is an error. END-EVALUATE is the optional scope terminator for EVALUATE.
The second format for EVALUATE is shown in this box.

SYNTAX   **Format 2**

EVALUATE condition

WHEN $\left\{ \begin{array}{c} \underline{TRUE} \\ \underline{FALSE} \end{array} \right\}$ imperative-statement-1 . . .

[WHEN OTHER imperative-statement-2]
[END-EVALUATE]

The following is an example:

```
EVALUATE PRINCIPAL > 1000
    WHEN TRUE  PERFORM 200-COMPUTE-INTEREST
    WHEN FALSE PERFORM 300-PENALTY.
```

Any condition, simple or compound, may follow EVALUATE with this format. However, since this format for EVALUATE is similar in meaning to an IF-statement, it is not commonly used.

```
...
      05  INTEGER-PRINCIPAL         PIC 9(07).
 PROCEDURE DIVISION.
 100-MAIN-MODULE.
*****************************************************************************
*   100-MAIN-MODULE:  CONTROLS OPENING AND CLOSING OF FILES AND           *
*   DIRECTION OF PROGRAM LOGIC.                                           *
*****************************************************************************
      OPEN INPUT  ACCOUNT-IN
           OUTPUT ACCOUNT-OUT.
      PERFORM 300-WRITE-HEADERS.
      READ ACCOUNT-IN,
           AT END MOVE 'NO' TO MORE RECORDS.
      PERFORM 200-PROCESS-RECORD
           UNTIL MORE-RECORDS = 'NO'.
      CLOSE ACCOUNT-IN
            ACCOUNT-OUT.
      STOP RUN.
 200-PROCESS-RECORD.
*****************************************************************************
*   200-PROCESS-RECORD:  PERFORMED FROM 100-MAIN-MODULE. PROCESSES        *
*   LATEST ACCOUNT-IN RECORD. COMPUTES INTEREST AND NEW PRINCIPAL AND     *
*   PRINTS REPORT LINE.                                                   *
*****************************************************************************
      MOVE AR-PRINCIPAL-RATE-IN TO WS-PRINCIPAL-RATE.
      MOVE AR-PRINCIPAL-IN TO INTEGER-PRINCIPAL.
      EVALUATE INTEGER-PRINCIPAL
           WHEN     0 THRU     99 MOVE ZERO TO WS-PRINCIPAL-RATE
           WHEN   100 THRU    999 ADD 0 TO WS-PRINCIPAL-RATE
           WHEN  1000 THRU   9999 ADD 0.25 TO WS-PRINCIPAL-RATE
           WHEN 10000 THRU  49999 ADD 0.50 TO WS-PRINCIPAL-RATE
           WHEN OTHER            ADD 0.75 TO WS-PRINCIPAL-RATE.
      COMPUTE INTEREST-ON-PRINCIPAL
           = (AR-PRINCIPAL-IN * WS-PRINCIPAL-RATE / 100) / 12.
      COMPUTE INTEREST-ON-DEPOSIT
           = ((AR-DEPOSIT-IN * AR-DEPOSIT-RATE-IN / 100)
              * AR-DEPOSIT-DAYS-IN) / 365.
      ADD AR-PRINCIPAL-IN, AR-DEPOSIT-IN, TOTAL-INTEREST
                               GIVING NEW-PRINCIPAL-COMPUTED.
      MOVE AR-CUSTOMER-NAME-IN     TO     DL-CUSTOMER-NAME-OUT.
      MOVE AR-PRINCIPAL-IN         TO     DL-OLD-PRINCIPAL-OUT.
      MOVE AR-DEPOSIT-IN           TO     DL-DEPOSIT-OUT.
      MOVE TOTAL-INTEREST          TO     DL-INTEREST-OUT.
      MOVE NEW-PRINCIPAL-COMPUTED TO     DL-NEW-PRINCIPAL-OUT.
      WRITE REPORT-RECORD-OUT FROM DETAIL-LINE-OUT
                     AFTER ADVANCING 1 LINE.
      READ ACCOUNT-IN
               AT END MOVE 'NO' TO MORE RECORDS.
 300-WRITE-HEADERS.
 ...
```

Figure 5.11 SAMPLE6 program using EVALUATE.

A program example using EVALUATE

This example again uses the processing of the file ACCOUNT-IN which contains records describing retirement savings accounts. Recall that, for each input record, the processing involved computing the interest on both the old principal and the deposit, and adding both the deposit and total interest to the old principal to get the new principal at month end.

The rate of interest applicable to the principal could depend on the size of the old principal. Suppose that the following decision table applied to the computation of interest on the old principal:

OLD PRINCIPAL	ACTION
$0.00–$99.99	Interest is zero.
$100.00–$999.99	Use interest given by principal rate.
$1,000.00–$9,999.99	Use principal rate + 0.25.
$10,000.00–$49,999.99	Use principal rate + 0.50.
Other	Use principal rate + 0.75. The principal cannot be negative.

You can use the procedure in Figure 5.11. It uses the same identifiers as in Figure 5.4, except for the new identifier INTEGER-PRINCIPAL. This identifier holds an integer version of the old principal (cents removed), and is needed with the EVALUATE statement.

If you wanted to do without the EVALUATE statement, you could use either a set of five separate IF-statements or a single composite IF-statement. Try to construct these, as an exercise.

Summary

1. The IF-statement is a conditional statement, as opposed to an imperative statement. It is used to decide which of two sets of statements will be executed; If the condition following IF is true, the THEN set of statements is executed; otherwise, the ELSE set of statements executes. The THEN and ELSE statements should always be on separate lines and should be indented to show intent.
2. The condition in an IF-statement can be simple or compound. A simple condition compares two quantities; a quantity compared can be either a literal or the value in an identifier. A compound condition involves two or more simple conditions connected by the logical connectives AND and OR. Parentheses should be used to ensure intent when more than three simple conditions occur in a compound condition. When NOT is used with a compound condition, take care that De Morgan's Rules are obeyed.

3. A THEN or ELSE statement within an IF-statement can also be an IF-statement. Such nesting of IF-statements allows for selection among multiple alternatives. Care should be taken with nesting of IF-statements. The scope terminator END-IF is advised, to indicate clearly the end of a nested IF-statement. A decision table is also advised before construction of an IF-statement with nesting, to ensure there is a set of statements to be executed for every possible condition. To avoid ambiguity, the scope terminators for many statements, such as READ and the arithmetic statements, are often needed with THEN and ELSE statements.
4. The EVALUATE statement is used for implementing a CASE construction. It is useful whenever a simple integer value for a given identifier is associated with a set of statements to be executed. An EVALUATE statement can always be replaced by either a set of IF-statements or an IF-statement containing nested IFs.

Key Terms

collating sequences   sign conditions   condition name
nested IF-statements   class conditions   condition table

Concept Review Questions

1. Explain the semantics of an IF-statement.
2. Explain a simple condition.
3. Explain a compound condition.
4. Why is the END-IF scope terminator needed?
5. Show that De Morgan's Rules must always hold.
6. Make up a truth table for A AND B AND C.
7. Make up a truth table for (A OR B) AND C.
8. Make up a truth table for A OR (B AND C).
9. Make up a truth table for NOT A OR B.
10. Eliminate the parentheses in NOT (A OR NOT B).
11. Eliminate the parentheses in NOT (A AND (B OR C)).
12. In which collating sequence does 'a' come before (is lower than) 'l'?
13. In which collating sequence does 'Z' come before (is lower than) '9'?
14. In which collating sequence are the following true?

```
CD42 < 15BD
DF5E > DFB7
```

15. What is a sign condition?
16. What are class conditions and where are they used?
17. What are condition names and where are they used?
18. What is a condition table and what is it used for?
19. Why is the END-READ scope terminator sometimes needed with READ statements nested within IF-statements?
20. Explain the semantics of the EVALUATE statement.
21. What is a CASE statement in pseudocode?

REQUIRED TRUE CONDITIONS			ACTION
X = C	AND	G > D	PERFORM 200-P
X > C	AND	G > D	PERFORM 300-P
X < C	AND	G > D	PERFORM 400-P
X = C	AND	G NOT= D	PERFORM 500-P
X NOT= C	AND	G NOT= D	PERFORM 600-P

10. Construct the IF-statement for this condition table:

REQUIRED TRUE CONDITIONS			ACTION
X = C	AND	G > D	PERFORM 200-P
X NOT= C	AND	G > D	PERFORM 300-P
X = C	AND	G < D	PERFORM 400-P
X NOT= C	AND	G < D	PERFORM 500-P
All other			PERFORM 600-P

11. Construct the condition table for the following IF- statement:

```
IF A > B
     THEN IF X = Y
                  PERFORM 200-P
     ELSE
                  PERFORM 300-P
     END-IF
ELSE
     IF X < Y
                  PERFORM 400-P
     ELSE
                  PERFORM 500-P
     END-IF
END-IF.
```

12. Convert the IF-statement in question 11 to four separate IF-statements.

13. What is wrong with this?

```
01 A      PIC 99      VALUE 6.
01 B      PIC 99      VALUE 4.
01 X      PIC 99V99   VALUE 4.
...
    EVALUATE  QUANTITY-1
       WHEN A - B  PERFORM 300-P
       WHEN A + B  PERFORM 400-P
       WHEN A / X  PERFORM 500-P.
```

Fix it, using IF-statements.

14. What is wrong with the following?

```
01 A      PIC 99      VALUE 6.
01 B      PIC 99      VALUE 4.
       EVALUATE QUANTITY-1
          WHEN   A  PERFORM 300-P
          WHEN < B  PERFORM 400-P.
```

Fix it with IF-statements.

15. Replace the EVALUATE statement in the program in Figure 5.11 with a composite IF-statement.

Programming Assignments

1. **A program to bill hotel guests**

   Each record in the input file gives data about the stay of a guest at a hotel. Some records of the file are

   ```
   ---------1---------2---------3
   GREEN, J.K          04S1404215
   JONES, G.U.         15L2315542
   HARDCASTLE, P.F.    06D0004780
   ```

Columns 01–20	Guest name
21–22	Number of nights occupancy
23	Single room (S), double room (D), or luxury room (L)
24–25	Number of local phone calls
26–30	Long distance phone calls

   Output a report with this format:

   ```
   BILLING REPORT

   GUEST          NIGHTS  ROOM    TOTAL    TOTAL       TOTAL
   NAME                   TYPE    ROOM     TELEPHONE   CHARGE
                                  CHARGE   CHARGE      incl. 7%
                                                       state tax

   GREEN, J. K       4    SINGLE  160.00   44.65       218.98
   ```

   In computing the report, the following should be observed:

   - For every seven nights' occupancy, one night is charged at half price.
   - Daily room cost is
       Single $40.00
       Double $55.00
       Luxury $62.50
   - Charge for a local telephone call is 25 cents, but the first four calls are free.
   - State sales tax of 7% is charged.

   a. Make up a record layout for the input data.
   b. Make up a program spacing chart for the output data.
   c. Draw a flowchart and a hierarchy diagram for the processing.
   d. Write the program and run it.

2. **A program to bill customers of an automobile rental company**

   Each record of the input file gives details of a car rental by a customer. The input file is

```
---------1---------2---------3---------4
BROWN, G.H.        OLDS0850207
GREEN, P.F.        HOND1240417
RABINOVITCH, T.G.  VOLK0072001
ANDERSON, T.D.     CHEV0041402
```

Columns 01–20   Customer name
       21–24   Car make
       25–29   Mileage to one decimal place
       30–31   Integer number of days

The output file is

CAR RENTAL BILLING REPORT

CUSTOMER NAME	CAR MAKE	MILEAGE	DAYS	STATE TAX	TOTAL CHARGE
BROWN, G.H.	OLDSMOBILE	850.2	7	$ 10.98	$ 194.01
...					

The following conditions hold:

- An Oldsmobile costs $0.12 per mile and $15.50 per day.
- A Chevrolet costs $0.09 per mile and $13.00 per day.
- A Honda costs $0.07 per mile and $8.25 per day.
- A Volkswagen costs $0.10 per mile and $11.50 per day.
- The first 100 miles are free if you exceed 100, but if less than or equal to 100, only the first 50 are free.
- If you rent for more than 6 days you get 1 free day. If you rent for more than 12 days you get 2 free days and 200 additional free miles.
- State sales tax is 6%.

a. Draw up a record layout for the input.
b. Draw up a printer spacing chart for the output.
c. Draw a flowchart and a hierarchy diagram.
d. Write and run the program.

3. **Program for conditional record selection**
   Some data about certain ships, described in an input file, are to be printed in a report, provided the ships meet certain conditions.
   The input data are:

```
---------1---------2---------3---------4---------5
BONJOUR      25FRANCE    42KOREA     1982T22
DON JUAN     33SPAIN     25JAPAN     1979B27
EVENREST     15U.S.A.    17CANADA    1972C19
FRANCISCO    41SPAIN     21KOREA     1986T33
GRANADA      17SPAIN     26U.S.A     1962F25
GOODWILL     35U.S.A     31KOREA     1977B22

...
```

```
Columns 01–14        Ship name
       15–16        Deadweight (thousands of tons)
       17–26        Country of registration
       27–28        Number in crew
       29–38        Country built
       39–42        Year built
       43           Type of ship (F=freighter, T=tanker, B=bulk
                        carrier, C=container vessel)
       44–45        Horsepower (thousands)
```

The output data are:

```
---------1---------2---------3---------4
          SELECTED VESSEL REPORT


SHIP NAME        REGISTERED         CREW


EVENREST         U.S.A              17
GRANADA          SPAIN              26
```

A detail line is contructed in the report from each input record for which all the following conditions hold:

- Deadweight < 20
- Not built in Japan or Korea
- Ship is a container vessel or freighter
- Built before 1975
- Horsepower between 18 and 26 (thousands)

a. Increase the number of records in the input file to about 20.
b. Draw a record layout for the input file.
c. Draw a printer spacing chart for the output file.
d. Draw a flowchart and a hierarchy diagram for the process.
e. Develop and run the program.

4. **Program to bill stock investors**
   This program computes the cost of each stock purchase made by a customer, taking into account a set of rules for computing the broker's commission for each transaction. The input data are

```
---------1---------2---------3---------4
ABC042500500
BGH020000150
CFH009750300
CMV018250075
DFG141500200
```

```
Columns 01–03        Stock symbol
       04–08        Stock price
       09–12        Number of shares purchased (a round lot is a
                        multiple of 100 shares)
```

The output data are

```
---------1---------2---------3---------4---------5---------6---------7
                STOCK PURCHASE REPORT

STOCK   SHARES      MARKET    COST            COMMISSION  TOTAL
SYMBOL  PURCHASED   PRICE                     ADDED       COST

ABC     500         $42.50  $   21,250.00  $     212.50  $  21,462.50
...
```

The total cost of a purchase of stock is the cost, which is shares purchased times market price, plus the broker's commission. This commission is computed as follows:

- If total purchase is under $10,000
    2.0% if share price is < $8
    1.5% if share price is >= 8 and < 100
- If total purchase is $10,000 or over
    1.5% if share price is < $8
    1.0% if share price is >= $8 and < $100
    0.75% if share price > $100
- If an odd lot is included, an odd lot charge is further added, as follows:
    $8 if the share price < $8
    $14 if the share price is >= 8 and < $100
    $20 if the share price >= $100

a. Draw the record layout for the input data.
b. Draw the printer spacing chart for the output data.
c. Make up a condition table for the processing.
d. Make up a flowchart and hierarchy diagram for the processing.
e. Develop and run the program. You should add more records to the input file, to test all the conditions.

6

LOOPED INSTRUCTION SEQUENCES

Y OU HAVE SEEN that three major structures can be employed in writing programs for processing data. These are the straight sequence of instructions, the selection between alternative sets of instructions, and the looped instruction sequence.

This chapter examines looped instruction sequences in detail. There have been some examples of looped instruction sequences in earlier chapters, since most programs that process records from an input file have at least one major loop. Each iteration of the loop processes a record. This chapter looks again at PERFORM ... UNTIL, commonly used for repeated execution or iteration, of groups of instructions. It also looks at another version of PERFORM that can be used with iterations, namely the PERFORM ... TIMES instruction. Finally, nested loops (loops within loops) are discussed. Remember that in a program with a looped instruction sequence, a group of instructions is executed over and over again, as often as necessary, to carry out some processing task.

6.1
A PERFORM . . . UNTIL *loop is commonly used to process files*

T HE MOST COMMON use of a looped sequence of instructions is in processing a file of input records, where the same overall set of instructions is used to process each record. The most commonly used instruction for repeated execution of the sequence of instructions needed to process a single record is the PERFORM .. UNTIL instruction, introduced in Chapter 4. The instructions needed to process a record are placed in a separate paragraph that is executed when a PERFORM ... UNTIL instruction is executed. The resulting overall format of the program statements is fairly constant, no matter what the processing.

No matter what processing the records in a file need, when each input record is processed to form an output record, the general program structure used is as follows:

Main-paragraph.

1. Open input and output files.
2. Set More-records flag to 'YES'.
3. Read first record.
4. Perform paragraph Process-record until end-of-file flag (More-records) is 'NO'.
5. Close files and stop.

Process-record.

1. Carry out computations, if any, on input record.
2. Construct output record.
3. Write output record.
4. Read next input record, and if none left, set More-records flag to 'NO'.

Notice how the Read instruction fits in. It is first used in Main-paragraph to read the first record. Then the instructions in Process-record process this first record and read the next record. Then this record is processed by the instructions in Process-record, and the next record is read.

The placement of the Read instruction at the end of Process-record is necessary. You should become familiar with this important technique.

Placement of the Read instruction at the end of the processing paragraph has to do with what happens when the end of the input file is reached. Suppose that the Read has just been carried out and the last record is read. Process-record will be executed again and the record will be processed correctly. Then the Read at the end of the paragraph is executed again. The Read will be something such as this:

```
READ INPUT-FILE,
    AT END MOVE 'NO' TO MORE-RECORDS.
```

This time there is no record to read. So the AT END statement is executed, which causes the "flag" identifier MORE-RECORDS to receive the value 'NO'. This causes execution of Process-record to cease—exactly what is required, since in Main-paragraph (step 4), it was specified that Process-record execute repeatedly until MORE-RECORDS received the value 'NO'. Once MORE-RECORDS contains a value 'NO', no further processing of Process-record should take place.

Finally, once execution of Process-record has stopped, step 5 of Main-paragraph is carried out. This closes the files and stops the processing.

The obvious way to do it, with Read at the start of Process-record, is also the Wrong way to do it. Why this is so should now be easy to understand. Let us look at the Wrong way. Suppose the following pseudocode was used:

Main-paragraph. (Error!)

1. Open input and output files.
2. Set More-records flag to 'YES'.
3. Perform paragraph Process-record until more-records flag is 'NO'.
4. Close files and stop.

Process-record. (Error!)

1. Read next input record, and if none left, set More-records flag to 'NO'.
2. Carry out computations, if any, on input record.
3. Construct output record.
4. Write output record.

This will work fine until the end of the input file is reached. The last record will be read and processed without any problem. The trouble is there is nothing to indicate that the last record *is* the last record. Computer systems react only when an attempt is made to read beyond the last record, that is, to read a record that is not in the file. Thus, when the last record has been read and correctly processed, MORE-RECORDS still contains the value 'YES'. This means that Process-record will be executed once more, in an attempt to read and process the record after the last, which does not exist. During this execution of Process-record, the READ instruction does not succeed, but steps 2, 3, and 4 in Processing-record are still executed.

As a result, things go wrong. Depending on the computer, either the last record will be processed twice, or there will be a run error, with the program terminating abruptly (an ABEND).

Looped sequences are very common in COBOL programs

Programs in previous chapters illustrated COBOL techniques for processing an input file with records that described customers' retirement accounts. Let us now analyze this example in the light of the previous discussion, to get a better understanding of looping with PERFORM . . . UNTIL.

Recall that processing the input file ACCOUNT-IN was carried out every month and consisted of reading each record and outputting a corresponding detail line of a report. For each record read, the latest financial data (based on calculations of interest earned) were computed and output in a line of the report. Recall that the processing was repeated for each record.

The core of a COBOL looped sequence for processing a file, such as ACCOUNT-IN, to generate a printer file REPORT-OUT, is structured as in the flowchart in Figure 6.1, with a program skeleton as in Figure 6.2.

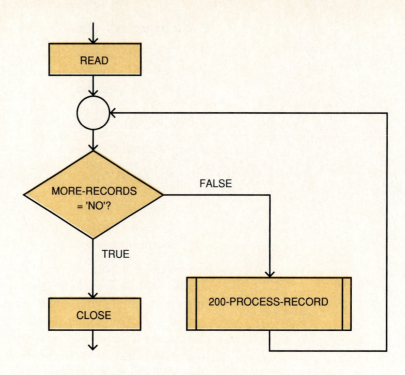

Figure 6.1 *The logic of the PERFORM statement. Note that the condition must be false for any execution of paragraph 200-PROCESS-RECORD.*

```
PROCEDURE DIVISION.
100-MAIN-MODULE.
    OPEN INPUT ACCOUNT-IN
        OUTPUT REPORT-OUT.
    MOVE 'YES' TO MORE-RECORDS.
    READ ACCOUNT-IN
            AT END display no input records message and stop.
    Write report headers, if any.
    PERFORM 200-PROCESS-RECORD
                UNTIL MORE-RECORDS = 'NO'.
    CLOSE ACCOUNT-IN
        REPORT-OUT.
    STOP RUN.
200-PROCESS-RECORD.
    Instructions involving computations with ACCOUNT-IN record.
    Instructions to form output fields in DETAIL-LINE-OUT.
    WRITE REPORT-RECORD-OUT FROM DETAIL-LINE-OUT
                AFTER ADVANCING 1 LINE.
    READ ACCOUNT-IN
            AT END MOVE 'NO' TO MORE-RECORDS.
```

Figure 6.2 *Program skeleton illustrating a looped sequence.*

In the skeleton of the COBOL routine, ACCOUNT-IN and REPORT-OUT are the names of the input and output files respectively. REPORT-RECORD-OUT and DETAIL-LINE-OUT are respectively the output buffer and working storage record structures for a record of REPORT-OUT.

The identifier MORE-RECORDS is used as a flag. As long as the value is 'YES', the PERFORM . . . UNTIL statement will cause repeated execution of the paragraph 200-PROCESS-RECORD.

Notice that there are two READ statements. The first READ causes the first record in ACCOUNT-IN to be read. If the file has no records (remotely possible), the AT END clause will cause suitable action to take place, involving cessation of the program.

The second READ causes all subsequent records to be read. An attempt to read beyond the end of the file will cause the AT END clause to be executed. This will give MORE-RECORDS the value 'NO', and end execution of the 200-PROCESS-RECORD.

Note carefully the sequence of execution of the instructions. Each instruction in 100-MAIN-MODULE is executed in sequence, including the PERFORM . . . UNTIL instruction. But the PERFORM . . . UNTIL instruction translates into repeated execution of the 200-PROCESS-RECORD. Thus the sequence of execution corresponds to that shown in the flowchart in Figure 6.1.

The PERFORM . . . UNTIL statement uses the same type of condition as IF-statements

The PERFORM . . . UNTIL statement causes repeated execution of 200-PROCESS-RECORD; it is crucial for constructing looped-sequence programs. The syntax for PERFORM . . . UNTIL was given in Chapter 4. Here it is again for your convenience:

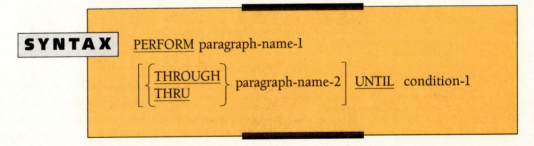

SYNTAX

PERFORM paragraph-name-1

$\left[\begin{Bmatrix} \text{THROUGH} \\ \text{THRU} \end{Bmatrix} \text{paragraph-name-2}\right]$ UNTIL condition-1

Notice that the condition used in PERFORM . . . UNTIL statements is exactly the same kind of condition used in IF-statements. Thus, compound conditions as well as simple conditions are allowed. Some valid statements are

```
PERFORM 600-RECORD-PROCESSING
          UNTIL MORE-RECORDS = 'NO'.

PERFORM 700-WRITE-ROUTINE
        UNTIL PAGE-NUMBER = 4 AND LINE-NUMBER = 20.

PERFORM P1 THRU P7
        UNTIL X > K OR Y < 15.4.
```

The most common type of PERFORM . . . UNTIL statement involves a single paragraph of instructions:

PERFORM P2 UNTIL condition-1.

The most important thing to remember about this PERFORM statement is that

The condition-1 is evaluated before each execution of P2; if condition-1 is false, P2 is executed; if it is true, the statement following PERFORM is executed.

Pseudocode is often used when planning looped sequences

Commonly used pseudocode for looped sequences is as follows:

```
...
Carry out instruction-1.
PERFORM . . . UNTIL condition.
    Instructions to be repeated.
END-PERFORM.
Carry out instruction-3.
...
```

In pseudocode the group of instructions to be repeated is sandwiched between PERFORM . . . UNTIL and END-PERFORM. This group of instructions is to be repeated as long as the condition is false.

Compound conditions are often used with PERFORM . . . UNTIL

The examples so far in this book have used only simple conditions with the PERFORM . . . UNTIL verb. The conditions that may be used with PERFORM . . . UNTIL are evaluated according to the same rules as conditions used with IF-statements. Thus, compound conditions may also be used. (You should be familiar with the sections on conditions in the previous chapter.)

Compound conditions are often used with the PERFORM verb. As a simple example, suppose you want to process all of the records of an input file ACCOUNT-IN if the file contains four or fewer records, but only the first four records if the file has more than four records.

You could use the flag MORE-RECORDS to signal the end of the file. You could also use the numeric identifier RECORDS-PROCESSED (defined with PIC 9(08), for example) to hold the number of records processed so far. The routine would be as shown in Figure 6.3.

```
PROCEDURE DIVISION.
100-MAIN-MODULE.
      OPEN INPUT ACCOUNT-IN
           OUTPUT REPORT-OUT.
      MOVE 'YES' TO MORE-RECORDS.
      MOVE ZERO TO RECORDS-PROCESSED.
      READ ACCOUNT-IN
           AT END MOVE 'NO' TO MORE-RECORDS.
      PERFORM 300-PRINT-HEADERS.
      PERFORM 200-PROCESS-RECORD
           UNTIL MORE-RECORDS = 'NO' OR RECORDS-PROCESSED = 4.
      CLOSE ACCOUNT-IN
            REPORT-OUT.
      STOP RUN.
200-PROCESS-RECORD.
```
Compute output record field values.

Form output record in DETAIL-LINE-OUT.
```
      WRITE REPORT-RECORD-OUT FROM DETAIL-LINE-OUT
           AFTER ADVANCING 1 LINE.
      ADD 1 TO RECORDS-PROCESSED.
      READ ACCOUNT-IN
           AT END MOVE 'NO' TO MORE-RECORDS.
```
. . .

Figure 6.3 *Program excerpt that processes all records where file contains four or fewer, but only first four if file has more than four records.*

Before processing of 200-PROCESS-RECORD can begin, the condition

```
MORE-RECORDS = 'NO' OR RECORDS-PROCESSED = 4
```

must be false. At the beginning, after the first record has been read, it will be false. Before the paragraph can be executed a second time, the condition is checked again. It will still be false if the file has at least two records.

Suppose the file has three records. When the paragraph has been executed three times, MORE-RECORDS will have the value 'NO'. Before the paragraph can be executed again, the compound condition will be checked. Since it will now be true, the paragraph is not executed again, and all the records in the file have been processed.

Now suppose that the file has 10 records. When the paragraph has been executed four times, the value of RECORDS-PROCESSED will be 4. Before the paragraph can be executed again, the condition in the PERFORM statement will be checked. It will be true, so that the paragaph will not be executed again, and exactly four records will have been processed.

Creating an infinite loop is easier than you might think

The PERFORM . . . UNTIL statement allows easy coding of looped sequences of instructions. The idea is for a group of instructions to be executed repeatedly, but a finite number of times. The condition in the PERFORM . . . UNTIL statement has to be constructed in such a way that,

```
PROCEDURE DIVISION.
100-MAIN-MODULE.
     OPEN INPUT ACCOUNT-IN
          OUTPUT REPORT-OUT.
     MOVE 'YES' TO MORE-RECORDS.
     MOVE ZERO TO RECORDS-PROCESSED.
     READ ACCOUNT-IN
          AT END MOVE 'NO' TO MORE-RECORDS.
     PERFORM 200-PROCESS-RECORD
          UNTIL MORE-RECORDS = 'NO' AND RECORDS-PROCESSED = 4.
     CLOSE ACCOUNT-IN
          REPORT-OUT.
     STOP RUN.
200-PROCESS-RECORD.
     Compute output record field values.
     Form output record in DETAIL-LINE-OUT.
     WRITE BUFFER-RECORD-OUT FROM DETAIL-LINE-OUT
               AFTER ADVANCING 1 LINE.
     ADD 1 TO RECORDS-PROCESSED.
     READ ACCOUNT-IN
          AT END MOVE 'NO' TO MORE-RECORDS.
```

Figure 6.4 *Program in Figure 6.3 with logical errors.*

after a finite number of loops, it will become true and stop the iteration. However, a programmer can easily set up the condition incorrectly so that it can never become true. As a result, the looping will continue forever, or at least as long as the computer is switched on. Such a condition is known as an *infinite loop*.

The problem with an infinite loop is that it is a run error; it will not be detected by the COBOL compiler before the program executes. It goes without saying that every effort must be made to avoid an infinite loop in a program. This usually means checking the logic behind the condition in a PERFORM . . . UNTIL statement very carefully.

It is easiest to get the condition wrong with compound conditions using the OR connective. As an example, recall the program in Figure 6.3, which processed the first four records of ACCOUNT-IN if there were more than four in the file, and all of the records if there were four or fewer. Suppose you coded it as shown in Figure 6.4.

The condition

```
MORE-RECORDS = 'NO' AND RECORDS-PROCESSED = 4.
```

could easily be coded for this case, if the programmer did not think too deeply about it. The simple condition

```
MORE-RECORDS = 'NO'
```

would work if you just wanted to process all the records. And the simple condition

```
RECORDS-PROCESSED = 4
```

would work if the file had four or more records and you just wanted to process the first four. A programmer might be forgiven for thinking that by combining the two simple conditions with an AND connective, the complex condition could be satisfied. But it is not, and worse, the program has an infinite loop if the file has more than four records.

Assume the file has 10,000 records. When four records have been processed, the condition is false, so processing continues. When 10,000 records have been processed, the condition is still false, so processing continues. When, in the next iteration, an attempt is made to read a record that is not there, 'NO' is placed in MORE-RECORDS, but the compound condition is still false, so processing continues. And, depending on the computer, the last record may be generated again. Following this, the condition will still be false, and, depending on the computer, processing will continue, and the last record will be printed over and over again.

The problem is that nothing can make the compound condition true and stop the loop. It is infinite. The correct condition, as you saw earlier, is

```
MORE-RECORDS = 'NO' OR RECORDS-PROCESSED = 4
```

Of course, the condition could also be correctly written as any of the three following examples:

```
MORE-RECORDS = 'NO' OR NOT (RECORDS-PROCESSED NOT = 4)

NOT (MORE-RECORDS = 'YES') OR RECORDS-PROCESSED = 4

NOT (MORE-RECORDS = 'YES' AND RECORDS-PROCESSED NOT = 4)
```

You may be able to see immediately that the last expression above is also correct. If you cannot, use De Morgan's first rule, in Chapter 5, to analyze it. You can see from this section that it is easy to get a compound condition wrong and cause an infinite loop.

6.2
The PERFORM . . . TIMES statement is used with a fixed number of iterations

THERE ARE TWO basic kinds of loops in programming: those where the number of iterations cannot be predicted in advance, and those where the number of iterations is known in advance. The PERFORM . . . UNTIL statement can be used with both types. However, it is best suited for cases where the number of iterations is not known in advance, such as processing the records of a file with an unknown number of records.

Where the number of iterations is known in advance, it is often easier to use another version of the PERFORM verb called PERFORM . . . TIMES.

Syntax for PERFORM . . . TIMES

The basic syntax for the PERFORM . . . TIMES statement is shown here:

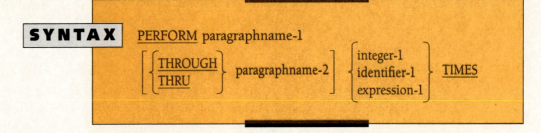

Some valid statements are as follows:

```
PERFORM 200-MODULE 10 TIMES.

PERFORM 500-PROCESS-RECORD RECORD-QUANTITY TIMES.

PERFORM 200-MODULE THRU 500-MODULE MONTHS TIMES.

PERFORM 200-MODULE (Q + 1) * D TIMES.
```

Note the following:

> Identifier-1 must be a numeric identifier specified in the data division and contain only a positive integer value of zero or greater. If an expression is used instead of an identifier, the value of the expression must be a positive integer.

Semantics for the PERFORM . . . TIMES Verb

The semantics for PERFORM . . . TIMES are relatively simple

- If the THRU/THROUGH option is used, the group of paragraphs from the first mentioned (paragraphname-1) to the last mentioned (paragraphname-2) is used.
- The single paragraph specified (paragraphname-1), or the group of paragraphs specified, is executed a number of times equal to the positive integer or value of the identifier coming before TIMES. If the identifier receives a new value during the iterations, the number of iterations is not affected.
- Following repeated execution of the paragraph or paragraphs specified, execution control returns to the statement that immediately follows the PERFORM . . . TIMES statement.

Example with PERFORM . . . TIMES

The PERFORM . . . TIMES statement is often used with repeated numeric calculations. It is not used much with repeated processing of input records, since even if you want to process an exact number of records, you can never be sure that the file does not contain less than that number. (It is also used with processing rows of a table where the number of rows is fixed. This will be covered in Chapter 11.)

A relevant example at this stage involves compound interest calculations. Let us review the basics.

Suppose you have a principal sum of $1000 and have it invested with annual interest compounded annually at 10 percent per annum. The principal sum will be

After 0 years: 1000
After 1 year: 1000 × (1 + 10/100)
After 2 years: 1000 × (1 + 10/100) × (1 + 10/100)
After 3 years: 1000 × (1 + 10/100) × (1 + 10/100) × (1 + 10/100)

This gives the results

PRINCIPAL	YEAR
1000	0
1100	1
1210	2
1331	3
...	...

In general, the new principal is given by

$$\text{new principal} = \text{original principal} \times (1 + \text{rate}/100)^{\text{years}}$$

With COBOL, given the obvious identifiers ORIGINAL-PRINCIPAL, RATE, YEARS, and NEW-PRINCIPAL, the new principal can be obtained by a single COMPUTE statement, as follows:

```
COMPUTE NEW-PRINCIPAL ROUNDED =
        ORIGINAL-PRINCIPAL * (1 + RATE / 100) ** YEARS.
```

This is very fast, but cannot be used if the new principal is needed at the end of each year during the investment period, as shown in the preceding table. In that case, you need a loop with a basic core such as the following:

```
100-MODULE.
    MOVE 0 TO YEAR-PROCESSED.
    MOVE ORIGINAL-PRINCIPAL TO NEW-PRINCIPAL.
    Write detail line showing initial principal.
    PERFORM 200-PROCESS-PRINCIPAL YEARS TIMES.
    ...
200-PROCESS-PRINCIPAL.
    COMPUTE NEW-PRINCIPAL = NEW-PRINCIPAL * (1 + RATE / 100).
    ADD 1 TO YEAR-PROCESSED.
    Write detail line containing data about the current
    new principal and the year processed.
```

If the value of YEARS was 5, you would get the initial principal, plus the principal for each of the subsequent five years.

Full Program Using PERFORM . . . TIMES

Let us take the preceding example and use it for a program to process a file CUSTOMER-IN that contains a single record. An example of the input data is given in Figure 6.5a. The record layout for the input data is in Figure 6.5b, and the structure of the matching input record is given in Figure 6.5c.

```
---------1---------2---------3---------4---------5
JOHN C. SMITH              000200000100004
<----------------------><-------><--><>
```

Figure 6.5a *Input data for file CUSTOMER-INFO.*

```
---------1---------2---------3---------4---------5
XXXXXXXXXXXXXXXXXXXXXXXXX999999999999999
```

Figure 6.5b *Spacing chart layout for input data.*

```
01    CUSTOMER-RECORD-IN.
      05   CR-CUSTOMER-NAME-IN          PIC X(25).
      05   CR-PRINCIPAL-IN              PIC 9(07)V9(02).
      05   CR-INTEREST-RATE-IN          PIC 9(02)V9(02).
      05   CR-YEARS-IN                  PIC 9(02).
```

Figure 6.5c *Structure of matching input area record.*

As usual, decimal points and spaces are left out in the input file. If some are put in, the data can be more easily understood by the reader:

```
JOHN C. SMITH              0002000.00   10.00    04
```

You want the value of the principal at the end of each year and at the beginning of the investment period. Suppose that the required output data are to go into a printer file called REPORT-OUT, with the format shown in Figure 6.6a. The printer spacing chart for the output is shown in Figure 6.6b and the structure of the output record used in the program is shown in Figure 6.6c.

```
---------1---------2---------3---------4---------5
JOHN C. SMITH               $0,002,000.00      00
JOHN C. SMITH               $0,002,200.00      01
JOHN C. SMITH               $0,002,420.00      02
JOHN C. SMITH               $0,002,662.00      03
JOHN C. SMITH               $0,002,928.20      04
```

Figure 6.6a *Output data for file REPORT-OUT.*

Figure 6.6b *Printer spacing chart for output data.*

```
01    DETAIL-LINE-OUT.
      05 FILLER                           PIC X(01)         VALUE SPACES.
      05 DL-CUSTOMER-NAME-OUT             PIC X(25).
      05 FILLER                           PIC X(02)         VALUE SPACES.
      05 DL-NEW-PRINCIPAL-OUT             PIC $9,999,999.99.
      05 FILLER                           PIC X(05)         VALUE SPACES.
      05 DL-YEAR-PROCESSED-OUT            PIC 9(02).
      05 FILLER                           PIC X(85)         VALUE SPACES.
```

Figure 6.6c *Structure of output record used.*

The program to carry out the processing is shown in Figure 6.7. Figure 6.8 shows the hierarchy structure diagram. Notice that the PERFORM . . . TIMES statements cause the interest computation to be performed CR-YEARS-IN times, where the value in CR-YEARS-IN is obtained from the input record.

```
IDENTIFICATION DIVISION.
PROGRAM-ID. S63.
ENVIRONMENT DIVISION.
INPUT-OUTPUT SECTION.
FILE-CONTROL.    SELECT CUSTOMER-IN  ASSIGN TO UT-S-CUST90.
                 SELECT REPORT-OUT   ASSIGN TO UR-S-SYSPRINT.
DATA DIVISION.
FILE SECTION.
FD  CUSTOMER-IN                      LABEL RECORDS ARE STANDARD.
01  CUSTOMER-RECORD-IN.
    05 CR-CUSTOMER-NAME-IN           PIC X(25).
    05 CR-PRINCIPAL-IN               PIC 9(07)V9(02).
    05 CR-INTEREST-RATE-IN           PIC 9(02)V9(02).
    05 CR-YEARS-IN                   PIC 9(02).
FD  REPORT-OUT                       LABEL RECORDS ARE OMITTED.
01  REPORT-RECORD-OUT                PIC X(133).
WORKING-STORAGE SECTION.
01 WS-WORK-AREAS.
    05 WS-NEW-PRINCIPAL              PIC 9(07)V9(06).
    05 WS-ROUNDED-PRINCIPAL          PIC 9(07)V9(02).
    05 WS-YEAR-PROCESSED             PIC 9(02).
01  DETAIL-LINE-OUT.
    05 FILLER                        PIC X(01)         VALUE SPACES.
    05 DL-CUSTOMER-NAME-OUT          PIC X(25).
    05 FILLER                        PIC X(02)         VALUE SPACES.
    05 DL-NEW-PRINCIPAL-OUT          PIC $9,999,999.99.
    05 FILLER                        PIC X(05)         VALUE SPACES.
    05 DL-YEAR-PROCESSED-OUT         PIC 9(02).
    05 FILLER                        PIC X(85)         VALUE SPACES.
```

```
      PROCEDURE DIVISION.
      100-MAIN-MODULE.
     ***************************************************************
     *  100-MAIN-MODULE:  CONTROLS OPENING AND CLOSING OF FILES AND     *
     *  DIRECTION OF PROGRAM LOGIC.                                     *
     ***************************************************************
          OPEN INPUT CUSTOMER-IN
               OUTPUT REPORT-OUT.
          READ CUSTOMER-IN
             AT END MOVE 'EMPTY FILE' TO REPORT-RECORD-OUT
                     WRITE REPORT-RECORD-OUT AFTER 1 LINE
                     STOP RUN.
          MOVE CR-PRINCIPAL-IN TO WS-ROUNDED-PRINCIPAL.
          MOVE CR-PRINCIPAL-IN TO WS-NEW-PRINCIPAL.
          MOVE CR-CUSTOMER-NAME-IN TO DL-CUSTOMER-NAME-OUT.
          MOVE ZERO TO WS-YEAR-PROCESSED.
          PERFORM 300-RECORD-GENERATION.
          PERFORM 200-PROCESS-PRINCIPAL CR-YEARS-IN TIMES.
          CLOSE CUSTOMER-IN
                REPORT-OUT.
          STOP RUN.
      200-PROCESS-PRINCIPAL.
     ***************************************************************
     *  200-PROCESS-PRINCIPAL:  PERFORMED FROM 100-MAIN-MODULE. COMPUTES   *
     *  NEW PRINCIPAL AT END OF YEAR FROM PREVIOUS YEAR'S PRINCIPAL.       *
     ***************************************************************
          COMPUTE WS-NEW-PRINCIPAL =
          WS-NEW-PRINCIPAL * (1 + CR-INTEREST-RATE-IN / 100).
          ADD 1 TO WS-YEAR-PROCESSED.
          COMPUTE WS-ROUNDED-PRINCIPAL ROUNDED = WS-NEW-PRINCIPAL.
          PERFORM 300-RECORD-GENERATION.
      300-RECORD-GENERATION.
     ***************************************************************
     *  300-RECORD-GENERATION:  PERFORMED FROM 100-MAIN-MODULE. ALSO      *
     *  PERFORMED FROM 200-PROCESS-PRINCIPAL AND PRINTS A DETAIL LINE OF  *
     *  THE REPORT.                                                       *
     ***************************************************************
          MOVE WS-YEAR-PROCESSED TO DL-YEAR-PROCESSED-OUT.
          MOVE WS-ROUNDED-PRINCIPAL TO DL-NEW-PRINCIPAL-OUT.
          WRITE REPORT-RECORD-OUT FROM DETAIL-LINE-OUT.
```

Figure 6.7 *Program that computes compound interest.*

Notice the first output record, which requires no computations, is generated outside the loop, using an initial execution of the paragraph 300-RECORD-GENERATION. Each of the subsequent output records is generated by an execution of both paragraph 200-PROCESS-PRINCIPAL and 300-RECORD-GENERATION.

Note that four identifiers are needed to hold the principal value at various stages in the processing. CR-PRINCIPAL-IN receives the incoming initial principal value. Both WS-NEW-PRINCIPAL and WS-ROUNDED-

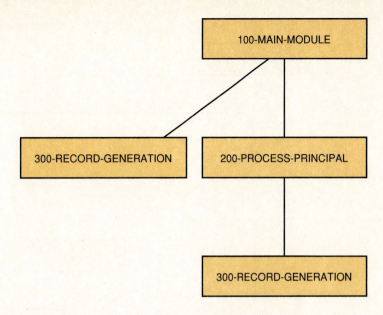

Figure 6.8 *Hierarchy diagram for program in Figure 6.7, which processes the record in Figure 6.5a and generates the data in Figure 6.6a.*

PRINCIPAL are used to hold values of the principal during processing. A WS-NEW-PRINCIPAL value can be computed to six decimal places and is used to compute the principal for the following year, which in turn becomes a WS-NEW-PRINCIPAL value. The identifier WS-ROUNDED-PRINCIPAL holds a rounded value of the current principal during the processing. This value is the one assigned to the edited identifier DL-NEW-PRINCIPAL-OUT for printing.

6.3
Nested loops
are important

LOOP CAN OCCUR anywhere within a program, even within another loop. A loop within a loop is referred to as a *nested loop*.

Mechanics of a Nested Loop

An example of a nested loop is illustrated in the flowchart in Figure 6.9 and in the following:

```
200-P.
      Statement-5.
      PERFORM 300-P 1000 TIMES.
      Statement-7.
      ...
300-P.
      Statement-40.
      PERFORM 400-P 80 TIMES.
      Statement-42.
400-P.
      Statement-600.
```

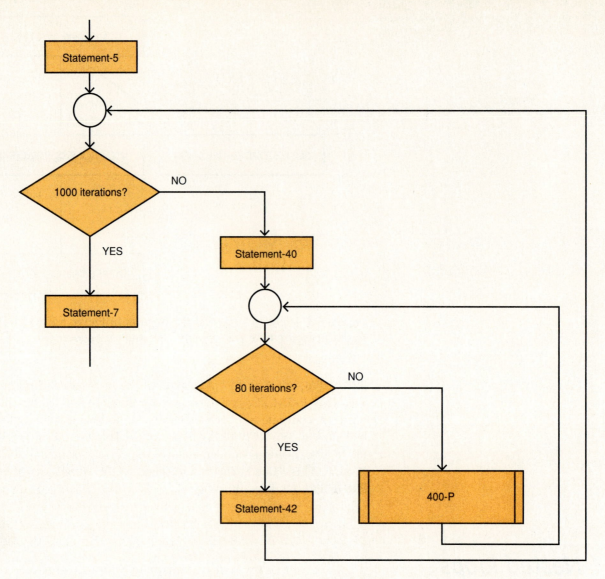

Figure 6.9 *A nested loop (a loop within a loop). Paragraph 400-P will be executed 80,000 times.*

The first PERFORM causes paragraph 300-P to be executed 1000 times. But each time P3 is executed, paragraph 400-P will be executed 80 times. Thus, paragraph 400-P and statement-600 will be executed 80,000 times. Using nested loops, you can easily make the computer carry out a great many instructions.

Example with a Nested Loop

Let us use the example in the previous section, which permitted only one input record, but this time without limiting the number of input records. Thus, the input file CUSTOMER-IN could have any number of records, such as the three records in Figure 6.10.

```
---------1---------2---------3---------4---------5
JOHN C. SMITH                000200000100003
MARY SAUNDERS               000150000090002
CATHERINE PETERSON          100500000100004
<------------------------><------><--><>
```

Figure 6.10a *Sample input records for file CUSTOMER-IN.*

```
---------1---------2---------3---------4---------5
XXXXXXXXXXXXXXXXXXXXXXXX999999999999999
```

Figure 6.10b *Record layout for input file.*

```
01    CUSTOMER-RECORD-IN.
      05   CR-CUSTOMER-NAME-IN          PIC X(24).
      05   CR-PRINCIPAL-IN              PIC 9(07)V9(02).
      05   CR-INTEREST-RATE-IN          PIC 9(02)V9(02).
      05   CR-YEARS-IN                  PIC 9(02).
```

Figure 6.10c *Structure of the matching input area record.*

As usual, in the input file decimal points and spaces are left out. If you put some in, the data can be more easily understood.

```
JOHN C. SMITH              0002000.00   10.00   03
MARY SAUNDERS             0001500.00   09.00   02
CATHERINE PETERSON        1005000.00   10.00   04
```

This time the processing consists of computing the principal for each year, for each customer. As before, for each year, the new principal is computed by adding the interest earned to the principal balance from the end of the previous year. The output data corresponding to the data in Figure 6.10 would be as shown in Figure 6.11.

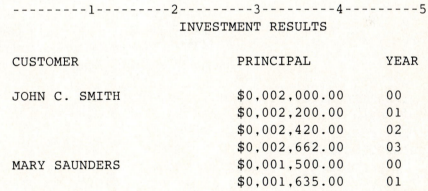

```
--------1---------2---------3---------4---------5
                  INVESTMENT RESULTS


CUSTOMER                    PRINCIPAL          YEAR

JOHN C. SMITH               $0,002,000.00      00
                            $0,002,200.00      01
                            $0,002,420.00      02
                            $0,002,662.00      03
MARY SAUNDERS               $0,001,500.00      00
                            $0,001,635.00      01
                            $0.001,782.15      02
CATHERINE PETERSON          $1,005,000.00      00
                            $1,105,500.00      01
                            $1,216,050.00      02
                            $1,337,655.00      03
                            $1,471,420.50      04

<------------------------><><-----------><---><><--
```

Figure 6.11a *Sample output data.*

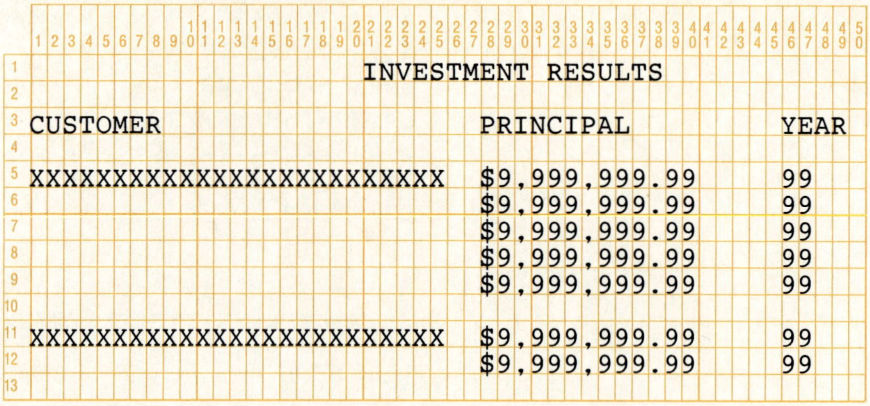

Figure 6.11b *Printer spacing chart for the output data.*

```
01    DETAIL-LINE-OUT.
      05 FILLER                      PIC X(01)       VALUE SPACES.
      05 DL-CUSTOMER-NAME-OUT        PIC X(25).
      05 FILLER                      PIC X(02)       VALUE SPACES.
      05 DL-NEW-PRINCIPAL-OUT        PIC $9,999,999.99.
      05 FILLER                      PIC X(05)       VALUE SPACES.
      05 DL-YEAR-PROCESSED-OUT       PIC 9(02).
      05 FILLER                      PIC X(85)       VALUE SPACES.
```

Figure 6.11c *Structure of the matching output area record. Blanks can be placed in DL-CUSTOMER-NAME-OUT when printing lines in which the name is suppressed.*

Program with a Nested Loop

In the program to process the records of CUSTOMER-IN (Figure 6.10), the techniques for processing more than one record need to be combined with the techniques for repeated arithmetic processing. The solution is to use a PERFORM . . . UNTIL for repeated processing of the records and PER-FORM . . . TIMES for repeated computation of the new principal. The program is shown in Figure 6.12.

```
IDENTIFICATION DIVISION.
PROGRAM-ID. MC2.
ENVIRONMENT DIVISION.
INPUT-OUTPUT SECTION.
FILE-CONTROL.    SELECT CUSTOMER-IN  ASSIGN TO UT-S-CUST90.
                 SELECT REPORT-OUT   ASSIGN TO UR-S-SYSPRINT.
DATA DIVISION.
FILE SECTION.
FD  CUSTOMER-IN                          LABEL RECORDS ARE STANDARD.
01  CUSTOMER-RECORD-IN.
    05  CR-CUSTOMER-NAME-IN    PIC X(24).
    05  CR-PRINCIPAL-IN        PIC 9(07)V9(02).
    05  CR-INTEREST-RATE-IN    PIC 9(02)V9(02).
    05  CR-YEARS-IN            PIC 9(02).
```

```
FD  REPORT-OUT                            LABEL RECORDS ARE OMITTED.
01  REPORT-RECORD-OUT              PIC X(133).
WORKING-STORAGE SECTION.
01 WS-WORK-AREAS.
    05    WS-NEW-PRINCIPAL         PIC 9(07)V9(06).
    05    WS-ROUNDED-PRINCIPAL     PIC 9(07)V9(02).
    05    WS-YEAR-PROCESSED        PIC 9(02).
    05    MORE-RECORDS             PIC X(03)            VALUE 'YES'.
01  REPORT-HEADER.
    05 FILLER                      PIC X(21)            VALUE SPACES.
    05 FILLER                      PIC X(18)            VALUE
                                                          'INVESTMENT RESULTS'.
    05 FILLER                      PIC X(94)            VALUE SPACES.
01  COLUMN-HEADERS.
    05 FILLER                      PIC X(01)            VALUE SPACES.
    05 FILLER                      PIC X(08)            VALUE 'CUSTOMER'.
    05 FILLER                      PIC X(19)            VALUE SPACES.
    05 FILLER                      PIC X(09)            VALUE 'PRINCIPAL'.
    05 FILLER                      PIC X(09)            VALUE SPACES.
    05 FILLER                      PIC X(04)            VALUE 'YEAR'.
    05 FILLER                      PIC X(83)            VALUE SPACES.
01  DETAIL-LINE-OUT.
    05 FILLER                      PIC X(01)            VALUE SPACES.
    05 DL-CUSTOMER-NAME-OUT        PIC X(25).
    05 FILLER                      PIC X(02)            VALUE SPACES.
    05 DL-NEW-PRINCIPAL-OUT        PIC $9,999,999.99.
    05 FILLER                      PIC X(05)            VALUE SPACES.
    05 DL-YEAR-PROCESSED-OUT       PIC 9(02).
    05 FILLER                      PIC X(85)            VALUE SPACES.
 01 ERROR-MESSAGE.
    05 MESSAGE                     PIC X(24)            VALUE
                                                        'NO RECORDS IN INPUT FILE'.
    05 FILLER                      PIC X(109)           VALUE SPACES.


 PROCEDURE DIVISION.
 100-MAIN-MODULE.
****************************************************************************
*  100-MAIN-MODULE:  CONTROLS OPENING AND CLOSING OF FILES AND            *
*  DIRECTION OF PROGRAM LOGIC.                                            *
****************************************************************************
    OPEN INPUT CUSTOMER-IN
         OUTPUT REPORT-OUT.
    READ CUSTOMER-IN
        AT END PERFORM 600-NO-RECORD.
    PERFORM 500-WRITE-HEADERS.
    PERFORM 200-PROCESS-RECORD
              UNTIL MORE-RECORDS = 'NO'.
    CLOSE CUSTOMER-IN
          REPORT-OUT.
    STOP RUN.
```

```
 200-PROCESS-RECORD.
 ******************************************************************************
 *   200-PROCESS-RECORD:  PERFORMED FROM 100-MAIN-MODULE. A SINGLE          *
 *   RECORD FROM THE INPUT FILE CUSTOMER-IN. MULTIPLE OUTPUT RECORDS        *
 *   ARE GENERATED FROM A SINGLE INPUT RECORD.                              *
 ******************************************************************************
     MOVE CR-PRINCIPAL-IN TO WS-ROUNDED-PRINCIPAL.
     MOVE CR-PRINCIPAL-IN TO WS-NEW-PRINCIPAL.
     MOVE ZERO TO WS-YEAR-PROCESSED.
     MOVE CR-CUSTOMER-NAME-IN TO DL-CUSTOMER-NAME-OUT.
     PERFORM 400-RECORD-GENERATION.
     MOVE SPACES TO DL-CUSTOMER-NAME-OUT.
     PERFORM 300-PROCESS-PRINCIPAL CR-YEARS-IN TIMES.
     MOVE SPACES TO REPORT-RECORD-OUT.
     WRITE REPORT-RECORD-OUT.
     READ CUSTOMER-IN
             AT END MOVE 'NO' TO MORE-RECORDS.
 300-PROCESS-PRINCIPAL.
 ******************************************************************************
 *   300-PROCESS-PRINCIPAL:  PERFORMED FROM 100-MAIN-MODULE. COMPUTES       *
 *   NEW PRINCIPAL AT END OF YEAR FROM PREVIOUS YEAR'S PRINCIPAL.           *
 ******************************************************************************
     COMPUTE WS-NEW-PRINCIPAL =
             WS-NEW-PRINCIPAL * (1 + CR-INTEREST-RATE-IN / 100).
     ADD 1 TO WS-YEAR-PROCESSED.
     COMPUTE WS-ROUNDED-PRINCIPAL ROUNDED = WS-NEW-PRINCIPAL.
     PERFORM 400-RECORD-GENERATION.
 400-RECORD-GENERATION.
 ******************************************************************************
 *   400-RECORD-GENERATION:  PERFORMED FROM 100-MAIN-MODULE. PERFORMED      *
 *   FROM 300-PROCESS-PRINCIPAL AND PRINTS A DETAIL LINE OF THE REPORT.     *
 ******************************************************************************
     MOVE WS-YEAR-PROCESSED TO DL-YEARS-PROCESSED-OUT.
     MOVE WS-ROUNDED-PRINCIPAL TO DL-NEW-PRINCIPAL-OUT.
     WRITE REPORT-RECORD-OUT FROM DETAIL-LINE-OUT AFTER ADVANCING 1 LINE.
 500-WRITE-HEADERS.
 ******************************************************************************
 *   500-WRITE-HEADERS:  PERFORMED FROM 100-MAIN-MODULE. WRITES THE         *
 *   REPORT AND COLUMN HEADER LINES FOR REPORT-OUT PRINTER FILE.            *
 ******************************************************************************
     WRITE REPORT-RECORD-OUT FROM REPORT-HEADER
             AFTER ADVANCING 1 LINE.
     WRITE REPORT-RECORD-OUT FROM COLUMN-HEADER
             AFTER ADVANCING 2 LINES.
     MOVE SPACES TO REPORT-RECORD-OUT.
     WRITE REPORT-RECORD-OUT
             AFTER ADVANCING 1 LINE.
 600-NO-RECORD.
 ******************************************************************************
 *   600-NO-RECORD: PERFORMED FROM 100-MAIN-MODULE. PRINTS A SIMPLE         *
 *   MESSAGE AND STOPS EXECUTION IF THERE ARE NO RECORDS IN THE             *
 *   INPUT FILE.                                                            *
 ******************************************************************************
```

```
WRITE REPORT-RECORD-OUT FROM ERROR-MESSAGE AFTER 1 LINE.
CLOSE CUSTOMER-IN
      REPORT-OUT.
STOP RUN.
```

Figure 6.12 Program with a nested loop.

The hierarchy diagram for the processing is shown in Figure 6.13, and the essential flowchart in Figure 6.14. Compare this program with the program in Figure 6.7, in which only one record was processed. Note the similarity. The essential difference is that the new paragraph 200-PROCESS-RECORD has been inserted to process each record in turn. A paragraph, executed in 100-MAIN-MODULE, for printing the report headers has also been introduced.

This leads to a practical technique for constructing programs with nested loops. It is often a good idea to write a preliminary version in which only the inner loop is needed. In this case, that would entail writing a program for the processing of a single record, as in Figure 6.7. It is then relatively easy to extend the program for many records, using an outer loop.

In addition to comparing the programs in Figures 6.7 and 6.12, you should also compare the hierarchy diagrams in Figures 6.8 and 6.13.

Notice how a customer name is blanked out once it has been output the first time (see Figure 6.11a). This is done by putting SPACES in DL-

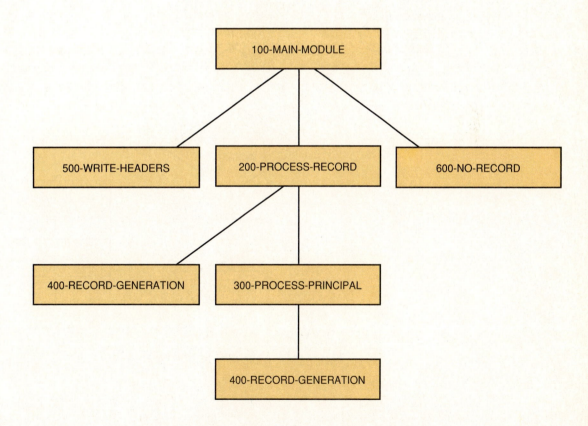

Figure 6.13 Hierarchy diagram for program in Figure 6.12.

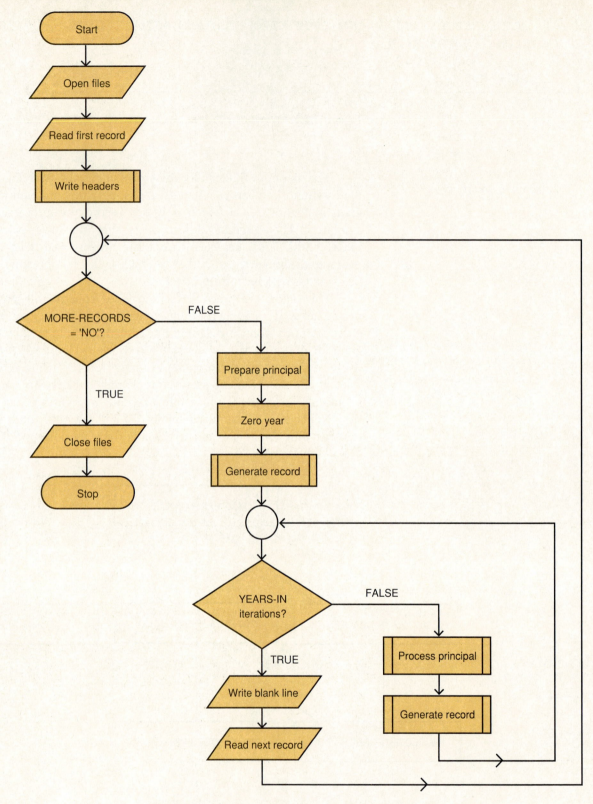

Figure 6.14 *Flowchart for the program in Figure 6.12.*

CUSTOMER-NAME-OUT just after the first output record for a customer has been written. Inspect the paragraph 200-PROCESS-RECORD in Figure 6.12 to see this.

Finally, a new paragraph called 600-NO-RECORD has been included. This paragraph is executed if the first READ statement finds no record in the file, that is, the end of the file is reached without a record being read. The paragraph causes a message to be printed explaining the problem and then stops the program.

Note that instead of the 600-NO-RECORD paragraph, the following could have been written:

```
READ CUSTOMER-IN
    AT END
        WRITE REPORT-RECORD-OUT FROM ERROR-MESSAGE
        CLOSE CUSTOMER-IN
              REPORT-OUT.
        STOP RUN
END-READ.
```

A sequence of statements is allowed in the AT END clause.

6.4
The in-line PERFORM can be convenient

WITH ALL THE PERFORM statements studied so far, execution of PERFORM causes at least one paragraph to be executed, as in

```
PERFORM 200-PROCESS-RECORD . . .
```

But, instead of having a paragraph executed repeatedly, it is possible to have an imperative statement (elementary or composite) following PERFORM executed. Thus, instead of writing

```
READ INFILE RECORD
        AT END . . .
PERFORM 200-PROCESS RECORD
        UNTIL MORE-RECORDS = 'NO'.
. . .
200-PROCESS-RECORD.
    MOVE INFILE-RECORD-IN TO OUTFILE-RECORD-OUT.
    WRITE OUTFILE-RECORD-OUT.
    READ INFILE RECORD
        AT END MOVE 'NO' TO MORE-RECORDS.
```

you could avoid the use of the paragraph 200-PROCESS-RECORD and write the following equivalent:

```
READ INFILE RECORD
        AT END . . .
PERFORM UNTIL MORE-RECORDS = 'NO'
    MOVE INFILE-RECORD-IN TO OUTFILE-RECORD-OUT
    WRITE OUTFILE-RECORD-OUT
    READ INFILE RECORD
        AT END MOVE 'NO' TO MORE-RECORDS
    END-PERFORM.
```

Note that END-PERFORM is the scope terminator. It cannot be omitted. This is called the in-line PERFORM . . . UNTIL statement; it is allowed with COBOL 85. It is useful where the number of statements to be repeated is small and using a paragraph to hold them serves little purpose.

There is also an in-line PERFORM . . . TIMES statement, which you can write as:

```
PERFORM QUANTITY-IN TIMES
     Statement-1
     Statement-2
     Statement-3
END-PERFORM.
```

Syntax for In-line PERFORM Statements

In-line PERFORM statements are available only with COBOL 85. The syntax for the two main in-line PERFORM statements is shown in the following syntax boxes:

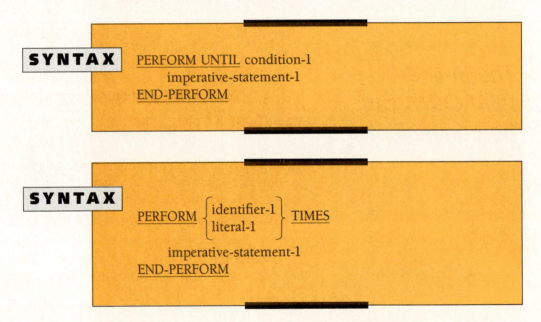

SYNTAX

PERFORM UNTIL condition-1
    imperative-statement-1
END-PERFORM

SYNTAX

$$\text{PERFORM} \begin{Bmatrix} \text{identifier-1} \\ \text{literal-1} \end{Bmatrix} \text{TIMES}$$
    imperative-statement-1
END-PERFORM

Notice that in both cases the END-PERFORM scope terminator is required.

There is a PERFORM with TEST AFTER option

With both the regular and in-line PERFORM . . . UNTIL, the condition following UNTIL is checked before each execution of the paragraph or in-line statements. This means that if the condition is true the first time the PERFORM is executed, the paragraph or in-line-statements are never executed, not even once. However, sometimes you want the paragraph to be executed the first time, no matter what. In such cases you can use the TEST AFTER

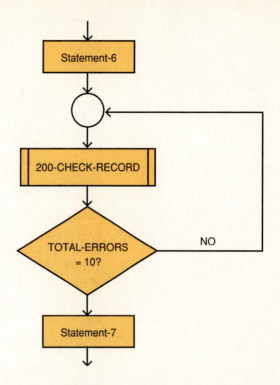

Figure 6.15 *Logic for PERFORM . . . UNTIL with TEST AFTER.*

option with the UNTIL clause to force a check of the condition after each execution of the paragraph or in-line statements.

For example, you could write

```
Statement-6.
PERFORM 200-CHECK-RECORD WITH TEST AFTER
    UNTIL TOTAL-ERRORS >= 10.
Statement-7.
...
200-CHECK-RECORD.
    ...
```

Even if the value of TOTAL-ERRORS is greater than or equal to 10 when the PERFORM is first executed, 200-CHECK-RECORD will be executed initially. At the end of execution of the paragraph, the condition will be tested. If the condition is true, the paragraph is not executed again, and statement-7 is executed. The logic for this is shown in the flowchart in Figure 6.15.

Summary

1. The PERFORM . . . UNTIL statement is used to repeatedly execute a paragraph as long as the UNTIL condition is false. Care should be taken to ensure that the condition will eventually become true and stop the iteration, and so avoid an infinite loop. The repeatedly executed paragraph is commonly used to process a record of an input file, so that PERFORM . . . UNTIL processes the entire file. Care should be taken with a compound UNTIL condition, particularly if the OR connective is used, as it is easy to get such a condition wrong and cause an infinite loop.
2. The PERFORM . . . UNTIL can be used whether or not the number of iterations is known in advance. In contrast, the PERFORM . . . TIMES statement is used to execute a paragraph a fixed number of times (a number of times known in advance).
3. Within a paragraph-2 repeatedly executed by means of a PERFORM statement in paragraph-1, there can be a further PERFORM statement causing repeated execution of a paragraph-3. In this way there can be a loop within a loop, or a nested loop.
4. There are in-line versions of both PERFORM . . . UNTIL and PERFORM . . . TIMES. The in-line version does not stipulate a paragraph to be repeatedly executed. Instead, a group of statements following the PERFORM statement and terminated by a scope terminator END-PERFORM is repeatedly executed.

Key Terms

nested loop   infinite loop   in-line PERFORM

Concept Review Questions

1. Explain how PERFORM paragraph UNTIL works, with respect to the condition.
2. In a loop that reads and processes records, explain why READ must be placed at the end of the repeated paragraph.
3. What is an infinite loop?
4. Explain how an infinite loop can occur.
5. Why could an infinite loop not occur with PERFORM . . . TIMES?
6. When should you use PERFORM . . . TIMES instead of PERFORM . . . UNTIL?
7. What is a nested loop?
8. Explain the difference between PERFORM . . . UNTIL and PERFORM . . . UNTIL with the TEST AFTER option.
9. Why are scope terminators needed with the PERFORM verbs? Give examples where they are needed.

COBOL Language Questions

1. Consider

```
        PERFORM 300-P 1000 TIMES.
300-P.
        PERFORM 400-P 5000 TIMES.
400-P.
        DISPLAY 'ONE MORE TIME'.
```

How many times will the DISPLAY statement be executed?

2. Consider

```
        MOVE 0 TO C-OUT.
        MOVE 0 TO C-IN.
        PERFORM UNTIL C-OUT > 25
            ADD C-IN TO C-OUT
            MOVE 0 TO C-IN
            PERFORM 300-P
                UNTIL C-IN > 6
        END-PERFORM.
        DISPLAY C-OUT.
300-P.
        ADD 1 TO C-IN.
```

What will be printed?

3. Suppose you have

```
        MOVE 'YES' TO MORE RECORDS.
        PERFORM 300-PROCESS-RECORD
            UNTIL MORE-RECORDS = 'NO'.
        ...
300-PROCESS-RECORD.
        ...
        WRITE REPORT-RECORD-OUT FROM DETAIL-LINE.
        ...
        READ DK-INFILE
                AT END MOVE 'YES' TO MORE-RECORDS.
```

What happens when this executes? What is wrong? Fix it.

4. How many iterations result from

```
        MOVE 0 TO N.
        PERFORM 300-P UNTIL N = 3.
300-P.
        ADD 1 TO N.
        DISPLAY N.
```

5. How many iterations result from

```
        MOVE 0 TO N.
        PERFORM UNTIL N > 7
                ADD 2 TO N
                DISPLAY N
        END-PERFORM.
```

6. Recall that 5 factorial is 5 * 4 * 3 * 2 * 1.

   a. Write a brief procedure to compute the factorial of an integer up to 10. An ACCEPT verb is used to read the input and DISPLAY for the output.
   b. Suppose you tried to compute the factorial of 20. What is likely to happen? (Hint: Consider how big it is.)

7. The growth of a rabbit colony follows the Fibonacci sequence: 1, 1, 2, 3, 5, 8, 13 . . . , where each item is the sum of the previous two. Write a routine to compute the series with integers less than 100. The routine should count the number of items in the sequence. (Leonardo Fibonacci was a thirteenth-century Italian mathematician.)

8. What happens if CNT changes during repeated execution of 300-P due to execution of

   `PERFORM 300-P CNT TIMES.`

9. In `PERFORM 300-P CNT TIMES.`
   what happens if CNT is zero?

Programming Assignments

1. **A program with a nested loop**

   In a college, there are classes in French, history, mathematics, and so on. The input file has class records and student records. A class record comes before the student records for the class. The class record gives the name and number of students in the class. The number of student records that follows will be equal to the number of students posted in the class record.

   The input data are

   ```
   ---------1---------2---------3
   FRENCH              12
   ABELSON, D.S.       47
   BARNEY, M.T.        82

   . . .
   TOWERS, S.M         23
   HISTORY             18
   BARNEY, M.T.        67
   BROWN, D.T.         89

   . . .
   VAUGHEN, J.R.       42
   MATHEMATICS         08
   ABELSON, D.S.       65

   . . .
   ```

The output data are

```
---------1---------2---------3---------4-----
            CLASS AVERAGE REPORT

    CLASS              TOTAL           AVERAGE
                       STUDENTS        SCORE

    FRENCH             12              67.9
    HISTORY            18              62.8
    MATHEMATICS        8               71.9
    . . . .
```

a. Draw up a record layout and a spacing chart for input and output data.
b. Draw a flowchart for the processing with a nested loop. The outer loop should be PERFORM . . . UNTIL and the inner loop (for the students of a single class) should be PERFORM . . . TIMES.
c. Write and run the program.

2. **Single loop program with extensive calculations**
   This time, write a program to generate the average score, maximum score, minimum score, and standard deviation for a single class of students. The input data are

```
---------1---------2---------3
FRENCH              06
ABELSON, D.S.       47
BROWN, D.T.         82
GREEN, F.G.         65
HARDY, W.M.         55
JOHNSON, P.F.       68
YEE, G.K.           69
```

   The first record gives the name of the class and the total students in the class.
   The output data are

```
---------1---------2---------3---------4---------5---------6---------7
            CLASS SCORE DATA

CLASS        TOTAL      MAX      MIN      AVERAGE     STANDARD
             STUDENTS   SCORE    SCORE    SCORE       DEVIATION

FRENCH       6          82       47       64.33       12.13
```

To compute the standard deviation use

$$[(\text{sum of squares of scores} - (\text{sum of scores})^2 / n) / (n - 1)]^{0.5}$$

where n is the number of students.

a. Draw up spacing charts for the input and output data.
b. Draw up a flowchart.
c. Write the program, using PERFORM . . . TIMES.

3. A nested loop program with extensive calculations

Use the input data from question 1. The processing will produce a report like this:

```
---------1---------2---------3---------4---------5---------6---------7
          CLASS SCORE DATA


CLASS               TOTAL      MAX      MIN      AVERAGE    STANDARD
                    STUDENTS   SCORE    SCORE    SCORE      DEVIATION


FRENCH              12          ...
HISTORY             18          ...
MATHEMATICS          8          ...
...
```

   a. Produce the spacing chart for the output.
   b. Combine the techniques used with the program in question 1 with those used in the program in question 2, to write a program to produce the report.

4. A nested loop program for computing time to reach an investment goal at a given annual yield

Different investors get a different annual return (yield, in percent) for their investment, as shown in the records of the input file. Each investor has a savings goal, to be obtained through annual compounding of their investments. The input file is

```
---------1---------2---------3---------4
BROWN, G.Y.         015000000750030000
GREEN, Y.P          206593851035500000
LITTLE, R.T.        000450850650002000
...
```

Columns	01–18	Investor name
	19–26	Principal sum invested (last two digits are cents)
	27–30	Annual yield (interest rate), in form dd.dd
	31–36	Savings goal

The input data are printed as a report. The report contains the number of years required to equal or exceed the savings goal.

```
---------1---------2---------3---------4---------5---------6---------7
          INVESTMENT PROJECTION (TAX FREE)


INVESTOR            PRINCIPAL      YIELD      SAVINGS      YEARS
                                   (% annum)  GOAL         NEEDED


BROWN, G.Y.         $ 15,000.00    7.50       $ 30,000     10
GREEN, Y.P          $206,593.85    10.35      $500,000     ?
LITTLE, R.T.        $     450.85   6.50       $  2,000     ?
...
```

In the processing, the years needed to reach the goal must be computed. If you have a principal P_0, at end of year 1 it will be worth $P_1 = P_0(1 + r/100)$ where r is the yield in percent. Similarly, at the end of year 2 the investment will be worth $P_2 = P_1(1 + r/100)$, and so on. By computing in this way and checking against the goal you can compute the number of years to reach or first exceed the goal.

a. Draw the spacing charts.
b. Draw a flowchart for the processing.
c.' Write and run the program.

5. **A nested loop program about rabbit pairs, rabbit farms, and Fibonacci numbers**
Each record in the input file has data about a new rabbit farm starting out with its first pair of rabbits. The farms can use different types of rabbits, so the cost of feeding a pair of rabbits for a day differs from one farm to another. The breeding period also varies from one type of rabbit to another. The breeding period is the number of days between birth of each new pair of rabbits with the same parents.

Each farm starts out with a pair of breeding rabbits that have just been born. It takes two breeding periods for a newly born pair to produce a new pair. After that they produce a pair every breeding period. The number of pairs of rabbits at the beginning of each new breeding period follows the Fibonacci sequence 1, 1, 2, 3, 5, 8, 13 . . . Each number of the sequence is the sum of the previous two.

In the processing, you have to compute the number of pairs of rabbits on each farm at the end of a given number of breeding periods and the total feeding bill for the farm since the first pair of rabbits was acquired.

The input data are

```
---------1---------2---------3
BONNYRABBIT   3015010
BUNNYSIDE     2819008
GREYRABBIT    3214014
HIGHFIELD     2709512
. . .
```

Columns 01–13   Farm name
       14–15   Breeding period (days)
       16–18   Feed cost per pair per day
       19–20   Number of breeding periods

The output data are

```
---------1---------2---------3---------4---------5---------6---------7
                  RABBIT BREEDING REPORT

FARM            BREEDING     DAILY     NUMBER OF    TOTAL     TOTAL
NAME            PERIOD       FEED      BREEDING     RABBIT    FEED
                (DAYS)       COST      PERIODS      PAIRS     COST

BONNYRABBIT     30           $1.50     10           89        $ 6,435.00
BUNNYSIDE       28           $1.90      8           34        $ 2,872.80
...
```

Use the following sample calculations to generate the first line of the report:

- Rabbits breed according to
  1 1 2 3 5 8 13 21 34 55 89 (10 breeding periods)
- At the end of the tenth breeding period, the last 34 rabbits have just been born and have cost nothing to feed.
- Total feed cost is
  $1.50 \times 30 \times (1 + 1 + 2 + 3 + 5 + 8 + 13 + 21 + 34 + 55)$
  $= \$6,435.00$

a. Draw spacing charts.
b. Draw a flowchart and hierarchy diagram.
c. Write the program, using a nested loop.

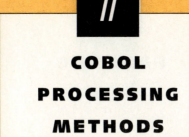

COBOL
PROCESSING
METHODS

7

PRINTING REPORTS

7.4 Printing headers is detailed but straightforward
The WRITE . . . ADVANCING statement is the key to printing headers
Be clear about WRITE . . . AFTER ADVANCING semantics
WRITE . . . BEFORE ADVANCING semantics are important too
Avoid mixing WRITE . . . BEFORE and WRITE . . . AFTER
WRITE . . . PAGE is used to control the printing of pages

7.5 COBOL report program examples
Use printer spacing charts to lay out reports
A program for a detail report
There is a convention for organizing paragraphs
Simple summary report program

R EMEMBER THAT all computer processing involves converting input data to output data. The output data can be in the form of a printed document, a display on a screen, or a file on disk or tape. When the output is another disk or tape file, the idea is to make it as concise as possible. There is no need for blank spaces between items of data or fields in an input file, since no human being will ever read them.

In contrast, with printed output clarity is what counts. The output should be designed so human beings can read and understand it with a minimum of effort. Thus, spaces between fields help, and with numbers, commas between sets of three digits are useful. A great deal of effort must therefore go into the design of printed output. Output sent to a screen also should be clear.

Printed output is normally called a report. You have already seen examples of reports in previous chapters. This chapter looks at the techniques needed to do a thorough job of generating a report. Some of the techniques have already been encountered. In brief, you need to know how to handle

- Report and column headers
- Edit identifiers
- Dates
- Page numbering and page headers
- Skipping lines

These will be examined in detail in this chapter. But first, an overview of the common types of reports should help put these techniques in perspective.

T HE TWO MAJOR kinds of reports are detail and summary reports. A less common type of report is the exception report. These types of reports are normally generated from an input file.

- **Detail report** A detail report typically prints one or more lines for each record of the input file. All the reports shown in previous chapters were detail reports. Each line printed as a result of processing an input record is called a *detail line*. At the top of each page of the report are *header lines*. Detail reports tend to be voluminous. People often find them hard to digest and they certainly use a lot of paper.

- **Exception reports** An exception report is like a detail report except that only detail lines satisfying some exceptional condition are printed. Consequently, these are much shorter than detail reports.

- **Summary reports** Summary reports mainly print lines that summarize data in groups of records of the input file. Some summary reports print only summary lines (with header lines). These reports tend to be short. Detail reports with summaries print detail lines followed by summary lines. These are often voluminous.

A typical example of an input file from which all three types of report could be generated is shown in the file MONTHLY-SALES in Figure 7.1. It gives the value and number of housing units sold in the month by each salesperson who works for a large real estate business. Each salesperson works in only one of four regions of a city. The file can be assumed to be on disk, and if printed in the format on disk would appear as in Figure 7.1, which would be all but useless to a human being.

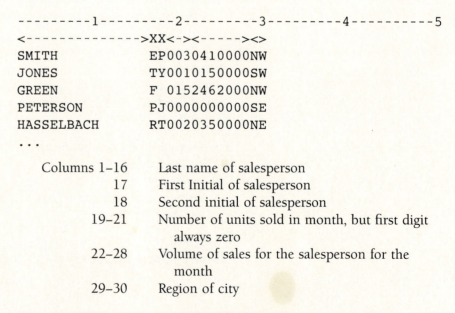

```
---------1---------2---------3---------4---------5
<-------------->XX<-><-----><>
SMITH            EP0030410000NW
JONES            TY0010150000SW
GREEN            F 0152462000NW
PETERSON         PJ0000000000SE
HASSELBACH       RT0020350000NE
...
```

Columns	
Columns 1–16	Last name of salesperson
17	First Initial of salesperson
18	Second initial of salesperson
19–21	Number of units sold in month, but first digit always zero
22–28	Volume of sales for the salesperson for the month
29–30	Region of city

Figure 7.1 *Input file MONTHLY-SALES.*

Detail reports have a line for each input record

The simplest detail report that could be generated from MONTHLY-SALES in Figure 7.1 would simply add in headers, put spaces between the fields, add edit symbols to numeric quantities, and insert date and page numbers. This is illustrated in Figure 7.2. In other words, the input file is simply copied into a format that is easy for human beings to understand.

Notice that the report and column headers are repeated at the top of each page. This is normal practice.

```
                      MONTHLY SALES REPORT
PAGE    1                                              02/09/91

SALESPERSON         UNITS          VOLUME         REGION
                    SOLD           OF SALES       OF CITY

E.P. SMITH          3              $   410,000    NW
T.Y. JONES          1              $   150,000    SW
F.   GREEN          15             $2,462,000     NW
P.J. PETERSON       0              $         0    SE
R.T. HASSELBACH     2              $   350,000    NE
...
T.H. GOODMAN        4              $   480,600    NW


                      MONTHLY SALES REPORT
PAGE    2                                              02/09/91

SALESPERSON         UNITS          VOLUME         REGION
                    SOLD           OF SALES       OF CITY

H.J. BROWN          1              $   113,000    SW
J.K. SHINFIELD      5              $6,459,200     SE
...
```

Figure 7.2 *Printing of the input file in Figure 7.1 as a detail report.*

A more common type of detail report involves printing out part or all of the data in the fields of the input file, plus some data computed from the fields.

Exception reports cut down on output

A variation on the theme of the detail report is the exception report. For example, suppose that the president of the real estate business was really interested in each salesperson who has sold two units or less. The report in Figure 7.2 would give the president this information, but not without much tedious page turning. A convenient exception report would print only the lines for salespersons who had sold two or fewer units.

Summary reports have one line for many input records

Often the amount of data in a detail report is so voluminous that it is difficult for human beings to digest it. In such cases, a summary report is often much more informative. A summary report is also generated from an input file. As an example, the summary report in Figure 7.3 gives a summary of sales in each region of the city.

```
                      MONTHLY SALES SUMMARY REPORT
     PAGE    1                                                 02/09/91

     REGION                  TOTAL UNITS           TOTAL VOLUME
     OF CITY                 SOLD                  OF SALES

     NE                      65                    $14,455,000
     NW                      51                    $ 9,890,500
     SE                      70                    $19,540,000
     SW                      59                    $12,300,900
               TOTALS        245                   $ 56,186,400
```

Figure 7.3 *Summary report generated from the input file in Figure 7.1.*

The report in Figure 7.3 is one of the simplest kinds of summary report and could easily be generated using the programming techniques learned so far, together with the editing techniques discussed later in this chapter.

However, summary reports can involve quite complex processing, especially when many levels of intermediate summaries are involved. Generating such summary reports involves more advanced techniques (such as control-break processing and sorting, covered later in the book.) This chapter concentrates on detail reports and simple summary reports.

The parts of a report have names

The lines on a report have commonly used names (refer to Figure 7.2). First is the report header line. This is followed by the date line, page line, or date/page line. Next come the two column header lines. Then, in the body of the report come the detail lines. Following a group of detail lines there may be one or more summary lines.

7.2
Edit symbols are used extensively with numeric output

A s you have already seen, there is a fundamental distinction between numeric identifiers that will be used in computations and those with contents that will be printed. With computational numeric identifiers, you can use only the symbols 9 (digit), V (implicit decimal point) and S (implicit sign) in the PICTURE clause. Thus the following are all valid identifiers for use in computations:

COMPREHENSIVE STRUCTURED COBOL

```
01  A    PIC 9(02).
01  B    PIC 9(03)V9(02)
01  C    PIC S9(03).
01  D    PIC S9(03)V9(02).
```

Space in memory is allocated only for PIC 9 specifications. Markers (1 bit long) are used for V and S, so that these take up no memory space in terms of characters.

In contrast, a fairly large number of edit symbols (or edit items) can be used to specify identifiers with contents that will be printed, that is, report items or edited identifiers. Table 7.1 gives a summary of these edit symbols. Each edit symbol, except CR and DB, occupies a character of memory space.

Table 7.1. *PICTURE Symbols*

Computational Numeric Identifiers

SYMBOL	
9	Digits
V	Implicit decimal point (not stored)
S	Implicit sign (not stored, one bit of the last digit is usually altered instead – a sign marker)

Edited Identifiers

SYMBOL	
9	Digit, leading zeros are printed
.	Decimal point
,	Comma, printed unless suppressed
Z	Blank, if leading zero
$	Dollar sign
*	Digit, but * printed if leading zero (used for check protection)
+	Plus sign for positive number, minus sign for negative number, plus sign for printed zero
-	Blank for positive number, minus sign for negative number, blank for printed zero
CR	CR (credit) symbol
DB	DB (debit) symbol
/	Slash
B	Blank (can also be used with alphanumeric identifier)
0	Zero (can also be used with alphanumeric identifier)

In the following discussion of these edit symbols, assume a MOVE statement

```
MOVE SF TO RF.
```

where SF will be a computational numeric identifier, and RF a printable numeric identifier or edited identifier. SF can be called the sending field and RF the receiving field. You may be interested to see how the contents of RF are affected by SF in the different kinds of PIC specifications.

Decimal points need edit symbols to be printed

The quantities in the sending field and receiving field are aligned on the decimal point as shown here:

SENDING FIELD SF	RECEIVING FIELD RF
PIC 99V99	PIC 99.99
42̲66	42.66
PIC 9999V999	PIC 9999.99
0678̲422	0678.42

Remember the V implicit decimal point specification in SF means that a decimal point is stored, but takes up no space in the identifier in memory. The explicit decimal point (.) in RF *is* physically stored in a byte (or character) of memory.

Commas also require edit symbols

A comma can be inserted to separate groups of three digits

SENDING FIELD SF	RECEIVING FIELD RF
PIC 9999999V99	PIC 9,999,999.99
275084̲87	2,750,842.87
PIC 9999999V99	PIC 9,999,999.99
000004̲277	0,000,042.77

Note the following:

> **RULES**   **Comma placement**
>
> A comma may be placed anywhere in a picture except the last position.

There is an edit symbol for the dollar sign ($)

A dollar sign can be arranged to print, as follows:

SENDING FIELD SF	RECEIVING FIELD RF
PIC 9999V99	PIC $9,999.99
4567̲67	$4,567.67
PIC 999999999	PIC $9,999,999.99
000006̲543	$0,000,065.43

The Z symbol suppresses leading zeros

The printing of leading zeros can be suppressed, as follows:

SENDING FIELD SF	RECEIVING FIELD RF
PIC 999V99	PIC ZZZ.99
00477	4.77
00034	.34
PIC 99999V99	PIC ZZ,ZZ9.99
0000089	0.89
0568942	5,689.42
PIC 9999V99	PIC $Z,ZZ9.99
234547	$2,345.47
004547	$ 45.47
000047	$ 0.47
PIC 999V99	PIC ZZZ.ZZ
00000	bbbbbb
00004	.04

Notice the last case—PIC ZZZ.ZZ. There is an important rule here.

RULES   **Zero suppression**

When all Z symbols are used both right and left of the decimal point, leading zero suppression does *not* occur on the right. However, if the value sent is zero, the entire number is suppressed and blanks result.

The check protection asterisk (*) is an edit symbol

Suppose that, as in the preceding example, RF has picture $Z,ZZ9.99 and we send it the value 5.50. The contents of RF become $ 5.50. This would be fine in most reports, but it would not be acceptable if the printer were printing checks (which are also reports as far as processing is concerned). It would be easy for a dishonest person to insert some additional digits before cashing the check. Accordingly, for printing dollar quantities on checks, leading zeros (and enclosed commas) are replaced with asterisks. The * edit symbol is used for this purpose

SENDING FIELD SF	RECEIVING FIELD RF
PIC 9999999V99	PIC $*,***,***.99
123456778	$1,234,567.78
000000548	$*******5.48
000000008	$*********.08
PIC 9999V99	PIC $*,***.**
123467	$1,234.67
000268	$****2.68
000008	$*****.08
000000	$*****.**

Notice the last example. If all asterisks are used, you get all asterisks, except for the decimal point, only if the value sent is zero.

The plus (+) and minus (-) edit symbols can be tricky

With + and -, bear in mind the following:

RULES   **Using + and - Edit Symbols**

Plus   If the + is used, a positive number prints with +, a negative number prints with -, and a zero prints with +, unless the whole number is zero suppressed, which gives no sign and a blank value.

Minus   If the - is used, a positive number prints with no sign, a negative number prints with -, and a zero prints with no sign.

Note that the + and - edit symbols can be placed either at the beginning or end of the picture. Some examples are

SENDING FIELD SF	RECEIVING FIELD RF
PIC S9999V99	PIC +9,999.99
(+) 067845	+0,678.45
(-) 005676	-0,056.76
PIC S9999V99	PIC +Z,ZZ9.99
(+) 007844	+ 78.44
(-) 000077	- 0.77
000000	+ 0.00
PIC S99999V99	PIC -99,999.99
(+) 3456756	34,567.56
(-) 0067887	-00,678.87
PIC S99999V99	PIC -ZZ,ZZ9.99
(+) 0004254	42.54
(-) 0000606	- 6.06
PIC S9999V99	PIC Z,ZZ9.99+
(+) 004477	44.77+
(-) 000566	5.66-
PIC S99V99	PIC 99.99-
(+) 4587	45.87
(-) 0334	03.34-
PIC S9999V99	PIC Z,ZZ9.99-
(+) 000589	5.89
(-) 001545	15.45-
000000	0.00
PIC S999	PIC ZZZ+
(+) 003	3+
000	b

The credit (CR) and debit (DB) work like the minus symbol

CR and DB work like the - symbol.

SENDING FIELD SF	RECEIVING FIELD RF
S999V99	PIC $ZZ9.99CR
(+) 05677	$ 56.77
(−) 00844	$ 8.44CR
00000	$ 0.00
PIC S9999.99	PIC $Z,ZZ9.99DB
(+) 008745	$ 87.45
(−) 000045	$ 0.45DB

Note that CR and DB each occupy two characters of space in memory.

The blank edit symbol (B) puts blanks between digits

B can be used for inserting blank spaces into numbers. For example, suppose you have a social security number stored as 034564756 in SF. You might frequently want it printed from RF as 034 56 4756, so you could specify it as follows:

SENDING FIELD SF	RECEIVING FIELD RF
PIC 999999999	PIC 999B99B9999
034564756	034 56 4756

The slash symbol (/) can be used in dates

The / can be used for inserting slashes into numbers. For example, you might have a date stored in SF as 02121990 and want it printed from RF as 02/12/1990. You could specify it as follows:

SENDING FIELD SF	RECEIVING FIELD RF
PIC 99999999	PIC 99/99/9999
02121990	02/12/1990

The zero symbol (0) is handy with megadollar quantities

The zero symbol is commonly used for adding 000 to the ends of numbers. For example, suppose the sending field SF contains the value 215, meaning 215 millions, which would mean you want $215,000,000 printed from the receiving field RF. RF would be specified with the necessary additional zeros, as follows:

SENDING FIELD SF	RECEIVING FIELD RF
PIC 999	PIC $999,000,000
215	$215,000,000

Watch out for the floating symbols ($, +, -)

As well as having the symbols $, +, - print in a specific position to the left of the number, whenever you want leading zero suppression it is possible to have these symbols "float" to the right to avoid blank spaces between the symbol and the number. Thus, instead of printing $ 40.56, you could get $40.56.

The three symbols $, +, and - all float to the right in the same way, as the following show.

SENDING FIELD SF	RECEIVING FIELD RF
PIC 99999V99	PIC $$$,$$$.99
3456743	$34,567.43
0004633	$46.33
0000044	$.44
PIC 99999V99	PIC $$$,$$$.$$
1234545	$12,345.45
0000587	$5.87
0000007	$.07
0000000	b
PIC S99999V99	PIC +++,+++.99
(+) 1234523	+12,345.23
(-) 0002724	-27.24
(+) 0000443	+4.43
(-) 0000002	-.02
PIC S99999V99	PIC ---,---.99
(+) 1234523	12,345.23
(-) 0034467	-344.67
(+) 0000087	.87
(-) 0000008	-.08

Caution: With the floating symbols, since they behave like Z symbols for zero suppression purposes, it is easy to forget that you need an extra one on the left for the +, -, or $ symbol when zero suppression does not take place. This is also shown in the preceding examples.

You can edit non-numeric pictures with B and 0 symbols

The edit symbols B and 0 can be used with alphabetic and alphanumeric pictures for insertion of blanks or zeros. For example, you might want to replace U.S.A. with U. S. A. or AB34 with AB3400. This is illustrated by the following examples:

SENDING FIELD SF	RECEIVING FIELD RF
PIC XXXXX	PIC XXBXXBXX
U.S.A.	U. S. A.
PIC XXXX	PIC XXXX00
AB34	AB3400

The group MOVE is an alphanumeric MOVE

We have seen that the identifiers in a group identifier can be moved to another group identifier in a single MOVE. Remember that one way to ensure the move is carried out correctly is for the pictures of the identifiers in the two groups to correspond. However, even if the pictures do not correspond, the move will still be carried out. The point is that with a group MOVE, the entire group identifier is treated as a single alphanumeric quantity. This can be very dangerous and is guaranteed to cause an error when edit symbols are used in the identifiers of the receiving group identifier. A good rule is never to use a group MOVE when the receiving field is a group identifier with edit symbols.

Use QUOTE to print quotation marks

In COBOL, an alphanumeric literal is enclosed in quotation marks as in

```
MOVE 'SMITH' TO NAME.
```

If the contents of NAME are then printed, only SMITH is printed, without the quotes. But suppose you actually wanted to print 'SMITH' *with* the quotes. You use the COBOL reserve constant QUOTE, which, depending on the computer system, always has either a single (') or a double (") quotation mark as its value.

Suppose you have the group identifier:

```
01 RECORD-OUT.
   05    ...
   05 FILLER    X     VALUE QUOTE.
   05 NAME      X(05).
   05 FILLER    X     VALUE QUOTE.
   05    ...
```

If SMITH is now moved to NAME and the contents of RECORD-OUT are printed, 'SMITH' (or "SMITH") will be printed.

Normally, when an alphanumeric literal is placed in an alphanumeric identifier, it is inserted left justified. However, there are times when you would like it right justified, such as when using a VALUE clause.

For example, suppose you wanted a report heading of MONTHLY SALES REPORT to begin on column 19 of the header line. You could arrange for the WORKING-STORAGE SECTION record REPORT-HEADER, as follows:

```
01 REPORT-HEADER.
    05   FILLER        PIC X       VALUE SPACE.
    05   FILLER        PIC X(18) VALUE SPACES.
    05   FILLER        PIC X(20) VALUE 'MONTHLY SALES REPORT'.
    05   FILLER        PIC X(94) VALUE SPACES.
```

The value MONTHLY SALES REPORT would be inserted into the third FILLER identifier left justified. However, you could also code it this way:

```
01 REPORT-HEADER.
    05   FILLER        PIC X(39) VALUE
                        'MONTHLY SALES REPORT' JUSTIFIED RIGHT.
    05   FILLER        PIC X(94) VALUE SPACES.
```

This would cause the literal to be inserted into an X(39) picture field right justified. The literal would thus be located in exactly the same place as in the earlier, more lengthy specification.

7.3
Special COBOL facilities are needed for the current date

THE IMPORTANT THING to understand about printing the current date on a report is that the date does not have to be input to the computer. Computers are equipped with internal clocks, so they always have the current date (and time) stored in memory.

In practice, to print the date it has to be in an identifier used in the program. To get the date into the identifier, it first has to be extracted from the special location in memory where it is kept and continually updated. There are two ways to extract the date and place it in a program identifier. These are

- The standard (American National Standard or ANS) method, available with many computers
- The IBM enhancement of the COBOL standard, available with most IBM computers

Let us look at these separately. The standard method is more elaborate, which is why IBM introduced its enhancement—to simplify things.

There is an ANS method for extracting the date

In the standard way, the date is kept in a reserve memory location or identifier called DATE. The date is in year-month-day format, so that July 4, 1991 is stored as PIC 910704.

Now suppose that you have a WORKING-STORAGE identifier arbitrarily named REPORT-DATE

```
01 REPORT-DATE  PIC 9(06).
```

To get the date from DATE to REPORT-DATE you must use the ACCEPT verb, as follows:

```
ACCEPT REPORT-DATE FROM DATE.
```

The format for this use of ACCEPT is

| SYNTAX | ACCEPT identifier-1 FROM DATE |

This is a special use of ACCEPT, and the identifier used, such as REPORT-DATE, must *not* be a group identifier. The identifier must be an unsigned numeric identifier with six digits, that is, the picture must be PIC 9(06).

If you now print the contents of REPORT-DATE, you get PIC 910704 — not the way people are used to seeing the date written. Accordingly, some additional processing is required before printing.

The processing depends on how you want the date to appear. Commonly, you would want PIC 910704 to appear in month/day/year format, that is, as 07/04/91. One way to do this is shown in Figure 7.4.

```
WORKING-STORAGE SECTION.
01  REPORT-DATE    PIC 9(06).
01  YEAR-MONTH-DAY.
    05 YEAR        PIC 9(02).
    05 MONTH       PIC 9(02).
    05 DAY         PIC 9(02).
01  RUN-DATE.
    05 RUN-MONTH   PIC 9(02).
    05 FILLER      PIC X(01) VALUE '/'.
    05 RUN-DAY     PIC 9(02).
    05 FILLER      PIC X VALUE '/'.
    05 RUN-YEAR    PIC 9(02).
...
PROCEDURE DIVISION.
    ...
    ACCEPT REPORT-DATE FROM DATE.
    MOVE REPORT-DATE TO YEAR-MONTH-DAY.

    MOVE MONTH TO RUN-MONTH.
    MOVE DAY TO RUN-DAY.
    MOVE YEAR TO RUN-YEAR.

    MOVE RUN-DATE TO BUFFER-RECORD-OUT.
    WRITE  BUFFER-RECORD-OUT.
```

Figure 7.4 *Processing for printing the date with slashes.*

Referring to Figure 7.4, assume that the date is July 4, 1991, so the date extracted from DATE and placed in REPORT-DATE is in the form PIC 910704. The contents of REPORT-DATE are then moved to the group identifier YEAR-MONTH-DAY. This is an alphanumeric move since it involves a group identifier. Note that the total length of REPORT-DATE matches that of YEAR-MONTH-DAY. Thus YEAR gets 91, MONTH gets 07 and DAY gets 04. The values of YEAR, MONTH, and DAY can then be individually moved to the identifiers of RUN-DATE, which are in the order month, day, and year. The group identifier RUN-DATE also has slashes inserted at the right places. Thus, when the contents of RUN-DATE are printed you get 07/04/91.

Admittedly, this seems like a lot of trouble just to get the date. But that is generally how it is done. A little less coding in the procedural division can be achieved if you use something called the REDEFINES clause, however.

You can use REDEFINES with the ANS method of extracting the date

You have seen that when an identifier is defined, for example, identifier N with picture PIC 9(06), N will take up six characters of space in a definite location in memory. However, it is possible to use the same location in memory for different identifiers. You do this by literally defining a second identifier on top of (or coincident with) the first identifier location in memory. Consider this:

```
01  N   PIC  9(6).
01  T   PIC  X(6) REDEFINES N.
```

You could now do the following:

```
MOVE '000015' TO T.
```

This would mean that T contains the alphanumeric quantity '000015', while at the same time N would contain the numeric quantity 000015. You could now carry out computations on N (but never on T).

```
COMPUTE N = N + 2.
```

As a result, N would now contain 17, whereas T would contain the alphanumeric quantity '000017'. (This facility is useful when you have to check if a numeric identifier did not contain alphanumeric data – which can happen, as explained in Chapter 8.)

You can use REDEFINES in another version of the code in Figure 7.4 to process the stored date to generate a date in month-day-year order with slashes. This version, using REDEFINES, is shown in Figure 7.5.

This time, when REPORT-DATE gets PIC 910704, it also automatically goes into the identifier YEAR-MONTH-DAY, since that is located coincident with REPORT-DATE in memory. Thus, the YEAR, MONTH, and DAY identifiers in YEAR-MONTH-DAY will get the values 91, 07, and 04, which can then be individually moved to RUN-YEAR, RUN-MONTH, and RUN-DAY.

```
WORKING-STORAGE SECTION.
01   REPORT-DATE      PIC 9(06).
01   YEAR-MONTH-DAY REDEFINES REPORT-DATE.
     05 YEAR          PIC 9(02).
     05 MONTH         PIC 9(02).
     05 DAY           PIC 9(02).
01   RUN-DATE.
     05 RUN-MONTH     PIC 9(02).
     05 FILLER        PIC X(01) VALUE '/'.
     05 RUN-DAY       PIC 9(02).
     05 FILLER        PIC X(01) VALUE '/'.
     05 RUN-YEAR      PIC 9(02).
...
PROCEDURE DIVISION.
     ...
     ACCEPT REPORT-DATE FROM DATE.
     MOVE MONTH TO RUN-MONTH.
     MOVE DAY TO RUN-DAY.
     MOVE YEAR TO RUN-YEAR.
     MOVE RUN-DATE TO BUFFER-RECORD-OUT.
     WRITE  BUFFER-RECORD-OUT.
```

Figure 7.5 *Processing for printing the date using REDEFINES.*

You do not have to use the REDEFINES facility for extracting the date, since the technique in Figure 7.4 is quite acceptable. But if you do decide to use it, note that the following is an error:

```
01   YEAR-MONTH-DAY REDEFINES REPORT-DATE.      error!
     05 YEAR      PIC 9(02).
     05 MONTH     PIC 9(02).
     05 DAY       PIC 9(02).
01   REPORT-DATE  PIC 9(6).
```

The error arises as follows: If identifier-2 is redefined on top of identifer-1, the definition of identifier-2, with the REDEFINES clause, must come immediately after the definition of identifier-1 in the WORKING-STORAGE SECTION.

You can use MOVE CORRESPONDING to extract the date

The multiple MOVEs shown in Figure 7.5 can be avoided by giving the elementary identifiers in the date group identifiers the same names, and using MOVE CORRESPONDING to transfer the elementary identifiers.

```
01   REPORT-DATE     PIC 9(06).
01   YEAR-MONTH-DAY REDEFINES REPORT-DATE.
     05 RUN-YEAR     PIC 9(02).
     05 RUN-MONTH    PIC 9(02).
     05 RUN-DAY      PIC 9(02).
01   RUN-DATE.
     05 RUN-MONTH    PIC 9(02).
     05 FILLER       PIC X(01) VALUE '/'.
     05 RUN-DAY      PIC 9(02).
     05 FILLER       PIC X(01) VALUE '/'.
     05 RUN-YEAR     PIC 9(02).
...
PROCEDURE DIVISION.

     ...
     ACCEPT REPORT-DATE FROM DATE.
     MOVE CORRESPONDING YEAR-MONTH-DAY TO RUN-DATE.
```

This is an acceptable use of MOVE CORRESPONDING.

There is an easy IBM enhancement for extracting the date

It is easier to use the IBM enhancement, where it is available. COBOL with IBM computers has a reserve word CURRENT-DATE, which is an identifier that names a memory location and contains the date in month/day/year format. Thus, July 4, 1991 would be stored in CURRENT-DATE as 07/04/91.

To extract the current date, you simply move the contents of CURRENT-DATE to any eight-character alphanumeric identifier, as illustrated in Figure 7.6.

```
WORKING-STORAGE SECTION.
...
01  RUN-DATE  PIC X(8).
...
PROCEDURE DIVISION.
...
     MOVE CURRENT-DATE TO RUN-DATE.

     MOVE RUN-DATE TO BUFFER-RECORD-OUT.
     WRITE BUFFER-RECORD-OUT.
```

Figure 7.6 Processing for extracting date with CURRENT-DATE (IBM enhancement).

7.4 Printing headers is detailed but straightforward

YOU HAVE ALREADY encountered some of the methods used for printing headers in reports. A report is a printer file and must have a buffer record specified in the file section of the data division. Typical specifications are

```
DATA DIVISION.
FILE SECTION.
FD   INFILE
     ...
FD   REPORT-FILE
     LABEL RECORDS ARE OMITTED.
01   REPORT-RECORD-OUT    PIC X(133).
```

The individual headers are then defined as records in the WORKING-STORAGE SECTION and moved to REPORT-RECORD-OUT prior to being written to the printer file. Each detail line of the report is also moved to REPORT-RECORD-OUT prior to being written to the file. Remember that the first space in REPORT-RECORD-OUT should be assigned only a space, since it may be involved in printer control. Most line printers have lines 133 spaces long, including the first, printer-control space.

Suppose you wanted to write the headings, plus some detail lines, for the report in Figure 7.7a. You would use the printer spacing chart in Figure 7.7b to construct the WORKING-STORAGE identifiers needed, as shown in Figure 7.7c. Then you could construct the statements needed to output these headers, including the current page numbers, as shown in Figure 7.7d.

```
                   MONTHLY SALES REPORT
PAGE   1                                              02/09/91

SALESPERSON          UNITS         VOLUME         REGION
                     SOLD          OF SALES       OF CITY
<----------------->X<><---------><--------><--><><----------
```

Figure 7.7a Part of report.

```
                   MONTHLY SALES REPORT
PAGE   Z9                                             XX/XX/XX

SALESPERSON          UNITS         VOLUME         REGION
                     SOLD          OF SALES       OF CITY

XXXXXXXXXXXXXXXXXX   Z9            $Z,ZZZ,ZZ9     XX
XXXXXXXXXXXXXXXXXX   Z9            $Z,ZZZ,ZZ9     XX
XXXXXXXXXXXXXXXXXX   Z9            $Z,ZZZ,ZZ9     XX
```

Figure 7.7b Printer spacing chart for part of the report.

```
WORKING-STORAGE SECTION.
01 PAGE-DATE-LINE-OUT.
       05   FILLER               PIC X            VALUE SPACE.
       05   FILLER               PIC X(06)        VALUE 'PAGE  '.
       05   PAGE-NUMB-OUT        PIC Z9           VALUE ZERO.
       05   FILLER               PIC X(50)        VALUE SPACES.
       05   RUN-DATE-OUT         PIC X(08).
       05   FILLER               PIC X(66)        VALUE SPACES.
01 REPORT-HEADER.
       05   FILLER               PIC X(39)        VALUE
                                 'MONTHLY SALES REPORT' JUSTIFIED RIGHT.
       05   FILLER               PIC X(94)        VALUE SPACES.
01 HEADER-1.
       05   FILLER               PIC X            VALUE SPACE.
       05   FILLER               PIC X(19)        VALUE 'SALESPERSON'.
       05   FILLER               PIC X(13)        VALUE 'UNITS'.
       05   FILLER               PIC X(14)        VALUE 'VOLUME'.
       05   FILLER               PIC X(06)        VALUE 'REGION'.
       05   FILLER               PIC X(80)        VALUE SPACES.
01 HEADER-2.
       05   FILLER               PIC X            VALUE SPACE.
       05   FILLER               PIC X(19)        VALUE SPACES.
       05   FILLER               PIC X(13)        VALUE 'SOLD'.
       05   FILLER               PIC X(14)        VALUE 'OF SALES'.
       05   FILLER               PIC X(07)        VALUE 'OF CITY'.
       05   FILLER               PIC X(79)        VALUE SPACES.
01 DETAIL-LINE-OUT.
       05   FILLER               PIC X            VALUE SPACE.
       05   DL-SALESPERSON-OUT   PIC X(18).
       05   FILLER               PIC X(01)        VALUE SPACES.
       05   DL-UNITS-OUT         PIC Z9.
       05   FILLER               PIC X(11)        VALUE SPACES.
       05   DL-VOLUME-OUT        PIC $Z,ZZZ,ZZ9.
       05   FILLER               PIC X(04)        VALUE SPACES.
       05   DL-REGION-OUT        PIC X(02).
       05   FILLER               PIC X(84)        VALUE SPACES.
...
```

Figure 7.7c WORKING-STORAGE *identifiers used to construct the headers in the report.*

```
PROCEDURE DIVISION.
      ...
      MOVE CURRENT-DATE TO RUN-DATE-OUT.
      MOVE REPORT-HEADER TO REPORT-RECORD-OUT.
      WRITE REPORT-RECORD-OUT
            AFTER ADVANCING 1 LINE.
      ADD 1 TO WS-PAGE-NUMBER.
      MOVE WS-PAGE-NUMBER TO PAGE-NUMB-OUT.
      WRITE REPORT-RECORD-OUT FROM PAGE-DATE-LINE-OUT
            AFTER ADVANCING 1 LINE
      MOVE HEADER-1 TO REPORT-RECORD-OUT.
      WRITE REPORT-RECORD-OUT
                  AFTER ADVANCING 2 LINES.
      MOVE HEADER-2 TO REPORT-RECORD-OUT.
      WRITE REPORT-RECORD-OUT
                  AFTER ADVANCING 1 LINE.
      MOVE SPACES TO REPORT-RECORD-OUT.
      WRITE REPORT-RECORD-OUT
                  AFTER ADVANCING 1 LINE.
      . . . .
```

Figure 7.7d *Statements needed to output the headers on a new page together with current page number. REPORT-RECORD-OUT is the output buffer identifier.*

The WRITE . . . ADVANCING statement is the key to printing headers

Note that the AFTER ADVANCING option is used with the WRITE statement to print a blank line, that is, to skip a line (Figure 7.7d). The format for WRITE with this option is:

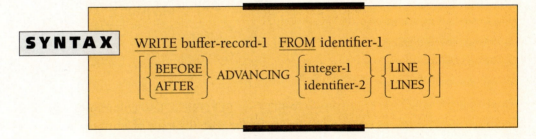

SYNTAX

WRITE buffer-record-1   FROM identifier-1

$\begin{Bmatrix} \text{BEFORE} \\ \text{AFTER} \end{Bmatrix}$ ADVANCING $\begin{Bmatrix} \text{integer-1} \\ \text{identifier-2} \end{Bmatrix} \begin{Bmatrix} \text{LINE} \\ \text{LINES} \end{Bmatrix}$

Some correct WRITE statements are as follows:

```
WRITE REPORT-RECORD-OUT
      BEFORE ADVANCING 3 LINES.

MOVE 4 TO LINE-COUNT.
WRITE REPORT-RECORD-OUT
      BEFORE ADVANCING LINE-COUNT LINES.

WRITE REPORT-RECORD-OUT FROM HEADER-6
      AFTER ADVANCING 2 LINES.
```

```
MOVE 5 TO LINE-COUNT.
WRITE REPORT-RECORD-OUT FROM HEADER-6
            AFTER LINE-COUNT LINES.
```

Be clear about WRITE . . . AFTER ADVANCING semantics

When a WRITE . . . AFTER ADVANCING 1 LINE is executed, the printer
then advances one line, and the value in the output buffer record is printed.
If WRITE . . . AFTER ADVANCING 1 LINE is executed again, the printer
advances another line and prints. In other words it prints on consecutive
lines, and does *not* skip a line.

Thus, repeated execution of WRITE . . . AFTER ADVANCING 1 LINE
causes single spacing. Repeated execution of WRITE . . . AFTER ADVANC-
ING 2 LINES causes double spacing (one blank line between printed lines);
so repeated execution of WRITE . . . AFTER ADVANCING *n* LINES causes *n*
minus 1 blank lines between printed lines. The following statements are
equivalent:

```
WRITE REPORT-RECORD-OUT.
```

and

```
WRITE REPORT-RECORD-OUT
            AFTER ADVANCING 1 LINE.
```

If either of these two statements is used repeatedly, single spacing will
result.

However, if you use ADVANCING with any WRITE in a program you
must use it with all WRITEs to the printer. For instance, you may not write

```
WRITE REPORT-RECORD-OUT
            AFTER ADVANCING 2 LINES.
...
WRITE REPORT-RECORD-OUT.                    error!
```

WRITE . . . BEFORE ADVANCING semantics are important too

WRITE . . . BEFORE is less commonly used than WRITE . . . AFTER. It is
more in step with the logic of a printer to advance and then print. Execution
of WRITE . . . BEFORE ADVANCING 1 LINE results in the printer printing
on the current line, and then advancing to the next (blank) line, and *not*
printing any further. Another execution of WRITE . . . BEFORE ADVANC-
ING 1 LINE causes printing on the current line and then advancing to the
next (blank) line without printing. Thus repeated execution of WRITE . . .
BEFORE ADVANCING 1 LINE results in single spacing.

Repeated execution of WRITE . . . BEFORE ADVANCING 2 LINES
causes double spacing (one blank line between printed lines). Repeated execution of WRITE . . . BEFORE ADVANCING *n* LINES causes n minus 1
blank lines between printed lines.

Avoid mixing WRITE . . . BEFORE and WRITE . . . AFTER

Remember that you cannot mix WRITE with either WRITE . . . BEFORE or WRITE . . . AFTER when writing to a printer file. However, you can mix WRITE . . . BEFORE and WRITE . . . AFTER, but you are strongly advised not to, unless you want overprinting. Things can go wrong if you mix the two. To see how, consider the following: Suppose the printer is positioned at line 10 and the following are executed:

```
WRITE REPORT-RECORD-OUT FROM H1
         AFTER ADVANCING 2 LINES.
```
prints on line 12, and remains positioned at line 12
```
...
WRITE REPORT-RECORD-OUT FROM H2
         BEFORE ADVANCING 2 LINES.
```
prints on line 12, and advances to blank line 14

The result is overprinting on line 12. The contents of H2 are written over the contents of H1. If H2 contained underscore characters, that would be fine, otherwise it is likely to result in incomprehensible output.

WRITE . . . PAGE is used to control the printing of pages

Most reports take up many pages. At the top of each new page there should be a page number and column headers. For example, page 5 of the report in Figure 7.2 could begin

```
                  MONTHLY SALES REPORT
PAGE   5                                          02/09/91

SALESPERSON          UNITS          VOLUME        REGION
                     SOLD           OF SALES      OF CITY

P. J. HARDY          4              $  590,000    SW
```

Thus, the program must keep track of the printer pages and arrange for the page number and column headers to be printed on each new page. If the program does not keep track of pages, the printer is likely to print detail lines regardless of the position of the print head on the paper; it may even print on the perforations between the pages.

The program keeps track as follows: First the programmer decides how many lines will be printed on each page in total. This is typically 55 lines, or less, including blank lines. As each line is printed, the instruction

```
        ADD 1 TO LINE-COUNT.
```

is carried out. When LINE-COUNT has the value 50, or whatever number of lines the programmer wants on the page, it is time for the line printer to advance (across the page perforation) to the first line of a fresh page. The report header will probably be printed first, followed by a line containing the incremented page number, as illustrated earlier. Thus, using the identifiers in Figure 7.7 you code

```
...
IF LINE-COUNT = 50
    THEN PERFORM 200-PRINT-HEADERS.
WRITE REPORT-RECORD-OUT FROM DETAIL-LINE-OUT
                 AFTER ADVANCING 1 LINE.
ADD 1 TO LINE-COUNT.
...
200-PRINT-HEADERS.
    WRITE REPORT-RECORD-OUT FROM REPORT-HEADER
                     AFTER ADVANCING PAGE.
    ADD 1 TO WS-PAGE-NUMBER.
    MOVE WS-PAGE-NUMBER TO PAGE-NUMB-OUT.
    WRITE REPORT-RECORD-OUT FROM PAGE-DATE-LINE-OUT
                     AFTER ADVANCING 1 LINE.
    MOVE HEADER-1 TO REPORT-RECORD-OUT.
    WRITE REPORT-RECORD-OUT
                     AFTER ADVANCING 2 LINES.
    MOVE HEADER-2 TO REPORT-RECORD-OUT.
    WRITE REPORT-RECORD-OUT
                     AFTER ADVANCING 1 LINE.
    MOVE SPACES TO REPORT-RECORD-OUT.
    WRITE REPORT-RECORD-OUT
                     AFTER ADVANCING 1 LINE.
    MOVE 6 TO LINE-COUNT.
```

The AFTER ADVANCING PAGE option is used with the WRITE statement to ensure that the report header line is printed at the top of the next page. The format for this version of WRITE is

SYNTAX

WRITE buffer-record-1 FROM identifier-1

$\left\{ \begin{array}{l} \underline{BEFORE} \\ \underline{AFTER} \end{array} \right\}$ ADVANCING PAGE

If the BEFORE ADVANCING option is used, the printer prints the buffer record, and then advances to the first line of the next page, ready to print the next line. Normally the AFTER ADVANCING option is used.
Note the following:

- Do not use the identifier LINE-COUNTER. It is a COBOL reserved word.
- The most common printer page size is 11 x 13 inches, which gives 66 lines at 6 lines per inch.

7.5
COBOL *report program examples*

T HIS SECTION USES the techniques explained in previous sections to develop some programs to print reports. Simple examples of a detail report and a summary report are shown.

Use printer spacing charts to lay out reports

In designing a layout for a report, a printer spacing chart is normally used, as described in Chapter 1. This consists of a squared sheet of paper, with each line divided into 132 character spaces (Figure 7.8b). This enables the designer to see at a glance the lengths of the various fields when specifying WORKING-STORAGE identifiers for headers and detail line fields.

Remember to include a blank character at the beginning of any record that will be printed so the record length will come to 133 characters.

```
---------1---------2---------3---------4---------5
SMITH           EP0030410000NW
JONES           TY0010150000SW
GREEN           F 0152462000NW
PETERSON        PJ0000000000SE
HASSELBACH      RT0020350000NE
...
<-------------->XX<-><-----><>
```

Columns	1–16	Last name of salesperson
	17	First initial of salesperson
	18	Second initial of salesperson
	19–21	Number of units sold in month, but first digit always zero
	22–28	Volume of sales for the salesperson for the month
	29–30	Region of city

Figure 7.8a *Input file MONTHLY-SALES.*

```
---------1---------2---------3---------4
XXXXXXXXXXXXXXXXXX99999999999XX
```

Figure 7.8b *Layout for an input record.*

```
01 SALES-RECORD-IN.
    05    SR-SURNAME-IN        PIC X(16).
    05    SR-INITIAL1-IN       PIC X.
    05    SR-INITIAL2-IN       PIC X.
    05    SR-UNITS-IN          PIC 9(03).
    05    SR-VOLUME-IN         PIC 9(07).
    05    SR-REGION-IN         PIC X(02).
```

Figure 7.8c *Input area record structure.*

```
---------1---------2---------3---------4---------5---------6---------7
               MONTHLY SALES REPORT
PAGE    1                                                  02/09/91


SALESPERSON        UNITS        VOLUME        REGION
                   SOLD         OF SALES      OF CITY

E.P. SMITH          3           $   410,000   NW
T.Y. JONES          1           $   150,000   SW
F.   GREEN         15           $2,462,000    NW
P.J. PETERSON       0           $         0   SE
R.T. HASSELBACH     2           $   350,000   NE
...
T.H. GOODMAN        4           $   480,600   SE


               MONTHLY SALES REPORT
PAGE    2                                                  02/09/91


SALESPERSON        UNITS        VOLUME        REGION
                   SOLD         OF SALES      OF CITY

H.J. BROWN          1           $   113,000   SW
J.K. SHINFIELD      5           $6,459,200    NE
...
```

Figure 7.9 Printing of the input file in Figure 7.8 as a detail report.

A program for a detail report

Suppose you have the input file MONTHLY-SALES, some initial records of which are shown in Figure 7.8 (this is the same file as in Figure 7.1.) The file is to be printed as a detail report, as shown in Figure 7.9, with the printer spacing chart shown earlier, in Figure 7.7b. The only fields printed are those in the input file. No additional fields are to be generated. The program to accomplish this is shown in Figure 7.10. The hierarchy diagram for the program is shown in Figure 7.11.

```
       IDENTIFICATION DIVISION.
       PROGRAM-ID. SR1.
*******************************************************************************
*   SR1:  THIS PROGRAM GENERATES A DETAIL LINE FOR EACH RECORD OF THE     *
*   INPUT FILE, WHICH DESCRIBES SALES OF HOMES.                           *
*******************************************************************************
       ENVIRONMENT DIVISION.
       INPUT-OUTPUT SECTION.
       FILE-CONTROL.   SELECT MONTHLY-SALES  ASSIGN TO UT-S-SALES011.
                       SELECT REPORT-FILE ASSIGN TO UR-S-SYSPRINT.
       DATA DIVISION.
       FILE SECTION.
       FD   MONTHLY-SALES                     LABEL RECORDS ARE STANDARD.
       01   SALES-RECORD-IN.
            05   SR-SURNAME-IN      PIC X(16).
            05   SR-INITIAL1-IN     PIC X.
            05   SR-INITIAL2-IN     PIC X.
            05   SR-UNITS-IN        PIC X(03).
            05   SR-VOLUME-IN       PIC 9(07).
            05   SR-REGION-IN       PIC X(02).
       FD   REPORT-FILE                        LABEL RECORDS ARE OMITTED.
       01   REPORT-RECORD-OUT       PIC X(133).
       WORKING-STORAGE SECTION.
       01 PAGE-DATE-LINE-OUT.
            05   FILLER             PIC X            VALUE SPACE.
            05   FILLER             PIC X(06)        VALUE 'PAGE  '.
            05   PAGE-NUMB-OUT      PIC Z9.
            05   FILLER             PIC X(50)        VALUE SPACES.
            05   RUN-DATE-OUT       PIC X(08).
            05   FILLER             PIC X(66)        VALUE SPACES.
       01 REPORT-HEADER.
            05   FILLER             PIC X(39)        VALUE
                                    'MONTHLY SALES REPORT' JUSTIFIED RIGHT.
            05   FILLER             PIC X(94)        VALUE SPACES.
       01 HEADER-1.
            05   FILLER             PIC X            VALUE SPACE.
            05   FILLER             PIC X(19)        VALUE 'SALESPERSON'.
            05   FILLER             PIC X(13)        VALUE 'UNITS'.
            05   FILLER             PIC X(14)        VALUE 'VOLUME'.
            05   FILLER             PIC X(06)        VALUE 'REGION'.
            05   FILLER             PIC X(80)        VALUE SPACES.
       01 HEADER-2.
            05   FILLER             PIC X            VALUE SPACE.
            05   FILLER             PIC X(19)        VALUE SPACES.
            05   FILLER             PIC X(13)        VALUE 'SOLD'.
            05   FILLER             PIC X(14)        VALUE 'OF SALES'.
            05   FILLER             PIC X(07)        VALUE 'OF CITY'.
            05   FILLER             PIC X(79)        VALUE SPACES.
```

```
 01 DETAIL-LINE-OUT.
        05  FILLER                   PIC X                 VALUE SPACE.
        05  DL-SALESPERSON-OUT  PIC X(18).
        05  FILLER                   PIC X(01)             VALUE SPACES.
        05  DL-UNITS-OUT         PIC Z9
        05  FILLER                   PIC X(11)             VALUE SPACES.
        05  DL-VOLUME-OUT        PIC $Z,ZZZ,ZZ9.
        05  FILLER                   PIC X(04)             VALUE SPACES.
        05  DL-REGION-OUT        PIC X(02).
        05  FILLER                   PIC X(84)             VALUE SPACES.
 01 WS-PERSON-NAME.
        05  WS-FIRST-INIT        PIC X.
        05  FILLER                   PIC X(02)             VALUE '.'
        05  WS-SECOND-INIT       PIC X.
        05  WS-PERIOD            PIC X(02).
        05  WS-LAST-NAME         PIC X(12).
 01 WS-WORK-AREAS.
        05  LINE-COUNT           PIC 9(02).
        05  MORE-RECORDS         PIC X(03)             VALUE 'YES'.
        05  WS-PAGE-NUMBER       PIC 9(02)             VALUE ZEROS.
 PROCEDURE DIVISION.
 100-MAIN-MODULE.
*****************************************************************************
*  100-MAIN-MODULE:  CONTROLS PROGRAM LOGIC.                              *
*****************************************************************************
       OPEN INPUT MONTHLY-SALES
            OUTPUT REPORT-FILE.
       MOVE CURRENT-DATE TO RUN-DATE-OUT.
       READ MONTHLY-SALES
            AT END MOVE 'NO' TO MORE-RECORDS.
       PERFORM 400-PAGE-HEADERS.
       PERFORM 200-PROCESS-RECORD UNTIL MORE-RECORDS = 'NO'.
       CLOSE MONTHLY-SALES
            REPORT-FILE.
       STOP RUN.
 200-PROCESS-RECORD.
*****************************************************************************
*  200-PROCESS-RECORD:  PERFORMED FROM 100-MAIN-MODULE. GENERATES AND   *
*  PRINTS A REPORT LINE FROM A RECORD OF MONTHLY SALES.                 *
*****************************************************************************
       PERFORM 300-GENERATE-NAME.
       MOVE SR-UNITS-IN TO DL-UNITS-OUT.
       MOVE SR-VOLUME-IN TO DL-VOLUME-OUT.
       MOVE SR-REGION-IN TO DL-REGION-OUT.
       IF LINE-COUNT = 50
            PERFORM 400-PAGE-HEADERS.
       WRITE REPORT-RECORD-OUT FROM DETAIL-LINE-OUT
                AFTER ADVANCING 1 LINE.
       ADD 1 TO LINE-COUNT.
       READ MONTHLY-SALES
            AT END MOVE 'NO' TO MORE-RECORDS.
```

```
    300-GENERATE-NAME.
***************************************************************
*   300 GENERATE NAME:  PERFORMED FROM 200-PROCESS-RECORD.  INSERTS    *
*   PERIODS WHERE NEEDED AND MOVES INITIALS TO BEFORE SURNAME.         *
***************************************************************
        MOVE SR-INITIAL1-IN TO WS-FIRST-INIT.
        MOVE SR-INITIAL2-IN TO WS-SECOND-INIT.
        IF WS-SECOND-INIT = SPACE
            THEN  MOVE SPACES TO WS-PERIOD
            ELSE MOVE '.' TO WS-PERIOD.
        MOVE SR-SURNAME-IN TO WS-LAST-NAME.
        MOVE WS-PERSON-NAME TO DL-SALESPERSON-OUT.
    400-PAGE-HEADERS.
***************************************************************
*   400-PAGE-HEADERS:  PERFORMED FROM 100-MAIN-MODULE AND FROM         *
*   200-PROCESS-RECORD. PRINTS PAGE HEADERS WITH CURRENT PAGE NUMBER.  *
***************************************************************
        WRITE REPORT-RECORD-OUT FROM REPORT-HEADER
                        AFTER ADVANCING PAGE.
        ADD 1 TO WS-PAGE-NUMBER.
        MOVE WS-PAGE-NUMBER TO PAGE-NUMB-OUT.
        WRITE REPORT-RECORD-OUT FROM PAGE-DATE-LINE-OUT
                        AFTER ADVANCING 1 LINE.
        WRITE REPORT-RECORD-OUT FROM HEADER-1
                        AFTER ADVANCING 2 LINES.
        WRITE REPORT-RECORD-OUT FROM HEADER-2
                        AFTER ADVANCING 1 LINE.
        MOVE SPACES TO REPORT-RECORD-OUT.
        WRITE REPORT-RECORD-OUT
                        AFTER ADVANCING 1 LINE.
        MOVE 6 TO LINE-COUNT.
```

Figure 7.10 *Program that prints a detail line for each record of input file in Figure 7.8.*

The logic for the program is given by the following pseudocode:

OPEN input file and output printer file.
Print page headers with date and page number.
READ first input record.
PERFORM until no records left:
      MOVE input data to WORKING-STORAGE record, and
      switch salesperson initials.
      IF line count is 50
          THEN print page headers with date and page number.
      WRITE record in WORKING STORAGE to printer file.
      ADD 1 to number of lines.
      READ next input record.
END-PERFORM.
CLOSE files and STOP.

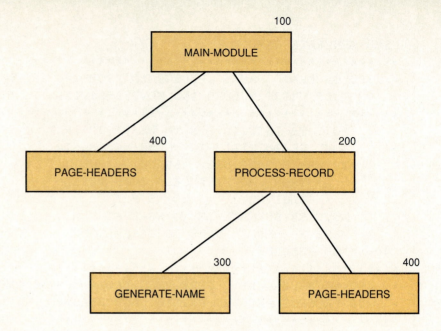

Figure 7.11 *Hierarchy diagram for program in Figure 7.10.*

Notice that some subsidiary processing (in 400-GENERATE-NAME) is needed to switch the initials from after the surname in the input file to before the surname with periods added. In many reports, the periods would be omitted.

The program, as shown, has a reasonable level of hierarchical structure. However, it can usefully be given more levels of hierarchy or, in other words, a greater degree of modularization. This is shown in a second version of the PROCEDURE DIVISION, in Figure 7.12. The hierarchy diagram for the routine in Figure 7.12 is shown in Figure 7.13.

```
PROCEDURE DIVISION.
100-MAIN-MODULE.
***********************************************************************
*   100-MAIN-MODULE:  CONTROLS PROGRAM LOGIC.                         *
***********************************************************************
      PERFORM 600-INITIALIZATION.
      PERFORM 500-PAGE-HEADERS.
      PERFORM 200-PROCESS-RECORD
                  UNTIL MORE-RECORDS = 'NO'.
      PERFORM 700-TERMINATION.
200-PROCESS-RECORD.
***********************************************************************
*   200-PROCESS-RECORD:  PERFORMED FROM 100-MAIN-MODULE.  GENERATES AND  *
*   PRINTS A REPORT LINE FROM A RECORD OF MONTHLY SALES.              *
***********************************************************************
      PERFORM 400-GENERATE-NAME.
      MOVE SR-UNITS-IN TO DL-UNITS-OUT.
      MOVE SR-VOLUME-IN TO DL-VOLUME-OUT.
      MOVE SR-REGION-IN TO REGION-OUT.
      PERFORM 300-PRINT-DETAIL-LINE.
      READ MONTHLY-SALES
            AT END MOVE 'NO' TO MORE-RECORDS.
300-PRINT-DETAIL-LINE.
***********************************************************************
*   300-PRINT-DETAIL-LINE:  PERFORMED FROM 200-PROCESS-RECORD. PRINTS  *
*   THE NEXT DETAIL RECORD. PAGE HEADERS ARE PRINTED FIRST IF THE      *
*   DETAIL RECORD IS PRINTED ON A NEW PAGE.                           *
***********************************************************************
      IF LINE-COUNT = 50
          PERFORM 500-PAGE-HEADERS.
      WRITE REPORT-RECORD-OUT FROM DETAIL-LINE-OUT
                        AFTER ADVANCING 1 LINE.
      ADD 1 TO LINE-COUNT.
400-GENERATE-NAME.
***********************************************************************
*   400-GENERATE-NAME:  PERFORMED FROM 200-PROCESS-RECORD.  MOVES      *
*   INITIALS TO BEFORE SURNAME AND INSERTS PERIODS WHERE NEEDED.       *
***********************************************************************
      MOVE SR-INITIAL1-IN TO WS-FIRST-INIT.
      MOVE SR-INITIAL2-IN TO WS-SECOND-INIT.
      IF WS-SECOND-INIT = SPACE
          THEN MOVE SPACES TO WS-PERIOD
          ELSE MOVE '.' TO WS-PERIOD
      END-IF.
      MOVE SR-SURNAME-IN TO WS-LAST-NAME.
      MOVE WS-PERSON-NAME TO DL-SALESPERSON-OUT.
```

```
 500-PAGE-HEADERS.
*****************************************************************
*  500-PAGE-HEADERS:  PERFORMED FROM 100-MAIN-MODULE AND FROM   *
*  300-PRINT-DETAIL-LINE. PRINTS PAGE HEADERS WITH CURRENT PAGE *
*  NUMBER.                                                      *
*****************************************************************
     WRITE REPORT-RECORD-OUT FROM REPORT-HEADER
                   AFTER ADVANCING PAGE.
     ADD 1 TO WS-PAGE-NUMBER.
     MOVE WS-PAGE-NUMBER TO PAGE-NUMB-OUT.
     WRITE REPORT-RECORD-OUT FROM PAGE-DATE-LINE-OUT
                   AFTER ADVANCING 1 LINE.
     WRITE REPORT-RECORD-OUT FROM HEADER-1
                   AFTER ADVANCING 2 LINES.
     WRITE REPORT-RECORD-OUT FROM HEADER-2
                   AFTER ADVANCING 1 LINE.
     MOVE SPACES TO REPORT-RECORD-OUT.
     WRITE REPORT-RECORD-OUT
                   AFTER ADVANCING 1 LINE.
     MOVE 6 TO LINE-COUNT.
 600-INITIALIZATION.
*****************************************************************
*  600-INITIALIZATION:  PERFORMED FROM 100-MAIN-MODULE. OPENS FILES,  *
*  EXTRACTS DATE, AND READS FIRST RECORD.                       *
*****************************************************************
     OPEN INPUT MONTHLY-SALES
          OUTPUT REPORT-FILE.
     MOVE CURRENT-DATE TO RUN-DATE-OUT.
     READ MONTHLY-SALES
             AT END MOVE 'NO' TO MORE-RECORDS.
 700-TERMINATION.
*****************************************************************
*  700-TERMINATION:  PERFORMED FROM 100-MAIN-MODULE. CLOSES FILES  *
*  AND TERMINATES PROGRAM.                                      *
*****************************************************************
     CLOSE MONTHLY-SALES, REPORT-FILE.
     STOP RUN.
```

Figure 7.12 PROCEDURE DIVISION *from Figure 7.10 with a more modularized structure.*

There is a convention for organizing paragraphs

A common paragraphing style is to place the initial OPEN statements, retrieval of the date, and the first READ statement in a paragraph called INITIALIZATION. Similarly, any statements connected with closing files and terminating processing are placed in a paragraph called TERMINATION. Details of printing a detail line are often placed in a separate paragraph as well, as in 300-PRINT-DETAIL-LINE in Figure 7.12.

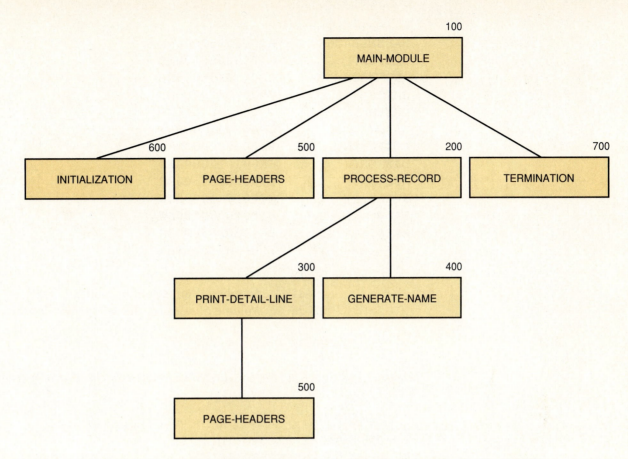

Figure 7.13 *Hierarchy diagram for the routine in Figure 7.12.*

There is a simple principle underlying grouping statements into paragraphs – each paragraph should carry out a single, well-defined function. Programs that are well-modularized in hierarchical fashion are said to be *structured*. Structured programs have been found to be the easiest to maintain; and students of COBOL programming are expected to write well-structured programs. Use Figure 7.12 as a guide when structuring your own programs.

Simple summary report program

This section shows a report program to generate a simple summary of data in the input file MONTHLY-SALES, used in the previous example. To make the processing easier at this stage, another version of MONTHLY-SALES, shown in Figure 7.14, is used. Records are sorted in ascending order by city region (that is, northeast (NE) sales first, then northwest (NW) sales, and so on). In addition, there are three salespeople for each region of the city, so the input file has exactly 12 records.

The summary report is shown in Figure 7.15. It gives a summary of the sales for each of the four regions of the city. Note that this is about the simplest summary report you can get. Nevertheless, the program illustrates the kind of programming needed for generating totals.

```
--------1--------2--------3--------4--------5
HASSELBACH         RT0020350000NE
BABSON             K 0030480000NE
ANDERSON           HG0010156000NE
SMITH              EP0030410000NW
GREEN              F 0010162000NW
HARDY              JP0020410000NW
PETERSON           PJ0000000000SE
DAWSON             GH0010120000SE
AUSTEN             ET0030365500SE
JONES              TY0010150000SW
BROWN              AK0040630000SW
BARNES             LP0020285600SW

<----------------><-><-----><>
```

Columns 01–18	Name of salesperson
19–21	Number of units sold in month
22–28	Volume of sales for the salesperson for the month
29–30	Region of city

Figure 7.14a *Input file MONTHLY-SALES, with records sorted in ascending order by city region.*

```
01   SALES-RECORD-IN.
     05   SR-NAME-IN              PIC X(18).
     05   SR-UNITS-IN             PIC X(03).
     05   SR-VOLUME-IN            PIC 9(07).
     05   SR-REGION-IN            PIC X(02).
```

Figure 7.14b *Structure of input area record.*

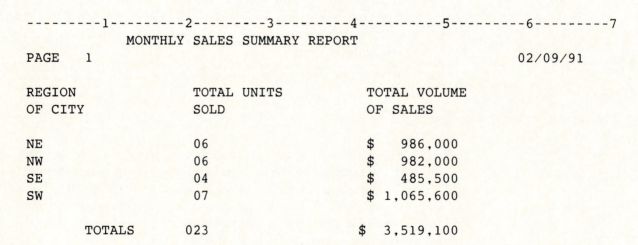

```
--------1--------2--------3--------4--------5--------6--------7
        MONTHLY SALES SUMMARY REPORT
PAGE   1                                                 02/09/91

REGION              TOTAL UNITS          TOTAL VOLUME
OF CITY             SOLD                 OF SALES


NE                  06                   $   986,000
NW                  06                   $   982,000
SE                  04                   $   485,500
SW                  07                   $ 1,065,600

        TOTALS      023                  $ 3,519,100
```

Figure 7.15a *Summary report generated from the input file in Figure 7.14.*

```
  1234567890123456789012345678901234567890123456789012345678901234567890
                    MONTHLY SALES SUMMARY REPORT
 2 PAGE   Z9                                                    XXXXXXXX

 4 REGION                  TOTAL UNITS             TOTAL VOLUME
 5 OF CITY                 SOLD                    OF SALES

 7 XX                        99                    $ZZ,ZZZ,ZZ9
 8 XX                        99                    $ZZ,ZZZ,ZZ9
 9 XX                        99                    $ZZ,ZZZ,ZZ9
10 XX                        99                    $ZZ,ZZZ,ZZ9

12        TOTALS            999                    $ZZZ,ZZZ,ZZ9
```

Figure 7.15b *Printer spacing chart for the output.*

```
01 TOTALS-LINE-OUT.
      05  FILLER                    PIC X          VALUE SPACE.
      05  TOT-REGION-OUT            PIC X(02).
      05  FILLER                    PIC X(18)      VALUE SPACES.
      05  TOT-UNITS-OUT             PIC 9(02).
      05  FILLER                    PIC X(19)      VALUE SPACES.
      05  TOT-VOLUME-OUT            PIC $ZZ,ZZZ,ZZ9.
      05  FILLER                    PIC X(80)      VALUE SPACES.
01 GRAND-TOTAL-LINE-OUT.
      05  FILLER                    PIC X          VALUE SPACE.
      05  FILLER                    PIC X(07)      VALUE SPACES.
      05  FILLER                    PIC X(12)      VALUE 'TOTALS'.
      05  GRAND-TOT-UNITS-OUT       PIC 9(03)
      05  FILLER                    PIC X(18)      VALUE SPACES.
      05  GRAND-TOT-VOLUME-OUT      PIC $ZZZ,ZZZ,ZZ9.
      05  FILLER                    PIC X(80)      VALUE SPACES.
```

Figure 7.15c *Structure of records for total and grand total lines.*

The program for generating the summary report is shown in Figure 7.16. It is highly modularized. The hierarchy diagram is shown in Figure 7.17.

```
        IDENTIFICATION DIVISION.
        PROGRAM-ID. SUM1.
        ***************************************************************
        *  SUM1:  THIS PROGRAM GENERATES A SUMMARY LINE FOR EACH GROUP OF   *
        *  THREE INPUT SALES RECORDS, THAT IS, FOR EACH REGION OF A CITY.   *
        ***************************************************************
        ENVIRONMENT DIVISION.
        INPUT-OUTPUT SECTION.
        FILE-CONTROL.    SELECT MONTHLY-SALES  ASSIGN TO UT-S-SALES011.
                         SELECT SUMMARY-FILE ASSIGN TO UR-S-SYSPRINT.
        DATA DIVISION.
        FILE SECTION.
        FD   MONTHLY-SALES                    LABEL RECORDS ARE STANDARD.
        01   SALES-RECORD-IN.
             05   SR-NAME-IN          PIC X(18).
             05   SR-UNITS-IN         PIC X(03).
             05   SR-VOLUME-IN        PIC 9(07).
             05   SR-REGION-IN        PIC X(02).
        FD   SUMMARY-REPORT                   LABEL RECORDS ARE OMITTED.
        01   REPORT-RECORD-OUT        PIC X(133).
        WORKING-STORAGE SECTION.
        01 PAGE-DATE-LINE-OUT.
             05   FILLER              PIC X.
             05   FILLER              PIC X(06)      VALUE 'PAGE  '.
             05   PAGE-NUMB-OUT       PIC Z9.
             05   FILLER              PIC X(50).
             05   RUN-DATE-OUT        PIC X(08).
             05   FILLER              PIC X(66)
        01 REPORT-HEADER.
             05   FILLER              PIC X(41)      VALUE
                               'MONTHLY SALES SUMMARY REPORT' JUSTIFIED RIGHT.
             05   FILLER              PIC X(92)      VALUE SPACES.
        01 HEADER-1.
             05   FILLER              PIC X          VALUE SPACE.
             05   FILLER              PIC X(20)      VALUE 'REGION'.
             05   FILLER              PIC X(21)      VALUE 'TOTAL UNITS'.
             05   FILLER              PIC X(12)      VALUE 'TOTAL VOLUME'.
             05   FILLER              PIC X(79)      VALUE SPACES.
        01 HEADER-2.
             05   FILLER              PIC X          VALUE SPACE.
             05   FILLER              PIC X(20)      VALUE 'OF CITY'.
             05   FILLER              PIC X(21)      VALUE 'SOLD'.
             05   FILLER              PIC X(08)      VALUE 'OF SALES'.
             05   FILLER              PIC X(83)      VALUE SPACES.
        01 TOTALS-LINE-OUT.
             05   FILLER              PIC X          VALUE SPACE.
             05   TOT-REGION-OUT      PIC X(02).
             05   FILLER              PIC X(18)      VALUE SPACES.
             05   TOT-UNITS-OUT       PIC 9(02).
             05   FILLER              PIC X(19)      VALUE SPACES.
             05   TOT-VOLUME-OUT      PIC $ZZ,ZZZ,ZZ9.
             05   FILLER              PIC X(80)      VALUE SPACES.
```

```
01  GRAND-TOTAL-LINE-OUT.
      05  FILLER                    PIC X          VALUE SPACE.
      05  FILLER                    PIC X(07)      VALUE SPACES.
      05  FILLER                    PIC X(12)      VALUE 'TOTALS'.
      05  GRAND-TOT-UNITS-OUT       PIC 9(03).
      05  FILLER                    PIC X(18)      VALUE SPACES.
      05  GRAND-TOT-VOLUME-OUT      PIC $ZZZ,ZZZ,ZZZ.
      05  FILLER                    PIC X(80)      VALUE SPACES.
01  WS-TOTAL-AREAS.
      05  WS-TOT-UNITS              PIC 9(02)      VALUE ZERO.
      05  WS-TOT-VOLUME             PIC 9(08)      VALUE ZERO.
      05  WS-GRAND-TOT-VOLUME       PIC 9(09)      VALUE ZERO.
      05  WS-GRAND-TOT-UNITS        PIC 9(03)      VALUE ZERO.
01  WS-WORK-AREAS.
      05  MORE-RECORDS              PIC X(03)      VALUE 'YES'.
      05  RECORD-COUNT              PIC 9(02)      VALUE ZERO.
      05  TOTAL-IN-GROUP            PIC 9(02)      VALUE 3.
      05  WS-PAGE-NUMBER            PIC 9(02)      VALUE ZERO.
PROCEDURE DIVISION.
100-MAIN-MODULE.
****************************************************************************
*   100-MAIN-MODULE:  CONTROLS PROGRAM LOGIC.                             *
****************************************************************************
      PERFORM 600-INITIALIZATION.
      PERFORM 500-PAGE-HEADERS.
      PERFORM 200-PROCESS-RECORD
               UNTIL MORE-RECORDS = 'NO'.
      PERFORM 400-PRINT-GRAND-TOTAL-LINE.
      PERFORM 700-TERMINATION.
200-PROCESS-RECORD.
****************************************************************************
*   200-PROCESS-RECORD:  PERFORMED FROM 100-MAIN-MODULE. GENERATES AND    *
*   PRINTS A REPORT LINE FROM A GROUP OF RECORDS OF MONTHLY-SALES.        *
****************************************************************************
      ADD 1 TO RECORD-COUNT.
      ADD SR-UNITS-IN TO WS-TOT-UNITS.
      ADD SR-VOLUME-IN TO WS-TOT-VOLUME.
      IF RECORD-COUNT = TOTAL-IN-GROUP
          THEN
              PERFORM 300-PRINT-TOTAL-LINE
              MOVE ZEROS TO RECORD-COUNT
              ADD WS-TOT-UNITS TO WS-GRAND-TOT-UNITS
              ADD WS-TOT-VOLUME TO WS-GRAND-TOT-VOLUME
              MOVE ZEROS TO WS-TOT-UNITS
              MOVE ZEROS TO WS-TOT-VOLUME
      END-IF.
      READ MONTHLY-SALES
              AT END MOVE 'NO' TO MORE-RECORDS.
```

```
 300-PRINT-TOTAL-LINE.
************************************************************************
*   300-PRINT-TOTAL-LINE:  PERFORMED FROM 200-PROCESS-RECORD.         *
*   PRINTS A TOTAL LINE.                                              *
************************************************************************
        MOVE SR-REGION-IN TO TOT-REGION-O
        MOVE WS-TOT-UNITS TO TOT-UNITS-OUT.
        MOVE WS-TOT-VOLUME TO TOT-VOLUME-OUT.
        WRITE REPORT-RECORD-OUT FROM TOTALS LINE-OUT
                  AFTER ADVANCING 1 LINE.
 400-PRINT-GRAND-TOTAL-LINE.
************************************************************************
*   400-PRINT-GRAND-TOTAL-LINE:  PERFORMED FROM 100-MAIN-MODULE.      *
*   PRINTS THE FINAL GRAND TOTAL LINE.                                *
************************************************************************
        MOVE SPACES TO REPORT-RECORD-OUT.
        WRITE REPORT-RECORD-OUT
                    AFTER-ADVANCING 1 LINE.
        MOVE WS-GRAND-TOT-UNITS TO GRAND-TOT-UNITS-OUT.
        MOVE WS-GRAND-TOT-VOLUME TO GRAND-TOT-VOLUME-OUT.
        MOVE GRAND-TOTALS-LINE-OUT TO REPORT-RECORD-OUT-OUT.
        WRITE REPORT-RECORD-OUT-OUT FROM GRAND-TOTAL-LINE-OUT
                AFTER ADVANCING 1 LINE.
 500-PAGE-HEADERS.
************************************************************************
*   500-PAGE-HEADERS:  PERFORMED FROM 100-MAIN-MODULE. PRINTS PAGE    *
*   HEADERS.                                                          *
************************************************************************
        WRITE REPORT-RECORD-OUT FROM REPORT-HEADER
                    AFTER ADVANCING PAGE.
        ADD 1 TO WS-PAGE-NUMBER.
        MOVE WS-PAGE-NUMBER TO PAGE-NUMB-OUT.
        WRITE REPORT-RECORD-OUT FROM PAGE-DATE-LINE-OUT
                    AFTER ADVANCING 1 LINE.
        MOVE HEADER-1 TO REPORT-RECORD-OUT.
        WRITE REPORT-RECORD-OUT
                    AFTER ADVANCING 2 LINES.
        MOVE HEADER-2 TO REPORT-RECORD-OUT.
        WRITE REPORT-RECORD-OUT
                    AFTER ADVANCING 1 LINE.
        MOVE SPACES TO REPORT-RECORD-OUT.
        WRITE REPORT-RECORD-OUT
                    AFTER ADVANCING 1 LINE.
```

```
 600-INITIALIZATION.
 ***************************************************************************
 *   600-INITIALIZATION:  PERFORMED FROM 100-MAIN-MODULE. OPENS FILES,    *
 *   EXTRACTS DATE, AND READS FIRST RECORD.                               *
 ***************************************************************************
        OPEN INPUT MONTHLY-SALES,
             OUTPUT REPORT-FILE.
        MOVE CURRENT-DATE TO RUN-DATE-OUT.
        READ MONTHLY-SALES,
                AT END MOVE 'NO' TO MORE-RECORDS.
 700-TERMINATION.
 ***************************************************************************
 *   700-TERMINATION:  PERFORMED FROM 100-MAIN-MODULE. CLOSES FILES       *
 *   AND TERMINATES PROGRAM.                                              *
 ***************************************************************************
        CLOSE MONTHLY-SALES, REPORT-FILE.
        STOP RUN.
```

Figure 7.16 *Program for generating the summary report.*

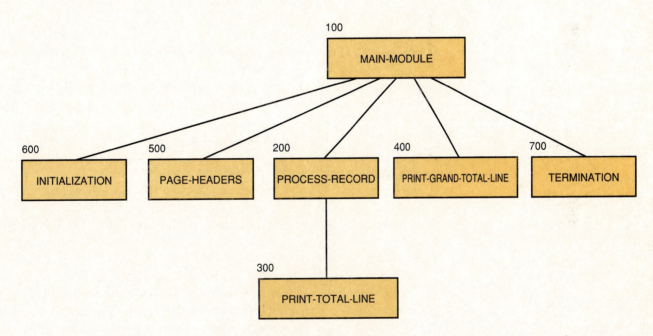

Figure 7.17 *Hierarchy diagram for the program in Figure 7.16 for printing a summary report.*

The logic for the processing is given by the following pseudocode:

OPEN input file and output printer file.
Print header lines, including page number and date.
READ first record.
PERFORM UNTIL no records left:
    Add 1 to record count
    Add values in record to city sector totals
    IF record count is 3 THEN
        Print city sector summary line
        ADD city sector totals to city totals
        MOVE zero to city sector totals
        MOVE zero to record count
    END-IF.
    READ next input record.
END-PERFORM.
Print city totals summary line.
CLOSE files and STOP.

Each record of the input file is read in sequence. There are only four possible SR-REGION-IN values, and each of these values occurs in three consecutive input records. For three consecutive records with the same SR-REGION-IN value, the number of DL-UNITS-OUT and DL-VOLUME-OUT of sales from each record are added to the identifiers WS-TOT-UNITS and WS-TOT-VOLUME, respectively. In this way the total lines are constructed.

When a total line has been constructed and output, the accumulated totals are added to the grand total, and the process is repeated for the next three input records. When all the records have been read, the grand total line can be output.

The first thing to notice about this program is the surprisingly large number of identifiers needed. This is partly due to the fact that a volume of sales quantity needs a numeric identifier version for computation (WS-TOT-VOLUME), that is, for accumulating regional totals. You also need a numeric identifier for the grand total (WS-GRAND-TOT-VOLUME), an edited numeric identifier from which the regional total value (TOT-VOLUME-OUT) can be printed, and an edited numeric identifier for printing the grand total volume (GRAND-TOT-VOLUME-OUT). Similarly, you need an equivalent set of identifiers for the number of units sold.

The number of records in the input file for each region of the city is the same (three). This assumption was made to keep the processing simple, and allow you to easily learn the essence of generating summary reports. If the number of records for each of the regions varies, you have to use a more sophisticated type of processing called control-break processing, described in Chapter 10. At this stage, you might think about what the program logic would be if the number of records differed among the regions.

Summary

1. The main types of reports are detail, summary, and exception reports. With a detail report, a line, called a detail line, is normally printed for each record in an input file. With a summary report, a summary line is printed for a group of records from the input report; detail lines may also be printed between the summary lines. An exception report is a detail report in which only detail lines meeting a predefined condition (exception), are printed.

2. Detail and summary lines are printed from identifiers that normally contain several edit symbols. When designing the report, a printer spacing chart should be made up, showing the edit symbols exactly where they are needed.

3. The date is stored internally in the computer and is extracted by an ACCEPT statement. With most computers it is stored in year-month-day format, which has to be edited into day/month/year format before printing. With IBM machines, the date is stored in day/month/year format so further processing is not normally necessary.

4. You print header lines by constructing them separately in WORKING-STORAGE group identifiers and then writing them out to the printer, each header line being output via the same output area (output buffer) identifier.

5. The AFTER PAGE option is used with WRITE to cause a line to be printed at the top of the next page. The program has to count the number of lines printed (including blank or skipped lines), to ensure that WRITE . . . AFTER PAGE can be executed when a satisfactory number of lines has been printed on the current page. The program has to count pages too, so the page number can be printed at the top of each page. Remember that the identifier LINE-COUNTER cannot be used, since it is a COBOL reserved word.

Key Terms

detail report	header line	summary report
detail line	exception report	summary line

Concept Review Questions

1. Explain the different kinds of reports.
2. Discuss the different possibilities with summary reports.
3. Why are exception reports convenient?
4. What does "a group MOVE is an alphanumeric MOVE" mean?
5. When is the JUSTIFIED RIGHT option useful?
6. Discuss the ANS and IBM methods of delivering the date to a program.
7. Explain what happens when an identifier is defined using REDEFINES.
8. Why does AFTER ADVANCING 1 LINE mean single spacing?

9. How is overprinting accomplished (for example, printing of a line with underscores)?
10. How do you skip to a new printer page?

COBOL Language Questions

1. For each quantity in a sending field SF below, decide what the value in the receiving field RF would be if you executed

   MOVE SF TO RF

   for each of the following:

SENDING FIELD SF	RECEIVING FIELD RF
a. PIC 9999V99	PIC Z,ZZZ.99
004387	
000042	
000001	
000000	
b. PIC 999V99	PIC ZZZ.ZZ
04387	
00042	
00001	
00000	
c. PIC 99999V99	PIC $**,***.Z9
1056756	
0000500	
0003404	
d. PIC 99999V99	PIC $**,***.**
2066736	
0001500	
0005407	
0000000	
e. PIC S99999V99	PIC +99,999.99
(+) 1056756	
(−) 0000500	
(+) 0003404	
f. PIC S9999V99	PIC +Z,ZZZ.ZZ
(+) 066736	
(−) 001500	
(+) 005407	
(−) 000000	
g. PIC S99999V99	PIC −99,999.99
(−) 0088757	
(−) 1234554	

SENDING FIELD SF	RECEIVING FIELD RF

```
h. PIC S9999V99      PIC Z,ZZ9.99+
   (+)   066736
   (-)   001500
   (+)   005407
   (-)   000000

i. PIC S9999V99      PIC 99,999.99-
   (+)   056756
   (-)   000500
   (+)   003404

j. PIC 999999        PIC /99/99/99
        44387

k. PIC 9999V99       PIC $$,$$9.99
        004583
        134523
        000025
        000000

l. PIC 9999V99       PIC ++,++9.99
        004583
        134523
        000025
        000000

m. PIC XXXXXX        PIC XXBXXBXXB
        I.B.M.
```
_____

2. What is wrong with

```
01 GPA.
     GA1   PIC 99       VALUE 56.
     GA2   PIC 9(04)    VALUE 0672
01 GPB.
     GB1   PIC 99.
     GB2   PIC $999.
MOVE GPA TO GPB.
```

3. If you have

```
01 A          PIC X(06)          VALUE '456ABC'.
01 B                             REDEFINES A.
     B-1   PIC 9(03).
     B-2   PIC X(03).
```

what is the value stored in B-2?

4. What is wrong with this?

```
01 B                             REDEFINES A.
     B-1   PIC 9(03).
     B-2   PIC X(03).
01 A          PIC X(06)          VALUE 'ABC123'.
```

5. What would be printed by the following?

```
MOVE 'AB  AB  AB' TO A.
MOVE '  12  12  ' TO B.
WRITE REPORT-RECORD-OUT FROM A
            AFTER ADVANCING 3 LINES.
WRITE REPORT-RECORD-OUT FROM B
            BEFORE ADVANCING 2 LINES.
```

6. What is wrong with this?

```
MOVE ZERO TO LINE-COUNTER.
```

Programming Assignments

1. **Multiple page detail report program**
   The input data are:

```
---------1---------2---------3---------4---------5---------6
BOEING                47720+1734
GENCORP               05134+0044
GENERAL DYNAMICS      24872+1124
GRUMMAN               10357+0241
KAMAN                 01815+0045
LOCKHEED              30124+1043
MARTIN MARIETTA       14557+0247
MCDONNELL DOUGLAS     43440+1479
NORTHROP              18236-0861
PARKER HANNIFIN       06216+0261
ROHR INDUSTRIES       02348+0069
SUNDSTRAND            04137-0184
UNITED TECHNOLOGIES   53784+1506
AMERCO                01836-0037
CHRYSLER              84573+4325
FORD MOTOR            24915+1154
GENERAL MOTORS        27893+1396
MACK TRUCKS           05668+0114
NAVISTAR INT          11268+0847
PACCAR                07894+0472
```

A report with the following format is to be constructed from the input file:

```
---------1---------2---------3---------4---------5---------6
         CORPORATE QUARTERLY SCORES
PAGE   1                                          05/06/92

CORPORATION           QUARTERLY          QUARTERLY
                      REVENUE ($ MIL.)   PROFITS ($ MIL.)

BOEING                4772.0             173.4
GENCORP                513.4               4.4
GENERAL DYNAMICS      2487.2             112.4
GRUMMAN               1035.7              24.1
KAMAN                  181.5               4.5
```

```
CORPORATION          QUARTERLY        QUARTERLY
                     REVENUE ($ MIL.) PROFITS ($ MIL.)


LOCKHEED             3012.4           104.3
MARTIN MARIETTA      1455.7            24.7
MCDONNELL DOUGLAS    4344.0           147.9
NORTHROP             1823.6            86.1  (LOSS)
PARKER HANNIFIN      0621.6            26.1
...
```

There should be five detail lines on each page.

    a. Make up the input record layout and printer spacing chart.

    b. Make up flowchart and hierarchy diagram.

    c. Write and run the program.

2. Summary report program

The input file is a modified version of the input file used in the previous exercise:

```
---------1---------2---------3---------4---------5---------6
AEROSPACE               00000+0000
BOEING                  47720+1734
GENCORP                 05134+0044
GENERAL DYNAMICS        24872+1124
GRUMMAN                 10357+0241
KAMAN                   01815+0045
LOCKHEED                30124+1043
MARTIN MARIETTA         14557+0247
MCDONNELL DOUGLAS       43440+1479
NORTHROP                18236-0861
PARKER HANNIFIN         06216+0261
ROHR INDUSTRIES         02348+0069
SUNDSTRAND              04137-0184
UNITED TECHNOLOGIES     53784+1506
AUTOMOTIVE              00000+0000
AMERCO                  01836-0037
CHRYSLER                84573+4325
FORD MOTOR              24915+1154
GENERAL MOTORS          27893+1396
MACK TRUCKS             05668+0114
NAVISTAR INT            11268+0847
PACCAR                  07894+0472
```

The input data include two types of companies, aerospace and automotive. In the following report, the quarterly revenues and profits are summarized in billions of dollars, rounded to the first decimal place.

```
---------1---------2---------3---------4---------5---------6
              QUARTERLY CORPORATE SUMMARY

INDUSTRY SECTOR      TOTAL QUARTERLY         TOTAL QUARTERLY
                     REVENUE ($ BIL.)        PROFITS ($ BIL)

AEROSPACE            ?                       ?
AUTOMOTIVE           ?                       ?
```

In your program, use the input record beginning 'AUTOMO-TIVE' to detect the end of the aerospace companies.

   a. Make up the input record layout and printer spacing chart.
   b. Draw the flowchart and hierarchy diagram.
   c. Write and run the program.

3. A detail report with summary lines
In this exercise, you will use the input file from the previous exercise. The output for each of the two industry sectors (aerospace and automotive) is to begin on a fresh page. A summary line is printed at the end of the detail records from each sector:

```
---------1---------2---------3---------4---------5---------6
              CORPORATE QUARTERLY SCORES
PAGE   1                                            05/06/92

AEROSPACE INDUSTRY

CORPORATION             QUARTERLY            QUARTERLY
                        REVENUE ($ MIL.)     PROFITS ($ MIL.)

BOEING                  4772.0               173.4
GENCORP                  513.4                 4.4
GENERAL DYNAMICS        2487.2               112.4
GRUMMAN                 1035.7               024.1
KAMAN                    181.5                 4.5


              CORPORATE QUARTERLY SCORES
PAGE   2                                            05/06/92
...


              CORPORATE QUARTERLY SCORES
PAGE   3                                            05/06/92
CORPORATION             QUARTERLY            QUARTERLY
                        REVENUE ($ MIL.)     PROFITS ($ MIL.)
ROHR INDUSTRIES         234.8                  6.9
SUNDSTRAND              413.7                 18.4   (LOSS)
UNITED TECHNOLOGIES     5378.4               150.6

AEROSPACE TOTALS        ?                      ?
($ BIL.)
```

a. Make up the input record layout and printer spacing chart.
b. Make up the flowchart and hierarchy diagram.
c. Write and run the program.

4. **A program to generate an exception report**
   In this exercise you will use the input file from Assignment 2. The program will select the data for companies that had a quarterly loss and print it in report format, followed by summary and average data, as shown here:

```
---------1---------2---------3---------4---------5---------6
               CORPORATE QUARTERLY LOSERS
PAGE   1                                            05/06/92


CORPORATION             QUARTERLY           QUARTERLY
                        REVENUE ($ MIL.)    LOSS ($ MIL.)

NORTHROP                1823.6              86.1
SUNDSTRAND              413.7               18.4
...
TOTALS ($ BIL)          ?                   ?
AVERAGES                ?                   ?
(87 COMPANIES)
```

In the program, assume there are many (about 1000) records in the input file, with about one loser in every 10 companies reporting.

In the report, a summary of revenue and losses is placed at the end followed by averages. The total number of losers is also printed.

a. Make up the input record layout and printer spacing chart.
b. Make up the flowchart and hierarchy diagram.
c. Write and run the program.

8

VALIDATION OF INPUT DATA

OBJECTIVES

- To emphasize the importance of data validation
- To illustrate the kinds of validation checks that need to occur
- To demonstrate the options available for dealing with records that fail validation tests

OUTLINE

8.1 Incorrect input data can often be detected

Use a checklist for input error detection when writing a program
Use the class test for detecting incorrect data type
Use the sign test for incorrectly signed data
Check for blanks as a missing data test
A reasonableness test involves checking ranges and limits
Bad data are repaired by counting and replacing characters
> Format-1 of INSPECT
> Format-2 of INSPECT
Condition codes must be checked
Checking for correct sequence is often necessary
Check digit computations help detect errors in numeric fields

8.2 A program can react to input errors in different ways

Use a checklist of possible program reactions to input errors when writing a program
Good error messages make the operator's life easier

8.3 Master files are created with built-in validation

Detecting errors is the basis of master file creation
Validity checks account for the complexity of master file creation programs

*I*N BUSINESS, a COBOL program tends to have a long life and is used on a regular basis, perhaps weekly or even daily. You should understand that each time such a program is run, a different set of input data will be used. For example, if a program generates a weekly sales report from an input file of sales data, each week the file will have different data. Typically, the amount of input data to be processed by a commercial program is very large.

As you have seen, before being processsed the data must be in an input file on disk or tape. This typically happens by someone manually entering the data from documents at a key-to-disk station (a computer running an editor program that accepts the input and places it on disk).

Because of the large amount of manually entered data, there will be undetected mistakes. As a result, it has to be anticipated that there will be errors in the input file being processed. And because of this, the program to process that data has to include routines to do the following two things:

- Detect as many input data errors as possible
- Correct the errors or output a listing of errors, and either continue processing or stop the program

This whole process is known as *data validation*, and is very important for any program that will be used repeatedly.

If no effort is made to detect input errors, one of two possible undesirable consequences will result:

- The incorrect data will result in incorrect output data. This is the well-known "garbage-in/garbage-out" (or GIGO) effect. Clearly, if a QUANTITY-IN value of 10 and a UNIT-COST-IN value of $20.45 are incorrect, a printed COST-OUT value of QUANTITY-IN * UNIT-COST-IN, $204.50, will be incorrect.

- The incorrect input data will give rise to a run error that causes the program to stop (abnormal ending or abend). For example, blanks in a numeric input field will cause an abend when an attempt is made to use the value in an arithmetic statement. Or, more obviously, the use of an incorrect input value of zero as the divisor in an arithmetic statement will cause an abend.

A program that has good data validation routines will minimize the output of incorrect results, even with bad input data. It will either correct bad input data or output an error listing. Furthermore, it will rarely abend, since much of the offending input data will have been detected before use in a statement that could cause an abend. This will enable the program to list the input data errors and carry on to the next record.

This chapter looks at techniques for detecting, dealing with, and sometimes correcting bad input data.

8.1
Incorrect input data can often be detected

THERE IS A fairly large number of methods used for detecting incorrect input data. These methods are meant to be used when writing a program used on a regular basis. However, it can be difficult for a student in a college course, writing programs solely as assignments, to seriously appreciate the need to detect incorrect input data. It will, in many cases, be a long time before you have to write or maintain a program for regular business use. As a result, material on detecting input errors may seem a bit tedious. It is a bit like architecture students having to learn fire prevention and retardation techniques. You naturally want to get on with designing elegant programs or edifices, not concentrating on what could go wrong.

With this in mind, this section has been organized for ready reference, assuming that error detection techniques are the least likely to be remembered of all COBOL programming techniques, despite their commercial importance.

Use a checklist for input error detection when writing a program

Let us begin with a summary list of the techniques used for detecting and correcting input errors. The idea is for this list to be used as a checklist when writing a program. You may want to make photocopies of this list and check the items against the input data used in any particular program.

You will now see the details of how the tests associated with these checks can be carried out. Again, much of this material is just for reference.

CHECKLIST | **Input Data Error**

1. **Incorrect data type**
   - **Class test** A numeric field may need to be checked to confirm that it does not contain alphanumeric data, especially spaces.
     An alphanumeric field may occasionally need to be checked to confirm that it does not contain numeric data.
   - **Sign test** If a numeric field is expected to contain either a positive or negative value, the sign of the value may need to be checked.
   - **Missing data test** Missing data normally are entered as blanks. It may be necesssary to check both numeric and alphanumeric fields for blanks.

2. **Unreasonable data values**
   - **Range test** It may be necessary to check that an input value, such as a salary, lies within a specified range, for instance, $8,000 to $125,000.
   - **Outer limit test** It may be necessary to check that a value does not exceed a certain limit. For example, if a business has eight warehouses, the number of warehouses with a certain part type must not exceed eight.

3. **Excess number of a particular character or digit**
   - It may be necessary to count the number or type of a particular character in a field, and even replace a particular type of character with another. For example, a product identification code may be correct only if it has exactly two alphabetic characters coming before a zero. As a further example, a zero in a numeric field may have been keyed in as a blank, which should be detected and replaced with a zero. This is an example of correction of input data, and is done using the INSPECT verb.

4. **Incorrect condition name values**
   - Single character codes, such as 'S' for SINGLE, 'M' for MARRIED are often used with condition names in input data to save keystrokes. It may be necessary to check that only allowed codes occur in the input data, for instance, 'S', 'M', 'D', or 'W' for MARITAL-STATUS.

5. **Out-of-sequence records**
   - Input records often have to appear in ascending or descending order by a particular field. The program may have to check for out-of-sequence records.

6. **Incorrect check digit computed**
   - Important numeric fields, such as Social Security numbers, often have an additional digit, called a *check digit*, with a value computed from the digits of the field. If the computed value does not match the value of the check digit, then an input error has occurred.

Use the class test for detecting incorrect data type

Suppose you have an input buffer record structure with these fields:

```
01 BUFFER-RECORD-IN.
   05 QUANTITY-IN   PIC 9(08).
   05 CUSTOMER-IN   PIC X(08).
```

When a READ has been executed for the input file, this group identifier will contain data. No abend will occur if the READ transfers alphabetic data from disk to QUANTITY-IN, or numeric data from disk to CUSTOMER-IN. Transfer of data from disk to buffer takes place like an alphanumeric MOVE in which BUFFER-RECORD-IN is treated as an alphanumeric identifier. Thus, following a READ, QUANTITY-IN could contain alphanumeric data and CUSTOMER-IN could contain numeric data. The problem with QUANTITY-IN will show up if you try to use that identifier in any arithmetic statement or move its contents to another numeric identifier, and will result in an abend. The problem with CUSTOMER-IN is unlikely to result in an abend, but will result in some kind of error in the output.

To detect such an error with QUANTITY-IN, you simply code something resembling:

```
IF QUANTITY-IN IS NOT NUMERIC
     PERFORM 1000-NON-NUMERIC-ERROR
ELSE
  ADD QUANTITY-IN TO TOTAL-QUANTITY
  ...
END-IF.
```

before using it in an arithmetic expression. It is considered good practice in commercial programs to make a check like this for every numeric input field before initial arithmetic use.

Similarly, you can check that CUSTOMER-IN contains only alphabetic characters with a statement such as:

```
IF CUSTOMER-IN IS NOT ALPHABETIC
     PERFORM 1100-NON-ALPHABETIC-ROUTINE
ELSE
     MOVE CUSTOMER-IN TO CUSTOMER-OUT
     ...
END-IF.
```

Use the sign test for incorrectly signed data

Suppose that the input record has the field ACCOUNT-BALANCE, as in

```
01 BUFFER-RECORD-IN.
   05 ACCOUNT-BALANCE   PIC S9(05)V99 SIGN LEADING SEPARATE.
      ...
```

and input records are expected to have negative values for ACCOUNT-BALANCE. The negative value should be checked before use by something like this:

```
IF ACCOUNT-BALANCE IS POSITIVE
      PERFORM 1000-POSITIVE-VALUE-ERROR
ELSE
      ADD 5.00 TO OVERDRAWN-PENALTY
      ...
END-IF.
```

Check for blanks as a missing data test

Suppose once more you have input records with the following structure:

```
01 BUFFER-RECORD-IN.
   05 QUANTITY-IN    PIC 9(08).
   05 CUSTOMER-IN    PIC X(08).
```

A common problem is that no value is keyed in for a particular field, so either QUANTITY-IN or CUSTOMER-IN could contain blanks. This is how missing data appear in the input record. Blanks in QUANTITY-IN will, of course, cause an abend if QUANTITY-IN is used in an arithmetic expression. Before such use, something resembling the following can be coded:

```
IF QUANTITY-IN IS NOT NUMERIC
      PERFORM 1000-MISSING-DATA
ELSE
   ADD QUANTITY-IN TO TOTAL-QUANTITY
   ...
END-IF.
```

A class test (for NUMERIC) with QUANTITY-IN can be used, since blanks make the contents of QUANTITY-IN alphanumeric. However, a class test could not be used with CUSTOMER-IN; there you would have to specifically test for blanks.

A reasonableness test involves checking ranges and limits

Reasonableness tests are very simple. The systems analyst, or programmer, decides what is a reasonable range of values for a given field, or what the upper or lower limit should be, and tests for it.

```
IF SALARY < 8000.00 OR SALARY > 125000.00
      PERFORM 1200-SALARY-OUT-OF-RANGE.
IF NUMBER-OF-WAREHOUSES > 8
      PERFORM 1300-TOO-MANY-WAREHOUSES.
```

A systems analyst often designs the system, that is, a collection of programs.

Within a field, it can be necessary to check individual characters. For example, certain characters in an alphanumeric value may have to be digits. As another example, a numeric value should have blanks replaced by zeros. These matters are accomplished using the INSPECT statement. The INSPECT verb allows

- A count of the number of times a given character occurs within the value of an identifier.
- Replacement of a specified number of occurrences of a character within the value of an identifier with another character.

There are two main formats of the INSPECT verb. The first is for counting characters; the second is for replacement of characters. They will be taken in turn.

Format-1 of INSPECT

The first format of INSPECT is used only for counting characters in the value of an identifer. It has the syntax shown in the following box.

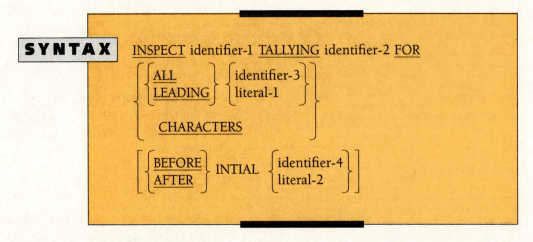

SYNTAX

```
INSPECT identifier-1 TALLYING identifier-2 FOR

    { ALL     } { identifier-3 }
    { LEADING }  { literal-1    }

      CHARACTERS

    [ { BEFORE } INTIAL { identifier-4 } ]
      { AFTER  }         { literal-2    }
```

Suppose again that you have the following input buffer record structure:

```
01 BUFFER-RECORD-IN.
   05 QUANTITY-IN  PIC 9(08).
   05 CUSTOMER-IN  PIC X(08).
```

Some examples of correct format-1 INSPECT statements are

```
MOVE ZERO TO COUNTER-1.
INSPECT QUANTITY-IN TALLYING COUNTER-1 FOR LEADING ZEROS.

MOVE ZERO TO COUNTER-2.
INSPECT CUSTOMER-IN TALLYING COUNTER-2 FOR ALL SPACES.

MOVE ZERO TO COUNTER-3.
INSPECT CUSTOMER-IN TALLYING COUNTER-3 FOR ALL SPACES
            BEFORE INITIAL ZERO.
```

```
MOVE ZERO TO COUNTER-4.
INSPECT QUANTITY-IN TALLYING COUNTER-4 FOR ALL ZEROS
             AFTER INITIAL '1'.

MOVE ZERO TO COUNTER-5.
INSPECT QUANTITY-IN TALLYING COUNTER-5  FOR ALL '1'
             BEFORE INITIAL '6'.

MOVE ZERO TO COUNTER-6.
INSPECT QUANTITY-IN TALLYING COUNTER-6 FOR ZERO
             AFTER INITIAL '4'.

MOVE ZERO TO COUNTER-7.
INSPECT QUANTITY-IN TALLYING COUNTER-7 FOR CHARACTERS.

MOVE ZERO TO COUNTER-8.
INSPECT QUANTITY-IN TALLYING COUNTER-7 FOR SPACES.
```

The identifier-2 that follows TALLYING is used for counting. It is a numeric identifier that should be initialized to zero before use, and is used for counting specific characters that occur in identifier-1.

Literal-2 (or the contents of identifier-3) must be a single character constant, such as 'A', '8', '%', or SPACES or ZEROS. The occurrences of this character constant that occur in identifier-1 are counted.

After FOR there are seven possibilities. Assume for the first four possibilities that you are counting a specific character, say '0'. The value being inspected is shown on the left, with the result in the counter shown in parentheses on the right:

b0000678	FOR LEADING ZERO	(4)
bb034020	FOR ALL ZERO	(3)
b0034000	FOR ALL ZERO BEFORE INITIAL '4'	(2)
00450003	FOR ALL ZERO AFTER INITIAL '5'	(3)
bb456bbb	FOR CHARACTERS	(3)
b0433676	FOR CHARACTERS BEFORE INITIAL 3	(2)
bb47457b	FOR CHARACTERS AFTER INITIAL 7	(3)

- LEADING means occurrences of the character to the left of any other character (except blanks), are counted.
- ALL means all occurrences of the character in the value are counted.
- ALL . . . BEFORE means all occurrences of the character before the first occurrence of another specified character are counted.
- ALL . . . AFTER means all occurrences of the character after the first occurrence of another specified character are counted.
- CHARACTERS means all characters in the value are counted (blanks do not count as characters).
- CHARACTERS BEFORE means all characters in the value before the first occurrence of a specified character are counted (blanks do not count as characters).
- CHARACTERS AFTER means all characters in the value after the first occurrence of a specified character are counted (blanks do not count as characters).

You could use the format 1 INSPECT to check values in BUFFER-RECORD-IN, as follows. QUANTITY-IN is rejected if it has any spaces in it.

```
MOVE ZERO TO COUNTER-1.
INSPECT QUANTITY-IN TALLYING COUNTER-1
        FOR ALL SPACES.
IF COUNTER-1 > 0
        PERFORM 1000-ERROR-ROUTINE.
```

Format 2 of INSPECT

The second format of INSPECT is used for replacing specific occurrences of a character in the value of an identifier with another character. It is commonly used to replace blanks in numeric quantities with zeros. It has the syntax shown in the following box:

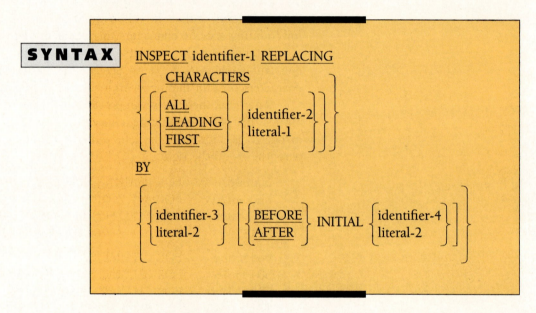

Suppose again you have the input buffer record structure

```
01 BUFFER-RECORD-IN.
    05 QUANTITY-IN  PIC 9(08).
    05 CUSTOMER-IN  PIC X(08).
```

Some correct Format 2 INSPECT statements, and their effects, are

```
INSPECT QUANTITY-IN
    REPLACING ALL SPACES BY ZEROS.          b9b99b60 becomes 09099060.

INSPECT QUANTITY-IN
    REPLACING LEADING ZEROS BY '1'.         00709878 becomes 11709878.

INSPECT QUANTITY-IN
    REPLACING ALL 'O' BY '9'
            BEFORE INITIAL '8'.             06080601 becomes 96980601.

INSPECT QUANTITY-IN
    REPLACING ALL SPACES BY ZEROS
            BEFORE INITIAL ZERO.            bb6b07b8 becomes 006007b8.
```

```
INSPECT QUANTITY-IN
   REPLACING FIRST '2' BY ZERO
              BEFORE INITIAL '6'.          02020602 becomes 00020602.

INSPECT QUANTITY-IN
   REPLACING ALL '8' BY ZEROS
              AFTER INITIAL '4'.           68788488 becomes 68788400.

INSPECT CUSTOMER-IN
   REPLACING FIRST SPACE BY '/'.           SMITHbKb becomes SMITH/Kb.

INSPECT CUSTOMER-IN
   REPLACING CHARACTERS BY ZERO.           G.bPECKb becomes 00b0000b.

INSPECT QUANTITY-IN
   REPLACING ALL SPACES BY '/.'            Error! Non-numeric replacement
```

Note that when characters in a numeric identifier are being replaced, the replacement character must be a digit. Any other character is an error.

The use of CHARACTERS, ALL, LEADING, BEFORE and AFTER is as in Format 1 of INSPECT. When FIRST is used, it means that the first occurrence of the specified character (in left to right order) is to be replaced.

INSPECT . . . REPLACE has other uses besides data validation. However, for data validation, the most common use would be to replace any blanks with zeros in an input field like QUANTITY-IN. To do this you would simply code

```
INSPECT QUANTITY-IN REPLACING ALL SPACES BY ZEROS.
```

It is a common syntax error to forget the ALL. Any other use of INSPECT . . . REPLACE for data validation purposes is rare.

Condition codes must be checked

Remember that condition names, defined as 88-level names, can be used as conditions in IF-statements. Suppose you have the WORKING-STORAGE definition

```
01 MARITAL-STATUS     PIC X.
       88 SINGLE          VALUE 'S'.
       88 MARRIED         VALUE 'M'.
       88 DIVORCED        VALUE 'D'.
       88 WIDOWED         VALUE 'W'.
```

In an IF-statement involving the value of the identifier MARITAL-STATUS, you can code

```
IF MARITAL-STATUS = 'M' OR MARITAL-STATUS = 'D'
     PERFORM 5090-MD-ROUTINE.
```

but it is more convenient to use condition names

```
IF MARRIED OR DIVORCED
     PERFORM 5090-MD-ROUTINE.
```

However, this is not the main advantage of condition names; that is in saving keystrokes when entering data for an input file.

Suppose a record of the input file has the structure

```
01 BUFFER-RECORD-IN.
      05 PERSON-NAME-IN      PIC X(20).
      05 OCCUPATION-IN       PIC X(10).
      05 MARITAL-STATUS-IN   PIC X.
```

In each record of the input file, instead of keying 'SINGLE', 'MARRIED' and so on, for the MARITAL-STATUS-IN field, many keystrokes are saved by only keying 'S', or 'M', 'D', or 'W' for each of very many input records.

When such codes are being used, it is advisable for the program to check each input record as it is read for the presence of one of the allowed codes, and no others. You could use the following to check

```
MOVE MARITAL-STATUS-IN TO MARITAL-STATUS.
IF SINGLE OR MARRIED OR DIVORCED OR WIDOWED
    NEXT SENTENCE
ELSE
    PERFORM 600-WRONG-MARITAL-ROUTINE
END-IF.
```

Alternatively, you could use

```
01 MARITAL-STATUS         PIC X.
   88 VALID-STATUS         VALUES 'S' 'M' 'D' 'W'.
...
  MOVE MARITAL-STATUS-IN TO MARITAL-STATUS.
  IF VALID-STATUS
      NEXT SENTENCE
  ELSE
      PERFORM 600-WRONG-MARITAL-ROUTINE
  END-IF.
```

Checking for correct sequence is often necessary

Input records often have to be in ascending or descending order by a specific sort field. A good example is an input file to be used for generating a summary report. You saw this at the end of Chapter 7, where the input file MONTHLY-SALES was sorted in ascending REGION-IN order. The simplest way to ensure records are in the right order is to have the input file sorted by a sort program.

Another way to perform sequence checking is to have the file read by a program that simply checks the sequence of the records, although it is not common to write a program to do that alone. Sequence checking is normally part of a program that performs some other function, such as printing a report. However, to illustrate the principles involved in sequence checking, this section looks at a separate program for sequence checking alone.

As an example of checking the sequence of records being read in, suppose input records have the structure

```
01 BUFFER-RECORD-IN.
      05 SORT-FIELD-IN    PIC X(4).
      05 B  ...
```

and belong to the file INFILE. They are supposed to be in ascending SORT-FIELD-IN order. Suppose also that the SORT-FIELD-IN values are unique. The following routine can be used to check that they are in ascending order. The sort field of any out-of-sequence record is output to a report file (called ERROR-REPORT), in a detail record with this structure:

```
01 DETAIL-LINE.
    05 FILLER            PIC X      VALUE SPACE.
    05 SORT-FIELD-OUT    PIC X(04).
    05 FILLER            PIC X      VALUE SPACE.
    05 MESSAGE-OUT       PIC X(15).
PROCEDURE DIVISION.
100-MAIN-MODULE.
    PERFORM 500-INITIALIZATION.
    PERFORM 200-CHECK-RECORD-SEQUENCE
        UNTIL MORE-RECORDS = 'NO'.
    PERFORM 600-TERMINATION.
200-CHECK-RECORD-SEQUENCE.
    IF SORT-FIELD-IN < CURRENT-SORT-FIELD
            MOVE 'SEQUENCE ERROR' TO MESSAGE-OUT
            PERFORM 300-ERROR
    ELSE
        IF SORT-FIELD-IN = CURRENT-SORT-FIELD
                MOVE 'DUPLICATE FIELD' TO MESSAGE-OUT
                PERFORM 300-ERROR
        ELSE
                MOVE SORT-FIELD-IN TO CURRENT-SORT-FIELD
                PERFORM 400-PROCESS-NORMAL-RECORD
        END-IF
    END-IF.
    READ INFILE
        AT END MOVE 'NO' TO MORE RECORDS.
300-ERROR.
    MOVE SORT-FIELD-IN TO SORT-FIELD-OUT.
    WRITE BUFFER-RECORD-OUT FROM DETAIL-LINE.
400-PROCESS-NORMAL-RECORD.
    Processing of a normal in sequence record takes place here.
500-INITIALIZATION.
    OPEN INPUT INFILE
         OUTPUT ERROR-REPORT.
    MOVE 'YES' TO MORE-RECORDS.
    MOVE SPACES TO CURRENT-SORT-FIELD.
    READ INFILE
        AT END MOVE 'NO' TO MORE-RECORDS.
600-TERMINATION.
    CLOSE INFILE
          ERROR-REPORT.
    STOP RUN.
```

As each new record is read, the sort field value from the preceding valid record has been kept in the field CURRENT-SORT-FIELD. By comparing the sort field value in the latest record, it can be decided if the latest record is out of sequence or has a duplicate sort field value. Before the next record is read, the sort field from the current record is moved to CURRENT-KEY, but only if that current record is in sequence. Thus, input such as

```
AC23
AG76
AA42      error!
BG56
BG56      error!
BJ00
BH20      error!
BI40      error! but note correct position with respect to BH20
BL34
```

would give output resembling

```
AA42 SEQUENCE ERROR
BG56 DUPLICATE FIELD
BH20 SEQUENCE ERROR
BI40 SEQUENCE ERROR
```

If the values of SORT-FIELD-IN were not required to be unique, so that duplicate values could occur, the IF-statement in the preceding excerpt would have to be changed to

```
IF SORT-FIELD-IN < CURRENT-SORT-FIELD
    MOVE 'SEQUENCE ERROR' TO MESSAGE-OUT
    PERFORM 300-ERROR
ELSE
    MOVE SORT-FIELD-IN TO CURRENT-SORT-FIELD
    PERFORM 400-PROCESS-NORMAL-RECORD
END-IF.
```

Check digit computations help detect errors in numeric fields

It is much easier for key operators to visually check alphanumeric data than numeric data. For example "NIXLN" is obviously meant to be "NIXON". However, there is no simple way for a key operator to visually check a field, such as a Social Security number, made up of a sequence of digits.

With important fields, such as Social Security numbers, employee numbers, and so on, a common technique is to include an additional digit as a check digit. If the value is entered correctly, then a computation, called a check digit routine, applied to the value, should give the value of the check digit.

As an example, suppose you have an n-digit employee number in which an additional final digit is a check digit. A common check digit computation uses the modulus-m method, where $m = n + 1$. Suppose a four-digit employee code, such as 59261, where the final 1 is the check digit. The check digit is computed as

$$5 * 5 + 9 * 4 + 2 * 3 + 6 * 2 = 79$$
$$\text{Remainder of } 79 / m \text{ (or } 79 / 5) = 4$$
$$m - 4 \text{ (or } 5 - 4) = 1$$

The check digit at the end is correct.

In addition to using check digits, with important codes checking procedures that require digits to obey other (possibly secret) rules may be used. There is no limit to the checking rules that can be devised.

When computing with individual digits of a field, it is often necessary to redefine a group identifier on the field. This group identifier is made up of elementary identifiers, each a single digit in length

```
05 EMPLOYEE-CODE                       PIC 9(04).
05 ECD REDEFINES EMPLOYEE-CODE
                 OCCURS 4 TIMES    PIC 9(01).
```

See Chapter 11 for an explanation of the OCCURS clause.

8.2
A program can react to input errors in different ways

THE PRECEDING SECTION examined how to detect the common input errors. To some extent, it also gave examples of what the program should do when an input error is detected. This section will take a brief look at common strategies for dealing with input errors, once they are detected.

Use a checklist of possible program reactions to input errors when writing a program

Common program reactions to input errors are given here, as an options list. You may want to make photocopies of this list to check off options when writing programs.

CHECKLIST   **Input Error Options**

1. Print an explanatory message and stop execution.
2. Print a message following, or within, a detail line and continue processing next input record. When the input record needed to produce a normal detail line is faulty, often only the key field from the input record would be printed in the detail line. The remainder would be the error message.
3. Skip the faulty record as far as normal processing is concerned, but list the record in a separate report at the end of the normal report.
4. Carry on normal processing, either skipping faulty input records or printing data based on them (plus an error message) in the normal report, as long as the number of faulty input records is less than a certain (reasonable) figure. Once this figure is reached, processing is stopped with a message explaining why.
5. Count all good and bad records in the input file, and, if relevant, in batches of input records. Print these totals at the end of processing, perhaps at the end of a normal report.

Good error messages make the operator's life easier

It is important that a clear and concise error message be printed when an input error occurs. The message should enable an operator or analyst to easily find the record that is causing the problem.

In particular, when an input error results in stopping execution of a program, easily understandable and practical information about the cause of the problem should be printed. Remember that the program may stop in the middle of the night, and the operator on duty who is running the program will probably understand little, if any, of the processing the program is carrying out. The operator would simply want to know if anything can be done to restart the program and have it execute without error. If there is, this should be printed when the program first stops.

8.3
Master files are created with built-in validation

A MASTER FILE is a file containing data of both current and long-term worth. An example might be a file containing accounts receivable data. Typically, a new master file is created from an input file that has been keyed in from document data. The complexity of the master file creation program depends solely on the amount of data validation required. The following minimum checks on the input data must be carried out:

- Numeric fields must have numeric quantities.
- Numeric fields should not contain any blanks.
- Alphanumeric fields should not be empty.
- Values should be reasonable.
- Primary key values should be in ascending order.
- Condition codes, if used, must be valid.

Where a record does not pass validation it is output to the control listing with a description of the problems. There may be several things wrong with the record and each problem should be listed. Typically, only a few records will fail validation. When these records have been corrected, they can be inserted into the master as an insertion update operation.

Now let us look at the creation of a master file containing accounts receivable data, called RECEIVABLES-MASTER, as an example. During the processing a control listing is output. The *control listing* lists the records that failed the validation tests.

Detecting errors is the basis of master file creation

The system diagram for the process of creating the master file RECEIVABLES-MASTER is shown in Figure 8.1. The format of records for the input file RECEIVABLES-IN is shown in Figure 8.2. The format for records of the master file will be exactly the same.

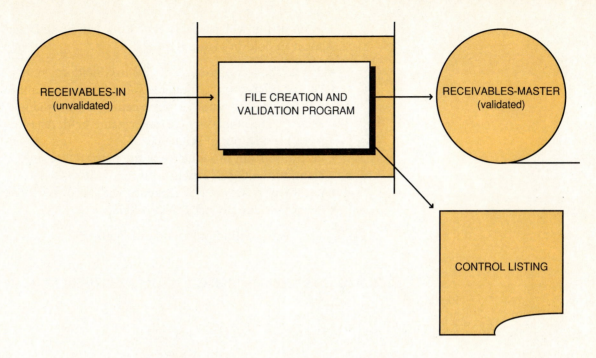

Figure 8.1 *System diagram for process of creating master file RECEIVABLES-MASTER.*

```
---------1---------2---------3---------4
ARTFIELD        145000
AVRILCORP       057500
BANKCORP        ABABAB
BUNTORAMO       078000
CALCOMP         267000
COMPUDISK       034000
bbbbbbbbbbbbbbb067500
DALCORP         134000
DADLOPCORP      023 00
DADLUGER        126000
DENCO           234000
DUBCORP         bbbbbb
CALCON          046500

Columns  1–15     Customer name
        16–21     Amount owing
```

Figure 8.2a *Format of input file RECEIVABLES-IN for creating master file RECEIVABLES-MASTER with same format. Invalid input records are shown in bold.*

```
---------1---------2---------3---------4
XXXXXXXXXXXXXXX999999
---------1---------2---------3---------4
```

Figure 8.2b *Record layout for an input record.*

```
01   RECEIVABLES-RECORD-IN.
     05   RR-CUSTOMER-IN      PIC X(15).
     05   RR-OWING-IN         PIC 9(06).
```

Figure 8.2c *Input area record structure.*

The input file will probably contain a few invalid records, such as those shown in bold in Figure 8.2a.

- Record 3 has a non-numeric OWING field
- Record 5 has an unreasonable value for the amount owing; it is assumed that no customer can owe more than $250,000.
- Record 7 has a missing customer name field. As a result, the record is also out of sequence.
- Record 9 is out of sequence with record 8. It also has a blank in the OWING field.
- Record 10 is also out of sequence with record 8.
- Record 12 has a blank OWING field.

The control listing will look like that in Figure 8.3.

```
          CONTROL LISTING ON CREATION OF RECEIVABLES-MASTER
PAGE  01                                                 12/15/91

RECORD#   INPUT RECORD               PROBLEM

0003      BANKCORP            ABABAB NON-NUMERIC OWING FIELD
0005      CALCOMP             267000 UNREASONABLE AMOUNT
0007                          067500 MISSING CUSTOMER FIELD
                                     OUT-OF-SEQUENCE RECORD
0009      DADLOPCORP          023 00 OUT-OF-SEQUENCE RECORD
                                     BLANKS IN NUMERIC FIELD
                                     NON-NUMERIC OWING FIELD
0010      DADLUGER            126000 OUT-OF-SEQUENCE RECORD
0012      DUBCORP                    BLANKS IN NUMERIC FIELD
                                     NON-NUMERIC OWING FIELD
...
TOTAL RECORDS:     GOOD:  98,678   INVALID:   1,367
```

Figure 8.3a *Control listing format.*

```
        CONTROL LISTING ON CREATION OF RECEIVABLES-MASTER
PAGE   99                                                XXXXXXXX

RECORD#   INPUT RECORD           PROBLEM

9999      XXXXXXXXXXXXXXXXXXXXX  XXXXXXXXXXXXXXXXXXXXXXXXX
9999      XXXXXXXXXXXXXXXXXXXXX  XXXXXXXXXXXXXXXXXXXXXXXXX
9999      XXXXXXXXXXXXXXXXXXXXX  XXXXXXXXXXXXXXXXXXXXXXXXX
9999      XXXXXXXXXXXXXXXXXXXXX  XXXXXXXXXXXXXXXXXXXXXXXXX
9999      XXXXXXXXXXXXXXXXXXXXX  XXXXXXXXXXXXXXXXXXXXXXXXX
...
TOTAL RECORDS:    GOOD:  ZZ,ZZ9   INVALID:  ZZ,ZZ9
```

Figure 8.3b *Printer spacing chart for control listing.*

```
01 DETAIL-LINE-OUT.
    05   FILLER              PIC X              VALUE SPACES.
    05   DL-REC-NUMB-OUT     PIC 9(04)
    05   FILLER              PIC X(05)          VALUE SPACES.
    05   DL-RECORDIN-OUT     PIC X(21).
    05   FILLER              PIC X(02)          VALUE SPACES.
    05   DL-MESSAGE-OUT      PIC X(25).
    05   FILLER              PIC X(75)          VALUE SPACES.
01 TOTAL-LINE-OUT.
    05   FILLER              PIC X              VALUE SPACE.
    05   FILLER              PIC X(23)          VALUE 'TOTAL RECORDS:    GOOD:'.
    05   FILLER              PIC X(02)          VALUE SPACES.
    05   TL-GOOD-RECS-OUT    PIC ZZ,ZZ9.
    05   FILLER              PIC X(03)          VALUE SPACE.
    05   FILLER              PIC X(08)          VALUE 'INVALID:'.
    05   FILLER              PIC X(02)          VALUE SPACE.
    05   TL-BAD-RECS-OUT     PIC ZZ,ZZ9.
    05   FILLER              PIC X(82)          VALUE SPACES.
```

Figure 8.3c Structure of detail and summary line records.

Notice that checking a record for faults does not stop when the first fault that would make the record invalid is detected. Every validity check coded in the program is carried out on each record. If there are multiple faults, these are listed.

A specific fault may cause a record to fail several checks. For example, a missing CUSTOMER field will cause the record to fail the check for a CUSTOMER field value that is not blank. It will also cause the record to fail the sequence check, since the blank CUSTOMER field will mean that the record is out of sequence. Both faults would be listed, as in the case of record 7 in Figure 8.3.

Validity checks account for the complexity of master file creation programs

The COBOL program for creating the master file RECEIVABLES-MASTER from the input file RECEIVABLES-IN (Figure 8.2) and generating a control listing of the kind shown in Figure 8.3, is shown in Figure 8.4. The hierarchy diagram is shown in Figure 8.5.

```
IDENTIFICATION DIVISION.
PROGRAM-ID. MAST1.
ENVIRONMENT DIVISION.
INPUT-OUTPUT SECTION.
FILE-CONTROL.    SELECT RECEIVABLES-IN   ASSIGN TO UT-S-MANDAT10.
                 SELECT RECEIVABLES-MASTER
                                    ASSIGN TO UT-S-RECEIV.
                 SELECT CONTROL-LISTING ASSIGN TO UR-S-SYSPRINT.
```

```
DATA DIVISION.
FILE SECTION.
FD    RECEIVABLES-IN                          LABEL RECORDS ARE STANDARD.
01    RECEIVABLES-RECORD-IN.
      05  RR-CUSTOMER-IN    PIC X(15).
      05  RR-OWING-IN       PIC 9(06).
FD    RECEIVABLES-MASTER                      LABEL RECORDS ARE STANDARD
                                              RECORD CONTAINS 21 CHARACTERS
                                              BLOCK CONTAINS 200 RECORDS.
01    MASTER-RECORD-OUT   PIC X(21).
FD    CONTROL-LISTING                         LABEL RECORDS ARE OMITTED.
01    PRINT-RECORD-OUT    PIC X(133).
WORKING-STORAGE SECTION.
01 WS-WORK-AREAS.
      05 LINE-COUNT        PIC 9(02).
      05 MORE-RECORDS      PIC X(03)     VALUE 'YES'.
      05 VALID-RECORD      PIC X(03).
      05 BAD-RECORD-COUNT  PIC 9(04)     VALUE ZEROS.
      05 RECORD-COUNT      PIC 9(05)     VALUE ZEROS.
      05 SEQUENCE-CONTROL  PIC X(15)     VALUE SPACES.
      05 COUNT-SPACES      PIC 9.
      05 ERROR-COUNT       PIC 9.
      05 WS-PAGE-NUMBER    PIC 9(02)     VALUE ZEROS.
01    PAGE-DATE-LINE-OUT.
      05  FILLER           PIC X         VALUE SPACE.
      05  FILLER           PIC X(06)     VALUE 'PAGE'.
      05  PD-PAGE-NUMB-OUT PIC 9(02).
      05  FILLER           PIC X(47)     VALUE SPACES.
      05  PD-RUN-DATE-OUT  PIC X(08).
      05  FILLER           PIC X(69)     VALUE SPACES.
01 REPORT-HEADER.
      05  FILLER           PIC X(09)     VALUE SPACES.
      05  FILLER           PIC X(124)    VALUE
              'CONTROL LISTING ON CREATION OF RECEIVABLES MASTER'.
01 HEADER-1.
      05  FILLER           PIC X         VALUE SPACES.
      05  FILLER           PIC X(32)     VALUE 'RECORD#  INPUT RECORD'.
      05  FILLER           PIC X(100)    VALUE 'PROBLEM'.
01 DETAIL-LINE-OUT.
      05  FILLER           PIC X         VALUE SPACES.
      05  DL-REC-NUMB-OUT  PIC 9(04).
      05  FILLER           PIC X(05)     VALUE SPACES.
      05  DL-RECORDIN-OUT  PIC X(21).
      05  FILLER           PIC X(02)     VALUE SPACES.
      05  DL-MESSAGE-OUT   PIC X(25).
      05  FILLER           PIC X(75)     VALUE SPACES.
```

```
01  WS-MESSAGE-DATA-OUT.
    05  NUMERIC-BLANKS       PIC X(25)      VALUE 'BLANKS IN NUMERIC FIELD'.
    05  NO-CUSTOMER          PIC X(25)      VALUE 'MISSING CUSTOMER FIELD'.
    05  WRONG-SEQUENCE       PIC X(25)      VALUE 'OUT OF SEQUENCE RECORD'.
    05  UNREASONABLE         PIC X(25)      VALUE 'UNREASONABLE AMOUNT'.
    05  NOT-NUMERIC          PIC X(25)      VALUE 'NON NUMERIC OWING FIELD'.
01  TOTAL-LINE-OUT.
    05  FILLER               PIC X          VALUE SPACE.
    05  FILLER               PIC X(23)      VALUE 'TOTAL RECORDS:    GOOD:'.
    05  FILLER               PIC X(02)      VALUE SPACES.
    05  TL-GOOD-RECS-OUT     PIC ZZ,ZZ9.
    05  FILLER               PIC X(03)      VALUE SPACE.
    05  FILLER               PIC X(08)      VALUE 'INVALID:'.
    05  FILLER               PIC X(02)      VALUE SPACE.
    05  TL-BAD-RECS-OUT      PIC ZZ,ZZ9.
    05  FILLER               PIC X(82)      VALUE SPACES.
PROCEDURE DIVISION.
100-MAIN-MODULE.
*******************************************************************************
*   DIRECTS PROGRAM LOGIC.                                                    *
*******************************************************************************
     PERFORM 200-INITIALIZATION.
     PERFORM 500-PROCESS-INPUT-RECORD
             UNTIL MORE-RECORDS = 'NO'.
     PERFORM 300-TERMINATION.
200-INITIALIZATION.
*******************************************************************************
*   PERFORMED FROM 100-MAIN-MODULE. OPENS FILES, EXTRACTS DATES, PRINTS       *
*   HEADERS, AND READS FIRST RECORD.                                          *
*******************************************************************************
     OPEN INPUT RECEIVABLES-IN
          OUTPUT CONTROL-LISTING
          OUTPUT RECEIVABLES-MASTER.
     MOVE CURRENT-DATE TO PD-RUN-DATE-OUT.
     PERFORM 400-PAGE-HEADERS.
     READ RECEIVABLES-IN
             AT END MOVE 'NO' TO MORE-RECORDS.
300-TERMINATION.
*******************************************************************************
*   PERFORMED FROM 100-MAIN-MODULE. PRINTS SUMMARY LINE. CLOSES FILES,        *
*   STOPS PROCESSING.                                                         *
*******************************************************************************
     PERFORM 600-TOTAL-LINE-OUT.
     CLOSE RECEIVABLES-IN
           RECEIVABLES-MASTER
           CONTROL-LISTING.
     STOP RUN.
```

```
    400-PAGE-HEADERS.
 ***************************************************************************
 *   PERFORMED FROM 200-INITIALIZATION, 900-PRINT-LINE. PRINTS HEADERS.   *
 ***************************************************************************
        WRITE PRINT-RECORD-OUT FROM REPORT-HEADER
                 AFTER ADVANCING PAGE.
        ADD 1 TO WS-PAGE-NUMBER.
        MOVE WS-PAGE-NUMBER TO PD-PAGE-NUMB-OUT.
        WRITE PRINT-RECORD-OUT FROM PAGE-DATE-LINE-OUT
                 AFTER ADVANCING 1 LINE.
        WRITE PRINT-RECORD-OUT FROM HEADER-1
                 AFTER ADVANCING 2 LINES.
        MOVE SPACES TO PRINT-RECORD-OUT.
        WRITE PRINT-RECORD-OUT
                 AFTER ADVANCING 1 LINE.
        MOVE 5 TO LINE-COUNT.
    500-PROCESS-INPUT-RECORD.
 ***************************************************************************
 *   PERFORMED FROM 100-MAIN-MODULE. CHECKS CURRENT RECORD. WRITES VALID   *
 *   RECORD TO DISK. TRACKS TOTAL AND INVALID RECORD COUNTS.               *
 *   READS NEXT RECORD.                                                    *
 ***************************************************************************
        ADD 1 TO RECORD-COUNT.
        MOVE 'YES' TO VALID-RECORD.
        PERFORM 700-CHECK-RECORD.
        IF VALID-RECORD = 'YES'
            WRITE MASTER-RECORD-OUT FROM RECEIVABLES-RECORD-IN
        ELSE
            ADD 1 TO BAD-RECORD-COUNT
        END-IF.
        READ RECEIVABLES-IN
            AT END MOVE 'NO' TO MORE-RECORDS.
    600-TOTAL-LINE-OUT.
 ***************************************************************************
 *   PERFORMED FROM 300-TERMINATION. PRINTS TOTAL LINE WHEN ENTIRE INPUT   *
 *   FILE HAS BEEN PROCESSED.                                              *
 ***************************************************************************
        MOVE BAD-RECORD-COUNT TO TL-BAD-RECS-OUT.
        SUBTRACT BAD-RECORD-COUNT FROM RECORD-COUNT
            GIVING TL-GOOD-RECS-OUT.
        WRITE PRINT-RECORD-OUT FROM TOTAL-LINE-OUT
            AFTER ADVANCING 2 LINES.
    700-CHECK-RECORD.
 ***************************************************************************
 *   PERFORMED FROM 500-PROCESS-INPUT RECORD. PERFORMS A SEQUENCE OF       *
 *   VALIDITY CHECKS. FOR EACH FAILURE A LINE APPEARS IN THE CONTROL       *
 *   LISTING. THUS, A SINGLE FAILING RECORD CAN CAUSE MANY LINES TO BE     *
 *   PRINTED IN THE CONTROL LISTING.  A RECORD LINE PRINTED INCLUDES       *
 *   THE FAILING RECORD ONLY FOR THE FIRST FAILURE. THE NUMBER OF          *
 *   FAILURES IS ALSO TRACKED.                                            *
 ***************************************************************************
```

```
        MOVE ZEROES TO ERROR-COUNT.
        IF RR-CUSTOMER-IN IS EQUAL TO SPACES
                    MOVE NO-CUSTOMER TO DL-MESSAGE-OUT
                    ADD 1 TO ERROR-COUNT
                    PERFORM 800-DETAIL-LINE-OUT
        END-IF.
        IF RR-CUSTOMER-IN <= SEQUENCE-CONTROL
                    MOVE WRONG-SEQUENCE TO DL-MESSAGE-OUT
                    ADD 1 TO ERROR-COUNT
                    PERFORM 800-DETAIL-LINE-OUT
        ELSE
                    MOVE RR-CUSTOMER-IN TO SEQUENCE-CONTROL
        END-IF.
        MOVE 0 TO COUNT-SPACES.
        INSPECT RR-OWING-IN TALLYING COUNT-SPACES FOR ALL SPACES.
        IF COUNT-SPACES > 0
                    MOVE NUMERIC-BLANKS TO DL-MESSAGE-OUT
                    ADD 1 TO ERROR-COUNT
                    PERFORM 800-DETAIL-LINE-OUT
        END-IF.
        IF RR-OWING-IN IS NOT NUMERIC
                    MOVE NOT-NUMERIC TO DL-MESSAGE-OUT
                    ADD 1 TO ERROR-COUNT
                    PERFORM 800-DETAIL-LINE-OUT
        END-IF.
        IF RR-OWING-IN IS NUMERIC
                    IF RR-OWING-IN > 250000
                        MOVE UNREASONABLE TO DL-MESSAGE-OUT
                        ADD 1 TO ERROR-COUNT
                        PERFORM 800-DETAIL-LINE-OUT
                    END-IF
        END-IF.
        IF ERROR-COUNT > 0
            MOVE 'NO' TO VALID-RECORD.
  800-DETAIL-LINE-OUT.
  ***************************************************************************
  *  PERFORMED FROM 700-CHECK-RECORD. PRINTS CONTROL LISTING LINE. FOR    *
  *  FIRST FAILURE A COMPLETE LINE IS PRINTED.  FOR ADDITIONAL FAILURES   *
  *  ONLY THE ERROR MESSAGE IS PRINTED.                                   *
  ***************************************************************************
        IF ERROR-COUNT = 1
            MOVE RECORD-COUNT TO DL-REC-NUMB-OUT
            MOVE RECEIVABLES-RECORD-IN TO DL-RECORDIN-OUT
            MOVE DETAIL-LINE-OUT TO PRINT-RECORD-OUT
            PERFORM 900-PRINT-LINE
            MOVE SPACES TO DETAIL-LINE-OUT
        ELSE
            PERFORM 900-PRINT-LINE
        END-IF.
```

```
        900-PRINT-LINE.
        *********************************************************************
        *   PERFORMED FROM 800-DETAIL-LINE-OUT. PRINTS NORMAL DETAIL LINE OF   *
        *   CONTROL LISTING. PRINTS HEADERS IF NEEDED.                          *
        *********************************************************************
                IF LINE-COUNT >= 45
                        PERFORM 400-PAGE-HEADERS
                END-IF.
                WRITE PRINT-RECORD-OUT
                        AFTER ADVANCING 1 LINE.
                ADD 1 TO LINE-COUNT.
```

Figure 8.4 *Program for creating master file RECEIVABLES-MASTER from the file RECEIVABLES-IN in Figure 8.2a. The program generates a control listing like that in Figure 8.3a.*

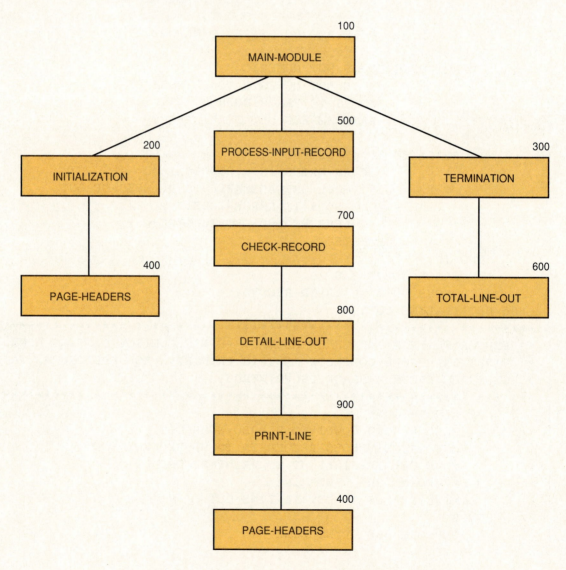

Figure 8.5 *Hierarchy diagram for program in Figure 8.4*

The core of the processing takes place in the paragraph 500-PROCESS-INPUT-RECORD. The paragraph processes a record just read. First the count of records is incremented and then the record is sent for a validity check. Each record receives five checks and a negative result for any check results in a detail line of the control listing.

If a record checked turns out to be valid, it is written as a master file record. If it is not valid, nothing except incrementing the count of invalid records is done. The next record is then read and processed by the next iteration of the paragraph 500-PROCESS-INPUT-RECORD.

This need to check the validity of each record is what complicates a master file creation program. In this example, the records of RECEIVABLES-IN have only two fields, yet it is reasonable to carry out five validity checks. If the record had many fields, as would be common in commercial practice, the paragraph for carrying out validity checks would be lengthy and would probably contain the better part of the program instructions.

Summary

1. When an input file is created manually, it must be assumed that it contains errors. Any program using such a file must contain extensive error checking routines. Each field in a record may have to be checked for (one or more of): the correct data type, reasonable data value, reasonable number of a certain character, correct condition name, and in-sequence field value.
2. One format of the INSPECT verb can be used to count the occurrences of a specific character in an identifier value. A second INSPECT verb format can be used to replace a certain character with another character; however, the INSPECT verb can replace a digit in a numeric identifier only with another digit.
3. When an input error is detected, there are many options open to the program. Most commonly, the record in which the fault is detected is listed in a report, along with an informative message explaining the problem. Processing of remaining records then continues normally. In some simple cases, the program will correct the error and continue normally. In cases in which the error is so severe that the program must be stopped, a message should be printed. This message should indicate clearly what can be done to restart the program and have it execute correctly.

Key Terms

data validation   check digit   control listing

Concept Review Questions

1. In any business organization, why must data, after manual entry, be exhaustively validated by the first program to use the data?
2. What are the two major tasks a data validation routine should perform?
3. How can incorrect input data cause a program to terminate abnormally?
4. List the major types of testing an incoming record field should be subjected to.
5. Suppose that data validation routines are in the paragraph 600-DV. 600-DV has six tests. If you have an input file of 100,000 records with 20 fields in each record, and it takes 0.05 milliseconds for the processor to carry out a test, how much time is spent by the processor in all to test the data in the file?
6. Explain the concept of testing for reasonableness.
7. What is a range test? How is it used?
8. Explain what out-of-sequence records are.
9. What type of test do you use to detect an incorrect data type?
10. Explain what a sign test is and how you use it.
11. How can a validation program repair bad data?
12. What are the two major functions of the INSPECT verb?
13. List common options for dealing with records that test faulty.
14. Why are good error messages important?
15. In a commercial program, if the program stops abnormally, what is the most important information that can be placed in an accompanying error message?

COBOL Language Questions

1. What is the difference, if any, between

   `IF A IS POSITIVE...`   and   `IF A > 0...`

2. Suppose you have the INSPECT statement

   `INSPECT AMOUNT-IN TALLYING TOT1 FOR-clause.`

   For the following values in AMOUNT-IN and FOR-clauses, give the results in TOT1:

AMOUNT-IN	FOR-CLAUSE	TOT1
b00045602	FOR ALL ZERO AFTER INITIAL 6	
00567000	FOR LEADING ZERO	
00560708	FOR ALL ZERO	
00560908	FOR ALL ZERO BEFORE INITIAL 9	
0578000	FOR ALL CHARACTERS	
059890	FOR ALL CHARACTERS BEFORE INITIAL 9	
00567023	FOR ALL CHARACTER AFTER INITIAL 7 .	

3. Suppose you have the INSPECT statement

   `05 AMOUNT-IN 9(08).`

   ...

   `INSPECT AMOUNT-IN REPLACING replacement-clause.`

For the following values in AMOUNT-IN and the replacement clauses, give the new values in AMOUNT-IN:

OLD NAME-IN	REPLACEMENT CLAUSE	NEW NAME-IN
00798004	LEADING ZEROS BY '2'	
bb890bb6	ALL SPACES BY '1'	
45658000	FIRST '5' BY ZERO BEFORE INITIAL 8	
7600892b	FIRST SPACE BY '/'	
00060060	ALL ZEROS BY '1' BEFORE INITIAL 6	

4. Suppose you have the INSPECT statement

    05 NAME-IN X(06).

    ...

    INSPECT NAME-IN REPLACING replacement-clause.

    For the following values in NAME-IN and the replacement clauses, give the new values in NAME-IN:

OLD NAME-IN	REPLACEMENT CLAUSE	NEW NAME-IN
PETERb	FIRST SPACE BY '.'	
ABbbAC	CHARACTERS BY 7	

Programming Assignments

1. **A program to list sequence errors**
    This input file has single field records giving the names of U.S. companies in ascending order:

    ```
    ABBOTT LABS
    ADVANCED MICROSYSTEMS
    ADVANCED SYSTEMS
    AETNA LIFE & CASUALTY
    AHMANSON
    AIRBORNE FREIGHT
    AIR PRODUCTS
    ALASKA AIR GROUP
    ALBERTO-CULVER
    ALBERTSON'S
    ALCOA
    ALCO STANDARD
    ALCO HEALTH SERVICES
    ALEXANDER & ALEX
    ALEXANDER & BALDWIN
    ALLEGHENY POWER
    ALLEGHENY
    ALLEGHENY INTERNATIONAL
    ALLEGHENY LUDLUM
    ALLIED-SIGNAL
    ALLTEL
    AM INTERNATIONAL
    ```

Enter the names exactly as shown and proof the list carefully. It contains subtle sequence errors. Write a program to list the sequence errors.

2. A program to print first word of a record
Using the same input file as in Assignment 1, write a program to print out the first word in each company name.

3. A program to print multi-word records
Using the same input file as in Assignment 1, write a program to print the company names that are more than one word (one or more spaces within the name). Use a single application of INSPECT with a record to do this.

4. Creation of a validated master file and output of the control listing
The input file is

SOURCE-FILE   Contains unvalidated master records
                            about very reliable electronic parts.

The output files are

NEW-MASTER   Newly created master file
CONTROL-LISTING   Printer file that lists the primary key of
                            every record in the master file. For each
                            key, it gives the status of the record,
                            either accepted or rejected. If rejected,
                            problems are listed.

Some input (SOURCE-FILE) records are

```
---------1---------2---------3
A019400157178J050
A025801594255B106
B4294    2750F155
C437310006025B00A
C346705004250L055
D01T502833X454199
D029405608280B140
D117612506530K230
E036900707250A185
E099401506640T130
E175802855500A178
E566714009265B340
F014909508500K160

...
---------1---------2---------3
```

Columns 01–05   Part type identification code, primary key
         06–09   Quantity in warehouse
         10–13   Price per unit ($dd.dd)
         14–17   Bin code (bin that contains the parts)

Beside the usual problems with input data, the following rules hold for certain fields:

- The part type codes must have a letter as the first character, with digits for the remaining characters.
- The first three digits used in the part type code must not form a number greater than 499.
- The sum of the last two digits of the part type code must be 13.
- The first character of the bin number must be a letter, with digits for the remaining characters.
- The three digits in a bin number must form a number not greater than 299.

The control listing for creating the master file has this format:

```
---------1---------2---------3---------4---------5---------6---------7
                 CONTROL LISTING FOR NEW-MASTER CREATION
PAGE    1                                               05/06/92

PART   QTY     PRICE  BIN         STATUS

A0194  0015    7178   J050        ACCEPTED
A0258  0159    4255   B106        ACCEPTED
B4294          2750   F155        REJECTED
     PROBLEMS:  NON NUMERIC QTY FIELD
C4373  1000    6025   B00A        REJECTED
     PROBLEMS:  INVALID FINAL DIGITS IN PART CODE
                INVALID CHARACTERS IN BIN CODE DIGITS
C3467  0500    4250   L055        ACCEPTED
D01T5  0283    3X45   4199        REJECTED
     PROBLEMS:  INVALID CHARACTERS IN PART CODE DIGITS
                NON NUMERIC PRICE FIELD
                INVALID CHARACTER IN BIN CODE LETTER
D0294  0560    8280   B140        ACCEPTED
D1176  1250    6530   K230        ACCEPTED
E0369  0070    7250   A185        REJECTED
     PROBLEMS:  INVALID FINAL DIGITS IN PART CODE
E0994  0150    6640   T130        ACCEPTED
E1758  0285    5500   A178        ACCEPTED
E5667  1400    9265   B340        REJECTED
     PROBLEMS:  INVALID DIGITS IN PART CODE
                INVALID DIGITS IN BIN CODE
F0149  0950    8500   K160        ACCEPTED
...
---------1---------2---------3---------4---------5---------6---------7
```

The output master file has records in exactly the same format as the input file.

a. Draw the input record layout and spacing chart for the files.
b. Make a list of error messages to be used.
c. Draw the flowchart and hierarchy diagram.
d. Write the program.

SORTING AND MERGING

9

*F*ILE RECORDS ON TAPE or disk frequently have to be sorted – on one or more fields – in either ascending or descending order before being input for processing. For example, to generate a summary report from an input file, the file has to be sorted on field X if you want to sum the values of one identifier for all records with the same X value. If you later want a summary of the values of an identifier for all records with the same field-Y value, then the file will have to be sorted again on field Y.

Thus, an existing file on disk or tape may need to be sorted in different ways for different uses. For example, suppose you have a file of records, each of which describes the amount owed to a business by a customer. Such an amount is usually called an "account receivable," and the file an "accounts receivable file." An input area identifier for an input record from this file could list the customer name and the amount owing, with this structure:

```
01 MASTER-RECORD.
   05 CUSTOMER    PIC X(15).
   05 OWING       PIC 9(06).
```

Typically, some field of a file has unique values and can be used to uniquely identify a record of the file. Such a field is called the primary key. CUSTOMER is an example of a primary key field. In addition, a file that is permanently maintained, frequently updated, and contains some important business data is called a master file. An accounts receivable file is one example of a master file.

In a master file, records would typically be sorted in ascending primary key order, as with the following accounts receivable records:

```
ABELSON        046500
DREXCORP       156000
NATIONALTEK    023000
TORDEK         004500
ZENCRAFT       135300
```

But management might be interested in reviewing the accounts receivable file with the customers who owe most coming first, as in

```
DREXCORP          156000
ZENCRAFT          135300
ABELSON           046500
NATIONALTEK       023000
TORDEK            004500
```

which is a version sorted in descending OWING order. As a result of such needs, it is important to be able to sort a file easily. Sorting a file is a very common operation.

There are two ways to sort a file

There are two main options when it comes to sorting files.

- Use a utility sort program. This will normally be available at your installation and is capable of sorting a wide variety of files once the parameters of the file have been specified for the sort program. No programming effort is needed with this option. It is good for sorting a very large file quickly, but lacks flexibility. Inquire about this option at your installation if you are interested.
- Use the COBOL SORT verb within a COBOL program written for the purpose of sorting a specific file. Programming effort is needed with this option, since a unique program has to be written for sorting a specific file. However, this approach is far more flexible than using a utility sort program.

The COBOL SORT verb is considered in this chapter. In addition, a later section looks at how two or more input files can be combined to produce a sorted output file. This process is called merging, and can be done with either the COBOL SORT or MERGE verb.

9.1
The COBOL SORT verb is used to sort a file

THE SORT VERB can be used in three main ways:

- You can simply sort an input file and generate a sorted output file. This is the simplest application—a straight sort.
- You can subject the file to a procedure prior to the sort. This procedure could, for example, select certain records, or otherwise process records from an input file, and then deliver these records for sorting and generation of a sorted output file. This is called using an *input procedure* with the sort.
- You can sort the input file and then subject the sorted file to a procedure to process the sorted records in some way. This is called use of an *output procedure* with the sort.

This section examines these three ways of using the SORT verb.

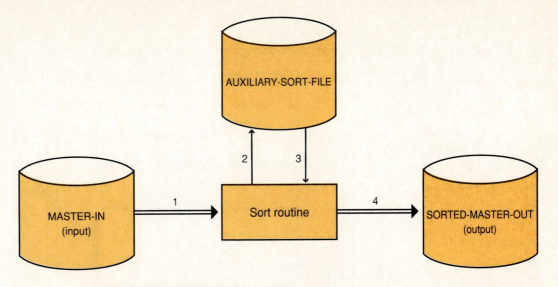

Figure 9.1 *Operation of the SORT verb in the simplest case. Records of the input file are first transferred to the auxiliary sort file, where they are sorted. Then they are transferred to the output file.*

The straight sort is a simple use of the SORT verb

Within a COBOL program, if you use the SORT verb in the simplest possible way, a single execution of the SORT command will accomplish the following:

- Transfer (or *release*) the records of an input file into another auxiliary file, called an *auxiliary sort file* or sort file, or work file
- Sort the auxiliary sort file
- Transfer (or *return*) the sorted records from the auxiliary sort file to a newly created output file

This process is diagrammed in Figures 9.1 and 9.2. The programmer decides the names of the existing input file, new output file, and the auxiliary sort file. The diagram uses the obvious names MASTER-IN, SORTED-MASTER-OUT, and AUXILIARY-SORT-FILE. The input and output files can be on tape or disk, although the auxiliary sort file is usually on disk.

The diagram in Figure 9.1 is a system diagram. It gives an overview of what happens when the SORT command is executed. Essentially, an auxiliary program of instructions, or sort routine, is executed. This is a standard routine that does not have to be written by the programmer.

Figure 9.2 gives more detail of the process. The sort routine has three components:

- A release component, which transfers records one by one from the input file to the auxiliary sort file
- A sort component, which sorts the records in the auxiliary sort file
- A return component, which returns the records one by one from the auxiliary sort file to the output file

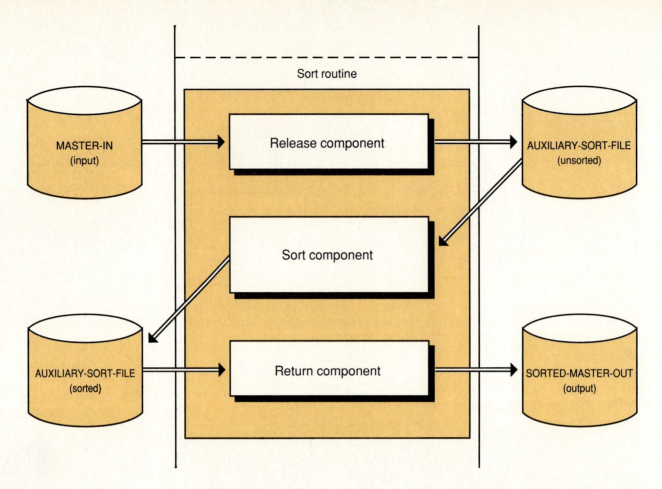

Figure 9.2 *Further details of the operation of the SORT verb. The SORT routine has three components. The release component delivers input records to the auxiliary SORT file. The SORT component sorts these records, producing a sorted version. The return component returns records from the auxiliary SORT file to the output file.*

The figure shows what these three components do. Note that the auxiliary sort file appears twice, first as the output (unsorted) of the release component and second as the output (sorted) of the sort component.

Elementary Sort Program

This section looks at a simple program to sort a receivables file, such as the one discussed earlier, in which records have the structure

```
01 MASTER-RECORD.
   05 CUSTOMER    PIC X(15).
   05 OWING       PIC 9(06).
```

The input file is assumed to be either unsorted or sorted in CUSTOMER order. The program sorts the output file in descending OWING order. The input and output files are MASTER-IN and SORTED-MASTER-OUT, and the auxiliary file is called AUXILIARY-SORT-FILE. Thus, Figures 9.1 and 9.2

apply to this sort. The sort program is shown in Figure 9.3. Statements and definitions associated with the SORT verb are shown in bold.

```
IDENTIFICATION DIVISION.
PROGRAM-ID. SORTA.
ENVIRONMENT DIVISION.
INPUT-OUTPUT SECTION.
FILE-CONTROL.
    SELECT MASTER-IN              ASSIGN TO UT-S-DISK10.
    SELECT SORTED-MASTER-OUT      ASSIGN TO UT-S-DISK11.
    SELECT AUXILIARY-SORT-FILE    ASSIGN TO UT-S-WORKSORT.
DATA DIVISION.
FILE SECTION.
FD   MASTER-IN                    LABEL RECORDS ARE STANDARD
                                  RECORD CONTAINS 21 CHARACTERS
                                  BLOCK CONTAINS 200 RECORDS.
01   MASTER-RECORD-IN             PIC X(21).
FD   SORTED-MASTER-OUT            LABEL RECORDS ARE STANDARD
                                  RECORD CONTAINS 21 CHARACTERS
                                  BLOCK CONTAINS 200 RECORDS.
01   SORTED-RECORD-OUT            PIC X(21).
SD   AUXILIARY-SORT-FILE          RECORD CONTAINS 21 CHARACTERS.
01   AUX-SORT-RECORD.
     05   FILLER                  PIC X(15).
     05   OWING                   PIC 9(06).
PROCEDURE DIVISION.
100-MAIN-MODULE.
    SORT                          AUXILIARY-SORT-FILE
        ON DESCENDING KEY         OWING
        USING                     MASTER-IN
        GIVING                    SORTED-MASTER-OUT.
    STOP RUN.
```

Figure 9.3 Simple sorting program to sort MASTER-IN and generate the sorted version SORTED-MASTER-OUT.

Apart from STOP RUN, the only verb needed in the PROCEDURE DIVISION is SORT. Here, execution of the SORT statement

```
SORT                  AUXILIARY-SORT-FILE
    ON DESCENDING KEY OWING
    USING             MASTER-IN
    GIVING            SORTED-MASTER-OUT.
```

does the following:

1. Opens MASTER-IN and SORTED-MASTER-OUT
2. Uses MASTER-IN as the input file, from which records are released to AUXILIARY-SORT-FILE

3. Sorts AUXILIARY-SORT-FILE on the field OWING (of the defined buffer record for the file) in descending order
4. Uses SORTED-MASTER-OUT as the output file, to which records are to be returned from the sorted AUXILIARY-SORT-FILE
5. Closes MASTER-IN and SORTED-MASTER-OUT

Notice that in the FILE SECTION of the DATA DIVISION, the auxiliary sort file is defined using SD, instead of FD:

```
SD   AUXILIARY-SORT-FILE    RECORD CONTAINS 21 CHARACTERS.
01   AUX-SORT-RECORD.
     05  FILLER             PIC X(15).
     05  OWING              PIC 9(06).
```

You must use SD. In addition, you must define fields for the buffer record (input area record) for the auxiliary sort file. Only the field or fields to be specified as the sort key or keys with the SORT verb, in this case OWING, must be named. Other fields can be called FILLER, or grouped together under the name FILLER. However, it is not wrong to name these other fields.

As a result of the processing by the program in Figure 9.3, the file MASTER-IN will be unchanged. A sorted version, in descending OWING order, will be in the newly created file SORTED-MASTER-OUT.

Notice that the SORT verb opens and closes the input file to the sort and the sorted output file. This means that, for example, if you wanted to use SORTED-MASTER-OUT for generating a report, following the sort, SORTED-MASTER-OUT would have to be opened again, this time with an OPEN statement. The following would be typical:

```
PROCEDURE DIVISION.
100-MAIN-MODULE.
    SORT                     AUXILIARY-SORT-FILE
      ON ASCENDING KEY       OWING
      USING                  MASTER-IN
      GIVING                 SORTED-MASTER-OUT.
    OPEN    INPUT SORTED-MASTER-OUT
            OUTPUT REPORT-FILE.
    READ SORTED-MASTER-OUT
            AT END MOVE 'NO' TO MORE-RECORDS.
    PERFORM 200-PROCESS-MASTER-RECORD
            UNTIL MORE-RECORDS = 'NO'.
    CLOSE SORTED-MASTER-OUT
          REPORT-FILE.
    STOP RUN.
200-PROCESS-MASTER-RECORD.
    ...
```

Syntax for a Simple SORT

There are three versions of the SORT verb, corresponding to the three main ways it can be used, as listed earlier. The simplest version was used in the program in Figure 9.3 and has the syntax shown here.

The Identifier-1 must be the name of an identifier of the buffer record structure defined for auxiliary-file-name (the auxiliary sort file). Some valid examples are:

Example 1: Sort on one field

```
SORT              SORT-FILE
   ON ASCENDING   CUSTOMER
   USING          CUSTOMER-FILE-IN
   GIVING         SORTED-CUSTOMER-MASTER.
```

Here, CUSTOMER would have to be a field of the buffer record for SORT-FILE. SORTED-CUSTOMER-MASTER records would be sorted in ascending CUSTOMER order.

Example 2: Sort on two fields

```
SORT              AUXILIARY-SORT-FILE
   ON ASCENDING   STATE
   ON ASCENDING   CITY
   USING          JOB-GROWTH-FILE-IN
   GIVING         SORTED-JOB-GROWTH-OUT.
```

Here, the output file SORTED-JOB-GROWTH-OUT would be sorted primarily in ascending STATE order and secondarily in ascending CITY order. The file is sorted primarily on the first sort key listed, secondarily on the second sort key listed, and so on. Some records of output file could be

```
ALABAMA    MOBILE         2.7
ALABAMA    MONTGOMERY     2.4
ALASKA     ANCHORAGE      3.6
ALASKA     FAIRBANKS      2.4
ALASKA     JUNEAU         2.7
   . . .
```

For a given group of records with the same STATE, the records are sorted in ascending CITY order.

Example 3: Sort direct to printer

```
SORT                  AUXILIARY-FILE
   ON DESCENDING KEY  EMPLOYEE-NUMBER
   USING              EMPLOYEE-FILE-IN
   GIVING             PRINTER-FILE-OUT
```

The final sorted file produced (PRINTER-FILE-OUT) does not have to be a tape or disk file; it can simply be a printer file, with the sorted records output to the printer. However, no editing of fields will have taken place; records will have the format of the input file records.

Example 4: Sort with multiple choice

```
SORT            SORT-FILE
   ON ASCENDING    CUSTOMER
   USING           CUSTOMER-FILE-IN
   GIVING          SORTED-CUSTOMER-MASTER
                   WORK-MASTER-1
                   WORK-MASTER-2.
```

You can get multiple copies of the sorted output file by specifying the names of the multiple copies after GIVING. The preceding codes generated three copies. (Note that, although this is a standard COBOL 85 feature, it was not included in COBOL 74, and so may not be available at your computer installation.)

The SORT verb can be used with an input procedure

Suppose you have an input file MASTER-IN with records that have not been validated and are also unsorted. What if you want to generate a master file SORTED-MASTER from this file, with records that are both validated and sorted in ascending order on the field CUSTOMER?

One way to proceed would be in two distinct steps, as follows:

1. Write a validation program and use it with MASTER-IN to generate a validated version of MASTER-IN called VALIDFILE.
2. In a separate part of the same program, sort VALIDFILE to generate SORTED-MASTER, using the SORT statement

```
SORT            AUXILIARY
   ON ASCENDING    CUSTOMER
   USING           VALIDFILE
   GIVING          SORTED-MASTER.
```

If you put these two steps in a single procedure, you would have something resembling this:

```
PROCEDURE DIVISION.
100-MAIN-MODULE.
    OPEN INPUT MASTER-IN
         OUTPUT VALIDFILE
         OUTPUT ERROR-REPORT.
    READ MASTER-IN
         AT END MOVE 'NO' TO MORE RECORDS.
    PERFORM 200-PROCESS-MASTER-RECORD
         UNTIL MORE-RECORDS = 'NO'.
```

```
      CLOSE MASTER-IN
            VALIDFILE          note, VALIDFILE must be closed
            ERROR-REPORT.
      SORT                AUXILIARY-SORT-FILE
         ON ASCENDING     CUSTOMER
         USING            VALIDFILE    note, SORT opens VALIDFILE
         GIVING           SORTED-MASTER.
      STOP RUN.
200-PROCESS-MASTER-RECORD.
   MOVE 'YES' TO VALID-RECORD.
   PERFORM 300-VALIDATE-RECORD.
   IF VALID-RECORD = 'YES'
   WRITE VALIDFILE-RECORD-OUT
         FROM MASTER-RECORD-IN
   ELSE
         PERFORM 400-LIST-IN-ERROR-REPORT
   END-IF.
   READ MASTER-IN,
         AT END MOVE 'NO' TO MORE-RECORDS.
300-VALIDATE-RECORD.
...
400-LIST-IN-ERROR-REPORT.
...
```

Note that VALIDFILE must be closed before applying the SORT verb, which opens the file again.

There is nothing wrong with this approach, except the need for an additional intermediate file VALIDFILE. If the file were large, this could mean tying up a lot of scarce storage space.

You can do without that intermediate VALIDFILE, however, if you use the input procedure feature of the SORT verb. This is the alternative way to proceed.

The syntax for the SORT verb with an input procedure is shown here:

SYNTAX

SORT auxiliary-file-name

ON $\left\{ \begin{array}{l} \underline{ASCENDING} \\ \underline{DESCENDING} \end{array} \right\}$ KEY identifier-1 ...

INPUT PROCEDURE IS procedure-name-1
GIVING output-sorted-file-name

A valid SORT statement is

```
      SORT                AUX-SORT-FILE
      ON ASCENDING        FIELD-A
      ON DESCENDING       FIELD-B
      INPUT PROCEDURE     200-VALIDATION-PARAGRAPH
      GIVING              MASTER-OUT.
```

Instead of the records being delivered directly from an input file to AUX-SORT-FILE on execution of the SORT statement, the input routine 200-VALIDATION-PARAGRAPH would be executed. This would deliver the input records to AUX-SORT-FILE, following some processing, for example, validation.

Let us take a specific example of the use of SORT with an input procedure. This example is similar to the preceding one without the use of an input procedure. Suppose you need to create a sorted master from input records that are both unsorted and not validated. The input file MASTER-IN contains receivables data, with this record structure

```
01 MASTER-RECORD-IN.
   05 CUSTOMER    PIC X(15).
   05 OWING       PIC 9(06).
```

and records such as

```
NATIONALTEK    023000
ZENCRAFT       ABABAB
ABELSON        046000
TORDEK         00  00
DREXCORP       156000

. . .
```

Let us assume the only thing that could invalidate an input record is a non-numeric OWING field. To generate the new sorted and validated master file SORTED-MASTER, with records sorted on CUSTOMER, you could use the program in Figure 9.4. The definitions and statements related to the use of the SORT verb are shown in bold.

The auxiliary sort file is used for the actual sorting, as before, and is defined with SD. The field CUSTOMER, defined with the buffer record structure AUX-SORT-RECORD, is used as the sort key.

This time, the SORT statement

```
SORT                AUXILIARY-SORT-FILE
   ON ASCENDING KEY CUSTOMER
   INPUT PROCEDURE  200-PRIOR-VALIDATION
   GIVING           SORTED-MASTER.
```

specifies an input procedure called 200-PRIOR-VALIDATION. The execution of this procedure causes valid records from MASTER-IN to be placed in AUXILIARY-SORT-FILE.

The execution of the SORT statement performs the following:

1. Opens SORTED-MASTER
2. Executes the procedure 200-PRIOR-VALIDATION. This procedure reads MASTER-IN records in sequence, then outputs the valid records to AUXILIARY-SORT-FILE and the invalid records to an error report file
3. Sorts AUXILIARY-SORT-FILE on the field CUSTOMER (of the defined buffer record for the file) in ascending order
4. Uses SORTED-MASTER as the final output file, to which records are to be returned from the sorted AUXILIARY-SORT-FILE
5. Closes SORTED-MASTER

```
IDENTIFICATION DIVISION.
PROGRAM-ID. SORT1.
*******************************************************************
*   SORT-1 USES AN INPUT PROCEDURE TO SELECT RECORDS FOR RELEASE TO AN   *
*   AUXILIARY SORT FILE FOR SORTING AND OUTPUT TO A NEW SORTED MASTER.   *
*******************************************************************
ENVIRONMENT DIVISION.
INPUT-OUTPUT SECTION.
FILE-CONTROL.
    SELECT MASTER-IN                    ASSIGN TO UT-S-DISK10.
    SELECT SORTED-MASTER                ASSIGN TO UT-S-DISK11.
    SELECT AUXILIARY-SORT-FILE          ASSIGN TO UT-S-WORKSORT.
    SELECT ERROR-REPORT                 ASSIGN TO UR-S-SYSPRINT.
DATA DIVISION.
FILE SECTION.
FD  MASTER-IN                   LABEL RECORDS ARE STANDARD
                                RECORD CONTAINS 21 CHARACTERS
                                BLOCK CONTAINS 200 RECORDS.
01  MASTER-RECORD-IN.
    05 CUSTOMER-IN              PIC X(15).
    05 OWING-IN                 PIC 9(06).
FD  SORTED-MASTER              LABEL RECORDS ARE STANDARD
                                RECORD CONTAINS 21 CHARACTERS
                                BLOCK CONTAINS 200 RECORDS.
01  SORTED-RECORD-OUT          PIC X(21).
FD  ERROR-REPORT               LABEL RECORDS ARE OMITTED.
01  ERROR-RECORD-OUT.
    05 FILLER                   PIC X(01) VALUE SPACES.
    05 ERRORDATA                PIC X(21).
SD  AUXILIARY-SORT-FILE        RECORD CONTAINS 21 CHARACTERS.
01  AUX-SORT-RECORD.
    05  CUSTOMER                PIC X(15).
    05  FILLER                  PIC 9(06).
WORKING-STORAGE SECTION.
01  WS-WORK-AREAS.
    05 MORE-RECORDS             PIC X(03)         VALUE 'YES'.
    05 VALID-RECORD             PIC X(03).
PROCEDURE DIVISION.
100-MAIN-MODULE.
*******************************************************************
*   100-MAIN-MODULE:  USES THE SORT VERB WITH A PROCEDURE TO SORT THOSE   *
*   RECORDS OF MASTER-IN REMAINING AFTER RECORDS HAVE BEEN REMOVED BY     *
*   THE PROCEDURE 200-PRIOR-VALIDATION.                                   *
*******************************************************************
SORT                AUXILIARY-SORT-FILE
    ON ASCENDING KEY    CUSTOMER
    INPUT PROCEDURE     200-PRIOR-VALIDATION
    GIVING              SORTED-MASTER.
STOP RUN.
```

```
   200-PRIOR-VALIDATION.
***************************************************************************
*   200-PRIOR-VALIDATION:   CALLED UP AT BEGINING OF EXECUTION OF SORT    *
*   IN 100-MAIN-MODULE.  DIRECTS LOGIC FOR ELIMINATING INVALID RECORDS    *
*   FROM MASTER-IN AND PASSING REMAINING RECORDS TO THE SORT ROUTINE      *
*   CONTROLLED BY SORT.                                                   *
***************************************************************************
       OPEN INPUT MASTER-IN
            OUTPUT ERROR-REPORT.
       READ MASTER-IN
               AT END MOVE 'NO' TO MORE-RECORDS.
       PERFORM 300-PROCESS-MASTER-RECORD
                   UNTIL MORE-RECORDS = 'NO'.
       CLOSE MASTER-IN
             ERROR-REPORT.
   300-PROCESS-MASTER-RECORD.
***************************************************************************
*   300-PROCESS-MASTER-RECORD:  PERFORMED FROM 200-PRIOR-VALIDATION.      *
*   CHECKS CURRENT MASTER-IN RECORD FOR VALIDITY AND READS NEXT           *
*   MASTER-IN RECORD.                                                     *
***************************************************************************
       MOVE 'YES' TO VALID-RECORD.
       PERFORM 400-VALIDATE-RECORD.
       IF VALID-RECORD = 'YES'
          RELEASE AUX-SORT-RECORD
                  FROM MASTER-RECORD-IN
        ELSE
          PERFORM 500-LIST-IN-ERROR-REPORT
       END-IF.
       READ MASTER-IN
           AT END MOVE 'NO' TO MORE-RECORDS.
   400-VALIDATE-RECORD.
***************************************************************************
*   400-VALIDATE-RECORD:  PERFORMED FROM 300-PROCESS-MASTER-RECORD.       *
*   CHECKS IF OWING FIELD CONTAINS ONLY DIGITS.                           *
***************************************************************************
       IF OWING-IN IS NOT NUMERIC
              MOVE 'NO' TO VALID-RECORD
       END-IF.
   500-LIST-IN-ERROR-REPORT.
***************************************************************************
*   500-LIST-IN-ERROR-REPORT:  PERFORMED FROM 300-PROCESS-MASTER-RECORD.  *
*   PRINTS INVALID MASTER-IN RECORD IN AN ERROR REPORT.                   *
***************************************************************************
       MOVE MASTER-RECORD-IN TO ERRORDATA.
       WRITE ERROR-RECORD-OUT.
```

Figure 9.4 Program that uses the SORT verb with an input procedure for validating the records of MASTER-IN before sorting them, to generate the sorted, validated master file, SORTED-MASTER.

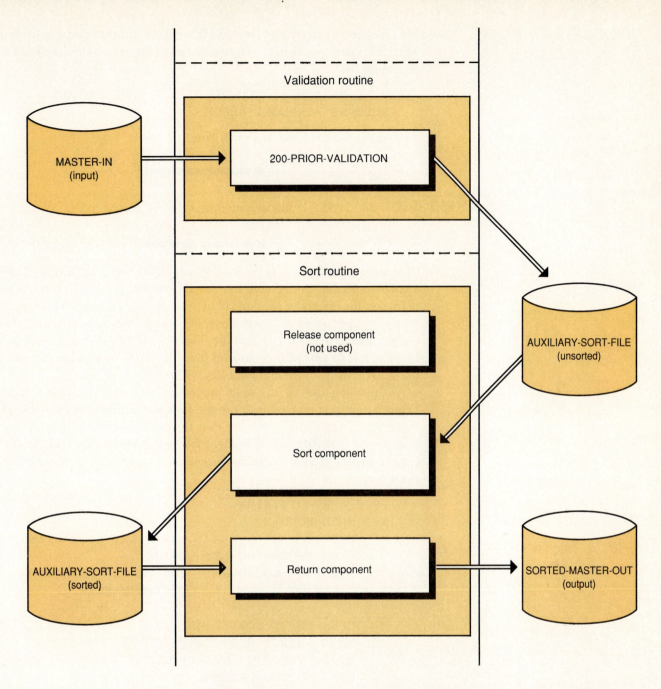

Figure 9.5 *Use of a programmer-written input routine (200-PRIOR-VALIDATION) to feed input records to the auxiliary sort file instead of the release component. The input routine can do such things as selecting only valid input records for transfer or release to the auxiliary sort file.*

This process is illustrated in Figure 9.5.

During the execution of 200-PRIOR-VALIDATION, valid records from MASTER-IN are written out to AUXILIARY-SORT-FILE. However, you *cannot* use WRITE here. You must use the RELEASE verb

```
RELEASE AUX-SORT-RECORD
        FROM MASTER-RECORD-IN.
```

This functions exactly like the WRITE verb, except that you use the word RELEASE instead of WRITE. Thus you can replace the preceding RELEASE statement with:

```
MOVE MASTER-RECORD-IN TO AUX-SORT-RECORD.
RELEASE AUX-SORT-RECORD.
```

The syntax for RELEASE is shown here:

SYNTAX RELEASE output-area-identifier FROM identifier-1

(If you are wondering why you cannot use WRITE to place a record in the auxiliary sort file, understand that all activities connnected with the auxiliary sort file are under the control of the sort routine. If WRITE were used, it would trigger use of the operating system's standard output routine, which cannot handle the auxiliary sort file. The word RELEASE triggers use of the sort routine. As you will see, to read from the auxiliary sort file you cannot use READ either, but must use a RETURN verb.)

Following use of an input procedure to preprocess input records before a sort, you may want to use the final sorted file, SORTED-MASTER. Once again, you must remember that the SORT statement execution will have closed SORTED-MASTER after placing the sorted records in it. If you want to use the file now, perhaps to generate a customer report, you have to open it again, as in

```
PROCEDURE DIVISION.
100-MAIN-MODULE.
    SORT                AUXILIARY-SORT-FILE
        ON ASCENDING KEY  OWING
        INPUT PROCEDURE   200-PRIOR-VALIDATION
        GIVING            SORTED-MASTER.

    OPEN INPUT SORTED-MASTER
         OUTPUT CUSTOMER-REPORT.
    MOVE 'YES' TO MORE-RECORDS.
    READ SORTED-MASTER,
         AT END MOVE 'NO' TO MORE-RECORDS.
    PERFORM 600-PROCESS-MASTER-RECORD
             UNTIL MORE-RECORDS = 'NO'.
    CLOSE SORTED-MASTER
          CUSTOMER-REPORT
    STOP RUN.
```

```
200-PRIOR-VALIDATION.
    OPEN INPUT MASTER-IN
         OUTPUT ERROR-REPORT.
    READ MASTER-IN
         AT END MOVE 'NO' TO MORE-RECORDS.
    PERFORM 300-PROCESS-MASTER-RECORD
            UNTIL MORE-RECORDS = 'NO'.
    CLOSE MASTER-IN
          ERROR-REPORT.
300-PROCESS-MASTER-RECORD.
...
    PERFORM 400-VALIDATE-RECORD.
...
    PERFORM 500-LIST-IN-ERROR-REPORT.
...
400-VALIDATE-RECORD.
...
500-LIST-IN-ERROR-REPORT.
...
600-PROCESS-MASTER-RECORD.
...
```

Study this excerpt carefully; at first glance it may appear that things are "back to front." But they are not. The SORT statement is executed first, which causes 200-PRIOR-VALIDATION and subsidiary routines to be executed. At the end of this, the sorted records are in SORTED-MASTER, which is now closed. Then the statements following the SORT statement are executed, which opens SORTED-MASTER again and processes it.

SORT can be used with an output procedure

Suppose you have a master file of receivables data called MASTER-IN, with the usual two fields CUSTOMER and OWING and with records sorted on the CUSTOMER field. Now you want a formal report (FORMAL-REPORT) that prints the records, with proper headings and page numbers, in descending OWING order.

You could go about this in two ways. One way involves using the SORT verb to generate a new version of the master, SORTED-MASTER, sorted in descending OWING order. Then you could open SORTED-MASTER and read the records one by one to generate the report. The core of the procedure would be

```
PROCEDURE DIVISION.
100-MAIN-MODULE.
    SORT                AUXILIARY-SORT-FILE
       ON DESCENDING KEY  OWING
       USING              MASTER-IN
       GIVING             SORTED-MASTER.

    OPEN INPUT SORTED-MASTER
         OUTPUT FORMAL-REPORT.
```
statements to generate FORMAL-REPORT report
from SORTED-MASTER . . .
```
    CLOSE SORTED-MASTER
          FORMAL-REPORT
    STOP RUN.
```

This is a perfectly correct method. However, you do need the intermediate sorted file SORTED-MASTER, and if this file is large it could mean tying up much scarce storage.

The alternative is to do without the file SORTED-MASTER and read the records out of the file AUXILIARY-SORT-FILE to generate the report. To do this, you must specify the output procedure involved in the SORT statement.

The syntax for SORT with an output procedure is shown here:

SYNTAX

SORT auxiliary-file-name

ON $\left\{\begin{array}{l}\underline{\text{ASCENDING}} \\ \underline{\text{DESCENDING}}\end{array}\right\}$ KEY identifier-1 . . .

<u>USING</u>   unsorted-input-file-name
<u>OUTPUT PROCEDURE</u> IS procedure-name-1

A valid SORT statement is

```
SORT                AUXILIARY-SORT-FILE
ON ASCENDING        A-FIELD
USING               MASTER-IN
OUTPUT PROCEDURE    200-PRODUCE-REPORT
```

When this SORT statement is executed, records of MASTER-IN are first placed in AUXILIARY-SORT-FILE and sorted. Then 200-PRODUCE-REPORT is executed. This procedure will have been designed to withdraw records one by one from AUXILIARY-SORT-FILE and use them to generate (in this case) a report.

You can apply this SORT verb to generating the report FORMAL-REPORT from a sorted version of the input file MASTER-IN. The essentials of the program are shown in Figure 9.6. The definitions and statements related to the use of the SORT verb in the program are shown in bold.

```
IDENTIFICATION DIVISION.
PROGRAM-ID. REP4.
**********************************************************************
*   REP4:   SORTS RECORDS OF MASTER-IN AND USES THE SORTED RECORDS TO   *
*   GENERATE A REPORT FORMAL-REPORT.                                    *
**********************************************************************
ENVIRONMENT DIVISION.
INPUT-OUTPUT SECTION.
FILE-CONTROL.
    SELECT MASTER-IN                    ASSIGN TO UT-S-DISK10.
    SELECT AUXILIARY-SORT-FILE          ASSIGN TO UT-S-WORKSORT.
    SELECT FORMAL-REPORT                ASSIGN TO UR-S-SYSPRINT.
DATA DIVISION.
FILE SECTION.
FD   MASTER-IN                  LABEL RECORDS ARE STANDARD
                                RECORD CONTAINS 21 CHARACTERS
                                BLOCK CONTAINS 200 RECORDS.
01   MASTER-RECORD-IN           PIC X(21).
FD   FORMAL-REPORT              LABEL RECORDS ARE OMITTED.
01   REPORT-RECORD-OUT          PIC X(133).
SD   AUXILIARY-SORT-FILE        RECORD CONTAINS 21 CHARACTERS.
01   AUX-SORT-RECORD.
     05   CUSTOMER              PIC X(15).
     05   OWING                 PIC 9(06).
WORKING-STORAGE SECTION.
...
     05   MORE-RECORDS          PIC X(3)        VALUE 'YES'.
PROCEDURE DIVISION.
100-MAIN-MODULE.
**********************************************************************
*   100-MAIN-MODULE:   USES SORT TO SORT INPUT FILE MASTER-IN AND       *
*   GENERATE A SORTED REPORT FROM THE AUXILIARY SORT FILE BY MEANS OF   *
*   AN OUTPUT PROCEDURE.                                                *
**********************************************************************
    SORT                    AUXILIARY-SORT-FILE
        ON DESCENDING KEY   OWING
        USING               MASTER-IN
        OUTPUT PROCEDURE    200-PRODUCE-REPORT.
    STOP RUN
200-PRODUCE-REPORT.
**********************************************************************
*   200-PRODUCE-REPORT:   CALLED UP BY EXECUTION OF SORT IN 100-MAIN-   *
*   MODULE. GENERATES REPORT FROM AUXILIARY SORT FILE.                  *
**********************************************************************
    OPEN OUTPUT FORMAL-REPORT.
    MOVE CURRENT-DATE TO RUN-DATE.
    PERFORM 500-HEADERS.
    RETURN AUXILIARY-SORT-FILE
            AT END MOVE 'NO' TO MORE-RECORDS.
    PERFORM 300-PROCESS-RECORD
            UNTIL MORE-RECORDS = 'NO'.
```

```
      CLOSE FORMAL-REPORT.
      300-PROCESS-RECORD.
      ****************************************************************
      *   300-PROCESS-RECORD:   PERFORMED FROM 200-PRODUCE-REPORT. PROCESSES   *
      *   CURRENT RECORD EXTRACTED FROM AUXILIARY SORT FILE AND EXTRACTS NEXT  *
      *   RECORD.                                                              *
      ****************************************************************
             PERFORM 400-PRODUCE-DETAIL-LINE.
             RETURN AUXILIARY-SORT-FILE
                  AT END MOVE 'NO' TO MORE-RECORDS.
      400-PRODUCE-DETAIL-LINE.
      ****************************************************************
      *   400-PRODUCE-DETAIL-LINE:   PERFORMED FROM 300-PROCESS-RECORD.   *
      *   GENERATES AND PRINTS DETAIL LINE OF REPORT FROM CURRENT RECORD  *
      *   EXTRACTED FROM AUXILIARY SORT FILE.  WILL PRINT HEADERS, AS NEEDED,  *
      *   AT TOP OF EACH NEW PAGE.                                       *
      ****************************************************************
             ...
      500-HEADERS.
      ...
```

Figure 9.6 *Essentials of a program that uses the SORT verb with an output procedure to process the records of AUXILIARY-SORT-FILE and generate a report FORMAL-REPORT. The input file MASTER-IN is first sorted on the OWING field, and the resulting sorted records are retained in AUXILIARY-SORT-FILE.*

The auxiliary sort file is used for the actual sorting, as before, and is defined with SD. The field OWING, defined with the buffer record structure AUX-SORT-RECORD, is to be used as the sort key.

This time the SORT statement

```
SORT                  AUXILIARY-SORT-FILE
   ON DESCENDING KEY  OWING
   USING              MASTER-IN
   OUTPUT PROCEDURE   200-PRODUCE-REPORT
```

specifies an output procedure called 200-PRODUCE-REPORT. The execution of this procedure causes records from AUXILIARY-SORT-FILE to be read one by one and used to construct the detail lines in the report file FORMAL-REPORT.

The execution of the SORT statement performs the following:

1. Opens MASTER-IN
2. Reads or releases MASTER-IN records in sequence into AUXILIARY-SORT-FILE
3. Sorts AUXILIARY-SORT-FILE on the field OWING (of the defined buffer record for the file) in descending order
4. Executes the procedure 200-PRODUCE-REPORT. This procedure reads (or returns) records from AUXILIARY-SORT-FILE in sequence and uses them to construct the detail lines in the report file FORMAL-REPORT
5. Closes MASTER-IN

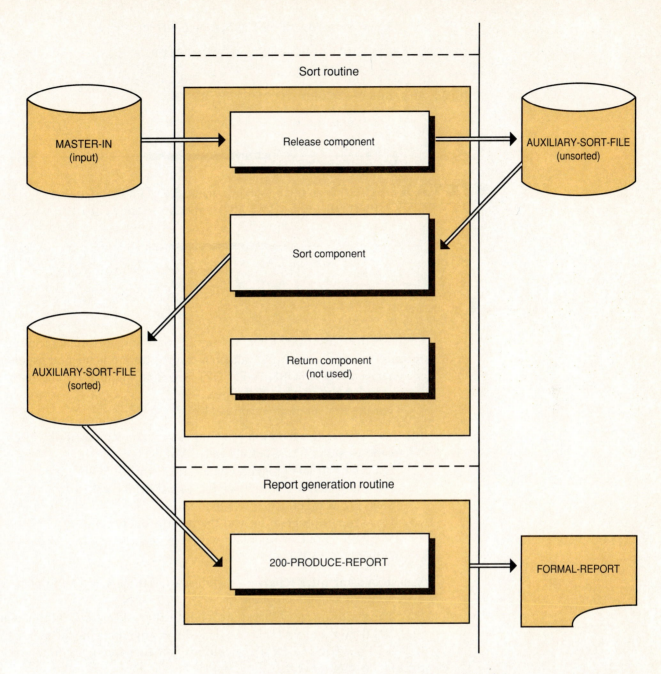

Figure 9.7 *Use of an output procedure instead of the return component to deliver, or return, records to the output file FORMAL-REPORT.*

This process is illustrated in Figure 9.7.

During the execution of 200-PRODUCE-REPORT, records are read, or returned, from the auxiliary sort file one by one. However, again, you cannot use READ here. You must use the RETURN verb

```
RETURN AUXILIARY-SORT-FILE
     AT END MOVE 'NO' TO MORE-RECORDS.
```

This verb functions exactly like the READ verb, except for the using of the word RETURN instead of READ. It places the next record from the auxiliary sorted file in the input area record for that file (AUX-SORT-RECORD).

Thus, the following RETURN statements are equivalent:

```
RETURN AUXILIARY-SORT-FILE INTO MASTER-RECORD,  AT END...

RETURN AUXILIARY-SORT-FILE,  AT END...
MOVE AUX-SORT-RECORD TO MASTER-RECORD.
```

The syntax for RETURN is shown here:

SYNTAX

RETURN auxiliary-sort-file-name-1 RECORD
[INTO identifier-1] AT END imperative-statement-1

SORT can be used with both input and output procedures

Suppose the file MASTER-IN has unvalidated and unsorted receivables records. You want to sort the validated records from this file and use them to generate a report FORMAL-REPORT. There are quite a few alternatives, but the two main ones are as follows.

For the first alternative you could:

1. Use a separate validation program to generate an unsorted valid version of MASTER-IN called VALIDFILE
2. Use a simple sort program containing a straight SORT statement to generate a sorted version of VALIDFILE called SORTED-MASTER-IN
3. Use a report program to read the records of SORTED-MASTER-IN to construct and write the detail lines of FORMAL-REPORT

Instead of using three separate programs, a variation would be to place all three steps in a single program.

The disadvantage of this approach is the need to use two intermediate files (VALIDFILE and SORTED-MASTER-IN) in generating the file FORMAL-REPORT from MASTER-IN. These intermediate files could be eliminated by the second alternative.

This second alternative involves using the SORT verb with both an input and output procedure, as follows:

```
PROCEDURE DIVISION.
100-MAIN-MODULE.
    SORT             AUXILIARY-SORT-FILE
    ON ASCENDING     CUSTOMER
    INPUT PROCEDURE  200-PRIOR-VALIDATION
    OUTPUT PROCEDURE 300-PRODUCE-REPORT.
    STOP RUN.
```

```
200-PRIOR-VALIDATION.
    OPEN INPUT MASTER-IN.
    ...
    READ MASTER-IN...
    ...
    RELEASE...  to auxiliary sort file
    ...
300-PRODUCE-REPORT.
    OPEN OUTPUT FORMAL-REPORT.
    ...
    RETURN AUXILIARY-SORT-FILE, AT END . . .
    ...
    WRITE REPORT-RECORD-OUT.
    ...
```

Execution of the SORT statement first causes 200-PRIOR-VALIDATION to be executed, which releases valid records from MASTER-IN to AUXILIARY-SORT-FILE. It then causes the auxiliary sort file to be sorted. Then 300-PRODUCE-REPORT executes, which takes records (returns records) from AUXILIARY-SORTED-FILE and uses them to generate the detail lines of FORMAL-REPORT.

The order of duplicates can be specified with SORT

Suppose that you are sorting the receivables file MASTER-IN on the OWING field. Now, the OWING field value is not unique and there could easily be two or more records with the value 025000, for example. In what order will a group of records with the same OWING value appear in the final sorted file? With the SORT verbs you have been using, this local order is not predictable. However, if you make use of the clause WITH DUPLICATES IN ORDER, as in

```
SORT              AUXILIARY-SORT-FILE
   ON DESCENDING  OWING, WITH DUPLICATES IN ORDER
   USING          MASTER-IN
   GIVING         SORTED-VERSION.
```

Records of a group with duplicate OWING values will appear in SORTED-VERSION in the order in which they were delivered from MASTER-IN to the auxiliary sort file.

9.2
Merging files requires use of either SORT or MERGE verbs

AN OPERATION that is related to sorting is merging, in which records of two different files are combined into one. However, merging is a much less common operation than sorting, which is used frequently. As an example of merging, suppose you have two master files of receivables data, for two different divisions of the company, as follows:

MASTER-1, DIVISION 1		MASTER-2, DIVISION 2	
ABELSON	046500	BACHDRIVE	075000
DREXCORP	156000	EVENDATA	189000
NATIONALTEK	023000	LASTFOOD	003700
TORDEK	004500	VALIANT	123000
ZENCRAFT	135300		

They could be merged to form a consolidated file for the whole company, called CONSOLIDATED-MASTER, as follows.

ABELSON	046500
BACHDRIVE	075000
DREXCORP	156000
EVENDATA	189000
LASTFOOD	003700
NATIONALTEK	023000
TORDEK	004500
VALIANT	123000
ZENCRAFT	135300

The merging consists of combining the two input files and arranging the records in an order, such as ascending CUSTOMER order.

With COBOL, files can be merged in two main ways:

- By using the SORT verb with an input procedure that delivers records from the files to be merged to the auxiliary sort file for sorting (this is the most common method).
- By using the MERGE verb (this method is occasionally used).

Let us look first at the use of the SORT verb for merging. This is the most important method.

The SORT verb is more flexible for merging

The idea behind using the SORT verb for merging is simple. Suppose you are to merge the files MASTER-1 and MASTER-2 to give the merged file CONSOLIDATED-MASTER, as illustrated before.

You use an input procedure to first deliver all the MASTER-1 records to the auxiliary sort file, and then all of the MASTER-2 records. Thus, at the end of the input procedure, the auxiliary sort file will contain MASTER-1 records coming first, followed by MASTER-2 records. Then the auxiliary sort file will be sorted and its contents delivered to CONSOLIDATED-MASTER, in ascending CUSTOMER order.

One advantage of this approach is that the number of records in the individual input files can be counted, which is usually required. They can also be validated. Another advantage is that the input files to be merged can be sorted, unsorted, or sorted in different ways.

Suppose that MASTER-1 is unsorted, and that MASTER-2 is sorted in descending OWING order, and you want the merged file CONSOLIDATED-MASTER to be sorted in ascending CUSTOMER order. The program to handle this merge is shown in Figure 9.8. Note that the technique used in this

```
IDENTIFICATION DIVISION.
PROGRAM-ID. MERGE1.
*******************************************************************
*   MERGE-1:  MERGES THE UNSORTED MASTER-1 AND SORTED MASTER-2 FILES    *
*   TO FORM A SORTED FILE CONSOLIDATED-MASTER.                          *
*******************************************************************
 ENVIRONMENT DIVISION.
 INPUT-OUTPUT SECTION.
 FILE-CONTROL.
     SELECT MASTER-1                 ASSIGN TO UT-S-DISK10.
     SELECT MASTER-2                 ASSIGN TO UT-S-DISK20.
     SELECT CONSOLIDATED-MASTER      ASSIGN TO UT-S-DISK11.
     SELECT AUXILIARY-SORT-FILE      ASSIGN TO UT-S-WORKSORT.
 DATA DIVISION.
 FILE SECTION.
 FD   MASTER-1                   LABEL RECORDS ARE STANDARD.
                                 RECORD CONTAINS 21 CHARACTERS
                                 BLOCK CONTAINS 200 RECORDS.
* THIS EXISTING FILE IS UNSORTED.
 01   MASTER-1-RECORD-IN         PIC X(21).
 FD   MASTER-2                   LABEL RECORDS ARE STANDARD.
                                 RECORD CONTAINS 21 CHARACTERS
                                 BLOCK CONTAINS 200 RECORDS.
* THIS EXISTING FILE IS SORTED IN DESCENDING OWING ORDER.
 01   MASTER-2-RECORD-IN         PIC X(21).
 FD   CONSOLIDATED-MASTER        LABEL RECORDS ARE STANDARD
                                 RECORD CONTAINS 21 CHARACTERS
                                 BLOCK CONTAINS 200 RECORDS.
* THIS FILE TO BE CREATED BY MERGING MASTER-1 AND MASTER-2 AND
* SORTING IN ASCENDING CUSTOMER ORDER.
 01   CON-MAST-RECORD-OUT   PIC X(21).
 SD   AUXILIARY-SORT-FILE     RECORD CONTAINS 21 CHARACTERS.
* THIS IS A TEMPORARY FILE IN WHICH THE SORTING TAKES PLACE.
 01   AUX-SORT-RECORD.
     05   CUSTOMER               PIC X(15).
     05   FILLER                 PIC 9(06).
 WORKING-STORAGE SECTION.
 01   WS-WORK-AREAS.
     05   MORE-RECORDS       PIC X(03) VALUE 'YES'.
     05   MASTER-1-COUNT     PIC 9(06) VALUE ZEROES.
     05   MASTER-2-COUNT     PIC 9(06) VALUE ZEROES.
 PROCEDURE DIVISION.
 100-MAIN-MODULE.
*******************************************************************
*   100-MAIN-MODULE:  USES THE SORT VERB WITH A PROCEDURE TO DELIVER   *
*   RECORDS OF MASTER-1 AND MASTER-2 FOR MERGING AND GENERATE A MERGED *
*   FILE.                                                              *
*******************************************************************
     SORT                       AUXILIARY-SORT-FILE
       ON ASCENDING KEY         CUSTOMER
       INPUT PROCEDURE          200-COLLECT-INPUT-RECORDS
       GIVING                   CONSOLIDATED-MASTER.
     STOP RUN.
```

```
 200-COLLECT-INPUT-RECORDS.
**********************************************************************
*   200-COLLECT-INPUT-RECORDS:   CALLED UP BY SORT VERB EXECUTION.    *
*  DELIVERS RECORDS OF MASTER-1 AND MASTER-2 FOR MERGING.             *
**********************************************************************
      OPEN INPUT MASTER-1
           INPUT MASTER-2.
      READ MASTER-1
           AT END MOVE 'NO' TO MORE-RECORDS.
      PERFORM 300-PROCESS-MASTER-1-RECORD
           UNTIL MORE-RECORDS = 'NO'.
      MOVE 'YES' TO MORE RECORDS.
      READ MASTER-2,
           AT END MOVE 'NO' TO MORE-RECORDS.
      PERFORM 400-PROCESS-MASTER-2-RECORD
           UNTIL MORE-RECORDS = 'NO'.
      CLOSE  MASTER-1
             MASTER-2.
      DISPLAY 'COUNT OF MASTER-1 RECORDS: ', MASTER-1-COUNT.
      DISPLAY 'COUNT OF MASTER-2 RECORDS: ', MASTER-2-COUNT.
 300-PROCESS-MASTER-1-RECORD.
**********************************************************************
*  300-PROCESS-MASTER-1-RECORD:  PERFORMED FROM 200-COLLECT-INPUT-    *
*  RECORDS.  DELIVERS MASTER-1 RECORDS TO THE AUXILIARY SORT FILE.    *
**********************************************************************
      ADD 1 TO MASTER-1-COUNT.
      RELEASE AUX-SORT-RECORD FROM MASTER-1-RECORD-IN.
      READ MASTER-1
           AT END MOVE 'NO' TO MORE-RECORDS.
 300-PROCESS-MASTER-2-RECORD.
**********************************************************************
*  300-PROCESS-MASTER-2-RECORD:  PERFORMED FROM 200-COLLECT-INPUT-    *
*  RECORDS.  DELIVERS MASTER-2 RECORDS TO THE AUXILIARY SORT FILE.    *
**********************************************************************
      ADD 1 TO MASTER-2-COUNT.
      RELEASE AUX-SORT-RECORD FROM MASTER-2-RECORD-IN.
      READ MASTER-2
           AT END MOVE 'NO' TO MORE-RECORDS.
```

Figure 9.8 *Program that uses the SORT verb with an input procedure to merge two input files MASTER-1 and MASTER-2 and generate the merged and sorted file CONSOLIDATED-MASTER.*

program could also merge more than two files. As usual, what is shown in bold relates to the use of SORT.

The flexibility of using the SORT verb with an input procedure is the reason for its popularity in business. With this approach, you can select specific records for merging from each of the input files and count and validate the input records.

Input files can be initially unsorted, or sorted differently from the output file. Finally, you can use an output procedure if the merged records are merely to be used immediately, as in the generation of a special report, instead of being stored in a new file, such as CONSOLIDATED-MASTER.

There are file format restrictions for merging with SORT

Note that you cannot feed just any files to the auxiliary sort file for sorting. In the preceding example, MASTER-1 and MASTER-2 records had identical format, so there was no problem. You *can* feed records from files with different formats to the auxiliary sort file, but you must observe the following:

- The records from all files that are to be fed to the auxiliary sort file should be the same length and equal in length to a record of the auxiliary sort file.
- The lengths, positions, and types of all fields to be used as sort keys must be the same in the files to be merged and in the auxiliary sort file. The other fields can be in different positions in the records of the different files; that is, they need not have the same format.

As an example, suppose you have two files with different types of records to be merged. Assume both files, RECEIV-1 and RECEIV-2, hold receivables data. The record structures for these files could be as follows:

```
01 RECEIV-1-RECORD.
    05   RECORD-TYPE-CODE   PIC 9.         value always 1
    05   CUSTOMER           PIC X(15).
    05   CITY               PIC X(20).
    05   OWING              PIC 9(06).
01 RECEIV-2-RECORD.
    05   RECORD-TYPE-CODE   PIC 9.         value always 2
    05   CUSTOMER           PIC X(15).
    05   OWING              PIC 9(06).
    05   FILLER             PIC X(20)
```

The two types of records have different formats, but both have the same length (42 characters). In addition, the field CUSTOMER has the same type, length, and position in both types of records.

Thus, both types of records could be delivered to the auxiliary sort file for merging and sorting in order by the CUSTOMER field. However, in turn, the buffer record for the auxiliary sort file would have to be defined with a length of 42 characters, and with a CUSTOMER field of the same type, length, and position:

```
SD    AUXILIARY-SORT-FILE      RECORD CONTAINS 42 CHARACTERS.
01    AUX-SORT-RECORD.
      05   FILLER              PIC X.
      05   CUSTOMER            PIC X(15).
      05   FILLER              PIC X(26).
```

When the auxiliary sort file is being sorted, the sorting routine checks only the sort key field and ignores the others. All records in the auxiliary sort file must be the same length, as well. Where input records are not the same length, the input procedure should be used to add blanks to the shorter types of record, so that all records ultimately sent (with the RELEASE verb) to the auxiliary sort file have the same length.

You could, thus, use SORT to merge the files RECEIV-1 and RECEIV-2 with records of unequal length

```
01  RECEIV-1-RECORD.
    05   RECORD-TYPE-CODE    PIC 9.          value always 1
    05   CUSTOMER            PIC X(15).
    05   CITY                PIC X(20).
    05   OWING               PIC 9(06).

                                             record length 42

01  RECEIV-2-RECORD.
    05   RECORD-TYPE-CODE    PIC 9.          value always 2
    05   CUSTOMER            PIC X(15).
    05   OWING               PIC 9(06).

                                             record length 22
```

by defining the records of the auxiliary sort file to be 42 bytes long and the records of the merged file to be 42 bytes long, that is, to match the input file with the longer record length. At the same time, you would define a 42-byte WORKING-STORAGE record:

```
01  WS-RECEIV-2-RECORD.
    05   DATA-COMPONENT.
         10   RECORD-TYPE-CODE    PIC 9.
         10   CUSTOMER            PIC X(15).
         10   OWING               PIC 9(06).
    05   FILLER                   PIC X(20)     VALUE SPACES.
```

Before you release a RECEIV-2 record to the auxiliary sort file, you would move RECEIV-2-RECORD to WS-RECEIVE-2-RECORD, and then release this blank-padded record to the auxiliary sort file

```
MOVE RECEIVE-2-RECORD TO DATA-COMPONENT IN WS-RECEIV-2-RECORD.
RELEASE AUX-SORT-RECORD FROM WS-RECEIV-2-RECORD.
```

In this way all the records involved have the same length of 42 bytes.

The MERGE verb is less flexible for merging

Instead of using SORT with an input routine, the special MERGE verb can sometimes be used. Unfortunately, there are so many restrictions on the use of MERGE that in practice programmers are usually forced to use the SORT verb with an input procedure, as just described.

The syntax for the MERGE statement is shown here:

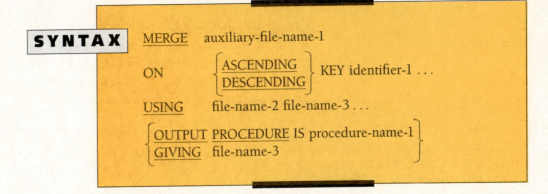

SYNTAX

MERGE   auxiliary-file-name-1

ON   { ASCENDING / DESCENDING } KEY identifier-1 . . .

USING   file-name-2 file-name-3 . . .

{ OUTPUT PROCEDURE IS procedure-name-1 / GIVING file-name-3 }

An example of a MERGE statement is

```
MERGE            AUXILIARY-MERGE-FILE
ON ASCENDING     FIELD-A
ON DESCENDING    FIELD-B
USING            MASTER-IN-1
                 MASTER-IN-2
GIVING           MERGED-FILE-OUT.
```

Here the records of MASTER-IN-1 and MASTER-IN-2 are merged to form MERGED-FILE-OUT, which is sorted primarily on FIELD-A and secondarily on FIELD-B. Just as sorting was carried out in an auxiliary sort file, so merging is carried out in an auxiliary merge file, which has been arbitrarily named AUXILIARY-MERGE-FILE in the preceding statement.

The following rules apply to the MERGE verb:

RULES   **Using MERGE**

1. Output from the auxiliary merge file can be either to an output file or a procedure.
2. Input to the auxiliary file can come only from two or more input files, never from a procedure.
3. Input files and output files must be closed before use of the MERGE statement, which opens them and closes them again afterwards.
4. The input files must all be sorted exactly as required for the output file.
5. Records of different input files must all have the same length, but may have different record formats. However, Rule 4 must hold.
6. If an output procedure is used instead of an output file, when extracting a record from the auxiliary merge file, a RETURN statement must be used.

Let us apply this MERGE verb to a practical problem. Suppose that the master files MASTER-1 and MASTER-2 have records with the structure

```
01    MASTER-RECORD.
      05    CUSTOMER              PIC X(15).
      05    FILLER                PIC 9(06).
```

and both are sorted in ascending CUSTOMER order. Using the program in Figure 9.9, you can merge these two files into a new file called CONSOLIDATED-MASTER, which is also sorted in ascending CUSTOMER order. You cannot count the number of input records from each input file, however.

```
IDENTIFICATION DIVISION.
PROGRAM-ID. MERGE2.
ENVIRONMENT DIVISION.
INPUT-OUTPUT SECTION.
FILE-CONTROL.
SELECT MASTER-1                  ASSIGN TO UT-S-DISK10.
SELECT MASTER-2                  ASSIGN TO UT-S-DISK20.
SELECT CONSOLIDATED-MASTER       ASSIGN TO UT-S-DISK11.
SELECT AUXILIARY-MERGE-FILE      ASSIGN TO UT-S-WORKMGE.
DATA DIVISION.
FILE SECTION.
FD    MASTER-1                   LABEL RECORDS ARE STANDARD.
                                 RECORD CONTAINS 21 CHARACTERS
                                 BLOCK CONTAINS 200 RECORDS.
* SORTED IN ASCENDING CUSTOMER ORDER.
01    MASTER-1-RECORD-IN         PIC X(21).
FD    MASTER-2                   LABEL RECORDS ARE STANDARD.
                                 RECORD CONTAINS 21 CHARACTERS
                                 BLOCK CONTAINS 200 RECORDS.
* SORTED IN ASCENDING CUSTOMER ORDER.
01    MASTER-2-RECORD-IN         PIC X(21).
FD    CONSOLIDATED-MASTER        LABEL RECORDS ARE STANDARD.
                                 RECORD CONTAINS 21 CHARACTERS
                                 BLOCK CONTAINS 200 RECORDS.
* TO BE CREATED SORTED IN ASCENDING CUSTOMER ORDER.
01    CON-MAST-RECORD-OUT        PIC X(21).
SD    AUXILIARY-MERGE-FILE       RECORD CONTAINS 21 CHARACTERS.
01    MERGE-FILE-RECORD.
      05    CUSTOMER             PIC X(15).
      05    FILLER               PIC 9(06).
PROCEDURE DIVISION.
100-MAIN-MODULE.
      MERGE                      AUXILIARY-MERGE-FILE
          ON ASCENDING KEY       CUSTOMER
          USING                  MASTER-1
                                 MASTER-2
          GIVING                 CONSOLIDATED-MASTER.
      STOP RUN.
```

Figure 9.9 *Program that uses the MERGE verb to merge two input files MASTER-1 and MASTER-2, which are sorted in ascending CUSTOMER order, and generates the merged file CONSOLIDATED-MASTER, also sorted in ascending CUSTOMER order.*

COMPREHENSIVE STRUCTURED COBOL

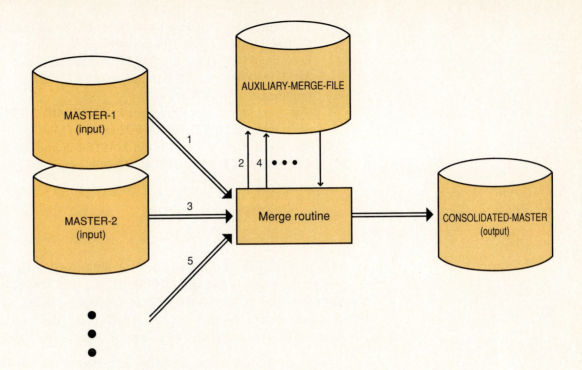

Figure 9.10 *Operation of the MERGE verb in the simplest case. The input files are first transferred to the auxiliary MERGE file, which is then sorted. Then the merged records are transferred to the output file.*

Note carefully that it would not be possible to use MERGE to do any of the following:

- Merge MASTER-1 and MASTER-2, already sorted in ascending CUSTOMER order, to generate CONSOLIDATED-MASTER sorted in descending CUSTOMER order.
- Merge unsorted MASTER-1 and MASTER-2 to generate CONSOLIDATED-MASTER sorted in any order.
- Merge MASTER-1 and MASTER-2, already sorted in ascending CUSTOMER order, to generate CONSOLIDATED-MASTER sorted in ascending OWING order.

The files MASTER-1 and MASTER-2 must be in the same sequence as required for the output file, in this case ascending CUSTOMER order. If you wanted to do any of the things in the preceding list, you would have to use the SORT verb with an input routine for merging.

The MERGE statement and related definitions in the program are shown in bold. The operation of MERGE is illustrated in Figure 9.10. The MERGE statement used in the program in Figure 9.9:

```
MERGE              AUXILIARY-MERGE-FILE
   ON ASCENDING KEY   CUSTOMER
   USING              MASTER-1
                      MASTER-2
   GIVING             CONSOLIDATED-MASTER.
```

carries out the following operations when executed:

1. The input files MASTER-1 and MASTER-2 and the output file CONSOLIDATED-MASTER are opened.
2. Records of MASTER-1 and MASTER-2 are read into AUXILIARY-MERGE-FILE in ascending CUSTOMER order, as required.
3. The merged and sorted records in AUXILIARY-MERGE-FILE are transferred to CONSOLIDATED-MASTER.
4. The input files MASTER-1 and MASTER-2, and the output file CONSOLIDATED-MASTER are closed.

There are also file restrictions for merging with MERGE

Note that you just cannot feed any files to the auxiliary merge file for merging. In the example in Figure 9.9, MASTER-1 and MASTER-2 records were both sorted on the CUSTOMER field in ascending order. Records of the files also had identical format. You can, however, use files with different formats as input files for merging, but you must observe the following:

- The records from input files to be fed to the auxiliary merge file must be the same length, the same length as records of the auxiliary merge file.
- The lengths, positions, and types of all fields to be used as sort fields must be the same in all the input files and in the auxiliary sort file. The other fields in the files to be merged can be different.

As an example of what you could do, suppose that you have two different files to be merged. Assume both files, RECEIV-1 and RECEIV-2, hold receivables data. The record structures for these files could be

```
01  RECEIV-1-RECORD.
    05   RECORD-TYPE-CODE     PIC 9.          value always 1
    05   CUSTOMER             PIC X(15).      sort field, ascending order
    05   CITY                 PIC X(20).
    05   OWING                PIC 9(06).
01  RECEIV-2-RECORD.
    05   RECORD-TYPE-CODE     PIC 9.          value always 2
    05   CUSTOMER             PIC X(15).      sort field, ascending order
    05   OWING                PIC 9(06).
    05   FILLER               PIC X(20).
```

The two types of records have different formats, but both have the same length (42 characters). In addition, the field CUSTOMER, on which both are already sorted, has the same type, length, and position in each type of record.

Both input files must be sorted, on the same field and in the same order as that specified for the output merge file. Thus, both files could serve as input files to the auxiliary merge file for merging in order of the field CUSTOMER. However, in turn, the buffer record for the auxiliary merge file would have to be defined with a length of 42 characters and with a CUSTOMER field of the same type, length, and position:

```
SD   AUXILIARY-MERGE-FILE        RECORD CONTAINS 42 CHARACTERS.
01   MERGE-FILE-RECORD.
        05   FILLER                PIC X
        05   CUSTOMER              PIC X(15).
        05   FILLER                PIC X(26).
```

When the input files are being merged into the auxiliary merge file, the merging routine involved checks only the sort key field and ignores other fields. In addition, it checks that incoming records are sorted in the way the auxiliary merge file is to be sorted. All input records must also be the same length.

Where input records are not the same length, you can always add blanks to the shorter types of record by means of a prior file processing program. The files generated from this prior processing, plus the file with the longest records, can then be used as input files with the MERGE statement. This is admittedly awkward, however, but if you use MERGE, there is no alternative.

If you have to merge records sorted one way into a file to be sorted another way, you have to use the SORT verb with an input routine as described earlier or, alternatively, use SORT to sort the files and then the MERGE verb to merge the sorted file.

COBOL can process a file containing records with different formats or variable length records

The merging process can create files with two or more different types of record formats. For example, if you merged records with the formats

```
01 RECEIV-1-RECORD.
    05   RECORD-TYPE-CODE    PIC 9.          value always 1
    05   CUSTOMER            PIC X(15).
    05   CITY                PIC X(20).
    05   OWING               PIC 9(06).
01 RECEIV-2-RECORD.
    05   RECORD-TYPE-CODE    PIC 9.          value always 2
    05   CUSTOMER            PIC X(15).
    05   OWING               PIC 9(06).
    05   FILLER              PIC X(20)
```

you could get a file CONSOLIDATED-MASTER with records such as:

```
2BRONSON          NEW YORK             006000
2BROWN & CO       DENVER               015000
1BRUNWALD         230500bbbbbbbbbbbbbbbbbbbb
2BRUSSELTECK      BOSTON               130000
1CODATA           001500bbbbbbbbbbbbbbbbbbbb
1COOLTASTECORP    023500bbbbbbbbbbbbbbbbbbbb
2CUVELER          SEATTLE              004000

. . .
```

but all correctly sorted in ascending CUSTOMER order.

Suppose, in later processing of CONSOLIDATED-MASTER, you needed to sum the OWING fields from the file. You would then have a problem, because the OWING fields are in different positions in the different types of record.

To process the file, you must know which type of record has just been read. Since you cannot know this in advance of reading the record, you must check the RECORD-TYPE-CODE field when the record first arrives in the input area record. If this field contains a 1, you move the record to the WORKING-STORAGE group identifier RECEIV-1-RECORD. If it contains a 2, you move the record to the WORKING-STORAGE group identifier RECEIV-2-RECORD; otherwise the record is listed in an error file. This is illustrated here:

```
...
FILE SECTION.
FD  CONSOLIDATED-MASTER          LABEL RECORDS STANDARD.
01  CON-MAST-RECORD.
    05   RECORD-TYPE-CODE-IN  PIC X.
    05   FILLER               PIC X(51).
WORKING-STORAGE SECTION.
01 RECEIV-1-RECORD.
    05   RECORD-TYPE-CODE     PIC 9.          value always 1
    05   CUSTOMER             PIC X(15).
    05   CITY                 PIC X(20).
    05   OWING                PIC 9(06).
01 RECEIV-2-RECORD.
    05   RECORD-TYPE-CODE     PIC 9.          value always 2
    05   CUSTOMER             PIC X(15).
    05   OWING                PIC 9(06).
    05   FILLER               PIC X(20)
01 WS-SUM                     PIC 9(7)            VALUE ZEROES.
01 MORE-RECORDS               PIC X(3)            VALUE 'YES'.
01 WS-SUM-OUT                 PIC $*,***,**9.
PROCEDURE DIVISION.
100-MAIN-MODULE.
    OPEN INPUT CONSOLIDATED-MASTER.
    READ CONSOLIDATED-MASTER,
        AT END MOVE 'NO' TO MORE-RECORDS.
    PERFORM 200-PROCESS-RECORD
        UNTIL MORE-RECORDS = 'NO'.
    MOVE WS-SUM TO WS-SUM-OUT.
    DISPLAY 'TOTAL AMOUNT RECEIVABLE IS: ', WS-SUM-OUT.
    CLOSE CONSOLIDATED-MASTER.
    STOP RUN.
200-PROCESS-RECORD.
    IF RECORD-TYPE-CODE-IN = 1
        MOVE CON-MAST-RECORD TO RECEIV-1-RECORD
        ADD OWING IN RECEIV-1-RECORD TO WS-SUM
```

```
FUQUA INDUSTRIES      02337-0148CONGLOMERATE
CHRYSLER              84573+4325AUTOMOTIVE
MARTIN MARIETTA       14557+0247AEROSPACE
ADVANCED MICRO        02481-0341SEMICONDUCTORS
GENCORP               05134+0044AEROSPACE
GENERAL DYNAMICS      24872+1124AEROSPACE
```

Columns 01–21   Company name
         22–26   Quarterly revenue ($ million), last digit fractional
         27–31   Quarterly profits ($ million), last digit fractional
         32–45   Industry sector

1. **Check writing program**
   Write a program, using the SORT verb, to sort the input file by
   ascending industry sector primarily, and descending revenue order
   secondarily. After the sort, the program should open the sorted file
   and print the contents as a check (no need for editing or a report
   format, unless your instuctor asks for it).

2. **Program that sorts on profit**
   Write a program, using the SORT verb to sort the input file on
   quarterly profit. Have the program print the resulting file. Study it
   carefully. Is the result satisfactory? What could be done about it?

3. **Program to print report of profit makers**
   Use an input procedure to sort, in ascending sector order primarily
   and descending company order secondarily, the records in the
   input file for which there is a quarterly profit. Have the program
   print the resulting file after the sort.

4. **Program to print report of losers**
   Use an output procedure to sort, in ascending sector order primarily and descending profit order secondarily, the records in the input
   file for which there is a quarterly loss. Have the program print the
   resulting file after the sort. (Why is use of an input procedure better in this case?)

5. **Simultaneous sort and output**
   Use an input procedure to sort, in ascending company order, the
   records in the input file for which there is a quarterly loss. At the
   same time, an output procedure should be used to have the program print the resulting file as a report, with the following format:

```
---------1---------2---------3---------4---------5---------6---------7
          COMPANIES WITH A QUARTERLY LOSS


COMPANY               REVENUE            LOSS            SECTOR
                      ($ mil.)           ($ mil.)


ADVANCED MICRO        $ 248.1            $ 34.1          SEMICONDUCTORS
...
```

10

CONTROL-BREAK PROCESSING

OBJECTIVES

- To explain the concept of a control break
- To demonstrate how to write single and multiple control-break programs
- To illustrate why a major control break must force a minor control break
- To show the structured programming concepts of module coherence and independence
- To demonstrate debugging techniques

OUTLINE

10.5 Debugging techniques with complex programs need to be mastered
The READY TRACE command lists executed paragraph names
DISPLAY outputs contents of one or more identifiers
EXHIBIT functions similarly to DISPLAY

CONTROL-BREAK PROCESSING is most commonly used to generate reports that contain summaries of data from a large number of groups of input records. In Chapter 7 there was an example in which four summaries had to be made, from four groups of input records. Control-break processing was not needed there because the number of records in each group was known in advance. When you do not know in advance how many input records are needed to generate a summary line, you must use *control-break processing*.

There are different levels of control-break processing. Single-level control-break processing is used where data in records is summarized for each group of input records that have the same value for a certain field, called the *control field*. Two-level control-break processing is used when summaries of data from groups of input records, plus summaries from subgroups within those groups, are needed; typically, two control fields are involved in two-level control-break processing. Similarly, three-level control-break processing involves three control fields and three levels of summaries, and so on. Up to four levels of control-break processing are common in business.

10.1 Single-level control-break processing is used with summary reports

THIS SECTION looks at single-level control-break processing. To understand control-break processing, it is best to look first at the results of such processing. After that the principles behind the processing will be explained.

Suppose you take a slightly altered version of the input file MONTHLY-SALES from Chapter 7. In the new version, each record gives the monthly housing sales of a salesperson at a national real estate business. Each salesperson sells units in only one city. The input file is shown in Figure 10.1

In this file, the records are arranged or sorted in order by the city field. This order is important, since the subsequent processing would be impossible without it. Thus, all the records of salespeople in Albany come first, followed by Boston, and so on. You can imagine this sorted version of MONTHLY-SALES was generated in a separate program that used the SORT verb (Chapter 9).

```
SMITH          EP0030410000ALBANY
JONES          TY0010150000ALBANY
GREEN          F 0152462000ALBANY
PETERSON       PJ0000000000BOSTON
HASSELBACH     RT0020350000BOSTON
. . .
```

Figure 10.1a *Records of input file MONTHLY-SALES.*

```
---------1---------2---------3---------4---------5
XXXXXXXXXXXXXXXX9999999999XXXXXXXXXXXXXXX
---------1---------2---------3---------4---------5
```

Figure 10.1b *Input record layout.*

```
01    SALES-RECORD-IN.
      05    SR-SURNAME-IN          PIC X(13).
      05    SR-INITIAL1-IN         PIC X.
      05    SR-INITIAL2-IN         PIC X.
      05    SR-UNITS-IN            PIC 9(03).
      05    SR-VOLUME-IN           PIC 9(07).
      05    SR-CITY-IN             PIC X(15).
```

Columns	
1–13	Last name of salesperson
14	First initial of salesperson
15	Second initial of salesperson
16–18	Number of units sold in month
19–25	Volume of sales for salesperson for month
26–40	City

Figure 10.1c *Input area record structure.*

Suppose you need a report that contains both a detail record for each input record, plus the total units and total volume for each city, as shown in Figure 10.2. You can see there has to be a break in the detailed reporting, each time the city changes, to allow for the printing of the summary data.

The report in Figure 10.2 would be generated by control-break processing. The SR-CITY-IN value from incoming records is used as a control

```
                   MONTHLY SALES REPORT
PAGE    1                                                 02/09/91

            SALESPERSON          UNITS       VOLUME        CITY
                                 SOLD        OF SALES

            E.P. SMITH            3          $  410,000    ALBANY
            T.Y. JONES            1          $  150,000    ALBANY
            F.   GREEN           15          $2,462,000    ALBANY

TOTALS FOR ALBANY                19         $ 3,022,000

            P.J. PETERSON         0          $        0    BOSTON
            R.T. HASSELBACH       2          $  350,000    BOSTON

TOTALS FOR BOSTON                 2         $   350,000
            ...
            H.P. DEARING          1          $  125,000    DALLAS
            J.L. BUSH             2          $  290,000    DALLAS

PAGE    2                                                 02/09/91

            SALESPERSON          UNITS       VOLUME        CITY
                                 SOLD        OF SALES

            E.F. JONES            4          $  530,000    DALLAS
            T.J. JOHNSON          2          $  350,000    DALLAS
            G.H. BLACK            9          $1,246,000    DALLAS

TOTALS FOR DALLAS                18         $ 2,541,000

            R.U. HARDY            4          $  467,000    DENVER
            ...
```

Figure 10.2a *Output file REPORT-FILE.*

```
 1                     MONTHLY SALES REPORT
 2 PAGE   Z9                                                XXXXXXXX
 3
 4            SALESPERSON          UNITS       VOLUME        CITY
 5                                 SOLD        OF SALES
 6
 7            XXXXXXXXXXXXXXX      Z9          $9,999,999    XXXXXXXXXXXXXXX
 8            XXXXXXXXXXXXXXX      Z9          $9,999,999    XXXXXXXXXXXXXXX
 9            XXXXXXXXXXXXXXX      Z9          $9,999,999    XXXXXXXXXXXXXXX
10            XXXXXXXXXXXXXXX      Z9          $9,999,999    XXXXXXXXXXXXXXX
11
12 TOTALS FOR XXXXXXXXXXXXXXX     ZZ9         $99,999,999
13
14            XXXXXXXXXXXXXXX      Z9          $9,999,999    XXXXXXXXXXXXXXX
15            XXXXXXXXXXXXXXX      Z9          $9,999,999    XXXXXXXXXXXXXXX
16
17
```

Figure 10.2b *Output records laid out on printer spacing chart.*

```
01  DETAIL-LINE-OUT.
     05   FILLER                   PIC X(13)          VALUE SPACES.
     05   DL-SALESPERSON-OUT       PIC X(15).
     05   FILLER                   PIC X(04)          VALUE SPACES.
     05   DL-UNITS-OUT             PIC Z9.
     05   FILLER                   PIC X(11)          VALUE SPACES.
     05   DL-VOLUME-OUT            PIC $9,999,999.
     05   FILLER                   PIC X(04)          VALUE SPACES.
     05   DL-CITY-OUT              PIC X(15).
     05   FILLER                   PIC X(59)          VALUE SPACES.
01  SUMMARY-LINE.
     05   FILLER                   PIC X              VALUE SPACE.
     05   FILLER                   PIC X(11)          VALUE 'TOTALS FOR '.
     05   SL-CITY-OUT              PIC X(15).
     05   FILLER                   PIC X(04)          VALUE SPACES.
     05   SL-TOT-UNITS-OUT         PIC ZZ9.
     05   FILLER                   PIC X(10)          VALUE SPACES.
     05   SL-TOT-VOLUME-OUT        PIC $99,999,999.
     05   FILLER                   PIC X(78)          VALUE SPACES.
```

Figure 10.2c Record structures for detail and summary lines.

identifier. Whenever the SR-CITY-IN value changes, a break in the processing takes place, in order to print the summary line.

This explains the name control-break processing. A change in the value of a control identifier causes a break in the normal processing, that is, a break from the printing of the normal detail lines.

When a control field changes, a summary line is printed

The principle behind control-break processing to generate the typical detail report with summaries shown in Figure 10.2, is illustrated in the file navigation diagram in Figure 10.3. On the left are the records of the input file; on the right the printed lines (or records) of the output report file.

The diagram represents the core of the processing—ignoring such things as page and column headers and new pages. You can see that the input records are read one by one, and are written out, in a clearer format, as detail lines of the report file. However, each time the SR-CITY-IN value in the input record changes, a summary line is printed.

The SR-CITY-IN value segregates the input records into groups. Notice that the first record of the next group has to be read before it can be determined that the SR-CITY-IN value has changed. Thus, SR-CITY-IN is the control field of the input records.

The current city value is kept in a control identifier (call it WS-CONTROL-CITY), which is compared with the control field SR-CITY-IN as each input record is read. When a record is read with its control field SR-CITY-IN that no longer matches the value in the control identifier WS-

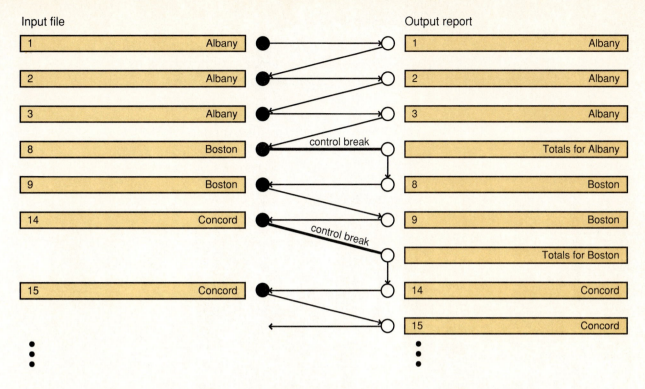

Figure 10.3 *File navigation for a single-level control-break processing.*

CONTROL-CITY, then the control break occurs and a summary line is printed.

Essential Control-Break Pseudocode

Pseudocode can be used to develop the basis of the code for handling control breaks, as shown in the diagram in Figure 10.3. This code ignores page and column headers and assumes an infinitely long page for printing the report.

Main-paragraph.

> OPEN files.
> MOVE 'YES' to More-records.
> READ first MONTHLY-SALES record,
>   at end print message and stop.
> MOVE City-in value in first record to WS-CONTROL-CITY.
> MOVE zero to Total-units and Total-volume.
> PERFORM Process-input-record until More-records = 'NO'.
> PERFORM Control-break-processing.
> CLOSE files.
> STOP.

Process-input-record.

```
IF WS-CONTROL-CITY NOT = City-in THEN
    PERFORM Control-break-processing.
Generate detail record.
Print detail record.
ADD Units-in to Total-units.
ADD Volume-in to Total-volume.
READ next record,
    at end MOVE 'NO' to More-records.
```

Control-break-processing.

```
Skip line.
Generate summary-line using WS-CONTROL-CITY,
    Total-units, and Total-volume.
Print summary-line.
Skip line.
IF More-records = 'YES' THEN
    MOVE City-in value in latest record read to
                WS-CONTROL-CITY
    MOVE zero to Total-units and Total-volume
END-IF.
```

End-of-file processing involves forcing a final control break

The preceding pseudocode routine handles the situation at the end of the file as illustrated in the file navigation diagram in Figure 10.4. When the last record has been read, the summary line for the previous group of records must be generated and printed. However, the necessary control-break processing will not be initiated because the SR-CITY-IN control field has not changed value. Therefore, the very last thing to do before closing the files (see Main-paragraph) is to call up the control-break processing for the last time.

This final use of control-break processing, even though strictly speaking there is no control break, is known as *forcing a control break*. In this final control-break processing, there is no need to reset the totals fields to zero or WS-CONTROL-CITY to the latest CITY-IN value. If you look at the paragraph control-break-processing, you will see that resetting will not occur if there are no records left in the input file.

Pseudocode for Headers with Single-level Control Breaks

There are different strategies for printing headers with control-break generated reports. A common strategy is simply to skip to a new page after a fixed number of lines have been printed 45 (for example) regardless of whether a group of detail lines is being interrupted. This is what is displayed for the page 1-boundary in Figure 10.2.

However, generally you would not want to separate the detail lines from the summary line. In other words, you do not want the detail lines for

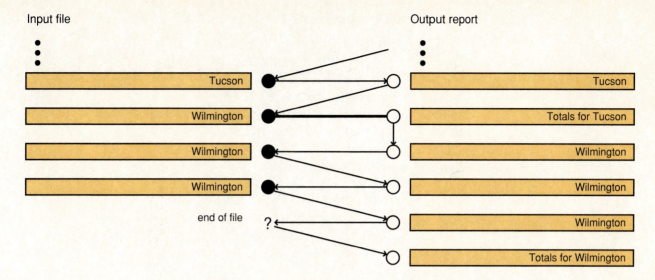

Figure 10.4 *End-of-file processing for a single-level control break. There is no control break to print the final total line. Instead, this is printed by a separate process.*

a city at the bottom of one page and the summary line on the next page, following the headers.

A solution to this is incorporated in the following version of the preceding pseudocode. If you wish, you may devise a different strategy for skipping to a new page and incorporate that as an exercise. A common alternative strategy is to begin a new page with each control break.

Main-paragraph.

    OPEN files.
    Extract date.
    MOVE 'YES' to More-records.
    READ first MONTHLY-SALES record,
           at end print message and stop.
    MOVE City-in value in record just read
      to WS-CONTROL-CITY.
    MOVE zero to Total-units and Total-volume.
    PERFORM Print-headings.
    MOVE 6 to Line-count.
    PERFORM Process-input-record until
      More-records = 'NO'.
    PERFORM Control-break-processing.
    CLOSE files.
    STOP.

Process-input record.

```
IF WS-CONTROL-CITY NOT = City-in THEN
    PERFORM Control-break-processing.
Generate detail record.
IF Line-count >= 45 THEN
    PERFORM Print-headings on new page,
    MOVE 6 to Line-count
END-IF.
Print detail record.
ADD 1 to LINE-COUNT.
ADD Units-in to Total-units.
ADD Volume-in to Total-volume.
READ next record,
    at end MOVE 'NO' to More-records.
```

Control-break-processing.

```
Skip line.
Generate summary-line using WS-CONTROL-CITY,
    Total-units, and Total-volume.
Print summary-line.
ADD 2 to Line-count.
IF Line-count < 45 THEN
    Skip line,
    Add 1 to Line-count
END-IF.
IF More-records = 'YES' THEN
    MOVE CITY-IN value in latest record to
                WS-CONTROL-CITY
    MOVE zero to Total-units and Total-volume.
END-IF.
```

Print-headings.

```
Print report heading.
Print date/page line.
Skip line.
Print column headers.
Skip line.
```

Consider the logic of this pseudocode carefully. Normally, when 45 lines have been printed, the next line is printed on a new page. Now suppose that the the city Houston has 10 detail lines, and that when the tenth of these lines has been printed, the line count shows 45. If there had been an eleventh detail line for Houston, it would have been printed on the next page. But, since there are no further detail lines for that city, the next line is empty and the following one is a summary line, which will be printed on line 47. Thus, here the next line is not printed on a new page.

An attempt to print a summary line when the line count is 45 or 46 does not result in a new page. But an attempt to print a detail line when the line count is 45 will result in a new page. Thus on most pages there will be 45 lines, but on a few pages there will be 46 or 47 lines, because a summary line has been printed at the bottom, as shown here.

	SALESPERSON	UNITS SOLD	VOLUME OF SALES	CITY
line				
...	. . .	. . .	. . .	. . .
42	E.T. JOHNS	3	$ 630,000	DENVER
43	T.Q. JUNDSEN	2	$ 390,000	DENVER
44	G.H. BROWN	8	$1,216,000	DENVER
45				
46	TOTALS FOR DENVER	18	$ 4,541,000	

Note also that in Figure 10.2 there is a blank line before and after the summary line. Naturally, there is no need for the blank line after the summary line if it is at the bottom of the page. This is the reason for the nested IF-statement in the paragraph control-break-processing.

A flowchart for the logic underlying the pseudocode routine is shown in Figure 10.5 on pages 364 and 365.

10.2
A single-level control-break program

THIS SECTION applies the principles from the previous section to write a single-level control-break COBOL program. Control-break programs can be quite complex, but structured programming principles help keep the complexity manageable. The program constructed should have a good level of modularization with a hierarchical structure.

As well as demonstrating single-level control-break programming, the modularization involved is used to demonstrate the concepts of module coherence and independence in structured programs.

Program for simple control-break processing

The program in Figure 10.6 is a COBOL version of the pseudocode routine in the previous section. It reads the input file MONTHLY-SALES (Figure 10.1) and generates the detail report with summary lines for each city, as shown in Figure 10.2. The program generates page and column headers for each page.

A group of records for a given city may span two pages or more. Pages normally have, at most, 45 lines of print. However, when a summary line would otherwise appear immediately after the column headers on a new page, it is instead printed on an extra line (line 46 or 47) of the previous page.

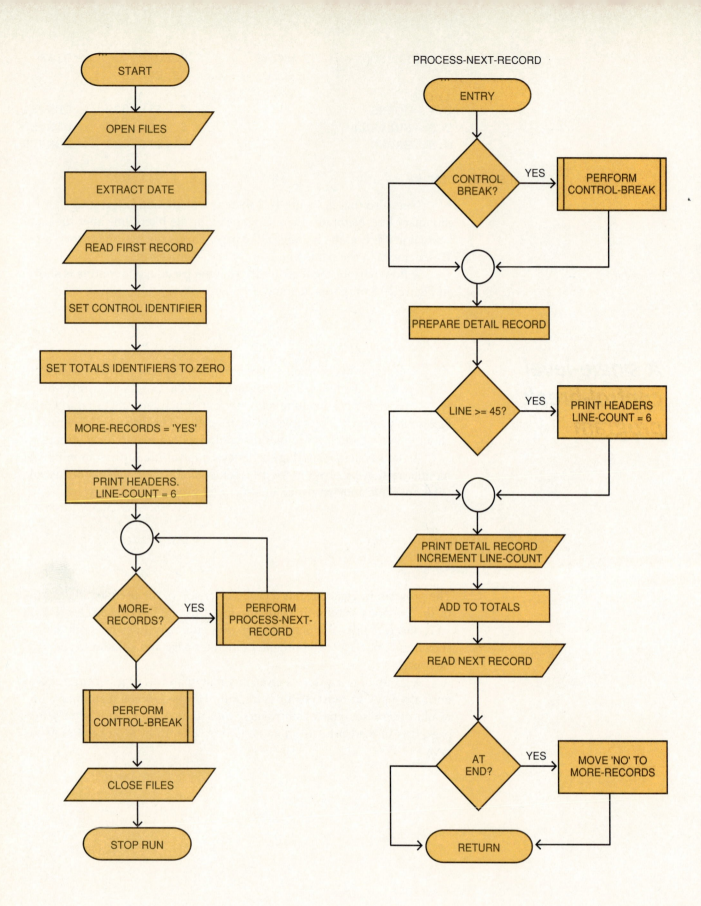

COMPREHENSIVE STRUCTURED COBOL

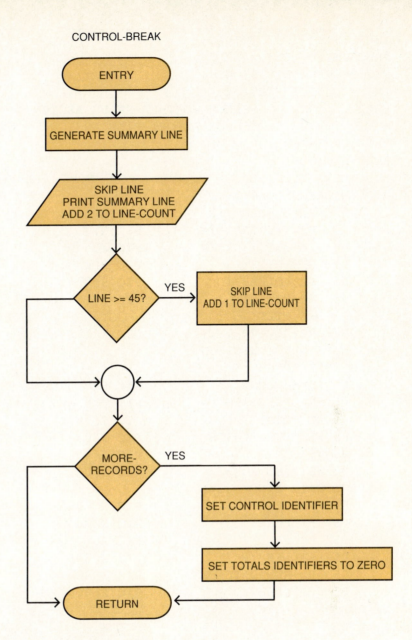

Figure 10.5 Flowchart showing logic of detail and summary line printing.

```
IDENTIFICATION DIVISION.
PROGRAM-ID. CB1.
ENVIRONMENT DIVISION.
INPUT-OUTPUT SECTION.
FILE-CONTROL.    SELECT MONTHLY-SALES ASSIGN TO UT-S-SALES08.
                 SELECT REPORT-FILE ASSIGN TO UR-S-SYSPRINT.
DATA DIVISION.
FILE SECTION.
FD    MONTHLY-SALES                         LABEL RECORDS ARE STANDARD.
01    SALES-RECORD-IN.
      05   SR-SURNAME-IN         PIC X(13).
      05   SR-INITIAL1-IN        PIC X.
      05   SR-INITIAL2-IN        PIC X.
      05   SR-UNITS-IN           PIC 9(03).
      05   SR-VOLUME-IN          PIC 9(07).
      05   SR-CITY-IN            PIC X(15).
FD    REPORT-FILE                           LABEL RECORDS ARE OMITTED.
01    REPORT-RECORD-OUT          PIC X(133).
WORKING-STORAGE SECTION.
01 WS-WORK-AREAS.
      05 LINE-COUNT              PIC 9(02).
      05 MORE-RECORDS            PIC X(03)      VALUE 'YES'.
      05 WS-TOTAL-VOLUME         PIC 9(08).
      05 WS-TOTAL-UNITS          PIC 9(03).
      05 WS-CONTROL-CITY         PIC X(15).
      05 WS-PAGE-NUMBER          PIC 9(02)      VALUE ZERO.
01 PAGE-DATE-LINE-OUT.
      05   FILLER                PIC X          VALUE SPACE.
      05   FILLER                PIC X(06)      VALUE 'PAGE  '.
      05   PD-PAGE-NUMB-OUT      PIC Z9.
      05   FILLER                PIC X(50)      VALUE SPACES.
      05   PD-RUN-DATE-OUT       PIC X(08).
      05   FILLER                PIC X(66)      VALUE SPACES.
01 REPORT-HEADER.
      05   FILLER                PIC X          VALUE SPACE.
      05   FILLER                PIC X(18)      VALUE SPACES.
      05   FILLER                PIC X(20)      VALUE 'MONTHLY SALES
                                                REPORT'.
      05   FILLER                PIC X(94)      VALUE SPACES.
01 COL-HEADER-1.
      05   FILLER                PIC X(13)      VALUE SPACES.
      05   FILLER                PIC X(19)      VALUE 'SALESPERSON'.
      05   FILLER                PIC X(13)      VALUE 'UNITS'.
      05   FILLER                PIC X(14)      VALUE 'VOLUME'.
      05   FILLER                PIC X(04)      VALUE 'CITY'.
      05   FILLER                PIC X(70)      VALUE SPACES.
01 COL-HEADER-2.
      05   FILLER                PIC X(32)      VALUE SPACES.
      05   FILLER                PIC X(13)      VALUE 'SOLD'.
      05   FILLER                PIC X(08)      VALUE 'OF SALES'.
      05   FILLER                PIC X(80)      VALUE SPACES.
```

```cobol
01  DETAIL-LINE-OUT.
    05  FILLER              PIC X(13)           VALUE SPACES.
    05  DL-SALESPERSON-OUT  PIC X(15).
    05  FILLER              PIC X(04)           VALUE SPACES.
    05  DL-UNITS-OUT        PIC Z9.
    05  FILLER              PIC X(11)           VALUE SPACES.
    05  DL-VOLUME-OUT       PIC $9,999,999.
    05  FILLER              PIC X(04)           VALUE SPACES.
    05  DL-CITY-OUT         PIC X(15).
    05  FILLER              PIC X(59)           VALUE SPACES.
01  SUMMARY-LINE.
    05  FILLER              PIC X               VALUE SPACE.
    05  FILLER              PIC X(11)           VALUE 'TOTALS FOR  '.
    05  SL-CITY-OUT         PIC X(15).
    05  FILLER              PIC X(04)           VALUE SPACES.
    05  SL-TOT-UNITS-OUT    PIC ZZ9.
    05  FILLER              PIC X(10)           VALUE SPACES.
    05  SL-TOT-VOLUME-OUT   PIC $99,999,999.
    05  FILLER              PIC X(78)           VALUE SPACES.
01  WS-PERSON-NAME.
    05 WSP-FIRST-INIT       PIC X.
    05 FILLER               PIC X               VALUE '.'.
    05 WSP-SECOND-INIT      PIC X.
    05 WSP-PERIOD           PIC X(02).
    05 WSP-LAST-NAME        PIC X(13).
PROCEDURE DIVISION.
100-MAIN-MODULE.
*****************************************************************************
*   CONTROLS OVERALL PROGRAM LOGIC.                                        *
*****************************************************************************
        PERFORM 200-INITIALIZATION.
        PERFORM 300-PROCESS-INPUT-RECORD UNTIL MORE-RECORDS = 'NO'.
        PERFORM 800-TERMINATION.
200-INITIALIZATION.
*****************************************************************************
*   OPENS FILES, EXTRACTS DATE, READS FIRST RECORD, SETS CONTROL AND       *
*   TOTALS IDENTIFIERS, AND PRINTS HEADERS ON FIRST PAGE.                  *
*****************************************************************************
        OPEN INPUT MONTHLY-SALES
            OUTPUT REPORT-FILE.
        MOVE CURRENT-DATE TO PD-RUN-DATE-OUT.
        READ MONTHLY-SALES,
            AT END MOVE ' NO FIRST RECORD' TO REPORT-RECORD-OUT
                   WRITE REPORT-RECORD-OUT AFTER 1 LINE
                   STOP RUN.
        MOVE SR-CITY-IN TO WS-CONTROL-CITY.
        MOVE ZERO TO WS-TOTAL-UNITS.
        MOVE ZERO TO WS-TOTAL-VOLUME.
        PERFORM 600-PAGE-HEADERS.
        MOVE 6 TO LINE-COUNT.
```

```
 300-PROCESS-INPUT-RECORD.
***********************************************************************
*   PERFORMED FROM 100-MAIN-MODULE. CONTROLS PRINTING OF DETAIL, LINES, *
*   PAGES, AND HEADINGS; READS LATEST INPUT RECORD.                   *
***********************************************************************
        IF SR-CITY-IN NOT EQUAL TO WS-CONTROL-CITY
            PERFORM 500-CONTROL-BREAK-PROCESSING.
        PERFORM 400-GENERATE-DETAIL-LINE.
        IF LINE-COUNT >= 45
            PERFORM 600-PAGE-HEADERS,
            MOVE 6 TO LINE-COUNT
        END-IF.
        ADD SR-UNITS-IN TO WS-TOTAL-UNITS.
        ADD SR-VOLUME-IN TO WS-TOTAL-VOLUME.
        WRITE REPORT-RECORD-OUT FROM DETAIL-LINE-OUT
                    AFTER ADVANCING 1 LINE.
        ADD 1 TO LINE-COUNT.
        READ MONTHLY-SALES
            AT END MOVE 'NO' TO MORE-RECORDS.
 400-GENERATE-DETAIL-LINE.
***********************************************************************
*   PERFORMED FROM 300-PROCESS-RECORD. PREPARES A DETAIL LINE FOR      *
*   PRINTING.                                                         *
***********************************************************************
        PERFORM 700-GENERATE-NAME.
        MOVE SR-UNITS-IN TO DL-UNITS-OUT.
        MOVE SR-VOLUME-IN TO DL-VOLUME-OUT.
        MOVE SR-CITY-IN TO DL-CITY-OUT.
 500-CONTROL-BREAK-PROCESSING.
***********************************************************************
*   PERFORMED FROM 300-PROCESS-RECORD AND 800-TERMINATION.  PRINTS     *
*   SUMMARY LINE AND RESETS CONTROL FIELD AND TOTALS.                 *
***********************************************************************
        MOVE SPACES TO REPORT-RECORD-OUT.
        WRITE REPORT-RECORD-OUT
                AFTER ADVANCING 1 LINE.
        MOVE WS-CONTROL-CITY TO SL-CITY-OUT IN SUMMARY-LINE.
        MOVE WS-TOTAL-UNITS TO SL-TOT-UNITS-OUT IN SUMMARY-LINE.
        MOVE WS-TOTAL-VOLUME TO SL-TOT-VOLUME-OUT IN SUMMARY-LINE.
        WRITE REPORT-RECORD-OUT FROM SUMMARY-LINE
                AFTER ADVANCING 1 LINE.
        ADD 2 TO LINE-COUNT.
        IF LINE-COUNT < 45
            MOVE SPACES TO REPORT-RECORD-OUT
            WRITE REPORT-RECORD-OUT
                AFTER ADVANCING 1 LINE
            ADD 1 TO LINE-COUNT
        END-IF.
        IF MORE-RECORDS = 'YES'
            MOVE SR-CITY-IN TO WS-CONTROL-CITY
            MOVE ZERO TO WS-TOTAL-UNITS
            MOVE ZERO TO WS-TOTAL-VOLUME
        END-IF.
```

```
 600-PAGE-HEADERS.
*****************************************************************************
*   PERFORMED FROM 200-INITIALIZATION AND 300-PROCESS-RECORD.   PRINTS    *
*   PAGE HEADERS WITH CURRENT PAGE NUMBER.                                *
*****************************************************************************
        WRITE REPORT-RECORD-OUT FROM REPORT-HEADER
                            AFTER ADVANCING PAGE.
        ADD 1 TO WS-PAGE-NUMBER.
        MOVE WS-PAGE-NUMBER TO PD-PAGE-NUMB-OUT.
        WRITE REPORT-RECORD-OUT FROM PAGE-DATE-LINE-OUT
                            AFTER ADVANCING 1 LINE
        WRITE REPORT-RECORD-OUT FROM COL-HEADER-1
                            AFTER ADVANCING 2 LINES.
        WRITE REPORT-RECORD-OUT FROM COL-HEADER-2
                            AFTER ADVANCING 1 LINE.
        MOVE SPACES TO REPORT-RECORD-OUT.
        WRITE REPORT-RECORD-OUT
                            AFTER ADVANCING 1 LINE.
 700-GENERATE-NAME.
*****************************************************************************
*   PERFORMED FROM 400-GENERATE-DETAIL-LINE-OUT. CONSTRUCTS OUTPUT        *
*   SALESPERSON FIELD WITH INITIALS COMING FIRST.                         *
*****************************************************************************
        MOVE SR-INITIAL1-IN TO WSP-FIRST-INIT.
        MOVE SR-INITIAL2-IN TO WSP-SECOND-INIT.
        IF WSP-SECOND-INIT = SPACE
            MOVE SPACES TO WSP-PERIOD
          ELSE
            MOVE '. ' TO WSP-PERIOD
        END-IF.
        MOVE SR-SURNAME-IN TO WSP-LAST-NAME.
        MOVE WS-PERSON-NAME TO DL-SALESPERSON-OUT.
 800-TERMINATION.
*****************************************************************************
*   PERFORMED FROM 100-MAIN-MODULE. PRINTS FINAL SUMMARY LINE             *
*   AND CLOSES FILES.                                                     *
*****************************************************************************
        PERFORM 500-CONTROL-BREAK-PROCESSING.
        CLOSE MONTHLY-SALES, REPORT-FILE.
        STOP RUN.
```

Figure 10.6 *Program that reads input file MONTHLY-SALES (Figure 10.1) and outputs summary report in Figure 10.2.*

The hierarchy diagram for this program is shown in Figure 10.7. The core of the logic is in the paragraphs 300-PROCESS-INPUT-RECORD and 500-CONTROL-BREAK-PROCESSING.

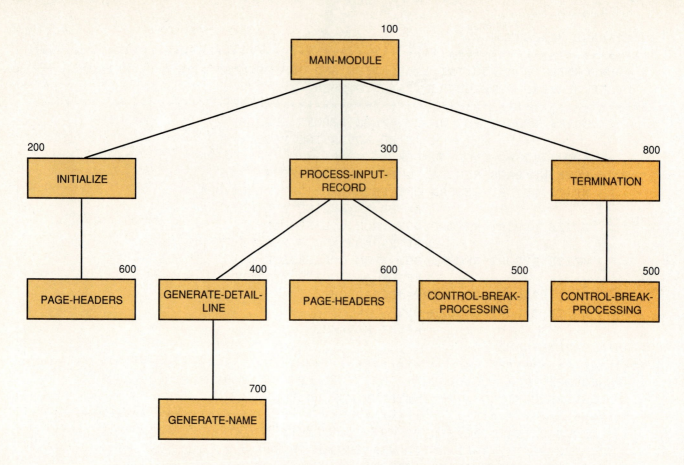

Figure 10.7 *Hierarchy diagram for the routine in Figure 10.6.*

Coherence and independence concepts are used with COBOL paragraphs

Paragraphs or modules in a COBOL program should have both a high degree of coherence and a high degree of independence.

- **Module coherence** A module is said to have a high degree of coherence if the tasks it performs all belong together.
- **Module independence** A module has a high degree of independence if the function it carries out can be altered without any need to alter other modules.

Coherence and independence considerations are at the core of structured programming. If modules in a COBOL program have a high degree of coherence and independence, the program can be much more easily maintained. Let us look at these two considerations separately in the context of the structured program in Figure 10.6.

Module Coherence

COBOL program module will have a high degree of coherence if it performs either a single function or a group of very closely related subfunctions. For example, the module 600-PAGE-HEADERS has a very high degree of coherence. All it does is print different headers.

Printing a report header is a different subfunction from printing column headers. However, all the headers are printed together, so these subfunctions belong together. Thus, the paragraph 400-PAGE-HEADERS is coherent.

Note that the module 600-PAGE-HEADERS does not update LINE-COUNT. Suppose the statement MOVE 6 TO LINE-COUNT was included at the end of this module, so LINE-COUNT was properly updated each time the headers were printed. Would that reduce or weaken the coherence of the module? It would not do so in the program, in Figure 10.6. If you examine the program, you will see that each time 600-PAGE-HEADERS is performed, the statement MOVE 6 TO LINE-COUNT is carried out immediately afterwards. Thus, this statement and the function it represents belong with the module 600-PAGE-HEADERS. The program would consequently be more coherent if the statement was placed within and at the end of 600-PAGE-HEADERS.

Module Independence

For a module to have a high degree of independence, it must be possible to alter it extensively without it being necessary to alter other modules. For example, the module 600-PAGE-HEADERS could undergo extensive alterations without the rest of the program being affected. These alterations would largely consist of changes to the headers.

The independence of the module 600-PAGE-HEADERS could be improved, however. Suppose the module was altered so that the headers printed took up eight lines, instead of the current six. Could that alteration be made independently of the other modules? No—because in the module superior to 600-PAGE-HEADERS, the identifier LINE-COUNT is set to 6 each time 600-PAGE-HEADERS is performed. Thus, if the change were carried out without also altering the superior modules, the printing would go quite wrong.

If, instead of having the statement MOVE 6 TO LINE-COUNT outside of 600-PAGE-HEADERS, it was placed at the end of the module 600-PAGE-HEADERS, the independence of the module would be improved. Suppose you did this, and that the number of header lines printed by the module was changed to eight. The last statement of the module would have to be changed to MOVE 8 TO LINE-COUNT. But this additional change would be internal to the module, so it could take place without having to alter other modules. In addition, it would be more obvious to any programmer making this change that a different setting would be needed for LINE-COUNT, and thus a change to the MOVE statement. This increased independence would therefore result in easier maintenance of the program during its life.

(Note that, in programs using a paragraph n00-PAGE-HEADERS in earlier chapters, a MOVE statement for setting an initial value to LINE-COUNT was correctly placed at the end of the paragraph, and not, as in the previous program, in a module superior to the paragraph.)

Two-level control-break processing is used for reports with two summary levels

WITH SINGLE-LEVEL control-break processing, the records of the input file must be arranged in the order of, (sorted on) the control field. In the input file MONTHLY-SALES in Figure 10.1, the control field was SR-CITY-IN. Thus, the records were arranged in SR-CITY-IN order.

With two-level control-break processing, the records of the input file must be sorted on two fields—primarily on one and secondarily on another. The primary sort field is called the *major control field* for the control-break processing. The the secondary sort field is called the *minor control field*.

Identify the primary and secondary sort fields

Figure 10.8 shows an example of a file with records sorted according to both primary and secondary sort fields. Each record gives the number of units and the dollar volume of sales by a salesperson. The city and state where the salesperson works are also given in the record. The records are sorted primarily in ascending state order; thus, records for Alabama come first and those for Wyoming last. The STATE field is therefore the primary sort field.

For a group of records with a given state value, the records are further sorted in ascending CITY order. Thus, for the Alaska records, Anchorage records come first and Juneau records last. The CITY field is therefore a secondary sort field.

SALESPERSON	UNITS	VOLUME	CITY	STATE
DREW	002	146,000	BIRMINGHAM	ALABAMA
TULLY	001	73,000	BIRMINGHAM	ALABAMA
JOHNSON	003	245,000	BIRMINGHAM	ALABAMA
GREEN	004	345,000	MONTGOMERY	ALABAMA
PECKFORD	001	87,000	MONTGOMERY	ALABAMA
FORD	001	86,000	ANCHORAGE	ALASKA
CRAWFORD	002	167,000	ANCHORAGE	ALASKA
DREXEL	003	380,000	FAIRBANKS	ALASKA
BROWN	002	235,000	FAIRBANKS	ALASKA
SCHMITT	001	98,000	JUNEAU	ALASKA
BRAUN	002	178,000	JUNEAU	ALASKA
DEVRY	003	355,000	JUNEAU	ALASKA
GETTY	001	85,000	LITTLE ROCK	ARKANSAS
...	...	...	...	...
TELFORD	002	168,000	CHEYENNE	WYOMING

Figure 10.8 *Display of records sorted on two fields.*

Suppose that the data in Figure 10.8 were stored in an input file called MONTHLY-SALES in the format in Figure 10.9. Now suppose you wanted to produce a detail report with summaries of units sold and dollar volume for each city, as was done earlier, but also for each state. The first few pages of this detail report are shown in Figure 10.10.

```
---------1---------2---------3---------4---------5---------6
DREW            GH002146000BIRMINGHAM      ALABAMA
TULLY           TK001073000BIRMINGHAM      ALABAMA
JOHNSON         SF003245000BIRMINGHAM      ALABAMA
GREEN           EL004345000MONTGOMERY      ALABAMA
PECKFORD        RK001087000MONTGOMERY      ALABAMA
FORD            TB001086000ANCHORAGE       ALASKA
CRAWFORD        AK002167000ANCHORAGE       ALASKA
DREXEL          SH003380000FAIRBANKS       ALASKA
BROWN           K 002235000FAIRBANKS       ALASKA
SCHMITT         HD001098000JUNEAU          ALASKA
BRAUN           G 002178000JUNEAU          ALASKA
DEVRY           YP003355000JUNEAU          ALASKA
GETTY           PH001085000LITTLE ROCK     ARKANSAS
...             ...   ...       ...          ...
```

Figure 10.9a *Records of input file MONTHLY-SALES.*

```
---------1---------2---------3---------4---------5---------6
XXXXXXXXXXXXXXX999999999XXXXXXXXXXXXXXXXXXXXXXXXXXXXXXX
```

Figure 10.9b *Input record layout.*

```
01   SALES-RECORD-IN.
     05   SR-SURNAME-IN          PIC X(13).
     05   SR-INITIAL1-IN         PIC X.
     05   SR-INITIAL2-IN         PIC X.
     05   SR-UNITS-IN            PIC 9(03).
     05   SR-VOLUME-IN           PIC 9(06).
     05   SR-CITY-IN             PIC X(15).
     05   SR-STATE-IN            PIC X(15).
```

Columns 1–13   Last name of salesperson
         14   First initial of salesperson
         15   Second initial of salesperson
         16–18   Number of units sold in month
         19–24   Volume of sales for salesperson for month
         25–39   City
         40–54   State

Figure 10.9c *Structure of input area record for the input file.*

MONTHLY SALES REPORT

SALESPERSON	UNITS SOLD	VOLUME OF SALES	CITY	STATE
G.H. DREW	2	$ 146,000	BIRMINGHAM	ALABAMA
T.K. TULLY	1	$ 73,000	BIRMINGHAM	ALABAMA
S.F. JOHNSON	3	$ 245,000	BIRMINGHAM	ALABAMA
TOTAL BIRMINGHAM	6	$ 464,000		
E.L. GREEN	4	$ 345,000	MONTGOMERY	ALABAMA
R.K. PECKFORD	1	$ 87,000	MONTGOMERY	ALABAMA
TOTAL MONTGOMERY	5	$ 432,000		
TOTAL ALABAMA	11	$ 896,000		
T.B. FORD	1	$ 86,000	ANCHORAGE	ALASKA
A.K. CRAWFORD	2	$ 167,000	ANCHORAGE	ALASKA
TOTAL ANCHORAGE	3	$ 253,000		
S.H. DREXEL	3	$ 380,000	FAIRBANKS	ALASKA
K. BROWN	2	$ 235,000	FAIRBANKS	ALASKA
TOTAL FAIRBANKS	5	$ 615,000		
H.D. SCHMITT	1	$ 98,000	JUNEAU	ALASKA

MONTHLY SALES REPORT

SALESPERSON	UNITS SOLD	VOLUME OF SALES	CITY	STATE
G. BRAUN	2	$ 178,000	JUNEAU	ALASKA
Y.P. DEVRY	3	$ 355,000	JUNEAU	ALASKA
TOTAL JUNEAU	6	$ 631,000		
TOTAL ALASKA	14	$ 1,499,000		
P.H. GETTY	1	$ 85,000	LITLE ROCK	ARKANSAS
...	...	...	...	...

Figure 10.10a Output file REPORT-FILE.

```
    MONTHLY SALES REPORT
PAGE  Z9                                              XXXXXXXX

      SALESPERSON          UNITS  VOLUME      CITY            STATE
                           SOLD   OF SALES

        XXXXXXXXXXXXXXX    Z9     $9,999,999  XXXXXXXXXXXXXXX XXXXXXXXXXXXXXX
        XXXXXXXXXXXXXXX    Z9     $9,999,999  XXXXXXXXXXXXXXX XXXXXXXXXXXXXXX
        XXXXXXXXXXXXXXX    Z9     $9,999,999  XXXXXXXXXXXXXXX XXXXXXXXXXXXXXX

    TOTAL XXXXXXXXXXXXXXX ZZ9     $99,999,999

        XXXXXXXXXXXXXXX    Z9     $9,999,999  XXXXXXXXXXXXXXX XXXXXXXXXXXXXXX
        XXXXXXXXXXXXXXX    Z9     $9,999,999  XXXXXXXXXXXXXXX XXXXXXXXXXXXXXX

    TOTAL XXXXXXXXXXXXXXX ZZ9     $99,999,999

TOTAL XXXXXXXXXXXXXXX    ZZZ9     $999,999,999
```

Figure 10.10b *Printer spacing chart for the output file.*

```
01 DETAIL-LINE-OUT.
    05  FILLER                    PIC X(08)          VALUE SPACES.
    05  DL-SALESPERSON-OUT        PIC X(15).
    05  FILLER                    PIC X(04)          VALUE SPACES.
    05  DL-UNITS-OUT              PIC Z9.
    05  FILLER                    PIC X(05)          VALUE SPACES.
    05  DL-VOLUME-OUT             PIC $9,999,999.
    05  FILLER                    PIC X(02)          VALUE SPACES.
    05  DL-CITY-OUT               PIC X(15).
    05  FILLER                    PIC X              VALUE SPACE.
    05  SR-STATE-OUT              PIC X(15).
    05  FILLER                    PIC X(56)          VALUE SPACES.
01 CITY-SUMMARY-LINE.
    05  FILLER                    PIC X(04)          VALUE SPACES.
    05  FILLER                    PIC X(06)          VALUE 'TOTAL'.
    05  CS-CITY-OUT               PIC X(15).
    05  FILLER                    PIC X              VALUE SPACES.
    05  CS-TOTAL-UNITS-OUT        PIC ZZ9.
    05  FILLER                    PIC X(04)          VALUE SPACES.
    05  CS-TOTAL-VOLUME-OUT       PIC $99,999,999.
    05  FILLER                    PIC X(89)          VALUE SPACES.
01 STATE-SUMMARY-LINE.
    05  FILLER                    PIC X              VALUE SPACE.
    05  FILLER                    PIC X(06)          VALUE 'TOTAL'.
    05  SS-STATE-OUT              PIC X(15).
    05  FILLER                    PIC X(03)          VALUE SPACE.
    05  SS-TOTAL-UNITS-OUT        PIC ZZZ9.
    05  FILLER                    PIC X(03)          VALUE SPACES.
    05  SS-TOTAL-VOLUME-OUT       PIC $999,999,999.
    05  FILLER                    PIC X(89)          VALUE SPACES.
```

Figure 10.10c *Structure of records for detail, city summary, and state summary lines.*

To generate this report you need minor and major control breaks. As each input record is read, a minor control break will occur if the SR-CITY-IN value in the latest record is different from a WS-CONTROL-CITY control identifier value. The control identifier holds the SR-CITY-IN value from the previous input record, and thus the city value for the latest group of records for the same city. The SR-CITY-IN field is the minor control field and the corresponding WS-CONTROL-CITY identifier is the minor control-break identifier. A minor control break will cause a summary line for the records with the WS-CONTROL-CITY value to be generated and printed.

A major control break will occur only if the SR-STATE-IN value in the latest input record differs from a WS-CONTROL-STATE control identifier value. This control identifier holds the SR-STATE-IN value from the previous input record, and thus the state value for the latest group of records for the same state. The SR-STATE-IN field is the major control field and the corresponding WS-CONTROL-STATE identifier is the major control-break identifier. A major control break will first cause a minor control break, and then cause a summary line for the records with the value in the major control-break identifier to be generated and printed.

With two-level control-break logic, the major control field is tested first

The logic for two-level control-break processing is illustrated by the file navigation diagram in Figure 10.11. On the left are the records of the input file and on the right the lines printed as the output file. You can see that a record with a new city value must be read before the city summary line is printed and, in addition, the record must have a new state value before the state summary line is printed.

The essential logic for a two-level control break is therefore, as follows:

Read latest input record.
If major control field not = major control identifier
    perform major control-break processing.
If minor control field not = minor control identifier
    perform minor control-break processing.

You should test for the major control break first. You could test for the minor break first—in most cases this would work—but in a few cases it would go wrong, for example, in the unlikely event the last city in Alabama and the first city in Alaska had the same name. However, the equivalent situation with business codes, such as department numbers, product codes, and so on, is much more likely.

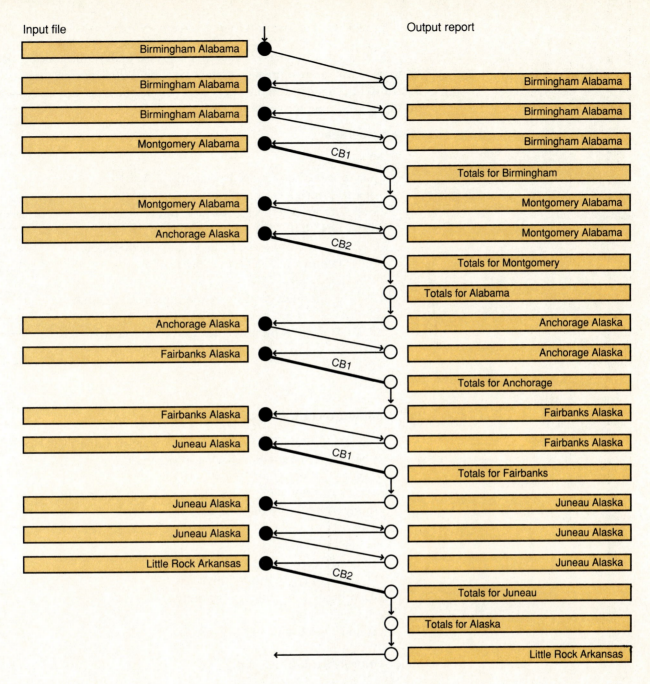

Figure 10.11 *File navigation diagram for a two-level control-break procedure. See also the program in Figure 10.12.*

Pseudocode for Two-level Control-break Processing

Pseudocode can be used to develop the essentials of the code for handling two-level control breaks, as shown in the file navigation diagram in Figure 10.11. This code ignores page and column headers and assumes an infinitely long page for printing the report.

Main-paragraph.

```
OPEN files.
READ first MONTHLY-SALES record,
    at end print message and stop.
MOVE City-in value in record just read to
    WS-CONTROL-CITY.
MOVE zero to City-total-units and City-total-volume.
MOVE State-in value in record just read to
    WS-CONTROL-STATE.
MOVE zero to State-total-units and State-total-volume.
MOVE 'YES' to More-records.
PERFORM Process-input-record until More-records = 'NO'.
PERFORM Major-control-break-processing.
CLOSE files.
STOP.
```

Process-input-record.

```
IF WS-CONTROL-STATE value NOT = State-in value THEN
    PERFORM Major-control-break-processing
END-IF.
IF WS-CONTROL-CITY value NOT = City-in value THEN
    PERFORM Minor-control-break-processing
END-IF.
Generate detail record.
Print detail record.
ADD Units-in to City-total-units.
ADD Volume-in to City-total-volume.
READ next record,
    at end MOVE 'NO' to More-records.
```

Major-control-break-processing.

```
PERFORM Minor-control-break-processing
Generate State-summary-line using WS-CONTROL-STATE,
    State-total-units and State-total-volume.
Print summary-line.
Skip line.
IF More-records = 'YES' THEN
    MOVE State-in value in latest record to
        WS-CONTROL-STATE,
    MOVE zero to State-total-units and State-total-volume
END-IF.
```

Minor-control-break-processing.

Skip line.
Generate City-summary-line using WS-CONTROL-CITY,
    City-total-units and City-total-volume.
Print summary-line.
Skip line.
ADD City-total-units to State-total-units.
ADD City-total-volume to State-total-volume.
IF More-records = 'YES' THEN
    MOVE City-in value in latest record to
        WS-CONTROL-CITY,
    MOVE zero to City-total-units and City-total-volume
END-IF.

Notice this pseudocode program takes care of the final city and state summary lines at the end of the report. When the attempt to read beyond the end of the input file causes More-records to get the value 'NO', processing input records stops, but no control breaks are generated by the paragraph process-input-record. Instead, the final city and state summary lines are written by the direct calling up of the minor and major control-break paragraphs at the end of Main-paragraph.

Note that the major control break always forces a minor control break. This is the proper approach. When the city changes, but not the state, you get a minor control break. When the state changes (even if the city does not, which could happen) there must be a major control break, which consists of a minor control break for the city summary, followed by the state summary. Hence a major break must contain a minor break.

Pseudocode for Two-level Control-break Processing with Page Headers

Once more, there are many different strategies for dealing with new pages. The strategy adopted here is a common one, shown in Figure 10.10a. Each page is allowed a fixed number of lines for printing. This number should be about five lines less than the number you think is adequate. (You have 66 lines per page available with most printers.) Assume 45 lines are allowed per page. Whenever detail lines are being printed, if the next detail line is to be printed on line 46, a new page is started and report and column headers printed at the top. Thus, the strategy allows for interruption of printing of detail lines to skip to a new page.

However, it is not acceptable to have a city summary line, or any following state summary line, on a page separate from the preceding city detail lines. Thus, these summary lines will be printed without skipping to a new page, even if it is necessary to print beyond line 45.

This strategy is incorporated in the following version of pseudocode shown earlier. It corresponds to the report in Figure 10.10a. If you wish, you may devise a different strategy for skipping to a new page and incorporate that as an exercise. A common alternative strategy is to begin the data for each new state on a fresh page.

Note that great care has to be taken in counting lines.

Main-paragraph.

OPEN files.
READ first MONTHLY-SALES record,
  at end print message and stop.
MOVE City-in value in record just read to
  WS-CONTROL-CITY.
MOVE zero to City-total-units and City-total-volume.
MOVE State-in value in record just read to
  WS-CONTROL-STATE.
MOVE zero to State-total-units and State-total-volume.
MOVE 'YES' to More-records.
PERFORM Process-input-record until More-records = 'NO'.
PERFORM Major-control-break-processing.
CLOSE files.
STOP.

Process-input-record.

IF WS-CONTROL-STATE value NOT = State-in value
  THEN PERFORM Major-control-break-processing
END-IF
IF WS-CONTROL-CITY value NOT = City-in value
  THEN PERFORM Minor-control-break-processing
END-IF.
IF Line-count >= 45 THEN
  PERFORM Print-headings,
END-IF.
Generate detail record.
Print detail record.
ADD 1 to Line-count.
ADD Units-in to City-total-units.
ADD Volume-in to City-total-volume.
READ next record,
  at end set More-records to 'NO'.

Minor control-break-processing.

Skip line.
Generate City-summary-line using WS-CONTROL-CITY,
  City-total-units and City-total-volume.
Print summary-line.
ADD 2 to Line-count.
IF Line-count < 45 or State-in value NOT =
    WS-CONTROL-STATE value THEN
  Skip line,
  ADD 1 to Line-count,
END-IF.
ADD City-total-units to State-total-units.
ADD City-total-volume to State-total-volume.

IF MORE-RECORDS = 'YES' THEN
    MOVE City-in value in latest record to
        WS-CONTROL-CITY,
    MOVE zero to City-total-units and City-total-volume.
END-IF.

Major-control-break-processing.

PERFORM Minor-control-break-processing.
Generate State-summary-line using WS-CONTROL-STATE,
    State-total-units and State-total-volume.
Print State-summary-line.
ADD 1 to Line-count.
IF Line-count < 45 THEN
    Skip line
    ADD 1 to Line-count
END-IF.
IF More-records = 'YES' THEN
    MOVE State-in value in latest record to
        WS-CONTROL-STATE,
    MOVE zero to State-total-units and State-total-volume.
END-IF.

Print-headings.

Print report heading.
Print date/page line.
Skip line.
Print column headers.
Skip line.
MOVE 6 to Line-count.

Observe the logic for handling headers and end of page processing carefully. The next detail line will go to a new page, after the headers, if the line count is 45. A city summary line never goes to a new page. In addition, when a city summary line has been printed on or beyond line 45, the line after it will be skipped only if a state summary line follows (since otherwise the page would end). Similarly, a state summary line never goes to a new page, and if it is printed on or beyond line 45, a line after it will not be skipped.

10.4
A two-level control-break program

THIS SECTION applies the principles explained previously to write a two-level control-break COBOL program. The program constructed is as complex as any you will find in this book. However, structured programming principles help keep the complexity manageable. The program has a good level of modularization with a hierarchical structure.

COBOL program for two-level control-break processing

The COBOL program that corresponds to the preceding pseudocode and would generate the report in Figure 10.10 is shown in Figure 10.12. The input file MONTHLY-SALES was shown in Figure 10.9. The program gives subsidiary summaries of total housing units sold and total dollar volume of sales for each city. It also gives these summaries by state.

```
IDENTIFICATION DIVISION.
PROGRAM-ID. CB2.
ENVIRONMENT DIVISION.
INPUT-OUTPUT SECTION.
FILE-CONTROL.    SELECT MONTHLY-SALES  ASSIGN TO UT-S-DISK50.
                 SELECT REPORT-FILE ASSIGN TO UR-S-SYSPRINT.
DATA DIVISION.
FILE SECTION.
FD    MONTHLY-SALES                       LABEL RECORDS ARE STANDARD.
01    SALES-RECORD-IN.
      05   SR-SURNAME-IN         PIC X(13).
      05   SR-INITIAL1-IN        PIC X.
      05   SR-INITIAL2-IN        PIC X.
      05   SR-UNITS-IN           PIC 9(03).
      05   SR-VOLUME-IN          PIC 9(06).
      05   SR-CITY-IN            PIC X(15).
      05   SR-STATE-IN           PIC X(15).
FD    REPORT-FILE                          LABEL RECORDS ARE OMITTED.
01    REPORT-RECORD-OUT          PIC X(133).
WORKING-STORAGE SECTION.
01 WS-WORK-AREAS.
      05   LINE-COUNT            PIC 9(02).
      05   MORE-RECORDS          PIC X(03)        VALUE 'YES'.
      05   WS-CONTROL-CITY       PIC X(15).
      05   WS-CONTROL-STATE      PIC X(15).
      05   WS-PAGE-NUMBER        PIC 9(02)        VALUE ZERO.
01 WS-TOTAL-AREAS.
      05   WS-CITY-TOTAL-VOLUME  PIC 9(08).
      05   WS-CITY-TOTAL-UNITS   PIC 9(03).
      05   WS-STATE-TOTAL-VOLUME PIC 9(09).
      05   WS-STATE-TOTAL-UNITS  PIC 9(03).
01 PAGE-DATE-LINE-OUT.
      05   FILLER                PIC X            VALUE SPACE.
      05   FILLER                PIC X(06)        VALUE 'PAGE '.
      05   PD-PAGE-NUMB-OUT      PIC Z9.
      05   FILLER                PIC X(50).
      05   PD-RUN-DATE-OUT       PIC X(08).
      05   FILLER                PIC X(66)        VALUE SPACES.
01 REPORT-HEADER.
      05   FILLER                PIC X            VALUE SPACE.
      05   FILLER                PIC X(18)        VALUE SPACES.
```

```
            05   FILLER                      PIC X(20)                   VALUE
                                                                         'MONTHLY SALES REPORT'.
            05   FILLER                      PIC X(94)                   VALUE SPACES.
       01 COL-HEADER-1.
            05   FILLER                      PIC X(08)                   VALUE SPACES.
            05   FILLER                      PIC X(19)                   VALUE 'SALESPERSON'.
            05   FILLER                      PIC X(07)                   VALUE 'UNITS'.
            05   FILLER                      PIC X(12)                   VALUE 'VOLUME'.
            05   FILLER                      PIC X(16)                   VALUE 'CITY'.
            05   FILLER                      PIC X(05)                   VALUE 'STATE'.
            05   FILLER                      PIC X(66)                   VALUE SPACES.
       01 COL-HEADER-2.
            05   FILLER                      PIC X(27)                   VALUE SPACES.
            05   FILLER                      PIC X(07)                   VALUE 'SOLD'.
            05   FILLER                      PIC X(08)                   VALUE 'OF SALES'.
            05   FILLER                      PIC X(91)                   VALUE SPACES.
       01 DETAIL-LINE-OUT.
            05   FILLER                      PIC X(08)                   VALUE SPACES.
            05   DL-SALESPERSON-OUT          PIC X(15).
            05   FILLER                      PIC X(04)                   VALUE SPACES.
            05   DL-UNITS-OUT                PIC Z9.
            05   FILLER                      PIC X(05)                   VALUE SPACES.
            05   DL-VOLUME-OUT               PIC $9,999,999.
            05   FILLER                      PIC X(02)                   VALUE SPACES.
            05   DL-CITY-OUT                 PIC X(15).
            05   FILLER                      PIC X                       VALUE SPACE.
            05   DL-STATE-OUT                PIC X(15).
            05   FILLER                      PIC X(56)                   VALUE SPACES.
       01 CITY-SUMMARY-LINE.
            05   FILLER                      PIC X(04)                   VALUE SPACES.
            05   FILLER                      PIC X(06)                   VALUE 'TOTAL  '.
            05   CS-CITY-OUT                 PIC X(15).
            05   FILLER                      PIC X                       VALUE SPACES.
            05   CS-TOTAL-UNITS-OUT          PIC ZZ9.
            05   FILLER                      PIC X(04)                   VALUE SPACES.
            05   CS-TOTAL-VOLUME-OUT         PIC $99,999,999.
            05   FILLER                      PIC X(89)                   VALUE SPACES.
       01 STATE-SUMMARY-LINE.
            05   FILLER                      PIC X                       VALUE SPACE.
            05   FILLER                      PIC X(06)                   VALUE 'TOTAL  '.
            05   SS-STATE-OUT                PIC X(15).
            05   FILLER                      PIC X(03)                   VALUE SPACE.
            05   SS-TOTAL-UNITS-OUT          PIC ZZZ9.
            05   FILLER                      PIC X(03)                   VALUE SPACES.
            05   SS-TOTAL-VOLUME-OUT         PIC $999,999,999.
            05   FILLER                      PIC X(89)                   VALUE SPACES.
       01 WS-PERSON-NAME.
            05 WSP-FIRST-INIT                PIC X.
            05 FILLER                        PIC X                       VALUE '.'.
            05 WSP-SECOND-INIT               PIC X.
            05 WSP-PERIOD                    PIC X(02).
            05 WSP-LAST-NAME                 PIC X(13).
```

```
 PROCEDURE DIVISION.
 100-MAIN-MODULE.
 **************************************************************************
 *   DIRECTS PROGRAM LOGIC.                                             *
 **************************************************************************
         PERFORM 200-INITIALIZATION.
         PERFORM 300-PROCESS-RECORD
                            UNTIL MORE-RECORDS = 'NO'.
         PERFORM 900-TERMINATION.
 200-INITIALIZATION.
 **************************************************************************
 *   PERFORMED FROM 100-MAIN-MODULE. OPENS FILES, EXTRACTS DATE, READS  *
 *   FIRST RECORD, SETS CONTROL AND TOTALS IDENTIFIERS, AND PRINTS      *
 *   HEADERS ON FIRST PAGE.                                             *
 **************************************************************************
         OPEN INPUT MONTHLY-SALES
              OUTPUT REPORT-FILE.
         MOVE CURRENT-DATE TO PD-RUN-DATE-OUT.
         READ MONTHLY-SALES,
              AT END MOVE ' NO FIRST RECORD' TO REPORT-RECORD-OUT
                       WRITE REPORT-RECORD-OUT AFTER 1 LINE
                       STOP RUN.
         MOVE SR-CITY-IN TO WS-CONTROL-CITY.
         MOVE ZERO TO WS-CITY-TOTAL-UNITS.
         MOVE ZERO TO WS-CITY-TOTAL-VOLUME.
         MOVE SR-STATE-IN TO WS-CONTROL-STATE.
         MOVE ZERO TO WS-STATE-TOTAL-UNITS.
         MOVE ZERO TO WS-STATE-TOTAL-VOLUME.
         PERFORM 700-PAGE-HEADERS.
 300-PROCESS-RECORD.
 **************************************************************************
 *   PERFORMED FROM 100-MAIN-MODULE. CHECKS FOR CONTROL BREAK, AND, IF  *
 *   FOUND, CARRIES OUT. ALSO CONSTRUCTS AND PRINTS DETAIL LINE, WITH   *
 *   PRIOR PAGE HEADERS IF NEEDED.  MAINTAINS TOTALS AND READS NEXT     *
 *   RECORD.                                                            *
 **************************************************************************
         IF SR-STATE-IN NOT EQUAL TO WS-CONTROL-STATE
             PERFORM 400-MAJOR-CONTROL-BREAK
         END-IF.
         IF SR-CITY-IN NOT EQUAL TO WS-CONTROL-CITY
             PERFORM 500-MINOR-CONTROL-BREAK
         END-IF.
         PERFORM 600-GENERATE-DETAIL-LINE-OUT.
         IF LINE-COUNT >= 45
             PERFORM 700-PAGE-HEADERS
         END-IF.
         WRITE REPORT-RECORD-OUT FROM DETAIL-LINE-OUT.
         ADD 1 TO LINE-COUNT.
         ADD SR-UNITS-IN TO WS-CITY-TOTAL-UNITS.
         ADD SR-VOLUME-IN TO WS-CITY-TOTAL-VOLUME.
         READ MONTHLY-SALES
              AT END MOVE 'NO' TO MORE-RECORDS.
```

```
400-MAJOR-CONTROL-BREAK.
**********************************************************************
*   PERFORMED FROM 300-PROCESS-RECORD AND 900-TERMINATION. DIRECTS    *
*   PRINTING OF STATE SUMMARY LINE WITH IMMEDIATELY PRIOR CITY SUMMARY *
*   LINE. RESETS STATE TOTALS AND STATE CONTROL IDENTIFIER.           *
**********************************************************************
        PERFORM 500-MINOR-CONTROL-BREAK.
        MOVE WS-CONTROL-STATE TO SS-STATE-OUT.
        MOVE WS-STATE-TOTAL-UNITS TO SS-TOTAL-UNITS-OUT.
        MOVE WS-STATE-TOTAL-VOLUME TO SS-TOTAL-VOLUME-OUT.
        WRITE REPORT-RECORD-OUT FROM STATE-SUMMARY-LINE
                AFTER ADVANCING 1 LINE.
        ADD 1 TO LINE-COUNT.
        IF LINE-COUNT < 45
            MOVE SPACES TO REPORT-RECORD-OUT
            WRITE REPORT-RECORD-OUT
                    AFTER ADVANCING 1 LINE
            ADD 1 TO LINE-COUNT
        END-IF.
        IF MORE-RECORDS = 'YES'
            MOVE SR-STATE-IN TO WS-CONTROL-STATE
            MOVE ZERO TO WS-STATE-TOTAL-UNITS
            MOVE ZERO TO WS-STATE-TOTAL-VOLUME
        END-IF.
 500-MINOR-CONTROL-BREAK.
**********************************************************************
*   PERFORMED FROM 400-MAJOR-CONTROL-BREAK. DIRECTS PRINTING OF CITY   *
*   SUMMARY LINE, ADDS CITY TOTALS TO STATE TOTALS AND RESETS CITY    *
*   TOTALS AND CITY CONTROL IDENTIFIER.                              *
**********************************************************************
        MOVE SPACES TO REPORT-RECORD-OUT.
        WRITE REPORT-RECORD-OUT
                AFTER ADVANCING 1 LINE.
        ADD 1 TO LINE-COUNT.
        MOVE WS-CONTROL-CITY TO CS-CITY-OUT.
        MOVE WS-CITY-TOTAL-UNITS TO CS-TOTAL-UNITS-OUT.
        MOVE WS-CITY-TOTAL-VOLUME TO CS-TOTAL-VOLUME-OUT.
        WRITE REPORT-RECORD-OUT FROM CITY-SUMMARY-LINE
                            AFTER ADVANCING 1 LINE.
        ADD 1 TO LINE-COUNT.
        IF LINE-COUNT < 45 OR SR-STATE-IN NOT = WS-CONTROL-STATE
            MOVE SPACES TO REPORT-RECORD-OUT
            WRITE REPORT-RECORD-OUT
                        AFTER ADVANCING 1 LINE
            ADD 1 TO LINE-COUNT
        END-IF.
        ADD WS-CITY-TOTAL-UNITS TO WS-STATE-TOTAL-UNITS.
        ADD WS-CITY-TOTAL-VOLUME TO WS-STATE-TOTAL-VOLUME.
        IF MORE-RECORDS = 'YES'
            MOVE SR-CITY-IN TO WS-CONTROL-CITY
            MOVE ZERO TO WS-CITY-TOTAL-UNITS
            MOVE ZERO TO WS-CITY-TOTAL-VOLUME
        END-IF.
```

```
 600-GENERATE-DETAIL-LINE-OUT.
*********************************************************************
*   PERFORMED FROM 300-PROCESS-RECORD. PREPARES A DETAIL LINE       *
*   FOR PRINTING.                                                   *
*********************************************************************
        PERFORM 800-GENERATE-NAME.
        MOVE SR-UNITS-IN TO DL-UNITS-OUT.
        MOVE SR-VOLUME-IN TO DL-VOLUME-OUT.
        MOVE SR-CITY-IN TO DL-CITY-OUT.
        MOVE SR-STATE-IN TO DL-STATE-OUT.
 700-PAGE-HEADERS.
*********************************************************************
*   PERFORMED FROM 200-INITIALIZATION AND FROM 300-PROCESS-RECORD.  *
*   PRINTS PAGE HEADERS WITH CURRENT PAGE NUMBER.                   *
*********************************************************************
        WRITE REPORT-RECORD-OUT FROM REPORT-HEADER
              AFTER ADVANCING PAGE.
        ADD 1 TO WS-PAGE-NUMBER.
        MOVE WS-PAGE-NUMBER TO PD-PAGE-NUMB-OUT.
        WRITE REPORT-RECORD-OUT FROM PAGE-DATE-LINE-OUT
              AFTER ADVANCING 1 LINE.
        WRITE REPORT-RECORD-OUT FROM COL-HEADER-1
              AFTER ADVANCING 2 LINES.
        WRITE REPORT-RECORD-OUT FROM COL-HEADER-2
              AFTER ADVANCING 1 LINE.
        MOVE SPACES TO REPORT-RECORD-OUT.
        WRITE REPORT-RECORD-OUT
              AFTER ADVANCING 1 LINE.
        MOVE 6 TO LINE-COUNT.
 800-GENERATE-NAME.
*********************************************************************
*   PERFORMED FROM 400-GENERATE-DETAIL-LINE-OUT. CONSTRUCTS OUTPUT  *
*   SALESPERSON FIELD WITH INITIALS COMING FIRST.                   *
*********************************************************************
        MOVE SR-INITIAL1-IN TO WSP-FIRST-INIT.
        MOVE SR-INITIAL2-IN TO WSP-SECOND-INIT.
        IF WSP-SECOND-INIT = SPACE
            MOVE SPACES TO WSP-PERIOD
          ELSE
            MOVE '.' TO WSP-PERIOD
        END-IF.
        MOVE SR-SURNAME-IN TO WSP-LAST-NAME.
        MOVE WS-PERSON-NAME TO DL-SALESPERSON-OUT.
 900-TERMINATION.
*********************************************************************
*   PERFORMED FROM 100-MAIN-MODULE. PRINTS FINAL CITY AND STATE SUMMARY  *
*   LINES. CLOSES FILES.                                            *
*********************************************************************
        PERFORM 400-MAJOR-CONTROL-BREAK.
        CLOSE MONTHLY-SALES
              REPORT-FILE.
        STOP RUN.
```

Figure 10.12 *Program that produces output file REPORT-FILE shown in Figure 10.10.*

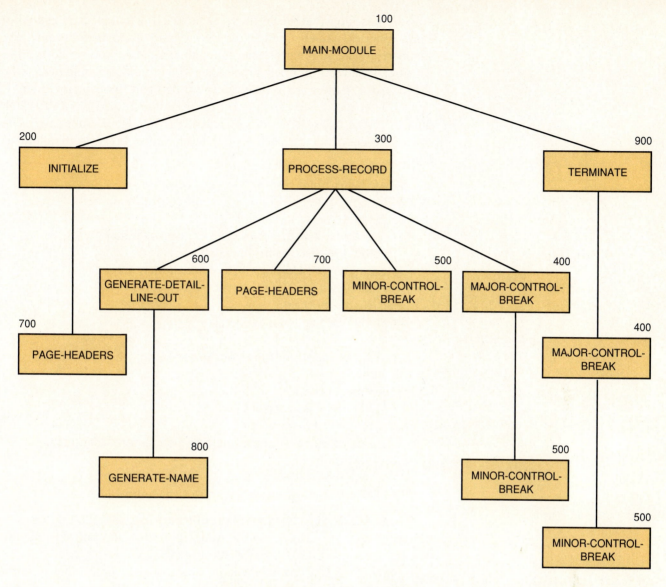

Figure 10.13 *Hierarchy diagram for the two-level control-break program in Figure 10.12.*

Notice that this program, in contrast to that in Figure 10.6, includes the update to the LINE-COUNT at the end of the module 700-PAGE-HEADERS.

The hierarchy diagram for this program is shown in Figure 10.13. The core of the logic is in the paragraphs 300-PROCESS-RECORD, 400-MAJOR-CONTROL-BREAK, and 500-MINOR-CONTROL-BREAK.

Higher-level control-break processing is common

The processing example used in this chapter concerned a real estate business. First single 1-level control break processing was used to generate sales summaries for each city. Then two-level control-break processing was used to get sales summaries for each city, and state.

Suppose now that the business operated in the three federal nations of North America, namely Canada, the U.S.A., and Mexico. If you wanted city summaries, state summaries, and national summaries, you would need to use three-level control-break processing. The input data would need to be sorted first in nation order, then in state order, and third in city order.

You would need three control identifiers: NATION-CONTROL (major), STATE-CONTROL (minor), and CITY-CONTROL (subminor). The essential pseudocode for such a three-level control break is, therefore, as follows:

```
READ latest input record.
IF Nation-control-field not = Nation-control-identifier
    PERFORM Nation-control-break.
IF State-control-field not = State-control-identifier
    PERFORM State-control-break.
IF City-control-field not = City-control-identifier
    PERFORM City-control-break.
Nation-control-break.
    PERFORM State-control-break.
    ...
    MOVE latest Nation-control-field to Nation-control-
identifier.
State-control-break.
    PERFORM City-control break.
    ...
    MOVE latest State-control-field to State-control-identifier.
City-control-break.
    ...
    MOVE latest City-control-field to City-control-identifier.
```

Note that with the nation-control-break paragraph, the first instruction will force a state control break. And within the state control break, the first instruction will force a city control break.

Three-level, and even four-level, control-break processing is fairly common. Nevertheless, the majority of control-break programs probably involve one or two levels. However, if you can write two-level control-break programs, it takes only slight additional effort to write three-level control-break programs, as the preceding logic demonstrates. Four-level control-break programs would be written according to the same system.

10.5
Debugging techniques with complex programs need to be mastered

You saw in Chapter 1 that programs can have three kinds of errors: syntax errors, logical errors, and run errors. Syntax errors are detected by the compiler at compile time. Logical errors can often be corrected by a desk check of the program before it executes. However, all too frequently subtle logical errors remain in programs at run time. Run errors, of course, cause the program to stop execution, that is, an abnormal ending or abend.

Thus, many logical errors and all run errors can be detected only by running the program. With complex programs, containing many modules, it can sometimes be difficult to find out exactly where in the program the error is located. Two COBOL commands can help here. These are the READY TRACE command and the DISPLAY command.

The READY TRACE command lists executed paragraph names

This command is normally placed right at the beginning of the 100-MAIN-MODULE paragraph in test versions of the program. It is used to determine in what paragraph, and in which execution of the paragraph, an abend occurs. When the program has stopped executing, whether normally or because of an abend, the command causes output of a list of the names of all paragraphs, in the sequence in which they are executed.

As an example, suppose you have the following:

```
PROCEDURE DIVISION.
100-MAIN-MODULE.
    READY TRACE.
    PERFORM 200-INITIALIZATION.
    PERFORM 300-PROCESS-RECORD
            UNTIL MORE-RECORDS = 'NO'.
    PERFORM 900-TERMINATION.
200-INITIALIZATION.
    ...
    PERFORM 700-PAGE-HEADERS.
    ...
300-PROCESS-RECORD.
    ...
    PERFORM 400-MINOR-CONTROL-BREAK.
    PERFORM 500-MAJOR-CONTROL-BREAK.
    ...
    PERFORM 600-GENERATE-DETAIL-LINE-OUT.
    ...
    PERFORM 700-PAGE-HEADERS.
    ...
400-MINOR-CONTROL-BREAK.
    ...
500-MAJOR-CONTROL-BREAK.
    ...
600-GENERATE-DETAIL-LINE-OUT.
    ...
    PERFORM 800-GENERATE-NAME.
    ...
700-PAGE-HEADERS.
...
800-GENERATE-NAME.
...
900-TERMINATION.
...
```

Suppose this program abends on the third execution of 300-PROCESS-RECORD. The output caused by READY TRACE could be the following:

```
100-MAIN-MODULE
200-INITIALIZATION
700-PAGE-HEADERS
300-PROCESS-RECORD
600-GENERATE-DETAIL-LINE-OUT
800-GENERATE-NAME
300-PROCESS-RECORD
600-GENERATE-DETAIL-LINE-OUT
800-GENERATE-NAME
300-PROCESS-RECORD
600-GENERATE-DETAIL-LINE-OUT
800-GENERATE-NAME
300-PROCESS-RECORD
600-GENERATE-DETAIL-LINE-OUT
```

This would clearly pinpoint the problem as being in 600-GENERATE-DETAIL-LINE-OUT and occuring in the third execution of that module. Note that READY TRACE always outputs the sequence of paragraphs executed, even if the program terminates correctly.

With a complex program involving many paragraphs, not all paragraphs are executed with specific input data. When testing a new program, READY TRACE can be used to check that a specific paragraph was executed. It can also be used to check the specific sequence in which paragraphs were executed.

READY TRACE can also be used more locally in a program. Instead of being placed at the beginning, it can be placed later in the program. Executed paragraph names will be output only after READY TRACE has executed. At a later point in the program you can have the output stopped, with the command RESET TRACE.

```
500-X-MODULE.
    ...
    READY TRACE.
    ...
900-Y-MODULE.
    ...
    RESET TRACE.
    ...
```

Thus, executed paragraph names are output between execution of READY TRACE and RESET TRACE.

READY TRACE is not part of COBOL 85. However most compilers have it as an enhancement.

DISPLAY outputs contents of one or more identifiers

The DISPLAY verb can be used to print the contents of one or more identifiers, and also for printing literals. The syntax is shown here:

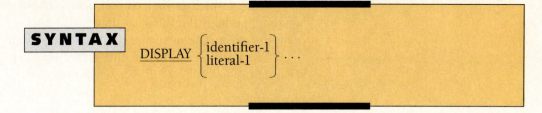

$$\text{DISPLAY} \begin{Bmatrix} \text{identifier-1} \\ \text{literal-1} \end{Bmatrix} \ldots$$

Some examples of correct DISPLAY statements are

```
DISPLAY FINAL-TOTAL.
DISPLAY 'TERMINATION OF PROGRAM'.
DISPLAY QUANTITY, COST.
DISPLAY 'COST OF UNITS IS:', COST, 'QUANTITY BOUGHT IS:', QUANTITY.
```

You can see that you can output a mixture of literals and identifier values with a single DISPLAY statement, if desired.

The DISPLAY command is often used to locate the exact statement where an error has taken place. You recall from Chapter 1 that a desk check involves tracing through the values each identifier receives as the instructions of the program are executed. DISPLAY enables you to get the actual values an identifier received during execution. This means you can compare these actual values with the values you expected, so you can find exactly where an error involving that identifier takes place.

For example, suppose you wanted to check the values identifier X received during execution of a program, because you suspect it is getting a wrong value somewhere. In the test version of the program, you would insert a DISPLAY statement after every statement that altered the value of X, perhaps as follows:

```
READ . . .
DISPLAY 'X value: ', X.
...
COMPUTE X = X * (TAX - 1.10).
DISPLAY 'X value: ', X.
...
COMPUTE X = X + 4 - DISCOUNT * RATE-INCREASE.
DISPLAY 'X value: ', X.
...
ADD REBATE TO X.
DISPLAY 'X value: ', X.
...
```

When the program executed, interspersed among the output would be something resembling:

```
...
X value: 45.90
...
X value: 68.87
...
X value: 47.45            error!
...
X value: 56.25
...
```

If your suspicions were correct, you will notice that one of these values is wrong, perhaps the third, as shown above. This will enable you to pinpoint the exact statement where the error is occurring.

When you have found the error, you can remove the DISPLAY statements.

EXHIBIT functions similarly to DISPLAY

Instead of DISPLAY, with some compilers the EXHIBIT command can be used. It does the same as DISPLAY except that, it has some additional options.

The following pairs of commands give the same output:

```
DISPLAY X, Y, Z.
EXHIBIT X, Y, Z.

DISPLAY 'THE VALUE OF X IS: ', X.

EXHIBIT 'THE VALUE OF X IS: ', X.
```

Thus, DISPLAY and EXHIBIT can be used interchangeably. However, you can use the NAMED option with EXHIBIT, but not with DISPLAY. Thus

```
EXHIBIT NAMED X, Y, Z.
```

could give the output

```
X = 0789   Y = 1345   Z = 4879
```

This is very convenient for debugging. Unfortunately, not all compilers allow for the EXHIBIT verb.

Summary

1. Single-level control-break processing is used to generate summary lines from each group of input file records that have a constant value in one field, called the control field. As records are read, the current control field value is kept in a separate control identifier. When the first record is read that has a different control field value, a control break occurs. The control break permits execution of a paragraph that causes the summary line to be printed.
2. Two-level control-break processing involves two control fields: major and minor. When a minor control field changes, a minor control break occurs, so that a summary line for the records with that minor control field value is printed. When a major control field changes, a major control break occurs, so that a summary line for the records with that major control field value is printed. A

major control field is tested before a minor control field, and a major control break forces a minor control break.

3. A paragraph within a structured program should have a high degree of both coherence and independence. A paragraph has a high degree of coherence if all the subfunctions performed by the paragraph naturally belong together. A paragraph has a high degree of independence if changes to it do not involve making changes to other paragraphs.

4. When debugging complex programs, the READY TRACE command can be used to output the sequence in which paragraphs are executed. The DISPLAY and EXHIBIT verbs can be used to output the sequence of values of identifiers.

Key Terms

control-break processing
control field
forcing a control break
coherence

independence
major control field
minor control field

Concept Review Questions

1. Explain the idea of a single-level control break.
2. What is a control field?
3. Why must the input file be sorted on the control field for single-level control-break processing?
4. Explain the idea of forcing a control break.
5. Explain the concept of module coherence.
6. Explain the concept of module independence.
7. Explain the idea of two-level control-break processing.
8. Explain why a major control field must be tested before a minor control field.
9. Describe some page break strategies for use with control-break processing.
10. Explain how the DISPLAY verb can be used for debugging.

COBOL Language Questions

1. If READY TRACE is placed in 100-P module of a program, what will happen?

2. What is the effect of the following?

```
READY TRACE.
PERFORM 600-P 10 TIMES.
RESET TRACE.
```

3. What is the effect of this?

```
EXHIBIT A, B, C.
```

4. What is the effect of the following?

```
EXHIBIT NAMED A, B, C.
```

Programming
Assignments

1. Single-level control-break processing (sorted input file)
The input file describes U.S. companies

```
---------1---------2---------3---------4---------5
BOEING                47720+1734AEROSPACE
GENCORP               05134+0044AEROSPACE
GENERAL DYNAMICS      24872+1124AEROSPACE
LOCKHEED              30124+1043AEROSPACE
MARTIN MARIETTA       14557+0247AEROSPACE
MCDONNELL DOUGLAS     43440+1479AEROSPACE
NORTHROP              18236-0861AEROSPACE
CHRYSLER              84573+4325AUTOMOTIVE
FORD MOTOR            24915+1156AUTOMOTIVE
GENERAL MOTORS        27893+1396AUTOMOTIVE
AMERICAN CYNAMID      12046+0627CHEMICALS
DU PONT               84710+5000CHEMICALS
ENGELHARD             06951+0193CHEMICALS
FUQUA INDUSTRIES      02337-0148CONGLOMERATE
PENN CENTRAL          04686+0193CONGLOMERATE
TENNECO               35899-1684CONGLOMERATE
ADVANCED MICRO        02481-0341SEMICONDUCTORS
INTEL                 07864+0834SEMICONDUCTORS
NATIONAL SEMI         07067-0267SEMICONDUCTORS
```

Columns 01–21   Company name
         22–26   Quarterly revenue ($ millions, last digit fractional)
         27–31   Quarterly profits ($ millions, last digit fractional)
         32–50   Industry sector
         The output data will look like this:

```
---------1---------2---------3---------4---------5---------6---------7
               U.S. INDUSTRY QUARTERLY RESULTS
PAGE  01                                                  05/06/91

        COMPANY              REVENUE        PROFITS        SECTOR

        BOEING               $4,772.0       $173.4         AEROSPACE
        GENCORP              $  513.4       $  4.4         AEROSPACE
        GENERAL DYNAMICS     $2,487.2       $112.4         AEROSPACE
        ...
        NORTHROP             $1,823.6       $ 86.1(LOSS)   AEROSPACE

TOTALS FOR AEROSPACE     $?,???,???.?  $??,???.?(????)

        CHRYSLER             $8,457.3       $432.5         AUTOMOTIVE
                ...
```

Assume that the normal number of lines available for headers and detail lines is 14 (in order to have multiple pages with limited data).

a. Make up the record layout and spacing chart for input and output.
b. Write a pseudocode program for the processing.
c. Draw a flowchart and hierarchy diagram.
d. Write and run the program.

2. **Single-level control-break processing (unsorted input file)**

The records of the input file describe ship cargos:

```
---------1---------2---------3---------4---------5
ARROWHEAD          OIL        050002040
ASTONHEAD          WHEAT      143500322
BULKFELLOW         IRON ORE   022603547
CRANSTON           COPPER     045607289
DEVONSHIRE         OIL        256002572
DOVEBIRD           WHEAT      189700754
DUSTY              IRON ORE   007563798
EVERYMAN           WHEAT      089670321
FORWARDBOUNTY      COPPER     007857382
FUNNELHEAD         OIL        200002176
GOODWILL           OIL        150002174
GOVERNOR           WHEAT      045200376
GULLLAKE           OIL        150002019
HALIFAXGULL        OIL        010002260
HEAVYSIDE          IRON ORE   006003422
HOODDOWN           COPPER     067007598
IVANHOE            IRON ORE   065003542
KARLSTAD           COPPER     002407486
KINGSTON           OIL        195002056
KUNGHU             WHEAT      200540342
```

Columns 01–20   Ship name
         21–30   Cargo type
         31–35   Units of cargo (tons, bushels, etc.)
         36–39   Cost per unit (pennies in last two digits)

The output show the data sorted in ascending cargo order, with summaries for each type of cargo.

```
---------1---------2---------3---------4---------5---------6---------7
                    SHIPPING DATA BY CARGO
     PAGE   1                                              06/05/92
                    SHIPMENTS OF COPPER

         SHIP NAME              UNITS        COST PER     CARGO
                                ON BOARD     UNIT         VALUE

         CRANSTON               4,560        $72.89       $   332,378
         FORWARDBOUNTY            785        $73.82       $     ?
         HOODDOWN               6,700        $75.98       $     ?
         KARLSTAD                 240        $74.86       $     ?

     TOTAL SHIPMENT           ??,???,???                $???,???,???

                    SHIPMENTS OF IRON ORE

         SHIP NAME              UNITS        COST PER     CARGO
                                ON BOARD     UNIT         VALUE

         BULKFELLOW             2,260        $35.47       $     ?
         ...
```

a. Make up the spacing chart for input and output.
b. Write a pseudocode program for the processing.
c. Draw a flowchart and hierarchy diagram.
d. Write and run the program using single-level control-break processing.

3. **Two-level control-break processing**
   The input and output file are shown here:

```
---------1---------2---------3---------4---------5
ARROWHEAD          OIL         050002040KOREA
ASTONHEAD          WHEAT       143500322PANAMA
BULKFELLOW         IRON ORE    022603547KOREA
CRANSTON           COPPER      045607289KOREA
DEVONSHIRE         OIL         256002572PANAMA
DOVEBIRD           WHEAT       189700754PANAMA
DUSTY              IRON ORE    007563798PANAMA
EVERYMAN           WHEAT       089670321KOREA
FORWARDBOUNTY      COPPER      007857382PANAMA
FUNNELHEAD         OIL         200002176PANAMA
GOODWILL           OIL         150002174KOREA
GOVERNOR           WHEAT       045200376KOREA
GULLLAKE           OIL         150002019KOREA
HALIFAXGULL        OIL         010002260PANAMA
HEAVYSIDE          IRON ORE    006003422PANAMA
HOODDOWN           COPPER      067007598KOREA
IVANHOE            IRON ORE    065003542KOREA
KARLSTAD           COPPER      002407486PANAMA
KINGSTON           OIL         195002056PANAMA
KUNGHU             WHEAT       200540342KOREA
```

```
                    Columns 01–20    Ship name
                            21–30    Cargo type
                            31–35    Units of cargo (tons, bushels, etc.)
                            36–39    Cost per unit (pennies in last two digits)
                            40–50    Registration of vessel
---------1---------2---------3---------4---------5---------6---------7
          SHIPPING DATA BY VESSEL REGISTRATION AND CARGO
   PAGE   1                                              06/05/92


            SHIP NAME          UNITS          COST PER       CARGO
                               ON BOARD       UNIT           VALUE


            CRANSTON           4,560          $72.89         $   332,378
            HOODDOWN           6,700          $75.98         $         ?

   TOTAL SHIPMENT        ??,???,???                      $???,???,???
          (IRON ORE)


            BULKFELLOW         2,260          $35.47         $         ?
            ...
            ...
   TOTAL CARGO VALUE                                 $??,???,???,???
          (KOREA REGISTERED VESSELS)
```

In the processing, you will not know in advance how many nations register vessels.

a. Make up the record layout and spacing chart for input and output.
b. Write a pseudocode program for the processing.
c. Draw a flowchart and hierarchy diagram.
d. Write and run the program using two-level control-break processing. Use registration as the major control field, and cargo as the minor control field.

4. **Two-level control-break processing**
   In this assignment, reuse the input file from Assignment 3. The output report is similar, but this time the major summary is for cargo type and the minor summary is for country of registration.

   a. Make up the record layout and spacing chart for input and output.
   b. Write a pseudocode program for the processing.
   c. Draw a flowchart and hierarchy diagram.
   d. Write and run the program using two-level control-break processing. Use cargo as the major control field and registration as the minor control field.

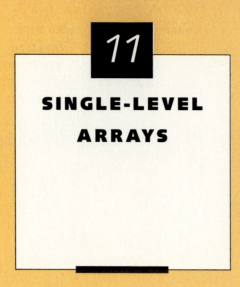

SINGLE-LEVEL ARRAYS

OBJECTIVES

- To demonstrate how to specify an array using an OCCURS clause
- To show how to load data into and manipulate data in an array
- To explain how to search an array using linear and binary searches

OUTLINE

Initializing numeric arrays
  Use PERFORM . . . VARYING
  Use a VALUE clause
  Use REDEFINES
There are rules for referring to subscripted identifiers

11.3 An array can be used for histogram generation
Histograms and arrays go together
Histogram development involves a specific technique
COBOL program for developing a histogram
There is a problem with a zero subscript

11.4 An array is used with repeating groups of fields
Move the repeating groups into an array for manipulation
A program for manipulation of repeating groups

11.5 Arrays can be used as look-up tables
Example of a look-up table for product data
A look-up table has to be initialized with data in a specific order
You can use either linear or binary searches
  Linear search
  Binary search
You can use PERFORM . . . VARYING for a linear table search
The SEARCH verb is used for a linear search of an array
  Using SEARCH for a linear table search
An index identifier contains a memory address offset value
You must use SET to manipulate an index value
  Use SET to assign a value
  Use SET to increase or decrease the value
  Use SET to transfer a value
The differences between an index identifier and a subscript identifier are
  very important
You can also use an index identifier with PERFORM . . . VARYING
You use SEARCH ALL for a binary search of a table
You must define a search key and an index to use SEARCH ALL

With COBOL, as with most other computer languages, it is possible to have an array of identifiers of the same type. The identifiers of the array are distinguished only by a *subscript* (a number that follows the identifier inside parentheses). For example, SCORE (1), SCORE (2), SCORE (3) . . . SCORE (100) could be identifiers in an array of 100 identifiers.

Arrays have many uses, but the ones most common are

- To store input data that need repeated processing within a single program
- To create multiple totals and histograms
- To handle repeating groups of fields in records
- To store tables that need to be accessed repeatedly within a single program

Let us take the first use of arrays, storage of input data that need repeated processing, to gain familiarity with the array concept. The other uses of arrays will be examined later.

Note that there are single-level arrays and multiple-level arrays. A multiple-level array has identifiers that require two or more subscripts. In this chapter when the term *array* is used, it means a single-level array.

11.1
The array concept is illustrated by repeated processing of a short input file

SUPPOSE YOU HAVE the following problem. A small input file gives student scores in an examination, as follows:

```
ARROWSMITH, F.G.      55
AXEWORTHY, R.E.       47
BARTON, J.P.          86
BURTON, Y.J           67
...
```

There are 1000 students and you want to print out the names and scores of students who score above average. You can read the records one by one and add each score to an identifier SUM-OF-SCORES. When all the records have been read, division by 1000 will give the average, which can be placed in an identifier AVERAGE.

But to get the above-average students you would have to close the file, open it again, then reread the records and print those with a score greater than the value in AVERAGE. However, it is preferable not to read the records twice, since reading records from a file is slow. In that case, the only alternative is to keep the records in working storage after the first reading of the file. The question is how to do that.

You use OCCURS to define an array of identifiers

You can specify space for all 1000 records in working storage using the OCCURS clause, as follows:

```
01  RECORD-COLLECTION-ARRAY.
    05  RCA-STUDENT-RECORD                    OCCURS 1000 TIMES.
        10  RCA-STUDENT-NAME    PIC X(21).
        10  RCA-SCORE           PIC 9(02).
```

The use of OCCURS means that 1000 RCA-STUDENT-RECORD identifiers have been specified. Each one of these identifies a distinct location in the working storage part of memory, and each one can be referred to uniquely by using a numeric subscript, which follows RCA-STUDENT-RECORD, inside parentheses. Thus, the following identifiers have actually been specified:

```
RCA-STUDENT-RECORD (1)
RCA-STUDENT-RECORD (2)
RCA-STUDENT-RECORD (3)
...
RCA-STUDENT-RECORD (999)
RCA-STUDENT-RECORD (1000)
```

This group of identifiers is an array of identifiers with 1000 elements. An element, such as RCA-STUDENT-RECORD (87), is a distinct identifier with a distinct memory location. A diagram of the array can often be drawn, such as that in Figure 11.1.

RCA-STUDENT-RECORD

Subscript	STUDENT-NAME	SCORE
1	ARROWSMITH, F.G.	55
2	AXWORTHY, R.E.	47
3	BARTON, J.P.	86
• • •		
999	ZENTAPH, A.K.	72
1000	ZUNPHOR, P.L.	56

Figure 11.1 *The array STUDENT-RECORD with 1000 elements, each containing two identifiers.*

A subscript distinguishes the different identifiers of an array

An array can be either an array of group identifiers or an array of elementary identifiers. However, in all cases the identifiers of the array have the same name and are distinguished only by the subscript. A subscript can be either a numeric literal or a numeric identifier containing a positive integer. Suppose you have an identifier

```
01 SUB  PIC 9(04).
```

In the PROCEDURE DIVISION the following is correct:

```
MOVE 467 TO SUB.
MOVE RCA-STUDENT-RECORD (SUB) TO REPORT-RECORD-OUT.
WRITE REPORT-RECORD-OUT.
```

This would be exactly equivalent to

```
MOVE RCA-STUDENT-RECORD (467) TO REPORT-RECORD-OUT.
WRITE REPORT-RECORD-OUT.
```

In both cases it would cause the contents of the 467th element of the array to be printed.

You put data into an element by using the subscript

Suppose the file containing the student scores is called SCORE-FILE and the input buffer record identifier for the file is SCORE-RECORD-IN. Suppose also that the identifier SUB is used as the subscript. To read the records of the input file SCORE-FILE into the array, you could write

```
100-MAIN-MODULE.
    ...
    MOVE 'YES' TO MORE-RECORDS.
    READ SCORE-FILE
      AT END  MOVE 'NO' TO MORE-RECORDS.
    MOVE 1 TO SUB.
    PERFORM 200-PROCESS-RECORD UNTIL MORE-RECORDS = 'NO'.
    ...
200-PROCESS-RECORD.
    MOVE SCORE-RECORD-IN TO RCA-STUDENT-RECORD (SUB).
    ADD 1 TO SUB.
    READ SCORE-FILE,
         AT END MOVE 'NO' TO MORE RECORDS.
    ...
```

As each record is read, it is placed in the next element of the array. The array has 1000 elements. Suppose that the file has 997 records. When the last record has been read, the first 997 elements of the array will have data. The last three will have no data. If the file had 1001 records, you would get an error at the last record when an attempt was made to place the last record in element RCA-STUDENT-RECORD (1001). There is no element RCA-STUDENT-RECORD (1001).

You could also use an in-line PERFORM (in COBOL 85) to read the records into the array, as follows:

```
100-MAIN-MODULE.
    ...
    MOVE 'YES' TO MORE-RECORDS.
    READ SCORE-FILE
         AT END MOVE 'NO' TO MORE-RECORDS.
    MOVE 1 TO SUB.
    PERFORM UNTIL MORE-RECORDS = 'NO'
         MOVE SCORE-RECORD-IN TO RCA-STUDENT-RECORD (SUB)
         ADD 1 TO SUB
         READ SCORE-FILE
              AT END MOVE 'NO' TO MORE RECORDS
    END-PERFORM.
```

Elements of an array are processed one by one using the subscript

Now suppose that the average score has been computed and is in the identifier AVERAGE. Assume there are 997 records. To print the records of students with a score above average, you would write

```
100-MAIN-MODULE.
    ...
    MOVE 1 TO SUB.
    PERFORM 300-PRINT-ABOVE-AVERAGE UNTIL SUB > 997.
    ...
```

```
300-PRINT-ABOVE-AVERAGE.
    IF RCA-SCORE (SUB) > AVERAGE
        WRITE REPORT-RECORD-OUT FROM RCA-STUDENT-RECORD (SUB)
                                AFTER ADVANCING 1 LINE
    END-IF.
    ADD 1 TO SUB.
```

Subscripts can be used with elementary identifiers of an array of group identifiers

In addition to demonstrating the use of a subscript to refer to an element of the (group) identifier RCA-STUDENT-RECORD, the preceding excerpt shows you can also use a subscript with an elementary identifier that is part of a subscripted group identifier. Thus, if you have the group identifier

```
05  SPECIAL-STUDENT.
    10  NAME    PIC X(21).
    10  MARKS   PIC 9(02).
```

the statement

```
MOVE 456 TO SUB.
MOVE RCA-STUDENT-RECORD (SUB) TO SPECIAL-STUDENT.
```

would be exactly equivalent to

```
MOVE 456 TO SUB.
MOVE RCA-STUDENT-NAME (SUB) TO NAME.
MOVE RCA-SCORE (SUB) TO MARKS.
```

COBOL program using an array for repeated processing of a short input file

Let us now look at the complete program to output the names and scores of students who have scored above average. The input data are in the file SCORE-FILE, as shown in Figure 11.2.

```
---------1---------2---------3---------4---------5
ARROWSMITH, F.G.      55
AXEWORTHY, R.E.       47          About 1,000 records
BARTON, J.P.          86          Maximum possible 1,050
BURTON, Y.J           67
         ...

Columns 1–21     Student name
        2–23     Score
```

Figure 11.2a *Initial records of SCORE-FILE.*

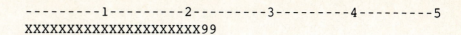
```
---------1---------2---------3---------4---------5
XXXXXXXXXXXXXXXXXXXXX99
```

Figure 11.2b *Input record layout for SCORE-FILE.*

```
01  SCORE-RECORD-IN.
    05   SR-STUDENT-NAME-IN        PIC X(21).
    05   SR-SCORE-IN               PIC 9(02).
```

Figure 11.2c *Input area record structure for SCORE-FILE records.*

The output data are to appear in the form of a simple report, as shown in Figure 11.3.

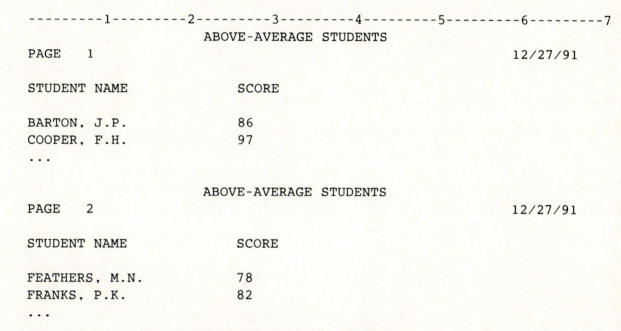

```
---------1---------2---------3---------4---------5---------6---------7
                    ABOVE-AVERAGE STUDENTS
PAGE    1                                              12/27/91

STUDENT NAME                   SCORE

BARTON, J.P.                   86
COOPER, F.H.                   97
...


                    ABOVE-AVERAGE STUDENTS
PAGE    2                                              12/27/91

STUDENT NAME                   SCORE

FEATHERS, M.N.                 78
FRANKS, P.K.                   82
...
```

Figure 11.3a *Format of report generated.*

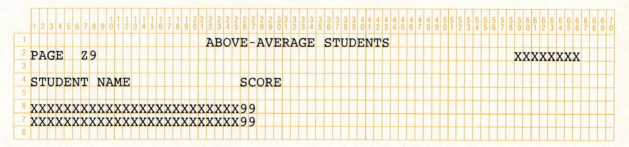

Figure 11.3b *Printer spacing chart for report.*

```
01 DETAIL-LINE-OUT.
   05   FILLER                      PIC X          VALUE SPACE.
   05   DL-STUDENT-OUT              PIC X(25).
   05   DL-SCORE-OUT                PIC 9(02).
   05   FILLER                      PIC X(105)     VALUE SPACES.
```

Figure 11.3c *Structure of detail line record for report.*

The program uses the principles discussed in the previous section. Essential pseudocode for the processing, excluding header printing, is as follows:

```
OPEN files.
READ first record.
MOVE 0 to Subscript.
PERFORM until no records left
     ADD 1 to Subscript
     ADD Score to Sum-of-scores
     MOVE record just read to Array (Subscript)
     READ next record
END-PERFORM.
MOVE subscript to Total-students.
DIVIDE Sum-of-scores by Total-students to give Average.
MOVE 1 to Subscript.
PERFORM until Subscript > Total-students
     IF Score (subscript) > Average THEN
        Print row (Subscript)
     END-IF
     ADD 1 to Subscript
END-PERFORM.
CLOSE files and STOP.
```

However, the actual number of records in the input file is not known exactly. But suppose it is known that the number cannot exceed 1050; so an array with 1050 elements is used. In most executions of the program, not all of these elements will be filled with data. However, since access to an empty element is an error, the program must know how many elements are filled. This information is obtained from the value of the subscript when the last record has been read. This is shown in the program in Figure 11.4.

```
IDENTIFICATION DIVISION.
PROGRAM-ID. SR1.
ENVIRONMENT DIVISION.
INPUT-OUTPUT SECTION.
FILE-CONTROL.   SELECT SCORE-FILE   ASSIGN UT-S-SC400.
                SELECT REPORT-FILE ASSIGN TO UR-S-SYSPRINT.
DATA DIVISION.
FILE SECTION.
FD   SCORE-FILE                     LABEL RECORDS ARE STANDARD.
01 SCORE-RECORD-IN.
     05   SR-STUDENT-NAME-IN   PIC X(21).
     05   SR-SCORE-IN          PIC 9(02).
FD   REPORT-FILE                    LABEL RECORDS ARE OMITTED.
01   REPORT-RECORD-OUT       PIC X(133).
WORKING-STORAGE SECTION.
01 WS-AREA.
     05 LINE-COUNT            PIC 9(02).
     05 MORE-RECORDS          PIC X(03)     VALUE 'YES'.
     05 SUB                   PIC 9(02).
     05 AVERAGE               PIC 9(02)V99.
     05 TOTAL-STUDENTS        PIC 9(04)V999 VALUE ZERO.
     05 SUM-OF-SCORES         PIC 9(07)     VALUE ZERO.
     05 WS-PAGE-NUMB          PIC 9(02)     VALUE ZERO.
01 PAGE-DATE-LINE-OUT.
     05   FILLER              PIC X         VALUE SPACE.
     05   FILLER              PIC X(06)     VALUE 'PAGE '.
     05   PD-PAGE-NUMB-OUT    PIC Z9.
     05   FILLER              PIC X(50)     VALUE SPACES.
     05   PD-RUN-DATE-OUT     PIC X(08).
     05   FILLER              PIC X(66)     VALUE SPACES.
01 REPORT-HEADER.
     05   FILLER              PIC X         VALUE SPACE.
     05   FILLER              PIC X(21)     VALUE SPACES.
     05   FILLER              PIC X(22)     VALUE
                                           'ABOVE-AVERAGE STUDENTS'.
     05   FILLER              PIC X(89)     VALUE SPACES.
01 COL-HEADER-1.
     05   FILLER              PIC X         VALUE SPACE.
     05   FILLER              PIC X(25)     VALUE 'STUDENT NAME'.
     05   FILLER              PIC X(05)     VALUE 'SCORE'.
     05   FILLER              PIC X(102)    VALUE SPACES.
01 DETAIL-LINE-OUT.
     05   FILLER              PIC X         VALUE SPACE.
     05   DL-STUDENT-OUT      PIC X(25).
     05   DL-SCORE-OUT        PIC 9(02).
     05   FILLER              PIC X(105)    VALUE SPACES.
01 RECORD-COLLECTION-ARRAY.
     05   RCA-STUDENT-RECORD                OCCURS 1050 TIMES.
       10   RCA-STUDENT-NAME  PIC X(21).
       10   RCA-SCORE         PIC 9(02).
PROCEDURE DIVISION.
```

```
 100-MAIN-MODULE.
****************************************************************************
*    DIRECTS PROGRAM LOGIC.                                              *
****************************************************************************
      PERFORM 200-INITIALIZATION.
      MOVE ZERO TO SUB.
      PERFORM 300-PROCESS-INPUT-RECORD UNTIL MORE-RECORDS = 'NO'.
      MOVE SUB TO TOTAL-STUDENTS.
      PERFORM 600-COMPUTE-AVERAGE.
      MOVE 1 TO SUB.
      PERFORM 400-PRINT-ABOVE-AVERAGE UNTIL SUB > TOTAL-STUDENTS.
      PERFORM 700-TERMINATION.
 200-INITIALIZATION.
****************************************************************************
*    PERFORMED FROM 100-MAIN-MODULE. OPENS FILES, READS FIRST RECORD,    *
*    EXTRACTS DATE, AND PRINTS INITIAL HEADERS.                          *
****************************************************************************
      OPEN INPUT SCORE-FILE
           OUTPUT REPORT-FILE.
      READ SCORE-FILE
              AT END MOVE 'NO' TO MORE-RECORDS.
      MOVE CURRENT-DATE TO PD-RUN-DATE-OUT.
      PERFORM 500-PAGE-HEADERS.
 300-PROCESS-INPUT-RECORD.
****************************************************************************
*    PERFORMED FROM 100-MAIN-MODULE. PLACES CURRENT RECORD IN ARRAY AND  *
*    READS NEXT RECORD.                                                  *
****************************************************************************
      ADD 1 TO SUB.
      ADD SR-SCORE-IN TO SUM-OF-SCORES.
      MOVE SCORE-RECORD-IN TO RCA-STUDENT-RECORD (SUB).
      READ SCORE-FILE
              AT END MOVE 'NO' TO MORE RECORDS.
 400-PRINT-ABOVE-AVERAGE.
****************************************************************************
*    PERFORMED FROM 100-MAIN-MODULE. CHECKS CURRENT RECORD IN ARRAY. IF  *
*    SCORE IS ABOVE AVERAGE, THE RECORD IS PRINTED.  INCREMENTS          *
*    SUBSCRIPT TO POINT TO NEXT RECORD IN ARRAY.  PRINTS PAGE HEADERS,   *
*    IF NECESSARY, BEFORE PRINTING A RECORD.                             *
****************************************************************************
      IF RCA-SCORE (SUB) > AVERAGE
          MOVE RCA-STUDENT-NAME (SUB) TO DL-STUDENT-OUT
          MOVE RCA-SCORE (SUB) TO DL-SCORE-OUT
          IF LINE-COUNT >= 45
              PERFORM 500-PAGE-HEADERS
          END-IF
          WRITE REPORT-RECORD-OUT FROM DETAIL-LINE-OUT
              AFTER ADVANCING 1 LINE
          ADD 1 TO LINE-COUNT
      END-IF.
      ADD 1 TO SUB.
```

```
 500-PAGE-HEADERS.
***************************************************************************
*   PERFORMED FROM 200-INITIALIZATION AND 400-PRINT-ABOVE-AVERAGE.       *
*   PRINTS REPORT HEADERS, PAGE NUMBER AND DATE, AND COLUMN HEADERS.     *
***************************************************************************
     WRITE REPORT-RECORD-OUT FROM REPORT-HEADER
               AFTER ADVANCING PAGE.
     ADD 1 TO WS-PAGE-NUMB.
     MOVE WS-PAGE-NUMB TO PD-PAGE-NUMB-OUT.
     WRITE REPORT-RECORD-OUT FROM PAGE-DATE-LINE-OUT
               AFTER ADVANCING 1 LINE.
     WRITE REPORT-RECORD-OUT FROM COL-HEADER-1
               AFTER ADVANCING 2 LINES.
     MOVE SPACES TO REPORT-RECORD-OUT
     WRITE REPORT-RECORD-OUT
               AFTER ADVANCING 1 LINE.
     MOVE 5 TO LINE-COUNT.
 600-COMPUTE-AVERAGE.
***************************************************************************
*   PERFORMED FROM 100-MAIN-MODULE. COMPUTES AVERAGE SCORE.              *
***************************************************************************
     DIVIDE TOTAL-STUDENTS INTO SUM-OF-SCORES
                         GIVING AVERAGE ROUNDED.
 700-TERMINATION.
***************************************************************************
*   PERFORMED FROM 100-MAIN-MODULE. CLOSES FILES, STOPS PROGRAM         *
*   EXECUTION.                                                           *
***************************************************************************
     CLOSE SCORE-FILE
           REPORT-FILE.
     STOP RUN.
```

Figure 11.4 Program to output names and scores of above-average students.

If you look at the paragraph 400-PRINT-ABOVE-AVERAGE, you will see that the elements of the array RCA-STUDENT-RECORD are examined one by one, beginning with RCA-SCORE (1), by incrementing the subscript SUB with each iteration of the paragraph. However, not all elements are examined. The subscript of the last element examined has a subscript value equal to TOTAL-STUDENTS, which was the number of records counted in the input file SCORE-FILE. Thus, records with a subscript higher than the value in TOTAL-STUDENTS are not examined. In fact, to attempt it would be an error, since these array elements contain no values.

The PERFORM . . . VARYING verb is used to scan an array

There is a version of the PERFORM verb designed for scanning through the elements of an array when the beginning and end subscripts for the scan are known. This is the PERFORM . . . VARYING verb. The basic syntax is given here:

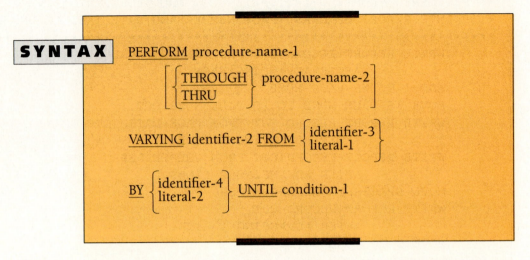

SYNTAX

PERFORM procedure-name-1

$$\left[\left\{ \begin{array}{l} \underline{THROUGH} \\ \underline{THRU} \end{array} \right\} \text{procedure-name-2} \right]$$

$$\underline{VARYING} \text{ identifier-2 } \underline{FROM} \left\{ \begin{array}{l} \text{identifier-3} \\ \text{literal-1} \end{array} \right\}$$

$$\underline{BY} \left\{ \begin{array}{l} \text{identifier-4} \\ \text{literal-2} \end{array} \right\} \underline{UNTIL} \text{ condition-1}$$

Some examples of correct syntax are

```
PERFORM 300-MODULE
    VARYING SUB FROM 4 BY 1 UNTIL SUB > 11.

PERFORM 300-MODULE THRU 500-MODULE
    VARYING SUBSCRIPT FROM 1 BY 1 UNTIL SUB > TOTAL-STUDENTS.

PERFORM 300-MODULE
    VARYING SUB FROM START BY 3 UNTIL SUB > 50.
```

The PERFORM . . . VARYING verb allows automatic increases for the subscript identifier used to scan the array. Normally the subscript will be increased by 1 (the BY 1 option). However, in a few cases you would want the subscript to increase by a value other than 1, so you would instead use that value following BY.

The first subscript value for the scan of an array is normally 1, but any value can be written in the FROM clause, so you can start the scan anywhere with the array. The condition following UNTIL determines where the scan will stop.

To use PERFORM . . . VARYING, you must know how many array elements to process

When scanning the elements of an array, you can always use PERFORM . . . UNTIL, as was illustrated in the program in Figure 11.4. However, where PERFORM . . . UNTIL is used, there has to be an instruction within the repeated paragraph for incrementing the subscript identifier. Figure 11.4 had the statement ADD 1 TO SUB in both paragraphs that were used to scan the elements of the array.

You can use the PERFORM . . . VARYING statement only where it is known exactly how many elements of the array will be accessed. Refer again to Figure 11.4. The first time the array is scanned is in paragraph 300-PROCESS-INPUT-RECORD. Each execution of the paragraph places the current record in the next empty space in the array of STUDENT-RECORD elements and then reads the next record. Here you cannot use PER-FORM . . . VARYING; you must use PERFORM . . . UNTIL, since you do not know beforehand how many records are in the file and thus how many elements of the array will be accessed.

The next time the array is scanned is in the paragraph 400-PRINT-ABOVE-AVERAGE. Each execution of the paragraph compares the score value in the current array element and prints that element if the score is above average. This time you know exactly how many elements of the array will be accessed, since this number is exactly equal to the number of records in the input file, counted earlier. Thus you could use either PER-FORM . . . UNTIL or PERFORM . . . VARYING.

The version of 400-PRINT-ABOVE-AVERAGE using PERFORM . . . VARYING is

```
100-MAIN-MODULE.
    ...
    MOVE 0 TO SUB
    PERFORM 300-PROCESS-INPUT-RECORD UNTIL MORE-RECORDS = 'NO'.
    MOVE SUB TO TOTAL-STUDENTS.
    PERFORM 600-COMPUTE-AVERAGE.
    PERFORM 400-PRINT-ABOVE-AVERAGE
        VARYING SUB FROM 1 BY 1 UNTIL SUB > TOTAL-STUDENTS.
    CLOSE SCORE-FILE, REPORT-FILE.
    STOP RUN.
...
400-PRINT-ABOVE-AVERAGE.
    IF RCA-SCORE (SUB) > AVERAGE
        MOVE RCA-STUDENT-NAME (SUB) TO DL-STUDENT-OUT
        MOVE RCA-SCORE (SUB) TO DL-SCORE-OUT
        IF LINE-COUNT >= 45
            PERFORM 500-PAGE-HEADERS
        END-IF
        WRITE REPORT-RECORD-OUT FROM DETAIL-LINE-OUT
                AFTER ADVANCING 1 LINE
        ADD 1 TO LINE-COUNT
    END-IF.
```

An in-line PERFORM . . . VARYING is also available

There is an in-line PERFORM . . . VARYING verb in COBOL 85. It is useful where the repeated paragraph involves only a few lines and there is little to be gained in terms of clarity in placing these few lines in a separate paragraph. The syntax for the in-line version is shown here:

$$\underline{\text{PERFORM VARYING}} \text{ identifier-2 } \underline{\text{FROM}} \begin{Bmatrix} \text{identifier-3} \\ \text{literal-1} \end{Bmatrix}$$

$$\underline{\text{BY}} \begin{Bmatrix} \text{identifier-4} \\ \text{literal-2} \end{Bmatrix} \underline{\text{UNTIL}} \text{ condition-1}$$

$$\text{imperative-statement-1 } \underline{\text{END-PERFORM}}$$

As an example, you might write

```
PERFORM ... VARYING SUB FROM 1 BY 1 UNTIL SUB > 10
          Statements to be repeated
END-PERFORM.
```

You could use the in-line PERFORM ... VARYING verb with the program in Figure 11.4. The paragraph 400-PRINT-ABOVE-AVERAGE is eliminated and the statements to be repeated placed in-line, after the PERFORM ... VARYING verb

```
100-MAIN-MODULE.
    ...
    MOVE 0 TO SUB.
    PERFORM 300-PROCESS-INPUT-RECORD UNTIL MORE-RECORDS = 'NO'.
    MOVE SUB TO TOTAL-STUDENTS.
    PERFORM 600-COMPUTE-AVERAGE.
    PERFORM VARYING SUB FROM 1 BY 1
                UNTIL SUB > TOTAL-STUDENTS
        IF RCA-SCORE (SUB) > AVERAGE
            MOVE RCA-STUDENT-NAME (SUB) TO DL-STUDENT-OUT
            MOVE RCA-SCORE (SUB) TO DL-SCORE-OUT
            IF LINE-COUNT >= 45
                PERFORM 500-PAGE-HEADERS
            END-IF
            WRITE REPORT-RECORD-OUT FROM DETAIL-LINE-OUT
                AFTER ADVANCING 1 LINE
            ADD 1 TO LINE-COUNT
        END-IF
    END-PERFORM.
    PERFORM 700-TERMINATION.
```

Watch out for a wrong UNTIL condition when scanning the elements of an array

A common error with array processing is to use equality in the UNTIL condition, instead of greater than. The following excerpt for processing 997 elements of the array STUDENT-RECORD, with each element containing an identifier SCORE, is wrong:

```
          MOVE 1 TO SUB.
          PERFORM 300-PRINT-ABOVE-AVERAGE UNTIL SUB = 997.      error!
          ...
      300-PRINT-ABOVE-AVERAGE.
          IF RCA-SCORE (SUB) > AVERAGE
             WRITE REPORT-RECORD-OUT FROM RCA-STUDENT-RECORD (SUB)
                                AFTER ADVANCING 1 LINE
          END-IF.
          ADD 1 TO SUB.
```

This will cause only 996 elements of the array to be processed. The UNTIL condition is tested before each execution of 300-PRINT-ABOVE-AVERAGE, so when SUB gets the value 997 the condition is true and the paragraph is not processed again.

11.2
There are array technicalities to be mastered

T HERE ARE A fair number of technical details to know when working with arrays. These mainly concern specifying arrays in working storage, putting initial values in arrays, and using subscripts.

There are rules for specifying arrays

Notice the array of RCA-STUDENT-RECORD elements was specified as a 05 level in a group identifier called RECORD-COLLECTION-ARRAY

```
01  RECORD-COLLECTION-ARRAY.
    05   RCA-STUDENT-RECORD              OCCURS 1000 TIMES.
        10   RCA-STUDENT-NAME            PIC X(21).
        10   RCA-SCORE                   PIC 9(02).
```

It could not have been specified as

```
01  RCA-STUDENT-RECORD                   OCCURS 1000 TIMES.    error!
    05   RCA-STUDENT-NAME                PIC X(21).
    05   RCA-SCORE                       PIC 9(02).
```

Note the following:

- The OCCURS clause can never be used with a 01 level identifier. It must be used with a level greater than 01, but not with a level 88 identifier.
- There may be a PICTURE specification with an OCCURS clause. This is used whenever each element of the array consists of a single elementary identifier, as in the first two examples that follow.

The following are examples of array specifications:

Example 1: A four-element array

```
01 SALES-RECORD.
   05 SALESPERSON                              PIC X(15).
   05 PRODUCT-TYPE                             PIC X(06).
   05 QUANTITY-OF-UNITS    OCCURS 4 TIMES      PIC 9(03).
```

The group identifier here consists of six elementary identifiers:

```
SALESPERSON
PRODUCT-TYPE
QUANTITY-OF-UNITS (1)
QUANTITY-OF-UNITS (2)
QUANTITY-OF-UNITS (3)
QUANTITY-OF-UNITS (4)
```

Thus, QUANTITY-OF-UNITS is an array consisting of four elements.

Example 2: A 10-element array

```
01 PRODUCT-CATEGORIES.
      10 CATEGORY    OCCURS 10 TIMES           PIC 9(02).
```

This gives an array CATEGORY with elements CATEGORY (1), CATEGORY (2) . . . CATEGORY (10).

Example 3: Two types of four-element arrays

The following specifications are not the same:

```
01 QUARTERLY-SALES-DATA.
   05  PRODUCT     OCCURS 4 TIMES      PIC X(06).
   05  QUANTITY    OCCURS 4 TIMES      PIC 9(02).
01 QUARTERLY-SALES-DATA.
   05 QUARTER         OCCURS 4 TIMES.
      10 PRODUCT                       PIC X(06).
      10 QUANTITY                      PIC 9(02).
```

In the first case are two distinct four-element arrays, PRODUCT and QUANTITY. If you printed contents of QUARTERLY-SALES-DATA, for this case, the contents of the identifiers would print in this order:

```
PRODUCT (1),  PRODUCT (2),  PRODUCT (3),  PRODUCT (4),
QUANTITY (1), QUANTITY (2), QUANTITY (3), QUANTITY (4).
```

In the second case is a single four-element group identifier array QUARTER, in which each element consists of two elementary identifiers. Thus, QUARTER (3) consists of PRODUCT (3) and QUANTITY (3). If you printed the contents of QUARTERLY-SALES-DATA in this case, the contents of the identifiers would print in this order:

```
PRODUCT (1),  QUANTITY (1),  PRODUCT (2),  QUANTITY (2),
PRODUCT (3),  QUANTITY (3),  PRODUCT (4), QUANTITY (4).
```

Each element of an array is either an elementary identifier or a group identifier in its own right. Thus, each element of an array has to be initialized before its value can be used in a statement. Often you would like an alphanumeric array to be initialized with spaces and a numeric array to be initialized with zero values. There are several ways to do this.

Initializing Alphanumeric Arrays

Suppose you have the array

```
01 PRODUCTS.
    05 PRODUCT-CODE OCCURS 6 TIMES        PIC X(04).
```

You have the following options for initializing this array:

Use PERFORM . . . VARYING Suppose you want to put spaces in each element. You could use a PERFORM . . . VARYING at the beginning of the procedure division

```
PERFORM 600-INITIALIZE-SPACES
    VARYING SUB FROM 1 BY 1 UNTIL SUB > 6.
...
600-INITIALIZE-SPACES.
    MOVE SPACES TO PRODUCT-CODE (SUB).
```

However, the in-line PERFORM (COBOL 85 only) is better

```
PERFORM VARYING SUB FROM 1 BY 1 UNTIL SUB > 6
    MOVE SPACES TO PRODUCT-CODE (SUB)
END-PERFORM.
```

Use a VALUE clause To insert spaces in each identifier, you could also use a VALUE clause. An identifier specification with an OCCURS clause can also have a VALUE clause, as can a specification subordinate to one with an OCCURS clause.

You could have originally defined PRODUCT-CODE as

```
01 PRODUCTS.
    05 PRODUCT-CODE OCCURS 6 TIMES    PIC X(04) VALUE SPACES.
```

All elements of the array are assigned the value spaces. Note that this is a COBOL 85 feature; it was not part of COBOL 74.

Use MOVE SPACES Another way to initialize all the elements of an array to blanks is to use a MOVE SPACES statement

```
MOVE SPACES TO PRODUCTS.
```

Note that some compilers do not allow this.

Use REDEFINES Suppose you had wanted to initialize the six identifiers of PRODUCT-CODE with CT11, CT12, CT13, CT14, CT15, and CT16. You could do it as follows:

```
01 PRODUCTS.
    05 INITIAL-DATA.
        10 FILLER                      PIC X(4)  VALUE 'CT11'.
        10 FILLER                      PIC X(4)  VALUE 'CT12'.
        10 FILLER                      PIC X(4)  VALUE 'CT13'.
        10 FILLER                      PIC X(4)  VALUE 'CT14'.
        10 FILLER                      PIC X(4)  VALUE 'CT15'.
        10 FILLER                      PIC X(4)  VALUE 'CT16'.
    05 PRODUCT-CODE
        REDEFINES INITIAL-DATA
            OCCURS 6 TIMES             PIC X(04).
```

Note that you can use an array, such as PRODUCT-CODE, to redefine an identifier, such as INITIAL-DATA. However, it is an error to use an identifier to redefine an array (that is, it is an error to have the array first, then the redefining identifier).

The REDEFINES clause is commonly used with a group of identifiers since you cannot use a VALUE clause with a group identifier, only with an elementary identifier. But note that an elementary identifier defined with an OCCURS clause can have a VALUE clause.

Initializing Numeric Arrays

Suppose you have the following array:

```
01 QUARTERLY-SALES.
    05 QUANTITY        OCCURS 4 TIMES           PIC 9(02)
```

You could initialize it as follows:

Use PERFORM . . . VARYING To put zero in each element, you could use PERFORM . . . VARYING in the PROCEDURE DIVISION

```
PERFORM 400-INITIALIZATION
      VARYING SUB FROM 1 BY 1 UNTIL SUB > 4.
...
400-INITIALIZATION.
    MOVE ZERO TO QUANTITY (SUB).
```

or alternatively, using an in-line PERFORM (in COBOL 85)

```
PERFORM . . . VARYING SUB FROM 1 BY 1 UNTIL SUB > 4
    MOVE ZERO TO QUANTITY (SUB).
END-PERFORM.
```

Use a VALUE clause To put zero in each element, you could write

```
01 QUARTERLY-SALES.
    05 QUANTITY OCCURS 4 TIMES          PIC 9(02)    VALUE ZEROS.
```

Use REDEFINES To put the values 14, 67, 89, and 56 in the elements, you could write

```
01 QUARTERLY SALES.
   05 INIT-DATA.
      10 FILLER          PIC 9(02) VALUE  14.
      10 FILLER          PIC 9(02) VALUE  67.
      10 FILLER          PIC 9(02) VALUE  89.
      10 FILLER          PIC 9(02) VALUE  56.
   05 QUANTITY REDEFINES INIT-DATA
                         OCCURS 4 TIMES       PIC 9(02).
```

There are rules for referring to subscripted identifiers

Suppose you have the following array:

```
01   SALES-DATA.
     05   QTY          PIC 9(02) OCCURS 100 TIMES.
```

In the PROCEDURE DIVISION, you can refer to

```
QTY (4)
```

or

```
QTY (SUB)
```

where SUB is an integer numeric identifier. You can also refer to

```
QTY (SUB - 4)
QTY (SUB + 6)
QTY (SUB + J)
QTY (SUB - J)
```

The subscript can consist of the sum or difference of any two integer numeric identifiers or literals (a COBOL 85 feature).

Note that with most compilers, you cannot write either of the following:

```
QTY(SUB)        error! – must be space before left parenthesis
QTY ( SUB )     error! – no spaces allowed before or after subscript
```

Note that a subscript may not have the value zero. Thus,

```
QYT (0)         error!
```

is not valid.

Finally, if you have

```
01 X-ARRAY.
   05 X      PIC 9(03) OCCURS 10 TIMES.
```

It is an error to use a subscript greater than 10. Thus, the following is wrong:

```
MOVE ZEROS TO X (11).            error!
```

There is no X (11). The maximum subscript value allowed is the number following OCCURS in the definition of the array.

An array can be used for histogram generation

A HISTOGRAM CAN be generated about any property of a large population. Properties commonly listed are height, weight, exam score, and age. Let us take the example of a histogram regarding the age of aircraft at an airline. At this airline, aircraft age is measured in years, rounded up to the nearest integer. Suppose that aircraft are retired after reaching 20 years; then the oldest aircraft will be 20 years old and the youngest 1 year old. The histogram will give the number of aircraft of each age.

The airline has a fleet of about 1000 aircraft. Suppose management wants a display of how many aircraft there are at each age, as shown in Figure 11.5, a histogram of the age of aircraft.

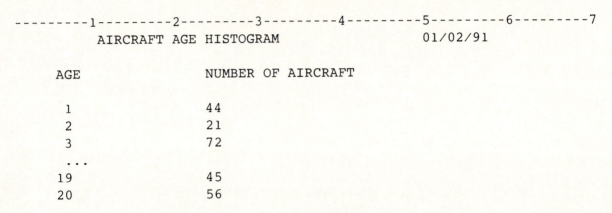

```
---------1---------2---------3---------4---------5---------6---------7
          AIRCRAFT AGE HISTOGRAM                   01/02/91

      AGE                   NUMBER OF AIRCRAFT

       1                    44
       2                    21
       3                    72
      ...
      19                    45
      20                    56
```

Figure 11.5 Aircraft age histogram.

You could also have a histogram of the age of people in a city or in a company. Starting at age 18, you give the number of people who are 18, followed by the number who are 19, 20, and so on.

Or you could have a histogram of the weight of people in a company. If you started at a weight of 120 pounds, you would give the number of people weighing 120, then the number weighing 121, then the number weighing 122, and so on. Similarly, you could have a histogram of any other measurable property of a population, such as height, rank, score on an exam, no sick days taken, and so on.

Histograms and arrays go together

Arrays work well for holding histograms. The data for the histogram in Figure 11.5 could be placed in the following array:

```
01 AGE-HISTOGRAM.
    05  NUMBER-OF-AIRCRAFT  OCCURS 20 TIMES          PIC 9(03).
```

The histogram in the array can be illustrated as shown in Figure 11.6. The value of the subscript identifies the age and the value of the identifier holds the number of aircraft of that age. Thus,

```
NUMBER-OF-AIRCRAFT (3)
```

will hold the number of aircraft that are three years old, which is 72.

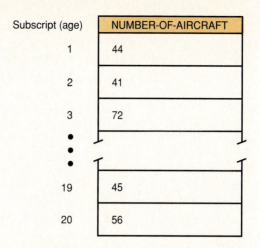

Subscript (age)

	NUMBER-OF-AIRCRAFT
1	44
2	41
3	72
⋮	
19	45
20	56

Figure 11.6 *Use of an array to hold a histogram. Element NUMBER-OF-AIRCRAFT (3), for example, holds the number of aircraft of age 3. Similarly, an array element COMPANY (567) could give the number of companies with 567 employees, and the element PERSON (155) could give the number of people weighing 155 pounds.*

Histogram development involves a specific technique

Suppose you have the input file FLEET-IN in Figure 11.7, which lists each aircraft in the fleet of an airline. Our goal is the development of a COBOL program to process this input file, in order to generate the output file in Figure 11.5.

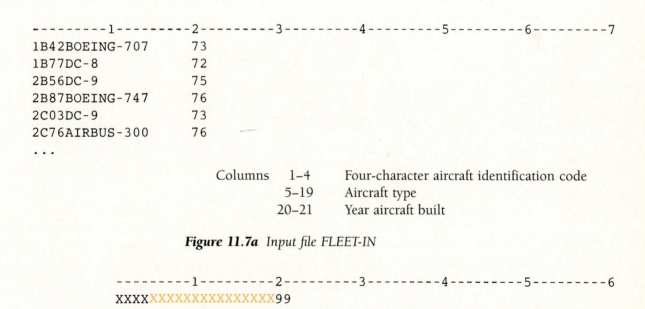

```
---------1---------2---------3---------4---------5---------6---------7
1B42BOEING-707    73
1B77DC-8          72
2B56DC-9          75
2B87BOEING-747    76
2C03DC-9          73
2C76AIRBUS-300    76
...
```

Columns	1–4	Four-character aircraft identification code
	5–19	Aircraft type
	20–21	Year aircraft built

Figure 11.7a *Input file FLEET-IN*

```
---------1---------2---------3---------4---------5---------6
XXXXXXXXXXXXXXXXXXX99
```

Figure 11.7b *Input record layout for FLEET-IN.*

```
01 AIRCRAFT-RECORD-IN.
    05 AIRCRAFT-ID-IN           PIC X(04).
    05 AIRCRAFT-TYPE-IN         PIC X(15).
    05 AIRCRAFT-YEAR-BUILT-IN   PIC 9(02).
```

Figure 11.7c *Input area record structure for FLEET-IN records.*

If the printer spacing chart for the histogram in Figure 11.5 is

```
         1111111111222222222233333333334444444444555555555566666666667
1234567890123456789012345678901234567890123456789012345678901234567890
1          AIRCRAFT AGE HISTOGRAM                         XXXXXXXX
2
3     AGE                 NUMBER OF AIRCRAFT
4
5     Z9                  Z9
6     Z9                  Z9
7
8
```

you can use the group identifier DETAIL-LINE-OUT to hold a detail line of the histogram,

```
01 DETAIL-LINE-OUT.
    05 FILLER                        PIC X(06)       VALUE SPACES.
    05 DL-AGE-OUT                    PIC Z9.
    05 FILLER                        PIC X(16)       VALUE SPACES.
    05 DL-NUMB-AIRCRAFT-OUT          PIC Z9.
    05 FILLER                        PIC X(107)      VALUE SPACES.
```

with the corresponding output buffer record

```
01 REPORT-RECORD-OUT                 PIC X(133).
```

If you use

```
01 SUB                               PIC 9(02).
01 AGE-HISTOGRAM.
    05  NUMBER-OF-AIRCRAFT
           OCCURS 20 TIMES           PIC 9(03) VALUE ZEROS.
```

as a subscript and array, the essential pseudocode for generating the histogram in Figure 11.5 is

Main-module.

```
OPEN files.
Print headers
READ first input record.
PERFORM until More-records is 'NO'
   COMPUTE Age as Current year - Year built in
   ADD 1 to Number-of-aircraft (Age)
   READ next input record
END-PERFORM.
PERFORM Print-detail-line-out varying SUB from 1 by 1 to 20.
CLOSE files.
STOP.
```

Print-detail-line-out.

> MOVE SUB to DL-AGE-OUT.
> MOVE Number-of-aircraft (SUB)
>   to DL-NUMB-AIRCRAFT-OUT.
> Print-detail-line-out.

The core of the method is in the in-line PERFORM statement. Make sure you understand it. To get the age of an aircraft, you subtract the year built from the current year (91). You use this age value to select which element of the array is to be incremented. In that way, an element of the array collects the total number of aircraft with an age equal to its subscript value. This is the essence of the technique for using an array to accumulate a histogram. The idea is also illustrated in Figure 11.6.

To print the histogram, each element of the array and its subscript value is used to construct a detail line, as illustrated in the module PRINT-DETAIL-LINE-OUT.

COBOL program for developing a histogram

The COBOL program corresponding to the pseudocode in the previous section, to generate the histogram output in Figure 11.5 from the input file FLEET-IN in Figure 11.7, is shown in Figure 11.8.

```
IDENTIFICATION DIVISION.
PROGRAM-ID. AGEHIST.
ENVIRONMENT DIVISION.
INPUT-OUTPUT SECTION.
FILE-CONTROL.    SELECT FLEET-IN  ASSIGN UT-S-FLEET91.
                 SELECT REPORT-FILE ASSIGN TO UR-S-SYSPRINT.
DATA DIVISION.
FILE SECTION.
FD    FLEET-IN                            LABEL RECORDS ARE STANDARD.
01 AIRCRAFT-RECORD-IN.
    05   AIRCRAFT-ID-IN         PIC X(04).
    05   AIRCRAFT-TYPE-IN       PIC X(16).
    05   AIRCRAFT-YEAR-BUILT-IN PIC 9(02).
FD    REPORT-FILE                         LABEL RECORDS ARE OMITTED.
01    REPORT-RECORD-OUT         PIC X(133).
WORKING-STORAGE SECTION.
01 WORK-AREAS.
    05   MORE-RECORDS           PIC X(03)    VALUE 'YES'.
    05   SUB                    PIC 9(02).
    05   CUR-YEAR               PIC 9(02)    VALUE 91.
    05   AIRCRAFT-AGE           PIC 9(02).
```

```cobol
 01 REPORT-HEADER.
      05  FILLER                      PIC X(11)    VALUE SPACES.
      05  FILLER                      PIC X(22)    VALUE
                                                   'AIRCRAFT AGE  HISTOGRAM'.
      05  FILLER                      PIC X(17)    VALUE SPACES.
      05  RUN-DATE-OUT                PIC X(08).
      05  FILLER                      PIC X(75)    VALUE SPACES.
 01 COL-HEADER-1.
      05  FILLER                      PIC X(06)    VALUE SPACES.
      05  FILLER                      PIC X(03)    VALUE 'AGE'.
      05  FILLER                      PIC X(15)    VALUE SPACES.
      05  FILLER                      PIC X(18)    VALUE 'NUMBER OF AIRCRAFT'.
      05  FILLER                      PIC X(91)    VALUE SPACES.
 01 DETAIL-LINE-OUT.
      05  FILLER                      PIC X(06)    VALUE SPACES.
      05  DL-AGE-OUT                  PIC Z9.
      05  FILLER                      PIC X(16)    VALUE SPACES.
      05  DL-NUMB-AIRCRAFT-OUT        PIC Z9.
      05  FILLER                      PIC X(107)   VALUE SPACES.
 01 AGE-HISTOGRAM.
      05  NUMBER-OF-AIRCRAFT
          OCCURS 20 TIMES             PIC 9(02)    VALUE ZEROS.
 PROCEDURE DIVISION.
 100-MAIN-MODULE.
************************************************************************
*   DIRECTS PROGRAM LOGIC.                                            *
************************************************************************
      PERFORM 200-INITIALIZATION.
      PERFORM 400-PROCESS-INPUT-RECORD
                  UNTIL MORE-RECORDS = 'NO'.
      PERFORM 500-PRINT-DETAIL-LINE-OUT
              VARYING SUB FROM 1 BY 1 UNTIL SUB > 20.
 200-INITIALIZATION.
************************************************************************
*   PERFORMED FROM 100-MAIN-MODULE. OPENS FILES, READS FIRST RECORD,  *
*   EXTRACTS DATE, AND PRINTS HEADERS.                                *
************************************************************************
      OPEN INPUT FLEET-IN,
           OUTPUT REPORT-FILE.
      READ FLEET-IN
              AT END MOVE 'NO' TO MORE-RECORDS.
      MOVE CURRENT-DATE TO PD-RUN-DATE-OUT.
      PERFORM 300-PAGE-HEADERS.
 300-PAGE-HEADERS.
************************************************************************
*   PERFORMED FROM 200-INITIALIZATION. PRINTS HEADERS.                *
************************************************************************
      WRITE REPORT-RECORD-OUT FROM REPORT-HEADER
              AFTER ADVANCING PAGE.
      WRITE REPORT-RECORD-OUT FROM COL-HEADER-1
              AFTER ADVANCING 2 LINES.
```

```
        MOVE SPACES TO REPORT-RECORD-OUT.
        WRITE REPORT-RECORD-OUT
                AFTER ADVANCING 1 LINE.
 400-PROCESS-INPUT-RECORD.
 ********************************************************************
 *   PERFORMED FROM 100-MAIN-MODULE.  ADDS 1 TO NUMBER OF AIRCRAFT WITH   *
 *   THE AIRCRAFT AGE IN THE CURRENT RECORD.  READS NEXT RECORD.          *
 ********************************************************************
        SUBTRACT AIRCRAFT-YEAR-BUILT-IN FROM CUR-YEAR
                     GIVING AIRCRAFT-AGE.
        ADD 1 TO NUMBER-OF-AIRCRAFT (AIRCRAFT-AGE).
        READ FLEET-IN
             AT END MOVE 'NO' TO MORE-RECORDS.
 500-PRINT-DETAIL-LINE-OUT.
 ********************************************************************
 *   PERFORMED FROM 100-MAIN-MODULE.  CONSTRUCTS AND PRINTS DETAIL LINE   *
 *   OF HISTOGRAM.                                                        *
 ********************************************************************
        MOVE SUB TO DL-AGE-OUT.
        MOVE NUMBER-OF-AIRCRAFT (SUB) TO DL-NUMB-AIRCRAFT-OUT.
        WRITE REPORT-RECORD-OUT FROM DETAIL-LINE-OUT
                     AFTER ADVANCING 1 LINE.
 600-TERMINATION.
 ********************************************************************
 *   PERFORMED FROM 100-MAIN-MODULE. CLOSES FILES, STOPS PROGRAM.         *
 ********************************************************************
        CLOSE FLEET-IN
              REPORT-FILE.
        STOP RUN.
```

Figure 11.8 Program AGEHIST, which generates histogram in Figure 11.5 from data in Figure 11.7.

There is a problem with a zero subscript

In listing the age of the aircraft, age values rounded up to the nearest integer were used. Thus, the youngest aircraft would be age 1. The example was constructed this way to avoid the possibility of age 0. But suppose age 0 was a possibility, so that the histogram could be something such as

AGE	NUMBER OF AIRCRAFT
0	23
1	44
2	21
3	72
...	
19	45
20	56

Then this histogram could not have been put into the array NUMBER-OF-AIRCRAFT, specified with OCCURS 21 TIMES, where the age corresponded to the subscript. You cannot have a zero subscript, so that the element NUMBER-OF-AIRCRAFT (0) is not a valid identifier.

But suppose you want the above histogram, with age 0. There are two techniques that can be used. Unfortunately, neither is elegant.

The first method involves letting age n correspond to subscript $n + 1$. Thus the number of aircraft for age 0 is in NUMBER-OF-AIRCRAFT (1), the number of aircraft for age 1 is in NUMBER-OF-AIRCRAFT (2), and so on. The PROCEDURE DIVISION for the program in Figure 11.8 would then have to be altered as follows:

```
100-MAIN-MODULE.
    ...
    PERFORM 400-PROCESS-INPUT-RECORD
                UNTIL MORE-RECORDS = 'NO'.
    PERFORM 500-PRINT-DETAIL-LINE-OUT
                VARYING SUB FROM 1 BY 1 UNTIL SUB > 21.
    ...
400-PROCESS-INPUT-RECORD.
    SUBTRACT AIRCRAFT-YEAR-BUILT-IN FROM CUR-YEAR
                GIVING AIRCRAFT-AGE.
    ADD 1 TO AIRCRAFT-AGE.
    ADD 1 TO NUMBER-OF-AIRCRAFT (AIRCRAFT-AGE).
    READ FLEET-IN
            AT END MOVE 'NO' TO MORE-RECORDS.
500-PRINT-DETAIL-LINE-OUT.
    COMPUTE DL-AGE-OUT = SUB - 1.
    MOVE NUMBER-OF-AIRCRAFT (SUB) TO DL-NUMB-AIRCRAFT-OUT.
    WRITE REPORT-RECORD-OUT FROM DETAIL-LINE-OUT
            AFTER ADVANCING 1 LINE.
```

You have to add 1 to the age in the input record when collecting totals and subtract 1 from the subscript identifier SUB when printing ages.

The other alternative is to use a special identifier ZERO-ELEMENT to take the place of the invalid NUMBER-OF-AIRCRAFT (0). You could then alter the program in Figure 11.8 as follows:

```
100-MAIN-MODULE.
    ...
    MOVE ZERO TO ZERO-ELEMENT.
    PERFORM 400-PROCESS-INPUT-RECORD
                UNTIL MORE-RECORDS = 'NO'.
    PERFORM 500-PRINT-AGE-ZERO-LINE.
    PERFORM 600-PRINT-DETAIL-LINE-OUT
                VARYING SUB FROM 1 BY 1 UNTIL SUB > 20.
    ...
400-PROCESS-INPUT-RECORD.
    SUBTRACT AIRCRAFT-YEAR-BUILT-IN FROM CUR-YEAR
                GIVING AIRCRAFT-AGE.
    IF AIRCRAFT-AGE = 0
        THEN ADD 1 TO ZERO-ELEMENT
    ELSE
        ADD 1 TO NUMBER-OF-AIRCRAFT (AIRCRAFT-AGE).
```

```
      END-IF.
      READ FLEET-IN AT END MOVE 'NO' TO MORE-RECORDS.
500-PRINT-AGE-ZERO-LINE.
      MOVE ZERO TO DL-AGE-OUT.
      MOVE ZERO-ELEMENT TO DL-NUMB-AIRCRAFT-OUT.
      WRITE REPORT-RECORD-OUT FROM DETAIL-LINE-OUT.
600-PRINT-DETAIL-LINE-OUT.
      MOVE NUMBER-OF-AIRCRAFT (SUB) TO DL-NUMB-AIRCRAFT-OUT.
      WRITE REPORT-RECORD-OUT FROM DETAIL-LINE-OUT
                  AFTER ADVANCING 1 LINE.
```

There is not much to choose between these two methods. However, the second may be clearer.

11.4
An array is used with repeating groups of fields

A RECORD in a file can have groups of similar fields. These are called *repeating groups* of fields. For example, suppose each record of a file YEARLY-SALES contains sales data for a real estate salesperson for each month of the year. Some sample records of YEARLY-SALES are shown in Figure 11.9a, with the record layout shown in 11.9b. The buffer record to hold a YEARLY-SALES record could have the structure shown in Figure 11.9c.

The group of fields UNITS-IN and VOLUME-IN repeats 12 times, once for each month of the year. This is a repeating group of fields. These repetitions can be easily handled by the 12-element array MONTHLY-DATA-IN (Figure 11.9c).

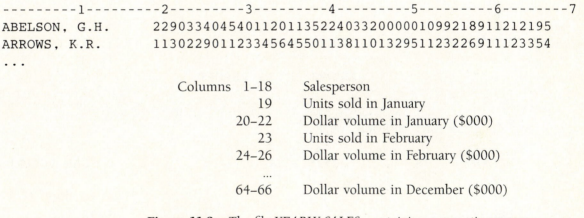

```
--------1---------2---------3---------4---------5---------6-------7
ABELSON, G.H.     229033404540112011352240332000010992189112121 95
ARROWS, K.R.      113022901123345645501138110132951123226911123354
...
```

Columns 1–18 Salesperson
         19   Units sold in January
         20–22 Dollar volume in January ($000)
         23   Units sold in February
         24–26 Dollar volume in February ($000)
                ...
         64–66 Dollar volume in December ($000)

Figure 11.9a *The file YEARLY-SALES, containing a repeating group.*

```
--------1---------2---------3---------4---------5---------6-------7
XXXXXXXXXXXXXXXXXX9999 9999 9999 9999 9999 9999 9999 9999 9999 9999 9999 9999
```

Figure 11.9b *Input record layout for YEARLY-SALES.*

```
01 SALES-RECORD-IN.
    05 SR-SALESPERSON-IN               PIC X(18).
    05 SR-MONTHLY-DATA-IN
          OCCURS 12 TIMES.
        10  SR-UNITS-IN                PIC 9.
        10  SR-VOLUME-IN               PIC 9(03).
```

Figure 11.9c *Input area record structure for YEARLY-SALES.*

Move the repeating groups into an array for manipulation

Repeating groups are not difficult to manipulate. You read each record into the input buffer record, which will have a suitable array as part of its structure. Once the input data are in this array, it can be processed using straightforward array manipulation. As an example, suppose you wanted to use the input file in Figure 11.9 to generate a report like that in Figure 11.10.

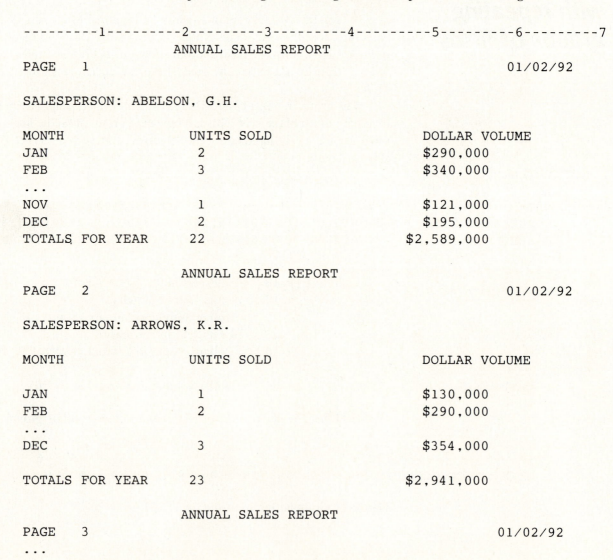

```
---------1---------2---------3---------4---------5---------6---------7
              ANNUAL SALES REPORT
PAGE    1                                                  01/02/92


SALESPERSON: ABELSON, G.H.


MONTH               UNITS SOLD              DOLLAR VOLUME
JAN                 2                       $290,000
FEB                 3                       $340,000
...
NOV                 1                       $121,000
DEC                 2                       $195,000
TOTALS FOR YEAR     22                      $2,589,000


              ANNUAL SALES REPORT
PAGE    2                                                  01/02/92


SALESPERSON: ARROWS, K.R.


MONTH               UNITS SOLD              DOLLAR VOLUME

JAN                 1                       $130,000
FEB                 2                       $290,000
...
DEC                 3                       $354,000

TOTALS FOR YEAR     23                      $2,941,000


              ANNUAL SALES REPORT
PAGE    3                                                  01/02/92
...
```

Figure 11.10a *Report generated from Figure 11.9.*

```
    1 2 3 4 5 6 7 8 9 0 1 2 3 4 5 6 7 8 9 0 1 2 3 4 5 6 7 8 9 0 1 2 3 4 5 6 7 8 9 0 1 2 3 4 5 6 7 8 9 0 1 2 3 4 5 6 7 8 9 0 1 2 3 4 5 6 7 8 9 0
 1                          ANNUAL SALES REPORT
 2  PAGE  Z9                                                                      XXXXXXXX
 3
 4  SALESPERSON: XXXXXXXXXXXXXXXXXX
 5
 6  MONTH                    UNITS SOLD                         DOLLAR VOLUME
 7
 8  XXX                         Z9                                $Z99,000
 9  XXX                         Z9                                $Z99,000
10  XXX                         Z9                                $Z99,000
11  XXX                         Z9                                $Z99,000
12  . . .
13  TOTALS FOR YEAR          ZZ9                                 $Z,Z99,000
14
```

Figure 11.10b *Printer spacing chart for the report.*

```
01 MONTH-DATA-ARRAY.
   05   MDL-MONTHLY-DATA-OUT
             OCCURS 12 TIMES.
        10   FILLER                PIC X            VALUE SPACES.
        10   MDL-MONTH-OUT         PIC X(03).
        10   FILLER                PIC X(17)        VALUE SPACES.
        10   MDL-UNITS-OUT         PIC Z9.
        10   FILLER                PIC X(26)        VALUE SPACES.
        10   MDL-VOLUME-OUT        PIC $Z99,000.
        10   FILLER                PIC X(76)        VALUE SPACES.
01 TOTALS-LINE.
   05   FILLER                     PIC X            VALUE SPACE.
   05   FILLER                     PIC X(19)        VALUE 'TOTALS FOR YEAR'.
   05   TOTAL-UNITS-OUT            PIC ZZ9.
   05   FILLER                     PIC X(24)        VALUE SPACES.
   05   TOTAL-VOLUME-OUT           PIC $Z,Z99,999.
   05   FILLER                     PIC X(76)        VALUE SPACES.
```

Figure 11.10c *Each element of the array MDL-MONTHLY-DATA-OUT holds a detail line of the report (MDL denotes monthly-detail line). The group identifier TOTALS-LINE holds a summary line.*

ARRAY MDL-MONTHLY-DATA-OUT

	MD-MONTH-OUT( )	MD-UNITS-OUT( )	MD-VOLUME-OUT( )
(1)	XXX	Z9	$Z99,000
(2)	XXX	Z9	$Z99,000
(3)	XXX	Z9	$Z99,000
(4)	XXX	Z9	$Z99,000
(5)	XXX	Z9	$Z99,000
(6)	XXX	Z9	$Z99,000
(7)	XXX	Z9	$Z99,000
(8)	XXX	Z9	$Z99,000
(9)	XXX	Z9	$Z99,000
(10)	XXX	Z9	$Z99,000
(11)	XXX	Z9	$Z99,000
(12)	XXX	Z9	$Z99,000

Figure 11.10d *Structure of array MDL-MONTHLY-DATA-OUT.*

Each record from the input file is used to generate a complete page of the report. The 12 monthly detail lines can be generated from the array MDL-MONTHLY-DATA-OUT, shown in Figure 11.10c and 11.10d.

Each of the 12 elements of the array is printed as a detail line of the report, as follows:

```
PERFORM 400-PRINT-DETAIL-LINE-OUT
    VARYING SUB FROM 1 BY 1 UNTIL SUB > 12.
...
400-PRINT-DETAIL-LINE-OUT.
    MOVE MDL-MONTHLY-DATA-OUT (SUB) TO REPORT-RECORD-OUT.
    WRITE REPORT-RECORD-OUT.
```

Notice (in Figure 11.9) that the names of the months are not part of the input data. You can include month names by defining an additional array MONTH-NAME, which will redefine a string containing the month values

```
01 AUXILIARY.
    05 INITIAL-DATA.
        10 FILLER                               PIC X(03) VALUE 'JAN'.
        10 FILLER                               PIC X(03) VALUE 'FEB'.
        10 FILLER                               PIC X(03) VALUE 'MAR'.
        10 FILLER                               PIC X(03) VALUE 'APR'.
        10 FILLER                               PIC X(03) VALUE 'MAY'.
        10 FILLER                               PIC X(03) VALUE 'JUN'.
        10 FILLER                               PIC X(03) VALUE 'JUL'.
        10 FILLER                               PIC X(03) VALUE 'AUG'.
        10 FILLER                               PIC X(03) VALUE 'SEP'.
        10 FILLER                               PIC X(03) VALUE 'OCT'.
        10 FILLER                               PIC X(03) VALUE 'NOV'.
        10 FILLER                               PIC X(03) VALUE 'DEC'.
    05 MONTH-NAME
        REDEFINES INITIAL-DATA
            OCCURS 12 TIMES                     PIC X(03).
```

You can then move the elements MONTH-NAME to the identifiers MDL-MONTH-OUT in the 12-element array MDL-MONTHLY-DATA-OUT in readiness for printing

```
        PERFORM 300-INITIALIZE-MONTH-NAMES
            VARYING SUB FROM 1 BY 1 UNTIL SUB > 12.
    ...
    300-INITIALIZE-MONTH-NAMES.
        MOVE MONTH-NAME (SUB) TO MDL-MONTH-OUT (SUB).
```

The other important array manipulation technique used to generate the report in Figure 11.10 involves scanning the array holding the incoming repeating groups, that is, SR-MONTHLY-DATA-IN, to get the total units sold and the total dollar volume for the year. This would be accomplished by

```
        MOVE ZEROS TO WS-TOTAL-UNITS, WS-TOTAL-VOLUME.
        PERFORM  600-COLLECT-TOTALS
            VARYING SUB FROM 1 BY 1 UNTIL SUB > 12.
    ...
```

```
600-COLLECT-TOTALS.
        ADD SR-UNITS-IN (SUB) TO WS-TOTAL-UNITS.
        ADD SR-VOLUME-IN (SUB) TO WS-TOTAL-VOLUME.
```

Let us now examine a complete program for processing an input file in which records contain a repeating group of fields.

A program for manipulation of repeating groups

The program in Figure 11.11 processes the input file in Figure 11.9 and generates the report in Figure 11.10. The hierarchy diagram for the program is shown in Figure 11.12.

```
IDENTIFICATION DIVISION.
PROGRAM-ID. MONTHLY4.
ENVIRONMENT DIVISION.
INPUT-OUTPUT SECTION.
FILE-CONTROL.    SELECT YEARLY-SALES  ASSIGN UT-S-AB25.
                 SELECT REPORT-FILE ASSIGN TO UR-S-SYSPRINT.
DATA DIVISION.
FILE SECTION.
FD   YEARLY-SALES               LABEL RECORDS ARE STANDARD.
01 SALES-RECORD-IN.
     05 SR-SALESPERSON-IN        PIC X(18).
     05 SR-MONTHLY-DATA-IN
           OCCURS 12 TIMES.
        10  SR-UNITS-IN          PIC 9.
        10  SR-VOLUME-IN         PIC 9(03).
FD   REPORT-FILE                 LABEL RECORDS ARE OMITTED.
01   REPORT-RECORD-OUT           PIC X(133).
WORKING-STORAGE SECTION.
01 WS-WORK-AREAS.
     05 MORE-RECORDS             PIC X(03)     VALUE 'YES'.
     05 WS-TOTAL-VOLUME          PIC 9(7).
     05 WS-TOTAL-UNITS           PIC 9(03).
     05 SUB                      PIC 9(02).
     05 WS-PAGE-NUMB             PIC 9(02)     VALUE ZERO.
01 PAGE-DATE-LINE-OUT.
     05    FILLER                PIC X         VALUE SPACES.
     05    FILLER                PIC X(06)     VALUE 'PAGE  '.
     05    PD-PAGE-NUMB-OUT      PIC 9(02).
     05    FILLER                PIC X(50)     VALUE SPACES.
     05    PD-RUN-DATE-OUT       PIC X(08).
     05    FILLER                PIC X(66)     VALUE SPACES.
01 REPORT-HEADER.
     05    FILLER                PIC X         VALUE SPACE.
     05    FILLER                PIC X(18)     VALUE SPACES.
     05    FILLER                PIC X(19)     VALUE 'ANNUAL SALES REPORT'.
     05    FILLER                PIC X(95)     VALUE SPACES.
```

```
01 SALESPERSON-HEADER.
    05  FILLER                      PIC X        VALUE SPACES.
    05  FILLER                      PIC X(13)    VALUE 'SALESPERSON: '.
    05  SALESPERSON-OUT             PIC X(18).
    05  FILLER                      PIC X(101)   VALUE SPACES.
01 COL-HEADER-1.
    05  FILLER                      PIC X        VALUE SPACES.
    05  FILLER                      PIC X(20)    VALUE 'MONTH'.
    05  FILLER                      PIC X(28)    VALUE 'UNITS SOLD'.
    05  FILLER                      PIC X(13)    VALUE 'DOLLAR VOLUME'.
    05  FILLER                      PIC X(71)    VALUE SPACES.
01 MONTH-DATA-ARRAY.
    05  MDL-MONTHLY-DATA-OUT
            OCCURS 12 TIMES.
        10  FILLER                  PIC X        VALUE SPACES.
        10  MDL-MONTH-OUT           PIC X(03).
        10  FILLER                  PIC X(17)    VALUE SPACES.
        10  MDL-UNITS-OUT           PIC Z9.
        10  FILLER                  PIC X(26)    VALUE SPACES.
        10  MDL-VOLUME-OUT          PIC $Z99,000.
        10  FILLER                  PIC X(76)    VALUE SPACES.
01 TOTALS-LINE.
    05  FILLER                      PIC X        VALUE SPACE.
    05  FILLER                      PIC X(19)    VALUE 'TOTALS FOR YEAR'.
    05  TOTAL-UNITS-OUT             PIC ZZ9.
    05  FILLER                      PIC X(24)    VALUE SPACES.
    05  TOTAL-VOLUME-OUT            PIC $Z,Z99,999.
    05  FILLER                      PIC X(76)    VALUE SPACES.
01 AUXILIARY.
    05  INITIAL-DATA.
        10 FILLER                   PIC X(03)    VALUE 'JAN'.
        10 FILLER                   PIC X(03)    VALUE 'FEB'.
        10 FILLER                   PIC X(03)    VALUE 'MAR'.
        10 FILLER                   PIC X(03)    VALUE 'APR'.
        10 FILLER                   PIC X(03)    VALUE 'MAY'.
        10 FILLER                   PIC X(03)    VALUE 'JUN'.
        10 FILLER                   PIC X(03)    VALUE 'JUL'.
        10 FILLER                   PIC X(03)    VALUE 'AUG'.
        10 FILLER                   PIC X(03)    VALUE 'SEP'.
        10 FILLER                   PIC X(03)    VALUE 'OCT'.
        10 FILLER                   PIC X(03)    VALUE 'NOV'.
        10 FILLER                   PIC X(03)    VALUE 'DEC'.
    05 MONTH-NAME
        REDEFINES INITIAL-DATA
            OCCURS 12 TIMES      PIC X(03).
```

```
PROCEDURE DIVISION.
100-MAIN-MODULE.
*****************************************************************************
*   DIRECTS PROGRAM LOGIC.                                                   *
*****************************************************************************
      PERFORM 200-INITIALIZATION.
      PERFORM 300-PROCESS-INPUT-RECORD UNTIL MORE-RECORDS = 'NO'.
      PERFORM 700-TERMINATION.
 200-INITIALIZATION.
*****************************************************************************
*   PERFORMED FROM 100-MAIN-MODULE. OPENS FILES, READS FIRST RECORD         *
*   EXTRACTS DATE, AND PLACES MONTH NAMES IN ARRAY CONTAINING A             *
*   DETAIL LINE FOR EACH MONTH.                                            *
*****************************************************************************
      OPEN INPUT YEARLY-SALES
           OUTPUT REPORT-FILE.
      READ YEARLY-SALES
              AT END MOVE 'NO' TO MORE-RECORDS.
      MOVE CURRENT-DATE TO PD-RUN-DATE-OUT.
      PERFORM VARYING SUB FROM 1 BY 1
                         UNTIL SUB > 12
          MOVE MONTH-NAME (SUB) TO MDL-MONTH-OUT (SUB)
      END-PERFORM.
 300-PROCESS-INPUT-RECORD.
*****************************************************************************
*   PERFORMED FROM 100-MAIN-MODULE. PRINTS A SINGLE PAGE.  STARTS WITH      *
*   PAGE HEADERS. TRANSFERS MONTHLY DATA FROM CURRENT INPUT RECORD TO       *
*   ARRAY CONTAINING DETAIL LINES.  PRINTS DETAIL LINES FOR 12 MONTHS.      *
*   SUMS MONTHLY DATA AND PRINTS DETAIL LINE FOR YEAR. READS INPUT          *
*   RECORD FOR NEXT SALESPERSON.                                           *
*****************************************************************************
      PERFORM 400-PAGE-HEADERS.
      PERFORM VARYING SUB FROM 1 BY 1
                      UNTIL SUB > 12
          MOVE SR-UNITS-IN (SUB) TO MDL-UNITS-OUT (SUB)
          MOVE SR-VOLUME-IN (SUB) TO MDL-VOLUME-OUT (SUB).
      END-PERFORM.
      PERFORM 500-PRINT-DETAIL-LINE
              VARYING SUB FROM 1 BY 1 UNTIL SUB > 12.
      MOVE ZEROS TO WS-TOTAL-UNITS, WS-TOTAL-VOLUME.
      PERFORM VARYING SUB FROM 1 BY 1
                         UNTIL SUB > 12
          ADD SR-UNITS-IN (SUB) TO WS-TOTAL-UNITS
          ADD SR-VOLUME-IN (SUB) TO WS-TOTAL-VOLUME
      END-PERFORM.
      PERFORM 600-PRINT-TOTALS-LINE.
      READ YEARLY-SALES
              AT END MOVE 'NO' TO MORE-RECORDS.
```

```
 400-PAGE-HEADERS.
*************************************************************************
*   PERFORMED FROM 300-PROCESS-INPUT-RECORD. PRINTS REPORT HEADER, PAGE   *
*   AND DATE LINE, SALESPERSON HEADER AND COLUMN HEADER.                   *
*************************************************************************
     WRITE REPORT-RECORD-OUT FROM REPORT-HEADER
                    AFTER ADVANCING PAGE.
     ADD 1 TO WS-PAGE-NUMB.
     MOVE WS-PAGE-NUMB TO PD-PAGE-NUMB-OUT.
     WRITE REPORT-RECORD-OUT FROM PAGE-DATE-LINE-OUT
                    AFTER ADVANCING 1 LINE.
     MOVE SR-SALESPERSON-IN TO SALESPERSON-OUT.
     WRITE REPORT-RECORD-OUT FROM SALESPERSON-HEADER
                    AFTER ADVANCING 2 LINES.
     WRITE REPORT-RECORD-OUT FROM COL-HEADER-1
                    AFTER ADVANCING 2 LINES.
     MOVE SPACES TO REPORT-RECORD-OUT.
     WRITE REPORT-RECORD-OUT
                    AFTER ADVANCING 1 LINE.
 500-PRINT-DETAIL-LINE.
*************************************************************************
*   PERFORMED FROM 300-PROCESS-RECORD. PRINTS A DETAIL LINE FROM AN       *
*   ARRAY ELEMENT.                                                        *
*************************************************************************
     MOVE MDL-MONTHLY-DATA-OUT (SUB) TO REPORT-RECORD-OUT.
     WRITE REPORT-RECORD-OUT
                AFTER ADVANCING 1 LINE.
 600-PRINT-TOTALS-LINE.
*************************************************************************
*   PERFORMED FROM 300-PROCESS-RECORD. COLLECTS TOTALS FOR YEAR AND       *
*   PRINTS SUMMARY LINE.                                                  *
*************************************************************************
          MOVE WS-TOTAL-UNITS TO TOTAL-UNITS-OUT.
          MOVE WS-TOTAL-VOLUME TO TOTAL-VOLUME-OUT.
          WRITE REPORT-RECORD-OUT FROM TOTALS-LINE
                    AFTER ADVANCING 2 LINES.
 700-TERMINATION.
*************************************************************************
*   PERFORMED FROM 100-MAIN-MODULE.  CLOSES FILES, STOPS PROGRAM.         *
*************************************************************************
     CLOSE YEARLY-SALES, REPORT-FILE.
     STOP RUN.
```

Figure 11.11 Program MONTHLY4, which generates report in Figure 11.10 from input data in Figure 11.9.

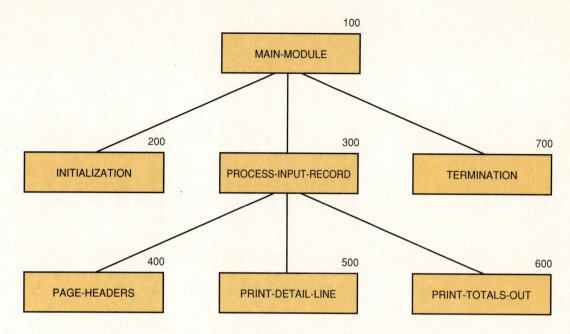

Figure 11.12 *Hierarchy diagram for program in Figure 11.11.*

11.5
Arrays can be used as look-up tables

DATA IN AN ARRAY can be used to supplement data coming from an input file in the generation of a report, since it is often not practical to include in an input file all the data necessary for generating a report. The data in an input file will normally vary each time a report-generating program is run, but some data will stay constant for a long period. Examples are the sales tax rate in each state, the unit price for each type of product, and the tax rate for each salary level. This data can be held in an array as a *look-up table*, and used as needed to generate the report from the input data. When the report-generating program executes, the first thing it does is put data into the look-up table. A specific example using a look-up table will help you understand these ideas.

Example of a look-up table for product data

Suppose a company sells about 1000 different products, each with its own unit price. Every day, customers are sent different quantities of these products. At the end of the day, the customers' orders are keyed into a computer to form the input file CUSTOMER-PURCHASE, as shown in Figure 11.13.

```
---------1---------2---------3---------4---------5
SMITH, K.J.            0200EX34
JONES, Y.T.           0050RT56
GREEN, J.R.           1000TY25
BURTON, T.L.          0015HJ34
...
```

Columns 1–19   Customer name
         21–24   Quantity purchased
         25–28   Product identification code

Figure 11.13a *Input file CUSTOMER-PURCHASE.*

```
---------1---------2---------3---------4---------5
XXXXXXXXXXXXXXXXXXXX9999XXXX
```

Figure 11.13b *Input record layout for CUSTOMER-PURCHASE.*

```
01 PURCHASE-RECORD-IN.
    05 CUSTOMER-IN           PIC X(19)
    05 QUANTITY-IN           PIC 9(04).
    05 ID-CODE-IN            PIC X(04).
```

Figure 11.13c *Input area record structure for CUSTOMER-PURCHASE records.*

On the basis of this input file, a report has to be generated that shows the value and type of the products purchased by each customer, as shown in Figure 11.14.

It should be clear that there is not enough information in the input file to generate this report. Information about the unit price and product type for each product code is needed. This information is fairly constant and can be kept in a separate input file.

The problem is, when processing each input record in CUSTOMER-PURCHASE, the product code from the record will have to be used to determine the product type and unit price. The most efficient way to do this is to keep the information about corresponding type and price for each product code in an array. This array can then serve as a look-up table. As each CUSTOMER-PURCHASE record is processed, the product code is looked up in the table and the unit price and product type data extracted, to generate the detail line in the report.

The data for the table could be kept in a permanent input file TABLE-DATA and read into the array PRODUCT-TABLE at the beginning of processing, ready for look-up operations as the main input file CUSTOMER-PURCHASE is processed. Some data for the input file TABLE-DATA and the array PRODUCT-TABLE are shown in Figure 11.15.

```
---------1---------2---------3---------4---------5---------6--------7-
                    CUSTOMER PURCHASES REPORT
PAGE    1                                              07/18/92


CUSTOMER                  PRODUCT    PRODUCT    QUANTITY  UNIT      COST
                          CODE       TYPE                 PRICE


SMITH, K.J.               EX34       BOLT       0200      001.10    $   220.00
JONES, Y.T.               RT56       CAMSHAFT   0050      025.00    $ 1,250.00
GREEN, J.R.               TY25       RAWLPLUG   1000      002.50    $ 2,500.00
BURTON, T.L.              HJ34       SCREW      0015      001.25    $    18.75
...
```

Figure 11.14a *Report generated from CUSTOMER-PURCHASE in Figure 11.13, using look-up table in Figure 11.15.*

Figure 11.14b *Printer spacing chart for report.*

```
01 DETAIL-LINE-OUT.
    05 FILLER                       PIC X            VALUE SPACE.
    05 DL-CUSTOMER-OUT              PIC X(19).
    05 FILLER                       PIC X            VALUE SPACE.
    05 DL-IDCODE-OUT                PIC X(04).
    05 FILLER                       PIC X(05)        VALUE SPACES.
    05 DL-PRODUCT-TYPE-OUT          PIC X(10).
    05 FILLER                       PIC X            VALUE SPACES.
    05 DL-QUANTITY-OUT              PIC 9(04).
    05 FILLER                       PIC X(06)        VALUE SPACES.
    05 DL-UNIT-PRICE-OUT            PIC 9(03).99.
    05 FILLER                       PIC X(04)        VALUE SPACES.
    05 DL-COST-OUT                  PIC $ZZ,ZZ9.99.
    05 FILLER                       PIC X(62)        VALUE SPACES.
```

Figure 11.14c *Structure of detail line record for the report.*

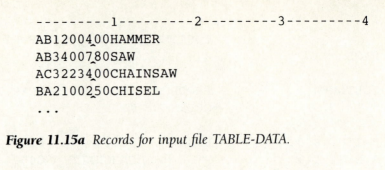

```
- - - - - - - - - 1 - - - - - - - - - 2 - - - - - - - - - 3 - - - - - - - - 4
AB1200400HAMMER
AB3400780SAW
AC3223400CHAINSAW
BA2100250CHISEL
...
```

Figure 11.15a *Records for input file TABLE-DATA.*

```
- - - - - - - - - 1 - - - - - - - - - 2 - - - - - - - - - 3 - - - - - - - - - 4
XXXX99999XXXXXXXXXX
```

Figure 11.15b *Input record layout for TABLE-DATA.*

```
01  LOOK-UP-TABLE.
    05  LU-PRODUCT-TABLE
            OCCURS 1000 TIMES.
        10  LU-IDCODE                 PIC X(04).
        10  LU-UNIT-PRICE             PIC 9(03)V99.
        10  LU-PRODUCT-TYPE           PIC X(10).
```

Figure 11.15c *An array to hold all the records from TABLE-DATA. (LU denotes look-up.)*

```
                        LU-PRODUCT-TABLE


    subscript   LU-IDCODE      LU-UNIT-PRICE      PRODUCT-TYPE

        1          AB12           00400              HAMMER
        2          AB34           00780              SAW
        3          AC32           23400              CHAINSAW
        4          BA21           00250              CHISEL

       ...          ...
```

Figure 11.15d *A view of the array LU-PRODUCT-TABLE as filled from TABLE-DATA records. Data are stored in ascending LU-IDCODE order. (Spaces between columns are not contained in the actual array.)*

A look-up table has to be initialized with data in a specific order

The first thing to do in a program that uses a look-up table is put the necessary data into the table. If the table is a short one or does not vary, this can be done using VALUE clauses and the REDEFINES option. This approach was used earlier to put the names of months into an array.

If there are many rows to the table, or if the table contents vary, the data would be read from an input file. In the case of the table LU-PRODUCT-TABLE in Figure 11.15, 1000 rows are assumed and the data would be taken from the input file TABLE-DATA. Normally the number of rows in a look-up table would be known exactly.

Suppose the buffer record for the input file TABLE-DATA is TABLE-BUFFER-RECORD, specified as:

```
01   TABLE-BUFFER-RECORD          PIC X(19).
```

and the array LU-PRODUCT-TABLE is specified in working storage as:

```
01 LOOK-UP-TABLE.
   05 LU-PRODUCT-TABLE
          OCCURS 1000 TIMES.
      10   LU-IDCODE              PIC X(04).
      10   LU-UNIT-PRICE          PIC 9(03)V99.
      10   LU-PRODUCT-TYPE        PIC X(10).
```

To make searching convenient, data are usually stored in a look-up table in ascending order of the values used for searching. Since the product code will be used for searching, data should be ordered in ascending LU-IDCODE order. You can assume that the data in the input file TABLE-DATA, used as the data source for the table, are also in ascending product code order. Thus, if the records are loaded one by one into the array, in ascending subscript order, the resulting array data will be in ascending LU-IDCODE order.

To load the contents of the table input file TABLE-DATA in Figure 11.15a into the array LU-PRODUCT-TABLE, you simply write the following:

```
MOVE 'YES' TO MORE-RECORDS.
MOVE 1 TO SUB.
READ TABLE-DATA
     AT END MOVE 'NO' TO MORE-RECORDS.
PERFORM 300-FILL-TABLE-ROW
     UNTIL MORE-RECORDS = 'NO' OR SUB > 1000.
IF SUB > 1000 PERFORM 800-TABLE-OVERFLOW
     ELSE PERFORM 900-UNUSED-ELEMENTS
          VARYING SUB2 FROM SUB BY 1 UNTIL SUB2 > 1000.
  ...
300-FILL-TABLE-ROW.
   MOVE TABLE-BUFFER-RECORD TO LU-PRODUCT-TABLE (SUB).
   READ TABLE-DATA
        AT END MOVE 'NO' TO MORE-RECORDS.
   ADD 1 TO SUB.
800-TABLE-OVERFLOW.
   IF MORE-RECORDS = 'YES'
     DISPLAY 'OVERFLOW OF ARRAY; TOO MANY INPUT RECORDS:'
     STOP RUN.
900-UNUSED-ELEMENTS.
   MOVE HIGH-VALUES TO LU-IDCODE (SUB2).
   MOVE ZEROS TO LU-UNIT-PRICE (SUB2).
   MOVE SPACES TO LU-PRODUCT-PRICE (SUB2).
```

In this iteration you cannot use PERFORM ... VARYING to put the input data into array elements, since you do not know beforehand how many records there are in TABLE-DATA. If there should be more than 1000 records, it is a serious error that will stop the program with a message. If there are less than 1000, SPACES or even HIGH-VALUES are often put into the remaining unused alphanumeric identifiers, and ZEROS are put into unused numeric identifiers. Sometimes unused identifiers are simply left with no data assigned to them. However, remember that it is a serious error to attempt to use the contents of an unassigned identifier in a COBOL statement, whether an array element or not. The contents of the look-up table are shown in Figure 11.15d.

You can use either linear or binary searches

Typically, you look up a table to find the data corresponding to a certain value, called the *search key* or target value. For example, if you want the unit price and product type data for product code BA21, you search through the array until you come to the element with LU-IDCODE value equal to BA21. BA21 is the search key.

There are three ways to look up a table with COBOL.

- Using PERFORM . . . VARYING with a linear search
- Using SEARCH with a linear search
- Using SEARCH ALL with a binary search, if elements of the array are in ascending or descending order

Linear Search

A *linear search* involves looking at element 1, then element 2, then element 3, and so on, until the element sought is encountered. Use of PERFORM . . . VARYING and SEARCH verbs is similar, except that SEARCH is more efficient. On average, if the table has n elements you will need $n/2$ element accesses to find a specific element with a linear search. Ascending order of the identifier values being searched is not required, but is usual.

Binary Search

A *binary search* involves the use of the SEARCH ALL verb. Binary searching is normally much faster than linear searching, but requires that the set of identifier values being searched be in ascending or descending order. You could use binary searching of the array LU-PRODUCT-DATA for a particular LU-IDCODE value, since the elements are ordered in ascending LU-IDCODE. The SEARCH ALL verb automatically looks after the details of the binary search.

With a binary search of an array with 1000 elements, element 500 could be accessed first; if its value is too low, then element 750 would be next. If the value in element 750 is too high, element 625 is checked next. If its value is too low, then element 687 is next; if it is too high, then perhaps element 656 is checked (depending on the machine), which might be the target element.

To determine which element to access next, you split differences. For example, suppose you have accessed elements 500 and 750, in that order. The next access would be 750 plus or minus 125, depending on whether the value in element 750 is too low or too high. If too low, you check element 750 plus 125; if too high, you check element 750 minus 125.

On average it takes $ln_2(n) - 1$ accesses to binary search an array with n elements. That works out to about nine accesses to search an array of 1000 elements, as compared with 1000/2 or 500 accesses, on average, for a linear search. Thus, where the number of elements in the array exceeds about 25, a binary search should be used if the order of elements allows it.

If you are still not convinced, look at it this way: Suppose you want to look up P. F. Jones in the telephone book. You could start at the A's, work through them in sequence, then at the B's, and so on, until you came to the Jones entries. That is a linear search, and would obviously take a long time. Alternatively, you open the phone book at about the middle and look. Too far. So you go back half way and look. Too far back. So you go forward a bit. Too far again. Back a bit, and so on. In no time you have found the right entry. You carry out that kind of search every day. It approximates a binary search and is obviously far superior to a linear search.

Bearing in mind the superiority of binary searching, let us look at the COBOL coding details for each of the three methods. Assume the input file CUSTOMER-PURCHASE in Figure 11.13, the report file in Figure 11.14, and the table in Figure 11.15. Also assume the following array definition:

```
01  LOOK-UP-TABLE.
        05  LU-PRODUCT-TABLE   OCCURS  1000 TIMES.
            10   LU-IDCODE              PIC X(04).
            10   LU-UNIT-PRICE         PIC 9(03)V99.
            10   LU-PRODUCT-TYPE       PIC X(10).
```

The definition for the buffer record structure for the input file CUSTOMER-PURCHASE is

```
01  PURCHASE-RECORD-IN.
        05  PR-CUSTOMER-IN            PIC X(19).
        05  PR-QUANTITY-IN            PIC 9(04).
        05  PR-IDCODE-IN              PIC X(04).
```

and the detail line structure for the report is

```
01  DETAIL-LINE-OUT.
        05  FILLER                   PIC X            VALUE SPACE.
        05  DL-CUSTOMER-OUT          PIC X(19).
        05  FILLER                   PIC X            VALUE SPACE.
        05  DL-IDCODE-OUT            PIC X(04).
        05  FILLER                   PIC X(05)        VALUE SPACES.
        05  DL-PRODUCT-TYPE-OUT      PIC X(10).
        05  FILLER                   PIC X            VALUE SPACES.
        05  DL-QUANTITY-OUT          PIC 9(04).
        05  FILLER                   PIC X(06)        VALUE SPACES.
        05  DL-UNIT-PRICE-OUT        PIC 9(03).99.
        05  FILLER                   PIC X(04)        VALUE SPACES.
        05  DL-COST-OUT              PIC $ZZ,ZZ9.99.
        05  FILLER                   PIC X(62)        VALUE SPACES.
```

The WORKING-STORAGE identifier WS-COST, for holding computed cost values to be output in DL-COST-OUT, is

```
01  WS-COST                          PIC 9(05)V99.
```

(Cost is quantity times unit price, for a given purchase.)

As each record of CUSTOMER-PURCHASE is read, the PR-IDCODE-IN value is used as the target value in the search of the LU-IDCODE column in the array LU-PRODUCT-TABLE (Figure 11.15d) for a matching value. When a match is found, the data in that row are used to put data in DETAIL-LINE-OUT, which are then output. If a match is not found, a message "NOT FOUND" is placed in the DL-PRODUCT-TYPE-OUT field in DETAIL-LINE-OUT, for which information is missing. A zero quantity is placed in the unit price and cost fields in DETAIL-LINE-OUT as well, if no matching row was found in the table.

The essential code to process records from the input file CUSTOMER-PURCHASE is as follows:

```
MOVE 'YES' TO MORE-RECORDS.
READ CUSTOMER-PURCHASE
            AT END MOVE 'NO' TO MORE-RECORDS.
PERFORM 400-PROCESS-INPUT-RECORD
            UNTIL MORE-RECORDS = 'NO'.
    . . .
400-PROCESS-INPUT-RECORD.
    MOVE 'NO' TO MATCH-FOUND.
    PERFORM 500-CHECK-TABLE-ROW
        VARYING SUB FROM 1 BY 1
        UNTIL SUB > 1000 OR MATCH-FOUND = 'YES'.
    IF MATCH-FOUND = 'NO'
        PERFORM 600-NO-MATCH-ROUTINE
    END-IF.
    MOVE PR-CUSTOMER-IN TO DL-CUSTOMER-OUT.
    MOVE PR-IDCODE-IN TO DL-IDCODE-OUT.
    MOVE PR-QUANTITY-IN TO DL-QUANTITY-OUT.
    WRITE REPORT-RECORD-OUT FROM DETAIL-LINE-OUT
                    AFTER ADVANCING 1 LINE.
    READ CUSTOMER-PURCHASE,
            AT END MOVE 'NO' TO MORE-RECORDS.
500-CHECK-TABLE-ROW.
    IF LU-IDCODE (SUB) = PR-IDCODE-IN
        MOVE 'YES' TO MATCH-FOUND
        MOVE LU-PRODUCT-TYPE (SUB) TO DL-PRODUCT-TYPE-OUT
        MOVE LU-UNIT-PRICE (SUB) TO DL-UNIT-PRICE-OUT
        MULTIPLY LU-UNIT-PRICE (SUB) BY PR-QUANTITY-IN
                                GIVING WS-COST
        MOVE WS-COST TO DL-COST-OUT
    END-IF.
600-NO-MATCH-ROUTINE.
    MOVE 'NOT FOUND' TO DL-PRODUCT-TYPE-OUT.
    MOVE 0.00 DL-UNIT-PRICE-OUT.
    MOVE 0.00 TO DL-COST-OUT.
```

Notice the PERFORM verb is used to search the table. As each element of the table is checked, SUB is incremented. However, when a match is found, the control identifier MATCH-FOUND becomes 'YES', which causes the condition after UNTIL to become true, even though not all elements of the table have been searched. This means that the search stops when a match is found.

If no match is found, eventually SUB exceeds 1000 and the search stops. But MATCH-FOUND stays with the value 'NO' it had before the search began. An appropriate message is then printed with the output detail line, instead of the necessary data based on information that should have been in the table, for example:

```
GREEN, J.R.      TY25    RAWLPLUG   1000    002.50    $ 2,500.00
BURTON, T.L.     HJ34    SCREW      0015    001.25    $    18.75
BROWN, G.K.      ASK1    NOT FOUND  0100    000.00    $     0.00
```

Study the logic of the preceding search very carefully, and make sure you fully understand all aspects of it. Remarkably, it is very easy to make subtle logical errors when using only PERFORM for searching. It is less easy to go wrong when using the SEARCH verb.

The SEARCH verb is used for a linear search of an array

You can use a SEARCH verb for searching the contents of an array; the search mechanism is similar to that of PERFORM . . . UNTIL. The search is linear, checking each element in turn, from a low to high subscript values. The difference is that a subscript identifier, such as SUB, is not used. Instead an index identifier, not defined in WORKING-STORAGE, is used. The syntax for the SEARCH verb is as shown here:

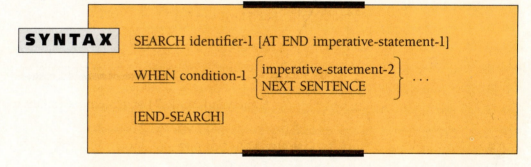

SYNTAX

SEARCH identifier-1 [AT END imperative-statement-1]

WHEN condition-1 { imperative-statement-2 / NEXT SENTENCE } . . .

[END-SEARCH]

The identifier-1 must be an identifier declared with an OCCURS clause and an index identifier. Thus, to use the array LU-PRODUCT-TABLE with the SEARCH verb, it would have to be declared with an index identifier, such as EX1, as follows:

```
01 LOOK-UP-TABLE.
   05 LU-PRODUCT-TABLE  OCCURS 1000 TIMES INDEXED BY EX1.
      10  LU-IDCODE              PIC X(04).
      10  LU-UNIT-PRICE          PIC 9(03)V99.
      10  LU-PRODUCT-TYPE        PIC X(10).
```

There is an implicit declaration of the index identifier EX1 here. It should not be declared elsewhere in the WORKING-STORAGE section. Any name complying with COBOL identifier naming rules can be used for an index identifier. Because there are 1000 elements in the array, EX1 will have the equivalent of a PIC 9(04) specification. An index identifier does *not* hold a subscript value, however, only a value that corresponds to a subscript value. Actually, an index identifier holds a value called a memory address offset or memory address displacement, which is quite different. (This will be explained later.)

A search of an array can start at any subscript position for the array. But no matter where it begins, the start position must be specified using a SET verb. You may not use ADD, SUBTRACT, COMPUTE, or MOVE to place a numeric literal or numeric identifier value in an index identifier, since it does not hold a subscript value.

There are three versions of SET. The first SET verb version (also called the initialization SET verb) is used to place an initial value in an index identifier, that is, for initializing an index identifier. The second SET verb version is used to increase or decrease the value in an index identifier. The third version is for transferring a value from an index identifier to a normal numeric identifier.

The syntax for SET is shown here:

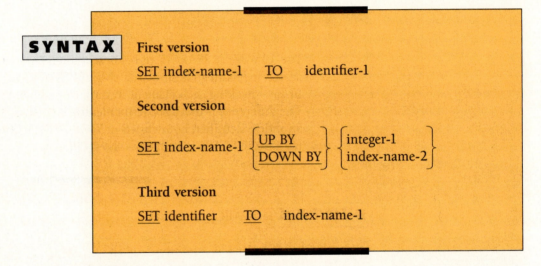

SYNTAX

First version

SET index-name-1   TO   identifier-1

Second version

SET index-name-1 $\left\{ \begin{array}{l} \text{UP BY} \\ \text{DOWN BY} \end{array} \right\}$ $\left\{ \begin{array}{l} \text{integer-1} \\ \text{index-name-2} \end{array} \right\}$

Third version

SET identifier   TO   index-name-1

Some valid SEARCH statements, with an appropriate SET statement are

```
MOVE 100 TO SUB.
SET EX1 TO SUB.          EX1 value corresponds to subscript 100
...
SET EX1 DOWN BY 60.     Search starts at subscript 40
SEARCH LU-PRODUCT-TABLE
     AT END PERFORM 700-NO-MATCH-ROUTINE
   WHEN PR-IDCODE-IN = LU-IDCODE (EX1)
   MOVE LU-PRODUCT-TYPE (EX1) TO DL-PRODUCT-TYPE-OUT
   MOVE LU-UNIT-PRICE (EX1) TO DL-UNIT-PRICE-OUT
   MULTIPLY LU-UNIT-PRICE (EX1) BY PR-QUANTITY-IN
                              GIVING WS-COST
   MOVE WS-COST TO DL-COST-OUT
END-SEARCH.
```

```
SET EX1 TO 1.
...
SET EX1 UP BY 4.          Search starts at subscript 5.
SEARCH LU-PRODUCT-TABLE
    WHEN PR-IDCODE-IN = LU-IDCODE (EX1)
            NEXT SENTENCE
END-SEARCH.
PERFORM 900-MATCH-FOUND-ROUTINE.    Not part of SEARCH
                                    statement!
```

When SEARCH is executed, the EX1 identifier will automatically get values in sequence, pointing first to the subscript specified in the most recent SET statement and finally pointing to subscript 1000, since this is the subscript range declared for LU-PRODUCT-TABLE.

Note the following:

- If a match is reached, the WHEN statements are executed.
- If no match is reached, the AT END statement is executed.

Thus, there must be two clear alternatives. But if you are not careful, you can write the SEARCH statement such that both alternatives are carried out—usually not what was intended, as in

```
SET EX1 UP BY 4.
SEARCH LU-PRODUCT-TABLE
        AT END PERFORM 700-NO-MATCH-ROUTINE
    WHEN PR-IDCODE-IN = LU-IDCODE (EX1)
            NEXT SENTENCE.
PERFORM 900-MATCH-FOUND-ROUTINE.        error!
```

Here both NO-MATCH-ROUTINE and MATCH-FOUND-ROUTINE would be carried out if no match was found.

Using SEARCH for a Linear Table Search

Let us now use SEARCH instead of PERFORM . . . VARYING in the search of the table LU-PRODUCT-TABLE. Once more, as each record of CUSTOMER-PURCHASE is read, the PR-IDCODE-IN value is used as the target value in the search of the LU-IDCODE column in the array LU-PRODUCT-TABLE (Figure 11.15d) for a matching value. When a match is found, the data in that row are used to put data in DETAIL-LINE-OUT, which are then output. If a match is not found, the message "NOT FOUND" is placed in the DL-PRODUCT-TYPE-OUT field in DETAIL-LINE-OUT for which information is missing. A zero quantity is also placed in the unit price and cost fields in DETAIL-LINE-OUT, if no matching row was found in the table. The essential code is as follows:

```
MOVE 'YES' TO MORE-RECORDS.
READ CUSTOMER-PURCHASE
        AT END STOP RUN.
PERFORM 400-PROCESS-INPUT-RECORD
        UNTIL MORE-RECORDS = 'NO'.
...
```

```
400-PROCESS-INPUT-RECORD.
        SET EX1 TO 1.
        SEARCH LU-PRODUCT-TABLE
        AT END PERFORM 500-NO-MATCH-ROUTINE
        WHEN PR-IDCODE-IN = LU-IDCODE (EX1)
              MOVE LU-PRODUCT-TYPE (EX1) TO DL-PRODUCT-TYPE-OUT
              MOVE LU-UNIT-PRICE (EX1) TO DL-UNIT-PRICE-OUT
              MULTIPLY LU-UNIT-PRICE (EX1) BY PR-QUANTITY-IN
                                      GIVING WS-COST
              MOVE WS-COST TO DL-COST-OUT
        END-SEARCH.
        MOVE PR-CUSTOMER-IN TO DL-CUSTOMER-OUT.
        MOVE PR-IDCODE-IN TO DL-IDCODE-OUT.
        MOVE PR-QUANTITY-IN TO DL-QUANTITY-OUT.
        WRITE REPORT-RECORD-OUT FROM DETAIL-LINE-OUT.
                          AFTER ADVANCING 1 LINE.
        READ CUSTOMER-PURCHASE,
              AT END MOVE 'NO' TO MORE-RECORDS.
500-NO-MATCH-ROUTINE.
        MOVE 'NOT FOUND' TO DL-PRODUCT-TYPE-OUT.
        MOVE 0.00 DL-UNIT-PRICE-OUT.
        MOVE 0.00 TO DL-COST-OUT.
```

The search stops when a match is found and the index identifier EX1 has a value corresponding to the subscript value of the matching element. The matching element is then used to partly construct DETAIL-LINE-OUT. When the rest of DETAIL-LINE-OUT has been constructed from the current input CUSTOMER-PURCHASE record, DETAIL-LINE-OUT is written out.

If no match is found, the search goes all the way to the end. Then the AT END statement PERFORM 500-NO-MATCH-ROUTINE is carried out. This places a "NOT FOUND" message near the end of DETAIL-LINE-OUT, and other fields for which there is no data are set to zero. Execution control then returns to the next statement after SEARCH. Then the rest of DETAIL-LINE-OUT is filled with data from the current input CUSTOMER-PURCHASE record. DETAIL-LINE-OUT is then output, with the same error-message results as with the PERFORM . . . VARYING version shown earlier.

An index identifier contains a memory address offset value

It is generally accepted that it is more efficient to use SEARCH than PER-FORM . . . VARYING with a subscript. This is largely because the index identifier usually holds a memory address offset or memory address displacement (or close equivalent) for each array element, resulting in the use of fewer machine language instructions.

To understand what a memory address offset is, let us take this array:

```
01 ARRAY-DATA.
   05 EL   PIC X(04) OCCURS 10 TIMES INDEXED BY EX1.
```

The elements of array EL are fixed in memory. Suppose the first element, EL (1), is located at address 1000. In that case EL (2) will be located at address

1004, with an offset of 4 bytes from address 1000, EL (3) will be at address 1008, with an offset of 8, and so on. Finally EL (10) will be at address 1036, with an offset of 36.

A subscript identifier thus holds integer subscript values, but an index identifier will hold the amount in bytes by which an element is offset from the address of the first element of the array. This is further illustrated by this table:

SUBSCRIPT (SUB) VALUE	ARRAY ELEMENT	MEMORY ADDRESS (BYTES)	MEMORY ADDRESS OFFSET (BYTES)	INDEX (EX1) VALUE
1	EL (1)	1000	0	0
2	EL (2)	1004	4	4
3	EL (3)	1008	8	8
...				
10	EL (10)	1036	36	36

You must use SET to manipulate an index value

Suppose that with array EL, index identifier EX1 contains offset value 12, so that it corresponds to subscript 4. You want to move the corresponding subscript value 4 to the identifier SUB. Since EX1 actually contains 12 and not 4, it would be pointless to allow use of MOVE. SET is used instead and the computation necessary to convert offset 12 to subscript 4 is carried out before the value in EX1 is transferred to SUB (and vice versa).

Because an index identifier contains a memory address offset instead of just a subscript value, you cannot use MOVE to transfer values between an index identifier and a normal numeric identifier. For the same reason, you cannot use ADD, SUBTRACT, or COMPUTE to alter the value in an index identifier. You must use SET for that as well.

In summary, you can do the following with an index identifier:

Use SET to Assign a Value

You can assign a value to an index identifier with the first version of SET. This initialization value can come from an ordinary numeric identifier, an integer, or another index identifier, as in:

```
SET EX1 TO SUB.          initialize to value in SUB
SET EX1 TO 10.           initialize to value 10
SET EX1 TO EX-4.         initialize EX1 to value in
                         index identifier EX-4
```

Remember that a conversion to the proper offset value will take place with this use of set. Thus if SUB contains 6 and an element of the array is 4 bytes in size, SET EX1 TO SUB will place 5 times 4, or 20 in EX1.

Use SET to Increase or Decrease the Value

The second version of set is used to increase or decrease the value in an index identifier. Remember that an index identifier holds an offset value. Now consider

```
SET EX1 UP BY 3.
```

This does not mean that the value in EX1 will increase by 3. EX1 holds an offset value. Thus, if an element of the array is 4 bytes, the value in EX1 will increase by 3 times 4, or 12 bytes. Similarly

```
SET EX1 DOWN BY 6.
```

means that the value in EX1 will fall by 6 times 4 bytes.

Use SET to Transfer a Value

The third version of SET is used to transfer the value in an index identifier, with proper conversion, to a numeric identifier. Thus, if the value in EX1 indexes the third element of an array, and you needed to use that number 3 in computations, you would first adjust the value in a numeric identifier to the subscript value corresponding to the index value in the index identifier, as in

```
SET SUB TO EX1.
```
SUB gets the subscript value corresponding to the index value in EX1

Here SUB is an ordinary numeric identifier. Note that SUB comes first in the expression. If you write

```
SET EX1 TO SUB.
```
error!

which is easy to do, since it is a valid first SET statement, it means that you are initializing EX1 to the value corresponding to the subscript in SUB.

The differences between an index identifier and a subscript identifier are very important

Note the following differences between index and subscript identifiers:

- An index identifier is defined by an INDEXED BY clause when an array is defined, and nowhere else. A subscript identifier is defined by a normal numeric identifier definition.
- An index identifier contains the amount in bytes by which an element is offset in memory from the first element of the array, that is, by a memory address offset. A subscript identifier contains a subscript value. An index identifier is usually more efficient than a subscript identifier.
- To move values to or from an index identifier, you must use the SET verb. The computational verbs ADD, SUBTRACT, MULTIPLY, DIVIDE, and COMPUTE cannot be used with an

index identifier. SET is also used to add a value to, or subtract a value from, an index identifier.

- An index identifier must be used with the SEARCH and SEARCH ALL verbs and may also be used with PERFORM . . . VARYING.

You can also use an index identifier with PERFORM . . . VARYING

You can use an index identifier with PERFORM . . . VARYING, instead of a subscripted identifier (defined separately). With many computer systems this use of an index identifier with PERFORM . . . VARYING is more efficient. The equivalent code to process input CUSTOMER-PURCHASE records by a search of the array LU-PRODUCT-TABLE for each input record, is as follows:

```
01 LOOK-UP-TABLE.
    05 LU-PRODUCT-TABLE   OCCURS 1000 TIMES INDEXED BY EX1.
        10   LU-IDCODE                 PIC X(04).
        10   LU-UNIT-PRICE             PIC 9(03)V99.
        10   LU-PRODUCT-TYPE           PIC X(10).
...
        MOVE 'YES' TO MORE-RECORDS.
        READ CUSTOMER-PURCHASE
                    AT END STOP RUN.
        PERFORM 400-PROCESS-INPUT-RECORD
                    UNTIL MORE-RECORDS = 'NO'.
        ...
400-PROCESS-INPUT-RECORD.
        MOVE 'NO' TO MATCH-FOUND.
        PERFORM 500-CHECK-TABLE-ROW
            VARYING EX1 FROM 1 BY 1
                UNTIL EX1 > 1000 OR MATCH-FOUND = 'YES'.
        IF MATCH-FOUND = 'NO'
            PERFORM 600-NO-MATCH-ROUTINE
        END-IF.
        MOVE PR-CUSTOMER-IN TO DL-CUSTOMER-OUT.
        MOVE PR-IDCODE-IN TO DL-IDCODE-OUT.
        MOVE PR-QUANTITY-IN TO DL-QUANTITY-OUT.
        WRITE REPORT-RECORD-OUT FROM DETAIL-LINE-OUT
                    AFTER ADVANCING 1 LINE.
        READ CUSTOMER-PURCHASE,
                AT END MOVE 'NO' TO MORE-RECORDS.

500-CHECK-TABLE-ROW.
    IF LU-IDCODE (EX1) = PR-IDCODE-IN
        MOVE 'YES' TO MATCH-FOUND
        MOVE LU-PRODUCT-TYPE (EX1) TO DL-PRODUCT-TYPE-OUT
        MOVE LU-UNIT-PRICE (EX1) TO DL-UNIT-PRICE-OUT
        MULTIPLY LU-UNIT-PRICE (EX1) BY PR-QUANTITY-IN
                                GIVING WS-COST
        MOVE WS-COST TO DL-COST-OUT
    END-IF.
```

```
600-NO-MATCH-ROUTINE.
        MOVE 'NOT FOUND' TO DL-PRODUCT-TYPE-OUT.
        MOVE 0.00 DL-UNIT-PRICE-OUT.
        MOVE 0.00 TO DL-COST-OUT.
```

You use SEARCH ALL for a binary search of a table

In practice, you write a SEARCH ALL statement exactly as you write a SEARCH statement. The syntax of SEARCH ALL is essentially the same as for SEARCH, except for a limitation on condition-1 following WHEN. The SEARCH ALL syntax is shown in the following box. Note that data-name-1 and data-name-2 cannot be subscripted with most compilers.

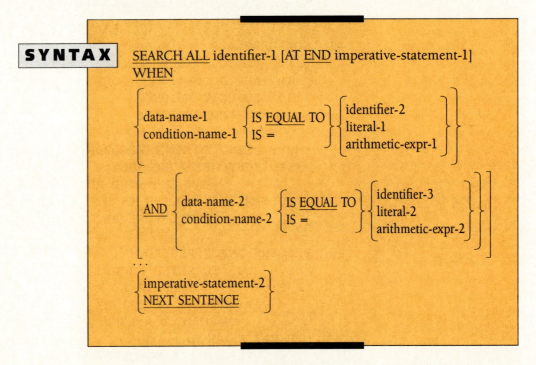

SYNTAX

SEARCH ALL identifier-1 [AT END imperative-statement-1]
WHEN

$\left\{ \begin{array}{l} \text{data-name-1} \\ \text{condition-name-1} \end{array} \right\} \left\{ \begin{array}{l} \text{IS EQUAL TO} \\ \text{IS =} \end{array} \right\} \left\{ \begin{array}{l} \text{identifier-2} \\ \text{literal-1} \\ \text{arithmetic-expr-1} \end{array} \right\}$

$\left[\text{AND} \left\{ \begin{array}{l} \text{data-name-2} \\ \text{condition-name-2} \end{array} \right\} \left\{ \begin{array}{l} \text{IS EQUAL TO} \\ \text{IS =} \end{array} \right\} \left\{ \begin{array}{l} \text{identifier-3} \\ \text{literal-2} \\ \text{arithmetic-expr-2} \end{array} \right\} \right]$

...

$\left\{ \begin{array}{l} \text{imperative-statement-2} \\ \text{NEXT SENTENCE} \end{array} \right\}$

In addition, you do not use a SET statement before SEARCH ALL. This is a typical SEARCH ALL statement:

```
SEARCH ALL LU-PRODUCT-TABLE
        AT END PERFORM 700-NO-MATCH-ROUTINE
    WHEN PR-IDCODE-IN = LU-IDCODE (EX1)
        MOVE LU-PRODUCT-TYPE (EX1) TO DL-PRODUCT-TYPE-OUT
        MOVE LU-UNIT-PRICE (EX1) TO DL-UNIT-PRICE-OUT
        MULTIPLY LU-UNIT-PRICE (EX1) BY PR-QUANTITY-IN
                                    GIVING WS-COST
        MOVE WS-COST TO DL-COST-OUT
END-SEARCH.
```

In the condition following WHEN, you can use only IS EQUAL TO or =, because anything other than equality would confuse the binary search mechanism. In addition, if the condition is a compound condition, the simple conditions must be connected by AND, never by OR, again because an OR would confuse the binary search mechanism.

Except for the elimination of the SET statement and the replacement of SEARCH by SEARCH ALL, the code for the binary search of the table LU-PRODUCT-TABLE using SEARCH ALL is the same as for the linear search of LU-PRODUCT-TABLE (given at the end of the previous section) using SEARCH.

Note that it is possible to use multiple WHEN clauses with both SEARCH and SEARCH ALL, as, for example, in

```
SET EX1 TO 1.
SEARCH LU-PRODUCT-TABLE
        AT END PERFORM 700-NO-MATCH-ROUTINE
    WHEN LU-IDCODE (EX1) =  'RT12'
                PERFORM 500-RT-MATCH-ROUTINE
    WHEN LU-IDCODE (EX1) =  'ZW30'
                PERFORM 600-ZW-MATCH-ROUTINE.
```

The 700-NO-MATCH-ROUTINE is carried out only if neither RT12 nor ZW30 occurs in the LU-IDCODE column of the table. If both occur, the match routine for whichever occurs first is carried out. If only one of them occurs, the corresponding match routine is carried out.

You must define a search key and an index to use SEARCH ALL

Note that in the definition of an array for binary searching with SEARCH ALL, you would have to specify which elementary identifier is to be used in searching for a match. That is, you must specify which elementary identifier is the search key identifier. You need to use LU-IDCODE as the search key identifier. You must also specify if the order of the data in the LU-IDCODE search key identifier is descending or ascending.

In addition, you need to specify an index identifier, even if you make no use of it in the SEARCH ALL statement. Thus, the declaration for LU-PRODUCT-TABLE needed for SEARCH ALL would be

```
01 LOOK-UP-TABLE.
   05 LU-PRODUCT-TABLE   OCCURS 1000 TIMES
               ASCENDING KEY IS LU-IDCODE INDEXED BY EX1.
      10   LU-IDCODE                 PIC X(04).
      10   LU-UNIT-PRICE             PIC 9(03)V99.
      10   LU-PRODUCT-TYPE           PIC X(10).
```

This specifies that the index identifier is EX1 and the search key identifier is LU-IDCODE, with values in ascending order. ASCENDING would be replaced by DESCENDING, if LU-IDCODE values were in descending order. Note that the ASCENDING clause must come before the INDEXED clause. The syntax for this is shown here:

Also note that you cannot index a level-1 identifier.

Summary

1. A single-level array is a subscripted collection of identifiers in memory. A single-level array is defined using an OCCURS clause, which cannot be used with a 01-level identifier. A subscripted identifier can be either an elementary or group identifier. The elementary identifiers of a subscripted group identifier are subscripted identifiers. A subscript can be a numeric non-zero integer literal or the non-zero integer value of a subscript identifier.

2. Single-level arrays are commonly used to hold histograms or input data that need repeated processing, to process repeating groups of fields in input records, and as look-up tables.

3. Arrays are commonly processed using either the PERFORM . . . UNTIL verb or the PERFORM . . . VARYING verb. The PERFORM . . . VARYING verb can be used only when it is known in advance how many elements of the array are to be processed.

4. An array can be searched with either a linear or a binary search. A linear search can be conducted using either of the PERFORM verbs or the SEARCH verb. The SEARCH verb uses an index identifier instead of a subscript identifier. An index identifier usually holds the memory address offset of an array element instead of a subscript, so processing with an index identifier is faster. The PERFORM . . . VARYING verb can use either a subscript identifier or an index identifier. To carry out a binary search of an array, you need to use the SEARCH ALL verb and the elements of the array must be ordered in ascending or descending order. An index identifier is needed with SEARCH ALL. To transfer a value to or from an index identifier, you must use the SET verb; the MOVE verb is illegal.

Key Terms

array	look-up table	linear search
subscript	search key	binary search
repeating groups		

Concept Review Questions

1. Give a single example showing why arrays are necessary.
2. Suppose you had to read in a long list of names from a file, in ascending order, and print them in descending order. Explain how you could use an array to do it.
3. Explain why it would be unreasonable to allow the use of OCCURS with a level-01 identifier.
4. Why is the PERFORM . . . VARYING verb particularly useful for processing arrays?
5. When should the in-line PERFORM . . . VARYING verb be used?
6. In processing an array of elements X (n), with 10 elements in which only the first 7 contain data, why is the following wrong?

```
MOVE 1 TO SUB.
PERFORM UNTIL SUB = 7
     MOVE X (SUB) TO . . .
END-PERFORM.
```

7. List methods of initializing an alphanumeric array to spaces.
8. List methods of initializing a numeric array to zeros.
9. Suppose an array has both alphanumeric and numeric elements. List methods of initializing the alphanumeric elements to spaces and the numeric elements to zeros.
10. What is needed to hold a histogram in a COBOL program?
11. Give the method for constructing a histogram about the heights of people from records in an input file in which each record gives the height of an individual person.
12. What is to be done when an application dictates use of an array with a zero subscript?
13. What is a repeating group of fields?
14. What is the standard method of handling a repeating group in an input record?
15. When is a look-up table useful?
16. List two methods of initializing a look-up table in an array in a program.
17. Explain the difference between a linear and a binary search.
18. Suppose you have an array with 256 elements, on average how long will it take to search it
    a. with linear searching?
    b. with binary searching?
19. Explain why the elements of an array have to be ordered before binary searching can be carried out.
20. Why must the search condition be restricted to equality with binary searching?
21. Why, with many computers, is the SEARCH verb more efficient for searching a look-up table than the PERFORM . . . VARYING verb with a numeric subscript?
22. Each element of an array is 7 bytes long. If element-1 starts at address 600 and index identifier EX1 points to element-6, what is the actual value held in EX1?
23. Why must SET and not MOVE be used in transferring data into and out of index identifiers?

24. Explain the difference between an index identifier and a subscript identifier.

25. Explain the difference between the SEARCH ALL and SEARCH verbs.

COBOL Language Questions

1. What is wrong with this?

```
01 DATA-ARRAY    PIC 9(04)    OCCURS 10 TIMES.
```

2. What is wrong with the following?

```
01 A.
   05 B         PIC X(10).
   05 C                      OCCURS 10 TIMES.
      10 CX  PIC 9(04).
      10 CT  PIC X(10).
   05 D         PIC X(10).
...
MOVE 11 TO SUB.
MOVE CT (SUB) TO B.
```

3. Suppose you have the numeric array elements Y (*n*), in which *n* can go up to 100. What does the following code do?

```
MOVE 1 TO Y (1).
MOVE Y (1) TO Y (2).
MOVE 3 TO SUB.
PERFORM UNTIL SUB = 101
     COMPUTE Y (SUB) = Y (SUB - 1) + Y (SUB - 2)
     ADD 1 TO SUB
END-PERFORM.
```

4. Suppose the histogram for the weights of employees at a company is in array elements W (*n*), where *n* goes from 1 to 400 (pounds). Write a routine to compute the average weight of the employees.

5. Rewrite the routine in question 3 using PERFORM . . . VARYING with a separate paragraph.

6. Rewrite the routine in question 3 using the in-line PERFORM . . . VARYING.

7. The array with elements T (*n*) has 100 elements, only the first 15 of which have been assigned data. To print the array contents, you write

```
MOVE 1 TO SUB.
PERFORM VARYING SUB FROM 1 BY 1
                     UNTIL SUB = 15
     MOVE T (SUB) TO REPORT-RECORD-OUT
     WRITE REPORT RECORD-OUT
END-PERFORM.
```

Find the bug.

8. How many identifiers are specified in the following?

```
01 A.
   05 Y     PIC 9(04).
   05 Y                        OCCURS 6 TIMES.
      10 R PIC X(04).
      10 S PIC X(02).
   05 W                        OCCURS 3 TIMES.
      10 T PIC 9(05).
```

9. What is wrong with this?

```
01 ARRAY6          VALUE SPACES.
   05 T  PIC X(04) OCCURS 10 TIMES.
```

10. What is wrong with this?

```
01 TAX-DATA.
   05  COMP    OCCURS 10 TIMES VALUE 0.
      10  COMPA   PIC 9(03).
      10  COMPB   PIC 9(04).
```

11. Suppose you have a look-up table, defined as

```
01 LUT.
   05 LUT-EMPLOYEE-TABLE OCCURS 100 TIMES INDEXED BY EX1.
      10 LUT-EMPNUMBER     PIC X(06).
      10 LUT-SALARY        PIC 9(07).
```

with

```
01 SUB                PIC 9(03).
```

a. Write a routine using PERFORM . . . VARYING to find the salary of employee E45600.
b. Write a routine using SEARCH to find the salary of employee E45600.
c. Write a routine to find the average salary of employees.
d. If data in the array are in ascending employee-number order, alter the array definition to permit a binary search for the salary of employee E45600 and write the routine for the binary search.

Programming Assignments

1. **Array to reverse the order of input data**
The input file EMPLOYEE-IN has data about 12 employees of a consulting company in descending salary order:

```
---------1---------2---------3
SMITH, P.F.             7956764
JONES, G.              7587900
GREEN, K.L.            7178367
KAZUK, K.F.            6489231
ALEXANDROVITCH, P.H.5789268
LEE, P.J.              5478967
GRIMES, H.P.           5389700
TANGENT, R.U.          5278970
PACKARD, W.H.          4978665
FRANKS, H.D.           4735965
DUROSHENSKY, R.D.      4505689
ZAVIER, M.             3656982
```

Use an array to output the data in ascending salary order, as in this report:

```
---------1---------2---------3---------4
EMPLOYEE NAME          SALARY

ZAVIER, M.            $36,569.82
DUROSHENSKY, R.D.     $45,056.89
. . .
```

a. Draw the input record layout and spacing chart.
b. Draw the flowchart and hierarchy diagram.
c. Write the program.

2. **Array to select input records for processing**
Use the same input file as in Assignment 1 but sorted in ascending employee-name order

```
---------1---------2---------3---------4
ALEXANDROVITCH, P.H.5789268
DUROSHENSKY, R.D.      4505689
FRANKS, H.D.           4735965
GREEN, K.L.            7178367
GRIMES, H.P.           5389700
JONES, G.              7587900
KAZUK, K.F.            6489231
LEE, P.J.              5478967
PACKARD, W.H.          4978665
SMITH, P.F.            7956764
TANGENT, R.U.          5278970
ZAVIER, M.             3656982
```

Use an array to output full data about employees who earn less than employee Lee, P.J. The output data should be in the form of a report, as follows:

```
---------1---------2---------3---------4
EMPLOYEE NAME          SALARY


ZAVIER, M.             $36,569.82
DUROSHENSKY, R.D.      $45,056.89
...
```

a. Draw the input record layout and the spacing chart.
b. Draw the flowchart and hierarchy diagram.
c. Write the program.

3. **Program to create and output a histogram**
Because of their great popularity, a library places certain cookbooks on restricted circulation. A record is kept of who has borrowed these cookbooks; it forms an input file, as follows:

```
---------1---------2---------3---------4---------5
02BON APPETIT       PIERRE LAMANCHESMITH, J.P
04GOOD FOODS COOKING JULIET CROW    GREEN, H.K.
01BEEFSTEAK DELIGHTS JOHN BULL       GOODMAN. P.P.
02BON APPETIT       PIERRE LAMANCHEFARVER,L.
03CHICKEN FOR HEALTH JOHN BIRD       GREEN, H.K.
04GOOD FOODS COOKING JULIET CROW    LEE, P.F
05MACROBIOTIC COOKINGTERI KOMATSU   BROWN, P.R.
06THE VEGETARIAN    THATCHER STRAW YEE, E.T.
05MACROBIOTIC COOKINGTERI KOMATSU   HARVEY, J.K.
02BON APPETIT       PIERRE LAMANCHEDEARING, H.J.
06THE VEGETARIAN    THATCHER STRAW LOOSE, H.P.
01BEEFSTEAK DELIGHTS JOHN BULL       FREEMAN. F.P.
04GOOD FOODS COOKING JULIET CROW    HARDY, U.P.
02BON APPETIT       PIERRE LAMANCHEJOHNSON, K.J.
05MACROBIOTIC COOKINGTERI KOMATSU   BRONSON, M.
06THE VEGETARIAN    THATCHER STRAW BENSON, K.P.
03CHICKEN FOR HEALTH JOHN BIRD       DEARING, H.J.
```

The first two digits in a record give the book identification number. The program uses an array to hold and output a histogram of the borrowing of these six books.

```
---------1---------2---------3---------4---------5---------6---------7
BOOK TITLE           AUTHOR             NUMBER OF BORROWINGS

BEEFSTEAK DELIGHTS   JOHN BULL          2
BON APPETIT          PIERRE LAMANCHE    4
...
```

a. Draw the input record layout and spacing chart.
b. Draw the flowchart and hierarchy diagram.
c. Write a program, using an array for the histogram.

4. **Program to output two histograms from a single input file**
National park officers have placed harmless identification rings on bears that tend to visit campsites in a large park. Each ring carries an easily visible two-digit identification number. During a test

period of one week, officers did not chase bears away from campsites (as long as no one was in danger) but simply recorded the day (number) and duration (in minutes) of each visit. These data form an input file, as follows:

```
---------1---------2--------3
03STONEY CREEK      14
07SANDY LAKE        13
09STONEY CREEK      12
12FLAT BOTTOMS      23
05VALLEY VIEW       22
01SANDY LAKE        24
03VALLEY VIEW       21
10FLAT BOTTOMS      32
08CEDAR RIDGE       35
04VALLEY VIEW       31
02CEDAR RIDGE       42
06STONEY CREEK      41
12SANDY LAKE        43
11VALLEY VIEW       45
06FLAT BOTTOMS      57
02CEDAR RIDGE       52
01SANDY LAKE        53
05FLAT BOTTOMS      55
09SANDY CREEK       61
10VALLEY VIEW       63
06FLAT BOTTOMS      62
01CEDAR RIDGE       64
12SANDY LAKE        72
02VALLEY VIEW       74
```

Columns	
01–02	Bear identification number
03–19	Campsite
20	Day of visit (1 to 7)
21	Duration of visit (minutes)

The program will output two histograms. The first is for the number of visits by a given bear

```
---------1---------2---------3---------4---------5
              VISITS BY EACH BEAR
```

BEAR ID	NUMBER OF VISITS	TOTAL MINUTES
01	3	11
02	2	6
...		

The second is for the number of bears that stay a given length of time.

```
---------1---------2---------3---------4---------5---------6
          BEARS VISITING FOR EACH VISIT DURATION

     MINUTES IN VISIT        NUMBER OF BEARS        TOTAL MINUTES

     1                       4                      4
     2                       6                      12
     3                       4                      12
     ...
```

a. Draw the input record layout and spacing charts.
b. Draw the flowchart and hierarchy diagram.
c. Write a program, using two distinct arrays for the histograms.

5. Output of multiple histograms

The same input file as in Assignment 4 applies. This time, the pair of histograms are to be output for each of the six campsites in the park, that is, 12 histograms in all. The data for a new campsite should begin on a new page, since it will be distributed to the officer on duty at that campsite, as an indication of what to expect.

6. Program to handle repeating groups in an input file

Each of three stock exchanges keeps track of the total number of stocks gaining in price and the number losing in price on each of the five trading days of a week. The data for a week form an input file, as follows:

```
---------1---------2---------3---------4---------5
NYSE0777038206470554034208970525075098750294
AMEX0478039702360532024503210432018903920245
NASD1234098709350934086513320956113212450899
```

In the numeric part, each group of eight digits gives the gainers (four digits) and losers (four digits) for the day.
The output data are

```
---------1---------2---------3---------4---------5---------6---------7
          NEW YORK STOCK EXCHANGE (NYSE)

DAY         NUMBER ADVANCING      NUMBER DECLINING     NUMBER UNCHANGED

MONDAY      777                   382                  391
TUESDAY     647                   554                  349
...


          AMERICAN EXCHANGE (AMEX)

DAY         NUMBER ADVANCING      NUMBER DECLINING     NUMBER UNCHANGED

MONDAY      478                   397                  325
...
```

DAY	NUMBER ADVANCING	NUMBER DECLINING	NUMBER UNCHANGED
MONDAY	...		

The total number of stocks listed on the NYSE can be taken as 1550, on AMEX as 1200, and on NASDAQ as 4500.

a. Draw the input record layout and spacing chart.
b. Draw a flowchart and hierarchy diagram for the processing.
c. Write the program using at least one array.

7. **Program using a look-up table**
A record of the main input file describes the cargo carried by a ship. The first field is the ship name, the second the cargo type, the third (numeric) the number of units of that cargo on board, and the last field is the country of registration.

```
---------1---------2---------3---------4---------5
ARROWHEAD          OIL         05000GREECE
ASTONHEAD          SUGAR       14350PANAMA
BULKFELLOW         IRON ORE    02260GREECE
CRANSTON           BUTANE      04560KOREA
DEVONSHIRE         OIL         25600PANAMA
DOVEBIRD           WHEAT       18970BRAZIL
DUSTY              IRON ORE    00756PANAMA
EVERYMAN           SUGAR       08967KOREA
FORWARDBOUNTY      COPPER      00785BRAZIL
FUNNELHEAD         OIL         20000PANAMA
GOODWILL           RUBBER      15000GREECE
GOVERNOR           WHEAT       04520GREECE
GULLLAKE           RUBBER      15000KOREA
HALIFAXGULL        OIL         01000PANAMA
HEAVYSIDE          TIMBER      00600BRAZIL
HOODDOWN           COPPER      067007KOREA
IVANHOE            IRON ORE    065003GREECE
KARLSTAD           BUTANE      002407PANAMA
KINGSTON           OIL         195002JAPAN
KUNGHU             WHEAT       200540KOREA
```

A subsidiary file gives information about the current price (in dollars and cents) per unit for bulk quantities of the various commodities on board the ships:

```
---------1---------2
BUTANE    0040
COPPER    0075
IRON ORE1050
OIL       2123
RUBBER    1080
SUGAR     0815
TIMBER    0046
WHEAT     0240
```

In processing the main input file, use is made of the price data in the subsidiary file to generate an output report, as shown here:

```
---------1---------2---------3---------4---------5---------6---------7
             CURRENT CARGO VALUE REPORT

SHIP NAME               CARGO       UNITS   TOTAL CARGO    REGISTRATION
                        ON BOARD            VALUE          NATION

ARROWHEAD               OIL         05000   $  106,150.00  GREECE
ASTONHEAD               SUGAR       14350   $  116,952.50  PANAMA
...
```

To carry out the assignment, the contents of the subsidiary file should be placed in a look-up table.

a. Draw the input record layouts and spacing chart.
b. Design the look-up table.
c. Draw the flowchart and hierarchy diagram.
c. Write the program and carry out the search of the look-up table with PERFORM . . . VARYING.

8. **Use of SEARCH with a look-up table**
Modify the program in Assignment 7 so that the SEARCH verb is used in searching the look-up table.

9. **Binary search of a look-up table**
Modify the program in Assignment 7 so that binary searches of the look-up table are conducted instead of linear searches.

12

MULTIPLE-LEVEL ARRAYS

IN THE SPECIFICATION of a group identifier, several levels of OCCURS clauses may be used. Thus, you might specify 10 occurrences of identifier X, each of which could consist of 20 occurrences of identifier Y. In all you would have specified 20 × 10 occurrences of Y. As a result, Y is said to be a two-dimensional or two-level, 10 × 20 array.

With COBOL 85, you may specify up to seven levels of OCCURS clauses, although more than two levels is less common in commercial practice. Most of this chapter will be devoted to techniques for dealing with two levels of OCCURS clauses.

12.1
The technicalities of two-level arrays must be learned

SUPPOSE A STORE has five salespersons (salesperson 1, salesperson 2, and so on), and is open six days a week, from Monday (day 1) to Saturday (day 6). On any given day each salesperson will have rung up a certain sales total. Since there are six days and five salespersons, there will be 6 × 5 sales totals in all, one for each salesperson for each day.

Suppose you want to have an identifier for each of the 30 sales totals. One way to specify the identifiers would be

```
01  MONDAY.
    05 SALES-TOT-MON   PIC 9(4)V99 OCCURS 5 TIMES.
01  TUESDAY.
    05 SALES-TOT-TUE   PIC 9(4)V99 OCCURS 5 TIMES.
01  WEDNESADY.
    05 SALES-TOT-WED   PIC 9(4)V99 OCCURS 5 TIMES.
01  THURSDAY.
    05 SALES-TOT-THU   PIC 9(4)V99 OCCURS 5 TIMES.
01  FRIDAY.
    05 SALES-TOT-FRI   PIC 9(4)V99 OCCURS 5 TIMES.
01  SATURDAY.
    05 SALES-TOT-SAT   PIC 9(4)V99 OCCURS 5 TIMES.
```

This might just be acceptable. But suppose you wanted the sales totals for each day of the year; this method would clearly be too cumbersome. You can more easily get the needed 30 identifiers for the case of five salespersons for six days with two levels of OCCURS.

```
01 TB-WEEKLY-SALES-TOTS.
   05 TB-DAY-ROW OCCURS 6 TIMES.
      10 TB-SALES OCCURS 5 TIMES          PIC 9(4)V99.
```

In memory 30 locations have been specified, which will normally be contiguous, that is, beside one another.

To be precise, the following have been specified:

group identifier TB-DAY-ROW (1) consisting of

`TB-SALES (1, 1)  TB-SALES (1, 2)  TB-SALES (1, 3)  TB-SALES (1, 4)  TB-SALES (1, 5)`

group identifier TB-DAY-ROW (2) consisting of

`TB-SALES (2, 1)  TB-SALES (2, 2)  TB-SALES (2, 3)  TB-SALES (2, 4)  TB-SALES (2, 5)`

group identifier TB-DAY-ROW (3) consisting of

`TB-SALES (3, 1)  TB-SALES (3, 2)  TB-SALES (3, 3)  TB-SALES (3, 4)  TB-SALES (3, 5)`

group identifier TB-DAY-ROW (4) consisting of

`TB-SALES (4, 1)  TB-SALES (4, 2)  TB-SALES (4, 3)  TB-SALES (4, 4)  TB-SALES (4, 5)`

group identifier TB-DAY-ROW (5) consisting of

`TB-SALES (5, 1)  TB-SALES (5, 2)  TB-SALES (5, 3)  TB-SALES (5, 4)  TB-SALES (5, 5)`

group identifier TB-DAY-ROW (6) consisting of

`TB-SALES (6, 1)  TB-SALES (6, 2)  TB-SALES (6, 3)  TB-SALES (6, 4)  TB-SALES (6, 5)`

TB-DAY-ROW (1) consists of the five identifiers that hold the sales totals for each salesperson for day 1. Thus TB-SALES (1, 1) holds the total sales for day 1 and salesperson 1, TB-SALES (1, 2) holds the sales totals for day 1 and salesperson 2, and so on. Of the two subscripts used with TB-SALES, the first gives the day number and the second the salesperson number.

It is conventional to visualize the 30 TB-SALES (n, m) identifiers arranged as rows and columns of a two-dimensional array called TB-SALES, as illustrated In Figure 12.1. Row 1, or TB-DAY-ROW (1), holds the five identifiers for day 1; row 2, or TB-DAY-ROW (2), holds the five identifiers for day 2, and so on.

	1	2	3	4	5	
1	058078	003500	056767	147637	037800	[TB-DAY-ROW (1)]
2	487950	397820	005439	007843	189087	[TB-DAY-ROW (2)]
3	045600	004535	023467	234578	003849	[TB-DAY-ROW (3)]
4	002588	027844	126724	389000	326566	[TB-DAY-ROW (4)]
5	089067	004334	002525	016956	003400	[TB-DAY-ROW (5)]
6	056778	006569	259848	308929	006782	[TB-DAY-ROW (6)]

Figure 12.1 *The two-dimensional array TB-SALES, displayed as a matrix. There are 6 × 5, or 30, identifiers in the array. In the array element TB-SALES (r,c), the first subscript always indicates a row, that is, the highest-level OCCURS identifier. Thus, TB-DAY-ROW (r) indicates the five identifiers of the rth row. The value in the identifier TB-SALES (2,3), for example, is 005439.*

In general, if you declare the array

```
01 TWO-D-ARRAY.
   05 ROW   OCCURS 50 TIMES
      10 POSITION OCCURS 100 TIMES           PIC X(4).
```

then the identifier POSITION (32, 87) is the identifier at column 87 of row 32 of the array of 50 × 100 identifiers.

Two subscripts are used with a two-dimensional array

An identifier of a two-dimensional array must have two subscripts. These are the row subscript and the column subscript. The row subscript must come first, so that TB-SALES (4, 3) is the identifier at row 4 and column 3 of the array. Alternatively, the first subscript results from the higher-level OCCURS, and the second from the lower-level OCCURS.

A subscript can be either a positive integer or an identifier holding a positive integer. Note the syntax for writing subscripts. There must be a space between the comma that follows the first subscript and the second subscript. There cannot be a space after the left parenthesis or before the right parenthesis. Also, there must be a space between the identifier and the left parenthesis. The following are wrong:

```
TB-SALES(2, 4)              error! space missing
TB-SALES (2,4)             error! space missing
TB-SALES ( SUBROW, SUBCOL)  error! space too many
TB-SALES (6, 6)            error! subscript out of bounds
TB-SALES (SUBROW,SUBCOL)   error! space missing
```

These are correct:

```
TB-SALES (2, 4)
TB-SALES (SUBDAY, SUBPERSON)
```

12.2 Accumulating totals is a common two-dimensional array activity

LET US CONTINUE with the example of TB-SALES. Suppose your problem is to print out the contents of TB-SALES at the end of the week, that is, you want the total sales for each salesperson for each day. The report looks as shown in Figure 12.2.

```
---------1---------2---------3---------4---------5---------6---------7
                    WEEKLY SALES FIGURES
                                                   11/25/91
DAY                            SALESPERSON
         1          2          3           4          5

1          580.78      35.00     567.67   1,456.37     378.00
2        4,879.58   3,978.28      54.39      78.43   1,890.87
...                 ...
6          567.78      65.69   2,598.48   3,089.29      67.82

TOTALS:  9,786.44  12,765.46   8,693.89  14,987.60  11,784.43

            TOTAL SALES FOR WEEK:    67,804.26
```

Figure 12.2a *The report resulting from the input file SALES-EVENT in Figure 12.3.*

```
1                  WEEKLY SALES FIGURES
2                                                    11/25/91
3
4  DAY                         SALESPERSON
5           1          2          3          4          5
6
7  9        Z,ZZ9.99   Z,ZZ9.99   Z,ZZ9.99   Z,ZZ9.99   Z,ZZ9.99
8  9        Z,ZZ9.99   Z,ZZ9.99   Z,ZZ9.99   Z,ZZ9.99   Z,ZZ9.99
9  9        Z,ZZ9.99   Z,ZZ9.99   Z,ZZ9.99   Z,ZZ9.99   Z,ZZ9.99
10 9        Z,ZZ9.99   Z,ZZ9.99   Z,ZZ9.99   Z,ZZ9.99   Z,ZZ9.99
11 9        Z,ZZ9.99   Z,ZZ9.99   Z,ZZ9.99   Z,ZZ9.99   Z,ZZ9.99
12 9        Z,ZZ9.99   Z,ZZ9.99   Z,ZZ9.99   Z,ZZ9.99   Z,ZZ9.99
13
14 TOTALS: ZZ,ZZ9.99  ZZ,ZZ9.99  ZZ,ZZ9.99  ZZ,ZZ9.99  ZZ,ZZ9.99
15
16           TOTAL SALES FOR WEEK:  ZZZ,ZZ9.99
17
18
```

Figure 12.2b *Printer spacing chart for report.*

```
01  DETAIL-LINE-OUT.
    05  FILLER                        PIC X.
    05  DL-DAY-OUT                    PIC 9.
    05  FILLER                        PIC X(09).
    05  DL-PERSON-DATA-OUT
              OCCURS 5 TIMES.
        10  DL-PERSON-SALES-OUT       PIC Z,ZZ9.99.
        10  FILLER                    PIC X(03).
    05  FILLER                        PIC X(67).
01  COLUMN-TOT-LINE-OUT.
    05  FILLER                        PIC X.
    05  CTL-TEXT-OUT                  PIC X(09)      VALUE 'TOTALS:'.
    05  CTL-COL-SUM-DATA-OUT
                OCCURS 5 TIMES.
        10  CTL-COL-TOT-OUT           PIC ZZ,ZZ9.99.
        10  FILLER                    PIC X(02).
    05  FILLER                        PIC X(68).
01  GRAND-SUMMARY-LINE-OUT.
    05  FILLER                        PIC X(14)      VALUE SPACES.
    05  FILLER                        PIC X(23)      VALUE
                                              'TOTAL SALES FOR WEEK '.
    05  GRAND-TOT-OUT                 PIC ZZZ,ZZ9.99 .
    05  FILLER                        PIC X(86)      VALUE SPACES.
```

Figure 12.2c Record structures for detail and total lines of the report.

Each time a salesperson makes a sale, a record is created in the input file SALES-EVENT. The record created gives the day number, salesperson number, and the amount of the sale. A record of SALES-EVENT has the format shown in Figure 12.3.

```
---------1
14001500
14003575
12002700
15034500
14000675
15002450
11021875
...
25020000
21001000
25000999
...
32002300
34012400

Columns 1      Day number
        2      Salesperson number
        3-8    Amount rung up
```

Figure 12.3a Some records of input file SALES-EVENT.

```
------ ---1
999999V99
```

Figure 12.3b Input record layout.

```
01  SALES-RECORD-IN.
    05  SR-DAY-IN                 PIC 9.
    05  SR-SALESPERSON-IN         PIC 9.
    05  SR-AMOUNT-IN              PIC 9(04)V99.
```

Figure 12.3c Input area record structure.

The pseudocode for the processing is as follows:

1. Initialize each element of TB-SALES to zero.
2. READ first record
   PERFORM until no records left.
   > For the record of SALES-EVENT read, for day *d* and
   > salesperson *s*, add the amount rung up to TB-SALES (*d*, *s*)
   > READ next record
   END-PERFORM
3. MOVE each row of the array TB-SALES to a one-dimensional array made up of edit identifiers, and print.
4. Get the total for each sales person by scanning each column of TB-SALES.
   MOVE these totals to a one-dimensional array with edit identifiers, and print.
5. Scan through TB-SALES to get the total sales for the week, and print.

Let us look at each of these steps individually, before putting them together as a program. These activities will show you a great deal about how two-dimensional arrays are used.

First you initialize a two-dimensional array (step 1)

In the processing, you will use the array TB-SALES, defined as

```
01  TB-SALES-TOTS.
    05  TB-DAY-ROW OCCURS 6 TIMES.
        10  TB-SALES OCCURS 5 TIMES      PIC 9(04)V99.
```

Since you will be adding quantities to each element of TB-SALES, you need to initialize them all to zero. The simplest way to do this is to define the array with VALUE ZEROS, as follows:

```
01  TB-SALES-TOTS.
    05  TB-DAY-ROW OCCURS 6 TIMES VALUE ZEROS.
        10  TB-SALES OCCURS 5 TIMES      PIC 9(04)V99.
```

You must use ZEROS here, not 0. You are dealing with an alphanumeric group MOVE here for the entire group identifier. The literal zero would place a single zero, left justified, in the group identifier. VALUE ZEROS will place a zero in every space of the group identifier, and thus also in every element of TB-SALES. (Unfortunately, not all compilers allow this use of VALUE with an array. Check if yours does.)

If you cannot initialize the array to zero using VALUE, you can use a PERFORM ... VARYING to do it.

```
PERFORM 300-INITIALIZE-ZERO
    VARYING DAY-SUB FROM 1 BY 1 UNTIL DAY-SUB > 6
    AFTER PERSON-SUB FROM 1 BY 1 UNTIL PERSON-SUB > 5.
300-INITIALIZE-ZERO.
    MOVE ZEROS TO TB-SALES (DAY-SUB, PERSON-SUB).
```

Note that an extended version of PERFORM ... VARYING has been used. This use of PERFORM ... VARYING causes DAY-SUB first to have the value 1, with PERSON-SUB having the values 1, 2, 3, 4, and 5 in sequence; then DAY-SUB gets the value 2, with PERSON-SUB having the values 1, 2, 3, 4, and 5 in sequence, and so on.

Alternatively, it could be said that for each row in sequence, the elements are visited one by one. Or more simply, the subscript specified following AFTER moves fastest, and this normally will be the column subscript, since the elements of an array are usually visited primarily in row order, and secondarily in column order.

The more complete syntax for PERFORM ... VARYING, showing the AFTER clause, is given here:

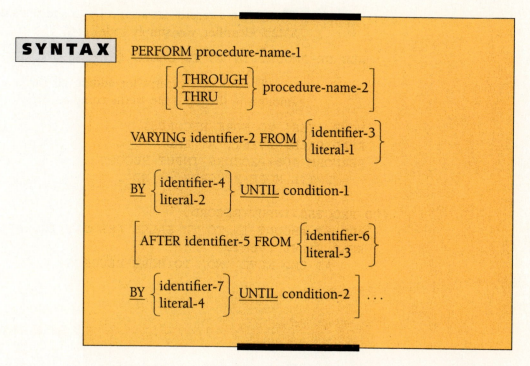

You could also use an in-line version of PERFORM ... VARYING ... AFTER here (with COBOL 85), as follows:

```
PERFORM
    VARYING DAY-SUB FROM 1 BY 1 UNTIL DAY-SUB > 6
    AFTER PERSON-SUB FROM 1 BY 1 UNTIL PERSON-SUB > 5
             MOVE ZEROS TO TB-SALES (DAY-SUB, PERSON-SUB)
END-PERFORM.
```

Then accumulate totals in the two-dimensional array (step 2)

Again you will use the array TB-SALES, defined earlier as

```
01 TB-SALES-TOTS.
   05 TB-DAY-ROW OCCURS 6 TIMES.
      10 TB-SALES OCCURS 5 TIMES              PIC 9(04)V99.
```

In each record of the input file SALES-EVENT in Figure 12.3, the first two fields are the day number and the salesperson number. These values can be used for the subscripts of the TB-SALES identifier to which the amount rung up in the input record will be added. Suppose that the buffer record for the input file is defined as

```
01 SALES-RECORD-IN.
   05 SR-DAY-IN                   PIC 9.
   05 SR-SALESPERSON-IN           PIC 9.
   05 SR-AMOUNT-IN                PIC 9(04)V99.
```

Thus, when a record has been read, to add the amount to the proper TB-SALES identifier, you simply code

```
ADD SR-AMOUNT-IN TO TB-SALES (SR-DAY-IN, SR-SALESPERSON-IN).
```

The relevant excerpt for adding all the amounts rung up, that is, amounts in the input file, to the complete array of TB-SALES identifiers is

```
MOVE 'YES' TO MORE-RECORDS.
READ SALES-EVENT, AT END . . .
PERFORM 400-PROCESS-INPUT-RECORD
    UNTIL MORE-RECORDS = 'NO'.
...
400-PROCESS-INPUT-RECORD.
   ADD SR-AMOUNT-IN TO TB-SALES (SR-DAY-IN, SR-SALESPERSON-IN).
   READ SALES-EVENT,
       AT END MOVE 'NO' TO MORE-RECORDS.
```

Then print contents of the two-dimensional array as a report (step 3)

Here again you use the array TB-SALES, defined earlier as

```
01 TB-SALES-TOTS.
   05 TB-DAY-ROW OCCURS 6 TIMES.
      10 TB-SALES OCCURS 5 TIMES              PIC 9(04)V99.
```

To print the array TB-SALES as the set of six detail lines in Figure 12.2, you need an additional one-dimensional array to hold a row of data from the two-dimensional array. This one-dimensional array will be printed as part of a detail line. The definition required for a detail line will therefore be

```
01 DETAIL-LINE-OUT.
    05 FILLER                               PIC X.
    05 DL-DAY-OUT                           PIC 9.
    05 FILLER                               PIC X(9).
    05 DL-PERSON-DATA-OUT OCCURS 5 TIMES.
       10 DL-PERSON-SALES-OUT               PIC Z,ZZ9.99 .
       10 FILLER                            PIC X(03).
    05 FILLER                               PIC X(67).
```

Notice the use of the second to last FILLER. Although DL-PERSON-DATA-OUT holds a row of data from the two-dimensional array TB-SALES, between each TB-SALES figure there are two spaces, to make the data more readable, as was shown in the report in Figure 12.2.

In the printing process, elements of the first row of TB-SALES will be transferred one by one to the elements of DL-PERSON-SALES-OUT and printed. This will be repeated for the second row of TB-SALES, and so on for all six rows. Thus, you need two loops: an inner loop to transfer the elements of an individual row of TB-SALES to DETAIL-LINE-OUT and an outer loop for the repetition for each detail line:

```
MOVE SPACES TO DETAIL-LINE-OUT.
PERFORM 500-TRANSFER-ROW
    VARYING DAY-SUB FROM 1 BY 1 UNTIL DAY-SUB > 6.
...
500-TRANSFER-ROW.
    PERFORM 600-TRANSFER-ELEMENT
        VARYING PERSON-SUB FROM 1 BY 1
        UNTIL PERSON-SUB > 5.
    MOVE DAY-SUB TO DL-DAY-OUT.
    WRITE REPORT-RECORD-OUT FROM DETAIL-LINE-OUT
        AFTER ADVANCING 1 LINE.
600-TRANSFER-ELEMENT.
    MOVE TB-SALES (DAY-SUB, PERSON-SUB)
            TO DL-PERSON-SALES-OUT (PERSON-SUB).
```

Notice that DAY-SUB, for holding the day number (see Figure 12.2), automatically receives the correct day number from the execution of the PERFORM . . . VARYING statement.

Notice also that spaces have been put in the FILLER fields by the MOVE SPACES statement. Because the array DL-PERSON-DATA-OUT contains FILLER fields, you cannot use VALUE clauses to do this.

Instead of using the preceding two conventional PERFORM statements above to print the array contents, you could make one of the PERFORM statements an in-line PERFORM (in COBOL 85). If the inner PERFORM is in-line, you have

```
      MOVE SPACES TO DETAIL-LINE-OUT.
      PERFORM 500-TRANSFER-ROW
         VARYING DAY-SUB FROM 1 BY 1 UNTIL DAY-SUB > 6.
      ...
   500-TRANSFER-ROW.
      PERFORM VARYING PERSON-SUB FROM 1 BY 1
                                      UNTIL PERSON-SUB > 5
           MOVE TB-SALES (DAY-SUB, PERSON-SUB)
                   TO DL-PERSON-SALES-OUT (PERSON-SUB)
      END-PERFORM.
      MOVE DAY-SUB TO DL-DAY-OUT.
      WRITE REPORT-RECORD-OUT FROM DETAIL-LINE-OUT
              AFTER ADVANCING 1 LINE.
```

Alternatively, the outer PERFORM could be in-line. If an in-line PER-FORM statement is used, it seems to be easier to read when the inner PER-FORM is the in-line statement. It is also possible to make both PERFORM statements in-line.

Then generate column totals from the two-dimensional array (step 4)

Once again, you use the array TB-SALES, defined earlier as

```
01 TB-SALES-TOTS.
   05 TB-DAY-ROW OCCURS 6 TIMES.
      10 TB-SALES OCCURS 5 TIMES                  PIC 9(04)V99.
```

To form the column totals line at the bottom of the report in Figure 12.2, you need a record defined as

```
01 COLUMN-TOT-LINE-OUT.
   05 FILLER                            PIC X.
   05 CTL-TEXT-OUT                      PIC X(9).
   05 CTL-COL-SUM-DATA-OUT OCCURS 5 TIMES.
      10 CTL-COL-TOT-OUT                PIC ZZ,ZZ9.99 .
      10 FILLER                         PIC X(02).
   05 FILLER                            PIC X(68).
```

Begin by scanning the first column of the array TB-SALES, and add each TB-SALES (n, m) value of the column to a summation identifier, COLUMN-SUM, defined as:

```
01 COLUMN-SUM      PIC 9(5)V99.
```

When you have the sum of the values in the first column in COLUMN-SUM, move them to the first CTL-COL-TOT-OUT identifier of the array CTL-COL-SUM-DATA-OUT. Repeat this for the next column of TB-SALES, and so on for all five columns.

Again you need a loop within a loop. For each outer iteration, an entire column of TB-SALES is processed. For each inner iteration, a single element of TB-SALES is added to the COLUMN-SUM identifier. The essential program excerpt is

```
          MOVE SPACES TO COLUMN-TOT-LINE-OUT.
          PERFORM 700-SUM-COLUMN
                    VARYING PERSON-SUB FROM 1 BY 1 UNTIL PERSON-SUB > 5.
          WRITE REPORT-RECORD-OUT FROM COLUMN-TOT-LINE-OUT
                    AFTER ADVANCING 2 LINES.
      700-SUM-COLUMN.
          MOVE ZEROS TO COLUMN-SUM.
          PERFORM 800-PROCESS-COLUMN-ELEMENT
                    VARYING DAY-SUB FROM 1 BY 1 UNTIL DAY-SUB > 6.
          MOVE COLUMN-SUM TO CTL-COL-TOT-OUT (PERSON-SUB).
      800-PROCESS-COLUMN-ELEMENT.
          ADD TB-SALES (DAY-SUB, PERSON-SUB) TO COLUMN-SUM.
```

Notice that in this processing, the array TB-SALES is not processed one row at a time, as is common, but one column at a time, because you want column sums. Thus, in the statement

```
          ADD TB-SALES (DAY-SUB, PERSON-SUB) TO COLUMN-SUM.
```

in this case it is the DAY-SUB subscript that moves fastest.

You could use in-line PERFORMS with either the outer or inner PERFORM, or with both. As mentioned, if an in-line PERFORM is used, an inner in-line statement seems easier to read.

Finally, sum the entire two-dimensional array (step 5)

You are still using the array TB-SALES, defined earlier as

```
01 TB-SALES-TOTS.
   05 TB-DAY-ROW OCCURS 6 TIMES.
      10 TB-SALES OCCURS 5 TIMES          PIC 9(04)V99.
```

To get the sum of all the elements of TB-SALES, one way would be to sum the column totals, generated to print the column totals line in the previous section. Instead, let us use the conventional method of summing an entire array. This method involves visiting each element, primarily in row order and secondarily in column order, and adding the values to a grand total identifier. The relevant program excerpt is

```
      MOVE ZEROS TO GRAND-TOT.
      PERFORM 900-ADD-ELEMENT
          VARYING DAY-SUB FROM 1 BY 1 UNTIL DAY-SUB > 6
          AFTER PERSON-SUB FROM 1 BY 1 UNTIL PERSON-SUB > 5.
      900-ADD-ELEMENT.
          ADD TB-SALES (DAY-SUB, PERSON-SUB) TO GRAND-TOT.
```

The contents of GRAND-TOT can then be printed. You can conveniently use an in-line version here instead.

```
        MOVE ZEROS TO GRAND-TOT.
        PERFORM VARYING DAY-SUB FROM 1 BY 1
                                          UNTIL DAY-SUB > 6
              AFTER PERSON-SUB FROM 1 BY 1
                                        UNTIL PERSON-SUB > 5
           ADD TB-SALES (DAY-SUB, PERSON-SUB) TO GRAND-TOT
        END-PERFORM.
```

A complete program with a two-dimensional array

The program in Figure 12.4 will carry out the processing of the input file SALES-EVENT (from Figure 12.3) and generate the report in Figure 12.2. It does so using the techniques and arrays described in previous sections. Paragraphs used in the program are the same as those used in these earlier explanatory sections. The only part of the program not explained earlier is the generation of the headers; this should give you no difficulty. There are no in-line PERFORMS in this program. You may insert them as an exercise, along the lines already explained, if desired.

```
IDENTIFICATION DIVISION.
PROGRAM-ID. WR1.
ENVIRONMENT DIVISION.
INPUT-OUTPUT SECTION.
FILE-CONTROL.    SELECT SALES-EVENT  ASSIGN TO UT-S-DISK90.
                 SELECT REPORT-FILE ASSIGN TO UR-S-SYSPRINT.

DATA DIVISION.
FILE SECTION.
FD   SALES-EVENT              LABEL RECORDS ARE STANDARD.
01 SALES-RECORD-IN.
     05 SR-DAY-IN             PIC 9.
     05 SR-SALESPERSON-IN     PIC 9.
     05 SR-AMOUNT-IN          PIC 9(04)V99.
FD   REPORT-FILE               LABEL RECORDS ARE OMITTED.
01   REPORT-RECORD-OUT        PIC X(133).
WORKING-STORAGE SECTION.
01 WORK-AREAS.
     05 MORE-RECORDS          PIC X(03)      VALUE 'YES'.
     05 DAY-SUB               PIC 9.
     05 PERSON-SUB            PIC 9.
     05 GRAND-TOT             PIC 9(06)V99   VALUE ZEROS.
     05 COLUMN-SUM            PIC 9(05)V99.
```

```
01 DATE-LINE.
    05  FILLER                         PIC X(58)       VALUE SPACES.
    05  RUN-DATE                       PIC X(08).
    05  FILLER                         PIC X(67)       VALUE SPACES.
01 REPORT-HEADER.
    05  FILLER                         PIC X(22)       VALUE SPACES.
    05  FILLER                         PIC X(20)       VALUE
                                                       'WEEKLY SALES FIGURES'.
    05  FILLER                         PIC X(91)       VALUE SPACES.
01 HEADER-1.
    05  FILLER                         PIC X           VALUE SPACE.
    05  FILLER                         PIC X(29)       VALUE 'DAY'.
    05  FILLER                         PIC X(11)       VALUE 'SALESPERSON'.
    05  FILLER                         PIC X(92)       VALUE SPACES.
01 HEADER-2.
    05  FILLER                         PIC X(11)       VALUE SPACES.
    05  FILLER                         PIC X(45)       VALUE
                           '1         2         3         4         5'.
    05  FILLER                         PIC X(77)       VALUE SPACES.
01 DETAIL-LINE-OUT.
    05 FILLER                          PIC X.
    05 DL-DAY-OUT                      PIC 9.
    05 FILLER                          PIC X(09).
    05 DL-PERSON-DATA-OUT
            OCCURS 5 TIMES.
        10 DL-PERSON-SALES-OUT         PIC Z,ZZ9.99.
        10 FILLER                      PIC X(03).
    05 FILLER                          PIC X(67).
01 COLUMN-TOT-LINE-OUT.
    05 FILLER                          PIC X.
    05 CTL-TEXT-OUT                    PIC X(09)       VALUE 'TOTALS:'.
    05 CTL-COL-SUM-DATA-OUT
                OCCURS 5 TIMES.
        10 CTL-COL-TOT-OUT             PIC ZZ,ZZ9.99.
        10 FILLER                      PIC X(02).
    05 FILLER                          PIC X(68).
01 GRAND-SUMMARY-LINE-OUT.
    05  FILLER                         PIC X(14)       VALUE SPACES.
    05  FILLER                         PIC X(23)       VALUE
                                                       'TOTAL SALES FOR WEEK'.
    05  GRAND-TOT-OUT                  PIC ZZZ,ZZ9.99.
    05  FILLER                         PIC X(86)       VALUE SPACES.
01 TB-SALES-TOTS.
    05 TB-DAY-ROW OCCURS 6 TIMES.
        10 TB-SALES
            OCCURS 5 TIMES             PIC 9(04)V99.
```

```
PROCEDURE DIVISION.
 100-MAIN-MODULE.
 ***************************************************************
 *   DIRECTS PROGRAM LOGIC.                                    *
 ***************************************************************
        PERFORM 200-INITIALIZATION.
        PERFORM 500-PROCESS-INPUT-RECORD UNTIL MORE-RECORDS = 'NO'.
        PERFORM 600-TRANSFER-ROW
               VARYING DAY-SUB FROM 1 BY 1 UNTIL DAY-SUB > 6.
        PERFORM 800-SUM-COLUMN
               VARYING PERSON-SUB FROM 1 BY 1 UNTIL PERSON-SUB > 5.
        WRITE REPORT-RECORD-OUT FROM COLUMN-TOT-LINE-OUT
                       AFTER ADVANCING 2 LINES.
        PERFORM 1000-ADD-ELEMENT
            VARYING DAY-SUB FROM 1 BY 1 UNTIL DAY-SUB > 6
            AFTER PERSON-SUB FROM 1 BY 1 UNTIL PERSON-SUB > 5.
        MOVE GRAND-TOT TO GRAND-TOT-OUT.
        WRITE REPORT-RECORD-OUT FROM GRAND-SUMMARY-LINE-OUT
               AFTER ADVANCING 2 LINES.
        PERFORM 1100-TERMINATION.
 200-INITIALIZATION.
 ***************************************************************
 *   PERFORMED FROM 100-MAIN-MODULE. OPENS FILES, PRINTS PAGE HEADERS, *
 *   ZEROS TB-SALES ARRAY, BLANKS DETAIL AND COLUMN SUM IDENTIFIERS,   *
 *   AND READS FIRST RECORD.                                           *
 ***************************************************************
        OPEN INPUT SALES-EVENT,
            OUTPUT REPORT-FILE.
        MOVE CURRENT-DATE TO RUN-DATE.
        PERFORM 300-PAGE-HEADERS.
        PERFORM 400-INITIALIZE-ZERO
               VARYING DAY-SUB FROM 1 BY 1 UNTIL DAY-SUB > 6
               AFTER PERSON-SUB FROM 1 BY 1 UNTIL PERSON-SUB > 5.
        MOVE SPACES TO DETAIL-LINE-OUT.
        MOVE SPACES TO COLUMN-TOT-LINE-OUT.
        READ SALES-EVENT,
            AT END MOVE 'NO' TO MORE-RECORDS.
 300-PAGE-HEADERS.
 ***************************************************************
 *   PERFORMED FROM 200-INITIALIZATION. PRINTS PAGE HEADERS.   *
 ***************************************************************
        WRITE REPORT-RECORD-OUT FROM REPORT-HEADER
               AFTER ADVANCING 1 LINE.
        WRITE REPORT-RECORD-OUT FROM DATE-LINE
               AFTER ADVANCING 1 LINE.
        WRITE REPORT-RECORD-OUT FROM HEADER-1
               AFTER ADVANCING 2 LINES.
        WRITE REPORT-RECORD-OUT FROM HEADER-2
               AFTER ADVANCING 1 LINE.
        MOVE SPACES TO REPORT-RECORD-OUT.
        WRITE REPORT-RECORD-OUT
               AFTER ADVANCING 1 LINE.
```

```
400-INITIALIZE-ZERO.
**********************************************************************
*   PERFORMED FROM 200-INITIALIZATION. ZEROS A SINGLE ELEMENT OF      *
*   ARRAY TB-SALES.                                                   *
**********************************************************************
        MOVE ZEROS TO TB-SALES (DAY-SUB, PERSON-SUB).
500-PROCESS-INPUT-RECORD.
**********************************************************************
*   PERFORMED FROM 100-MAIN-MODULE. ADDS SALES IN CURRENT RECORD TO   *
*   ELEMENT OF ARRAY TB-SALES FOR CORRECT DAY AND SALESPERSON. READS  *
*   NEXT RECORD.                                                      *
**********************************************************************
        ADD SR-AMOUNT-IN TO TB-SALES (SR-DAY-IN, SR-SALESPERSON-IN).
        READ SALES-EVENT,
                AT END MOVE 'NO' TO MORE-RECORDS.
600-TRANSFER-ROW.
**********************************************************************
*   PERFORMED FROM 100-MAIN-MODULE. TRANSFERS ROW OF TB-SALES TO      *
*   DETAIL-LINE-OUT AND PRINTS.                                       *
**********************************************************************
        PERFORM 700-TRANSFER-ELEMENT
                VARYING PERSON-SUB FROM 1 BY 1 UNTIL PERSON-SUB > 5.
        MOVE DAY-SUB TO DL-DAY-OUT.
        WRITE REPORT-RECORD-OUT FROM DETAIL-LINE-OUT
                AFTER ADVANCING 1 LINE.
700-TRANSFER-ELEMENT.
**********************************************************************
*   PERFORMED FROM 600-TRANSFER-ROW. MOVES ELEMENT IN A ROW TB-SALES TO *
*   AN ELEMENT IN  DETAIL-LINE-OUT.                                   *
**********************************************************************
        MOVE TB-SALES (DAY-SUB, PERSON-SUB)
                        TO DL-PERSON-SALES-OUT (PERSON-SUB).
800-SUM-COLUMN.
**********************************************************************
*   PERFORMED FROM 100-MAIN-MODULE. SUMS A COLUMN OF ARRAY TB-SALES AND *
*   TRANSFERS RESULT TO COLUMN TOTAL LINE.                            *
**********************************************************************
        MOVE ZEROS TO COLUMN-SUM.
        PERFORM 900-PROCESS-COLUMN-ELEMENT
                VARYING DAY-SUB FROM 1 BY 1 UNTIL DAY-SUB > 6.
        MOVE COLUMN-SUM TO CTL-COL-TOT-OUT (PERSON-SUB).
900-PROCESS-COLUMN-ELEMENT.
**********************************************************************
*   PERFORMED FROM 800-SUM-COLUMN. ADDS ELEMENT OF COLUMN OF ARRAY    *
*   TB-SALES TO SUMMATION IDENTIFIER COLUMN-SUM.                      *
**********************************************************************
        ADD TB-SALES (DAY-SUB, PERSON-SUB) TO COLUMN-SUM.
```

```
 1000-ADD-ELEMENT.
 ****************************************************************
 *   PERFORMED FROM 100-MAIN-MODULE. ADDS ELEMENT OF TB-SALES TO   *
 *   SUMMATION IDENTIFIER GRAND-TOT.                               *
 ****************************************************************
         ADD TB-SALES (DAY-SUB, PERSON-SUB) TO GRAND-TOT.
 1100-TERMINATION.
 ****************************************************************
 *   PERFORMED FROM 100-MAIN-MODULE. CLOSES FILES, STOPS PROGRAM.  *
 ****************************************************************
         CLOSE SALES-EVENT
                REPORT-FILE.
         STOP RUN.
```

Figure 12.4 *Program to generate report in Figure 12.2 from input file Figure 12.3.*

12.3
Two-level arrays sometimes have to be searched

OCCASIONALLY, IT IS necessary to search the elements of a two-level array, looking for a particular target value. As an example, suppose that each element of a two-level array consists of an employee identification number and the employee's hourly rate. Suppose also that each record of an input file contains the employee's identification number and the hours worked in the current week, with this record structure:

```
01 EMPLOYEE-RECORD-IN.
   05 EMPLOYEE-ID-IN          PIC X(05).
   05 HOURS-WORKED-IN         PIC 9(02).
```

Now, if you want to process the input file to print out (among other things) the gross pay earned by the employee in the week, for each input record the hourly rate has to be looked up in the array. Hence, you need a search of the array.

Suppose the array is two-level, because an employee can work at any of 20 plants, where each plant has at most 100 employees. Thus, the data about each employee (employee identification number and hourly rate) can be held in the array TB-EMPLOYEE, defined as follows:

```
01 TB-EMPLOYEE-DATA.
   05  TB-PLANT                          OCCURS   20 TIMES.
       10 TB-EMPLOYEE                     OCCURS 100 TIMES.
          15 TB-EMPLOYEE-ID   PIC X(05).
          15 TB-HOURLY-RATE   PIC 9(02)V99.
```

Each TB-PLANT group identifier (or row of the array) has 100 elements. Each of these elements will consist of two identifiers, which will either contain employee data or spaces and zeros. A plant can have less than 100 employees. Where there are unused elements, in initializing the array, it is to be assumed that these unneeded elements were originally assigned spaces (in the case of the TB-EMPLOYEE-ID identifier), and zero (in the case of the TB-HOURLY-RATE identifier). Some data for part of the array are shown in Figure 12.5.

```
                    EMPLOYEE
PLANT|      (1)              (2)              (3)              (100)
     |   ID    RATE       ID    RATE       ID    RATE ...    ID    RATE
-----------------------------------------------------------------------------
(01) |  EA00   1642      EA03   1786      EA04   1275 ...   ET46   1047
     |
(02) |  EA01   1586      EA03   1610      EB05   0895 ...   bbbb   0000
     |
(03) |  EA13   1489      EA12   1234      EC12   1015 ...   EX34   1589
 ... |  ...    ...       ...    ...       ...    ...        ...    ...
     |
(20) |  EA09   1289      EB07   1485      EB01   0856 ...   bbbb   0000
```

Figure 12.5 *Contents of TB-EMPLOYEE*

Let us now examine the options for searching this array to find the hourly rate of an employee whose employee identification occurs in the latest input record. There are two basic techniques available:

- Use of PERFORM . . . VARYING
- Use of both PERFORM . . . VARYING and SEARCH

These will be examined in turn.

You can search a two-level array using PERFORM . . . VARYING

You can search the array in either row first, column second order, or the converse. Other things being equal, it is normal to search in row first, column second order. Assume that the input records are being read from the file EMPLOYEE-FILE. The following code shows how each record would be read and the information about hourly rate obtained by searching the array:

```
MOVE 'YES' TO MORE-RECORDS.
READ EMPLOYEE-FILE AT END . . .
PERFORM 300-PROCESS-INPUT-RECORD
        UNTIL MORE-RECORDS = 'NO'.
    . . .
```

```
300-PROCESS-INPUT-RECORD.
     MOVE 'NO' TO MATCH-FOUND.
     PERFORM 400-SCAN-ARRAY
        VARYING PLANT-SUB FROM 1 BY 1 UNTIL PLANT-SUB > 20
                                       OR MATCH-FOUND = 'YES'
           AFTER EMPLOYEE-SUB FROM 1 BY 1 UNTIL EMPLOYEE-SUB > 100
                      OR MATCH-FOUND = 'YES'.
     IF MATCH-FOUND = 'NO'
           PERFORM 600-NO-MATCH-ROUTINE.
     PERFORM 500-PRINT-DETAIL-LINE-OUT.
     READ EMPLOYEE-FILE
        AT END MOVE 'NO' TO MORE-RECORDS.
400-SCAN-ARRAY.
     IF EMPLOYEE-ID-IN = TB-EMPLOYEE-ID (PLANT-SUB, EMPLOYEE-SUB)
           MOVE 'YES' TO MATCH-FOUND
           COMPUTE GROSS-PAY =
              TB-HOURLY-RATE (PLANT-SUB, EMPLOYEE-SUB)
                                    * HOURS-WORKED-IN

     END-IF.
500-PRINT-DETAIL-LINE-OUT.
        generate and print detail line (detail line may contain a not-found message)
```

During the search, note that the EMPLOYEE-SUB subscript moves faster than the PLANT-SUB subscript.

It is a common mistake to use the MATCH-FOUND = 'YES' condition only in the AFTER clause, for example:

```
PERFORM 400-SCAN-ARRAY
   VARYING PLANT-SUB FROM 1 BY 1 UNTIL PLANT-SUB > 20
   AFTER EMPLOYEE-SUB FROM 1 BY 1 UNTIL EMPLOYEE-SUB > 100
           OR MATCH-FOUND = 'YES'.        error!
```

The program will go wrong if you do this. Suppose a match is found at row 10, column 40. The inner loop will stop, but the outer loop will not, and so the program will go wrong.

You can search a two-level array using both PERFORM . . . VARYING and SEARCH

Remember that with SEARCH you have to use an index identifier instead of a subscript identifier. With a SEARCH command, you can only have a single index incremented as the search proceeds. Therefore, SEARCH is used to search the elements of a row of a two-level array, and PERFORM . . . VARYING is used to scan through the rows.

Because you need to use an index with the SEARCH verb, it is convenient to use an index with PERFORM . . . VARYING as well. Thus, the array TB-EMPLOYEE is best defined as

```
01  TB-EMPLOYEE-DATA.
    05   TB-PLANT               OCCURS  20 TIMES INDEXED BY PLANT-EX.
         10  TB-EMPLOYEE        OCCURS 100 TIMES INDEXED BY EMPLOYEE-EX.
             15  TB-EMPLOYEE-ID    PIC X(05).
             15  TB-HOURLY-RATE    PIC 9(02)V99.
```

Again, assume that an input record of EMPLOYEE-FILE has the structure

```
01  EMPLOYEE-RECORD-IN.
    05  EMPLOYEE-ID-IN     PIC X(05).
    05  HOURS-WORKED-IN    PIC 9(02)V99.
```

As each record of EMPLOYEE-FILE is read, the employee identification number in the input record is used to find the appropriate hourly rate in the array TB-EMPLOYEE. The code is as follows:

```
MOVE 'YES' TO MORE-RECORDS.
READ EMPLOYEE-FILE
     AT END STOP RUN.
PERFORM 300-PROCESS-INPUT-RECORD
     UNTIL MORE-RECORDS = 'NO'.
...
300-PROCESS-INPUT-RECORD.
    MOVE 'NO' TO MATCH-FOUND.
    PERFORM 400-SCAN-ARRAY
       VARYING PLANT-EX FROM 1 BY 1 UNTIL PLANT-EX > 20
                                    OR MATCH-FOUND = 'YES'.
    IF MATCH-FOUND = 'NO' PERFORM 600-NO-MATCH.
    PERFORM 500-PRINT-DETAIL-LINE-OUT.
    READ EMPLOYEE-FILE,
         AT END MOVE 'NO' TO MORE-RECORDS.
400-SCAN-ARRAY.
    SET EMPLOYEE-EX TO 1.
    SEARCH TB-EMPLOYEE            use lowest level OCCURS identifier
    WHEN EMPLOYEE-ID-IN = TB-EMPLOYEE-ID (PLANT-EX, EMPLOYEE-EX)
        MOVE 'YES' TO MATCH-FOUND
        COMPUTE GROSS-PAY =
            TB-HOURLY-RATE (PLANT-EX, EMPLOYEE-EX) * HOURS-WORKED-IN
    END-SEARCH.
500-PRINT-DETAIL-LINE-OUT.
        generate and print detail line (detail line may contain not-found message)
```

Notice the use of the identifier MATCH-FOUND. When a match is found, the value in this identifier switches to YES. This stops both the scanning of the current row by the SEARCH verb and the scanning from one row to the next by the PERFORM . . . VARYING verb.

Sometimes you retrieve just the position of a target element

In the previous example, the array was searched until a matching employee identification number was found, and then the associated hourly rate was used to compute that employee's gross pay. In some applications, however, it is the position of the target within the array that is wanted. For example, suppose you needed to find the position of the employee with identification number EK15. That would mean that you would have to search the entire array looking for this value. As soon as you have found it, you would want the search to stop. You could code as follows:

```
        MOVE 'NO' TO MATCH-FOUND.
        PERFORM 400-SCAN-ARRAY
            VARYING PLANT-EX FROM 1 BY 1 UNTIL PLANT-EX > 20
                                       OR MATCH-FOUND = 'YES'.
        IF MATCH-FOUND = 'NO'
            PERFORM 500-NO-MATCH.
        ...
400-SCAN-ARRAY.
        SET EMPLOYEE-EX TO 1.
        SEARCH TB-EMPLOYEE          use lowest level OCCURS identifier
        WHEN 'EK15' = TB-EMPLOYEE-ID (PLANT-EX, EMPLOYEE-EX)
            MOVE 'YES' TO MATCH-FOUND.
            SET ROW-OUT TO PLANT-EX
            SET COL-OUT TO EMPLOYEE-EX
            DISPLAY 'FOUND AT ROW: ', ROW-OUT, 'COLUMN: ', COL-OUT.
500-NO-MATCH.
        DISPLAY 'EK15', ' NOT FOUND'.
```

Note that you cannot print out the indexes PLANT-EX and EMPLOYEE-EX for the position where the target is found. You use SET to place these values in ordinary numeric identifiers, which are then printed.

12.4
Three-level arrays are needed too

SOMETIMES a three-level array is convenient. For example, to extend the array of the previous section, for each of five states a company could have up to 10 plants, each with up to 100 employees. A three-level array could be used.

```
01 TB-EMPLOYEE-DATA-3.
   05  TB-STATE  OCCURS 5 TIMES.
       10  TB-PLANT    OCCURS  10 TIMES.
           15 TB-EMPLOYEE  OCCURS 100 TIMES.
               20 TB-EMPLOYEE-ID     PIC X(04).
               20 TB-HOURLY-RATE     PIC 9(02)V99.
```

The elements of the array thus range from TB-EMPLOYEE (1, 1, 1) to TB-EMPLOYEE (5, 10, 100), giving 5 × 10 × 100 or 5000 elements in all.

Such an array is manipulated similarly to a two-level array, except that typically three levels of iteration are required. You can either use PERFORM ... VARYING with two AFTER clauses or PERFORM ... VARYING with one AFTER clause and a nested SEARCH. For example, to find the total number of employees in the array (where some elements are filled with spaces instead of employee data), you could code

```
MOVE ZEROS TO COUNT-EMPLOYEES.
PERFORM 300-COUNT-EMPLOYEE
        VARYING STATE-SUB FROM 1 BY 1 UNTIL STATE-SUB > 5
        AFTER PLANT-SUB FROM 1 BY 1 UNTIL PLANT-SUB > 10
        AFTER EMPLOYEE-SUB FROM 1 BY 1 UNTIL EMPLOYEE-SUB > 100.
DISPLAY 'NUMBER OF EMPLOYEES IS: ', COUNT-EMPLOYEES.
...
300-COUNT-EMPLOYEE.
    IF TB-EMPLOYEE-ID (STATE-SUB, PLANT-SUB, EMPLOYEE-SUB)
                                        NOT EQUAL TO SPACES
            ADD 1 TO COUNT-EMPLOYEES.
```

As a final example, to find the position in the array of the data for employee EK15, you could use PERFORM . . . VARYING . . . AFTER plus SEARCH, as follows:

```
PERFORM 400-SCAN-ARRAY
    VARYING STATE-EX FROM 1 BY 1 UNTIL STATE-EX > 5
                                OR MATCH-FOUND = 'YES'
        AFTER PLANT-EX FROM 1 BY 1 UNTIL PLANT-EX > 10
                                OR MATCH-FOUND = 'YES'.
IF MATCH-FOUND = 'NO' PERFORM 500-NO-MATCH.
...
400-SCAN-ARRAY.
    SET EMPLOYEE-EX TO 1.
    SEARCH EMPLOYEE            use lowest level OCCURS identifier
    WHEN 'EK15' =
            TB-EMPLOYEE-ID (STATE-EX, PLANT-EX, EMPLOYEE-EX)
        SET STATE-OUT TO STATE-EX
        SET ROW-OUT TO PLANT-EX
        SET COL-OUT TO EMPLOYEE-EX
        DISPLAY 'FOUND AT POSITION: ',
                    STATE-OUT, ROW-OUT, COL-OUT.
500-NO-MATCH.
    DISPLAY 'EK15', ' NOT FOUND'.
```

Note that the array would have to be defined with the index identifiers STATE-EX, PLANT-EX, and EMPLOYEE-EX for this excerpt to work, as follows:

```
01 TB-EMPLOYEE-DATA.
   05  TB-STATE OCCURS 5 TIMES INDEXED BY STATE-EX.
   05  TB-PLANT   OCCURS  10 TIMES INDEXED BY PLANT-EX.
       10 TB-EMPLOYEE OCCURS 100 TIMES INDEXED BY EMPLOYEE-EX.
          15 TB-EMPLOYEE-ID     PIC X(04).
          15 TB-HOURLY-RATE     PIC 9(02)V99.
```

Remember that you must use an index identifier with SEARCH. You can use either an index or subscript identifier with PERFORM . . . VARYING. However, if you use both PERFORM . . . VARYING and SEARCH to manipulate a higher-level array, as in the preceding case, you should use index identifiers with PERFORM, and, of course, an index identifier with the SEARCH verb.

Summary

1. A multiple-level array is a collection of identifiers, each identified by a fixed number of subscripts. A two-level array has identifiers identified by two subscripts, and can be visualized as a matrix or two-dimensional table. The first subscript identifies the row and the second the column. Two levels of OCCURS clauses are used to define a two-level array, the first OCCURS defining a number of rows and the second a number of elements with a row.

2. Two-level arrays are commonly processed in row first, column second order. A PERFORM ... VARYING ... AFTER statement can be used to process all the elements of a two-level array. In searching a two-level array, PERFORM ... VARYING ... AFTER can be used with either subscripts or indexes. An outer PERFORM ... VARYING for the rows with a nested SEARCH (or SEARCH ALL) for the elements within a row can also be used.

Concept Review Questions

1. What is a two-dimensional array?
2. Is a two-dimensional array actually physically stored as a two-dimensional structure in memory, with physically identifiable rows and columns? Explain.
3. What are two-dimensional arrays used for? Give some examples.
4. Give two ways of initializing each element in a two-dimensional array to zero.
5. Explain how the contents of a two-dimensional array are printed, with each row printed as one line.
6. Explain how the contents of a two-dimensional array are printed, with each column printed as one line.
7. Explain how (a) row totals and (b) column totals of a two-dimensional array are obtained.
8. Give two ways of summing the entire contents of a numeric two-dimensional array.
9. List and explain the options for searching a two-dimensional array.
10. Give an example of a three-dimensional array.

COBOL Language Questions

Questions 1 through 4 refer to the following array.

```
01 A.
   05  B  OCCURS 9 TIMES.
       10 C PIC 9(04) OCCURS 5 TIMES.
```

1. How many elements does the array have?

2. Pick out the invalid references here:

```
   C (CSUB), C (BSUB, CSUB), B (BSUB, CSUB),
B (BSUB), B (CSUB), C (0, 2), B (0)
```

3. How many columns are there?

4. Write a routine to initialize all elements to zero,
   a. using a conventional PERFORM ... VARYING statement.
   b. using an in-line PERFORM ... VARYING statement.

5. Suppose you have a file MEASUREMENT, with nine records, in which a record fits the following input area identifier:

```
01 MEAS-RECORD-IN.
   05   MR-VEHICLE-ID      PIC 9.
   05   MR-MEAS-COST       PIC 9(04)  OCCURS 5 TIMES.
```

Each record describes the costs of five types of measurements (measurement types 1, 2, 3, 4, and 5, in that order) on one of nine vehicles. The vehicles are vehicle 1, 2, 3, and so on, and are ordered in ascending MR-VEHICLE-ID order in the file.
   a. Write a routine to place the data in an array.
   b. Write a routine to sum the costs for each measurement type for all vehicles and print as a detail line.
   c. Write a routine to sum the measurement costs for each vehicle and print as a detail line.
   d. Write a routine to print each row of the array as a detail line.
   e. Write a routine to search the array and output the vehicle number and measurement type number for the first measurement that costs less than $100. Search in row first, column second order, and use the SEARCH verb.
   f. Write a routine to search the array and output the vehicle number and measurement type number for each measurement that cost less than $100. Search in column first, row second order, and use only PERFORM ... VARYING.

Programming Assignments

1. **A program to load and print a two-dimensional table**
   Each of five parts is supplied all of four suppliers at a price that depends on the supplier and the part. The price data (prices all less than $100) for a part are given as a record of the input file

```
---------1---------2
47 86 23 45 16 98 17 23
46 82 22 98 15 77 18 42
46 44 21 27 17 83 18 56
47 68 22 56 17 42 19 27
45 25 23 39 18 21 17 99
```

The first record has the data for part 1, the next for part 2, and so on. The first price in a record is for supplier 1, the next for supplier 2, and so on.

The data are used to produce the following report:

```
---------1---------2---------3---------4---------5---------6---------7
              PRICES FOR INDUSTRIAL PARTS
PART                   SUPPLIER                          SUPPLIER
         1              2             3            4      AVERAGE

1       $47.86         $23.45        $16.98       $17.23  $26.38
2       $46.82         $22.98        $15.77       $18.42  ...
3       $46.44         $21.27        $17.83       $18.56
4       $47.68         $22.56        $17.42       $19.27
5       $45.25         $23.39        $18.21       $17.99
PART
AVERAGE: $46.81        ...
```

a. Define an array to hold the input data.
b. Draw spacing charts for input and output data.
c. Draw the flowchart and hierarchy diagram for the processing.
d. Write and run the program.

2. **A program to accumulate data on cattle in a two-dimensional array and print it, together with summary computations**

A cattle rancher weighs his 20 cattle every month for the first four months of the year. Each animal is identified by a two-digit number. For each animal, a measurement record is placed in the input file when the animal is weighed. Because animals are weighed randomly, the records are not placed in the input file in any order, but all measurements for month 1 come before those for month 2, and so on.

Some records in the input file are

```
---------1
1414671
2013428
0209864
0913457
0312346
...
0714823
0115032
...
0115426
...
0115794
...
```

Columns 01–02	Animal identification number
03–07	Weight in pounds, to one decimal place

The input file is used to output the following report:

```
---------1---------2---------3---------4---------5---------6---------7
                MONTHLY WEIGHT OF CATTLE REPORT (lb)
```

ANIMAL		MONTH			WEIGHT
	JAN	FEB	MAR	APR	GAIN
01	1,482.1	1,503.2	1,542.6	1,579.4	97.4
02	986.4	...	...	...	...
03	1,234.6	...	...	...	...
...	...	...	...	...	...
20	1,342.8	...	...	...	...
TOTAL WT. OF HERD	26,789.5	...	...	...	...
AVERAGE PER ANIMAL	1,234.7	...	...	...	...

a. Define an array to hold the input data.
b. Draw spacing charts for input and output data.
c. Draw the flowchart and hierarchy diagram for the processing.
d. Write and run the program.

3. **A program for searching a two-dimensional array**
The input file is:

```
---------1---------2---------3
P015P123P497P035P472P521
P124P952P284P755P862P321
P371P682P748P317P918P567
P345P987P459P840P211P447
P921P004P670P637P452P975
```

Each input record gives six part identification numbers (three characters) followed by a quantity (one digit). The first record gives inventory at warehouse 1, the second for warehouse 2, and so on. The first part/quantity group in a record is for bin 1, the second for bin 2, and so on.

The input data can be better understood when displayed as the output data as follows:

```
---------1---------2---------3---------4---------5---------6---------7
                    INVENTORIED PART LOCATION GUIDE


                              BIN NUMBER

          1            2            3            4            5            6

WARE-    PART QTY    PART QTY    PART QTY    PART QTY    PART QTY    PART QTY
HOUSE


1        P01 5       P12 3       P49 7       P03 5       P47 2       P52 1
2        P12 4       P95 2       P28 4       P75 5       P86 2       P32 1
3        P37 1       P68 2       P74 8       P31 7       P91 8       P56 7
4        P34 5       P98 7       P45 9       P84 0       P21 1       P44 7
5        P92 1       P00 4       P67 0       P63 7       P45 2       P97 5
```

In addition, in response to a query (input from the terminal) for information about a given part (for example, part P31), the output is

```
---------1---------2---------3
PART NUMBER  P31
QUANTITY ON HAND: 7
LOCATION:  BIN 4, WAREHOUSE 3
```

or, alternatively

```
---------1---------2---------3
PART NUMBER  P77
NOT FOUND IN INVENTORY
```

Just prior to entry of the query part number at the terminal, the program should display

```
PLEASE ENTER PART NUMBER
```

a. Define an array to hold the input data.
b. Draw spacing charts for input and output data.
c. Draw the flowchart and hierarchy diagram for the processing.
d. Search the array in row first, column second order.
e. Write and run the program to output the report and to respond to a query as shown. Use index identifiers with the search.

COBOL
FOR FILE AND
DATA BASE
PROCESSING

13

SEQUENTIAL FILES

OBJECTIVES

- To understand sequential and master files.
- To learn how to update a sequential master file.

OUTLINE

13.1 A sequential master file allows only sequential access

Sequential files were originally tape files

You can have both sequential and direct-access disk files

Speed of access depends on the storage device

Reading and writing records require input/output routines

Summary of discussion of sequential and direct-access files

You normally use blocks and buffers of records with sequential files

You normally use input and output buffers with sequential files

A buffer record is always defined in a COBOL program

    A buffer record is mobile within a buffer

Double buffers are standard

A master file is a business concept

A master file must be created with validated records

Control listing is generated with master file creation

    Master file creation example

13.2 The classical method of updating a sequential master file is standard practice

A control listing is common with master file updating

Classical change updating involves a basic principle

    Program for ideal classical change updating

        Use of separate paragraphs for updating options

    Duplicate transaction keys may occur with ideal change updating

        Rejection of duplicates may be necessary in ideal change updating

    Unmatched transaction records may occur with classical change updating

    Classical insertion updating example

T HROUGHOUT THIS BOOK so far, we have been dealing with processing where records from an input file on disk or tape are read in and used to output lines of a report. These simple input files are sequential files. They will consist of records keyed in at a terminal and stored on disk or tape using an editor, or of records keyed in at a key-to-disk or key-to-tape station, which amounts to the same thing. Such files can also be created with a program that writes the records on disk or tape.

Instead of creating a report with an input file, you can use it to make a more permanent and reliable version, on disk or tape, called a *master file*. A master file is typically used by a business to hold records about entities both of current importance and of importance over the long run. Reports and other important documents, such as invoices, can then be generated using master files as input files.

13.1
A sequential master file allows only sequential access

A MASTER FILE does not have to be a sequential file; it can also be a direct-access file. However, this chapter concerns master files that are sequential files. So we will first look at the concept of a sequential file and then at the idea of a master file.

Sequential files were originally tape files

In the early days of computing, as far back as the early 1950s, all computer files were sequential files, since the only storage medium in those days was the magnetic tape. Computer disks had not been invented.

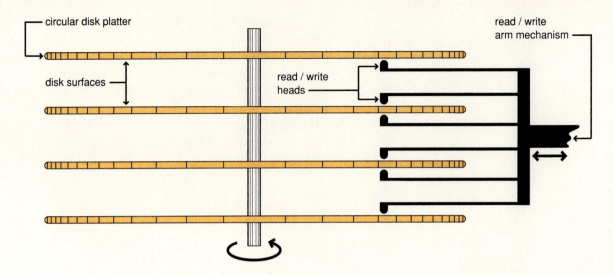

circular disk platter

read / write arm mechanism

disk surfaces

read / write heads

Figure 13.1 *Disk storage mechanism. The "comb" of read/write arms moves in and out. When turned on, the disk rotates continuously.*

A magnetic tape is a sequential medium – for records to be read on a tape, the tape has to unwind from a reel. Thus, records can be read only in the sequence in which they are recorded on the tape, and a file of records on tape has to be a sequential file. There is no other possibility with most tape devices. (It is possible with some tapes for microcomputers, but that is not relevant here.) Records must be read and written in a well-defined sequence. This is the essence of a sequential file.

In ancient times books were sequential as well, because they were written on scrolls. This meant that the lines could appear only as the scroll unwound. You could not just "open" it at page 120. First you had to scroll through all the lines before that page. So it is with sequential files. To read record number 10,000, records 1 through 9,999 must be read first.

You can have both sequential and direct-access disk files

It is important to understand that whereas with tapes you can have only sequential files, on a disk there can be both sequential and direct-access files. It is useful to examine how this is possible.

As we saw in Chapter 1, data are recorded magnetically on disk and tape. Tapes require only a single read/write head. However, since a disk storage unit has many disk platters, each with two surfaces, for disks there has to be at least one read/write head for each surface. In addition, these read/write heads are mobile and are all attached to a single arm, so they can move as a group. As a result, an individual read/write head can move to sit adjacent to any of the many tracks on a surface, as illustrated in Figure 13.1.

There can be many hundreds of tracks for a surface and many thousands of tracks for the entire disk pack, but the data on any track can be directly accessed and read without reading any other tracks. Thus, it is possible to have a file of many hundreds of thousands of records on disk and to read just one of them for processing, without having to read other

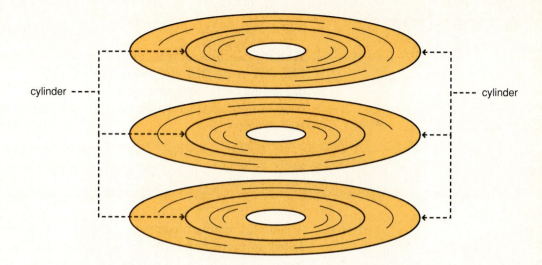

cylinder - - - -   - - - - cylinder

Figure 13.2 *The cylinder concept. All tracks of the same radius are said to form a cylinder. Data on the tracks making up a cylinder can be read without the read/write arm mechanism moving.*

records. If you want to read number 10,000 in a disk file, you may be able to read it directly, without first reading records 1 through 9999. A disk file for which this is possible is a direct-access file.

Disks can be used to hold sequential as well as direct-access files. Suppose a disk has 10 recording surfaces and 400 tracks per surface. When a disk is used for a sequential file, the first 100 records, for instance, could be on track 1 of surface 1, the next 100 records on track 1 of surface 2, and so on, so that the first 1000 records are on track 1 of each of the 10 surfaces. Then the next 1000 records would be on track 2 of each of the 10 surfaces, the next 1000 on track 3 of each of the 10 surfaces, and so on.

Records stored in this way are said to be recorded in ascending cylinder order. The concept of a cylinder is illustrated in Figure 13.2. All tracks of the same radius form a cylinder. Thus, in our disk with 400 tracks per surface and 10 surfaces, cylinder 1 would have 10 track 1s, cylinder 2 would have 10 track 2s, and so on, until cylinder 400, which would have 10 track 400s. In recording a new sequential file on an empty disk, the tracks of the first cylinder (cylinder 1) are filled first, then the tracks of the adjacent cylinder (cylinder 2), and so on.

Records are stored on disk in this ascending cylinder sequence to minimize movement of the read/write heads when the file is being read. The arms holding the read/write heads form a comb that moves in and out. When the read/write arms are in a given position, all the read/write heads will be adjacent to tracks of the same radius, that is, the tracks of a single cylinder. So all the tracks of a cylinder can be read (as they rotate past the heads) without it being necessary for the arms to move. This is essential because movement of the arms, to place each of the heads adjacent to a different track, is very slow. It takes about 25 milliseconds for each movement (called a *seek*) of the comb of arms, which is a very long time by computer standards. Thus, recording and reading in ascending cylinder order on a disk means much faster processing than any of the other ways it could be organized.

Speed of access depends on the storage device

Typically, the time to read a block of records is much the same with tape files and sequential disk files, although there will be some difference, depending on the disk and tape drives used. On average, a block of about 3000 bytes in a sequential file takes close to 10 milliseconds to read on both tape and disk.

Reading and writing records require input/output routines

A complex auxiliary computer program, or system software component, called an input/output routine or access method, is needed to enable a record in a sequential file to be read. (An input/output routine is called a "system software component" because it is supplied with the computer system. It does not have to be written for each application.) When a READ statement in a COBOL program reading a sequential file is executed, it is execution of the input/ouput routine that actually retrieves the record. A quite different input/output routine has to be used to read a record in a direct-access file.

The operating system provides the correct input/output routine to read and write records when READ and WRITE statements are executed in a program. The tasks that must be carried out when a record is read or written, in any kind of file, are too complex to be carried out by just one computer instruction. Many instructions are needed. Hence the need for the input/output routine.

A file defined in a program as a sequential file cannot be manipulated or accessed within that program as if it were a direct- access file. The operating system will not have the right input/output routine in place.

There is no need to explicitly define a file as a sequential file in a COBOL program. However, you must explicitly define a direct-access file (see Chapter 14). If the file is not defined as a direct-access file, the compiler assumes it to be a sequential file.

Summary of discussion of sequential and direct-access files

To summarize the discussion so far, remember the following:

- A sequential file can be on either disk or tape.
- Records of a sequential file on disk are recorded in ascending cylinder order.
- A direct-access file must be on a disk, never on tape.
- Either sequential or direct-access file organization is possible. There are several different ways to organize direct-access files.
- When a READ or WRITE statement is executed within a COBOL program, the operating system causes execution of a complex software component called an *access method*, or input/output routine, which looks after the details of reading and writing records.

- A different access method or input/output routine is used by the operating system to read or write records of a file (in response to COBOL READ or WRITE statement execution) for each type of file organization. File organizations are thus quite different.
- Sequential files on tape and disk can be read and written about equally fast, depending on the storage devices involved.
- In a COBOL program, if a disk file is not explicitly defined as a direct-access file, a sequential file organization is assumed, and the operating system will supply input/output routines for that file organization.

You normally use blocks and buffers of records with sequential files

As explained in Chapter 3, records on tape, that is, records of a tape-sequential file, are recorded in blocks, with a significant gap between blocks. This interblock gap is about half an inch, or the equivalent of about 1000 characters or more of storage space, depending on the type of tape. The gap is there to give the tape a place to stop between reading blocks of records.

Because of the large size of the gap, blocks of records should not be too small; otherwise too much space on the tape is wasted. For example, if each block is the size of the gap, then half the space on the tape will be occupied by gaps and thus unused for storage.

Records of a sequential disk file are also blocked, largely because records of tape files, which were in use many years before the advent of disk files, were blocked. With tape files, a block of records is a convenient unit for transmission between the buffer in main memory and the tape—blocks rather than individual records are moved between tape and buffer. Since it takes much the same time to move a block as an individual record, and with both that time is rather long by computer standards, it is more economical to transfer records in blocks. This economy applied equally well to disks, when they appeared, so records of sequential disk files were blocked as well.

In addition, with disks a track holds only an integer number of blocks. Because of this a poorly chosen block size can waste space at the end of a track. For example, if a track can hold 18,000 bytes and the block size is 6100, only two blocks can be stored, with almost 5800 bytes wasted.

Typically, blocks with tape and disks should be between 2000 and 6000 bytes. (A block size commonly used is 6000 bytes. This gives three blocks to a track, with little wasted track space, on IBM 3330 and 3350 disks, and gives seven blocks per track with little waste on the large capacity IBM 3380 disk.)

The number of records in a block of a new tape file being created can be defined in the file creation program, in the file section of the data division, as was explained in Chapter 3. For example, the specification

```
RECORD CONTAINS 100 CHARACTERS
BLOCK CONTAINS 40 RECORDS
```

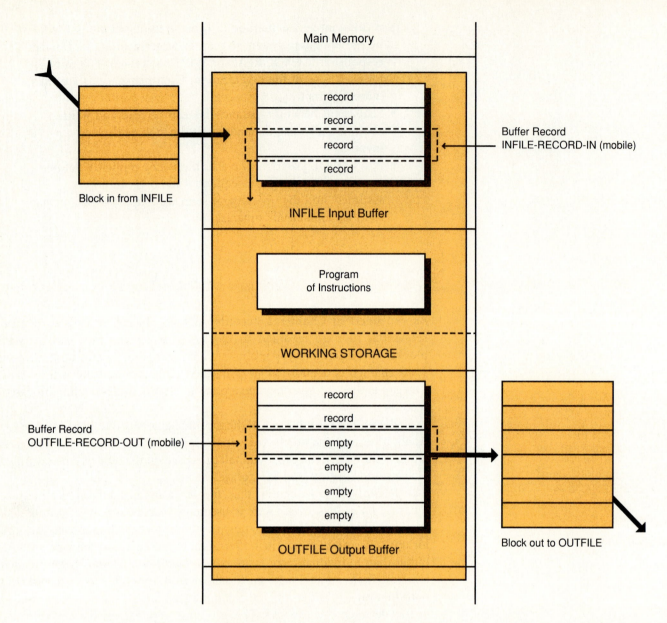

Figure 13.3 *Input and output buffers. Records are read and written from a file via transmission of blocks. An input buffer holds exactly one block of records. The buffer record specified in a COBOL program in the file section is mobile within the buffer: a READ causes the input buffer record to move coincident with the next record; a WRITE causes the output buffer record to move to the next empty record slot.*

will mean that the records of the new file will be grouped in blocks of 4000 bytes (characters) long, and that each block will have 40 records.

You normally use input and output buffers with sequential files

Because records are transferred between the storage medium and main memory in blocks, a part of main memory must receive blocks from an input file and transmit blocks to an output file. These parts of memory are input and output buffers, as illustrated in Figure 13.3.

An input buffer is exactly the same size as each block of the input file being processed. An output buffer is exactly the same size as each block of the output file. (When the output file is a printer file or report, the output buffer is typically 133 characters in size, capable of holding only one output record or printer line. Two output buffers are used with a printer file.)

A buffer record is always defined in a COBOL program

We have seen that in a COBOL program you must define an input buffer identifier, or input area identifier, for an input file, and an output buffer identifier, or output area identifier, for an output file. For example, given input and output files INFILE and OUTFILE, we might define the following:

```
DATA DIVISION.
FILE SECTION.
FD  INFILE                            LABEL RECORDS STANDARD
                                      RECORD CONTAINS 100 CHARACTERS
                                      BLOCK CONTAINS 4 RECORDS.
01 INFILE-RECORD-IN.
    05    CUSTOMER-IN     PIC  X(20).
    05    OTHER-IN        PIC  X(80).
FD  OUTFILE                           LABEL RECORDS STANDARD
                                      RECORD CONTAINS 80 CHARACTERS
                                      BLOCK CONTAINS 6 RECORDS.
01 OUTFILE-RECORD-OUT.
    05    CUSTOMER-OUT    PIC  X(20).
    05    OTHER-OUT       PIC  X(60).
```

Normally the number of records per block would be defined as being much larger (40 to 60), but here the blocking factor has been left small to conform with Figure 13.3.

A Buffer Record Is Mobile Within a Buffer

Notice that in the preceding program excerpt, we have defined just one input buffer record (INFILE-RECORD-IN). However, a block of input records and the input buffer will contain four INFILE records, as defined in the BLOCK CONTAINS clause in the excerpt and as illustrated in Figure 13.3. There is no inconsistency. INFILE-RECORD-IN is located in the input buffer, but its position varies as each READ INFILE statement is executed.

When OPEN INFILE is executed, the first block from the sequential file INFILE is transferred to the input buffer. When the first READ is executed, the buffer record INFILE-RECORD-IN is located coincident with record 1 of the block in the input buffer. When the next READ is executed, INFILE-RECORD-IN moves and is located coincident with record 2 of the block, and so on. In this way INFILE-RECORD-IN always contains the record read by the latest READ statement. When INFILE-RECORD-IN has contained the last record of the block, a new READ will move it coincident with record 1 of a new block.

The output buffer record OUTFILE-RECORD-OUT (shown in Figure 13.3) is also mobile in the output buffer. It always sits coincident with the next empty record slot in the output buffer. When a WRITE statement is executed, the record slot fills and OUTFILE-RECORD-OUT moves to the next empty slot. (This empty slot may not actually be empty, however, and may contain data. For this reason never MOVE, or otherwise utilize, the contents of an output buffer record after a WRITE statement has been executed. This is a common and subtle source of error.) When a WRITE fills the last empty slot in an output buffer, the entire buffer contents are transferred to the storage medium, and OUTFILE-RECORD-OUT moves to the first empty slot in an empty buffer.

The input/output routine, or access method, is responsible for transferring blocks between buffers and storage medium and for moving the buffer records INFILE-RECORD-IN and OUTFILE-RECORD-OUT to the next buffer locations as READ and WRITE statements are executed.

Double buffers are standard

Although single input and output buffers were shown in Figure 13.3, in practice the operating system assigns two buffers to each sequential file. This improves the efficiency of processing.

To understand this, suppose we have two input buffers, and suppose also that INFILE-RECORD-IN is coincident with the last record of one of these two input buffers. A new READ execution will move INFILE-RECORD-IN to the first location in the second buffer, which will have been filled earlier. Meanwhile, the input/output routine is filling the first buffer with the next block from the storage medium. In this way, when a READ is executed, there never has to be a lengthy wait for a new block to be transferred from the storage medium.

A similar efficiency improvement results from using two output buffers. When a WRITE is executed there is no wait while a block is being transferred.

It is possible to alter the normal allocation of two buffers per sequential file by an entry in the input/output section of the ENVIRONMENT DIVISION. For example, if we wanted three input buffers for INFILE, we could code "RESERVE 3 AREAS," as in

```
ENVIRONMENT DIVISION.
INPUT-OUTPUT SECTION.
FILE-CONTROL.
    SELECT INFILE    ASSIGN TO UT-S-DATA14N
                     RESERVE 3 AREAS.
```

Note that this RESERVE entry would probably increase efficiency only slightly, if at all, and so would rarely be included.

A master file is a business concept

You should understand by now that a sequential file is a specific type of computer file, on either tape or disk. A master file can be either a sequential file or a direct-access file.

A master file is defined more in terms of the business use to which it is put, not in terms of how it is organized on disk or tape. Master files contain records about entities important to the business, both currently and for the foreseeable future. For example, a file in which each record describes a customer of a business would be a master file, which might be called CUSTOMER-MASTER. A file that gives the details of how much each customer owes a business is a master file, and might be called RECEIVABLES-MASTER.

To illustrate a few points about a master file, let us take the simplest case of RECEIVABLES-MASTER. Suppose each record has fields CUSTOMER and OWING. OWING gives the amount currently owed to the business by a customer. Some records are shown in Figure 13.4 (spacing between fields is not important).

CUSTOMER	OWING
ARTFIELD	145,000
AVRILCORP	57,500
BANKCORP	134,000
BUNTORAMO	78,000
...	

Figure 13.4 Records in RECEIVABLES-MASTER file.

Typically, some field will have unique values so that it can be used to identify a record. This field is called the primary key. The primary key field of RECEIVABLES-MASTER would be CUSTOMER. In diagrams, such as Figure 13.4, the primary key is often underscored. With a sequential file, records are typically ordered in ascending primary key order.

A master file has to contain reliable data. Care therefore has to be taken in creating it, and also in updating it.

A master file must be created with validated records

In creating a new master, the records for the master are initially keyed in, to create an input file from which the master is created. In principle, creating a master file is merely a copying operation. During master file creation, each input record is read in and output to a master file that has labels and a carefully chosen blocking factor. Before an input record is written out to the master, however, the data in the record must be carefully validated. Thus, most of the code in a master file creation program is devoted to input data validation.

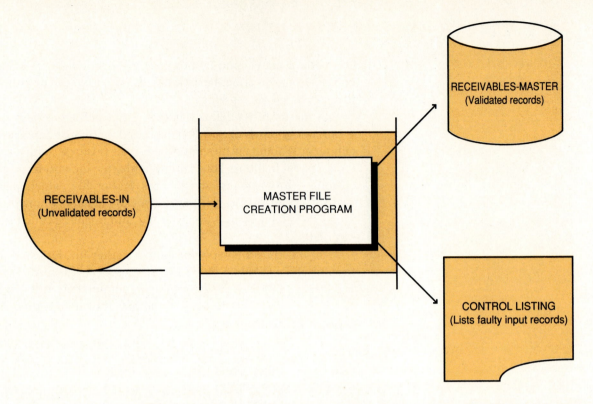

Figure 13.5 *System diagram for creation of the master file RECEIVABLES-MASTER.*

Control listing is generated with master file creation

At the same time the master file is created, a *control listing* is generated. This is a report on the status of the records read in, prior to validation. In the most comprehensive control listing, the fate of every record read in is listed. If a record is valid and placed in the master, it is also output to the control listing report with an "accepted" comment. If a record is invalid, it is output to the control listing with a list of its problems. Often a less comprehensive control listing is generated in which only the problem records are listed; these less comprehensive control listings are often called error reports.

Master File Creation Example

A master file is normally created from an input file that has been keyed in from document data. The complexity of the master file creation program depends solely on the amount of data validation required. A system diagram for creating a master file RECEIVABLES-MASTER is shown in Figure 13.5. The detailed program for creating this master file with validation checks using the input file RECEIVABLES-IN (Figure 13.6) was given in Chapter 8.

```
  ---------1---------2---------3---------4
        ARTFIELD       145000
        AVRILCORP      057500
        BANKCORP       ABABAB
        BUNTORAMO      078000
        CALCOMP        267000
        COMPUDISK      034000
        bbbbbbbbbbbbbbb067500
        DALCORP        134000
        DADLOPCORP     023 00
        DADLUGER       126000
        DENCO          234000
        DUBCORP        bbbbbb
        CALCON         046500
        . . .

        Columns  1–15    Customer name
                16–21    Amount owing
```

Figure 13.6a *Format of input file, RECEIVABLES-IN, for creating master file, RECEIVABLES-MASTER, with same format. (Invalid input records are shown in boldface.)*

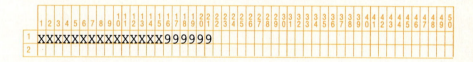

Figure 13.6b *Spacing chart for input record.*

```
01    RECEIVABLES-RECORD-IN.
      05   RR-CUSTOMER-IN      PIC X(15).
      05   RR-OWING-IN         PIC 9(06).
```

Figure 13.6c *Input area record structure.*

The input file shown in Figure 13.6a contains a few invalid records. These invalid records were detected by the program given earlier in Chapter 8. Apart from the need to check for invalid data, a master file creation program is essentially a copying operation, in which a record is read from the input file and written to an output file on disk or tape.

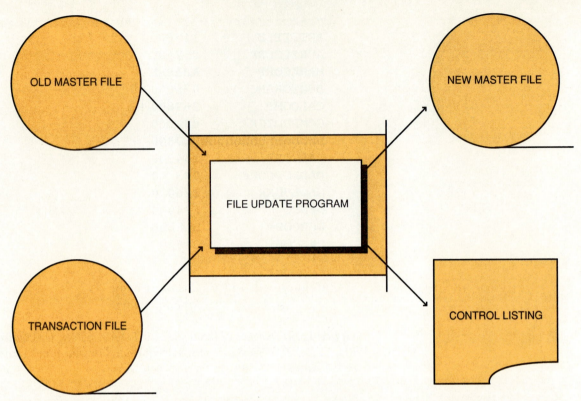

Figure 13.7 *Classical method of updating a master file from records in a transaction file. At the end of the processing there are two copies of the master file: the old copy and the new, updated copy.*

13.2
The classical method of updating a sequential master file is standard practice

THERE ARE FOUR kinds of master file updating:

- **Change updating**   values of record fields are changed
- **Insertion updating**   new records are inserted
- **Deletion updating**   some records are deleted
- **General updating**   any combination of change, insertion, and deletion updating

In most cases, updates use update data held in a *transaction file*. Each record in the transaction file

- Contains data to identify a specific master file record and change update some of its fields, or
- Contains data to identify and delete a specific master file record, or
- Is simply a new record to be inserted into the master file

Because the data are used to update master files, data in a transaction file must be carefully validated before use. The examples in this section assume this has been done earlier.

There is a common method for updating a sequential master file and an uncommon one. The common one is the *classical method*, which can be used with master files on either tape or disk. The classical method can be used for change, insertion, deletion, and general updating.

The classical method is illustrated in Figure 13.7. The important point is that the existing master, or old master, is actually not updated. Instead, the old master and the transaction file are used to create a new, updated version of the master, called the new master. In addition, any messages about the process are written out to a control listing. Thus, at the end of the processing, you have both the original file before updating and a new, updated version.

The other method is the *rewrite method* and can be used only with disks. It is more restricted than the classical method, being, for example, unsuitable for insertion updating. It is not commonly used with sequential files in business. We look briefly at the rewrite method at the end of the chapter.

A control listing is common with master file updating

As when a master file is created, during updating of a master file a control listing is generated. In this case it reports the status of transaction records. In a comprehensive control listing, the fate of every transaction record is listed; a transaction record that is used to update the master is listed as having been used; a transaction record that cannot be used is listed along with an explanation of the problem, or problems, with the record. Alternatively, an error report may be generated, listing the problem transaction records and their problems.

Classical change updating involves a basic principle

The essentials of classical change updating are illustrated in the file navigation diagram in Figure 13.8. Imagine you are updating the receivables master file from Figure 13.4. In the transaction file, each record contains the data needed to change update a record of the old master. Each transaction record has a primary key that matches the primary key of some record in the old master. As usual, records of both the transaction file and the master file are sorted in ascending primary key order.

Each record in the transaction file can be imagined to hold data about a payment made by a customer. The fields of the transaction file are TRANS-CUSTOMER and PAYMENT-IN. When a pair of transaction and old master records match, the updating consists of subtracting the PAYMENT-IN value from the OWING field in the old master record. This is the updating shown in Figure 13.8.

In the processing, the records of the old master are read in sequence, as are the records of the transaction file. The primary key of the latest old master record is continually compared with the primary key of the latest transaction record to find a match. Old master records that do not match any transaction records are written to the new master unchanged. Old master records that match a transaction record are updated before being written out to the new master.

In the ideal case, every record in the transaction file has a matching old master record. It is this case that is illustrated in Figure 13.8.

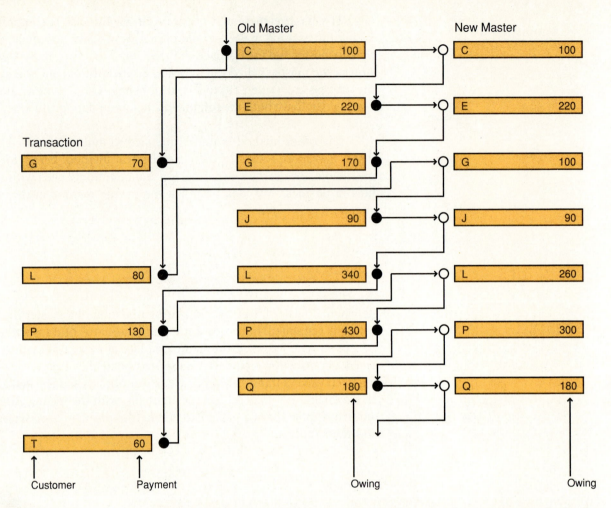

Old Master   New Master

C	100		C	100
E	220		E	220
G	170		G	100
J	90		J	90
L	340		L	260
P	430		P	300
Q	180		Q	180

Transaction

G	70
L	80
P	130
T	60

Customer   Payment   Owing   Owing

Figure 13.8 *File navigation diagram for change updating a master file by the classical method. In this example, where primary keys match, the transaction PAYMENT value is subtracted from the old master OWING value to give the new master OWING value. Notice that following a match, the new master record is not written out until the next transaction record has been read.*

Program for Ideal Classical Change Updating

Suppose we call the latest or current transaction record "cur-tr," and the current old master record "cur-om." The basic logic for the ideal case of classical change updating, where no unmatched transaction records can occur, is as follows:

Case A. customer in cur-tr > customer in cur-om

ACTION

1. Write out old master in working storage as next new master record.
2. Read next old master record into working storage.

Case B. customer in cur-tr = customer in cur-om

ACTION

1. Use current transaction record to update old master record in working storage.
2. Read next transaction record.

Notice that in the case of a match (Case B), the action merely involves updating the old master record in working storage, and does not include writing it out to the new master. That happens after the next comparison, which must involve Case A.

We can apply this logic in a COBOL program for the change updating depicted earlier in Figure 13.8. The files are the transaction file TRANS, and the old and new master files OLD-MASTER and NEW-MASTER. The program works as shown in Figure 13.9.

```
IDENTIFICATION DIVISION.
PROGRAM-ID. CH2.
*************************************************************************
*   CHANGE UPDATES OLD-MASTER FROM TRANS TO GENERATE NEW-MASTER.        *
*************************************************************************
ENVIRONMENT DIVISION.
INPUT-OUTPUT SECTION.
FILE-CONTROL.       SELECT OLD-MASTER        ASSIGN TO UT-S-REC006.
                    SELECT NEW-MASTER        ASSIGN TO UT-S-REC007.
                    SELECT TRANS             ASSIGN TO UT-S-DISK80.
                    SELECT CONTROL-LISTING   ASSIGN TO UR-S-SYSPRINT.
DATA DIVISION.
FILE SECTION.
FD   OLD-MASTER                        LABEL RECORDS ARE STANDARD
                                       RECORD CONTAINS 21 CHARACTERS
                                       BLOCK CONTAINS 200 RECORDS.
01   OLD-MAST-RECORD-IN      PIC X(21).
FD   NEW-MASTER                        LABEL RECORDS ARE STANDARD
                                       RECORD CONTAINS 21 CHARACTERS
                                       BLOCK CONTAINS 200 RECORDS.
01   NEW-MAST-RECORD-OUT     PIC X(21).
FD   TRANS                             LABEL RECORDS ARE STANDARD.
01   TRANS-RECORD-IN.
     05   TRANS-CUSTOMER-IN   PIC X(15).
     05   TRANS-PAYMENT-IN    PIC 9(06).
FD   CONTROL-LISTING                   LABEL RECORDS ARE OMITTED.
01   PRINT-RECORD-OUT        PIC X(133).
WORKING-STORAGE SECTION.
01 WS-WORK-AREAS.
     05    MORE-RECORDS       PIC X(03)      VALUE 'YES'.
     05    TRANS-COUNT        PIC 9(04)      VALUE ZEROS.
     05    MASTER-COUNT       PIC 9(05)      VALUE ZEROS.
01 WS-MASTER-RECORD.
     05   WS-MAST-CUSTOMER    PIC X(15).
     05   WS-MAST-OWING       PIC 9(06).
```

```
   01 TOTAL-LINE-OUT.
       05  FILLER                  PIC X         VALUE SPACES.
       05  FILLER                  PIC X(18)     VALUE 'TRANSACTION COUNT:'.
       05  FILLER                  PIC X(02)     VALUE SPACES.
       05  TL-TRANS-CNT-OUT        PIC Z,ZZ9.
       05  FILLER                  PIC X(02)     VALUE SPACES.
       05  FILLER                  PIC X(20)     VALUE 'MASTER RECORD COUNT:'.
       05  FILLER                  PIC X(02)     VALUE SPACES.
       05  TL-MASTER-CNT-OUT       PIC ZZ,ZZ9.
       05  FILLER                  PIC X(77)     VALUE SPACES.
   PROCEDURE DIVISION.
   100-MAIN-MODULE.
  ******************************************************************************
  *   DIRECTS PROGRAM LOGIC.                                                   *
  ******************************************************************************
        PERFORM 200-INITIALIZATION.
        PERFORM 400-COMPARE
               UNTIL MORE-RECORDS = 'NO'.
        PERFORM 300-TERMINATION.
   200-INITIALIZATION.
  ******************************************************************************
  *   PERFORMED FROM 100-MAIN-MODULE.  OPENS FILES, READS FIRST OLD            *
  *   MASTER AND TRANSACTION RECORDS.                                          *
  ******************************************************************************
        OPEN INPUT OLD-MASTER
             OUTPUT NEW-MASTER
             INPUT TRANS
             OUTPUT CONTROL-LISTING.
        READ OLD-MASTER INTO WS-MASTER-RECORD
                       AT END MOVE 'NO' TO MORE-RECORDS.

        READ TRANS
             AT END MOVE ' NO FIRST TRANS RECORD' TO PRINT-RECORD-OUT
                 WRITE PRINT-RECORD-OUT
                 STOP RUN.
   300-TERMINATION.
  ******************************************************************************
  *   PERFORMED FROM 100-MAIN-MODULE. PRINTS TOTALS, CLOSES FILES, AND         *
  *   STOPS PROGRAM.                                                           *
  ******************************************************************************
        MOVE TRANS-COUNT TO TL-TRANS-CNT-OUT.
        MOVE MASTER-COUNT TO TL-MASTER-CNT-OUT.
        WRITE PRINT-RECORD-OUT FROM TOTAL-LINE-OUT.
        CLOSE OLD-MASTER.
        CLOSE NEW-MASTER.
        CLOSE TRANS.
        CLOSE CONTROL-LISTING.
        STOP RUN.
```

```
      400-COMPARE.
*****************************************************************************
*  PERFORMED FROM 100-MAIN-MODULE.  COMPARES OLD MASTER AND        *
*  TRANSACTION RECORD PRIMARY KEYS. UPDATES MASTER RECORD ON MATCH   *
*  AND LEAVES MASTER RECORD UNCHANGED WHEN NO MATCH.                 *
*****************************************************************************
      IF TRANS-CUSTOMER-IN > WS-MAST-CUSTOMER
          WRITE NEW-MAST-RECORD-OUT FROM WS-MASTER-RECORD
          READ OLD-MASTER INTO WS-MASTER-RECORD
                AT END MOVE 'NO' TO MORE-RECORDS
          END-READ
          ADD 1 TO MASTER-COUNT
      END-IF.
      IF TRANS-CUSTOMER-IN = WS-MAST-CUSTOMER
          SUBTRACT TRANS-PAYMENT-IN FROM WS-MAST-OWING
          READ TRANS
             AT END MOVE 'ZZZ' TO TRANS-CUSTOMER-IN
          END-READ      'ZZZ' best replaced by HIGH-VALUES.
          ADD 1 TO TRANS-COUNT
      END-IF.
```

Figure 13.9 *Program for CH2, the ideal case of change updating illustrated in Figure 13.8. It is assumed that unmatched TRANS records cannot occur.*

The essential logic given earlier for this ideal case of classical change updating is incorporated in the module 400-COMPARE. A minor detail is that the transaction and master records are counted, and the totals printed in the report file for the process. (To help you concentrate on the essentials, output of headers to the control listing has been omitted.)

Notice that when there are no more transaction records, the value 'ZZZ' is placed in the primary key field of the transaction buffer record. This is needed to allow for end-of-file conditions.

Because we do not admit the possibility of an unmatched TRANS record, TRANS must end either before or at the same time as the old master. When TRANS ends before OLD-MASTER, we want the processing to continue and write out the remaining OLD-MASTER, records to NEW-MASTER, as illustrated in Figure 13.10. But before an old master record can be written out, its primary key must be less than the transaction record's primary key. Since there are no more TRANS records, giving TRANS-CUSTOMER-IN the very high value of ZZZ eliminates any possibility of the old master record's primary key being equal to it. In this way remaining old master records will always be written out to NEW-MASTER.

There can, however, be machine-dependent problems with using a high value such as ZZZ. The equivalent COBOL figurative constant HIGH-VALUES is much better, as in

```
READ TRANS
   AT END MOVE HIGH-VALUES TO TRANS-CUSTOMER-IN
END-READ
```

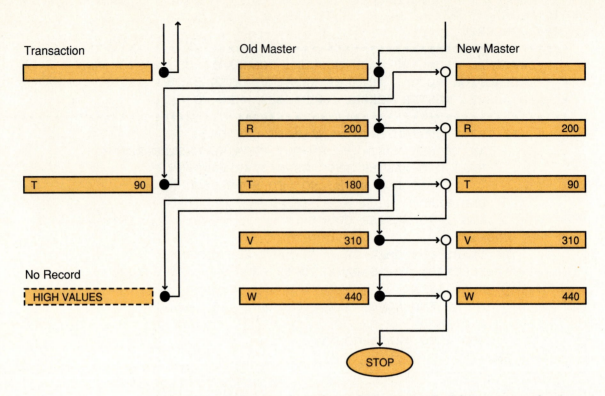

Transaction   Old Master   New Master

No Record
HIGH VALUES

STOP

Figure 13.10 *File navigation diagram showing end-of-file processing for classical change updating. When the transaction file ends first, a final imaginary record with primary key HIGH-VALUES is assumed to have been read. This causes output of the remaining old master records to the new master.*

The constant in HIGH-VALUES is the highest possible in the collating sequence for the computer. It cannot be printed.

Use of separate paragraphs for updating options In the paragraph 400-COMPARE in Figure 13.9, the two updating options (for no match and match) are carried out within the paragraph. Notice that if you do this you will have READ . . . AT END statements within IF-statements. This use of READ may require that you use END-READ to prevent error, as in 400-COMPARE. The following contains errors:

```
400-COMPARE.
IF TRANS-CUSTOMER-IN > WS-MAST-CUSTOMER
    WRITE NEW-MAST-RECORD-OUT FROM WS-MASTER-RECORD
    READ OLD-MASTER INTO WS-MASTER-RECORD
        AT END MOVE 'NO' TO MORE-RECORDS        error!
    ADD 1 TO MASTER-COUNT
  END-IF.
IF TRANS-CUSTOMER-IN = WS-MAST-CUSTOMER
    SUBTRACT TRANS-PAYMENT-IN FROM WS-MAST-OWING
    READ TRANS
        AT END MOVE HIGH-VALUES TO TRANS-CUSTOMER-IN   error!
    ADD 1 TO TRANS-COUNT
  END-IF.
```

You need END-READ with each read. Of course in this case, the error could be avoided if we place the ADD statements before the READs. The alternative, commonly used with COBOL 74, which did not allow use of END-READ, is to have a separate paragraph for each updating option, as in

```
400-COMPARE.
    IF TRANS-CUSTOMER-IN > WS-MAST-CUSTOMER
       PERFORM 500-NO-UPDATE.
    IF TRANS-CUSTOMER-IN = WS-MAST-CUSTOMER
       PERFORM 600-UPDATE-MASTER.
500-NO-UPDATE.
    WRITE NEW-MAST-RECORD-OUT FROM WS-MASTER-RECORD.
    READ OLD-MASTER INTO WS-MASTER-RECORD
            AT END MOVE 'NO' TO MORE-RECORDS.
    ADD 1 TO MASTER-COUNT.
600-UPDATE-MASTER.
    SUBTRACT TRANS-PAYMENT-IN FROM WS-MAST-OWING.
    READ TRANS
       AT END MOVE HIGH-VALUES TO TRANS-CUSTOMER-IN.
    ADD 1 TO TRANS-COUNT.
```

In this version we do not need to worry about an error caused by omission of an END-READ. Notice that records are counted correctly in all these versions; a master record is counted only when it is written. If we had organized the count to occur only after a READ, we would risk counting the final READ, which caused the AT END clause to be executed.

Duplicate Transaction Keys May Occur with Ideal Change Updating

For the program in Figure 13.9, the possibility of unmatched TRANS records was excluded. We shall deal with that possibility presently. However, the possibility of two or more transaction records with the same primary key value was not excluded. For example, a customer might send two or more payments, so that there would be several transaction records for that customer, and thus, with the same primary key value. The TRANS-PAYMENT-IN values in all of these transaction records would have to be deducted from the owing field in a single master record in order to correctly update it. This is illustrated by the record for BUNTORAMO in Figure 13.11.

You may now be surprised to learn that the simple program in Figure 13.9, and the essential logic of the update given earlier, will handle the case of TRANS records with duplicate keys used for multiple updates of the same master record, provided there is no possibility of unmatched TRANS records. The logic used in that program was more subtle than you might realize at first glance.

Refer to both Figure 13.11 and the paragraph 400-COMPARE in the program in Figure 13.10. Suppose that the latest OLD-MASTER record is the BUNTORAMO record, and that the latest TRANS record is the first BUNTORAMO record in that file.

The keys of the two records are now compared in an iteration of 400-COMPARE. Because the transaction and master keys match, the 15,000

CUSTOMER	PAYMENT		CUSTOMER	OWING		CUSTOMER	OWING
			ARTFIELD	145,000		ARTFIELD	145,000
AVRILCORP	10,000		AVRILCORP	57,500		AVRILCORP	47,500
			BANKCORP	134,000		BANKCORP	134,000
BUNTORAMO	15,000		BUNTORAMO	78,000		BUNTORAMO	43,000
BUNTORAMO	20,000						
			BUXITE	140,500		BUXITE	140,500.
CONCOMP	10,500						
...							

TRANS	OLD-MASTER	NEW-MASTER

Figure 13.11 *A single OLD-MASTER updated by multiple TRANS records (TRANS records with duplicate primary keys, for example, the BUNTORAMO records).*

TRANS-PAYMENT-IN value will be subtracted from the 78,000 value of WS-MAST-OWING, to give an WS-MAST-OWING value of 63,000. Then the next TRANS record is read, which is the second BUNTORAMO record.

Another iteration of 400-COMPARE now begins, at which point the record has not yet been written out to NEW-MASTER. Again the keys match, so the 20,000 TRANS-PAYMENT-IN value will be subtracted from the 53,000 value in WS-MAST-OWING, giving a WS-MAST-OWING value of 43,000. Then the next TRANS record is read, which is the CALCOMP record.

At the next iteration of 400-COMPARE, the master and transaction keys are different, so that WS-MASTER-RECORD, having been updated twice, is written out to NEW-MASTER.

Rejection of duplicates may be necessary in ideal change updating
Suppose it was an error to have two or more records in TRANS with the same primary key. For example, it might be that the data entry department made sure that a group of payments by a given WS-MAST-CUSTOMER were collected in the PAYMENT value in a single transaction record. In that case two records with the same primary key would be an error. For example, a mistake in data entry of the transaction records could make the WS-MAST-CUSTOMER values "CHANG" and "CHENG" the same (both "CHANG"), so that, with the program in Figure 13.9, Cheng's payment would update Chang's account. (Actually, in commercial practice, names are rarely used as primary keys because of difficulties of this kind; customer numbers would be used instead.)

The procedure given in the program in Figure 13.9 could be modified to reject duplicates. The modifications are shown in boldface. The minor matter of counting transaction and master records has been omitted from this version to allow you to concentrate on the essentials.

```
100-MAIN-MODULE.
    PERFORM 200-INITIALIZATION.
    PERFORM 400-COMPARE
            UNTIL MORE-RECORDS = 'NO'.
    PERFORM 300-TERMINATION.
200-INITIALIZATION.
    OPEN INPUT OLD-MASTER
         OUTPUT NEW-MASTER
         INPUT TRANS
         OUTPUT CONTROL-LISTING.
    READ OLD-MASTER INTO WS-MASTER-RECORD
                        AT END MOVE 'NO' TO MORE-RECORDS.
    READ TRANS
            AT END MOVE ' NO FIRST TRANS RECORD' TO PRINT-RECORD-OUT
                    WRITE PRINT-RECORD-OUT
                    STOP RUN.
    MOVE TRANS-CUSTOMER-IN TO CONTROL-KEY.
300-TERMINATION.
    CLOSE OLD-MASTER.
    CLOSE NEW-MASTER.
    CLOSE TRANS.
    CLOSE CONTROL-LISTING.
    STOP RUN.
400-COMPARE.
    IF TRANS-CUSTOMER-IN > WS-MAST-CUSTOMER
        WRITE NEW-MAST-RECORD-OUT FROM WS-MASTER-RECORD
        READ OLD-MASTER INTO WS-MASTER-RECORD
                AT END MOVE 'NO' TO MORE-RECORDS
    END-IF.
    IF TRANS-CUSTOMER-IN = WS-MAST-CUSTOMER
        SUBTRACT TRANS-PAYMENT-IN FROM WS-MAST-OWING
        READ TRANS
            AT END MOVE HIGH-VALUES TO TRANS-CUSTOMER-IN
        END-READ
        IF TRANS-CUSTOMER-IN < HIGH-VALUES
          PERFORM 500-DUPLICATE-CHECK
                UNTIL CONTROL-KEY < TRANS-CUSTOMER-IN
    END-IF
END-IF.
    500-DUPLICATE-CHECK.
        IF TRANS-CUSTOMER-IN = CONTROL-KEY
            PERFORM 600-LIST-DUPLICATE-RECORD
            READ TRANS
                AT END MOVE HIGH-VALUES TO TRANS-CUSTOMER-IN
        ELSE
            MOVE TRANS-CUSTOMER-IN TO CONTROL-KEY
        END-IF.
600-LIST-DUPLICATE-RECORD.
...
```

In this version, each time a new TRANS record is read, its primary key is checked against the primary key of the previous TRANS record, held in CONTROL-KEY. If the record has a duplicate key, the record is listed in a control listing, and the next TRANS record is read and checked. If that record, too, is a duplicate, it is also listed in a control listing. This process of rejecting a whole series of duplicates continues until a TRANS record with a different primary key value is read. Thus, the above program excerpt will use the first of a series of duplicates to update the master and will reject the remainder of the series.

Note that coding, such as the preceding, for detection of transaction records with duplicate primary keys is not very common, since it is usually not necessary to detect duplicate records in a transaction file during update of a master file. If necessary, you can always eliminate those records with prior processing of the transaction file. But often duplicates in the transaction file are wanted and will simply be used for multiple updates to a single master record, as explained earlier (Figure 13.11).

Unmatched Transaction Records May Occur with Classical Change Updating

Now suppose that there can be records in the transaction file that match no master record, that is, unmatched TRANS records. Obviously, an unmatched TRANS record would be an error, and each one would be listed in a control listing. In commercial practice the possibility of such unmatched TRANS records is usually assumed, since it is rarely possible to remove them by prior data validation processing.

And suppose that TRANS records with duplicate primary keys can also occur, and that all the TRANS records with the same primary key can be used to update the corresponding master record, in the manner illustrated in Figure 13.11. The essential logic for this common type of change updating is

Case A. customer in cur-tr > customer in cur-om

ACTION

1. Write out old master in working storage as next new master record.
2. Read next old master record into working storage.

Case B. customer in cur-tr = customer in cur-om

ACTION

1. Use current transaction record to update old master record in working storage.
2. Read in next transaction record.

Case C. customer in cur-tr < customer in cur-om

ACTION

1. List current transaction record in control listing.
2. Read in next transaction record.

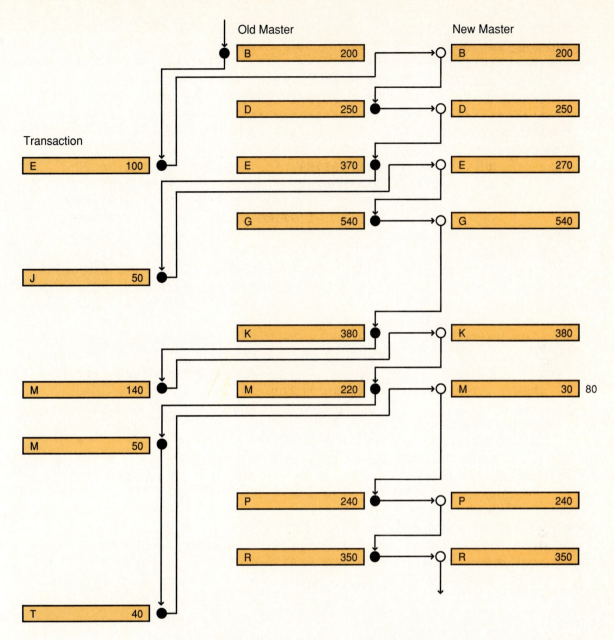

Figure 13.12 *File navigation diagram for classical change updating, where unmatched transactions can occur and duplicate matching transactions will be used.*

Using the example of receivable data presented earlier, in which a TRANS record contains details of a payment by a customer, this logic appears in action in the file navigation diagram in Figure 13.12. The control listing is not included, however.

The COBOL program to handle this case is given in Figure 13.13. An example of the control listing resulting from this program is shown in Figure 13.14.

```
       IDENTIFICATION DIVISION.
       PROGRAM-ID. CH3.
      *****************************************************************************
      *   CHANGE UPDATES OLD-MASTER FROM TRANS TO GENERATE NEW-MASTER            *
      *   UNMATCHED TRANS RECORDS LISTED IN CONTROL LISTING.                     *
      *****************************************************************************
       ENVIRONMENT DIVISION.
       INPUT-OUTPUT SECTION.
       FILE-CONTROL.    SELECT OLD-MASTER       ASSIGN TO UT-S-REC006.
                        SELECT NEW-MASTER       ASSIGN TO UT-S-REC007.
                        SELECT TRANS            ASSIGN TO UT-S-DISK47.
                        SELECT CONTROL-LISTING  ASSIGN TO UR-S-SYSPRINT.
       DATA DIVISION.
       FILE SECTION.
       FD    OLD-MASTER                          LABEL RECORDS ARE STANDARD
                                                 RECORD CONTAINS 21 CHARACTERS
                                                 BLOCK CONTAINS 200 RECORDS.
       01    OLD-MAST-RECORD-IN    PIC X(21).
       FD    NEW-MASTER                           LABEL RECORDS ARE STANDARD
                                                  RECORD CONTAINS 21 CHARACTERS
                                                  BLOCK CONTAINS 200 RECORDS.
       01    NEW-MAST-RECORD-OUT   PIC X(21).
       FD    TRANS                                LABEL RECORDS ARE STANDARD.
       01    TRANS-RECORD-IN.
             05    TRANS-CUSTOMER-IN  PIC X(15).
             05    TRANS-PAYMENT-IN   PIC 9(06).
       FD    CONTROL-LISTING                      LABEL RECORDS ARE OMITTED.
       01    PRINT-RECORD-OUT      PIC X(133).
       WORKING-STORAGE SECTION.
       01    WS-WORK-AREAS.
             05    MORE-RECORDS       PIC X(03)      VALUE 'NO'.
             05    TRANS-COUNT        PIC 9(03)      VALUE ZEROS.
             05    LINE-COUNT         PIC 9(02)      VALUE ZEROS.
             05    WS-PAGE-NUMBER     PIC 9(02)      VALUE ZEROS.
       01    WS-MASTER-RECORD.
             05    WS-MAST-CUSTOMER   PIC X(15).
             05    WS-MAST-OWING      PIC 9(06).
       01 PAGE-DATE-LINE-OUT.
             05    FILLER             PIC X          VALUE SPACE.
             05    FILLER             PIC X(06)      VALUE 'PAGE'.
             05    PD-PAGE-NUMB-OUT   PIC 9(02).
             05    FILLER             PIC X(50)      VALUE SPACES.
             05    PD-RUN-DATE-OUT    PIC X(08).
             05    FILLER             PIC X(66)      VALUE SPACES.
         01 REPORT-HEADER.
             05    FILLER             PIC X(19)      VALUE SPACES.
             05    FILLER             PIC X(114)     VALUE
                                      'CONTROL LISTING WITH CHANGE UPDATE'.
```

```
01  HEADER-1.
    05   FILLER                PIC X           VALUE SPACES.
    05   FILLER                PIC X(25)       VALUE
                                               'SEQUENCE#    TRANS-RECORD'.
    05   FILLER                PIC X(107)      VALUE SPACES.
01  DETAIL-LINE-OUT.
    05   FILLER                PIC X           VALUE SPACES.
    05   DL-REC-NUMB-OUT       PIC 9(03).
    05   FILLER                PIC X(10)       VALUE SPACES.
    05   DL-RECORDIN-OUT       PIC X(21).
    05   FILLER                PIC X(98)       VALUE SPACES.
 PROCEDURE DIVISION.
 100-MAIN-MODULE.
****************************************************************************
*   DIRECTS PROGRAM LOGIC.                                                *
****************************************************************************
     PERFORM 200-INITIALIZATION.
     PERFORM 400-COMPARE
             UNTIL WS-MAST-CUSTOMER  = HIGH-VALUES
                 AND TRANS-CUSTOMER-IN = HIGH-VALUES.
     PERFORM 300-TERMINATION.
 200-INITIALIZATION.
****************************************************************************
*   PERFORMED FROM 100-MAIN-MODULE. OPENS FILES, EXTRACTS DATE, PRINTS    *
*   CONTROL LISTING HEADINGS, READS FIRST TRANSACTION AND MASTER          *
*   RECORDS. BEGINS TRACKING SEQUENCE OF TRANSACTION RECORDS.             *
****************************************************************************
     OPEN INPUT OLD-MASTER
          OUTPUT NEW-MASTER
          INPUT TRANS
          OUTPUT CONTROL-LISTING.
     MOVE CURRENT-DATE TO PD-RUN-DATE-OUT.
     PERFORM 600-PAGE-HEADERS.
     READ OLD-MASTER INTO WS-MASTER-RECORD
                        AT END STOP RUN.
     READ TRANS
             AT END STOP RUN.
 300-TERMINATION.
****************************************************************************
*   PERFORMED FROM 100-MAIN-MODULE. CLOSES FILES, STOPS PROGRAM.          *
****************************************************************************
     CLOSE OLD-MASTER.
     CLOSE NEW-MASTER.
     CLOSE TRANS.
     CLOSE CONTROL-LISTING.
     STOP RUN.
```

```
      400-COMPARE.
     ****************************************************************************
     *   PERFORMED FROM 100-MAIN-MODULE.  COMPARES OLD MASTER AND TRANSACTION *
     *   RECORD PRIMARY KEYS. UPDATES MASTER ON MATCH AND LEAVES MASTER       *
     *   UNCHANGED WHEN NO MATCH. IF NO MATCH IS EVER FOUND (MASTER KEY       *
     *   > TRANSACTION KEY) THE TRANSACTION.                                  *
     ****************************************************************************
           IF TRANS-CUSTOMER-IN > WS-MAST-CUSTOMER
               WRITE NEW-MAST-RECORD-OUT FROM WS-MASTER-RECORD
               READ OLD-MASTER INTO WS-MASTER-RECORD
                   AT END MOVE HIGH-VALUES TO WS-MAST-CUSTOMER
           END-IF.
           IF TRANS-CUSTOMER-IN = WS-MAST-CUSTOMER
               SUBTRACT TRANS-PAYMENT-IN FROM WS-MAST-OWING
               READ TRANS
                   AT END MOVE HIGH-VALUES TO TRANS-CUSTOMER-IN
               END-READ
               ADD 1 TO TRANS-COUNT
           END-IF.
           IF TRANS-CUSTOMER-IN < WS-MAST-CUSTOMER
               PERFORM 500-PRINT-TRANS-RECORD
               READ TRANS
                   AT END MOVE HIGH-VALUES TO TRANS-CUSTOMER-IN
               END-READ
               ADD 1 TO TRANS-COUNT
           END-IF.
      500-PRINT-TRANS-RECORD.
     ****************************************************************************
     *   PERFORMED FROM 400-COMPARE. PRINTS UNMATCHED TRANS RECORD WITH PAGE  *
     *   HEADERS IF REQUIRED.                                                 *
     ****************************************************************************
           MOVE TRANS-RECORD-IN TO DL-RECORDIN-OUT.
           MOVE TRANS-COUNT TO DL-REC-NUMB-OUT.
           IF LINE-COUNT > 45
               PERFORM 600-PAGE-HEADERS
           END-IF.
           WRITE PRINT-RECORD-OUT FROM DETAIL-LINE-OUT
               AFTER ADVANCING 1 LINE.
           ADD 1 TO LINE-COUNT.
      600-PAGE-HEADERS.
     ****************************************************************************
     *   PERFORMED FROM 200-INITIALIZATION AND 500-PRINT-TRANS-RECORD.        *
     *   PRINTS PAGE HEADERS IN CONTROL LISTING.                             *
     ****************************************************************************
           MOVE REPORT-HEADER TO PRINT-RECORD-OUT.
           WRITE PRINT-RECORD-OUT
               AFTER ADVANCING PAGE.
           ADD 1 TO WS-PAGE-NUMBER.
           MOVE WS-PAGE-NUMBER TO PD-PAGE-NUMB-OUT.
           MOVE PAGE-DATE-LINE-OUT TO PRINT-RECORD-OUT.
```

```
            WRITE PRINT-RECORD-OUT
                AFTER ADVANCING 1 LINE.
            MOVE HEADER-1 TO PRINT-RECORD-OUT.
            WRITE PRINT-RECORD-OUT
                AFTER ADVANCING 2 LINES.
            MOVE SPACES TO PRINT-RECORD-OUT.
            WRITE PRINT-RECORD-OUT
                AFTER ADVANCING 1 LINE.
            MOVE 5 TO LINE-COUNT.
```

Figure 13.13 CH3 Program for change updating with the possibility of unmatched TRANS records (as illustrated in Figure 13.12). Unmatched TRANS records are listed in the control listing in Figure 13.14.

```
---------1---------2---------3---------4---------5---------6--------7
                    CONTROL LISTING WITH CHANGE UPDATE
        PAGE   01                                          12/15/91


        SEQUENCE#       TRANS-RECORD

        007             DREXCORP      010900
        015             EWING         005800
        ...
```

Figure 13.14a Control listing printed by program in Figure 13.12. Report contains a list of unmatched TRANS records.

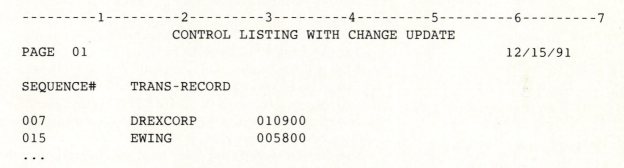

Figure 13.14b Printer spacing chart for control listing.

```
        01 DETAIL-LINE-OUT.
            05  FILLER              PIC X          VALUE SPACES.
            05  DL-REC-NUMB-OUT     PIC 9(03).
            05  FILLER              PIC X(10)      VALUE SPACES.
            05  DL-RECORDIN-OUT     PIC X(21).
            05  FILLER              PIC X(98)      VALUE SPACES.
```

Figure 13.14c Structure of record for detail line of report.

As before, the essentials of the processing, according to the logic given earlier, are carried out in the paragraph 400-COMPARE of the program. But notice that either of the two files TRANS and OLD-MASTER can end first.

The logic in 400-COMPARE and the PERFORM 400-COMPARE statement look after the end-of-file conditions. At the end of each file, HIGH-VALUES is placed in the primary key field in memory for the record for each file. The PERFORM 400-COMPARE statement ensures that iterations of 400-COMPARE stop only when the ends of both files have been reached. If TRANS ends first, each subsequent iteration of 400-COMPARE will output an OLD-MASTER record to NEW-MASTER. If OLD-MASTER ends first, each subsequent iteration of 400-COMPARE will output an unmatched TRANS record to the control listing.

You should carefully compare paragraph 400-COMPARE in the preceding program (Figure 13.13) with the 400-COMPARE in the program in Figure 13.9, where no unmatched records allowed. The two paragraphs are essentially the same, except that the program in Figure 13.13 has a final IF- statement to detect and handle unmatched TRANS records.

The paragraph 400-COMPARE in Figure 13.13 and the earlier one in Figure 13.9 will handle the case of matched TRANS records with duplicate primary keys (as for example in Figure 13.11) in exactly the same way. Thus, with the program in Figure 13.13, the PAYMENT fields in a series of TRANS records with the same primary key will be used to update a single OLD-MASTER record with a matching primary key.

Suppose you wanted to perform the change updating with the possibility of unmatched TRANS records. But suppose further that you did not want to accept multiple updates of a single OLD-MASTER record from a series of TRANS records with duplicate primary keys. Assuming that such unwanted duplicate TRANS records were possible, you would normally preprocess the TRANS file to remove them before using it in the change update. Alternatively, in a few cases, you could add code to the change update program to detect duplicate TRANS records and list them in the control listing, along the lines shown earlier.

Classical Insertion Updating Example

Now suppose that the transaction file contains new records to be inserted into the master file; you will use this transaction file for classical insertion updating. Once more, the old master is not actually updated; the transaction file and old master are used to create a new, updated file—the new master.

Both the transaction file and old master will be sorted in ascending primary key order. Since the transaction records are going to be added to the master file, a record in the transaction file with a duplicate primary key has to be an error—there can be only one record in the master file for a given primary key value. However, since duplicates in the transaction file can be detected by prior processing, we begin by excluding the possibility of records with duplicate primary key values.

Both the transaction file and old master files are processed in sequence, as with classical change updating described earlier. The processing is illustrated in Figure 13.15. Suppose the first pair of records has been

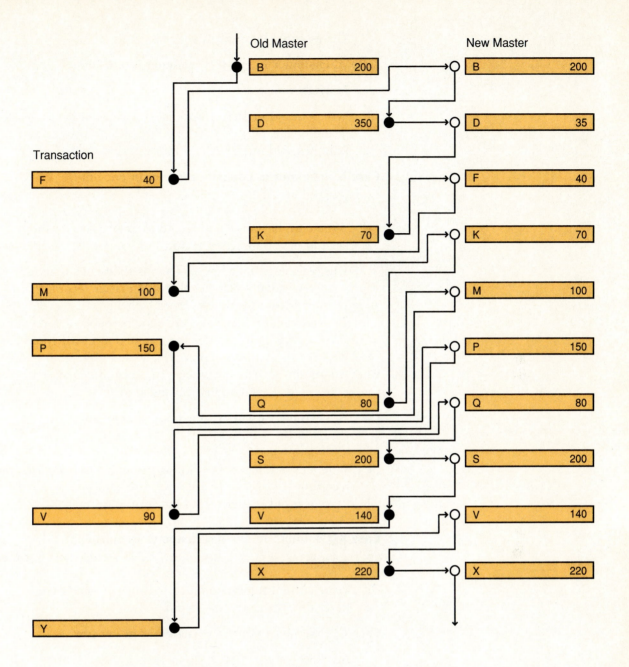

Figure 13.15 *File navigation diagram for classical insertion updating. Notice that the matching transaction with key V is rejected.*

read. If the old master record has a lower key it is written out to the new master, and the next old master record is read.

This reading and writing of old master records normally continues until the current old master has a key greater than the current transaction record. In that case that transaction record is written out to the new master file and the next transaction record read. Typically, another group of old master records will then be output, one by one, until once more the transaction record has a primary key lower than the old master key, enabling the transaction record to be output to the new master, and so on.

The essential logic for this processing is

Case A. customer in cur-tr > customer in cur-om

ACTION

1. Write out old master in working storage as next new master record.
2. Read next old master record into working storage.

Case B. customer in cur-tr < customer in cur-om

ACTION

1. Write current transaction record as new master record.
2. Read in next transaction record.

This logic does not allow for the possibility of a transaction record in which the key actually matches that of a master record, that is, when an attempt is made to insert a new record with a key that already exists in the master. Clearly, such a TRANS record should not occur, but in practice, due to an error in keying in data for the transaction file, it could happen.

We have to modify the preceding essential logic to handle the case when an unwanted match between a transaction and an old master record can be expected. This modified expanded logic is

Case A. customer in cur-tr > customer in cur-om

ACTION

1. Write out old master in working storage as next new master record.
2. Read next old master record into working storage.

Case B. Customer in cur-tr < customer in cur-om

ACTION

1. Write current transaction record as new master record.
2. Read in next transaction record.

Case C. customer in cur-tr = customer in cur-om

ACTION

1. List current transaction record in control listing.
2. Read in next transaction record.

The core COBOL processing with this expanded logic, for insertion updating with a transaction file TRANS and master files OLD-MASTER and NEW-MASTER is shown in the program excerpt in Figure 13.16.

Either the TRANS or OLD-MASTER file can end first. This time, if OLD-MASTER ends first, the subsequent 400-COMPARE iterations cause the remaining TRANS records to be output to NEW-MASTER. If TRANS ends first, the remaining OLD-MASTER records are also output to NEW-MASTER by the subsequent 400-COMPARE iterations. To ensure this, the primary key for the record in main memory for each of these files is given the value HIGH-VALUES as soon as the file ends. The PERFORM 400-COMPARE statement causes 400-COMPARE to be repeated until both files have ended.

```
DATA DIVISION.
FILE SECTION.
...
01  OLD-MAST-RECORD-IN              PIC X(21).
...
01  NEW-MAST-RECORD-OUT             PIC X(21).
...
01  TRANS-RECORD-IN.
    05  TRANS-CUSTOMER-IN           PIC X(15).
    05  TRANS-OWING-IN              PIC 9(06).
...
WORKING-STORAGE SECTION.
01  WS-MASTER-RECORD.
    05  WS-MAST-CUSTOMER            PIC X(15).
    05  WS-MAST-OWING               PIC 9(06).
...
PROCEDURE DIVISION.
100-MAIN-MODULE.
    OPEN ...
    READ OLD-MASTER INTO WS-MASTER-RECORD
                        AT END STOP RUN.
    READ TRANS
            AT END STOP RUN.
    PERFORM 400-COMPARE
            UNTIL WS-MAST-CUSTOMER  = HIGH-VALUES
            AND TRANS-CUSTOMER-IN = HIGH-VALUES.
    CLOSE...
    STOP RUN.
400-COMPARE.
    IF TRANS-CUSTOMER-IN > WS-MAST-CUSTOMER
        WRITE NEW-MAST-RECORD-OUT FROM WS-MASTER-RECORD
        READ OLD-MASTER INTO WS-MASTER-RECORD
            AT END MOVE HIGH-VALUES TO WS-MAST-CUSTOMER
        END-READ
    END-IF.
    IF TRANS-CUSTOMER-IN < WS-MAST-CUSTOMER
        WRITE NEW-MAST-RECORD-OUT FROM TRANS-RECORD-IN
        READ TRANS
            AT END MOVE HIGH-VALUES TO TRANS-CUSTOMER-IN
        END-READ
        ADD 1 TO TRANS-COUNT
    END-IF.
    IF TRANS-CUSTOMER-IN = WS-MAST-CUSTOMER
        PERFORM 600-PRINT-TRANS-RECORD
        READ TRANS
            AT END MOVE HIGH-VALUES TO TRANS-CUSTOMER-IN
        END-READ
        ADD 1 TO TRANS-COUNT
    END-IF.
    ...
```

Figure **13.16** *Essential processing for classical insertion updating, where unwanted matches can occur but duplicate TRANS primary keys cannot.*

Insertion Updating Can Involve
Transaction Records with Duplicate Keys

The program in Figure 13.16 assumed that no transaction records with duplicate primary keys were possible. A TRANS record with a duplicate primary key is a problem only if it does not match an OLD-MASTER primary key, since that would lead to insertion into the master of two records with the same primary key.

To eliminate such duplicate TRANS records, common practice is to preprocess the TRANS file to eliminate them. Occasionally, code is placed in the insertion update program to eliminate them, as already explained.

Classical deletion updating example

With classical deletion updating, the primary keys of the master records to be deleted are normally the only fields in the records of the transaction file. Both transaction and old master file are in ascending primary key order.

As with change and insertion updating, the old master file is not altered by the updating. Instead, a new master is generated, without the records that were to be deleted.

In the ideal case, every transaction record has a matching old master record, and there are no transaction records with duplicate primary keys. In the processing for this ideal case, the transaction file and old master are read in sequence, and current transaction and old master primary keys compared. Most of the keys will not match, so that an old master record just read is not deleted and is output to the new master. If the keys match, the old master record is simply not output to the new master.

The essential logic for the ideal case is

Case A. customer in cur-tr > customer in cur-om

ACTION

1. Write out old master in working storage as next new master record.
2. Read next old master record into working storage.

Case B. customer in cur-tr = customer in cur-om

ACTION

1. Read in next transaction record.
2. Read next old master record into working storage.

In practice, however, there can be transaction records that do not match any of the old master records. These unmatched records have to be rejected and listed in a control listing. The logic for this situation is

Case A. customer in cur-tr > customer in cur-om

ACTION

1. Write out old master in working storage as next new master record.
2. Read next old master record into working storage.

Case B. customer in cur-tr = customer in cur-om

ACTION

1. Read in next transaction record.
2. Read next old master record into working storage.

Case C. customer in cur-tr < customer in cur-om

ACTION

1. List current transaction record in control listing.
2. Read in next transaction record.

This logic automatically takes care of the case of transaction records with duplicate primary keys. The first of a sequence of duplicates (if it is a match) will delete a master record. The remaining duplicates of the sequence, since they cannot delete the record again, will simply be treated as unmatched records and listed in the control listing.

The essentials for the COBOL program for deletion updating of OLD-MASTER using TRANS to yield NEW-MASTER is shown in Figure 13.17. Note that this time, a TRANS record has a single field TRANS-CUSTOMER-IN. The program excerpt allows for unmatched TRANS records.

```
DATA DIVISION
FILE SECTION.
...
01  OLD-MAST-RECORD-IN                   PIC X(21).
...
01  NEW-MAST-RECORD-OUT                  PIC X(21).
...
01  TRANS-RECORD-IN.
    05  TRANS-CUSTOMER-IN                PIC X(15).
...
WORKING-STORAGE SECTION.
01  WS-MASTER-RECORD.
    05  WS-MAST-CUSTOMER                 PIC X(15).
    05  WS-MAST-OWING                    PIC 9(06).
...
PROCEDURE DIVISION.
100-MAIN-MODULE.
    OPEN ...
    READ OLD-MASTER INTO WS-MASTER-RECORD
                    AT END STOP RUN.
    READ TRANS
          AT END STOP RUN.
    MOVE 1 TO TRANS-COUNT.
    PERFORM 400-COMPARE
          UNTIL WS-MAST-CUSTOMER  = HIGH-VALUES
            AND TRANS-CUSTOMER-IN = HIGH-VALUES.
    CLOSE ...
    STOP RUN.
```

```
400-COMPARE.
    IF TRANS-CUSTOMER-IN > WS-MAST-CUSTOMER
        WRITE NEW-MAST-RECORD-OUT FROM WS-MASTER-RECORD
        READ OLD-MASTER INTO WS-MASTER-RECORD
            AT END MOVE HIGH-VALUES TO WS-MAST-CUSTOMER
    END-IF.
    IF TRANS-CUSTOMER-IN = WS-MAST-CUSTOMER
        READ TRANS
            AT END MOVE HIGH-VALUES TO TRANS-CUSTOMER-IN
        END-READ
        ADD 1 TO TRANS-COUNT
        READ OLD-MASTER INTO WS-MASTER-RECORD
            AT END MOVE HIGH-VALUES TO WS-MAST-CUSTOMER
    END-IF.
IF TRANS-CUSTOMER-IN < WS-MAST-CUSTOMER
    PERFORM 600-PRINT-TRANS-RECORD
    READ TRANS
        AT END MOVE HIGH-VALUES TO TRANS-CUSTOMER-IN
    END-READ
    ADD 1 TO TRANS-COUNT
    END-IF.
...
```

Figure 13.17 *Essential processing for classical deletion updating, where both unmatched and duplicate TRANS records can occur.*

Note that, once more, either TRANS or OLD-MASTER can end first. The end conditions are handled in this program excerpt as in insertion and change updating.

In commercial practice great care is taken when deleting records from a master file, and many checks are carried out. For example, it could be that in the case of the deletion of records from OLD-MASTER, notwithstanding the occurrence of the record's primary key in TRANS, the record would be deleted only if the owing value was also less than a certain small amount, say $1.00. This additional condition could be coded with

```
01 TRIVIAL-BALANCE      PIC 9V99    VALUE 1.00.
...
    IF TRANS-CUSTOMER-IN = WS-MAST-CUSTOMER
        IF WS-MAST-OWING >= TRIVIAL-BALANCE
          WRITE NEW-MAST-RECORD-OUT FROM WS-MASTER-RECORD
        END-IF
        READ TRANS
          AT END MOVE HIGH-VALUES TO TRANS-CUSTOMER-IN
        ADD 1 TO TRANS-COUNT
        READ OLD-MASTER INTO WS-MASTER-RECORD
          AT END MOVE HIGH-VALUES TO WS-MAST-CUSTOMER
    END-IF.
```

Since accounts must balance to the last cent, deletion of accounts receivable records with even trivial balances would probably have to be accompanied by corresponding updates to another file containing balancing accounting data. Note that it is also common practice to save deleted records in a separate file, in case the current master ever has to be regenerated from an earlier version (a recovery process).

Classical general updating is very common

Classical general updating involves carrying out two or more of change, insertion, and deletion updating in a single run. A transaction record is marked (typically with a 1, 2 or 3) in an update code field to indicate whether change, insertion, or deletion updating is to be performed. General updating often involves just a combination of change and insertion updating, with deletions being carried out separately. The latter is taken as an example, to illustrate the principles involved.

General Updating Involving Changes and Insertions

If we are carrying out combined change/insertion updating of the receivables file from previous sections, a transaction record would then have the structure

```
01 TRANS-RECORD-IN.
   05 TRANS-UPDATE-CODE-IN            PIC  9.
                          value 1, insertion, or 2, change
   05 TRANS-RECORD.
       10   TRANS-CUSTOMER-IN    PIC X(15).
       10   TRANS-AMOUNT-IN      PIC 9(06).
```

There are three main strategies for dealing with a transaction file such as this, which contains two types of update records.

1. Process the transaction file, and create one transaction file with update transaction records and another with insertion transactions. Then carry out separate insertion and change updates of the master using these two new transaction files, with insertion update first.
2. Sort the transaction file on the TRANS-UPDATE-CODE-IN field. The update program can then have two distinct parts. One part has the logic for insertion updating, as explained earlier; this part is used until all the insertion transaction records have been used up. The other part of the program has logic for change updating, as explained earlier, and is used with the remaining change transaction records.
3. Have the transaction file sorted primarily on the TRANS-CUSTOMER-IN field and, if duplicate TRANS-CUSTOMER-IN values can occur, sorted secondarily on TRANS-UPDATE-CODE-IN. Use this sorted version to update the master.

The first two strategies are straightforward. The third strategy can involve complex programming.

The logic of the programming for the third strategy will involve combining the logic for change and insertion updating given in earlier sections.

The combined logic required will depend on whether

- Change transaction records that do not match any master record can occur.
- Insertion transaction records that do match a master record can occur.
- Insertion and change transaction records with the same TRANS-CUSTOMER-IN value can occur in sequence.
- A sequence of change transaction records with the same TRANS-CUSTOMER-IN value can occur, and, if so, whether all the records of such a sequence should be used to update the master.
- A sequence of insertion transaction records with the same TRANS-CUSTOMER-IN value can occur.

As a result, there is no standard logic for combined change and insertion updating. The logic depends on what conditions apply. The more of the preceding conditions that apply, the more complex the logic.

Let us look at a fairly simple and common case, where only the first two of the conditions hold true. The only complexities for this case are:

- Change transaction records that do not match any master record can occur.
- Insertion transaction records that do match a master record can occur.

The logic for this case is

Case A. customer in cur-tr > customer in cur-om

ACTION

1. Write old WS-MAST-CUSTOMER in working storage to new master.
2. Read next old master record into working storage.

Case B. customer in cur-tr = customer in cur-om and update code indicates insertion

ACTION

1. List transaction record in control listing.
2. Read next transaction record.

Case C. customer in cur-tr = customer in cur-om and update code indicates change

ACTION

1. Update old master in working storage using transaction record.
2. Read next transaction record.

Case D. customer in cur-tr < customer in cur-om and update code indicates insertion

ACTION.

1. Write transaction record to new master.
2. Read next transaction record.

Case E. customer in cur-tr < customer in cur-om and update code indicates change

ACTION

1. List transaction in control listing.
2. Read next transaction record.

The essential COBOL code that incorporates this updating logic in the TRANS OLD-MASTER and NEW-MASTER files from previous sections is shown in Figure 13.18.

This program excerpt looks after end-of-file conditions. Either TRANS or OLD-MASTER can end first. If TRANS ends first, remaining OLD-MASTER records are written to NEW-MASTER. Conversely, remaining TRANS records are written to the control listing if they are change update records, and to NEW-MASTER if they are insertion update records.

```
DATA DIVISION.
FILE SECTION.
...
01   OLD-MAST-RECORD-IN          PIC X(21).
...
01   NEW-MAST-RECORD-OUT         PIC X(21).
...
01 TRANS-RECORD-IN.
     05  TRANS-UPDATE-CODE-IN     PIC  9.          value 1, insertion, or 2, change
     05  TRANS-RECORD.
         10   TRANS-CUSTOMER-IN    PIC X(15).
         10   TRANS-AMOUNT-IN      PIC 9(06).
...
WORKING-STORAGE SECTION.
01   WS-MASTER-RECORD.
     05  WS-MAST-CUSTOMER         PIC X(15).
     05  WS-MAST-OWING            PIC 9(06).
...
PROCEDURE DIVISION.
100-MAIN-MODULE.
    OPEN . . .
    READ OLD-MASTER INTO WS-MASTER-RECORD
                    AT END STOP RUN.
    READ TRANS
         AT END STOP RUN.
    PERFORM 400-COMPARE
         UNTIL WS-MAST-CUSTOMER  = HIGH-VALUES
           AND TRANS-CUSTOMER-IN = HIGH-VALUES.
    CLOSE...
    STOP RUN.
```

```
400-COMPARE.
    IF TRANS-CUSTOMER-IN > WS-MAST-CUSTOMER
        WRITE NEW-MAST-RECORD-OUT FROM WS-MASTER-RECORD
        READ OLD-MASTER INTO WS-MASTER-RECORD
            AT END MOVE HIGH-VALUES TO WS-MAST-CUSTOMER
    END-IF.
    IF TRANS-CUSTOMER-IN = WS-MAST-CUSTOMER
                AND TRANS-UPDATE-CODE-IN = 1                    insertion
        PERFORM 700-PRINT-TRANS-RECORD
        READ TRANS
            AT END MOVE HIGH-VALUES TO TRANS-CUSTOMER-IN
    END-IF.
    IF TRANS-CUSTOMER-IN = WS-MAST-CUSTOMER
                AND TRANS-UPDATE-CODE-IN = 2                    change
        PERFORM 600-CHANGE-UPDATE
    END-IF.
    IF TRANS-CUSTOMER-IN < WS-MAST-CUSTOMER
                AND TRANS-UPDATE-CODE-IN = 1                    insertion
        PERFORM 500-INSERTION-UPDATE
    END-IF.
    IF TRANS-CUSTOMER-IN < WS-MAST-CUSTOMER
                AND TRANS-UPDATE-CODE-IN = 2                    change
        PERFORM 700-PRINT-TRANS-RECORD
        READ TRANS
            AT END MOVE HIGH-VALUES TO TRANS-CUSTOMER-IN
    END-IF.
500-INSERTION-UPDATE.
    WRITE NEW-MAST-RECORD-OUT FROM TRANS-RECORD-IN.
    READ TRANS
        AT END MOVE HIGH-VALUES TO TRANS-CUSTOMER-IN.
600-CHANGE-UPDATE.
    SUBTRACT TRANS-AMOUNT-IN FROM WS-MAST-OWING.
    READ TRANS
            AT END MOVE HIGH-VALUES TO TRANS-CUSTOMER-IN.
700-PRINT-TRANS-RECORD.
    ...
```

Figure 13.18 *Essential processing for combined change and insertion updating,*
where TRANS records with duplicate customers cannot occur.

General Updating Involving Changes, Deletions, and Insertions

Updating a sequential file from a transaction file, where a transaction
record can cause a change update, a deletion update, or an insertion update,
is slightly more complex. However, it can be handled by the principles
described in the previous section.

13.3
Rewrite updating

*I*N THE PREVIOUS sections we examined the classical updating method for sequential files. Recall that the classical technique can be used with sequential master files on either disk or tape. The other method of updating is the rewrite method. However, this method can be used only with master files on disk; and it is suitable only for change updating. Consequently, rewrite updating of sequential files is not very common. (Note that some COBOL compilers may not allow rewrite updating with sequential files. It is allowed with COBOL 85. Check your manual.)

Basis of rewrite updating

In updating the master, each record is read in ascending primary key order. If the record does not need change updating (there is no transaction record with a matching key), nothing is done with it. When a master record is read whose key matches the key of the first transaction record, that master record is updated and written back, or rewritten, over the original master record on disk. The next transaction record is then read; and then master records are read one by one, and ignored, until again a master record is encountered that matches the latest transaction record. Once again, this record is updated and rewritten over the original record on disk, and so on.

Rewriting a record just read over the original copy in the file is normally possible only with records in disk files. It is not possible with normal tape files, since once a record is read, the tape has moved forward and the original record can no longer be accessed, much less overwritten. With a disk file, once a record is read from a track, that track is rotating, so the same record passes the read/write head about once every 15 milliseconds (the rotation time of the disk). Thus, with a sequential disk file, it is possible for a record just read to be rewritten later, so long as that is before the next record is read.

COBOL REWRITE verb

The command used to rewrite a record on disk that has just been read is the REWRITE verb, which, except for the word "REWRITE," has the same syntax as WRITE.

The following are valid REWRITE sentences:

```
REWRITE MASTER-RECORD-OUT.
REWRITE MASTER-RECORD-OUT FROM WS-MASTER-RECORD.
```

Remember that the record rewritten by a REWRITE statement will overwrite the record most recently read by a READ statement. Thus you can have

```
READ XFILE INTO B, AT END ...
REWRITE XFILE-RECORD-OUT FROM C.
```

Here a record from the file XFILE is read and placed in the working-storage structure B. Then the contents of an entirely different working-storage structure, C, are used to overwrite the record just read on the disk. (If you have studied the use of REWRITE with indexed files, covered in Chapter 14, note that you may not use the INVALID KEY clause with REWRITE in sequential files.)

When using rewrite updating you must have READ and REWRITE statements, so you must have both input and output of records with a single file. The OPEN statement is:

```
OPEN I-O XFILE.
```

You cannot open the file for either INPUT or OUTPUT; it must be opened for both, that is for I-O.

Summary

1. Tape files are always sequential files. Disk files can be either sequential or direct-access files. A master sequential file can thus be either a tape or disk file. Records of a sequential disk or tape file are recorded in blocks. A block of records is transmitted between buffer and storage medium. The input area identifier that holds an input record is mobile within the block of records in the input buffer. The output area identifier is similarly mobile. On creation, a sequential master file must be validated.
2. Sequential master files are commonly updated using the classic updating technique. Update data is stored in a transaction file, whose records are in ascending primary key order. Records from the transaction file and the original master file are used to generate a new master file.
3. Classic updating involves change updating, insertion updating, deletion updating, and any combination of these. Processing can be complicated by the need to reject unmatched transaction records in the case of change and deletion updating, and matching transaction records in the case of insertion updating.

Key Terms

control listing   classical method
transaction file   rewrite method

Concept Review Questions

1. Explain the concepts of master and transaction files.
2. Distinguish sequential and direct-access files.
3. When a sequential file is recorded on disk, how are the records placed with respect to tracks and surfaces?
4. Explain the concept of a disk cylinder.
5. What is an input/output routine?
6. Explain the concept of file organization using the concept of an input/output routine.

7. Explain why input and output area (buffer) identifiers have to be mobile in memory with a sequential file.
8. Why are double buffers more efficient with a sequential file?
9. Why is data validation important with the creation of a master file?
10. List the kinds of classical sequential file updating.
11. Distinguish rewrite and classical sequential file updating.
12. Why is rewrite updating little used with sequential files?
13. List the kinds of validation checks that are typically made on a field of a new master sequential file.
14. What are father and grandfather files, and what are they used for?
15. List some common unique sets of conditions that may apply to classical change updating.
16. When are transaction records most likely to contain duplicate primary keys?
17. Why should it not normally be necessary for a change update program to check for unwanted duplicate primary keys in transaction records?
18. Why should it not normally be necessary for a change update program to check for out-of-sequence transaction records?
19. List some common sets of conditions that may apply to classical insertion updating.
20. List some common sets of conditions that may apply to classical deletion updating.
21. How could you handle general updating that includes more than one of change, insertion, and deletion updating, triggered by an appropriate code in transaction records?
22. How does a disk permit rewrite change updating with a sequential file?
23. Why are rewrite insertion and deletion updating not practical with sequential files?
24. Explain two different kinds of control listing for classical updating.

COBOL Language Questions

1. What is wrong with

```
IF TRANS-KEY-IN = WS-MASTER-KEY
    SUBTRACT TRANS-AMOUNT-IN FROM WS-MASTER-AMOUNT
    READ TRANS-FILE
        AT END MOVE HIGH-VALUES TO TRANS-KEY-IN
    ADD 1 TO TRANS-COUNT
END-IF.
```

Fix it.

2. Write a routine to remove transaction records with duplicate keys from a transaction file TRANS, in which the input area identifier is

```
01 TRANS-RECORD-IN.
    05 TR-KEY-IN      PIC X(04).
    05 TR-AMOUNT1-IN  PIC 9(04)V99.
    05 TR-AMOUNT2-IN  PIC 9(02)V99.
```

3. Write a routine to remove out-of-sequence records from the transaction file in question 2.

4. Assume a sequential master file MASTER, in which the working-storage record identifier is

```
01 WS-MASTER-RECORD.
   01 WS-MASTER-KEY        PIC X(04).
   01 WS-MASTER-LOCATION   PIC X(10).
   01 WS-MASTER-TOTAL1     PIC 9(05)V99.
   05 WS-MASTER-TOTAL2     PIC 9(03)V99.
```

Assume a transaction file TRANS, in which the input area identifier is

```
01 TRANS-RECORD-IN.
   05 TR-KEY-IN       PIC X(04).
   05 TR-AMOUNT1-IN   PIC 9(04)V99.
   05 TR-AMOUNT2-IN   PIC 9(02)V99.
```

MASTER is change updated from TRANS by adding AMOUNT1 to TOTAL1, and AMOUNT2 to TOTAL2. Given this information, write the classical change update routine, assuming no duplicate TRANS records and no unmatched TRANS records.

5. Rewrite the routine in question 4 to allow for unmatched TRANS records.

6. Assume the MASTER and TRANS files in question 4. Write the classical deletion update routine, assuming no duplicate TRANS records and no unmatched TRANS records.

7. Rewrite the routine in question 6 to allow for some unmatched TRANS records.

Programming Assignments

1. **Classical change updating a master file**
A record of an established master file OLD-MASTER describes the inventory of a part in a warehouse. The master records are:

```
---------1---------2
A019400157178J050
A025801594255B106
B429405402750F155
C437610006025B007
C346705004250L055
D018502833045K199
D029405608280B140
D117612506530K230
E036700707250A185
E099401506640T130
E175802855500A178
E366714009265B240
F014909508500K160
```

Columns		
01–05	Part type identification code, primary key	
06–09	Quantity in warehouse	
10–13	Price per unit ($dd.dd)	
14–17	Bin code (bin contains the parts; only one bin can contain a given type of part)	

Records of the transaction file are:

```
---------1---------2
A02580100A
A02580050S
C23940100A
C43760074S
D01850100A
D02940700S
E09940100A
EO9940200S
E17581200A
```

Columns 01–05   Part type identification code, not unique
        06–09   Quantity removed from (S) or added to (A)
                           warehouse
        10   Add or Subtract code

Transaction records are sorted primarily on the transaction code and secondarily on the add/subtract code. Transaction records with duplicate transaction code values are processed normally (that is, each record of a group with duplicate transaction codes will cause an update to the same master record).

The transaction file is used to update the quantity field in the master. Assume that unmatched transaction records can occur. Unmatched records are to be printed in a control file.

Note: In the case of withdrawal of parts, if the quantity of parts on hand is less than the quantity in the transaction record, the transaction record is printed in the control file with an explanation of the problem. The control listing appears as follows:

```
---------1---------2---------3---------4---------5---------6---------7
            CHANGE UPDATE CONTROL LISTING (TRANS ERROR RECORDS)
PAGE   1                                                    07/12/92


PART   QTY   OPERATION   UPDATE        PROBLEM
                         STATUS

A0258  0100  ADD         DONE
A0258  0050  SUBTR.      DONE
C2394  0100  ADD         REJECTED   UNMATCHED PART CODE
C4376  0074  SUBTR.      DONE
D0185  0100  ADD         DONE
D0294  0700  SUBTR.      REJECTED   TOO FEW PARTS IN MASTER
E0994  0100  ADD         DONE
EO994  0200  SUBTR.      DONE
E1758  1200  ADD         DONE
```

  a. Draw spacing charts for the files.
  b. Make a list of error messages to be used.
  c. Draw a flowchart and hierarchy diagram.
  d. Write the program using classical change updating.

2. **Insertion updating assignment**

In this assignment the same master file as in Assignment 2 is used. This time new records are to be inserted into the master from a transaction file, in which the records are as follows:

```
---------1---------2---------3
A1185001035,47K188
B4294010027,80F155
C3467300754,0L055
C4449100085,40K173
E0994025065,40T130
E1267005025,30G149
F2094150034,60K143
F3494008055,25M280
```

Columns	01–05	Part type identification code, primary key
	06–09	Quantity in warehouse
	10–13	Price per unit ($dd.dd)
	14–17	Bin code (bin contains the parts)

Transaction records with matching keys can occur.

The control listing for the update appears as follows:

```
---------1---------2---------3---------4---------5---------6---------7
        INSERTION UPDATE CONTROL LISTING (TRANS ERROR RECORDS)
PAGE  1                                              07/12/92

PART  QTY   PRICE  BIN  INSERTION  PROBLEM
                        STATUS


A1185 0010  35.47  K188 ACCEPTED
B4294 0100  27.80  F155 REJECTED   MATCHING KEY
C3467 0300  75.40  L055 REJECTED   MATCHING KEY
C4449 1000  85.40  K173 ACCEPTED
E0994 0250  65.40  T130 REJECTED   MATCHING KEY
E1267 0050  25.30  G149 ACCEPTED
F2094 1500  34.60  K143 ACCEPTED
F3494 0080  55.25  M280 ACCEPTED
```

a. Draw spacing charts for the files.
b. Draw flowchart and hierarchy diagram.
c. Write the program.

3. **General classical updating**
   The master file to be updated is the same as in Assignment 2. The transaction file contains insertion records (update code I0) and change update records (update codes A0 and S0). Update codes are the first two characters of each transaction record. The transaction file is

```
---------1---------2---------3
A0A02580100bbbbbbbb
S0A02580050bbbbbbbb
I0A118500103547K188
I0B429401002780F155
A0C23940100bbbbbbbb
I0C346703007540L055
S0C43760074bbbbbbbb
I0C444910008540K173
S0C44490200bbbbbbbb
A0D01850100bbbbbbbb
S0D02940700bbbbbbbb
I0E099402506540T130
A0E09940100bbbbbbbb
S0E09940200bbbbbbbb
I0E126700502530G149
A0E17581100bbbbbbbb
I0F109415003460K143
I0F349400805525M280
```

Columns 01–02	Update code (I0 insertion, A0 change with addition, S0 change with subtraction)
03–07	Part type identification code, primary key
08–11	Quantity of parts
12–15	Price per unit ($dd.dd) or blanks
16–19	Bin code (bin contains the parts) or blanks

Note the following conditions:

- Insertion transaction records with matching keys can occur.
- For a given transaction code, insertion records come before change records, and addition change records come before subtraction change records.
- Change records with duplicate transaction code values are processed normally (that is, each change record of a group with duplicate transaction codes will cause an update to the same master record).

The update is accompanied by output of a control listing. There is a record in the control listing giving the fate of every transaction record.

a. Design the control listing.
b. Make a list of error messages to be used.
c. Draw spacing charts for the files.
d. Draw a flowchart and hierarchy diagram.
e. Write the program.

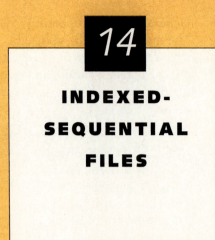

14
INDEXED-SEQUENTIAL FILES

OBJECTIVES

- To explain how indexed-sequential files are structured
- To demonstrate creating and updating indexed-sequential files
- To describe secondary keys and their manipulation.

OUTLINE

14.1 The index is the major feature of an indexed-sequential file

An index relates a primary key to a disk address
An index is searched by an input/output routine
You can have an index to an index: multiple-level indexes
ISAM and VSAM indexes are the most common
Record insertions cause problems
There are many ways to process an indexed-sequential file
You need a sample indexed-sequential file called INDEXED-MASTER
  Sequential-access mode (ACCESS SEQUENTIAL)
    OPEN OUTPUT
    OPEN INPUT
    OPEN I-O
  Direct-access mode (ACCESS RANDOM)
    OPEN I-O
    OPEN INPUT
    OPEN OUTPUT
  Dynamic-access mode (ACCESS DYNAMIC)
    OPEN INPUT
    OPEN OUTPUT
    OPEN I-O

14.2 An indexed-sequential file must first be created

A sample indexed-sequential file creation program
Control listing for indexed file creation is normal
Primary keys should be alphanumeric
The FILE STATUS clause works well for deciding the nature of errors

14.3 Indexed-sequential files permit flexible updating

14.4 Indexed-sequential files are often used for information retrieval

14.5 A secondary index permits direct-access on a non-primary key field

14.6 The START verb permits sequential processing from any position in the file

CHAPTER 13 pointed out that sequential and direct-access files are the two main types of files. With a sequential file, if you want to retrieve record number 10,000 from the file, you must first read record numbers 1 through 9999. With a direct-access file you can simply read record number 10,000 directly .

There are several kinds of direct-access file in use in commerce, but by far the most common is the indexed-sequential file. It is called an *indexed-sequential* file because it combines the properties of a sequential file and a direct-access file. Thus, when you want to read record number 10,000 in the file, if you like, you can first read records 1 through 9999. But you can also read record number 10,000 directly. A separately stored index is used to facilitate direct-access. An indexed-sequential file must be a disk file.

This chapter begins with the principles behind indexed-sequential files. Then it goes on to show how to create and update an indexed-sequential file and how to use one for information retrieval. Finally, it shows how a special type of index called a *secondary index* is useful for information retrieval.

14.1
The index is the major feature of an indexed-sequential file

AN INDEXED-SEQUENTIAL file is first of all a sequential file on disk. However, an additional structure is stored on disk, as well as the records of the file. This structure is an index to the records of the file and is used to permit direct-access to the records.

Cylinder	Track				
110	0	ABENDON	ABINDRON	ABURTON	ACABY
110	1	ACETURN	ACEVY	ACIDRON	ACIFUR
110	2	ACONTRON	ACOPPUR	ACUTCORP	AEFIRON
111	0	AFARON	AFATROP	AFAWAY	AFBRON
111	1	AFBRUN	AFCRON	AFDRUP	AFETRAP
111	2	AFEWAY	AFFAGON	AFFAKRON	AFFAVROFF
112	0	AFFOTRON	AFFOWAIT	AFFUDRA	AFFUFRON
112	1	AFGRAN	AFGRAP	AFGRASPAT	AFGRON
112	2	AFGROP	AFGRUP	AFGRUWAY	AFHADRON
113	0	AFJONSON	AFJOTRON	AFJUPRAY	AFKROP

⋮   ⋮   ⋮

Figure 14.1 *Records of an indexed-sequential file are laid out on tracks and cylinders, in increasing cylinder order. The file does not have to start at the first cylinder; the one shown here starts at cylinder 110. For this diagram, three tracks per cylinder and four records per track have been assumed. Records on a track are normally blocked (this is not shown).*

An index relates a primary key to a disk address

Records of an indexed-sequential file are stored on disk in ascending primary key order, starting on the track 0 of the lowest cylinder used. This is illustrated in Figure 14.1, in which four records per track have been assumed and three tracks per cylinder. In practice, there might be 15 tracks per cylinder.

In order to directly extract a record from the file, a read/write head has to be adjacent to the correct track. Thus, if you want to extract a record with primary key value of 'BORCORP', you must know at least the cylinder and track on which that record is stored in order to move the comb of read/write heads to the correct cylinder and select the correct read/write head.

The cylinder number, track number, and block number for where a record is stored is the record's *disk address*. However, Figure 14.1 just shows the cylinder number and track number for each record. With some systems, the disk address of a record is its cylinder number, track number, and sector number; with these systems each track is divided into sectors, instead of blocks. Each sector is typically 512 bytes. (Whether a disk address is considered to use sector numbers or block numbers is immaterial to the following discussion.)

The comb of read/write heads cannot be moved to the correct cylinder and track to retrieve a record unless the disk address of the record is known. This means there has to be a way of determining a record's disk address from its primary key before it can be directly accessed. The index is what enables the computer to determine the record's address given its primary key.

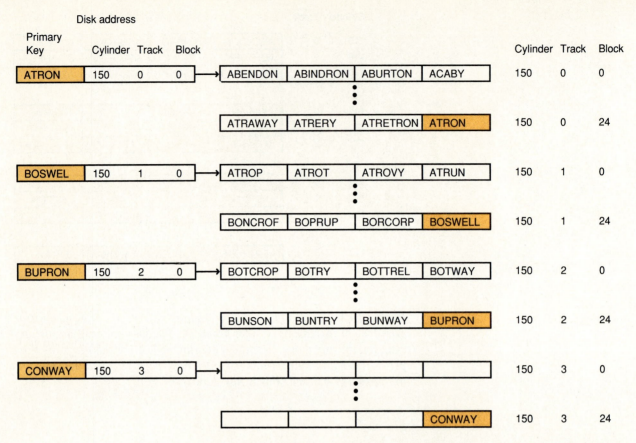

Disk address

Primary Key	Cylinder	Track	Block						Cylinder	Track	Block
ATRON	150	0	0	→	ABENDON	ABINDRON	ABURTON	ACABY	150	0	0
					ATRAWAY	ATRERY	ATRETRON	ATRON	150	0	24
BOSWEL	150	1	0	→	ATROP	ATROT	ATROVY	ATRUN	150	1	0
					BONCROF	BOPRUP	BORCORP	BOSWELL	150	1	24
BUPRON	150	2	0	→	BOTCROP	BOTRY	BOTTREL	BOTWAY	150	2	0
					BUNSON	BUNTRY	BUNWAY	BUPRON	150	2	24
CONWAY	150	3	0	→					150	3	0
								CONWAY	150	3	24

Figure 14.2 Indexed-sequential file with a one-level index. There is an index entry for each 100 records (the number of records on a track, with 25 blocks each containing four records). The index entry contains the primary key of the last record of a group of 100 records and the disk address of the first. Typically, there is an index entry for the group of records on each track, as in this example. However, any record grouping will do.

An index is a collection of index entries. A file with an index is called an indexed file. The records of an indexed file are divided into groups, such as the group of records on a track, or any other convenient group, depending on the computer system. An entry in an index for an indexed file will consist of the last primary key in such a group of records, plus the disk address of the first primary key of the group of records. This is illustrated in Figure 14.2 for the records of a file of receivables data, in which the primary key is the customer name. In this file, it is assumed there are four records to a block and 25 blocks to a track, for 100 records per track. Thus, there is an index entry for the group of records on each track.

An index is searched by an input/output routine

You learned in Chapter 13 that when a READ or WRITE statement in a COBOL program is executed to read or write a record in a file, a special subsidiary routine called an input/output routine (or access method, with IBM systems) is executed. The input/output routine does the work of reading or writing a record.

The input/output routine required for carrying out READ, WRITE, and REWRITE commands with an indexed-sequential file is complex and expensive, since it has to look after all the details of managing and searching the index. With most computer systems, an access method for managing indexed-sequential files is an optional extra, so a smaller computer installation may not have one.

To grasp the essentials of what the input/output routine does in retrieving a record from an indexed-sequential file, refer to the file and associated index in Figure 14.2. Suppose a READ statement is executed in a COBOL program for retrieval of a record with the key BUNTRY. The input/output routine would first access the index, in which each entry can be considered as a record of a sequential file. The input/output routine would read each "record," or entry, of the index in sequence, until it reads the first entry with a key greater than BUNTRY. This is the index entry for BUPRON.

The input/output routine would then take the disk address from that index entry and use it to examine the first of the group of records beginning at track 2 of cylinder 150. If that record did not have key BUNTRY, it would examine the next record, and the next, and so on, until it either comes to the BUPRON record at end of the group (in which case the record sought is not in the file) or it arrives at the target BUNTRY record. The BUNTRY record is then retrieved and delivered to the input buffer record for that file.

You can have an index to an index: multiple-level indexes

The index in Figure 14.2 is a one-level index. Suppose the file has 1,000,000 records, and there is an entry in the index for each 100 records, which would be typical in practice. Thus, the index would have 10,000 entries. To search this index looking for a key near to a specific target record, on average 5000 index entries would have to be accessed in sequence. This would be rather slow, but much faster than accessing half the records in the entire file (500,000 records).

Call the index in Figure 14.2 "index-level-1." To speed up the search, a further index could be added. This new index (index-level-2) is an index to the entries in index-level-1 (see Figure 14.3). For each 100 entries in index-level-1, there could be an entry in index-level-2, so that index-level-2 could have only 100 entries.

The original index-level-1 entries are divided into groups of 100 entries. For each group of entries there is an entry in index-level-2, consisting of the disk address of the first of the 100 entries and the primary key in the last. In Figure 14.3, disk addresses are shown as pointer arrows.

To search for a record now, the input/output routine would scan index-level-2 until it came to the first entry with a key greater than the target. This entry would point to a group of entries in index-level-1, which would then be scanned in sequence until the first entry with a key greater than the target record key was found. This entry would point to a group of records on the disk, which would in turn be scanned in sequence until either the target record was found or it was confirmed that the record was not in the file.

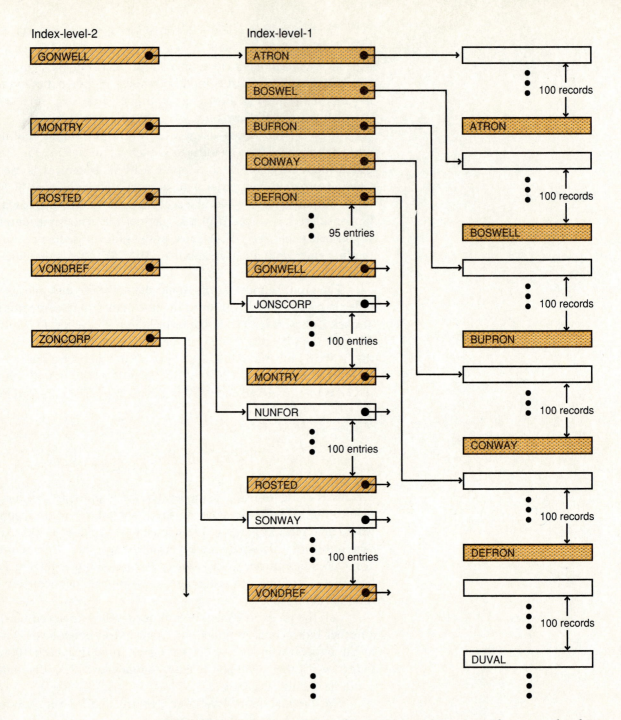

Figure 14.3 *Extension of the index in Figure 14.2, to provide a second index level called index-level-2. There are 100 entries in index-level-1 for each entry in index-level-2.*

Such a two-level index cuts down the number of index entries to be examined, and thus increases the speed with which a target record can be retrieved. In practice, with a large file an index with three or more index levels (a *multiple-level index*) would be used.

ISAM and VSAM indexes are the most common

The best known and most widely used input/output routine (or access method) for indexed-sequential files is VSAM from IBM (pronounced *vee-sam*). It is an acronym for "virtual sequential access method." VSAM is large; it can occupy as much as one million characters of memory space. Another common, but now somewhat obsolete access method for indexed-sequential files, is IBM's ISAM (pronounced *eyesam*), for "indexed sequential access method."

With ISAM, there is an index entry for each group of records on a track, and this lowest-level index is called a track index. The next index level is the cylinder index. There is a cylinder index entry for each cylinder of records. There are also higher-level index levels.

With VSAM the groupings of records for which there is an index entry can vary from one file to another. They are defined in Job Control Language statements for the file. For practical purposes, it is useful to regard the lowest level VSAM index as roughly equivalent to an ISAM track index, and the next level of a VSAM index as roughly equivalent to an ISAM cylinder index.

Record insertions cause problems

Recall that an indexed-sequential file is first of all a sequential file. The records must be stored in ascending primary key order to permit an index to be used. However, you saw that with sequential files, if you want to insert records (an insertion update), you have to create a new version of the file, containing the old records plus the new records. That is not acceptable with a direct-access file (you would have to copy the index too), so is it necessary to insert records straight into the existing file.

The problem with inserting a record into a file that has records ordered in increasing primary key order, is that there is normally no space between records. However, with indexed-sequential files, space is scattered systematically throughout the file when it is created. And further space is created as records are deleted. Thus, when a new record is inserted, by moving existing records up or down in the file to the nearest space, a new record can be placed in the correct ascending primary key order. Again, the input/output routine manages this when a WRITE command is executed that inserts a record into an existing indexed-sequential file. The input/output routine also uses the index to determine where in the file the record should go. At the same time, the input/output routine looks after any adjustments needed to the index as a result of the insertion.

What if there is no space left to insert new records? In that case the input/output routine takes drastic action. In the case of VSAM and similar systems, it literally splits portions of the file and moves them elsewhere on the disk in order to make room. This technique is known as block-splitting. However, the details do not concern a programmer writing a program to manipulate an indexed-sequential file. The access method looks after it all.

In contrast, with ISAM, such excess records are placed in a separate overflow area of disk, and connected to the rest of the file by identifiers that contain disk addresses (pointer fields). Since following pointers is a slow business, after many record insertions access to an ISAM file becomes slow and the file has to be reorganized. This reorganization consists of reading the records of the old ISAM file and using them to create a new ISAM file. This can be done by means of a utility program.

There are many ways to process an indexed-sequential file

Because an indexed-sequential file is a sequential file on disk, it can be processed sequentially. Because it is also a direct-access file, it can be processed by direct-access. The following discussion is based on VSAM. It also applies to ISAM, with only minor modifications, which will be pointed out.

To specify an indexed-sequential file called INDEXED-MASTER, with a primary key CUSTOMER, you must place the clause ORGANIZATION IS INDEXED and RECORD KEY IS CUSTOMER in the SELECT entry.

You can access an indexed-sequential file in one of three access modes. These are

- **Sequential-access mode** This permits the file to be processed as a sequential disk file, but with rewrite updating only. You code "ACCESS MODE IS SEQUENTIAL" with the SELECT statement.
- **Random- (or direct-) access mode** This permits only direct-access. You code "ACCESS MODE IS RANDOM" with the SELECT statement.
- **Dynamic-access mode** This permits both sequential and direct-access processing. You code "ACCESS MODE IS DYNAMIC" with the SELECT statement. (With ISAM there is no DYNAMIC access mode.)

For each of these access modes, the file can be opened in three ways:

```
OPEN INPUT ...
OPEN OUTPUT ...
OPEN I-O ...
```

Combining access modes with opening possibilities gives you nine different ways to process the file. For each of these ways, some or all of READ, WRITE, REWRITE, DELETE, and START statements can be used. You have already encountered READ, WRITE, and REWRITE with sequential files. DELETE is used to delete a record in an existing indexed-sequential file. START is used to begin sequential processing at a specific point in the file with both ACCESS SEQUENTIAL and ACCESS DYNAMIC. The START verb is covered in detail in Section 14.6.

You need a sample indexed-sequential file called INDEXED-MASTER

Let us now examine each of the three access modes—SEQUENTIAL, RANDOM and DYNAMIC—in more detail. An indexed sequential file INDEXED-MASTER will be used to illustrate the ideas. Each record of the file describes an account receivable. The fields are IM-CUSTOMER, which identifies a customer who owes money, and IM-OWING, which gives the amount owing. Some records are:

```
IM-CUSTOMER       IM-OWING

ARTFIELD          145000
AVRILCORP         057500
BANKCORP          155000
BUNTORAMO         078000
...
```

The field IM-CUSTOMER is the primary key and records of the file are always maintained in ascending IM-CUSTOMER order. The buffer record for the file would be specified as

```
FD    INDEXED-MASTER              LABEL RECORDS ARE STANDARD.
01    IM-MASTER-BUFFER-RECORD.
      05  IM-CUSTOMER     PIC X(15).
      05  IM-OWING        PIC 9(06).
```

A WORKING-STORAGE identifier to hold an INDEXED-MASTER record would be

```
WORKING-STORAGE.
01 WS-MASTER-RECORD.
    05 WS-MAST-CUSTOMER      PIC X(15).
    05 WS-MAST-OWING         PIC 9(06).
```

With an ISAM file, it is good practice to leave an additional one-character field (a delete byte) at the beginning of each record.

```
01 WS-MASTER-RECORD.
    05 DELETE-BYTE           PIC X.
    05 WS-MAST-CUSTOMER      PIC X(15).
    05 WS-MAST-OWING         PIC 9(06).
```

When a record is deleted, instead of removing the record from the disk, ISAM places HIGH-VALUES in the delete byte. A deleted ISAM record can be read by a direct-access READ statement, although this can be prevented by appropriate accompanying Job Control Language statements.

Sequential-Access Mode (ACCESS SEQUENTIAL)

For sequential-access mode, you specify ACCESS MODE IS SEQUENTIAL in the SELECT statement for the indexed-sequential file INDEXED-MASTER, as follows:

```
INPUT-OUTPUT SECTION.
FILE-CONTROL.
     SELECT INDEXED-MASTER
          ASSIGN TO MAST234
          ORGANIZATION IS INDEXED
          ACCESS MODE IS SEQUENTIAL
          RECORD KEY IS IM-CUSTOMER [IN IM-MASTER-BUFFER-RECORD].
```

Note that you also specify the primary key IM-CUSTOMER in the RECORD KEY clause. The primary key IM-CUSTOMER so specified must be defined within the buffer (input area) record definition (IM-MASTER-BUFFER-RECORD) for the file.

The preceding SELECT statement applies to VSAM. If an ISAM file were involved, you would have the following, with the differences shown in bold:

```
INPUT-OUTPUT SECTION.
FILE-CONTROL.
    SELECT INDEXED-MASTER
          ASSIGN TO DA-I-MAST234
          ACCESS MODE IS SEQUENTIAL
          NOMINAL KEY IS IM-CUSTOMER.
```

The ORGANIZATION IS INDEXED entry is not required.

OPEN OUTPUT   OPEN OUTPUT is used for creating the file originally. You must open the file with

```
OPEN OUTPUT INDEXED-MASTER.
```

You can use only WRITE statements and records must be written out in ascending CUSTOMER order. You can use WRITE statements of the form

```
WRITE IM-MASTER-BUFFER-RECORD FROM SOURCE-RECORD
    INVALID KEY PERFORM 800-ERROR-ROUTINE.
```

The INVALID KEY clause is optional, but will be executed if you try to write an out-of-sequence record or a record with a duplicate key. The index is created as the records are written out.

OPEN INPUT   OPEN INPUT is used for normal reading of the records in ascending primary key order, for such purposes as generating reports. You open the file with

```
OPEN INPUT INDEXED-MASTER.
```

You can use only READ . . . AT END . . . END-READ statements like those for sequential files. You may not use the INVALID KEY option here.

You can also use the START verb to begin reading at a point other than the beginning of the file.

OPEN I-O   OPEN I-O is used for change updating in the manner of rewrite updating with sequential files. You open with

```
OPEN I-O INDEXED-MASTER.
```

You can use READ and REWRITE statements, like those for rewrite updating with sequential disk files, except that you can use the INVALID KEY option with REWRITE. You read records in sequence with READ . . . AT END . . . END-READ statements. A REWRITE replaces, or overwrites, the record most recently read with a READ statement, as in

```
READ INDEXED-MASTER INTO WS-MASTER-RECORD
     AT END MOVE 'NO' TO MORE-RECORDS.
ADD TRANS-PAYMENT-IN TO WS-MAST-OWING.
```

```
REWRITE IM-MASTER-BUFFER-RECORD FROM WS-MASTER-RECORD
    [INVALID KEY PERFORM 900-WRONG-PRIMARY-KEY].
```

The INVALID KEY clause is executed if the primary key (IM-CUSTOMER) value in the buffer record does not match that of the most recently read record.

You may also use a DELETE statement to delete the most recently read record. You can use the INVALID KEY option with DELETE.

```
READ INDEXED-MASTER INTO WS-MASTER-RECORD
    AT END MOVE 'NO' TO MORE-RECORDS.
DELETE INDEXED-MASTER
        [INVALID KEY PERFORM 500-ERROR-ROUTINE].
```

The INVALID KEY clause is executed if the primary key (IM-CUSTOMER) value in the buffer record does not match that of the most recently read record.

You may not use WRITE to insert a new record, however:

```
READ TRANS INTO WS-MASTER-RECORD
        AT END ...
WRITE IM-MASTER-BUFFER-RECORD FROM WS-MASTER-RECORD.   error!
```

You can also use the START verb to begin reading at a specific record, instead of at the beginning of the file.

Direct-Access Mode (ACCESS RANDOM)

For direct-access mode, you must code ACCESS MODE IS RANDOM with the SELECT entry.

```
INPUT-OUTPUT SECTION.
FILE-CONTROL.
    SELECT INDEXED-MASTER
            ASSIGN TO MAST234
            ORGANIZATION IS INDEXED
            ACCESS MODE IS RANDOM
            RECORD KEY IS IM-CUSTOMER [IN IM-MASTER-BUFFER-RECORD].
```

You must specify the name of the primary key (IM-CUSTOMER) in the RECORD KEY clause. The primary key field so specified must appear in the specification of the buffer (input area record) IM-MASTER-BUFFER-RECORD for the indexed sequential file.

OPEN I-O   With this type of processing, you can retrieve a record directly with a READ, you can insert a record directly with a WRITE, you can update a record directly with a READ and REWRITE, and you can delete a record directly with a DELETE. You may not use the START verb.

1. Direct-access READ
   You can use a direct-access READ to retrieve a record directly.
   To retrieve the record with primary key value 'SMITH', you could code

```
01 TARGET-KEY      PIC  X(15)     VALUE 'SMITH'.
    ...
       MOVE TARGET-KEY TO IM-CUSTOMER.
       READ INDEXED-MASTER
           INVALID KEY PERFORM 500-NOT-FOUND.
```

This will directly read the record with primary key 'SMITH' into the buffer record for the file (IM-MASTER-BUFFER-RECORD). The INVALID KEY clause is normally used with the direct-access READ. It is executed if the record is not in the file. The primary key of the target record must be placed in the RECORD KEY identifier (IM-CUSTOMER). You may not use AT END with a direct-access READ.

Surprisingly, with ISAM a deleted record is read, so that the program must check the delete-byte value to distinguish between a normal and deleted record.

2. Direct-access WRITE
   You can use WRITE to insert a new record into the file by direct-access. To insert the record NEW-RECORD, which has a primary key, 'NEWTON', in the identifier NR-CUSTOMER, you would code

```
MOVE NR-CUSTOMER TO IM-CUSTOMER.
WRITE IM-MASTER-BUFFER-RECORD FROM NEW-RECORD
            INVALID KEY PERFORM 500-DUPLICATE-KEY.
```

The INVALID KEY clause is normally used with the direct-access WRITE. If a record with primary key 'NEWTON' is already in the file, the insertion will be rejected and the INVALID KEY clause executed.

3. Direct-access update with READ and REWRITE.
   To add the value 1000 (in identifier TRANS-PAYMENT-IN) to the amount owing for customer 'DREXEL', that is, primary key value 'DREXEL', read the record into a WORKING-STORAGE identifier, such as

```
01 WS-MASTER-RECORD.
    05 WS-MAST-CUSTOMER      PIC X(15).
    05 WS-MAST-OWING         PIC 9(6).
```

by direct-access. Then update that record and rewrite it as follows:

```
01 TARGET-KEY      PIC  X(15)     VALUE 'DREXEL'.
    ...
    MOVE TARGET-KEY TO IM-CUSTOMER.
    READ INDEXED-MASTER INTO MASTER-RECORD
            INVALID KEY PERFORM 500-NOT-FOUND.
    IF RECORD-FOUND = 'YES'
        ADD TRANS-PAYMENT-IN TO WS-MAST-OWING
                            IN WS-MASTER-RECORD
        REWRITE IM-MASTER-BUFFER-RECORD FROM WS-MASTER-RECORD
            INVALID KEY PERFORM 600-KEY-ERROR
    END-IF.
```

A direct-access REWRITE overwrites the record on disk that has a primary key in the RECORD KEY identifier (IM-CUSTOMER).

4. Direct-access DELETE
   You can delete a record by direct-access using DELETE. To delete a record with primary key 'BANKCORP', you use the DELETE verb, as follows:

```
01 TARGET-KEY      PIC  X(15)     VALUE 'BANKCORP'.
    . . .
    MOVE TARGET-KEY TO IM-CUSTOMER.
    DELETE INDEXED-MASTER
         INVALID KEY PERFORM 600-RECORD-NOT-FOUND.
```

The INVALID KEY clause is normally used with the direct-access DELETE. It will be executed if the record is not found.

OPEN INPUT You can use a direct-access READ to retrieve a record directly, and that is all. This is often used for retrieving records for responding to ad hoc queries, or to generate a report about a few selective records. To retrieve the record with primary key value 'SMITH', you could code

```
01 TARGET-KEY      PIC  X(15)     VALUE 'SMITH'.
    . . .
    MOVE TARGET-KEY TO IM-CUSTOMER.
    READ INDEXED-MASTER
         INVALID KEY PERFORM 500-NOT-FOUND.
```

This will directly read the record with primary key 'SMITH' into the buffer record for the file (IM-MASTER-BUFFER-RECORD).

The INVALID KEY clause is normally used with the direct-access READ. It is executed if the record is not in the file.

You cannot use AT END with a direct-access READ. Nor can you use START.

OPEN OUTPUT You can use WRITE to insert a new record into the file by direct-access, and that is all. To insert the record NEW-RECORD, with a primary key 'NEWTON' in the identifier NR-CUSTOMER, you would code

```
    MOVE NR-CUSTOMER TO IM-CUSTOMER.
    WRITE IM-MASTER-BUFFER-RECORD FROM NEW-RECORD
              INVALID KEY PERFORM 500-DUPLICATE-KEY.
```

The INVALID KEY clause is normally used with the direct-access WRITE. If a record with primary key 'NEWTON' is already in the file, the insertion will be rejected and the INVALID KEY clause executed. The primary key of the record being written must be in the RECORD KEY identifier (IM-CUSTOMER).

Dynamic-Access Mode (ACCESS DYNAMIC)

The dynamic-access mode is not as commonly used as the SEQUENTIAL and RANDOM modes; and is not allowed with ISAM. It permits both sequential and direct-access. For example, you might want to carry out a direct-access update of a few records, to be followed by output of all records (sequential processing) after a specific record, possibly even the first. In that case ACCESS DYNAMIC could be used.

OPEN INPUT   With OPEN INPUT, you can use the direct-access READ, a sequential-access READ ... NEXT ... AT END ... END-READ, and the START verb. The sequential access READ requires the use of the word NEXT. For example, to read records sequentially from INDEXED-MASTER, you would code

```
READ INDEXED-MASTER NEXT RECORD
        AT END MOVE 'NO' TO MORE RECORDS
END-READ.
```

The NEXT RECORD clause is necessary for a sequential READ when ACCESS DYNAMIC is coded. Sequential reading begins at either

- The record located by a START statement prior to the sequential READ
- The record following the last record read by a direct-access READ
- The beginning of the file, if there has been no START and no prior direct-access READ

OPEN OUTPUT   As with ACCESS RANDOM, with OPEN OUTPUT all you can use is the sequential WRITE ... INVALID KEY.

OPEN I-O   With OPEN I-O you can use all the verbs discussed so far. For sequential processing you can use

- START to define a first record to be read
- READ ... NEXT ... AT END ... END-READ, to read records in ascending primary key order
- REWRITE ... [INVALID KEY], to overwrite a record read by a READ ... NEXT ... AT END ... END-READ
- DELETE ... [INVALID KEY], to delete a record previously read by a READ ... NEXT ... AT END ... END-READ

For direct-access processing you can use

- READ ... [INVALID KEY], with a value in the primary key field in the buffer record for the indexed file, to retrieve the record with that primary key
- WRITE ... [INVALID KEY], to directly write out the record in the buffer record and use its primary key to correctly position it in the file
- REWRITE ... [INVALID KEY], to use the contents of the buffer record to directly overwrite the record in the file with a primary key the same as that in the RECORD KEY identifier (IM-CUSTOMER)
- DELETE ... [INVALID KEY], to directly delete the record with a primary key in the RECORD KEY identifier (IM-CUSTOMER).

If READ ... NEXT is used after any of these direct-access commands, the next record in ascending primary key sequence is read.

An indexed-sequential file must first be created

A N INDEXED-SEQUENTIAL file is frequently a master file. It must

- Be created in ascending primary key order using sequential processing, and no pair of records can have duplicate primary keys
- Be created with validated data

It makes little sense to create an indexed-sequential master file, instead of a sequential file, if the percentage of records accessed in updates and information retrieval programs is high, that is, if the hit rate is high. Indexed-sequential master files are normally created in anticipation of processing with very low hit rates.

A sample indexed-sequential file creation program

Suppose you want to create an indexed-sequential master file of receivables data, called INDEXED-MASTER, from a sequential file SOURCE-FILE-IN as shown in Figure 14.4.

```
---------1---------2---------3---------4
ARTFIELD        145000
AVRILCORP       057500
BANKCORP        155000
BANKCORP        144789
BUNTORAMO       078000
CALCOMP         167000
ARROWCORP       178900
COMPUDISK       034000

. . .

Columns  1–15     Customer name
        16–21     Amount owing
```

Figure 14.4a *Format of input file SOURCE-FILE-IN for creating the indexed-sequential master file INDEXED-MASTER with the same format.*

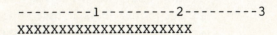

```
---------1---------2---------3
XXXXXXXXXXXXXXXXXXXXX
```

Figure 14.4b *Record layout for a SOURCE-FILE-IN record.*

```
01   SOURCE-RECORD-IN PIC X(21)
```

Figure 14.4c *Buffer record definition for SOURCE-FILE-IN.*

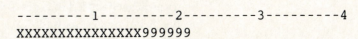

```
---------1---------2---------3---------4
XXXXXXXXXXXXXXX999999
```

Figure 14.4d *Record layout for an INDEXED-MASTER record.*

```
01    IM-MASTER-BUFFER-RECORD.
      05   IM-CUSTOMER   PIC X(15).
      05   IM-OWING      PIC 9(06).
```

Figure 14.4e Buffer record definition for an INDEXED-MASTER record.

```
---------1---------2---------3---------4---------5---------6---------7
         CONTROL LISTING ON CREATION OF INDEXED MASTER
PAGE   01                                               12/15/91


RECORD#   INPUT RECORD          PROBLEM

0004      BANKCORP     144789   DUPLICATE KEY
0007      ARROWCORP    178900   OUT-OF-SEQUENCE KEY
...
```

Figure 14.4f Control listing format.

Since INDEXED-MASTER is a master file, it must contain validated data. This allows us two alternatives.

- Incorporating the validation routine in the indexed-sequential file creation program
- Making sure that SOURCE-FILE-IN has been validated before use. This alternative is assumed since a validation routine for this kind of file was demonstrated earlier in the program in Figure 8.8.

The program to create INDEXED-MASTER is shown in Figure 14.5. Code specific to indexed-sequential file creation is shown in bold. Note that, in the case of a VSAM file, before the file can be created a VSAM utility routine that allocates disk space for the file must first be executed.

Notice that the field IM-CUSTOMER, selected as the primary key by the clause RECORD KEY IS IM-CUSTOMER, must be defined, with the same name, in the buffer record structure for the indexed-sequential file, in this case IM-BUFFER-RECORD. If other fields are not going to be used, as would be the case if the data had previously been validated, they can be defined collectively using FILLER entries in the buffer record definition.

As each record is written, the underlying input/output routine checks the IM-CUSTOMER primary key field. The records must be written out with unique primary keys, in ascending primary key (IM-CUSTOMER) order. If an attempt is made to write an out-of-sequence or duplicate primary key record, the INVALID KEY clause is executed and the record is rejected. Such an event is recorded in the control listing for the file creation. Note that primary key fields that contain digits are less likely to generate duplicates.

The input/output routine also uses the primary key IM-CUSTOMER in the construction of the index. At the end of the processing, not only have the records been stored in ascending primary key order, but an index to the file has been created as well.

Notice that no BLOCK CONTAINS clause was used with the indexed-sequential file INDEXED-MASTER. Like sequential files, the records of indexed-sequential files are blocked. However, the blocking factor is not under programmer control with the commonly used VSAM files; it is chosen by the input/output routine. Thus, you cannot specify a BLOCK CONTAINS clause with VSAM indexed-sequential files.

```
IDENTIFICATION DIVISION.
PROGRAM-ID. MASTER.
ENVIRONMENT DIVISION.
INPUT-OUTPUT SECTION.
FILE-CONTROL.
    SELECT SOURCE-FILE-IN
                  ASSIGN TO UT-3380-S-DATA.
    SELECT INDEXED-MASTER
                  ASSIGN TO MAST234
                  ORGANIZATION IS INDEXED
                  ACCESS MODE IS SEQUENTIAL
                  RECORD KEY IS IM-CUSTOMER.
    SELECT CONTROL-LISTING
                  ASSIGN TO UR-S-SYSPRINT.
DATA DIVISION.
FILE SECTION.
FD    INDEXED-MASTER              LABEL RECORDS ARE STANDARD.
01    IM-BUFFER-RECORD.
      05   IM-CUSTOMER     PIC X(15).       RECORD KEY field must be defined here.
      05   IM-OWING        PIC 9(06).
FD    SOURCE-FILE-IN              LABEL RECORDS ARE STANDARD
                                  RECORD CONTAINS 21 CHARACTERS
                                  BLOCK CONTAINS 200 RECORDS.
01    SOURCE-RECORD-IN   PIC X(21).
FD    CONTROL-LISTING            LABEL-RECORDS ARE OMITTED.
01    PRINT-RECORD-OUT   PIC X(133).
WORKING-STORAGE SECTION.
01  WS-WORK-AREAS.
      05   MORE-RECORDS    PIC X(03)        VALUE 'YES'.
      05   BAD-RECORD      PIC X(03).
      05   LINE-COUNT      PIC 9(02).
      05   WS-PAGE-NUMBER  PIC 9(02)        VALUE ZEROS.
      05   WS-CONTROL-KEY  PIC X(15)        VALUE SPACES.
      05   WS-RECORD-COUNT PIC 9(04)        VALUE ZEROS.
01  PAGE-DATE-LINE-OUT.
      05   FILLER          PIC X            VALUE SPACE.
      05   FILLER          PIC X(06)        VALUE 'PAGE'.
      05   PD-PAGE-NUMB-OUT PIC 9(02).
      05   FILLER          PIC X(50)        VALUE SPACES.
      05   PD-RUN-DATE-OUT PIC X(08).
      05   FILLER          PIC X(66)        VALUE SPACES
01  REPORT-HEADER.
      05   FILLER          PIC X(09)        VALUE SPACES.
      05   FILLER          PIC X(124)       VALUE
                  'CONTROL LISTING ON CREATION OF INDEXED MASTER'.
```

```
01  HEADER-1.
    05   FILLER              PIC X          VALUE SPACES.
    05   FILLER              PIC X(32)      VALUE 'RECORD#  INPUT RECORD'.
    05   FILLER              PIC X(100)     VALUE 'PROBLEM'.
01  DETAIL-LINE-OUT.
    05   FILLER              PIC X          VALUE SPACES.
    05   DL-REC-NUMB-OUT     PIC 9(04).
    05   FILLER              PIC X(05)      VALUE SPACES.
    05   DL-RECORDIN-OUT     PIC X(21)
    05   FILLER              PIC X(02)      VALUE SPACES.
    05   DL-MESSAGE-OUT      PIC X(100).
01  WS-MESSAGE-DATA-OUT.
    05   SEQUENCE-MESSAGE    PIC X(19)      VALUE 'OUT-OF-SEQUENCE-KEY'.
    05   DUPLICATE-MESSAGE   PIC X(13)      VALUE 'DUPLICATE KEY'.
PROCEDURE DIVISION.
100-MAIN-MODULE.
*****************************************************************************
*   DIRECTS PROGRAM LOGIC.                                                  *
*****************************************************************************
    PERFORM 200-INITIALIZATION.
    PERFORM 300-PROCESS-RECORD
             UNTIL MORE-RECORDS = 'NO'.
    PERFORM 400-TERMINATION.
200-INITIALIZATION.
*****************************************************************************
*   PERFORMED FROM 100-MAIN-MODULE. OPENS FILES AND READS FIRST RECORD.   *
*****************************************************************************
    OPEN INPUT SOURCE-FILE-IN
          OUTPUT INDEXED-MASTER
          OUTPUT CONTROL-LISTING.
    MOVE CURRENT-DATE TO PD-RUN-DATE-OUT.
    PERFORM 400-PAGE-HEADERS.
    READ SOURCE-FILE-IN RECORD
          AT END MOVE 'NO' TO MORE-RECORDS.
300-PROCESS-RECORD.
*****************************************************************************
*   PERFORMED FROM 100-MAIN-MODULE. WRITES CURRENT SOURCE RECORD TO       *
*   INDEXED FILE AND READS NEXT SOURCE RECORD.                            *
*****************************************************************************
    MOVE SOURCE-RECORD-IN TO IM-BUFFER-RECORD.
    MOVE 'NO' TO BAD-RECORD.
    ADD 1 TO WS-RECORD-COUNT.
    WRITE IM-BUFFER-RECORD
       INVALID KEY
          PERFORM 500-BAD-RECORD.
    IF BAD-RECORD = 'NO'
       MOVE IM-CUSTOMER TO WS-CONTROL-KEY
    END-IF.
    READ SOURCE-FILE-IN RECORD
          AT END MOVE 'NO' TO MORE-RECORDS.
```

```
 400-TERMINATION.
*************************************************************************
*   PERFORMED FROM 100-MAIN-MODULE. CLOSES FILES, STOPS PROGRAM.       *
*************************************************************************
     CLOSE SOURCE-FILE-IN.
     CLOSE INDEXED-MASTER.
     CLOSE CONTROL-LISTING.
     STOP RUN.
 400-PAGE-HEADERS.
*************************************************************************
*   PERFORMED FROM 200-INITIALIZATION AND 500-BAD-RECORD.  PRINTS      *
*   HEADERS FOR CONTROL LISTING.                                       *
*************************************************************************
     WRITE PRINT-RECORD-OUT FROM REPORT-HEADER
             AFTER ADVANCING PAGE.
     ADD 1 TO WS-PAGE-NUMBER.
     MOVE WS-PAGE-NUMBER TO PD-PAGE-NUMB-OUT.
     WRITE PRINT-RECORD-OUT FROM PAGE-DATE-LINE-OUT
             AFTER ADVANCING 1 LINE.
     WRITE PRINT-RECORD-OUT FROM HEADER-1
             AFTER ADVANCING 2 LINES.
     MOVE SPACES TO PRINT-RECORD-OUT.
     WRITE PRINT-RECORD-OUT
             AFTER ADVANCING 1 LINE.
     MOVE 5 TO LINE-COUNT.
 500-BAD-RECORD.
*************************************************************************
*   PERFORMED FROM 300-PROCESS-RECORD. DECIDES PROBLEM WITH REJECTED   *
*   RECORD AND PRINTS RECORD AND PROBLEM IN CONTROL LISTING.           *
*************************************************************************
     MOVE 'YES' TO BAD-RECORD.
     IF IM-CUSTOMER = WS-CONTROL-KEY
         MOVE DUPLICATE-MESSAGE TO DL-MESSAGE-OUT
     ELSE
         MOVE SEQUENCE-MESSAGE TO DL-MESSAGE-OUT
     END-IF.
     MOVE SOURCE-RECORD-IN TO DL-RECORDIN-OUT.
     MOVE WS-RECORD-COUNT TO DL-REC-NUMB-OUT.
     IF LINE-COUNT >= 45
             PERFORM 400-PAGE-HEADERS.
     WRITE PRINT-RECORD-OUT FROM DETAIL-LINE-OUT
                     AFTER ADVANCING 1 LINE.
```

Figure 14.5 Program to create an indexed-sequential file, INDEXED-MASTER, from a sequential-source file, SOURCE-FILE-IN, containing already validated records, and print problem records in a control listing.

Control listing for indexed file creation is normal

Usually a control listing showing both good records and unacceptable records is output at the file creation stage. For the program in Figure 14.5, to allow you to concentrate on the essentials, it was assumed that input records have been validated. But the possibility of both duplicate primary keys and out-of-sequence records has been allowed . The file creation program prints only these rejected records in the control listing. The format of the control listing is shown in Figure 14.4f.

Primary keys should be alphanumeric

COBOL 85 requires that the field specified as the RECORD KEY be defined with a PIC consisting of X's only, as in the preceding program. However, many systems permit all 9s to be used as well, as does VSAM.

The FILE STATUS clause works well for deciding the nature of errors

You have seen how to use the INVALID KEY clause for detecting input/output errors involving a primary key value. However, there is a more thorough method of handling errors of any kind, which involves the use of the FILE STATUS clause.

FILE STATUS can be used with all kinds of files, including both indexed-sequential and sequential. The FILE STATUS clause can be included at the end of the SELECT statement, as, for example, with the definition of the indexed-sequential file INDEXED-MASTER.

```
SELECT INDEXED-MASTER
                ASSIGN TO MAST234
                ORGANIZATION IS INDEXED
                ACCESS MODE IS SEQUENTIAL
                RECORD KEY IS IM-CUSTOMER.
                FILE STATUS IS F-STATUS.
WORKING-STORAGE SECTION.
...
     05 F-STATUS    PIC  X(02).
```

What has been done here is to specify that an arbitrarily named identifier F-STATUS, defined in the WORKING-STORAGE SECTION, be used as an input/output status identifier. This means that following each READ, WRITE, or REWRITE statement execution, the input/output routine will place, or return, a status code in F-STATUS, to indicate the degree of success or failure of the operation. The program can check the value in F-STATUS following each input/output operation and take appropriate action. The main status codes are

00	There are no errors of any kind.
02	Other records have the same secondary key value. This code can be returned when accessing on the basis of a secondary key.
04	The record has been read but is too long to fit the input area (buffer) record. (Does not apply to indexed-sequential files.)

UNSUCCESSFUL OPERATION

10	No records are left on attempt at a sequential read.
21	Sequence error: Primary key is out of sequence.
22	Duplicate primary key is used with a WRITE.
23	The record was not found.
30	There is a hardware problem – probably a defect on tape or disk.
91–99	These depend on the system you are using. Check your manual.

The status identifier is used in a program where specific information must be output about the cause of an input/output error. Instead of using the identifier WS-CONTROL-KEY in the indexed-sequential file creation program in Figure 14.5, instead F-STATUS could have used, as follows:

```
WRITE IM-BUFFER-RECORD
   INVALID KEY
        PERFORM 500-BAD-RECORD.
...
500-BAD-RECORD.
     MOVE 'YES' TO BAD-RECORD.
     IF F-STATUS = '22'
     MOVE DUPLICATE-MESSAGE TO DL-MESSAGE-OUT.
     END-IF.
     IF F-STATUS = '21'
     MOVE SEQUENCE-MESSAGE TO DL-MESSAGE-OUT
     END-IF.
     ...
```

14.3
Indexed-sequential files permit flexible updating

YOU HAVE SEEN that you can specify three different access modes for an indexed-sequential file: ACCESS IS SEQUENTIAL, ACCESS IS RANDOM, and ACCESS IS DYNAMIC.

If you specify ACCESS MODE IS SEQUENTIAL, you can process the file as a sequential file. Since you cannot generate a new copy of the file during update (because it would not have an index), you must update the existing file. That means you can only use rewrite updating. In addition, you can delete existing records. You cannot insert a new record with a WRITE statement.

Accordingly, sequentially updating an indexed-sequential file means rewrite change updating like that for a sequential disk file, or rewrite deletion updating. The only difference with rewrite change updating for sequential processing of an indexed file, as compared with a sequential file, is in the requirement for the additional clauses in the SELECT entry (see Section 14.1).

Rewrite deletion updating is not normally practical with sequential files, but is quite simple with sequential processing of indexed files. So this is a new possibility with indexed files.

The other new updating possibilities with an indexed-sequential file have to do with ACCESS MODE IS RANDOM. With this access mode, you can carry out direct-access versions of

- Change updating
- Insertion updating
- Deletion updating
- Generalized updating

A transaction file is needed to hold the changes, insertion, or deletions, or any combination of these, but the transaction records need not be sorted in the same sequence as the master (although they can be sorted). Let us look at these types of direct-access updating in turn, but begin with a brief look at change and deletion updating with sequential access.

Logic for rewrite change updating with sequential access

The essential logic for rewrite change updating with sequential access depends on whether records can occur in the transaction file that do not match any master record (unmatched transactions), and whether duplicate-key transactions can occur and whether they should be used as a group or rejected.

Let us we take the simple case where neither unmatched transaction records nor duplicate-key transaction records can occur. Suppose also that you are updating the receivables file from earlier sections, where the primary key is a customer name. If cur-tr is the latest or current transaction record and cur-mast is the latest master record read, the essential logic is

Case A. customer in cur-tr > customer in cur-mast

ACTION

1. Read next master record into working storage.

Case B. customer in cur-tr = customer in cur-mast

ACTION

1. Update current master in working storage using transaction record.
2. Rewrite working-storage master to master file.
3. Read next master record into working storage.
4. Read next transaction record into working storage.

If unmatched transaction records are allowed, but no duplicate-key transactions can occur, you also have to check for the possibility of the current master key being greater than the current transaction key. So the preceding logic has to be extended, as follows:

Case A. customer in cur-tr > customer in cur-mast

ACTION

1. Read next master record into working storage.

Case B. customer in cur-tr = customer in cur-mast

ACTION

1. Update current master in working storage using transaction record.
2. Rewrite working-storage master to master file.
3. Read next master record into working storage.
4. Read next transaction record into working storage.

Case C. customer in cur-tr < customer in cur-mast

ACTION

1. List transaction in control listing.
2. Read next transaction record.

The essentials of a COBOL program to carry out this update with the files TRANS and INDEXED-MASTER are as follows:

```
IDENTIFICATION DIVISION.
PROGRAM-ID. RWUPDATE.
ENVIRONMENT DIVISION.
INPUT-OUTPUT SECTION.
FILE-CONTROL.
    SELECT TRANS
                ASSIGN TO UT-S-D400.
    SELECT INDEXED-MASTER
                ASSIGN TO MAST234
                ORGANIZATION IS INDEXED
                ACCESS MODE IS SEQUENTIAL
                RECORD KEY IS IM-CUSTOMER.
    SELECT CONTROL-LISTING
                ASSIGN TO UR-S-SYSPRINT.
DATA DIVISION.
FILE SECTION.
FD  TRANS                      LABEL RECORDS ARE STANDARD.
01  TRANS-RECORD-IN.
    05 TRANS-CUSTOMER-IN    PIC X(15).
    05 TRANS-PAYMENT-IN     PIC 9(05).
FD  INDEXED-MASTER             LABEL RECORDS ARE STANDARD.
01  IM-BUFFER-RECORD.
    05  IM-CUSTOMER         PIC X(15).    RECORD KEY must be defined here.
    05  IM-OWING            PIC 9(06).
FD  CONTROL-LISTING            LABEL RECORDS OMITTED.
01  PRINT-RECORD-OUT        PIC X(133).
WORKING-STORAGE SECTION.
01  WS-MASTER-RECORD.
    05  WS-MAST-CUSTOMER    PIC X(15).
    05  WS-MAST-OWING       PIC 9(06).
...
```

details of control listing identifiers

```cobol
PROCEDURE DIVISION.
100-MAIN-MODULE.
    PERFORM 200-INITIALIZATION.
    PERFORM 300-COMPARE
            UNTIL TRANS-CUSTOMER-IN = HIGH-VALUES.
    PERFORM 500-TERMINATION.
200-INITIALIZATION.
    OPEN INPUT TRANS.
    OPEN I-O INDEXED-MASTER.
    OPEN OUTPUT CONTROL-LISTING.
    READ INDEXED-MASTER INTO WS-MASTER-RECORD
        AT END MOVE ' NO FIRST MASTER RECORD' TO PRINT-RECORD-OUT
                WRITE PRINT-RECORD-OUT
                STOP RUN.
    READ TRANS
        AT END MOVE ' NO FIRST TRANS RECORD' TO PRINT-RECORD-OUT
                WRITE PRINT-RECORD-OUT
                STOP RUN.
300-COMPARE.
    IF TRANS-CUSTOMER-IN > WS-MAST-CUSTOMER
        READ INDEXED-MASTER INTO WS-MASTER-RECORD
        AT END MOVE HIGH-VALUES TO WS-MAST-CUSTOMER
    END-IF.
    IF TRANS-CUSTOMER-IN = WS-MAST-CUSTOMER
        SUBTRACT TRANS-PAYMENT-IN FROM WS-MAST-OWING
        REWRITE IM-BUFFER-RECORD FROM WS-MASTER-RECORD
        READ INDEXED-MASTER INTO WS-MASTER-RECORD
          AT END MOVE HIGH-VALUES TO WS-MAST-CUSTOMER
        END-READ
        READ TRANS
          AT END MOVE HIGH-VALUES TO TRANS-CUSTOMER-IN
        END-READ
    END-IF.
    IF TRANS-CUSTOMER-IN < WS-MAST-CUSTOMER
        PERFORM 400-PRINT-TRANS-RECORD
        READ TRANS
          AT END MOVE HIGH-VALUES TO TRANS-CUSTOMER-IN
        END-READ
        ADD 1 TO TRANS-COUNT
    END-IF.
400-PRINT-TRANS-RECORD.
    prints record in control listing
    ...
500-TERMINATION.
    CLOSE  TRANS
           INDEXED-MASTER
           CONTROL-LISTING.
    STOP RUN.
```

The program handles end-of-file conditions. Either TRANS or INDEXED-MASTER can end first. If TRANS ends first, there is no need to continue reading and not writing MASTER records; thus processing is programmed to stop (see PERFORM 300-COMPARE statement) if TRANS ends first. If INDEXED-MASTER ends first, processing continues and the remaining TRANS records are listed in the control listing.

Note that this above program will not work if duplicate-key transaction records are to be used for updating. As it stands, the program will simply use the first of a sequence of matching duplicate transactions for updating and list the rest in the control listing. You are invited to consider how you would modify the preceding program excerpt above so that all of a sequence of duplicate-key TRANS records would be used to update the single matching INDEXED-MASTER record.

A control listing is common with indexed file updating

In commercial practice, a control listing is usually generated during updating of an indexed file. The control listing can range from comprehensive to minimal. With a comprehensive control listing, every transaction record and its fate are listed. In the minimal case, only problem transaction records, or just their keys, are listed, together with descriptions of the problems. Such a minimal control listing is often called an exception report.

Example of deletion updating with sequential access

Suppose you need to delete some records from the file INDEXED-MASTER. The primary keys of the records to be deleted are in the file TRANS. Some records of TRANS and INDEXED-MASTER are

```
TRANS-CUST-IN                         IM-CUSTOMER    IM-OWING
                                      ARTFIELD       145000
AVRIL CORP                            AVRILCORP      057500
                                      BANKCORP       155000
BUNTORAMO                             BUNTORAMO      078000
CALCOMP                               CALCOMP        167000
                                      COMPUDISK      034000
...                                   ...
        TRANS                              INDEXED-MASTER
```

TRANS and INDEXED-MASTER records are read in ascending primary key order. The current records of each file are compared, and if their keys match, an INDEXED-MASTER record is deleted with a DELETE statement. If cur-tr is the current TRANS record and cur-mr is the current INDEXED-MASTER record, the logic for the update is as follows:

Case A. primary key of cur-tr > primary key of cur-mr

ACTION

1. Read next master record.

Case B. primary key of cur-tr = primary key of cur-mr

ACTION

1. Delete master record.
2. Read next master.
3. Read next transaction.

CASE C. primary key of cur-tr < primary key of cur-mr

ACTION

1. List transaction record in control listing.
2. Read next transaction.

It is assumed there can be transaction records with primary keys that do not match any primary key in the master file. Duplicate transaction records are also assumed.

```
        SELECT TRANS
                   ASSIGN TO UT-S-D400.
        SELECT INDEXED-MASTER
                   ASSIGN TO MAST234
                   ORGANIZATION IS INDEXED
                   ACCESS MODE IS SEQUENTIAL
                   RECORD KEY IS IM-CUSTOMER.
        SELECT CONTROL-LISTING
                   ASSIGN TO UR-S-SYSPRINT.
DATA DIVISION.
FILE SECTION.
FD   TRANS                       LABEL RECORDS ARE STANDARD.
01   TRANS-RECORD-IN.
     05 TRANS-CUSTOMER-IN   PIC X(15).
FD   INDEXED-MASTER              LABEL RECORDS ARE STANDARD.
01   IM-BUFFER-RECORD.
     05  IM-CUSTOMER           PIC X(15).     RECORD KEY must be defined here.
     05  IM-OWING              PIC 9(06).
...
PROCEDURE DIVISION.
100-MAIN-MODULE.
     PERFORM 200-INITIALIZATION.
     PERFORM 300-COMPARE
             UNTIL TRANS-CUSTOMER-IN = HIGH-VALUES.
     PERFORM 400-TERMINATION.
200-INITIALIZATION.
     OPEN INPUT TRANS
          I-O INDEXED-MASTER
          OUTPUT CONTROL-LISTING.
     READ TRANS RECORD
             AT END MOVE HIGH-VALUES TO TRANS-CUSTOMER-IN.
     READ INDEXED-MASTER RECORD
             AT END MOVE HIGH-VALUES TO IM-CUSTOMER.
```

```
300-COMPARE.
    IF TRANS-CUSTOMER-IN > IM-CUSTOMER
        READ INDEXED-MASTER RECORD
            AT END MOVE HIGH-VALUES TO IM-CUSTOMER
    END-IF.
    IF TRANS-CUSTOMER-IN = IM-CUSTOMER
        DELETE INDEXED-MASTER
        READ INDEXED-MASTER RECORD
            AT END MOVE HIGH-VALUES TO IM-CUSTOMER
        END-READ
        READ TRANS RECORD
            AT END MOVE HIGH-VALUES TO TRANS-CUSTOMER-IN
        END-READ
    END-IF.
    IF TRANS-CUSTOMER-IN < IM-CUSTOMER
        PERFORM 500-CONTROL-LIST-ENTRY
        READ TRANS RECORD
            AT END MOVE HIGH-VALUES TO TRANS-CUSTOMER-IN
        END-READ.
400-TERMINATION.
    CLOSE TRANS.
    CLOSE INDEXED-MASTER.
    CLOSE CONTROL-LISTING.
    STOP RUN.
500-CONTROL-LIST-ENTRY.
```
makes an entry in control listing for the update

The code specific to the processing of an indexed file is shown in bold.

Direct-access change updating example

Suppose each record of a transaction file TRANS contains details of a payment, recorded in IM-CUSTOMER, to reduce the outstanding debt listed in INDEXED-MASTER. Thus, a TRANS record will have the structure

```
01 TRANS-RECORD-IN.
    05 TRANS-CUSTOMER-IN        PIC X(15).
    05 TRANS-PAYMENT-IN         PIC 9(06).
```

which happens to be the same as that for an INDEXED-MASTER record, although this need not be the case.

If the records of TRANS

- are unsorted
- can have unmatched primary keys
- can have duplicate primary key fields

the update can be handled much more simply than with sequential files. The essential logic is ead next TRANS record.

se TRANS-CUSTOMER-IN value to directly read matching

IDEXED-MASTER record.

no matching master record is found,

HEN

    list record in control listing

LSE

    subtract payment from WS-MASTER-OWING in master
       record,

    rewrite master record just read onto the disk.

ND-IF.

he full COBOL program for such an update is shown in Figure 14.6.

at it is assumed that the data in TRANS has been validated in a prior

```
IDENTIFICATION DIVISION.
PROGRAM-ID. CHUD.
ENVIRONMENT DIVISION.
INPUT-OUTPUT SECTION.
FILE-CONTROL.
    SELECT TRANS
                    ASSIGN TO UT-S-D400.
    SELECT INDEXED-MASTER
                    ASSIGN TO MAST234
        ORGANIZATION IS INDEXED
        ACCESS MODE IS RANDOM
        RECORD KEY IS IM-CUSTOMER.
     SELECT CONTROL-LISTING
                    ASSIGN TO UR-S-SYSPRINT.
DATA DIVISION.
FILE SECTION.
FD   TRANS                 LABEL RECORDS ARE STANDARD.
01   TRANS-RECORD-IN.
     05 TRANS-CUSTOMER-IN  PIC X(15).
     05 TRANS-PAYMENT-IN   PIC 9(06).
FD   INDEXED-MASTER        LABEL RECORDS ARE STANDARD.
01   IM-BUFFER-RECORD.
     05  IM-CUSTOMER       PIC X(15).        RECORD KEY must be defined here.
     05  FILLER            PIC 9(06).
FD   CONTROL-LISTING                  LABEL RECORDS OMITTED.
01   PRINT-RECORD-OUT      PIC X(133).
WORKING-STORAGE SECTION.
01   PAGE-DATE-LINE-OUT.
     05   FILLER           PIC X        VALUE SPACE.
     05   FILLER           PIC X(06)    VALUE 'PAGE'.
     05   PD-PAGE-NUMB-OUT PIC 9(02).
     05   FILLER           PIC X(50)    VALUE SPACES.
     05   PD-RUN-DATE-OUT  PIC X(08).
     05   FILLER           PIC X(66)    VALUE SPACES.
```

```
01  REPORT-HEADER.
    05  FILLER              PIC X(09)      VALUE SPACES.
    05  FILLER              PIC X(124)     VALUE
                        'CONTROL LISTING ON CHANGE UPDATE OF INDEXED MASTER'.
01  HEADER-1.
    05  FILLER              PIC X          VALUE SPACES.
    05  FILLER              PIC X(32)      VALUE 'RECORD#  TRANS RECORD'.
    05  FILLER              PIC X(100)     VALUE 'PROBLEM'.
01  DETAIL-LINE-OUT.
    05  FILLER              PIC X          VALUE SPACES.
    05  DL-REC-NUMB-OUT     PIC 9(04).
    05  FILLER              PIC X(05)      VALUE SPACES.
    05  DL-RECORDIN-OUT     PIC X(21).
    05  FILLER              PIC X(02)      VALUE SPACES.
    05  DL-MESSAGE-OUT      PIC X(100).
01  WS-MESSAGE-DATA-OUT.
    05  UNMATCHED-MESSAGE   PIC X(19)      VALUE 'UNMATCHED TRANS KEY'.
01  WS-MASTER-RECORD.
    05  WS-MASTER-CUSTOMER  PIC X(15).
    05  WS-MASTER-OWING     PIC 9(06).
01  WS WORK AREAS.
    05  MORE-RECORDS        PIC X(03)      VALUE 'YES'.
    05  RECORD-FOUND        PIC X(03).
    05  MORE-RECORDS        PIC X(03)      VALUE 'YES'.
    05  LINE-COUNT          PIC 9(02).
    05  WS-PAGE-NUMBER      PIC 9(02)      VALUE ZEROS.
    05  WS-RECORD-COUNT     PIC 9(04)      VALUE ZERO.
PROCEDURE DIVISION.
100-MAIN-MODULE.
********************************************************************************
*   DIRECTS PROGRAM LOGIC.                                                     *
********************************************************************************
    PERFORM 200-INITIALIZATION.
    PERFORM 300-PROCESS-TRANS-RECORD
                UNTIL MORE-RECORDS = 'NO'.
    PERFORM 400-TERMINATION.
200-INITIALIZATION.
********************************************************************************
*   PERFORMED FROM 100-MAIN-MODULE. OPENS FILES AND READS FIRST RECORD.  *
********************************************************************************
    OPEN INPUT TRANS
         I-O INDEXED-MASTER
         OUTPUT CONTROL-LISTING.
    MOVE CURRENT-DATE TO PD-RUN-DATE-OUT.
    PERFORM 500-PAGE-HEADERS.
    READ TRANS RECORD
                AT END MOVE 'NO' TO MORE-RECORDS.
```

```cobol
 300-PROCESS-TRANS-RECORD.
*****************************************************************************
*   PERFORMED FROM 100-MAIN-MODULE. USES TRANS KEY VALUE TO ACCESS AND    *
*   UPDATE MATCHING INDEXED-MASTER RECORD.                                *
*****************************************************************************
       ADD 1 TO WS-RECORD-COUNT.
       MOVE TRANS-CUSTOMER-IN TO IM-CUSTOMER.
       MOVE 'YES' TO RECORD-FOUND.
       READ INDEXED-MASTER INTO WS-MASTER-RECORD
           INVALID KEY
         MOVE 'NO' TO RECORD-FOUND.
       IF RECORD-FOUND = 'NO'
             PERFORM 600-PROCESS-UNMATCHED-TRANS
           ELSE
             SUBTRACT TRANS-PAYMENT-IN FROM WS-MASTER-OWING
             REWRITE IM-BUFFER-RECORD FROM WS-MASTER-RECORD
       END-IF.
       READ TRANS RECORD
                 AT END MOVE 'NO' TO MORE-RECORDS.
 400-TERMINATION.
*****************************************************************************
*   PERFORMED FROM 100-MAIN-MODULE. CLOSES FILES, STOPS PROGRAM.          *
*****************************************************************************
       CLOSE TRANS
             INDEXED-MASTER
             CONTROL-LISTING.
       STOP RUN.
 500-PAGE-HEADERS.
*****************************************************************************
*   PERFORMED FROM 200-INITIALIZATION. PRINTS HEADERS FOR LISTING.        *
*****************************************************************************
       MOVE REPORT-HEADER TO PRINT-RECORD-OUT.
       WRITE PRINT-RECORD-OUT
               AFTER ADVANCING PAGE.
       ADD 1 TO WS-PAGE-NUMBER.
       MOVE WS-PAGE-NUMBER TO PD-PAGE-NUMB-OUT.
       MOVE PAGE-DATE-LINE-OUT TO PRINT-RECORD-OUT.
       WRITE PRINT-RECORD-OUT
               AFTER ADVANCING 1 LINE.
       MOVE HEADER-1 TO PRINT-RECORD-OUT.
       WRITE PRINT-RECORD-OUT
               AFTER ADVANCING 2 LINES.
       MOVE SPACES TO PRINT-RECORD-OUT.
       WRITE PRINT-RECORD-OUT
               AFTER ADVANCING 1 LINE.
       MOVE 5 TO LINE-COUNT.
 600-PROCESS-UNMATCHED-TRANS.
*****************************************************************************
*   PERFORMED FROM 300-PROCESS-TRANS-RECORD.  PRINTS REJECTED TRANS       *
*   RECORD AND PROBLEM IN CONTROL LISTING.                                *
*****************************************************************************
```

```
MOVE UNMATCHED-MESSAGE TO DL-MESSAGE-OUT
MOVE TRANS-RECORD-IN TO DL-RECORDIN-OUT.
MOVE WS-RECORD-COUNT TO DL-REC-NUMB-OUT.
IF LINE-COUNT >= 45
          PERFORM 400-PAGE-HEADERS.
WRITE PRINT-RECORD-OUT FROM DETAIL-LINE-OUT
                    AFTER ADVANCING 1 LINE.
```

Figure 14.6. *Change updating the indexed-sequential file INDEXED-MASTER by direct access.*

If two TRANS records have the same TRANS-CUSTOMER-IN value, then the matching master record will simply be read twice and the TRANS-PAYMENT-IN value will be correctly subtracted from the WS-MASTER-OWING field in the master each time. If you did not want an update from a group of records with the same primary key, there would be no alternative to sorting the TRANS file on TRANS-CUSTOMER-IN prior to its use for updating. Then a record with a duplicate TRANS-CUSTOMER-IN value could be detected and rejected using techniques similar to those described in Chapter 13.

Notice how the INVALID KEY clause is used. The syntax for the clause is

SYNTAX   INVALID KEY imperative-statement

A common error is to attempt to do without the RECORD-FOUND identifier and use the following version, which is wrong:

```
300-PROCESS-TRANS-RECORD.
     ADD 1 TO WS-RECORD-COUNT.
     MOVE TRANS-CUSTOMER-IN TO IM-CUSTOMER.
     READ INDEXED-MASTER INTO WS-MASTER-RECORD
          INVALID KEY PERFORM 600-PROCESS-UNMATCHED-TRANS.
     SUBTRACT TRANS-PAYMENT-IN FROM WS-MASTER-OWING.
     REWRITE IM-BUFFER-RECORD FROM WS-MASTER-RECORD.
     READ TRANS RECORD
          AT END MOVE 'NO' TO MORE-RECORDS.
600-PROCESS-UNMATCHED-TRANS.
     ...
```

This is why it is wrong: Suppose a READ INDEXED-MASTER statement does not find a record. In that case, 600-PROCESS-UNMATCHED-TRANS will be executed. However, control returns to the SUBTRACT statement that follows where the value in the master record is the previous record read. This will thus cause an incorrect update. The preceding code would be correct only if no unmatched TRANS records were expected and 600-PROCESS-UNMATCHED-TRANS stopped the program, as in the following:

```
600-PROCESS-UNMATCHED-TRANS.
        DISPLAY 'UNEXPECTED UNMATCHED RECORD, EXECUTION STOPPED'.
        STOP RUN.
```

You can use a NOT INVALID KEY clause

In every verb usable with an indexed file, if an INVALID KEY clause is allowed, you can also use a NOT INVALID KEY clause, with the syntax

SYNTAX   <u>NOT INVALID</u> KEY imperative-statement

The NOT INVALID KEY clause is executed if there is a matching key and the original statement is carried out correctly. Thus, you can also conveniently write the 300-PROCESS-TRANS-RECORD in the previous program as

```
300-PROCESS-TRANS-RECORD.
    ADD 1 TO WS-RECORD-COUNT.
    MOVE TRANS-CUSTOMER-IN TO IM-CUSTOMER IN IM-BUFFER-RECORD.
    READ INDEXED-MASTER INTO WS-MASTER-RECORD
        INVALID KEY
            PERFORM 600-PROCESS-UNMATCHED-TRANS
        NOT INVALID KEY
            SUBTRACT TRANS-PAYMENT-IN FROM WS-MASTER-OWING
            REWRITE IM-BUFFER-RECORD FROM WS-MASTER-RECORD
    END-READ.
    READ TRANS RECORD
            AT END MOVE 'NO' TO MORE-RECORDS.
```

This is a much simpler way to eliminate the RECORD-FOUND identifier and has much to recommend it. The NOT INVALID KEY clause first became available in COBOL 85.

Program using direct-access insertion updating

The only way to carry out insertion updating on an indexed sequential file is by direct-access, commonly with random-access mode, although you can also do it with dynamic-access mode. You cannot do it with sequential-access mode.

Again, TRANS is used as the transaction file. This time TRANS will contain records to be inserted into the file, with the following structure:

```
01 TRANS-RECORD-IN.
    05 TRANS-CUSTOMER-IN      PIC X(15).
    05 OWING-IN               PIC 9(06).
```

It is assumed the records of TRANS

- Are unsorted, but can occur sorted
- Can contain records with duplicate TRANS-CUSTOMER-IN values
- Can contain records with TRANS-CUSTOMER-IN values that already match the IM-CUSTOMER value in INDEXED-MASTER records, that is, unwanted matches

Once again, the essential logic is straightforward.

1. Read next TRANS record.
2. Use the TRANS-CUSTOMER-IN primary key value to insert the record into the master file. If the record is rejected, list it in a control listing as having a primary key already occurring in the master.

A program to insertion update INDEXED-MASTER from TRANS is shown in Figure 14.7.

```
IDENTIFICATION DIVISION.
PROGRAM-ID. INSERT2.
ENVIRONMENT DIVISION.
INPUT-OUTPUT SECTION.
FILE-CONTROL.
    SELECT TRANS
                    ASSIGN TO UT-S-D400.
    SELECT INDEXED-MASTER
                    ASSIGN TO MAST234
                    ORGANIZATION IS INDEXED
                    ACCESS MODE IS RANDOM
                    RECORD KEY IS IM-CUSTOMER.
    SELECT CONTROL-LISTING
                    ASSIGN TO UR-S-SYSPRINT.
DATA DIVISION.
FILE SECTION.
FD  TRANS                          LABEL RECORDS ARE STANDARD.
01  TRANS-RECORD-IN.
    05 TRANS-CUSTOMER-IN  PIC X(15).
    05 OWING-IN           PIC 9(06).
FD  INDEXED-MASTER                 LABEL RECORDS ARE STANDARD.
01  IM-BUFFER-RECORD.
    05  IM-CUSTOMER       PIC X(15).        RECORD KEY must be defined here.
    05  FILLER            PIC 9(06).
FD  CONTROL-LISTING                LABEL RECORDS ARE OMITTED.
01  PRINT-RECORD-OUT      PIC X(133).
WORKING-STORAGE SECTION.
01 WS-WORK-AREAS.
    05  MORE-RECORDS      PIC X(03)     VALUE 'YES'.
    05  LINE-COUNT        PIC 9(02).
    05  WS-PAGE-NUMBER    PIC 9(02)     VALUE ZEROS.
    05  WS-RECORD-COUNT   PIC 9(04)     VALUE ZEROS.
```

```
01   PAGE-DATE-LINE-OUT.
     05   FILLER               PIC X              VALUE SPACE.
     05   FILLER               PIC X(06)          VALUE 'PAGE'
     05   PD-PAGE-NUMB-OUT     PIC 9(02).
     05   FILLER               PIC X(50)          VALUE SPACES.
     05   PD-RUN-DATE-OUT      PIC X(08).
     05   FILLER               PIC X(66)          VALUE SPACES.
01 REPORT-HEADER.
     05   FILLER               PIC X(09)          VALUE SPACES.
     05   FILLER               PIC X(124)         VALUE
                'CONTROL LISTING ON INSERTION UPDATE OF INDEXED MASTER'.
01 HEADER-1.
     05   FILLER               PIC X              VALUE SPACES.
     05   FILLER               PIC X(32)          VALUE 'RECORD#  TRANS RECORD'.
     05   FILLER               PIC X(100)         VALUE 'PROBLEM'.
01 DETAIL-LINE-OUT.
     05   FILLER               PIC X              VALUE SPACES.
     05   DL-REC-NUMB-OUT      PIC 9(04).
     05   FILLER               PIC X(05)          VALUE SPACES.
     05   DL-RECORDIN-OUT      PIC X(21).
     05   FILLER               PIC X(02)          VALUE SPACES.
     05   DL-MESSAGE-OUT       PIC X(100).
01 WS-MESSAGE-DATA-OUT.
     05   MATCHED-MESSAGE      PIC X(17)          VALUE 'MATCHED TRANS KEY'.
01   WS-MASTER-RECORD.
     05 WS-MASTER-CUSTOMER PIC X(15).
     05 WS-MASTER-OWING       PIC 9(06).
PROCEDURE DIVISION.
100-MAIN-MODULE.
**************************************************************************
*   DIRECTS PROGRAM LOGIC.                                             *
**************************************************************************
     PERFORM 200-INITIALIZATION.
     PERFORM 300-PROCESS-TRANS-RECORD
               UNTIL MORE-RECORDS = 'NO'.
     PERFORM 400-TERMINATION.
200-INITIALIZATION.
**************************************************************************
*   PERFORMED FROM 100-MAIN-MODULE. OPENS FILES AND READS FIRST RECORDS. *
**************************************************************************
     OPEN INPUT TRANS
          I-O INDEXED-MASTER
          OUTPUT CONTROL-LISTING.
     MOVE CURRENT-DATE TO PD-RUN-DATE-OUT.
     PERFORM 500-PAGE-HEADERS.
     READ TRANS RECORD
               AT END MOVE 'NO' TO MORE-RECORDS.
```

```
     300-PROCESS-TRANS-RECORD.
*****************************************************************************
*   PERFORMED FROM 100-MAIN-MODULE. INSERTS CURRENT TRANS RECORD            *
*   DIRECTLY INTO INDEXED FILE. READS NEXT TRANS RECORD.                    *
*****************************************************************************
         ADD 1 TO WS-RECORD-COUNT.
         MOVE TRANS-RECORD-IN TO IM-BUFFER-RECORD.
         WRITE IM-BUFFER-RECORD
               INVALID KEY
               PERFORM 600-MATCHING-TRANS-RECORD.
         READ TRANS RECORD
                   AT END MOVE 'NO' TO MORE-RECORDS.
     400-TERMINATION.
*****************************************************************************
*   PERFORMED FROM 100-MAIN-MODULE. CLOSES FILES, STOPS PROGRAM.            *
*****************************************************************************
         CLOSE TRANS
               INDEXED-MASTER
               CONTROL-LISTING.
         STOP RUN.
     500-PAGE-HEADERS.
*****************************************************************************
*   PERFORMED FROM 200-INITIALIZATION.  PRINTS HEADERS FOR CONTROL          *
*   LISTING.                                                                *
*****************************************************************************
         WRITE PRINT-RECORD-OUT FROM REPORT-HEADER
                   AFTER ADVANCING PAGE.
         ADD 1 TO WS-PAGE-NUMBER.
         MOVE WS-PAGE-NUMBER TO PD-PAGE-NUMB-OUT.
         WRITE PRINT-RECORD-OUT FROM PAGE-DATE-LINE-OUT
                   AFTER ADVANCING 1 LINE.
         WRITE PRINT-RECORD-OUT FROM HEADER-1
                   AFTER ADVANCING 2 LINES.
         MOVE SPACES TO PRINT-RECORD-OUT.
         WRITE PRINT-RECORD-OUT
                   AFTER ADVANCING 1 LINE.
         MOVE 5 TO LINE-COUNT.
     600-MATCHING-TRANS-RECORD.
*****************************************************************************
*   PERFORMED FROM 300-PROCESS-TRANS-RECORD.  PRINTS REJECTED TRANS         *
*   RECORD AND PROBLEM IN CONTROL LISTING.                                  *
*****************************************************************************
         MOVE MATCHED-MESSAGE TO DL-MESSAGE-OUT.
         MOVE TRANS-RECORD-IN TO DL-RECORDIN-OUT.
         MOVE WS-RECORD-COUNT TO DL-REC-NUMB-OUT.
         IF LINE-COUNT >= 45
                   PERFORM 400-PAGE-HEADERS.
         WRITE PRINT-RECORD-OUT FROM DETAIL-LINE-OUT
                          AFTER ADVANCING 1 LINE.
```

Figure 14.7 *Insertion updating by direct access.*

If you have two TRANS records with duplicate primary keys, the first will be inserted. The second will not, because by the time a WRITE is executed for it there will already be a record in the master with the same primary key.

Direct-access deletion update example

Direct-access deletion is common with indexed-sequential files, although, as you saw earlier, you can also do it using sequential processing. This time it is assumed that a TRANS record contains the primary key of a record to be deleted, and has the following structure:

```
01 TRANS-RECORD-IN.
   05 TRANS-CUSTOMER-IN      PIC X(15).
```

You can assume that the records of TRANS

- Are unsorted, but can occur sorted
- Can have duplicate values
- Can contain records that do not match any master record, that is, unmatched transactions

The essential logic for the update is

1. Read next TRANS record.
2. Use the TRANS-CUSTOMER-IN primary key value to delete a record in the master file. If the deletion is rejected, list the record in a control listing as having a primary key that is not in the master.

A program to deletion update INDEXED-MASTER from TRANS is shown in Figure 14.8.

```
IDENTIFICATION DIVISION.
PROGRAM-ID. DELETE-2.
ENVIRONMENT DIVISION.
INPUT-OUTPUT SECTION.
FILE-CONTROL.
   SELECT TRANS
               ASSIGN TO UT-S-D400.
   SELECT INDEXED-MASTER
               ASSIGN TO MAST234
               ORGANIZATION IS INDEXED
               ACCESS MODE IS RANDOM
               RECORD KEY IS IM-CUSTOMER.
   SELECT CONTROL-LISTING
               ASSIGN TO UR-S-SYSPRINT.
DATA DIVISION.
```

```
     FILE SECTION.
     FD   TRANS                             LABEL RECORDS ARE STANDARD.
     01   TRANS-RECORD-IN.
          05 TRANS-CUSTOMER-IN   PIC X(15).
     FD   INDEXED-MASTER                    LABEL RECORDS ARE STANDARD.
     01   IM-BUFFER-RECORD.
          05  IM-CUSTOMER        PIC X(15).        RECORD KEY must be defined here.
          05  FILLER             PIC 9(06).
     ...
     WORKING-STORAGE SECTION.
     ...
     01   WS-MASTER-RECORD.
          05 WS-MASTER-CUSTOMER  PIC X(15).
          05 WS-MASTER-OWING     PIC 9(06).
     01   MORE-RECORDS           PIC X(03) VALUE 'YES'.
     PROCEDURE DIVISION.
     100-MAIN-MODULE.
     ***************************************************************************
     *   DIRECTS PROGRAM LOGIC.                                                 *
     ***************************************************************************
          PERFORM 200-INITIALIZATION.
          PERFORM 300-PROCESS-TRANS-RECORD
                     UNTIL MORE-RECORDS = 'NO'.
          PERFORM 400-TERMINATION.
     200-INITIALIZATION.
     ***************************************************************************
     *   PERFORMED FROM 100-MAIN-MODULE. OPENS FILES AND READS FIRST            *
     *   TRANSACTION RECORD.                                                    *
     ***************************************************************************
          OPEN INPUT TRANS
               I-O INDEXED-MASTER
               OUTPUT CONTROL-LISTING.
          ...
          READ TRANS RECORD
               AT END MOVE 'NO' TO MORE-RECORDS.
     300-PROCESS-TRANS-RECORD.
     ***************************************************************************
     *   PERFORMED FROM 100-MAIN-MODULE. USES PRIMARY KEY OF CURRENT TRANS      *
     *   RECORD TO DIRECTLY ACCESS AND DELETE A MASTER RECORD. READS NEXT       *
     *   TRANS RECORD.                                                          *
     ***************************************************************************
          ADD 1 TO WS-RECORD-COUNT.
          MOVE TRANS-CUSTOMER-IN TO IM-CUSTOMER IN IM-BUFFER-RECORD.
          DELETE INDEXED-MASTER
               INVALID KEY
                  PERFORM 600-UNMATCHED-TRANS-RECORD.
          READ TRANS RECORD
                  AT END MOVE 'NO' TO MORE-RECORDS.
```

```
400-TERMINATION.
**************************************************************************
*   PERFORMED FROM 100-MAIN-MODULE. CLOSES FILES, STOPS PROGRAM.       *
**************************************************************************
      CLOSE TRANS
            INDEXED-MASTER
            CONTROL-LISTING.
      STOP RUN.
          ...
  500-PAGE-HEADERS.
  ...
  600-PROCESS-UNMATCHED-TRANS.
          lists record in control listing
```

Figure 14.8 Program using the transaction file TRANS to delete records from the indexed-sequential file INDEXED-MASTER by direct access.

If there are two TRANS records with duplicate but matching primary keys, the first will cause a master record deletion. The second will not, because by the time it has been read in, there will be no record in the master with the same primary key.

Programs using generalized updating

This time it is assumed that each record of TRANS contains an UPDATE-CODE field to distinguish three different types of transaction record: insertion update (code 1), change update (code 2), and deletion update (code 3). A record of TRANS can have the structure:

```
01 TRANS-RECORD-IN.
   05 TRANS-UPDATE-CODE              PIC 9.     values 1, 2, or 3
   05 TRANS-DATA.
      10   TRANS-CUSTOMER-IN         PIC X(15).
      10   AMOUNT-IN                 PIC 9(06).
```

Some records of TRANS could be

```
1AVROCORP        096000
3BANKCORP        bbbbbb
2BUNTORAMO       004000
2CONDATA         023000
2CONDATA         007000
1DEXCORP         125000
2DEXCORP         006000
3DUVAL           bbbbbb
    ...
```

Update code 1 means that the TRANS record is to be inserted into INDEXED-MASTER. Code 2 means the AMOUNT-IN field is to be used to change update the master. And Code 3 means the corresponding master record is to be deleted.

Assume that the records have been sorted on the TRANS-CUSTOMER-IN value primarily, and secondarily on the TRANS-UPDATE-CODE field. (They have to be sorted on TRANS-UPDATE-CODE at least; otherwise there is no way to handle the updates for DEXCORP, where a new record must first be inserted and then updated.)

It is also assumed that

- Change and deletion update TRANS records with unmatched primary key values can occur
- TRANS insertion records with matched primary key values can occur
- TRANS records with the same update code can have the same TRANS-CUSTOMER-IN value

The essential pseudocode for the update is

```
READ next TRANS record.
IF update code is 1
        PERFORM Insertion-update.
IF update code is 2
        PERFORM Change-update.
IF update code is 3
        PERFORM Deletion-update.
```

Insertion-Update

Use the TRANS-CUSTOMER-IN primary key value to insert the record into the master file. If the record is rejected, list it in a control listing as having a primary key already occurring in the master.

Change-Update

1. Use TRANS-CUSTOMER-IN value to directly read matching INDEXED-MASTER record.
2. IF no matching master record is found,
   THEN
           list record as an error record
   ELSE
           subtract payment from WS-MASTER-OWING in master
               record,
           rewrite master record just read onto the disk.
   END-IF.

Deletion-Update

Use the TRANS-CUSTOMER-IN primary key value to delete a record in the master file. If the deletion is rejected, list the record in a control listing as having a primary key that is not in the master.

A program for carrying out this update is shown in Figure 14.9.

```cobol
IDENTIFICATION DIVISION.
PROGRAM-ID. CHUPDATE.

ENVIRONMENT DIVISION.
INPUT-OUTPUT SECTION.
FILE-CONTROL.
    SELECT TRANS
                    ASSIGN TO UT-S-D400.
    SELECT INDEXED-MASTER
                    ASSIGN TO MAST234
                    ORGANIZATION IS INDEXED
                    ACCESS MODE IS RANDOM
                    RECORD KEY IS IM-CUSTOMER.
    SELECT CONTROL-LISTING
                    ASSIGN TO UR-S-SYSPRINT.
DATA DIVISION.
FILE SECTION.
FD  TRANS                            LABEL RECORDS ARE STANDARD.
01  TRANS-RECORD-IN.
    05 TRANS-UPDATE-CODE      PIC 9.          values 1, 2, or 3
    05 TRANS-DATA-IN.
        10 TRANS-CUST-IN      PIC X(15).
        10 TRANS-AMOUNT-IN    PIC 9(06).
FD  INDEXED-MASTER                   LABEL RECORDS ARE STANDARD.
01  IM-BUFFER-RECORD.
    05  IM-CUSTOMER           PIC X(15).      RECORD KEY must be defined here.
    05  FILLER                PIC 9(06).
FD  CONTROL-LISTING                  LABEL RECORDS ARE OMITTED.
01  PRINT-RECORD-OUT          PIC X(133).
WORKING-STORAGE SECTION.
01 WS-WORK-AREAS.
    05   MORE-RECORDS         PIC X(03)     VALUE 'YES'.
    05   LINE-COUNT           PIC 9(02).
    05   WS-PAGE-NUMBER       PIC 9(02)     VALUE ZEROS.
    05   WS-RECORD-COUNT      PIC 9(04)     VALUE ZERO.
01 PAGE-DATE-LINE-OUT.
    05   FILLER               PIC X         VALUE SPACE.
    05   FILLER               PIC X(06)     VALUE 'PAGE'.
    05   PD-PAGE-NUMB-OUT     PIC 9(02).
    05   FILLER               PIC X(50)     VALUE SPACES.
    05   PD-RUN-DATE-OUT      PIC X(08).
    05   FILLER               PIC X(66)     VALUE SPACES.
01 REPORT-HEADER.
    05   FILLER               PIC X(09)     VALUE SPACES.
    05   FILLER               PIC X(124)    VALUE
                    'CONTROL LISTING ON GENERAL UPDATE OF INDEXED MASTER'.
01 HEADER-1.
    05   FILLER           PIC X          VALUE SPACES.
    05   FILLER           PIC X(32)      VALUE 'RECORD#  TRANS RECORD'.
    05   FILLER           PIC X(100)     VALUE 'PROBLEM'.
```

```
01 DETAIL-LINE-OUT.
    05  FILLER              PIC X            VALUE SPACES.
    05  DL-REC-NUMB-OUT     PIC 9(04).
    05  FILLER              PIC X(05)        VALUE SPACES.
    05  DL-RECORDIN-OUT     PIC X(22).
    05  FILLER              PIC X(02)        VALUE SPACES.
    05  DL-MESSAGE-OUT      PIC X(99).
01 WS-MESSAGE-DATA-OUT.
    05  MATCHED-MESSAGE     PIC X(17)        VALUE 'MATCHED TRANS KEY'.
    05  UNMATCHED-MESSAGE   PIC X(19)        VALUE 'UNMATCHED TRANS KEY'.
    05  CODE-MESSAGE        PIC X(19)        VALUE 'INVALID UPDATE CODE'.
01 WS-MASTER-RECORD.
    05 WS-MASTER-CUSTOMER   PIC X(15).
    05 WS-MASTER-OWING      PIC 9(06).
PROCEDURE DIVISION.
100-MAIN-MODULE.
****************************************************************************
*   DIRECTS PROGRAM LOGIC.                                               *
****************************************************************************
    PERFORM 200-INITIALIZATION.
    PERFORM 300-PROCESS-TRANS-RECORD
            UNTIL MORE-RECORDS = 'NO'.
    PERFORM 700-TERMINATION.
200-INITIALIZATION.
****************************************************************************
*   PERFORMED FROM 100-MAIN-MODULE. OPENS FILES AND READS FIRST RECORDS. *
****************************************************************************
    OPEN INPUT TRANS
         I-O INDEXED-MASTER
         OUTPUT CONTROL-LISTING.
    MOVE CURRENT-DATE TO PD-RUN-DATE-OUT.
    PERFORM 800-PAGE-HEADERS.
    READ TRANS RECORD
        AT END MOVE 'NO' TO MORE-RECORDS.
300-PROCESS-TRANS-RECORD.
****************************************************************************
*   PERFORMED FROM 100-MAIN-MODULE. DECIDES KIND OF ACTION WITH TRANS    *
*   RECORD AND CARRIES IT OUT. READS NEXT TRANS RECORD.                  *
****************************************************************************
    ADD 1 TO WS-RECORD-COUNT.
    EVALUATE TRANS-UPDATE-CODE
            WHEN 1 PERFORM 400-INSERTION-UPDATE
            WHEN 2 PERFORM 500-CHANGE-UPDATE
            WHEN 3 PERFORM 600-DELETION-UPDATE
            WHEN OTHER
                PERFORM 900-PROBLEM-TRANS-RECORD.
    READ TRANS RECORD
            AT END MOVE 'NO' TO MORE-RECORDS.
```

```
400-INSERTION-UPDATE.
*********************************************************************
*   PERFORMED FROM 300-PROCESS-TRANS-RECORD. PLACES CURRENT TRANS DATA   *
*   IN CORRECT POSITION IN INDEXED FILE.                                 *
*********************************************************************
      MOVE TRANS-DATA-IN TO IM-BUFFER-RECORD.
      WRITE IM-BUFFER-RECORD
          INVALID KEY
          PERFORM 900-PROBLEM-TRANS-RECORD.
 500-CHANGE-UPDATE.
*********************************************************************
*   PERFORMED FROM 300-PROCESS-TRANS-RECORD. USES PRIMARY KEY IN CURRENT *
*   TRANS RECORD TO DIRECTLY ACCESS AND UPDATE MATCHING MASTER RECORD.   *
*********************************************************************
      MOVE TRANS-CUST-IN TO IM-CUSTOMER.
      READ INDEXED-MASTER INTO WS-MASTER-RECORD
          INVALID KEY
              PERFORM 900-PROBLEM-TRANS-RECORD
          NOT INVALID KEY
            SUBTRACT TRANS-AMOUNT-IN FROM WS-MASTER-OWING
            REWRITE IM-BUFFER-RECORD FROM WS-MASTER-RECORD
      END-READ.
 600-DELETION-UPDATE.
*********************************************************************
*   PERFORMED FROM 300-PROCESS-TRANS-RECORD. USES PRIMARY KEY IN         *
*   CURRENT TRANS RECORD TO DIRECTLY ACCESS AND DELETE THE MATCHING      *
*   MASTER RECORD.                                                       *
*********************************************************************
      MOVE TRANS-CUST-IN TO IM-CUSTOMER.
      DELETE INDEXED-MASTER
          INVALID KEY
          PERFORM 900-PROBLEM-TRANS-RECORD.
 700-TERMINATION.
*********************************************************************
*   PERFORMED FROM 100-MAIN-MODULE. CLOSES FILES, STOPS PROGRAM.         *
*********************************************************************
      CLOSE TRANS.
      CLOSE INDEXED-MASTER.
      CLOSE CONTROL-LISTING.
      STOP RUN.
 800-PAGE-HEADERS.
*********************************************************************
*   PERFORMED FROM 200-INITIALIZATION. PRINTS HEADERS FOR CONTROL       *
*   LISTING.                                                            *
*********************************************************************
      WRITE PRINT-RECORD-OUT FROM REPORT-HEADER
              AFTER ADVANCING PAGE.
      ADD 1 TO WS-PAGE-NUMBER.
      MOVE WS-PAGE-NUMBER TO PD-PAGE-NUMB-OUT.
      WRITE PRINT-RECORD-OUT FROM PAGE-DATE-LINE-OUT
              AFTER ADVANCING 1 LINE.
```

```
        WRITE PRINT-RECORD-OUT FROM HEADER-1
                AFTER ADVANCING 2 LINES.
        MOVE SPACES TO PRINT-RECORD-OUT.
        WRITE PRINT-RECORD-OUT
                AFTER ADVANCING 1 LINE.
        MOVE 5 TO LINE-COUNT.
    900-PROBLEM-TRANS-RECORD.
    ************************************************************************
    *   PERFORMED FROM 300-PROCESS-TRANS-RECORD.  PRINTS REJECTED TRANS   *
    *   RECORD AND PROBLEM IN CONTROL LISTING.                            *
    ************************************************************************
        EVALUATE TRANS-UPDATE-CODE
                WHEN 1 MOVE MATCHED-MESSAGE TO DL-MESSAGE-OUT
                WHEN 2 MOVE UNMATCHED-MESSAGE TO DL-MESSAGE-OUT
                WHEN 3 MOVE UNMATCHED-MESSAGE TO DL-MESSAGE-OUT
                WHEN OTHER
                        MOVE CODE-MESSAGE TO DL-MESSAGE-OUT.
        MOVE TRANS-RECORD-IN TO DL-RECORDIN-OUT.
        MOVE WS-RECORD-COUNT TO DL-REC-NUMB-OUT.
        IF LINE-COUNT >= 45
                PERFORM 400-PAGE-HEADERS.
        WRITE PRINT-RECORD-OUT FROM DETAIL-LINE-OUT
                        AFTER ADVANCING 1 LINE.
```

Figure 14.9 *Generalized updating of the indexed-sequential file INDEXED-MASTER by direct access.*

Any rejected TRANS records are listed in the control listing, along with an explanation of the problem.

14.4
Indexed-sequential files are often used for information retrieval

INFORMATION RETRIEVAL with an indexed-sequential file can involve either sequential processing or direct-access processing. With sequential processing, a typical information retrieval task would involve generation of a report by control-break processing of the master, where the master is processed as a sequential input file. This task was discussed in Chapter 10.

With direct-access processing, a typical information retrieval task involves retrieving some records with primary keys that are either listed in a query file or are entered directly at the keyboard. Let us look next at an example of this.

You can use a query file for information retrieval

Suppose that a query file, QUERYFILE, to be used with the file INDEXED-MASTER from previous sections has records with the structure

```
01 QUERY-BUF-REC-IN.
    05 QUERY-CUSTOMER        PIC X(15).
```

Each record could list the primary key of a delinquent IM-CUSTOMER record, that is, that of a customer who has not made any payments towards reducing the amount owing. You need to know the total WS-MASTER-OWING values of such delinquent customers.

To carry out the processing, the primary key of each record in QUERY-FILE is used to retrieve a record from INDEXED-MASTER, and the WS-MASTER-OWING value in each record retrieved is added to a summation identifier SUM-OWING. Records not found are listed in a control listing. The essentials of the processing are

```
ENVIRONMENT DIVISION.
FILE-CONTROL.
   SELECT QUERY-FILE
                 ASSIGN UT-S-QUE34.
   SELECT INDEXED-MASTER
                 ASSIGN TO MAST234
        ORGANIZATION IS INDEXED
        ACCESS MODE IS RANDOM
        RECORD KEY IS IM-CUSTOMER.
DATA DIVISION.
FILE SECTION.
FD  QUERY-FILE               LABEL RECORDS ARE STANDARD.
01  QUERY-RECORD-IN.
    05 QUERY-CUSTOMER    PIC X(15).
FD   INDEXED-MASTER          LABEL RECORDS ARE STANDARD.
01   IM-BUFFER-RECORD.
     05  IM-CUSTOMER     PIC X(15.     RECORD KEY must be defined here.
     05  FILLER          PIC 9(06).
WORKING-STORAGE SECTION.
01 WS-WORK-AREAS.
    05   MORE-RECORDS    PIC X(03)      VALUE 'YES'.
    05   SUM-OWING       PIC 9(7)       VALUE ZERO.
    05   EDIT-SUM        PIC $Z,ZZZ,ZZ9.
01  WS-MASTER-RECORD.
    05 WS-MASTER-CUSTOMER  PIC X(15).
    05 WS-MASTER-OWING     PIC 9(06).
01  DETAIL-LINE ...
PROCEDURE DIVISION.
100-MAIN-MODULE.
************************************************************************
*   DIRECTS PROGRAM LOGIC.                                           *
************************************************************************
    PERFORM 200-INITIALIZATION.
    PERFORM 300-PROCESS-QUERY-RECORD
              UNTIL MORE-RECORDS = 'NO'
    PERFORM 400-TERMINATION.
```

```
 200-INITIALIZATION.
********************************************************************
*  PERFORMED FROM 100-MAIN-MODULE. OPENS FILES AND READS FIRST RECORD.  *
********************************************************************
     OPEN INPUT QUERY-FILE,
             I-O INDEXED-MASTER.
     READ QUERY-FILE RECORD
             AT END MOVE 'NO' TO MORE-RECORDS.
 300-PROCESS-QUERY-RECORD.
********************************************************************
*  PERFORMED FROM 100-MAIN-MODULE. USES PRIMARY KEY FROM QUERY-FILE  *
*  RECORD TO DIRECTLY ACCESS THE MATCHING MASTER AND ADD ITS AMOUNT  *
*  OWING VALUE TO A TOTAL IDENTIFIER SUM-OWING.                      *
********************************************************************
     MOVE QUERY-CUSTOMER TO IM-CUSTOMER IN IM-BUFFER-RECORD.
     READ INDEXED-MASTER INTO WS-MASTER-RECORD
         INVALID KEY
         PERFORM 500-CONTROL-LIST-ENTRY.
         NOT INVALID KEY
            ADD WS-MASTER-OWING TO SUM-OWING
     END-READ.
     READ QUERY-FILE RECORD
             AT END MOVE 'NO' TO MORE-RECORDS.
 400-TERMINATION.
********************************************************************
*  PERFORMED FROM 100-MAIN-MODULE. DISPLAYS TOTAL SUM OWING, CLOSES  *
*  FILES, AND STOPS EXECUTION.                                       *
********************************************************************
     MOVE SUM-OWING TO EDIT-OWING.
     DISPLAY 'TOTAL DELINQUENT AMOUNT:  ', EDIT-OWING.
     CLOSE QUERY,
             INDEXED-MASTER.
     STOP RUN.
 500-CONTROL-LIST-ENTRY.
 ...
```

You can query the file from a terminal

Indexed-sequential files are very well suited for responding to a query entered via a terminal. For example, suppose that an accountant wants to quickly retrieve the amount owing for any customer, simply by entering the customer name at a terminal. The essentials of the procedure for a program to do this are as follows:

```
FD   INDEXED-MASTER            LABEL RECORDS ARE STANDARD.
01   IM-BUFFER-RECORD.
     05   IM-CUSTOMER      PIC X(15).              RECORD KEY must be defined here.
     05   FILLER           PIC 9(06).
...
01   QUERY-CUSTOMER        PIC X(15).
PROCEDURE DIVISION.
     100-MAIN-MODULE.
     PERFORM 200-INITIALIZATION.
     PERFORM 300-PROCESS-QUERY.
     PERFORM 400-TERMINATION.
200-INITIALIZATION.
     OPEN I-O INDEXED-MASTER.
     DISPLAY 'SYSTEM READY FOR QUERYING ACCOUNTS RECEIVABLE DATA'.
     DISPLAY 'ENTER CUSTOMER NAME'.
300-PROCESS-QUERY.
     ACCEPT QUERY-CUSTOMER.
     MOVE QUERY-CUSTOMER TO IM-CUSTOMER.
     READ INDEXED-MASTER INTO WS-MASTER-RECORD
       INVALID KEY
           DISPLAY 'CUSTOMER: ', IM-CUSTOMER, ' NOT IN FILE'
       NOT INVALID KEY
           DISPLAY 'AMOUNT OWING FOR CUSTOMER: ', IM-CUSTOMER,
                   ' IS: ', IM-OWING
     END-READ.
400-TERMINATION.
     DISPLAY 'PROGRAM TERMINATED'.
     CLOSE INDEXED-MASTER.
     STOP RUN.
```

This short program allows only one query before terminating. A modified version, involving repeated execution of 300-PROCESS-QUERY, can be written to permit a user to enter a sequence of requests one after another from a terminal.

The preceding is an example of an interactive program. A more efficient way to execute interactive programs is by means of a system called a *teleprocessing monitor*, which allows many users at different terminals to execute the same program concurrently. This topic is covered in Chapter 18.

The primary key limits information retrieval

With a straight indexed-sequential file, the user must know the primary key of a record in order to have it retrieved. This limits the types of retrievals that can be carried out. With many indexed-sequential files, in addition to the normal index for retrieval on the basis of a primary key value, it is possible to have secondary indexes constructed for direct-access retrieval on the basis of non-primary key fields.

14.5
A secondary index permits direct-access on a non-primary key field

A SECONDARY INDEX allows direct-access to the records of a disk file on the basis of a non-primary key field, that is, on the basis of a *secondary key* field. A secondary key field will normally have values that are not unique.

In order for a field to be used as a secondary key, a secondary key index must be constructed for that specific field. Thus an indexed sequential file with two secondary key fields will require three indexes: a primary index for the primary key and a distinct secondary index for each of the secondary keys.

With the VSAM access method, when an indexed-sequential file is created, a primary index for the primary key is constructed automatically. However, if one or more secondary keys are specified in the SELECT statement, VSAM will construct secondary indexes for these fields as well.

Let us begin with the concept of a secondary index. Then you will see how to create a file with one and how to make use of it.

The secondary index idea is ingenious

Suppose you have an indexed-sequential master file IS-EMPLOYEE, with records that describe employees of a large company with business locations in many cities. The structure of a record is

```
01  IS-EMPLOYEE-BUFFER-RECORD.
    05  IS-EMPNUMB      PIC X(06).      employee number, primary  key
    05  IS-SALARY       PIC 9(05).
    05  IS-CITY         PIC X(15).
    05  IS-SKILL        PIC X(15).
```

For the sake of the discussion, suppose you have only a few records in IS-EMPLOYEE, as shown in Figure 14.10a (with extra spacing between fields).

IS-EMPNUMB	IS-SALARY	IS-CITY	IS-SKILL
E00001	24000	MIAMI	PROGRAMMER
E00003	33500	DENVER	ENGINEER
E00004	18000	MIAMI	SECRETARY
E00006	37000	SEATTLE	PROGRAMMER
E00009	23000	DENVER	PROGRAMMER
E00012	17500	DENVER	SECRETARY
. . .			

IS-EMPLOYEE

Figure 14.10a Indexed-sequential file IS-EMPLOYEE with primary key IS-EMPNUMB.

X-CITY	REFERENCE-1	REFERENCE-2	REFERENCE-3	REFERENCE-4
DENVER	E00003	E00009	E00012	-
MIAMI	E00001	E00004	-	-
SEATTLE	E00006	-	-	

CITY-INDEX

Figure 14.10b *Secondary index for the secondary key IS-CITY. This index is also an indexed-sequential file with primary key X-CITY.*

X-SKILL	REFERENCE-1	REFERENCE-2	REFERENCE-3	REFERENCE-4
ENGINEER	E00003	-	-	-
PROGRAMMER	E00001	E00006	E00009	-
SECRETARY	E00004	E00012	-	-

SKILL-INDEX

Figure 14.10c *Secondary index for the secondary key IS-SKILL. This index is also an indexed-sequential file with primary key X-SKILL.*

Figure 14.10b shows a simple secondary index called CITY-INDEX for the field IS-CITY of the IS-EMPLOYEE file. This secondary index is a file in its own right. It is typically organized as an indexed-sequential file. The primary key of this file is X-CITY, and there is an X-CITY value for each IS-CITY value in IS-EMPLOYEE. The primary index for CITY-INDEX is not shown.

For each IS-CITY value in IS-EMPLOYEE there is a record in CITY-INDEX. This record contains the IS-CITY value (in X-CITY) and the primary key IS-EMPNUMB field value for each IS-EMPLOYEE record with that particular IS-CITY value. Thus, the CITY-INDEX record for 'MIAMI', for example, lists 'E00001' and 'E00004' as the primary keys of records in IS-EMPLOYEE that have a IS-CITY value 'MIAMI'.

Figure 14.10c shows another secondary index, called SKILL-INDEX, for the field IS-SKILL in IS-EMPLOYEE. The SKILL-INDEX record for SECRETARY, for example, lists 'E00004' and 'E00012' as the primary keys for IS-EMPLOYEE records with the IS-SKILL value 'SECRETARY'.

Use of a secondary index for direct-access with a given secondary key value

You can use a secondary index for direct-access to records with a given secondary key value. For example, suppose you want to know the salaries of employees in Miami. You could proceed as follows:

1. Read the record of the indexed-sequential file CITY-INDEX by presenting 'MIAMI' as the primary key and place it in CITY-INDEX-RECORD.
2. Take the value E00001 from CITY-INDEX-RECORD and use it to directly access the indexed-sequential file IS-EMPLOYEE. Output the $24,000 value extracted for the IS-SALARY value.

3. Take the value E00004 from CITY-INDEX-RECORD and use it to directly access the indexed-sequential file IS-EMPLOYEE. Output the $18,000 value extracted for the IS-SALARY value.

Notice that for a given secondary key field value

- There has to be a secondary index for the field.
- More than one record will likely be retrieved from IS-EMPLOYEE with that field value.

Secondary indexes are useful for arbitrary information retrieval requests involving large files.

The VSAM access method will handle secondary indexes

With VSAM indexed-sequential files, one or more secondary indexes can be constructed automatically by the VSAM input/output routine (access method) as the records of the file are written out. Later, to retrieve a group of records with a given secondary key value from the file, VSAM permits the records of this group to be retrieved one by one, simply by issuing a direct-access READ statement for the first of this group of records and a sequential READ NEXT statement for each of the remaining records of the group. Thus, VSAM shields the programmer from the details of how a secondary index is managed.

Creating a VSAM Indexed-Sequential File with Secondary Keys

Suppose you want to create the indexed-sequential master file IS-EMPLOYEE in Figure 14.10a, but with associated secondary indexes for the fields IS-CITY and IS-SKILL, in addition. Assume that validated source records are available in the sequential file SOURCE-FILE-IN. You proceed exactly as if you were creating an ordinary indexed-sequential file, except for ALTERNATE KEY entries. The VSAM term for a secondary key is ALTERNATE KEY. The file creation program is shown in Figure 14.11.

To allow you to better concentrate on the essentials, details concerning the control listing have been omitted. A control listing would be essential in commercial practice; instead, here DISPLAY has been used for any problem with a source record.

```
        IDENTIFICATION DIVISION.
        PROGRAM-ID. SECINDX.
        ENVIRONMENT DIVISION.
        INPUT-OUTPUT SECTION.
        FILE-CONTROL.
            SELECT SOURCE-FILE-IN
                            ASSIGN TO UT-S-SFDATA12.
            SELECT IS-EMPLOYEE
                            ASSIGN TO MAST234
                            ORGANIZATION IS INDEXED
                            ACCESS MODE IS SEQUENTIAL
                            RECORD KEY IS IS-EMPNUMB
                            ALTERNATE RECORD KEY IS IS-CITY
                                    WITH DUPLICATES
                            ALTERNATE RECORD KEY IS IS-SKILL
                                    WITH DUPLICATES.
        DATA DIVISION.
        FILE SECTION.
        FD    SOURCE-FILE-IN              LABEL RECORDS ARE STANDARD
                                          RECORD CONTAINS 41 CHARACTERS
                                          BLOCK CONTAINS 200 RECORDS.

        01    SOURCE-RECORD-IN    PIC X(41).
        FD    IS-EMPLOYEE                 LABEL RECORDS ARE STANDARD.
        01    IS-EMPLOYEE-BUFFER-RECORD.
              05 IS-EMPNUMB       PIC X(06).    employee number, primary key
              05 IS-SALARY        PIC 9(05).
              05 IS-CITY          PIC X(15).    secondary key
              05 IS-SKILL         PIC X(15).    secondary key
        WORKING-STORAGE SECTION.
        01  MORE-RECORDS          PIC X(03)     VALUE 'YES'.
        PROCEDURE DIVISION.
        100-MAIN-MODULE.
        ****************************************************************
        *   DIRECTS PROGRAM LOGIC.                                    *
        ****************************************************************
            PERFORM 200-INITIALIZATION.
            PERFORM 300-PROCESS-RECORD
                        UNTIL MORE-RECORDS = 'NO'.
            PERFORM 400-TERMINATION.
        200-INITIALIZATION.
        ****************************************************************
        *   PERFORMED FROM 100-MAIN-MODULE. OPENS FILES AND READS FIRST RECORD   *
        ****************************************************************
            OPEN INPUT SOURCE-FILE-IN,
                    OUTPUT IS-EMPLOYEE.
            READ SOURCE-FILE-IN RECORD
                        AT END MOVE 'NO' TO MORE-RECORDS.
```

```
 300-PROCESS-RECORD.
****************************************************************************
*   PERFORMED FROM 100-MAIN-MODULE. WRITES CURRENT SOURCE RECORD TO         *
*   INDEXED FILE. READS NEXT SOURCE RECORD.                                 *
****************************************************************************
      MOVE SOURCE-RECORD-IN TO IS-EMPLOYEE-BUFFER-RECORD.
      WRITE IS-EMPLOYEE-BUFFER-RECORD
       INVALID KEY
         DISPLAY 'DUPLICATE OR OUT-OF-SEQUENCE KEY:  ', IS-EMPNUMB.
      READ SOURCE-FILE-IN RECORD
              AT END MOVE 'NO' TO MORE-RECORDS.
 400-TERMINATION.
****************************************************************************
*   PERFORMED FROM 100-MAIN-MODULE. CLOSES FILES, STOPS PROGRAM.            *
****************************************************************************
      CLOSE SOURCE-FILE-IN
            IS-EMPLOYEE.
      STOP RUN.
```

Figure 14.11 *Program to create an indexed-sequential file IS-EMPLOYEE with secondary keys from a sequential source file SOURCE-FILE-IN containing already validated records.*

Execution of this program would place the records of IS-EMPLOYEE on disk, in addition to a primary index for the IS-EMPNUMB field and a secondary index for each of the IS-CITY and IS-SKILL fields.

In the SELECT statement, the ALTERNATE RECORD clauses

```
ALTERNATE RECORD KEY IS IS-CITY
                    WITH DUPLICATES
ALTERNATE RECORD KEY IS IS-SKILL
                    WITH DUPLICATES.
```

give the names of the secondary keys. These must be defined in the buffer record for the file (IS-EMPLOYEE-BUFFER-RECORD).

The WITH DUPLICATES clause can be omitted in the (rare) case where the secondary key field will have unique values. In that case, the secondary key index would have the same structure as the primary key index. An example would be a file with records that describe insured automobiles at an insurance company. Policy number could be the primary key (RECORD KEY) and would have unique values. However, access might also be required on engine number, which would also be unique for each automobile and therefore each record.

COBOL 85 requires that the secondary keys be alphanumeric. This restriction is of little importance since, in practice, almost all secondary key fields are alphanumeric. However, some compilers allow numeric secondary keys.

Retrieval of Information Using a Secondary Key

Suppose an accountant was accustomed to retrieving the total payroll for a given city, such as 'DENVER', by entering the city value at a terminal. A program to do this would have to retrieve the records for Denver and add the IS-SALARY values to a TOTAL-PAY identifier, which would then be printed.

Each Denver record can be retrieved by a READ statement, but, as mentioned earlier, both direct-access and sequential READs are needed. The direct-access READ retrieves the first record of the group of DENVER records, and this READ must specify which secondary key is involved, since it could be either IS-CITY or IS-SKILL. You would code as follows:

```
MOVE 'DENVER' TO IS-CITY.
READ IS-EMPLOYEE RECORD,
         KEY IS IS-CITY,
         INVALID KEY PERFORM 500-ROUTINE.
```

This will retrieve the record for IS-EMPLOYEE E00003 (see Figure 14.10).

To retrieve the remaining Denver records, you repeatedly execute a sequential READ statement with a NEXT RECORD clause.

```
READ IS-EMPLOYEE NEXT RECORD,
         AT END MOVE 'NO' TO MORE-TARGET-RECORDS.
```

When eventually a record is read (in this context called the *record of reference*) that has an IS-CITY value different from 'DENVER', the AT END clause is executed. The complete program for such a retrieval is shown in Figure 14.12.

```
IDENTIFICATION DIVISION.
PROGRAM-ID. QUERYPGM.
ENVIRONMENT DIVISION.
INPUT-OUTPUT SECTION.
FILE-CONTROL.
    SELECT IS-EMPLOYEE
                ASSIGN TO MAST234
                ORGANIZATION IS INDEXED
                ACCESS MODE IS DYNAMIC
                RECORD KEY IS IS-EMPNUMB
                ALTERNATE RECORD KEY IS IS-CITY
                            WITH DUPLICATES.
DATA DIVISION.
FILE SECTION.
FD   IS-EMPLOYEE         LABEL RECORDS ARE STANDARD.
01   IS-EMPLOYEE-BUFFER-RECORD.
     05  IS-EMPNUMB          PIC X(06).    employee number, primary key
     05  IS-SALARY           PIC 9(05).
     05  IS-CITY             PIC X(15).    secondary key
     05  IS-SKILL            PIC X(15).
```

```
 WORKING-STORAGE SECTION.
 01 WS-WORKING-STORAGE.
      05   MORE-T-RECORDS      PIC X(03)     VALUE 'YES'.
      05   RECORD-FOUND        PIC X(03)     VALUE 'NO'.
      05   TOTAL-PAY           PIC 9(07).
      05   TOTAL-PAY-OUT       PIC $Z,Z99,999.
      05   QUERY-CITY          PIC X(15).
 PROCEDURE DIVISION.
 100-MAIN-MODULE.
 ****************************************************************************
 *   DIRECTS PROGRAM LOGIC.                                                *
 ****************************************************************************
      PERFORM 200-INITIALIZATION.
      PERFORM 300-PROCESS-QUERY.
      PERFORM 500-TERMINATION.
 200-INITIALIZATION.
 ****************************************************************************
 *   PERFORMED FROM 100-MAIN-MODULE. OPENS FILES AND DISPLAYS MESSAGES.    *
 ****************************************************************************
      OPEN INPUT IS-EMPLOYEE.
      DISPLAY 'SYSTEM READY FOR QUERYING IS-EMPLOYEE DATA'.
      DISPLAY 'ENTER IS-CITY'.
 300-PROCESS-QUERY.
 ****************************************************************************
 *   PERFORMED FROM 100-MAIN-MODULE. READS CITY VALUE FROM KEYBOARD OF     *
 *   TERMINAL AND USES IT TO DIRECTLY ACCESS THE FIRST RECORD WITH THAT    *
 *   CITY VALUE. IF THERE IS SUCH A RECORD, REMAINING RECORDS WITH THAT    *
 *   VALUE ARE ACCESSED IN SEQUENCE.                                       *
 ****************************************************************************
      ACCEPT QUERY-CITY.
      MOVE QUERY-CITY TO IS-CITY.
      READ IS-EMPLOYEE RECORD
        KEY IS IS-CITY
          INVALID KEY
             DISPLAY 'CITY: ', IS-CITY, ' NOT IN FILE'
          NOT INVALID KEY
                PERFORM 400-TOTAL-SALARIES
                    UNTIL MORE-T-RECORDS = 'NO'
             MOVE 'YES' TO RECORD-FOUND
      END-READ.
 400-TOTAL-SALARIES.
 ****************************************************************************
 *   PERFORMED FROM 300-PROCESS-QUERY. ADDS THE SALARY FROM RECORD         *
 *   RETRIEVED TO A TOTALS IDENTIFIER.                                     *
 ****************************************************************************
      ADD IS-SALARY TO TOTAL-PAY.
      READ IS-EMPLOYEE NEXT RECORD,
             AT END MOVE 'NO' TO MORE-T-RECORDS.
```

```
 500-TERMINATION.
 ***********************************************************************
 *   PERFORMED FROM 100-MAIN-MODULE. DISPLAYS RESULTS, CLOSES MASTER    *
 *   FILE, AND STOPS PROGRAM.                                           *
 ***********************************************************************
     IF RECORD-FOUND = 'YES'
         MOVE TOTAL-PAY TO TOTAL-PAY-OUT
         DISPLAY 'PAYROLL FOR ', IS-CITY, 'IS ', TOTAL-PAY-OUT.
     DISPLAY 'PROGRAM TERMINATED'.
     CLOSE IS-EMPLOYEE.
     STOP RUN.
```

Figure 14.12 *Direct access using a secondary key.*

The program structure assumes that the city value is entered at a terminal and taken up by an ACCEPT statement.

Note that ACCESS MODE IS DYNAMIC must be used here. DYNAMIC must be specified anytime you want to open a file for both direct and sequential access.

Recall that a NEXT RECORD clause is needed with any (sequential) READ . . . AT END statement when ACCESS MODE IS DYNAMIC is used.

Watch out for the order of secondary key retrieval

VSAM records with the same secondary key are retrieved in the order of insertion, or chronological order, whereas they are stored in the IS-EMPLOYEE file in ascending primary key order, because it is an indexed-sequential file. It may thus be necessary to sort records retrieved by secondary key access.

Updating is slower with secondary keys

A secondary key is specified when an indexed-sequential file is created only after careful consideration of whether it can be done without. The problem is that during updating of the file, the input/output routine will have to maintain both the primary index and any secondary index.

Ideally, a secondary index would be created only for a field that is used for direct-access, but is never updated, so that the secondary index would never need updating. In practice, you choose fields that are used a great deal for direct-access retrievals and less for updating.

14.6
The START verb permits sequential processing from any position in the file

*T*HE START VERB can be used with either primary or secondary key access to begin sequential retrieval at a specific point in the file. This point is decided by the value of the *start key*, or *key of reference*, which is the key specified in the KEY clause of the START verb, or, by default, the primary key. The START statement has the syntax

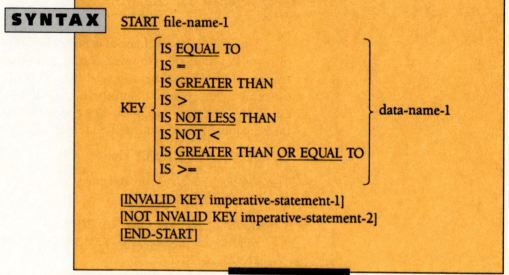

SYNTAX

START file-name-1

KEY
  IS EQUAL TO
  IS =
  IS GREATER THAN
  IS >
  IS NOT LESS THAN
  IS NOT <
  IS GREATER THAN OR EQUAL TO
  IS >=
data-name-1

[INVALID KEY imperative-statement-1]
[NOT INVALID KEY imperative-statement-2]
[END-START]

The following rules hold:

RULES   **Using START**

1. When the KEY clause is omitted, the start key, or key of reference, is assumed to be the primary key defined by the RECORD KEY clause in the SELECT statement.
2. If the KEY clause is included, the start key is data-name-1.
3. Data-item-1 should be either the primary key (defined by the RECORD KEY clause of the SELECT statement), or a secondary key, defined by an ALTERNATE RECORD KEY clause in the SELECT statement.

You must be clear about the following:

*   If the key of reference is the primary key, subsequent sequential READ statements will retrieve records in ascending primary key order.
*   If the key of reference is a secondary key, subsequent sequential READ statements will retrieve records in ascending secondary key order, right to the end of the file if enough sequential READs are executed.

Using the file IS-EMPLOYEE in Figure 14.10a as an example, some valid START statements, with explanations, are

Example 1:   No KEY Clause

```
MOVE 'E00006' TO IS-EMPNUMB.
START IS-EMPLOYEE
INVALID KEY
     PERFORM 200-NO-START-RECORD-FOUND.
NOT INVALID KEY
    READ IS-EMPLOYEE
              AT END ...
```

The read/write mechanism is positioned ready to read the record with primary key 'E00006'. However, the record is not read. It takes the next sequential READ statement to read the 'E00006' record. If no record with the primary key 'E00006' is in the file, the INVALID-primary key clause is executed. Continued execution of sequential READ statements will read all the remaining records in the file, in ascending primary key order.

Example 2:   Using a KEY clause

There is no KEY clause in the preceding START statement. That excerpt could be rewritten as

```
MOVE 'E00006' TO IS-EMPNUMB.
START IS-EMPLOYEE KEY = IS-EMPNUMB
INVALID KEY
     PERFORM 200-NO-START-RECORD-FOUND.
NOT INVALID KEY
     READ IS-EMPLOYEE
         AT END ...
```

Here a KEY clause has been inserted. The KEY clause is not needed when the start key is the primary key, that is, the key defined by the RECORD KEY clause in the SELECT statement, in this case IS-EMPNUMB.

Example 3:   Primary key as the START key

```
MOVE 'E00006' TO IS-EMPNUMB.
START IS-EMPLOYEE KEY >= IS-EMPNUMB
    INVALID KEY PERFORM 200-NO-START-RECORD-FOUND
    NOT INVALID KEY PERFORM 300-SCAN.
```

Here the start key is the primary key. You must use a KEY clause because a start position greater than or equal to the value held by the start key identifier has been specified. As a result of execution of this statement, the read/write mechanism is positioned before the record in the file with a primary key 'E00006' or, if no such record, the first record with a greater primary key. Then the paragraph 300-SCAN is executed. The START statement itself does not read a record. The next sequential READ will do that, presumably in 300-SCAN. Records will be read by sequential READ statements in ascending primary key order.

Example 4: Secondary key as the START key

```
MOVE 'MIAMI' TO IS-CITY.
   START IS-EMPLOYEE KEY = IS-CITY
      INVALID KEY PERFORM 200-NO-START-RECORD-FOUND
      NOT INVALID KEY PERFORM 300-SCAN.
```

Here a secondary key, IS-CITY, has been used as the start key. Note that for IS-CITY to be used as the start key, the field IS-CITY must be defined as a secondary (alternate) key.

The read/write mechanism is placed so that the first record with secondary key IS-CITY value 'MIAMI' can be read. The next sequential READ . . . AT END statement (within 300-SCAN) will actually read the record. If sequential READ . . . AT END statements continue to be executed, *all* the remaining records in the file will be read in ascending IS-CITY order, *not* just Miami records. AT END will be used to detect the end of the file.

Summary

1. An indexed-sequential file has records stored initially like a sequential file on disk, but always in ascending primary key order. Associated with the file is a separately stored sparse multiple-level index. When the file is created, records must be written out in ascending primary key order. The underlying input/output routine looks after creation of the index. VSAM is a commonly used input/output routine for manipulating indexed-sequential files.

2. In a COBOL program, the access mode for an indexed-sequential file can be specified as sequential, random, or dynamic. Sequential mode means sequential processing; rewrite updating, not classical updating, must be used with sequential processing. Random mode means direct-access on presentation of a primary key. Dynamic mode allows both sequential and direct-access to be carried out.

3. For each of the three processing modes, the file can be open for input, output, and input/output (I-O). Thus, the file can be processed in nine different ways. For each of these ways of processing, various READ, WRITE, REWRITE, DELETE, and START statements can be used. Remember that with SEQUENTIAL I-O, you cannot use WRITE (for record insertion updates). Record insertion updating is carried out with RANDOM I-O.

4. With an indexed-sequential file, direct-access on the basis of the primary key is possible. If you need direct-access on the basis of a non-primary key field, that is, a secondary key field, a special secondary index must exist for that secondary key. Some indexed-sequential file input/output routines, such as VSAM, will construct and manipulate a secondary key index, and so permit direct-access on the basis of a secondary key field. Since there will normally be many records with a given secondary key value, a direct-access READ is used to access the first record of the group, and a READ NEXT is used to access the remainder sequentially.

Key Terms

Concept Review Questions

1. Distinguish single and multiple-level indexes.
2. Why are indexes used with indexed-sequential files?
3. Why are multiple-level indexes used with indexed-sequential files?
4. What is a disk address?
5. Distinguish access modes SEQUENTIAL, RANDOM, and DYNAMIC.
6. What does it mean if an indexed file with mode SEQUENTIAL is open for I-O?
7. What does it mean if an indexed file with mode RANDOM is open for I-O?
8. Explain the difference between a direct-access READ and a sequential READ statement.
9. What does it mean if an indexed file with mode DYNAMIC is open for I-O?
10. If you have to change update a file with 10,000 records from a transaction file of 200 records, what is the hit rate?
11. Why is direct-access updating efficient with a low hit rate?
12. Why is a control listing essential when creating an indexed-sequential file?
13. List the kinds of updating that can be performed with
    a. sequential processing of an indexed file
    b. direct-access processing of an indexed file
14. Explain how an indexed-sequential file can be used for responding to random queries.
15. Explain the concept of a secondary key.
16. What is a secondary index, and how does it work?
17. Why should a secondary key be a field that is infrequently updated?
18. What is an ALTERNATE KEY?
19. Explain how all the records with a given secondary key value can be retrieved from an indexed file by direct-access.
20. Explain the use of the FILE STATUS clause.

COBOL Language Questions

1. What is wrong with the following?

```
        ACCESS MODE SEQUENTIAL
 . . .
    OPEN INPUT INDEX-CUSTOMER.
 . . .
    READ INDEX-CUSTOMER
        AT END MOVE 'NO' TO MORE-RECORDS
        INVALID KEY PERFORM 800-CONTROL-LIST.
```

2. What is wrong with this?

```
                    ACCESS MODE SEQUENTIAL
        ...
            OPEN I-O INDEX-CUSTOMER.
        ...
            WRITE INDEX-CUSTOMER-RECORD FROM WS-RECORD.
```

3. What is wrong with the following?

```
                    ACCESS MODE RANDOM
        ...
            OPEN INPUT INDEX-CUSTOMER.
        ...
            READ INDEX-CUSTOMER INTO WS-CUSTOMER-RECORD
                INVALID KEY PERFORM 800-UNMATCHED.
            ADD TRANS-PAYMENT-IN TO WS-CUSTOMER-AMOUNT.
            REWRITE...FROM WS-CUSTOMER-RECORD.
```

4. Rewrite the code in question 3 using the NOT INVALID KEY clause.

5. What is wrong with the following code for retrieval of records with the secondary key value in QUERY-CITY?

```
ACCEPT QUERY-CITY.
MOVE QUERY-CITY TO IS-CITY IN IS-EMPLOYEE-BUFFER-RECORD.
READ IS-EMPLOYEE RECORD
    KEY IS IS-CITY
        INVALID KEY
            DISPLAY 'IS-CITY: ', IS-CITY, ' NOT IN FILE'
        NOT INVALID KEY
            PERFORM UNTIL MORE-TARGET-RECORDS = 'NO'
                    ADD IS-SALARY TO TOTAL-PAY
                    READ IS-EMPLOYEE RECORD,
                        AT END MOVE 'NO' TO MORE-TARGET-RECORDS
                    END-READ
            END-PERFORM
            MOVE 'YES' TO RECORD-FOUND
    END-READ.
```

Programming Assignments

1. **Creation of an indexed-sequential master file and output of the control listing**

   The input file is

   SOURCE-FILE   Contains validated master records about very
                  reliable electronic parts. The file can contain
                  records that are out of sequence or have dupli-
                  cate primary keys

   The output files are

   NEW-MASTER   Newly created indexed master file
   CONTROL-LISTING   Printer file that lists the primary key of
                     every record in the master file. For each

key, it gives the status of the record, either accepted or rejected. If rejected, problems are listed

Some input (SOURCE-FILE) records are

```
---------1---------2
A0194001571.78J050
A025801594.255B106
A025805402.750T130
C4376100006.025B106
C045605004.250J050
D018502833.045T130
D029405608.280B106
D117612506.530T130
E036700707.250J050
E099401506.640T130
E175802855.500J050
E366714009.265B106
F014909508.500T130
```

Columns 01–05	Part type identification code, primary key
06–09	Quantity in warehouse
10–13	Price per unit ($dd.dd)
14–17	Bin code (a bin can hold many types of parts)

The control listing for creating the master file has the following format:

```
---------1---------2---------3---------4---------5---------6---------7
```

COMPREHENSIVE CONTROL LISTING
INDEXED-SEQUENTIAL MASTER FILE CREATION

PAGE   1   05/06/92

PART	QTY	PRICE	BIN	STATUS	PROBLEM
A0194	0015	7178	J050	ACCEPTED	
A0258	0159	4255	B106	ACCEPTED	
A0258	0540	2750	T130	REJECTED	DUPLICATE KEY
C4376	1000	6025	B106	ACCEPTED	
C0456	0500	4250	J050	REJECTED	OUT-OF-SEQUENCE KEY
D0185	0283	3045	T130	ACCEPTED	

. . .

The output indexed-sequential master file has records in exactly the same format as the input file.

a. Draw record layouts and spacing charts for the files.
b. Draw the flowchart and hierarchy diagram.
c. Write the program.

2. Classical change updating a master file
The master file is the one created in Assignment 1, with corrections made to the invalid records. A record describes the inventory of a part in a warehouse. The master records are

```
----------1----------2
A019400157178J050
A025801594255B106
B025805402750T130
C437610006025B106
C445605004250J050
D018502833045T130
D029405608280B106
D117612506530T130
E036700707250J050
E099401506640T130
E175802855500J050
E366714009265B106
F014909508500T130
```

Columns 01–05	Part type identification code, primary key
06–09	Quantity in warehouse
10–13	Price per unit ($dd.dd)
14–17	Bin code (a bin can hold many types of parts)

Corrections were made to the data from Assignment 1, as a result of the output of the control listing during master file creation.

Records of the transaction file are

```
----------1----------2
E09940100A
C43760074S
EO9940200S
A02580100A
C23940100A
C43760074S
A02580050S
D01850100A
E17581200A
D02940700S
```

Columns 01–05	Part type identification code, not unique
06–09	Quantity removed from (S) or added to (A) warehouse
10	Add or subtract code

Transaction records are used to change update the quantity of parts in a master record.

Transaction records are unsorted. Transaction records with duplicate transaction code values are processed normally (that is, each record of a group with duplicate transaction codes will cause an update to the same master record).

The transaction file is used to update the quantity field in the master. Assume that unmatched transaction records can occur. Unmatched records are to be printed in a control listing.

Note: In the case of withdrawal of parts, if the quantity of parts on hand is less than the quantity in the transaction record, the transaction record is printed in the control file with an explanation of the problem. The control listing appears as follows:

```
--------1---------2---------3---------4---------5---------6---------7
              CHANGE UPDATE CONTROL LISTING (TRANSACTION ERROR RECORDS)
       PAGE    1                                              07/12/92

       PART    QTY    OPERATION    UPDATE       PROBLEM
                                   STATUS

       E0994   0100   ADD          DONE
       C4376   0074   SUBTR.       DONE
       EO994   0200   SUBTR.       DONE
       A0258   0100   ADD          DONE
       C2394   0100   ADD          REJECTED    UNMATCHED PART CODE
       A0258   0050   SUBTR.       DONE
       D0185   0100   ADD          DONE
       E1758   1200   ADD          DONE
       D0294   0700   SUBTR.       REJECTED    TOO FEW PARTS IN MASTER
```

a. Draw record layouts and spacing charts for the files.
b. Make a list of error messages to be used.
c. Draw the flowchart and hierarchy diagram.
d. Write the program using direct-access change updating.

3. **General classical updating**

The master file to be updated is the same as in Assignment 2. The transaction file contains insertion records (update code 'I0'), change-update records (update codes 'A0' for addition and 'B0' for subtraction), and deletion records (update code 99). Update codes are the first two characters of each transaction record. The transaction file is

```
---------1---------2
A0E09940100bbbbbbbb
I0E099402506540T130
99D0294bbbbbbbbbbbb
A0A02580100bbbbbbbb
I0C444910008540K173
99D0185bbbbbbbbbbbb
I0A118500103547K188
99C4456bbbbbbbbbbbb
I0F349400805525M280
B0E09940200bbbbbbbb
99C4376bbbbbbbbbbbb
B0C43760074bbbbbbbb
```

Column 01–02   Update code (I0 for insertion, A0 change for addition, B0 change for subtraction, 99 for deletion)
       03–07   Part type identification code, primary key
       08–11   Quantity of parts
       12–15   Price per unit ($dd.dd) or blanks
       16–19   Bin code (bin contains the parts) or blanks

Note the following conditions:

- Insertion transaction records with matching keys can occur.
- Deletion transaction records can be unmatched.
- Change transaction records can be unmatched.
- Change records with duplicate transaction code values are processed normally (that is, each change record of a group with duplicate transaction codes will cause an update to the same master record).
- If a change subtraction transaction cannot be carried out, the transaction record should be listed in the control listing.

The update is accompanied by output of a comprehensive control listing. There is a record in the control listing giving the fate of every transaction record.

a. Design the control listing.
b. Make of list of error messages to be used.
c. Draw record layouts and spacing charts for the files.
d. Draw the flowchart and hierarchy diagram.
e. Write the program.

4. **Creation of an indexed file with secondary keys**
   Repeat Assignment 1, making the bin number a secondary key.

5. **Use of a secondary key with a retrieval program**
   Use the file created in Assignment 4 to write a program for responding to queries. When a user gives the bin number, the program prints the contents of the bin, in accordance with the following dialogue (user input is boldface):

```
INFORMATION RETRIEVAL PROGRAM IN SESSION        07/10/92
ENTER BIN NUMBER BELOW:
T130
DATA FOR BIN T130 IS AS FOLLOWS:

PART    QTY      PRICE

B0258   0540    $27.50
D0185   0283    $30.45
D1176   1250    $65.30
E0994   0150    $66.40
F0149   0950    $85.00
SESSION ENDED
```

Or, alternatively

```
INFORMATION RETRIEVAL PROGRAM IN SESSION        07/10/92
ENTER BIN NUMBER BELOW:
T230
NO DATA FOR BIN T230.
SESSION ENDED.
```

15

RELATIVE
FILES

*I*N THE PREVIOUS chapter you dealt with one type of direct-access file – the indexed-sequential file. In this chapter you will deal with another – the relative file. Relative files are far less commonly used than indexed-sequential files, however. Two types of relative file are possible: the matched-key relative file and the hash file. This chapter will concentrate on the creation and manipulation of matched-key relative files, but will also introduce hash files, which are more advanced.

Recall that disks and indexed-sequential files were discussed early in Chapter 14. There it was pointed out that to gain direct access to a block of records on a disk, the input/output routine (or access method) that does the retrieval must have the block's disk address, in terms of cylinder and track number. This permits movement of the read/write heads to the right cylinder, selection of the correct head for the track, and selection of the correct block on the track. With an indexed-sequential file, the input/output routine obtains the disk address by scanning the index for an entry with a primary key value close to the primary key of the record sought.

With a *relative file*, no index is used. The input/output routine still needs the disk address to gain direct access to a given record, however. *With a relative file it is simply up to the program to supply the needed disk address.* Because it is not always convenient to do this, relative files are not as commonly used as indexed-sequential files.

Nevertheless, the great advantage of relative files is speed of access. Recall that the index of an indexed-sequential file is kept on disk, and requires one or two disk accesses to search it. This slows down direct access with indexed-sequential files. With a relative file, since an index does not have to be searched, direct access is much faster. For this reason relative files are frequently used in applications in which continual direct-access retrievals are made by users at many terminals.

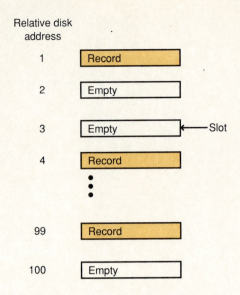

Relative disk
address

1   Record

2   Empty

3   Empty ←— Slot

4   Record

99   Record

100   Empty

Figure 15.1 *A relative file is a numbered sequence of slots; each slot can hold a record. The numbers that identify the slots are relative disk addresses. A record can be placed in any slot by a WRITE statement that cites the relative disk address of the slot. The file is very like an array on disk; the relative disk address corresponds to a subscript. The file above has 100 slots, not all of which contain records.*

15.1
Relative files permit direct access to a relative address

ONE SIMPLE WAY to understand the concept of a relative file is to consider it as akin to a one-dimensional array stored on disk (see Figure 15.1). Each element or slot of the "array" can contain a record of the file. The "subscript" to identify the record is the relative disk address. A relative disk address is a positive integer. In a typical relative file, some slots contain records and others are empty.

Relative file addresses are relative to the address of the first record

A relative disk address of a record is not the real disk address – in terms of cylinder, track, and block number. It is the address relative to the first record of the file. The input/output routine can get the address of the first record in the file from the disk (typically from a directory of all the files on the disk). If it is instructed to retrieve the record with relative address 1000, for example, that means that it must get the 999th record after the first. Since it has the actual disk address of the first record, the input/output routine can then easily deduce the actual disk address of the 999th. In this way, it is only necessary for a relative file processing program to work in terms of relative disk addresses, and not the much more cumbersome real or physical disk addresses.

With most computer systems, the relative disk addresses are integers beginning with 1. In some cases they are integers beginning with 0. Check the manual for your system. In this book relative addresses begin at relative address 1. (There can be other variations between the relative file features incorporated into your compiler and those of ANS COBOL. This chapter follows 1985 ANS COBOL. Check with your installation.)

There are three ways to create a relative file

Suppose you have two versions of a simple sequential file, EMPLOYEE-A and EMPLOYEE-B, as shown in Figure 15.2, in which the spaces shown between values do not matter. In both files, each record describes an employee. With EMPLOYEE-B records, the EMPNUMB (employee number) primary keys are longer than with EMPLOYEE-A records.

EMPNUMB	SALARY	CITY
01	24000	MIAMI
03	33500	DENVER
04	18000	MIAMI
06	37000	SEATTLE
07	23000	SEATTLE
09	17500	DENVER

EMPLOYEE-A

Figure 15.2a Sequential file EMPLOYEE-A, with primary key EMPNUMB.

EMPNUMB	SALARY	CITY
201	24000	MIAMI
306	37000	SEATTLE
504	18000	MIAMI
609	17500	DENVER
703	33500	DENVER
907	23000	SEATTLE

EMPLOYEE-B

Figure 15.2b Sequential file EMPLOYEE-B with primary key EMPNUMB.

You can create three types of relative files using the records in either EMPLOYEE-A or EMPLOYEE-B as source records, with the following input/output area (buffer area) structure:

```
01 SOURCE-RECORD-IN.
   05 EMPNUMB    PIC 999.
   05 SALARY     PIC 9(5).
   05 CITY       PIC X(15).
```

The three types of file are

- Simple relative file (trivial type)
- Matched-key relative file
- Hash (or hashed key) file

The differences between these three types of files will shortly be explained, using examples.

No matter what type of relative file you want, to create any relative file RELFILE, generally the file is specified as follows in the INPUT-OUTPUT and FILE sections:

```
ENVIRONMENT DIVISION.
INPUT-OUTPUT SECTION.
FILE-CONTROL.
     SELECT RELFILE          ASSIGN TO DA-R-DISK001
                             ORGANIZATION IS RELATIVE
                             ACCESS IS SEQUENTIAL
                             [RELATIVE KEY IS REL-DISK-ADDRESS].
...
DATA DIVISION.
FILE SECTION.
FD RELFILE                   RECORD CONTAINS 23 CHARACTERS
                             LABEL RECORDS ARE STANDARD.
01  RELFILE-RECORD-OUT   PIC X(23).
...
WORKING-STORAGE SECTION.
[01  REL-DISK-ADDRESS     PIC 9(3).]
...
```

The clause RELATIVE KEY IS REL-DISK-ADDRESS specifies that the identifier REL-DISK-ADDRESS is to be used for delivering a relative disk address to the input/output routine when a WRITE statement is used (or a READ statement is used when an existing relative file is being read). The identifier REL-DISK-ADDRESS should be defined as an integer identifier in the WORKING-STORAGE SECTION.

The RELATIVE KEY clause can be omitted when the relative file is being created, in which case there will be no need for a relative disk address identifier like REL-DISK-ADDRESS. However, whether or not a relative disk address identifier is used when the file is created makes a difference to the resulting file, as you will see in the examples that follow. If you want either a matched-key relative file or a hash file, you must make use of the relative disk address identifier specified in the RELATIVE KEY clause. (Note that with IBM systems the RELATIVE KEY clause is replaced by NOMINAL KEY IS . . .)

Simple Relative File

Let us begin with creation of a trivial type of relative file that may be called a *simple relative file*. The records inserted are simply packed as closely as possible into the first slots of the file, as illustrated in Figure 15.3. Notice that the employee number values do not match the relative address values. Thus, if you later want to retrieve the record for employee 07, for example, you will not be able to obtain the relative address from the EMPNUMB value 07 to permit direct access; the record is in address 05.

RELATIVE ADDRESS	EMPNUMB	SALARY	CITY
001	001	24000	MIAMI
002	003	33500	DENVER
003	004	18000	MIAMI
004	006	37000	SEATTLE
005	007	23000	SEATTLE
006	009	17500	DENVER

```
                                        PACKED-REL
```

Figure 15.3a *Perspective on the relative file PACKED-REL created from EMPLOYEE-A source records in Figure 15.2a. Spaces between fields are not stored in the file.*

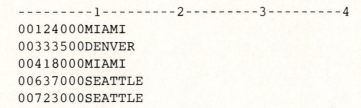

```
---------1---------2---------3---------4
00124000MIAMI
00333500DENVER
00418000MIAMI
00637000SEATTLE
00723000SEATTLE
```

Figure 15.3b *The actual source records to create PACKED-REL. PACKED-REL records are identical to the source EMPLOYEE-A records.*

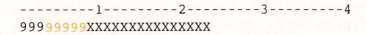

```
---------1---------2---------3---------4
99999999XXXXXXXXXXXXXXX
```

Figure 15.3c *Record layout for a source record or relative record.*

```
01    SR-SOURCE-RECORD-IN.
      05 SR-EMPNUMB-IN        PIC 9(03).
      05 SR-SALARY-IN         PIC 9(05).
      05 SR-CITY-IN           PIC X(15).
01    REL-RECORD-OUT          PIC X(23).
```

Figure 15.3d *The buffer record structure for the source records and the relative file records. The records are the same.*

The program to create the relative file in Figure 15.3 is shown in Figure 15.4 on pages 604–605.

Records are simply output in sequence to addresses 1, 2, 3, and so on, which means the relative disk address for a record will not match the record's primary key (see Figure 15.3a). This form of relative file is not useful, since, for later retrieval by direct access, there has to be a way to deduce a record's relative disk address from its primary key value. This is possible only with either a matched-key relative file or a hash file.

```
IDENTIFICATION DIVISION.
PROGRAM-ID. REL1.
ENVIRONMENT DIVISION.
INPUT-OUTPUT SECTION.
FILE-CONTROL.
    SELECT EMPLOYEE-A
                    ASSIGN TO UT-S-RDATA80.
    SELECT PACKED-REL
                    ASSIGN TO DA-R-MAST234
                    ORGANIZATION IS RELATIVE
                    ACCESS MODE IS SEQUENTIAL.
DATA DIVISION.
FILE SECTION.
FD    EMPLOYEE-A                      LABEL RECORDS ARE STANDARD
                                      RECORD CONTAINS 23 CHARACTERS.
01    SR-SOURCE-RECORD-IN.
   05 SR-EMPNUMB-IN    PIC 9(03).
   05 SR-SALARY-IN     PIC 9(05).
   05 SR-CITY-IN       PIC X(15).
FD    PACKED-REL                      LABEL RECORDS ARE STANDARD
                                      RECORD CONTAINS 23 CHARACTERS.
01    REL-RECORD-OUT    PIC X(23).

WORKING-STORAGE SECTION.
01  MORE-RECORDS        PIC X(3)      VALUE 'YES'.
PROCEDURE DIVISION.
100-MAIN-MODULE.
*****************************************************************************
*   DIRECTS PROGRAM LOGIC.                                                 *
*****************************************************************************
    PERFORM 200-INITIALIZATION.
    PERFORM 300-PROCESS-RECORD
                UNTIL MORE-RECORDS = 'NO'.
    PERFORM 400-TERMINATION.
200-INITIALIZATION.
*****************************************************************************
*  PERFORMED FROM 100-MAIN-MODULE. OPENS FILES, READS FIRST SOURCE        *
*  RECORD.                                                                 *
*****************************************************************************
    OPEN INPUT EMPLOYEE-A
         OUTPUT PACKED-REL.
    READ EMPLOYEE-A
             AT END MOVE 'NO' TO MORE-RECORDS.
300-PROCESS-RECORD.
*****************************************************************************
*  PERFORMED FROM 100-MAIN-MODULE. WRITES CURRENT RECORD TO RELATIVE      *
*  FILE. READS NEXT SOURCE RECORD.                                        *
*****************************************************************************
    WRITE REL-RECORD-OUT FROM SR-SOURCE-RECORD-IN.
    READ EMPLOYEE-A
             AT END MOVE 'NO' TO MORE-RECORDS.
```

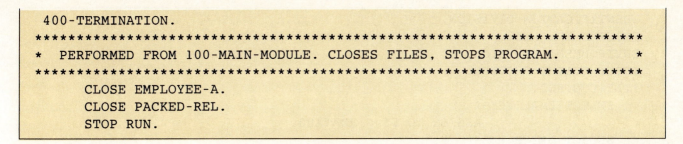

```
      400-TERMINATION.
      **************************************************************
      *   PERFORMED FROM 100-MAIN-MODULE. CLOSES FILES, STOPS PROGRAM.      *
      **************************************************************
             CLOSE EMPLOYEE-A.
             CLOSE PACKED-REL.
             STOP RUN.
```

Figure 15.4 Program for creating a relative file in which the records are output in sequence to the slots of the relative file, leaving no blank slots.

Matched-Key Relative File

With a *matched-key relative file* the employee number value of a record is matched to the relative disk address of the record. In other words, the primary key value of a record is also the relative disk address of a record.

You use the RECORD KEY clause and a relative disk address identifier when the file is created to do this. You can thus use EMPLOYEE-A records to create the relative file MATCH-REL shown in Figure 15.5.

RELATIVE ADDRESS	EMPNUMB	SALARY	CITY
001	001	24000	MIAMI
002	high values		
003	003	33500	DENVER
004	004	18000	MIAMI
005	high values		
006	006	37000	SEATTLE
007	007	23000	SEATTLE
008	high values		
009	009	17500	DENVER

MATCH-REL

Figure 15.5 Relative file created from EMPLOYEE-A records in Figure 15.2a. Record keys match the relative addresses, but there are slots that contain no records.

Records must be output in ascending primary key order to this file, and the slot where a record is to go must be indicated. This is done by placing the required relative disk address in REL-DISK-ADDRESS before WRITE is executed. Thus, if you want to place the record in SR-SOURCE-RECORD-IN in the slot with relative address 5, you would code

```
      MOVE 5 TO REL-DISK-ADDRESS.
      WRITE REL-RECORD-OUT FROM SR-SOURCE-RECORD-IN
             INVALID KEY....
```

The program to create the file MATCH-REL in Figure 15.5 is shown in Figure 15.6.

```
       IDENTIFICATION DIVISION.
       PROGRAM-ID. REL2.
       ENVIRONMENT DIVISION.
       INPUT-OUTPUT SECTION.
       FILE-CONTROL.
           SELECT EMPLOYEE-A
                        ASSIGN TO UT-S-RDATA80.
           SELECT MATCH-REL
                        ASSIGN TO DA-R-MAST234
                        ORGANIZATION IS RELATIVE
                        ACCESS MODE IS SEQUENTIAL
                        RELATIVE KEY IS REL-DISK-ADDRESS.
```
With IBM systems use NOMINAL KEY IS REL-DISK-ADDRESS
```
       DATA DIVISION.
       FILE SECTION.
       FD    EMPLOYEE-A                    LABEL RECORDS ARE STANDARD
                                          RECORD CONTAINS 23 CHARACTERS.
       01    SR-SOURCE-RECORD-IN.
             05 SR-EMPNUMB-IN     PIC 9(03).
             05 SR-SALARY-IN      PIC 9(05).
             05 SR-CITY-IN        PIC X(15).
       FD    MATCH-REL                     LABEL RECORDS ARE STANDARD
                                          RECORD CONTAINS 23 CHARACTERS.
       01    REL-RECORD-OUT        PIC X(23).
       WORKING-STORAGE SECTION.
       01 WS-WORK-AREAS.
             05   MORE-RECORDS     PIC X(03)        VALUE 'YES'.
             05   REL-DISK-ADDRESS PIC 9(03).
       PROCEDURE DIVISION.
       100-MAIN-MODULE.
      ****************************************************************************
      *   DIRECTS PROGRAM LOGIC.                                               *
      ****************************************************************************
             PERFORM 200-INITIALIZATION.
             PERFORM 300-PROCESS-RECORD
                        UNTIL MORE-RECORDS = 'NO'.
             PERFORM 400-TERMINATION.
       200-INITIALIZATION.
      ****************************************************************************
      *   PERFORMED FROM 100-MAIN-MODULE. OPENS FILES, READS FIRST SOURCE      *
      *   RECORD.                                                              *
      ****************************************************************************
             OPEN INPUT EMPLOYEE-A
                        OUTPUT MATCH-REL.
             READ EMPLOYEE-A
                        AT END MOVE 'NO' TO MORE-RECORDS.
```

```
300-PROCESS-RECORD.
**************************************************************************
*  PERFORMED FROM 100-MAIN-MODULE. WRITES CURRENT RECORD TO RELATIVE    *
*  FILE. READS NEXT SOURCE RECORD.                                      *
**************************************************************************
      MOVE SR-EMPNUMB-IN TO REL-DISK-ADDRESS.
      WRITE REL-RECORD-OUT FROM SR-SOURCE-RECORD-IN
            INVALID KEY DISPLAY 'ERROR IN WRITING RECORD: ',
                                           REL-DISK-ADDRESS.
      READ EMPLOYEE-A
            AT END MOVE 'NO' TO MORE-RECORDS.
400-TERMINATION.
**************************************************************************
*  PERFORMED FROM 100-MAIN-MODULE. CLOSES FILES, STOPS PROGRAM.         *
**************************************************************************
      CLOSE EMPLOYEE-A
            MATCH-REL.
      STOP RUN.
```

Figure 15.6 Program for creating a relative file in which each record is placed in a slot with a relative address equal to the primary key value, leaving blank slots where there are no corresponding primary keys.

The records of EMPLOYEE must be available in ascending primary key order so the records will be output in ascending relative disk address order. As the records are written, if a slot is skipped the input/output routine marks that slot as empty (possibly by placing a HIGH VALUES constant in the first character, depending on the computer system.)

If a record cannot be written, there is a write error. A typical reason for a write error would be an out-of-order primary key (not in ascending order). A write error will trigger the INVALID KEY clause. If there is no INVALID KEY clause and there is a write error, the program will terminate abnormally (abend). Normally the INVALID KEY clause execution will cause the record to be output to the control listing for the file creation. (This was omitted in the preceding program to keep the essentials simple).

For retrieval purposes, the file MATCH-REL is decidedly useful. Primary key values match relative disk address values. Thus retrieval of a record by direct access is very efficient. For example, if you want to retrieve the record for employee 06, you would code

```
MOVE 06 TO REL-DISK-ADDRESS.
READ MATCH-REL INTO RECORD-IN
        INVALID-KEY....
```

There is no need for the input/output routine to search an index to find the relative disk address of the record. The program delivers the needed relative disk address.

RELATIVE ADDRESS	SR-EMPNUMB-IN	SR-SALARY-IN	SR-CITY-IN
001	201	24000	MIAMI
002	high values		
003	703	33500	DENVER
004	504	18000	MIAMI
005	high values		
006	306	37000	SEATTLE
007	907	23000	SEATTLE
008	high values		
009	609	17500	DENVER

HASH-REL

Figure 15.7 *Hash file created from EMPLOYEE-B records. Notice that the last two digits of each primary key match the relative address.*

Hash File

The file MATCH-REL in Figure 15.5 is all very well, but what if the primary key values are either not numeric or are so large that a great many empty spaces would be left between records if the primary key values were used for relative disk addresses? An example of this is the file EMPLOYEE-B in Figure 15.2b. If this file was used to create MATCH-REL there would be hundreds of empty slots between each record and the next, which would be very wasteful. In practice, there could be thousands of empty slots between records if you just used the primary key as the relative disk address.

The solution is to use a routine to convert the primary key values into a set of values that better match the relative disk addresses of the relative file. Such a routine is called a *hashing routine*. For example, you could divide each SR-EMPNUMB-IN value in an EMPLOYEE-B record by 100 and take the remainder as the relative disk address. Thus, you would have

PRIMARY KEY	DISK ADDRESS
201	01
703	03
504	04
306	06
907	07
609	09

This would enable you to generate the file HASH-REL from EMPLOYEE-B records, as shown in Figure 15.7. The range of record keys no longer match the range of relative disk addresses, but the results of applying the hashing routine (last two digits of each primary key) do match the range of relative disk addresses.

The routine to convert an SR-EMPNUMB-IN primary key value to a relative disk address could be placed in the paragraph 500-HASHING-ROUTINE

```
500-HASHING-ROUTINE.
    DIVIDE SR-EMPNUMB-IN BY 100 GIVING QUOT
                    REMAINDER REL-DISK-ADDRESS.
```

Thus, to place the record with key 307 in HASH-REL (Figure 15.7), you could code:

```
MOVE 307 TO EMPNUMB.
PERFORM 500-HASHING-ROUTINE.
WRITE REL-RECORD-OUT FROM SR-SOURCE-RECORD-IN
     INVALID KEY....
```

The program to create the file HASH-REL from EMPLOYEE-B records is shown in Figure 15.8. This time the records are not written out in ascending relative disk address order, since hashing the primary keys generates relative disk addresses in an unpredictable order. Consequently, the file has to be created with ACCESS IS RANDOM, so that records can be written out in any order.

Hash files with collisions   There is a major complication with hash files, not encountered in creating HASH-REL from EMPLOYEE-B records. The complication appears when the same relative disk address is generated by the hashing routine from two different primary keys.

Consider the case of EMPLOYEE-B records with primary key values 806 and 306, for example. If you use the hashing routine that divides the primary key by HASH-DIVISOR and takes the remainder as the relative disk address, then for both records a relative disk address of 6 will be generated. This situation is called a *collision*, and must be dealt with by the program. Dealing with collisions is a major aspect of hash file techniques. If there was a collision during execution of the program in figure 15.8, the file would not be created correctly, since the INVALID KEY clause would be executed when the second of the pair of colliding records (or synonyms) is written.

The details of the subject of hash files with collisions is an advanced topic and beyond the scope of this book. However, the basic idea for dealing with collisions is as follows:

Suppose three records, with keys 806, 306, and 506 all hashed to the same address, 6. The first record, record 806, is placed in address 6, and is said to be in its home address. Record 306, when it later also hashes to address 6, is placed in a nearby empty address, perhaps address 7, 8, or 9. Record 506 in turn is also placed in an empty slot near address 6. Records 306 and 506 are said to be overflow records.

When retrieving a record you do not know beforehand whether it is in its home address. Suppose you have to retrieve record 506. You hash the key and get 6, the home address. Then you look in address 6 and discover that it does not contain the record sought. Now you must look in nearby slots for a possible overflow record. How do you know where to look? Typically you follow a chain of addresses until the end of the chain, using a technique called chained progressive overflow management.

When the hash file is created, a chain is constructed for all the records belonging to a given home address, such as address 6. Each record in the chain has a field at the end giving the address of the next overflow record in the chain. Thus, record 806 in address 6 might have the address 10 in its address field. If you look in address 10 you find record 306, which in turn has the address 17 in its address field. If you look in address 17, you find record 506, with a null value in its address field, signifying the end of the

```
IDENTIFICATION DIVISION.
PROGRAM-ID. REL3.
ENVIRONMENT DIVISION.
INPUT-OUTPUT SECTION.
FILE-CONTROL.
    SELECT EMPLOYEE-B
                    ASSIGN TO UT-S-RDATA80.
    SELECT HASH-REL
                    ASSIGN TO DA-R-MAST234
                    ORGANIZATION IS RELATIVE
                    ACCESS MODE IS RANDOM
                    RELATIVE KEY IS REL-DISK-ADDRESS.
                    NOMINAL KEY IS with IBM systems
DATA DIVISION.
FILE SECTION.
FD    EMPLOYEE-B              LABEL RECORDS ARE STANDARD
                             RECORD CONTAINS 23 CHARACTERS.

01    SR-SOURCE-RECORD-IN.
      05 SR-EMPNUMB-IN        PIC 9(03).
      05 SR-SALARY-IN         PIC 9(05).
      05 SR-CITY-IN           PIC X(15).
FD    HASH-REL               LABEL RECORDS ARE STANDARD
                             RECORD CONTAINS 23 CHARACTERS.

01    REL-RECORD-OUT          PIC X(23).
WORKING-STORAGE SECTION.
01  WS-WORK-AREAS.
    05   MORE-RECORDS         PIC X(03)       VALUE 'YES'.
    05   REL-DISK-ADDRESS     PIC 9(03).
    05   QUOT                 PIC 9(03)V99.
    05   HASH-DIVISOR         PIC 9(03)       VALUE 100.
```

chain. Thus, when searching for a record with home address 6, you search along the chain to the end. If you do not find the record, it is not in the file.

There are other ways of arranging for overflow records to be found easily, that is, other overflow (or collision) management techniques. The idea is always to keep the search to the minimum number of disk accesses. The method described here, called *chained progressive overflow*, gives quite good results, however. More efficient methods tend to be even more complicated.

The advantage of hash files is speed. However, programming to handle collisions and the resulting overflow records is complex, and for this reason hash files are uncommon in normal business file processing; they are simply too expensive to write and maintain. Even if indexed-sequential files are slower, it is much easier, and therefore much cheaper, to write programs to process them. Nevertheless, if the keys in the file lend themselves to constructing a matched-key relative file, then you have the best of both worlds, since the file will be both very fast and easy to manipulate.

A variation on the hash file is the *direct file*, described in more detail at the end of the chapter. This is a special kind of relative file, in which each slot is a track, which can hold many records. As a result, more than one record with the same home address can be inserted into an address.

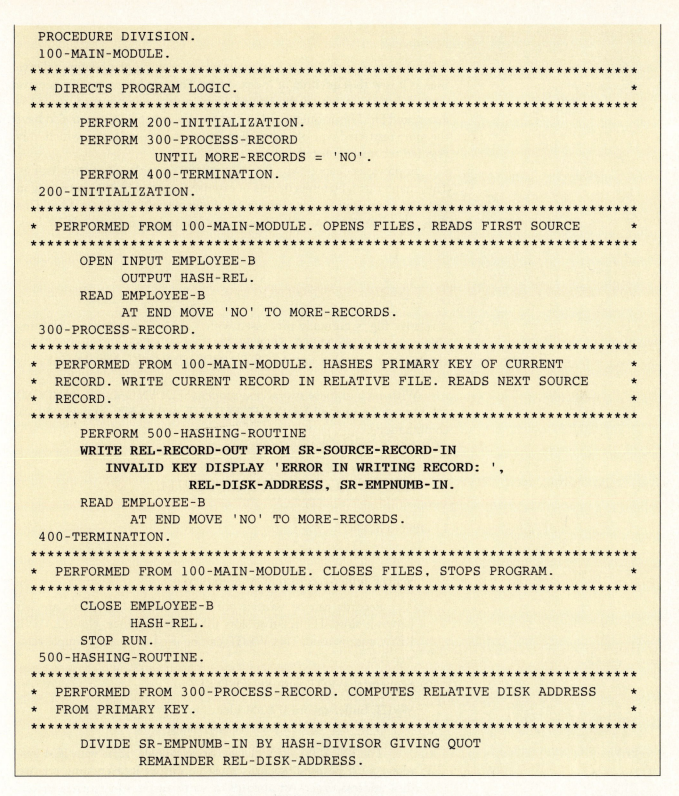

```
     PROCEDURE DIVISION.
      100-MAIN-MODULE.
     ******************************************************************
     *   DIRECTS PROGRAM LOGIC.                                       *
     ******************************************************************
          PERFORM 200-INITIALIZATION.
          PERFORM 300-PROCESS-RECORD
                   UNTIL MORE-RECORDS = 'NO'.
          PERFORM 400-TERMINATION.
      200-INITIALIZATION.
     ******************************************************************
     *   PERFORMED FROM 100-MAIN-MODULE. OPENS FILES, READS FIRST SOURCE  *
     ******************************************************************
          OPEN INPUT EMPLOYEE-B
               OUTPUT HASH-REL.
          READ EMPLOYEE-B
               AT END MOVE 'NO' TO MORE-RECORDS.
      300-PROCESS-RECORD.
     ******************************************************************
     *   PERFORMED FROM 100-MAIN-MODULE. HASHES PRIMARY KEY OF CURRENT    *
     *   RECORD. WRITE CURRENT RECORD IN RELATIVE FILE. READS NEXT SOURCE *
     *   RECORD.                                                      *
     ******************************************************************
          PERFORM 500-HASHING-ROUTINE
          WRITE REL-RECORD-OUT FROM SR-SOURCE-RECORD-IN
               INVALID KEY DISPLAY 'ERROR IN WRITING RECORD: ',
                    REL-DISK-ADDRESS, SR-EMPNUMB-IN.
          READ EMPLOYEE-B
               AT END MOVE 'NO' TO MORE-RECORDS.
      400-TERMINATION.
     ******************************************************************
     *   PERFORMED FROM 100-MAIN-MODULE. CLOSES FILES, STOPS PROGRAM.    *
     ******************************************************************
          CLOSE EMPLOYEE-B
                HASH-REL.
          STOP RUN.
      500-HASHING-ROUTINE.
     ******************************************************************
     *   PERFORMED FROM 300-PROCESS-RECORD. COMPUTES RELATIVE DISK ADDRESS  *
     *   FROM PRIMARY KEY.                                            *
     ******************************************************************
          DIVIDE SR-EMPNUMB-IN BY HASH-DIVISOR GIVING QUOT
                 REMAINDER REL-DISK-ADDRESS.
```

Figure 15.8 *Program for creating a simple hash file in which a record's relative disk address is computed by applying a standard routine (the hashing routine) to its primary key value.*

Control listings are necessary with relative files

A good control listing is as important when creating or updating relative files as it is with sequential or indexed files. You can have a comprehensive control listing, in which the fate of every source or transaction record is accounted for. This is often used in commercial practice. You can also have the more restricted type of control listing, or error report file, in which only rejected records are listed.

In previous chapters you have seen many examples of control listings. This chapter usually omits details of extensive control listing processing in order to allow you to concentrate on the essentials of relative files. This does not mean that control listings are any less important with relative files.

Certain verbs are used for processing relative files

A relative file is normally processed with a SELECT statement containing either an ACCESS MODE SEQUENTIAL or ACCESS MODE RANDOM clause. (You can also use ACCESS MODE DYNAMIC, but this is rarely done.)

With each of these two access modes (SEQUENTIAL and RANDOM) the file can be opened for INPUT, OUTPUT, or I-O, which gives you six combinations.

Verbs with ACCESS MODE SEQUENTIAL

1. OPEN OUTPUT

   a. Sequential WRITE

   <u>WRITE</u> buffer-record [<u>FROM</u> identifier]

   Records can be written out in any order. No spaces are left between slots. The relative slots fill up in sequence. No RELATIVE KEY clause is used. This WRITE can be used to create a simple relative file.

   b. Sequential WRITE with RECORD KEY

   <u>WRITE</u> buffer-record [<u>FROM</u> identifier]
      [<u>INVALID KEY</u> imperative-statement]

   The RELATIVE KEY clause (or NOMINAL KEY, with IBM systems) must be used. Records must be output in ascending relative disk address order. An attempt to write an out-of-sequence record causes the INVALID KEY clause to be executed. A record is placed in the slot with a relative address in the RECORD KEY identifier. Unused slots are marked as empty. This can be used to create a matched-key relative file.

2. OPEN INPUT

a. Sequential READ

<u>READ</u> file-name [<u>INTO</u> identifier]
    [<u>AT END</u> imperative-statement]

Records are read in ascending relative disk address order. No RECORD KEY clause is used. Empty slots are normally not read, but check with your installation to confirm this for your system.

3. OPEN I-O

a. Sequential READ

<u>READ</u> file-name [<u>INTO</u> identifier]
    [<u>AT END</u> imperative-statement]

Records are read in ascending relative disk address order. No RECORD KEY clause is used. Empty slots are normally not read, but check with your installation to confirm this for your system.

b. Sequential REWRITE statement

<u>REWRITE</u> buffer-record [<u>FROM</u> identifier]
    [<u>INVALID KEY</u> imperative-statement]

REWRITE overwrites the record on disk that was most recently read. RECORD KEY clause is used. This is used for sequential change updating.

c. Sequential DELETE statement

<u>DELETE</u> file-name
    [<u>INVALID KEY</u> imperative-statement]

The most recently read record is deleted. An attempt to delete anything else causes the INVALID KEY clause to be executed. The RECORD KEY clause must be used. This is used for sequential deletion updating.

Verbs with ACCESS MODE RANDOM

1. OPEN INPUT

a. Sequential READ

<u>READ</u> file-name <u>NEXT</u> RECORD [<u>INTO</u> identifier]
    [<u>AT END</u> imperative-statement]

Records are read in ascending relative disk address order. Reading begins either at the start of the file or immediately following the point where the previous direct-access READ accessed the file. No RECORD KEY clause is used. Empty slots are normally not read, but check with your installation to confirm this for your system. Note that NEXT must be used to distinguish between direct access and sequential access.

b. Direct-access READ

READ file-name [INTO identifier]
    [INVALID KEY imperative-statement]

An attempt to read an empty slot causes the INVALID KEY clause to be executed. The RECORD KEY clause must be used. The record read is the one whose relative address is in the RECORD KEY identifier.

2. OPEN OUTPUT
    a. Direct-access WRITE

WRITE buffer-record [FROM identifier]
    [INVALID KEY imperative-statement]

An attempt to write a record into an occupied slot causes the INVALID KEY clause to be executed. The RECORD KEY clause must be used. The record goes into the slot whose relative address is in the identifier specified in the RECORD KEY clause. This WRITE can be used to create a hash file. Records will be scattered over the relative address space.

3. OPEN I-O
    a. Sequential READ.

READ file-name NEXT RECORD [INTO identifier]
    [AT END imperative-statement]

Records are read in ascending relative disk address order. Reading begins either at the start of the file or immediately following the point where the previous direct access READ accessed the file. No RECORD KEY clause is used. Empty slots are normally not read, but check with your installation to confirm this for your system. Note that NEXT must be used to distinguish between direct access and sequential access.

    b. Direct-access READ

READ file-name [INTO identifier]
    [INVALID KEY imperative-statement]

An attempt to read an empty slot causes the INVALID KEY clause to be executed. The RECORD KEY clause must be used. The record read is the one whose relative address is in the RECORD KEY identifier.

    c. Direct-access WRITE

WRITE buffer-record [FROM identifier]
    [INVALID KEY imperative-statement]

An attempt to write a record into an occupied slot causes the INVALID KEY clause to be executed. The RECORD KEY clause must be used. The record goes into the slot whose relative address is in the identifier specified in the RECORD KEY clause. This WRITE can be used for direct-access insertion updating.

d. Direct-access REWRITE statement

REWRITE buffer-record [FROM identifier]
[INVALID KEY imperative-statement]

REWRITE overwrites the record on disk whose relative address is in the RECORD KEY identifier. The RECORD KEY clause is used. This is used for direct-access change updating.

e. Direct-access DELETE statement

DELETE file-name
[INVALID KEY imperative-statement]

The record whose relative address is in the RECORD KEY clause is deleted. An attempt to delete an empty slot causes the INVALID KEY clause to be executed. The RECORD KEY clause must be used. This DELETE is used for direct-access deletion updating.

15.2 Matched-key relative files use straightforward updating techniques

THE PREVIOUS SECTION showed how a matched-key relative file (MATCH-REL in Figure 15.5) was created by the program REL-2 in Figure 15.6. This section will show how MATCH-REL can be updated. A matched-key relative file can be updated using either sequential access (ACCESS MODE SEQUENTIAL) or direct access (ACCESS MODE RANDOM).

A matched-key relative file can be sequentially change updated

Suppose you want to change update MATCH-REL in Figure 15.5 using a transaction file TRANS. A TRANS record could hold the TRANS-EMPNUMB-IN primary key and a salary increase TRANS-INCREASE-IN:

```
01  TRANS-RECORD-IN.
    05  TRANS-EMPNUMB          PIC 9(03).
    05  TRANS-INCREASE-IN      PIC 9(05).
```

During the updating the TRANS-INCREASE-IN value is added to the TRANS-SALARY-IN value in a MATCH-REL record with the same primary key value.

The updating is carried out almost exactly as is rewrite updating for sequential files. TRANS records must be in ascending primary key order, and both TRANS and MATCH-REL records are read in sequence. An important point is that, as each READ is executed with the relative file it is the next record that is read. Slots with no records in them are not read; that is, they are skipped over.

The program to carry out the change updating, shown in Figure 15.9, allows for the general case where some records in TRANS will not have keys that match any master file records. The logic for this situation was explained in Chapter 14, for sequential processing using the rewrite method.

```
IDENTIFICATION DIVISION.
PROGRAM-ID. RELSEQ1.
ENVIRONMENT DIVISION.
INPUT-OUTPUT SECTION.
FILE-CONTROL.
    SELECT CONTROL-LISTING
                    ASSIGN TO UR-R-SYSPRINT.
    SELECT TRANS
                    ASSIGN TO UT-S-INFO90F.
    SELECT MATCH-REL
                    ASSIGN TO DA-R-MAST234
                    ORGANIZATION IS RELATIVE
                    ACCESS MODE IS SEQUENTIAL.
DATA DIVISION.
FILE SECTION.
FD   CONTROL-LISTING               LABEL RECORDS ARE OMITTED.
01   PRINTER-RECORD-OUT.
     05 FILLER             PIC X       VALUE SPACE.
     05 PR-DATA-OUT        PIC X(132).
FD   TRANS                          LABEL RECORDS ARE STANDARD
                                    RECORD CONTAINS 8 CHARACTERS.
01   TRANS-RECORD-IN.
     05 TRANS-EMPNUMB-IN   PIC 9(03).
     05 TRANS-INCREASE-IN  PIC 9(05).
FD   MATCH-REL                      LABEL RECORDS ARE STANDARD
                                    RECORD CONTAINS 23 CHARACTERS.

01   REL-BUF-REC          PIC X(23).
WORKING-STORAGE SECTION.
01   REL-MASTER-RECORD.
     05 REL-EMPNUMB        PIC 9(03).
     05 REL-SALARY         PIC 9(05).
     05 REL-CITY           PIC X(15).
PROCEDURE DIVISION.
100-MAIN-MODULE.
*****************************************************************************
*   DIRECTS PROGRAM LOGIC.                                                *
*****************************************************************************
    PERFORM 200-INITIALIZATION.
    PERFORM 300-COMPARE
            UNTIL TRANS-EMPNUMB-IN = HIGH-VALUES.
    PERFORM 600-TERMINATION.
200-INITIALIZATION.
*****************************************************************************
*   PERFORMED FROM 100-MAIN-MODULE. OPENS FILES, READS FIRST TRANSACTION *
*   AND MASTER RECORDS. PRINTS REPORT HEADER.                            *
*****************************************************************************
        OPEN INPUT TRANS
             I-O MATCH-REL
             OUTPUT CONTROL-LISTING.
```

```
          READ TRANS
               AT END MOVE 'NO FIRST TRANSACTION RECORD' TO PR-DATA-OUT
                    WRITE PRINTER-RECORD-OUT
                    STOP RUN.
          READ MATCH-REL
               AT END MOVE 'NO FIRST MASTER RECORD' TO PR-DATA-OUT
                    WRITE PRINTER-RECORD-OUT
                    STOP RUN.
          PERFORM 500-REPORT-HEADER.
      300-COMPARE.
  ************************************************************************
  *   PERFORMED FROM 100-MAIN-MODULE. COMPARES PRIMARY KEYS OF CURRENT   *
  *   TRANSACTION AND MASTER RECORDS. WHEN KEYS MATCH, MASTER IS UPDATED. *
  *   IF TRANSACTION KEY IS GREATER, THE NEXT MASTER IS READ. IF         *
  *   TRANSACTION KEY IS LESS, IT MEANS THERE IS NO MATCH FOR THAT       *
  *   TRANSACTION RECORD, AND IT IS LISTED IN THE CONTROL LISTING FILE.  *
  ************************************************************************
          IF TRANS-EMPNUMB-IN > REL-EMPNUMB
              READ MATCH-REL INTO REL-MASTER-RECORD
                       AT END MOVE HIGH-VALUES TO REL-EMPNUMB
          END-IF.
          IF TRANS-EMPNUMB-IN = REL-EMPNUMB
              ADD TRANS-INCREASE-IN TO REL-SALARY
              REWRITE REL-BUF-REC FROM REL-MASTER-RECORD
              READ MATCH-REL INTO REL-MASTER-RECORD
                   AT END MOVE HIGH-VALUES TO REL-EMPNUMB
              END-READ
              READ TRANS
                 AT END MOVE HIGH-VALUES TO TRANS-EMPNUMB-IN
              END-READ
          END-IF.
          IF TRANS-EMPNUMB-IN < REL-EMPNUMB
              PERFORM 400-PRINT-TRANS-RECORD
              READ TRANS
                 AT END MOVE HIGH-VALUES TO TRANS-EMPNUMB-IN
          END-IF.
      400-PRINT-TRANS-RECORD.
  ************************************************************************
  *   PERFORMED FROM 300-COMPARE. PRINTS UNMATCHED TRANS RECORD.         *
  ************************************************************************
          MOVE TRANS-RECORD-IN TO PR-DATA-OUT.
          WRITE PRINTER-RECORD-OUT.
      500-REPORT-HEADER.
  ************************************************************************
  *   PERFORMED FROM 200-INITIALIZATION. PRINTS SINGLE INITIAL REPORT    *
  *   HEADER. IN A MORE THOROUGH VERSION OF THE PROGRAM, THIS PARAGRAPH   *
  *   WOULD ALSO BE PERFORMED FROM 400-PRINT-RECORD FOR EACH NEW PAGE.    *
  ************************************************************************
          MOVE '      CONTROL LISTING' TO PR-DATA-OUT.
          WRITE PRINTER-RECORD-OUT.
```

```
    600-TERMINATION.
 **********************************************************************
 *   PERFORMED FROM 100-MAIN-MODULE. CLOSES FILES, STOPS PROGRAM.      *
 **********************************************************************
        CLOSE TRANS
              MATCH-REL
              CONTROL-LISTING.
        STOP RUN.
```

Figure 15.9 *Change updating a matched-key relative file using sequential access. Unmatched TRANS records are printed in the error file.*

Notice there is no RELATIVE KEY clause to specify a relative disk address identifier. No use is made of a relative disk address identifier in the program.

Incidentally, when a relative file is read sequentially, as in the program in Figure 15.9, if a relative disk address identifier (REL-DISK-ADDRESS) is defined, then when a READ is executed, the input/output routine will place the relative disk address of the record read in REL-DISK-ADDRESS. This can sometimes be useful.

The control listing generated by the program for the unmatched TRANS records has a very simple format, to help you concentrate on the essentials. In practice, a more extensive control listing would be generated.

A matched-key relative file can be change updated by direct access

Suppose that you repeat the change update from the previous section using direct access. In that case, the TRANS records no longer have to be in ascending primary key order. Each TRANS record is still read in sequence, however. The primary key of a TRANS record is used to retrieve the matching master record from the relative file, if it exists. If there is a matching master record, it is updated, otherwise the TRANS record is listed in a control listing. The program to carry out the update is in Figure 15.10.

```
 IDENTIFICATION DIVISION.
 PROGRAM-ID. DIR1.
 ENVIRONMENT DIVISION.
 INPUT-OUTPUT SECTION.
 FILE-CONTROL.
     SELECT CONTROL-LISTING
                   ASSIGN TO UR-R-SYSPRINT.
     SELECT TRANS
                   ASSIGN TO UT-S-RELINFO.
     SELECT MATCH-REL
                   ASSIGN TO DA-R-MAST234
                   ORGANIZATION IS RELATIVE
                   ACCESS MODE IS RANDOM
                   RELATIVE KEY IS REL-DISK-ADDRESS.
```

```
DATA DIVISION.
FILE SECTION.
FD    CONTROL-LISTING                        LABEL RECORDS ARE OMITTED.
01    PRINTER-RECORD-OUT.
      05 FILLER                  PIC X          VALUE SPACE.
      05 PR-DATA-OUT             PIC X(132).
FD    TRANS                                   LABEL RECORDS ARE STANDARD
                                              RECORD CONTAINS 8 CHARACTERS.
01    TRANS-RECORD-IN.
      05 TRANS-EMPNUMB-IN        PIC 9(03).
      05 TRANS-INCREASE-IN       PIC 9(05).
FD    MATCH-REL                               LABEL RECORDS ARE STANDARD
                                              RECORD CONTAINS 23 CHARACTERS.
01    REL-BUF-REC                PIC X(23).
WORKING-STORAGE SECTION.
01 WS-WORK-AREAS.
      05 MORE-RECORDS            PIC X(03)      VALUE 'YES'.
      05 REL-DISK-ADDRESS        PIC X(03).
01    REL-MASTER-RECORD.
      05 REL-EMPNUMB             PIC 9(03).
      05 REL-SALARY              PIC 9(05).
      05 REL-CITY                PIC X(15).
PROCEDURE DIVISION.
100-MAIN-MODULE.
**************************************************************************
*   DIRECTS PROGRAM LOGIC.                                             *
**************************************************************************
      PERFORM 200-INITIALIZATION.
      PERFORM 300-PROCESS-TRANSACTION
            UNTIL MORE-RECORDS = 'NO'.
      PERFORM 600-TERMINATION.
200-INITIALIZATION.
**************************************************************************
*  PERFORMED FROM 100-MAIN-MODULE. OPENS FILES, READS FIRST TRANSACTION *
*  AND MASTER RECORDS. PRINTS REPORT HEADER.                           *
**************************************************************************
      OPEN INPUT TRANS
           I-O MATCH-REL
           OUTPUT CONTROL-LISTING.
      READ TRANS
           AT END MOVE 'NO FIRST TRANSACTION RECORD' TO PR-DATA-OUT
                WRITE PRINTER-RECORD-OUT
                STOP RUN.
      PERFORM 500-REPORT-HEADER.
```

```
     300-PROCESS-TRANSACTION.
     *********************************************************************
     *  PERFORMED FROM 100-MAIN-MODULE. PRIMARY KEY OF CURRENT TRANSACTION   *
     *  IS USED AS RELATIVE DISK ADDRESS TO ACCESS MATCHING MASTER RECORD.   *
     *  MASTER IS UPDATED FROM TRANS AND REWRITTEN. IF NO MATCHING MASTER    *
     *  IS FOUND, UNMATCHED RECORD IS WRITTEN TO ERROR FILE. READS NEXT      *
     *  TRANS RECORD.                                                        *
     *********************************************************************
             MOVE TRANS-EMPNUMB-IN TO REL-DISK-ADDRESS.
             READ MATCH-REL INTO REL-MASTER-RECORD
               NOT INVALID KEY
                 ADD TRANS-INCREASE-IN TO REL-SALARY
                 REWRITE REL-BUF-REC FROM REL-MASTER-RECORD
               INVALID KEY
                 PERFORM 400-PRINT-TRANS-RECORD
             END-READ.
             READ TRANS
                 AT END MOVE 'NO' TO MORE-RECORDS.
      400-PRINT-TRANS-RECORD.
     *********************************************************************
     *  PERFORMED FROM 300-PROCESS-RECORD. PRINTS UNMATCHED TRANS RECORDS.  *
     *********************************************************************
             MOVE TRANS-RECORD-IN TO PR-DATA-OUT.
             WRITE PRINTER-RECORD-OUT.
      500-REPORT-HEADER.
     *********************************************************************
     *  PERFORMED FROM 200-INITIALIZATION. PRINTS SINGLE INITIAL REPORT     *
     *  HEADER. IN A MORE THOROUGH VERSION OF THE PROGRAM, THIS PARAGRAPH    *
     *  WOULD ALSO BE PERFORMED FROM 400-PRINT-RECORD FOR EACH NEW PAGE.     *
     *********************************************************************
             MOVE '        CONTROL LISTING' TO PR-DATA-OUT.
             WRITE PRINTER-RECORD-OUT.
      600-TERMINATION.
     *********************************************************************
     *  PERFORMED FROM 100-MAIN-MODULE. CLOSES FILES, STOPS PROGRAM.        *
     *********************************************************************
             CLOSE TRANS
                   MATCH-REL
                   CONTROL-LISTING.
             STOP RUN.
```

Figure 15.10 *Change updating a matched-key relative file using direct access. Unmatched TRANS records are printed in the error file.*

Note the use of the INVALID KEY clause following a direct-access READ. The INVALID KEY clause will be executed if

- The relative disk address in REL-DISK-ADDRESS is for a slot that does not contain a record
- The relative disk address used is beyond the boundary of the file

An INVALID KEY clause that follows a direct-access WRITE or DELETE statement will be executed for the same reasons.

You need not rely wholly on the INVALID KEY clause with direct-access READ, WRITE, and DELETE statements. As was explained for indexed-sequential files, a file-status identifier can be defined for the file, as in

```
SELECT MATCH-REL
            ASSIGN TO DA-R-MAST234
            ORGANIZATION IS RELATIVE
            ACCESS MODE IS RANDOM
            RELATIVE KEY IS REL-DISK-ADDRESS
            STATUS IS F-STATUS.
```

Following each direct-access READ, WRITE or DELETE, the F-STATUS can be checked using an IF-statement. With relative files, the most important codes returned are those shown in Table 15.1.

Table 15.1. *File-Status Codes for Relative Files.*

STATUS CODE	MEANING
00	Operation completed successfully
22	Disk address is valid, but is the address of an occupied slot, in the case of a WRITE. INVALID KEY clause executed if coded
23	Disk address is valid, but is the address of an empty slot, in the case of a READ or DELETE. INVALID KEY clause executed if coded
24	Relative disk address is beyond bounds of file. INVALID KEY clause executed if coded
30	Hardware error

Insertion updating of a matched-key relative file involves direct access

Suppose that TRANS contains records to be inserted into the master file MATCH-REL, where each TRANS record has the structure

```
01    TRANS-RECORD-IN.
      05 TRANS-EMPNUMB-IN              PIC 9(03).
      05 TRANS-SALARY-IN               PIC 9(05).
      05 TRANS-CITY-IN                 PIC X(15).
```

The insertions would be carried out by direct access, so that the order of records in TRANS would not matter. Thus, ACCESS IS RANDOM will be specified and a relative key identifier (REL-DISK-ADDRESS) defined. The essence of the insertion update is given in Figure 15.11. Apart from the TRANS-RECORD-IN structure, which is modified as shown earlier to hold a complete MATCH-REL record, the definitions used in the program are the same as those in Figure 15.10.

```
PROCEDURE DIVISION.
100-MAIN-MODULE.
     PERFORM 200-INITIALIZATION.
     PERFORM 300-PROCESS-TRANSACTION
               UNTIL MORE-RECORDS = 'NO'.
     PERFORM 600-TERMINATION.
200-INITIALIZATION.
     OPEN INPUT TRANS
          I=O MATCH-REL
          OUTPUT CONTROL-LISTING.
     READ TRANS
          AT END MOVE 'NO FIRST TRANSACTION RECORD' TO PR-DATA-OUT
                  WRITE PRINTER-RECORD-OUT
                  STOP RUN.
     PERFORM 500-REPORT-HEADER.
300-PROCESS-TRANSACTION.
     MOVE TRANS-EMPNUMB-IN TO REL-DISK-ADDRESS.
     WRITE REL-BUF-REC FROM TRANS-RECORD-IN
        INVALID KEY
     PERFORM 400-PRINT-TRANS-RECORD.
     READ TRANS
     AT END MOVE 'NO' TO MORE-RECORDS.
400-PRINT-TRANS-RECORD.
     MOVE TRANS-RECORD-IN TO PR-DATA-OUT.
     WRITE PRINTER-RECORD-OUT.
500-REPORT-HEADER.
     MOVE '       ERROR REPORT' TO PR-DATA-OUT.
     WRITE PRINTER-RECORD-OUT.
600-TERMINATION.
     CLOSE TRANS
           MATCH-REL
           CONTROL-LISTING.
     STOP RUN.
```

Figure 15.11 *Insertion updating a matched-key relative file using direct access.*
TRANS records with a key already in the master file MATCH-REL are printed
in the error file.

If a TRANS record has a primary key value that already occurs in
MATCH-REL, this is detected when a direct-access WRITE uses that primary key value, in REL-DISK-ADDRESS. An already occupied slot will cause
the INVALID KEY clause to be executed, which will prohibit insertion of the
new record. This will result in the TRANS record being placed in the control listing instead of the master file.

Suppose that each TRANS record contains the key of a record to be deleted from the master file MATCH-REL and has the structure:

```
01   TRANS-RECORD-IN.
     05 TRANS-EMPNUMB-IN            PIC 9(03).
```

The deletions would typically be carried out by direct access, so the order of records in TRANS would not matter. (Sequential access is possible if the transaction records are sorted in ascending primary key order.) Once more, ACCESS IS RANDOM will be specified and a relative key identifier (REL-DISK-ADDRESS) defined. The essence of the deletion update is given in Figure 15.12. Apart from the TRANS-RECORD-IN structure, which is modified as shown earlier to hold a complete MATCH-REL primary key value only, the definitions used in the program are the same as those in Figure 15.10.

```
PROCEDURE DIVISION.
100-MAIN-MODULE.
    PERFORM 200-INITIALIZATION.
    PERFORM 300-PROCESS-TRANSACTION
            UNTIL MORE-RECORDS = 'NO'.
    PERFORM 600-TERMINATION.
200-INITIALIZATION.
    OPEN INPUT TRANS
         I-O MATCH-REL
         OUTPUT CONTROL-LISTING.
    READ TRANS
         AT END STOP RUN.
    PERFORM 500-REPORT-HEADER.
300-PROCESS-TRANSACTION.
    MOVE TRANS-EMPNUMB-IN TO REL-DISK-ADDRESS.
    DELETE MATCH-REL
      INVALID KEY MOVE
         PERFORM 400-PRINT-TRANS-RECORD.
    READ TRANS
       AT END MOVE 'NO' TO MORE-RECORDS.
400-PRINT-TRANS-RECORD.
    MOVE TRANS-RECORD-IN TO PR-DATA-OUT.
    WRITE PRINTER-RECORD-OUT.
500-REPORT-HEADER.
    MOVE '      ERROR REPORT' TO PR-DATA-OUT.
    WRITE PRINTER-RECORD-OUT.
600-TERMINATION.
    CLOSE TRANS
          MATCH-REL
          CONTROL-LISTING.
    STOP RUN.
```

Figure 15.12 *Insertion updating a matched-key relative file using direct access. TRANS records with a key already in the master file MATCH-REL are printed in the error file.*

The number of slots in a relative file must be specified

The number of slots available in a relative file is not normally defined in the file creation program, but in an operating system command that accompanies the program. Check your manual for the proper method.

With a matched-key relative file, the number of slots should exceed the largest primary key value likely to occur in the file. If you have defined the number of slots as 499 and you later use a direct access WRITE statement to try to insert a record with a relative address 503, the INVALID KEY clause will be executed.

Relative files are much faster than indexed files

If the primary keys of a collection of records are such that it is convenient to create a matched-key relative file, then manipulation of the file will be much more efficient than for a comparable indexed-sequential file. To retrieve a record from the relative file, for example, only one access to the disk will be needed. In the case of the indexed file, several accesses will be needed, since the input/output routine has to access different levels of the index first, which are also on disk.

Remember that a disk access is very time-consuming by computer standards—about 25 milliseconds per access, on average. If you needed three disk accesses for each record of a 150,000-record indexed-sequential file, it would take about 11,250 seconds, or more than three hours, just to access the records. Thus, when considering creating an indexed-sequential file, it is a good idea to consider whether the keys and the use of the file would allow a matched-key relative file to be used instead. If they do not, another possible alternative is the use of the direct file.

Direct files are hash files that avoid the collision problem

As you have seen, hash files are normally considered too complex for everyday use. At the same time, however, you can use a matched-key relative file only if the primary key values lend themselves to it. A variation on the hash file is the direct file, which is available on many IBM systems. It lies outside the ANSI standard.

A direct file is a special kind of relative file where each slot is a track, which can hold many records. As a result, more than one record with the same home address can be inserted into an address. In addition, should there be too many records for the slot, the access method puts the overflow records in the nearest vacant space automatically, so that the program does not have to contain instructions for handling overflow records. A hashing routine is still needed to compute each record's home address from the primary key, however.

Instead of using a relative address alone to retrieve a record, you must present a combined relative (track) address and primary key, called an *actual key*. Remember that two or more records may have the same track address, as generated by the hashing routine. Thus, presentation of the relative track address to the access method is not enough to retrieve a record, since the track may hold several records—you must also present the primary key of the record. Both relative track address and primary key are presented using an actual key group identifier as follows (assuming you were creating [or using] a direct file called DIR-FILE built with the source records in the file EMPLOYEE-B in Figure 15.2):

```
SELECT DIR-FILE
          ASSIGN TO DA-D-DIRMAST
          ACCESS MODE IS RANDOM
          ACTUAL KEY IS REL-ADDRESS-KEY-COMBINATION
          TRACK-LIMIT IS 10 TRACKS.
...
01   REL-ADDRESS-KEY-COMBINATION.
     05 REL-TRACK-ADDRESS        PIC 9(03) COMP.
     05 PRIMARY-KEY-PART.
          10 DELETE-BYTE         PIC X           VALUE LOW-VALUES.
          10 PRIMARY-KEY         PIC X(03).
```

The TRACK-LIMIT clause states the number of tracks in the file (used only with file creation). The actual key identifier REL-ADDRESS-KEY-COMBINATION holds the combined relative track address and primary key. The delete byte within this actual key is set to LOW-VALUES for a valid record. On deletion of a record, the record remains in the track, but its delete byte is set to HIGH-VALUES.

The program to create DIR-FILE from EMPLOYEE-B records is shown in Figure 15.13.

The file can be manipulated in the same manner as a matched-key file, except that direct access (ACCESS MODE RANDOM) should always be used. To retrieve a record with a READ statement, you must first place the record's actual key in the ACTUAL KEY identifier, that is, you must hash the primary key of the required record and place the resulting relative address in REL-TRACK-ADDRESS, and also place the primary key value itself in PRIMARY-KEY. The INVALID-KEY clause will be executed if the record is not found. (A LIMCT=integer clause is coded in the accompanying DD statement for the file, to specify the maximum number [an integer] of tracks that should be searched when looking for an overflow record. Note that it is LIMCT and not LIMIT.) You can use WRITE, REWRITE, and DELETE as with matched-key relative files, except that you must always use the actual key value in the ACTUAL KEY identifier.

A direct file can waste a lot of disk space if care is not taken. To avoid wasting space, the number of tracks specified for the file should be able to hold not much more than about 1.25 times the number of records in the file.

```
IDENTIFICATION DIVISION.
PROGRAM-ID. REL3.
ENVIRONMENT DIVISION.
INPUT-OUTPUT SECTION.
FILE-CONTROL.
    SELECT EMPLOYEE-B
                    ASSIGN TO UT-S-RDATA80.
    SELECT DIR-FILE
                    ASSIGN TO DA-D-DIRMAST
                    ACCESS MODE IS RANDOM
                    ACTUAL KEY IS REL-ADDRESS-KEY-COMBINATION
                    TRACK-LIMIT IS 10 TRACKS.
DATA DIVISION.
FILE SECTION.
FD    EMPLOYEE-B                    LABEL RECORDS ARE STANDARD
                                    RECORD CONTAINS 23 CHARACTERS.
01    SR-SOURCE-RECORD-IN.
      05 SR-EMPNUMB-IN         PIC 9(03).
      05 SR-SALARY-IN          PIC 9(05).
      05 SR-CITY-IN            PIC X(15).
FD    DIR-FILE                      LABEL RECORDS ARE STANDARD
                                    RECORD CONTAINS 23 CHARACTERS.
01    DIR-RECORD-OUT          PIC X(23).
WORKING-STORAGE SECTION.
01    WS-WORK-AREAS.
      05    MORE-RECORDS       PIC X(03)       VALUE 'YES'.
      05    QUOT               PIC 9(03)V99.
      05    HASH-DIVISOR       PIC 9(03)       VALUE 100.
01    REL-ADDRESS-KEY-COMBINATION.
      05 REL-TRACK-ADDRESS     PIC 9(03) COMP.
      05 PRIMARY-KEY-PART.
          10 DELETE-BYTE       PIC X           VALUE LOW-VALUES.
          10 PRIMARY-KEY       PIC X(03).
PROCEDURE DIVISION.
100-MAIN-MODULE.
****************************************************************************
*  DIRECTS PROGRAM LOGIC.                                                *
****************************************************************************
      PERFORM 200-INITIALIZATION.
      PERFORM 300-PROCESS-RECORD
              UNTIL MORE-RECORDS = 'NO'.
      PERFORM 400-TERMINATION.
200-INITIALIZATION.
****************************************************************************
*  PERFORMED FROM 100-MAIN-MODULE. OPENS FILES, READS FIRST SOURCE       *
*  RECORD.                                                               *
****************************************************************************
      OPEN INPUT EMPLOYEE-B
           OUTPUT DIR-FILE.
      READ EMPLOYEE-B
           AT END MOVE 'NO' TO MORE-RECORDS.
```

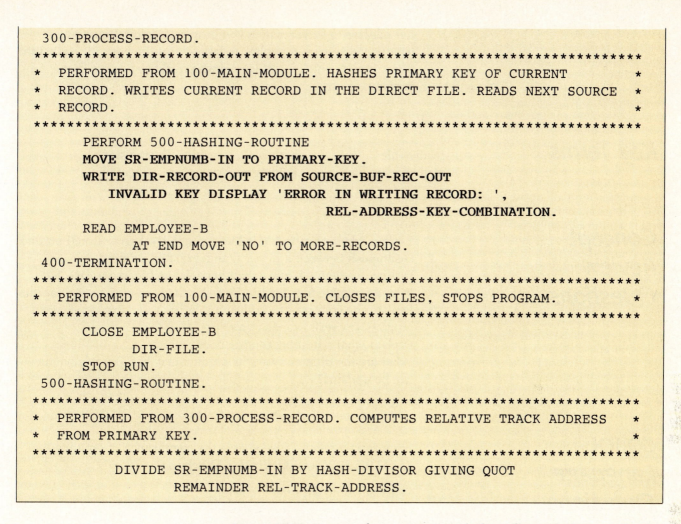

```
 300-PROCESS-RECORD.
*********************************************************************
*   PERFORMED FROM 100-MAIN-MODULE. HASHES PRIMARY KEY OF CURRENT     *
*   RECORD. WRITES CURRENT RECORD IN THE DIRECT FILE. READS NEXT SOURCE *
*   RECORD.                                                            *
*********************************************************************
       PERFORM 500-HASHING-ROUTINE
       MOVE SR-EMPNUMB-IN TO PRIMARY-KEY.
       WRITE DIR-RECORD-OUT FROM SOURCE-BUF-REC-OUT
           INVALID KEY DISPLAY 'ERROR IN WRITING RECORD: ',
                               REL-ADDRESS-KEY-COMBINATION.
       READ EMPLOYEE-B
            AT END MOVE 'NO' TO MORE-RECORDS.
 400-TERMINATION.
*********************************************************************
*   PERFORMED FROM 100-MAIN-MODULE. CLOSES FILES, STOPS PROGRAM.      *
*********************************************************************
       CLOSE EMPLOYEE-B
             DIR-FILE.
       STOP RUN.
 500-HASHING-ROUTINE.
*********************************************************************
*   PERFORMED FROM 300-PROCESS-RECORD. COMPUTES RELATIVE TRACK ADDRESS *
*   FROM PRIMARY KEY.                                                 *
*********************************************************************
             DIVIDE SR-EMPNUMB-IN BY HASH-DIVISOR GIVING QUOT
                   REMAINDER REL-TRACK-ADDRESS.
```

Figure 15.13 *Program for creating a simple direct file in which a record's relative track address is computed by applying a hashing routine to its primary key value.*

Summary

1. A relative file is like a one-level array stored on disk. The file consists of numbered slots, usually beginning with slot 1. The number of a slot is the relative address of a slot. A slot can hold a record.

2. Records can be placed sequentially in the numbered slots. With a matched-key relative file, the primary key has an integer value, and a record is placed in a slot with a relative address (slot number) equal to the primary key. The record can be retrieved by direct access on presentation of the slot number (the primary key). Matched-key relative files are faster than indexed-sequential files.

3. In a hash file, the primary key is subjected to what is called a *hashing routine*, which generates a relative address from the primary key. When two or more different primary keys cause the same rela-

tive address to be generated, you have a collision. Processing to handle collisions is complex. A variation of the hash file, called the direct file, in which a slot is an entire track, avoids the problem of overflow records.

Key Terms

relative file	hash file	collision
matched-key file	hashing routine	direct file

Concept Review Questions

1. Explain why a relative file is like a single-level array stored on disk.
2. Distinguish between a physical and a relative address.
3. Distinguish between a matched-key relative file and a hash file.
4. Why do relative files tend to be faster than indexed-sequential files?
5. Explain the concept of a collision in a hash file. Explain chained progressive overflow management.
6. Explain what a hashing routine does.
7. What are the different ways in which a matched-key relative file can be updated?

COBOL Language Questions

1. In creating a relative file, what is the significance of omitting the RELATIVE KEY (or NOMINAL KEY) clause?

2. What is wrong with the following

```
FILE-CONTROL.
  SELECT MASTER ASSIGN TO
                ORGANIZATION IS RELATIVE
                ACCESS IS RANDOM
                RELATIVE KEY RDA.
...
FD MASTER       LABEL RECORDS STANDARD.
01 MASTER-RECORD.
    05 RDA PIC X(8).
    05 ...
```

3. Where must the identifier that holds a relative address be defined?

4. Under what circumstances can INVALID KEY not be used with WRITE?

Programming Assignments

1. **Creation of a matched-key master file and output of the control listing.**
The input file is

SOURCE-FILE   Validated master records about very reliable electronic parts; can contain records that are out-of-sequence or have duplicate primary keys.

The output files are

NEW-MASTER   Newly created master file
CONTROL-LISTING   Printer file that lists the primary key of
every master file record. For each key, it
gives the status of the record, either
accepted or rejected; if rejected, problems
are listed

Some input (SOURCE-FILE) records are

```
---------1---------2---------3
0100157178J050
0301594255B106
0305402750T130
0710006025B106
0605004250J050
1002833045T130
1105608280B106
1212506530T130
1500707250J050
1901506640T130
2102855500J050
2214009265B106
2509508500T130
```

Columns 01–02   Part type identification code, primary key
03–06   Quantity in warehouse
07–10   Price per unit ($dd.dd)
11–14   Bin code (a bin can hold many types of parts).

The control listing for creating the master file has the following format:

```
---------1---------2---------3---------4---------5---------6---------7
            COMPREHENSIVE CONTROL LISTING
            RELATIVE MASTER FILE CREATION
PAGE   1                                          05/06/92

PART   QTY    PRICE   BIN        STATUS      PROBLEM

01     0015   7178    J050       ACCEPTED
03     0159   4255    B106       ACCEPTED
03     0540   2750    T130       REJECTED    DUPLICATE KEY
07     1000   6025    B106       ACCEPTED
06     0500   4250    J050       REJECTED    OUT-OF-SEQUENCE KEY
10     0283   3045    T130       ACCEPTED
...
```

The output matched-key relative master file has records in
exactly the same format as the input file.

a. Draw record layouts and spacing charts for the files.
b. Draw the flowchart and hierarchy diagram.
c. Write the program.

2. Classical change updating a master file

The master file is the one created in Assignment 1, with corrections made to the invalid records. A record describes the inventory of a part in a warehouse. The transaction and master records are

```
---------1---------2              ---------1---------2
080100A                           0100157178J050
030074S                           0301594255B106
220200S                           0405402750T130
120100A                           0710006025B106
130100A                           0805004250J050
190050S                           1002833045T130
220050S                           1105608280B106
110100A                           1212506530T130
041200A                           1500707250J050
250700S                           1901506640T130
                                  2102855500J050
                                  2214009265B106
                                  2509508500T130
```

Columns 01–02   Part type identification code, not unique
        03–06   Quantity removed from (S) or added to
                (A) warehouse
        07   Add or Subtract code.

Corrections were made to the data from Assignment 1, as a result of the output of the control listing during master file creation.

Transaction records are used to change update the quantity of parts in a master record. Transaction records are unsorted; those with duplicate transaction code values are processed normally (that is, each record of a group with duplicate transaction codes will cause an update to the same master record).

The transaction file is used to update the quantity field in the master. Assume that unmatched transaction records can occur. Unmatched records are to be printed in a control listing.

Note: In the case of withdrawal of parts, if the quantity of parts on hand is less than the quantity in the transaction record, the transaction record is printed in the control file with an explanation of the problem. The control listing appears as follows:

```
---------1---------2---------3---------4---------5---------6---------7
         CHANGE UPDATE CONTROL LISTING (TRANSACTION ERROR RECORDS)
PAGE   1                                                   07/12/92

PART   QTY   OPERATION    UPDATE       PROBLEM
                          STATUS

08     0100  ADD          DONE
03     0074  SUBTR.       DONE
22     0200  SUBTR.       DONE
12     0100  ADD          DONE
13     0100  ADD          REJECTED   UNMATCHED PART CODE
19     0050  SUBTR.       DONE
22     0100  ADD          DONE
11     1200  ADD          DONE
04     0700  SUBTR.       REJECTED   TOO FEW PARTS IN MASTER
```

a. Draw record layouts and spacing charts for the files.
b. Make of list of error messages to be used.
c. Draw the flowchart and hierarchy diagram.
d. Write the program using direct-access change updating.

3. **Insertion updating assignment**
In this assignment, the same master file as in Assignment 2 is used. This time, new records are to be inserted into the master from a transaction file, with these records:

```
---------1---------2
0910008540K173
0200103547K188
2300805525M280
1202506540T130
0703007540L055
2415003460K143
1400502530G149
1901002780F155
```

Columns	
01–02	Part type identification code, primary key
03–06	Quantity in warehouse
07–10	Price per unit ($dd.dd)
11–14	Bin code (bin contains the parts)

Transaction records are unsorted and matching keys can occur.
The control listing for the update appears as follows:

```
---------1---------2---------3---------4---------5---------6---------7
          INSERTION UPDATE CONTROL LISTING (TRANSACTION ERROR RECORDS)
PAGE    1                                                  07/12/92
```

PART	QTY	PRICE	BIN	INSERTION STATUS	PROBLEM
09	1000	85 40	K173	ACCEPTED	
02	0010	35 47	K188	ACCEPTED	
23	0080	55 25	M280	ACCEPTED	
12	0250	65 40	T130	REJECTED	MATCHING KEY
07	0300	75 40	L055	REJECTED	MATCHING KEY
24	1500	34 60	K143	ACCEPTED	
14	0050	25 30	G149	ACCEPTED	
19	0100	27 80	F155	REJECTED	MATCHING KEY

a. Draw record layouts and spacing chart for the files.
b. Draw the flowchart and hierarchy diagram.
c. Write the program using direct-access insertion.

RELATIONAL FILES AND DATA BASES

OBJECTIVES
- To explain the concepts of a relation, a relational data base, and a relationship between relations
- To demonstrate how to load and update a relational data base using SQL at a terminal

OUTLINE

16.1 A relational data base consists of relations that participate in relationships
A relation is a simple kind of file
A view is formed from a base table relation
A data base administrator is needed for managing a data base
There is a relationship between two relational files if they have a common field
You create a data base before you put records into it
Views lead to data independence

16.2 You can manipulate a relational data base from a terminal
The INSERT command is used for initial data base loading
The SELECT command can be used with a single relation

Retrieval 1	Retrieval 9
Retrieval 2	Retrieval 10
Retrieval 3	Retrieval 11
Retrieval 4	Retrieval 12
Retrieval 5	Retrieval 13
Retrieval 6	Retrieval 14
Retrieval 7	Retrieval 15
Retrieval 8	Retrieval 16

The SELECT command can be used with two or more relations

Retrieval 17	Retrieval 19
Retrieval 18	Retrieval 20

The UPDATE command can update multiple records
    Update 1
    Update 2
    Update 3
    Update 4 (may be skipped on first reading)
    Update 5
Exercise caution with the use of UPDATE
The DELETE command can delete multiple records
    Update 6
    Update 7
Exercise caution with the DELETE command

A COLLECTION OF master files that are related to one another in some way is called a *data base*. The most important type of data base is the *relational data base*. A master file that is part of a relational data base is called a *relational file* or just a *relation*. A relational file is also frequently called a *base table*. (Do not confuse a relation or relational file with the relative files covered in the previous chapter. They have nothing to do with each other.)

In the context of data bases, a relation or base table is a kind of file made up of records. Just as COBOL can be used to manipulate conventional files, that is, non–data base files, it can also be used to manipulate files in a data base, that is, base tables or relations. Thus, COBOL programs can manipulate a data base.

Similarly, as a COBOL program can be used to create a master file, either with or without data validation, a COBOL program can also be used to create (or "load") a relation or base table of a data base. Thus, COBOL programs can be used to load a data base with records.

Just as conventional files can be change, insertion, or deletion updated by COBOL programs using transaction files, so can data base files. Thus, a data base can be change, insertion, or deletion updated using a COBOL program and an appropriate transaction file.

Recall that in conventional file processing with COBOL, records are transferred between main memory and file storage devices using READ, WRITE, and REWRITE commands. When a READ, WRITE, or REWRITE statement is executed, an appropriate input/output routine or access method is executed and does the actual work of transferring the record.

When a relational data base is being manipulated with COBOL, instead of READ, WRITE, and REWRITE, quite different commands are used. Briefly, the commands used are SELECT (retrieve), INSERT (insert), DELETE (delete), and UPDATE (change) commands. Furthermore, it is not an input/output routine that is called up and executed when one of these commands is executed. Instead it is a more complex software component called a *data base management system* (DBMS) that is executed.

In order for you to create and manipulate an indexed-sequential file, for example, an indexed-sequential input/output routine or access method (such as VSAM) must be installed in your computer. Many smaller computer installations may not have an access method as sophisticated as VSAM installed for indexed-sequential files. The same is true for the input/output routine or access method needed for relative files.

Similarly, many smaller installations may not have a relational data base management system installed that permits you to create and manipulate a relational data base using COBOL. If this is the case, you can still learn about these techniques from this chapter and the next, but you will not be able to run COBOL programs for processing a data base. However, these chapters are written so as to permit you to learn, even if you do not have access to a data base management system.

Let us begin with some relational data base concepts. Then you will see a wide variety of different SELECT, UPDATE, INSERT, and DELETE commands that can be used with COBOL to manipulate a relational data base. The collection of these commands is considered to be a separate language and is called SQL for "structured query language."

When SQL commands are used within a COBOL program, they are said to be *embedded* in the COBOL program. SQL can also be used directly at a terminal without COBOL, however. Typically, SQL expressions are tested at a terminal before insertion into COBOL programs. Here, the initial study of SQL will involve its use at a terminal, and will not involve embedding it in COBOL. That will be tackled in the next chapter.

16.1
A relational data base consists of relations that participate in relationships

B EGINNING WITH the concept of a relation or relational file, this section will then look at how such files can be related to form data bases. It will also examine the advantages of data bases over conventional files.

A relation is a simple kind of file

Any computer file made up of records is a relation (or relational file or base table) if it satisfies all of the following conditions:

- No two records are alike.
- All records have the same number, type, and order of fields.
- All fields contain data of interest to users; that is, there are no fields used only by the computer system in storing the records.

A relation is thus a simple kind of computer file. Many of the files used in previous chapters could be considered to be relations. The file SUPPLIER in Figure 16.1 (ignoring spaces between the fields and commas in the OWING field) is a relation.

```
SNUMB     OWING     CITY
0445      10,500    DENVER
0589       5,400    MIAMI
0899      15,000    DENVER
1578         400    SEATTLE
2400      10,300    DENVER
2980       3,700    SEATTLE
                    SUPPLIER
```

Figure 16.1 *The relation (or relational file) SUPPLIER. Each record describes a supplier of parts to a company. SNUMB, the supplier number, is the primary key.*

The records of the file are unique, they all have the same length and format, and there are no auxiliary implementation fields. Each record describes a supplier of parts to the company. SNUMB, the supplier number, is the primary key. OWING gives the amount owing to the supplier and CITY gives the city in which the supplier is located.

A relation can be stored on disk as either an indexed-sequential file or a hash file. Usually it is an indexed-sequential file. However, the user, or COBOL programmer, need not be aware of exactly how the file is stored. The data base management system looks after all details of indexes, hashing routines, auxiliary pointers, and secondary indexes. Thus, a relation is really an abstract kind of file; it does not actually exist except in users' imaginations.

What does physically exist is what is stored on disk. The version on disk will probably be somewhat different and, with most computer systems, will have associated primary and secondary indexes to permit direct access. In a few cases, the relation may be stored as a hash file. The version stored on disk is called the *storage file*. Users never see the storage file; users manipulate relations. The data base management system manipulates both relations and underlying storage files.

A relation is not normally the same thing as the storage file, although in rare cases it could be. For example, if the storage file were a simple sequential file, then the relation and storage file would be the same. The relation directly abstracted from the storage file is often called a base table (as distinct from further relations derived from the base table). Thus, SUPPLIER, in Figure 16.1, would be a base table relation.

A view is formed from a base table relation

Although it was said earlier that users manipulate relations, a more exact statement would be that users manipulate views of base table relations. In

```
SNUMB     CITY
0445      DENVER
0589      MIAMI
0899      DENVER
1578      SEATTLE
2400      DENVER
2980      SEATTLE
          VIEW-SUP-CITY
```

Figure 16.2 *The view VIEW-SUP-CITY derived from SUPPLIER, in Figure 16.1, by removing the column of OWING fields.*

the simplest case, a *view* of a base table is the base table relation with zero or more columns removed (and any resulting duplicate records removed as well).

For example, one view of the base table relation SUPPLIER, in Figure 16.1, could be VIEW-SUP-CITY, in Figure 16.2. This view is formed by removing the OWING field from SUPPLIER. A trivial view could be the same as SUPPLIER, formed by removing no (zero) fields.

A user can manipulate a view from a terminal using SQL. A COBOL program with embedded SQL commands can also manipulate a view. In both cases, the data base management system is used to transfer data between memory and disk. However, it is really the underlying storage file that is involved in the manipulation. The view is only a view of a part of the storage file provided by the data base management system.

A data base administrator is needed for managing a data base

A data base in any organization will be administered by a *data base administrator* (DBA), who gives different user groups permission to use certain parts of the data base. These user groups will typically manipulate the data base both directly from a terminal and via COBOL programs. The view facility enables the data base administrator to screen out certain sensitive fields from certain user groups. Thus, it could be that a user group was not allowed to know how much the company owed each supplier (OWING field), but needed to know where the supplier was located. In that case the data base administrator could create the view VIEW-SUP-CITY for that particular user group.

Use of views thus increases the security of data in important data base files. The data base administrator employs views to ensure that you can only get at data, for either information retrieval or updating, for which you have a demonstrated need. Views have other important uses too, as you will see.

Do not be confused about the terms *relation* and *relationship*. In the context of data bases, a relation is a kind of file, made up of records. A relationship is something quite different. Loosely speaking, persons or things are related, or participate in a relationship, if they share something in common. Similarly, two files of a relational data base, that is, two relational files or relations, can participate in a relationship if they have at least a field in common.

Consider a simple data base with the basic relations or base table relations SUPPLIER and DELIVERY, in Figure 16.3a.

This data base has two basic relations, or base table relations. A record of SUPPLIER describes a supplier of parts to the company. A record of DELIVERY describes a delivery of part types to the company by a supplier.

The two relations are related because they have a field SNUMB in common. The relationship between the relations is said to be one-to-many ($1:n$), because for one record in SUPPLIER there can be zero or more related records in DELIVERY.

Any pair of SUPPLIER and DELIVERY records will be related if they have the same SNUMB value. Thus, the record for supplier 0445 is related to three records in DELIVERY. Each of these three records describes a delivery of part types by supplier 0445; for one supplier there can be zero or more deliveries. This is shown in Figure 16.3b. One-to-many relationships between data base relations are very common.

The SUPPLIER relation would often be called the *parent relation* of the related pair of relational files, and the DELIVERY relation would often be called the *child relation*. This convention has to do with the obvious $1:n$ relationship in a parent to child relationship—one parent can have zero or more children.

SNUMB	OWING	CITY
0445	10,500	DENVER
0589	5,400	MIAMI
0899	15,000	DENVER
1578	400	SEATTLE
2400	10,300	DENVER
2980	3,700	SEATTLE

SUPPLIER

SNUMB	PTNUMB	PRICE	QTY
0445	P34	15	100
2980	P67	10	40
0445	P88	12	100
0899	P34	14	200
2400	P71	3	300
0445	P67	9	50
2400	P55	21	100
2980	P71	4	100
2400	P88	11	250
2980	P34	16	100
0899	P55	20	50

DELIVERY

Figure 16.3a Relational data base made up of the two master files, or base table relations, SUPPLIER and DELIVERY. The files are related because they have the common field SNUMB (supplier number). A record of DELIVERY gives the price and quantity of a given type of part (PTNUMB) delivered by the supplier to the company. Note that different suppliers may have different prices for the same type of part.

SNUMB	OWING	CITY		SNUMB	PTNUMB	PRICE	QTY
0445	10,500	DENVER		0445	P34	15	100
				0445	P67	9	50
				0445	P88	12	100
0589	5,400	MIAMI					
0899	15,000	DENVER		0899	P34	14	200
				0899	P55	20	50
1578	400	SEATTLE					
2400	10,300	DENVER		2400	P55	21	100
				2400	P71	3	300
				2400	P88	11	250
2980	3,700	SEATTLE		2980	P34	16	100
				2980	P67	10	40
				2980	P71	4	100

SUPPLIER   **DELIVERY**

Figure 16.3b *There is a one-to-many relationship between SUPPLIER and DELIVER records. For a given SUPPLIER record, there can be zero or more related DELIVERY records.*

You create a data base before you put records into it

To create a new data base, two major steps are needed.

1. The data base must be defined, and the definition stored, for use by the data base management system. When this has been done the data base exists, but its relations contain no records. A data base is defined using the SQL CREATE command, outside of any program.
2. Next, the data base must be loaded with records; that is, records are placed in the empty relations. This is done using the SQL INSERT command. INSERT can either be used at a terminal or embedded within a COBOL program.

Unlike conventional computer files, a relational file (or base table relation) in a relational data base is defined outside of any program that will later manipulate that file. The files of a relational data base are defined by the data base administrator before any data goes into them.

The data base administrator defines the data base at a terminal by entering base table definition commands. These definitions are accepted by the data base management system and stored on disk. The data base management system is capable of managing more than one data base, but it must have access to a specification of any data base it is required to manipulate.

To define a data base, the data base administrator defines the basic relations of the data base, or base table relations. He or she also defines the underlying storage files on disk and any views derived from the base table relations.

For example, to define the base table relations SUPPLIER and DELIVERY, the data base administrator could enter the following:

```
CREATE TABLE SUPPLIER      (SNUMB        CHAR (4) NOT NULL,
                            OWING        SMALLINTEGER,
                            CITY         CHAR (15));
CREATE TABLE DELIVERY      (SNUMB        CHAR (4) NOT NULL,
                            PTNUMB       CHAR (3) NOT NULL,
                            PRICE        SMALLINTEGER,
                            QTY          SMALLINTEGER);
```

A field in a record of a base table relation is defined as capable of having a null value (value not known, but believed to exist), unless this is prohibited in the definitions of the relations, by means of the NOT NULL clause. A primary key field may not be defined as capable of having a null value.

The fields of the relations are defined with the notation of PL/1 and not COBOL. CHAR (n) is equivalent to PIC X(n). SMALLINTEGER is equivalent to about PIC 9(6). In any COBOL program to manipulate these files, pictures large enough to hold these fields would have to be defined.

To define the underlying storage files for SUPPLIER and DELIVERY, the data base administrator must decide which fields are to have primary indexes and which are to have secondary indexes. The data base administrator would probably define a primary index for SNUMB in SUPPLIER, as this is the primary key. Suppose the data base administrator calls this index SNUMB-INDEX. It would be defined as follows:

```
CREATE UNIQUE INDEX
        SNUMB-INDEX ON SUPPLIER (SNUMB);
```

The word UNIQUE defines the index as primary.

If the data base administrator decided there would be a great deal of direct access to the SUPPLIER relation on the basis of the CITY field, then he or she might define a secondary index, perhaps called CITY-INDEX, for the CITY field. This secondary index would be defined as follows:

```
CREATE INDEX
        CITY-INDEX ON SUPPLIER (CITY);
```

Omission of UNIQUE means that the index is secondary.

With the DELIVERY relation, the primary key is a combination of the SNUMB and PTNUMB fields, that is, SNUMB PTNUMB values taken together are unique. It is unlikely that direct access would be needed on the basis of the primary key. But direct access could certainly be needed on the basis of either SNUMB or PTNUMB, so that secondary indexes could be defined for these fields.

```
CREATE INDEX
        SNUMB-DEL-INDEX ON DELIVERY (SNUMB);
CREATE INDEX
        PTNUMB-DEL-INDEX ON DELIVERY (PTNUMB)
```

Once an index has been defined, the data base management system creates the necessary data structures on disk. When the files are later filled with records, the data base management system places appropriate entries in these indexes. The indexes are similar in structure to those described in Chapter 14.

The data base administrator could next define any needed views on the relations SUPPLIER and DELIVERY. A view on SUPPLIER, consisting of the fields SNUMB and CITY and called VIEW-SUP-CITY, could be defined as follows:

```
CREATE VIEW        VIEW-SUP-CITY (SNUMB, CITY)
AS                 SELECT (SNUMB, CITY) FROM SUPPLIER;
```

This view was illustrated in Figure 16.2.

The trivial view VIEW-SUPPLIER that is the same as the SUPPLIER relation could be defined.

```
CREATE VIEW        VIEW-SUPPLIER (SNUMB, OWING, CITY)
AS                 SELECT (SNUMB, OWING, CITY) FROM SUPPLIER;
```

The second step of placing records in the newly defined data base will be examined shortly.

Views lead to data independence

Using a view of a relation instead of the base table relation in a program, gives a benefit known as *data independence*. Suppose that the relation SUPPLIER had been defined as a conventional indexed-sequential file instead of as a data base file. In the course of time, if the file was used in a large company, perhaps many programs would make use of this file. Now suppose that one day it is necessary to extend each record of the existing file to four fields, by adding a new field. The new field could be CREDIT-LIMIT, for the credit limit offered by each supplier. Thus a new version of the file will be created with the CREDIT-LIMIT field.

None of the existing programs will be able to use this new version without alteration to the definitions in the environment and data divisions. Thus, the existing programs are not independent of the data structure of the file, that is, they are not data independent. Because it is expensive to change a large number of existing programs, the conventional solution is to live with two or more versions of the same file. Thus, you would start with a three-field version of SUPPLIER, but after some time there would be both a three-field and a four-field version. Later a five-field version could be introduced, and so on. This, unfortunately, would give rise to possibilities of the different file versions not being consistent, because of different updating schedules.

If SUPPLIER were defined as a data base file, all the programs using it could be data independent. Suppose these programs used the view VIEW-SUPPLIER as defined earlier. Later the data base administrator could add the new field CREDIT-LIMIT to the existing SUPPLIER relation, simply by entering the ALTER command.

```
ALTER TABLE SUPPLIER
              ADD        CREDIT-LIMIT   SMALLINTEGER;
```

The existing file, SUPPLIER, would immediately have the fourth field added, although the value of the field in each record would be null until a later update placed other values in the fields. Nevertheless, SUPPLIER would now have four fields instead of the original three. However, since all the existing programs would be based on the view VIEW-SUPPLIER, and not SUPPLIER, these programs would not be affected. The view VIEW-SUPPLIER would continue to have its original three fields. Thus, the programs would be data independent.

Programs using any view of a data base have data independence because they are insulated against any additions to the fields of the base table relations from which the views are derived. Data independence is one of the major reasons for using a data base instead of conventional files—it reduces program maintenance costs.

16.2 You can manipulate a relational data base from a terminal

A RELATIONAL data base can be manipulated in two distinct ways.

- From a terminal by entering SQL commands that are immediately executed
- By execution of COBOL programs in which SQL commands are embedded

Thus, it is important to learn how to formulate and use SQL commands. It is easiest to learn SQL commands by using them directly at a terminal—the subject of the remainder of this chapter. In the next chapter you will learn how to embed SQL in COBOL programs.

The SQL needed to fill a data base with records initially will be examined first, then the SQL for retrieving information from a data base and for updating a data base. SQL is an acronym for "structured query language"; this is a misnomer, however, since SQL is used for both information retrieval and updating.

The following is a brief summary of the SQL commands.

INSERT	Used for loading records into a relation initially and for insertion updating
SELECT	Used for information retrieval; complex retrieval conditions can be used with SELECT
UPDATE	Used for change updating; complex conditions can be used with the command to select the records from a relation for updating
DELETE	Used for deletion updating; complex conditions can be used with the command to select the records from a relation for deletion

Let us now examine these commands in some detail.

The INSERT command is used for initial data base loading

Once a relational file has been defined using the CREATE TABLE entry shown earlier and given all necessary index structures, records can be placed in the relation. With a small relation, it is convenient to enter the records one by one from a terminal, using the INSERT command, as follows:

```
INSERT
INTO  SUPPLIER (SNUMB, OWING, CITY)
VALUES ('0445', 10500, 'DENVER');
```

Alphanumeric values are enclosed in quotes. The preceding command places the first record of SUPPLIER, from Figure 16.3, in the data base. Repeated execution of the command for the different records can be used to fill the relation.

Large relations are best loaded by a COBOL program that contains embedded INSERT commands. The source records would be available in a conventional sequential file, read in one by one using READ statements, and output to the relational file using embedded INSERT commands. This aspect of inserting records is dealt with in more detail in the next chapter. For now, assume that the data base has been filled with the records shown in Figure 16.3.

The SELECT command can be used with a single relation

Very complex SELECT expressions can be constructed, depending on the complexity of the retrieval conditions. Let us look at simplest, or basic, SELECT command format first. The structure or format of the basic SELECT expression is

```
SELECT     fieldname-1, fieldname-2, . . .
FROM       relationname-1
WHERE      condition-1.
```

A simple SELECT expression retrieves the field values specified from each record of the relation specified for which the condition holds true. A condition is very like a condition in COBOL. The following examples illustrate this.

Retrieval 1

Find the supplier numbers for all Denver suppliers.

```
SELECT SNUMB
FROM SUPPLIER
WHERE CITY = 'DENVER';
```

This would retrieve

```
SNUMB
0445
0899
2400
```

If you did not have authorization from the data base administrator to use SUPPLIER, you might be required to use the view VIEW-SUP-CITY. The following expression would give the same result:

```
SELECT SNUMB
FROM VIEW-SUP-CITY
WHERE CITY = 'DENVER'
```

In most of these examples, information will be retrieved information from the base table relations SUPPLIER and DELIVERY. But bear in mind that SQL SELECT expressions can be applied equally well to views.

Retrieval 2

Retrieve all SUPPLIER records for suppliers who are owed less than $10,000.

```
SELECT SNUMB, OWING, CITY
FROM SUPPLIER
WHERE OWING < 10000;
```

The result is

```
SNUMB___OWING___CITY
0589     5400    MIAMI
1578      400    SEATTLE
2980     3700    SEATTLE
```

The condition following WHERE (the WHERE condition) is constructed like a condition in COBOL, except you must use an operator, =, <, >, <=, >=, or NOT =.

In carrying out the retrieval, the data base management system checks all records of SUPPLIER. Those records for which the condition is true are selected. Compound conditions can be used, just as in COBOL, as shown in Retrieval 3.

Note the preceding expression could be replaced by

```
SELECT *
FROM SUPPLIER
WHERE OWING < 10000;
```

The * symbol means all the fields in the records of the relation specified, that is, the complete records.

Retrieval 3

Retrieve the supplier numbers and amount owed for those suppliers in DENVER for which the amount owed does not exceed $15,000.

```
SELECT SNUMB, OWING
FROM SUPPLIER
WHERE CITY = 'DENVER' AND OWING <= 15000;
```

The result is

```
SNUMB  OWING
0445   10500
0899   15000
2400   10300
```

You may use AND and OR to connect conditions, with the same meaning as in COBOL. With complex conditions always use parentheses to clarify your intent.

Retrieval 4

Find the suppliers and the cities in which they are located.

```
SELECT SNUMB, CITY
FROM SUPPLIER;
```

The result is

```
SNUMB  CITY
0445   DENVER
0589   MIAMI
0899   DENVER
1578   SEATTLE
2400   DENVER
2980   SEATTLE
```

If no WHERE condition is included, all records are retrieved, but only the fields specified are selected.

Retrieval 5

Find the suppliers and their cities for which the amount owed is more than $3000, and display the data in descending CITY order.

```
SELECT SNUMB, CITY
FROM SUPPLIER
WHERE OWING > 3000
ORDER BY CITY DESC;
```

The result is

```
SNUMB  CITY
2980   SEATTLE
0589   MIAMI
0445   DENVER
0899   DENVER
2400   DENVER
```

In carrying out the command, the data base management system first retrieves the data and then sorts it.

If you wanted the data sorted in ascending CITY order, you could specify ORDER BY CITY ASC. If you wanted it sorted primarily in ascending CITY order, but secondarily in descending SNUMB order, you could specify ORDER BY CITY ASC, SNUMB DESC.

The order by clause is useful with SELECT expressions that are embedded in COBOL, since it often makes it possible to have records sorted without the use of the COBOL SORT verb.

Retrieval 6

How many suppliers are there in Denver?

```
SELECT COUNT (*)
FROM SUPPLIER
WHERE CITY = 'DENVER';
```

The result is 3. The system first retrieves the records and then the COUNT function counts them.

Retrieval 7

What is the total amount owed to suppliers in Denver?

```
SELECT SUM (OWING)
FROM SUPPLIER
WHERE CITY = 'DENVER';
```

The result is 35800. The Denver records are first retrieved and then the SUM function is applied to the OWING fields.

Retrieval 8

What is the average amount owed to Denver suppliers?

```
SELECT AVG (OWING)
FROM SUPPLIER
WHERE CITY = 'DENVER';
```

The result is 11933.34. The Denver records are first retrieved and then the AVG (average) function is applied to the OWING fields.

Instead of AVG (OWING), you could use MAX (OWING), which would give the maximum amount owing to Denver suppliers, or MIN (OWING), which would give the minimum amount owing.

Retrieval 9

What is the type of part, and the value of the order, for each type of part delivered by supplier 0899?

```
SELECT PTNUMB, QTY * PRICE
FROM DELIVERY
WHERE SNUMB = '0899';
```

The result is

```
PTNUMB _ _ _ _ _ _
P34      2800
P55      1000
```

Instead of displaying the field values retrieved from each record, they can be used in arithmetic operations for which the result is to be displayed, such as QTY * PRICE. Normal COBOL arithmetic expressions of the type found in a COMPUTE statement can be used.

Retrieval 10

What is the type of part, and the value of the order, including a 10 percent tax and a $1000 commission, for each order delivered from supplier 0899?

```
SELECT PTNUMB, QTY * PRICE * 1.10 + 1000
FROM DELIVERY
WHERE SNUMB = '0899';
```

The result is

```
PTNUMB _ _ _ _ _ _
P34      4080
P55      2100
```

For each record retrieved, the QTY and PRICE values are multiplied, the result is then multiplied by 1.10, and 1000 is added to that result. This final result is displayed for each record retrieved.

Retrieval 11

For each supplier, what is the total number of parts delivered that are priced over $10?

```
SELECT SNUMB, SUM (QTY)
FROM DELIVERY
WHERE PRICE > 10
GROUP BY SNUMB;
```

The result is

```
SNUMB _ _ _ _ _ _ _
0445     200
0899     250
2400     350
2980     100
```

Here the GROUP BY clause causes the relation DELIVERY to be partitioned into subrelations by SNUMB value (see Figure 16.3b). The sum of the QTY values is then retrieved for each group of records with the same SNUMB value. You can regard the GROUP BY field SNUMB as the equivalent of a control-break identifier.

Retrieval 12

Get the supplier numbers for suppliers in either Seattle or Miami.

```
SELECT SNUMB
FROM SUPPLIER
WHERE CITY = 'SEATTLE' OR CITY = 'MIAMI';
```

Compound conditions can be constructed using AND and OR. Parentheses should be used where there are three or more connectives, to avoid error.

Retrieval 13

Get the supplier numbers for suppliers in Chicago, Dallas, Seattle, or Miami.

```
SELECT SNUMB
FROM SUPPLIER
WHERE CITY IN ('CHICAGO', 'DALLAS', 'SEATTLE', 'MIAMI');
```

The result is

```
SNUMB
0589
1578
2980
```

The retrieval condition should be studied carefully. It is a perfectly valid condition and for any record of SUPPLIER will have the value TRUE or FALSE. It is a set inclusion condition. Thus, the statement

13 is in the set (9, 12, 13, 17)

is true. However, the statement

NEW YORK is in the set (PORTLAND, BALTIMORE, DALLAS, DENVER)

is false.

In the SQL expression, a set inclusion condition has the syntax:

 **SYNTAX**   fieldname [NOT] IN set

In executing the preceding SQL expression, the system checks each record of SUPPLIER in turn. If the CITY value is included in the set of cities specified, the record is retrieved.

Retrieval 14

Get the supplier numbers for those suppliers who are in Denver and are owed either $15,000 or $3700.

```
SELECT SNUMB
FROM SUPPLIER
WHERE CITY = 'DENVER' AND (OWING = 15000 OR OWING = 3700);
```

Without parentheses, the condition would be evaluated incorrectly as

```
(CITY = 'DENVER' AND OWING = 15000) OR OWING = 3700;
```

since AND evaluates before OR, as in a COBOL condition.

Retrieval 15

Get the cities in which there are suppliers who are owed less than $14,000.

```
SELECT CITY
FROM SUPPLIER
WHERE OWING < 14000;
```

The result is

```
CITY
DENVER
MIAMI
SEATTLE
DENVER
SEATTLE
```

Note that there are duplicates, since the CITY value is simply extracted from each record that fits the condition. If you want duplicates eliminated, the word DISTINCT should be inserted.

```
SELECT DISTINCT CITY
FROM SUPPLIER
WHERE OWING < 14000;
```

What you now get is

```
CITY
DENVER
MIAMI
SEATTLE
```

Retrieval 16

How many cities are there with a supplier owed less than $14,000?

```
SELECT COUNT (DISTINCT CITY)
FROM SUPPLIER
WHERE OWING < 14000;
```

The response is 3. DISTINCT must be used when the number of field values retrieved is counted, since otherwise duplicates would be counted.

This is an introduction to the more comprehensive use of SELECT. If you like, it may be skipped on first reading. Comprehensive coverage of the use of SELECT can be found in many data base management texts.

A SELECT expression can involve two or more relations. Generally you want to retrieve either

- Field values from a pair of related records or
- Field values from one record, where related records comply with a condition

A pair of records from SUPPLIER and DELIVERY are related if they have a common SNUMB value. Thus, the SUPPLIER record for supplier 0445 in Figure 16.3 is related to three DELIVERY records, each of which describes a delivery made by supplier 0445.

Retrieval 17

What are the prices of P67 parts and the cities and suppliers from which they were delivered?

```
SELECT SUPPLIER.SNUMB, CITY, PRICE
FROM SUPPLIER, DELIVERY
WHERE PTNUMB = 'P67'
  AND SUPPLIER.SNUMB = DELIVERY.SNUMB;
```

The result is

SNUMB	CITY	PRICE
0445	DENVER	9
2980	SEATTLE	10

In this case, every possible pair of SUPPLIER and DELIVERY records, paired by means of a common SNUMB value, is considered. Some such pairs are shown here:

SNUMB	OWING	CITY	SNUMB	PTNUMB	PRICE	QTY
0445	10,500	DENVER	0445	P34	15	100
0445	**10,500**	**DENVER**	**0445**	**P67**	**9**	**50**
0445	10,500	DENVER	0445	P88	12	100
0899	15,000	DENVER	0899	P34	14	200
0899	15,000	DENVER	0899	P55	20	50
...	...	...	...	...	...	...
2980	**3,700**	**SEATTLE**	**2980**	**P67**	**10**	**40**
2980	3,700	SEATTLE	2980	P71	4	100

Those pairs for which PTNUMB = 'P67' are selected and the SNUMB, CITY, and PRICE fields extracted are shown in bold. The condition

```
SUPPLIER.SNUMB = DELIVERY.SNUMB
```

ensures that related pairs of records are selected. (SUPPLIER.SNUMB means the SNUMB field in a SUPPLIER record, and is the PL/1 notation for the COBOL notation SNUMB IN SUPPLIER-RECORD.)

Retrieval 18

Give the cities from which parts priced under $10 have been delivered, and give the part types and quantities involved.

```
SELECT CITY, PTNUMB, QTY
FROM SUPPLIER, DELIVERY
WHERE PRICE < 10
   AND SUPPLIER.SNUMB = DELIVERY.SNUMB;
```

The result is

```
CITY_____PTNUMB__QTY
DENVER      P67       50
DENVER      P71      300
SEATTLE     P71      100
```

Pairs of related records for which the condition PRICE < 10 is true are selected.

Retrieval 19

Retrieve the supplier number and city for each supplier that supplies part type P88.

```
SELECT SNUMB, CITY
FROM SUPPLIER
WHERE SNUMB IN (SELECT SNUMB
                FROM DELIVERY
                WHERE PTNUMB = 'P88');
```

The result is

```
SNUMB_____CITY
0445       DENVER
2400       DENVER
```

In the preceding expression, what follows WHERE is a compound condition. The inner SELECT-FROM-WHERE gives the set of suppliers that have delivered P88. The outer SELECT-FROM-WHERE selects SUPPLIER records with SNUMB value in that set, that is, among those that have delivered P88.

The condition is a set inclusion condition, as explained in the previous section (see Retrieval 13). However, this time the set of values is the set of SNUMB values resulting from execution of the inner SELECT-FROM-WHERE. This mechanism is commonly used in SQL for retrieval of records from one file on condition that properties of related records in another file hold true.

Retrieval 20

Get the part type, price, and quantity for each part type delivered from Seattle.

```
SELECT PTNUMB, PRICE, QTY
FROM DELIVERY
WHERE SNUMB IN (SELECT SNUMB
                FROM SUPPLIER
                WHERE CITY = 'SEATTLE');
```

The result is

```
PTNUMB____PRICE_____QTY
P34        16       100
P67        10        40
P71         4       100
```

This time, the inner SELECT-FROM-WHERE retrieves the set of supplier numbers for Seattle suppliers (1578, 2980). The outer SELECT-FROM-WHERE selects DELIVERY records with an SNUMB value among the values in this set.

The UPDATE command can update multiple records

The UPDATE command is used for change updating existing records. It can be used to update a single record identified by a condition, a group of records identified by a condition, or every record in a relation.

Update 1

Change the amount owed to supplier 0589 to $6000.

```
UPDATE SUPPLIER
SET OWING = 6000
WHERE SNUMB = '0589';
```

The record for supplier 0589 is retrieved, its OWING field is changed to 6000, and the record is rewritten into the file. Because SNUMB is a primary key, only one record is selected and updated.

The rules for forming the WHERE condition here are the same as for the WHERE condition with SELECT.

Update 2

Increase the amount owed to supplier 0589 by 10 percent.

```
UPDATE SUPPLIER
SET OWING = OWING * 1.10
WHERE SNUMB = '0589';
```

If you wanted to add $500 to the existing owing value, the SET clause needed would be

```
SET OWING = OWING + 500
```

The SET clause is like the COMPUTE statement in COBOL.

Update 3

Add $1000 to the amount owed to each Denver supplier.

```
UPDATE SUPPLIER
SET OWING = OWING + 1000
WHERE CITY = 'DENVER'
```

This time, three Denver records are retrieved and the OWING field of each one of them has 1000 added. This is an example of a multiple-record update.

Update 4 (may be skipped on first reading)

Subtract $300 from the amount owed to each supplier that has delivered P88 parts.

```
UPDATE SUPPLIER
SET OWING = OWING - 300
WHERE SNUMB IN (SELECT SNUMB
                FROM DELIVERY
                WHERE PTNUMB = 'P88');
```

The inner SELECT-FROM-WHERE retrieves the set (0445, 2400). The outer expression retrieves the SUPPLIER records for suppliers 0445 and 2400 and subtracts 300 from their OWING fields. This is another multiple-record update.

Update 5

Reduce the amount owed to all suppliers by 20 percent.

```
UPDATE SUPPLIER
SET OWING = OWING * 0.80;
```

There is no WHERE condition, so all SUPPLIER records are retrieved and updated.

Exercise caution with the use of UPDATE

When UPDATE is used with a multiple-record update, great care must be taken. It is easy to get the WHERE condition wrong in an UPDATE (or SELECT expression), with the result that a large number of records could be updated incorrectly. For this reason, with many important data bases, update from a terminal is prohibited by the data base administrator. Only updating by means of programs containing embedded SQL commands is allowed, since the SQL commands needed can be thoroughly tested before the program is released for routine use.

Care also has to be taken when updating views. A view based on a base table relation must contain the primary key from the base table relation before it can be change updated. Otherwise, the data base management system cannot identify the underlying base table and storage record involved.

The DELETE command can delete multiple records

The DELETE command can also be used for deleting either a single record or a group of records that satisfy a condition.

Update 6

Delete supplier 0589.

```
DELETE
FROM SUPPLIER
WHERE SNUMB = '0589';
```

The WHERE condition determines which records are selected for deletion. In this case, SNUMB is a primary key field, so only a single record is selected and deleted. WHERE conditions in DELETE expressions are formulated using the same rules as for WHERE conditions with SELECT expressions.

Update 7

Delete all DELIVERY records for deliveries by supplier '2400'.

```
DELETE
FROM DELIVERY
WHERE SNUMB = '2400';
```

The condition is satisfied by three DELIVERY records, which are deleted. SNUMB is not a primary key in DELIVERY.

Exercise caution with the DELETE command

The cautions listed earlier for the use of UPDATE also apply to DELETE. The use of DELETE at a terminal to delete multiple records is risky. It is easy to get the WHERE condition wrong and delete large numbers of records incorrectly with a single DELETE command. DELETE with multiple records is best used within a COBOL program, in which the DELETE expression can be extensively tested before use.

DELETE can be used with a view only if the primary key from the underlying base table relation is included in the view.

Summary

1. A relational data base consists of a collection of relations, or base tables, that are related. Two base tables are related if they have a common field. In a one-to-many relationship between relations R1 and R2, for one R1 record there can be zero or more related R2 records.

2. Underlying a base table is a storage file on disk, with associated primary key and secondary key indexes. A base table consists only of records that contain useful data fields; all records of a base table have the same format and there cannot be duplicate records. A simple view is derived from a base table by removing zero or more fields. Views permit data independence, where the number of fields in a base table can be increased without affecting the ability of existing applications program to execute.

3. A data base management system is needed for manipulation of a relational data base. It functions somewhat like an input/output routine, but is much more powerful. SQL commands are used to manipulate a data base. SQL commands can be used directly at a terminal or embedded within a COBOL program. A single SQL command can retrieve or update multiple records that satisfy a condition specified with the command.

Key Terms

relational data base	view
relation	data base administrator
base table	relationship
storage file	data independence
data base management system	

Concept Review Questions

1. Compare a relational data base with conventional files.
2. Compare a data base management systems with an input/output routine (or access method).
3. Exactly what is a relation?
4. What is a storage file?
5. What is a view?
6. Explain why a view is a relation but not a base table.
7. Explain when a relation, or relational file, is a base table.
8. When is there a relationship between two relations?
9. Explain the concept of a 1:n relationship.
10. List the two major steps required to create a data base.
11. Explain the concept of data independence.
12. How are primary and secondary indexes for a new relation defined?
13. How is the primary key for a new relation defined?
14. Give two ways to load records into a data base.

All questions refer to the data base in Figure 16.3. Write SQL SELECT expressions for the following:

1. Find the prices of P34 parts.
2. Get full details about deliveries where the quantity was less than 100.
3. What Denver suppliers owe less than $12,000?
4. What suppliers have delivered P34 parts at less than $16?
5. Get full details on each delivery of less than 100 parts at a price of more than $10 per unit.
6. List all suppliers outside of Seattle, with their locations.
7. How many suppliers are there in Seattle?
8. What is the total quantity of parts delivered by all suppliers?
9. What is the total quantity of parts delivered by supplier 2400?
10. What is the average price of parts delivered by supplier 2980?
11. What is the average price of P34 parts?
12. How many deliveries did supplier 0899 make?
13. What is the average amount owing by Denver suppliers?
14. What is the total amount owed by suppliers outside of Miami?
15. What Denver supplier owes the least?
16. What supplier delivered the most expensive P34 parts?
17. List full details on deliveries in ascending part number order primarily and descending supplier number order secondarily, for deliveries of more than 60 parts.
18. What is the value of each order for P88 parts?
19. For each type of part delivered, what is the average price?
20. For each type of part delivered, find the total number of deliveries.
21. For each city, find the maximum amount owed by a supplier.
22. What suppliers have delivered any of the following parts: P67, P55, P71? (Use IN construct.)
23. Get the quantities of parts, with the suppliers and amount owing, that were delivered from Denver.
24. Get the cities from which P55 parts were delivered and the price of the parts.
25. Get the supplier and amount owing for each supplier that has delivered a batch of 200 parts.
26. Get the price and quantity for each delivery from Seattle.
27. Get the parts that do not come from Denver.
28. Deduct $1000 from the amount owing by all suppliers outside Miami.
29. Increase the price on all P34 parts by $3.
30. Double the quantities in all deliveries of parts by supplier 0899.
31. Delete all Seattle suppliers.
32. Delete all deliveries of P55 parts.
33. Delete all deliveries from Seattle.
34. Delete all suppliers who have never delivered P71 parts.

Programming
Assignment

1. **Creating a data base**
   Create the data base in Figure 16.3. Then enter as many of the SQL expressions as possible for the preceding questions and run them.

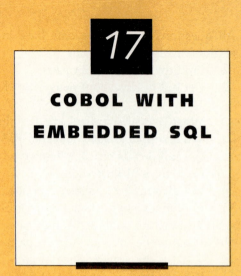

17

COBOL WITH
EMBEDDED SQL

*I*T IS POSSIBLE to embed SQL expressions within COBOL application programs; programmer productivity can be greatly increased this way. A few lines of SQL code can replace many tens of lines of COBOL code. Including SQL expressions in a COBOL program thus means the COBOL programmer needs to write fewer lines of COBOL instructions.

You have learned the rudiments of SQL, but there are additional skills to learn before you can embed SQL expressions in a COBOL program. The main skill needed is knowing how to interface SQL expressions with COBOL instructions. A specific skill must be acquired for this. It has to do with the fact that SQL expressions often manipulate many records at a time, unlike COBOL READ, WRITE, and REWRITE commands, which deal with a single record at a time.

17.1 A COBOL SQL program must be preprocessed before execution

*L*IKE ANY OTHER COBOL program, a COBOL source program with embedded SQL expressions (a COBOL SQL program), has to be translated into machine code before it can be executed. However, with a COBOL SQL program, translation to machine language requires an additional step, called a preprocessing step. Essentially, once the COBOL SQL program has been written, complete with embedded SQL expressions, and entered into an editor file using the system editor, it must be preprocessed before it can be compiled.

This section examines the nature of this preprocessing and shows how it affects the way a programmer prepares a program for execution.

Preprocessing COBOL SQL programs involves precompilation and translation of SQL expressions

The preprocessing is carried out by two sophisticated software components that are auxiliary components of the data base management system. These system components are

- **The SQL precompiler** The precompiler does not translate any COBOL code. Instead it extracts the SQL expressions and essentially replaces them with COBOL CALL statements to subprograms that will be generated from the SQL expressions.
- **The SQL bind system** This system takes the SQL expressions that have been extracted from the COBOL program by the precompiler and translates them into machine language subprograms. Each subprogram will be given a name, and the corresponding CALL statement placed in the COBOL program will call up this named subprogram. These subprograms are stored on disk.

The preprocessed source program, now containing COBOL CALL statements instead of embedded SQL expressions, is next translated into machine language by the COBOL compiler.

When the COBOL (object) program (in machine language format) executes, the CALL statements are executed, one by one. When a CALL statement is executed, the data base system carries out the commands contained within the corresponding subprogram stored on disk. This is illustrated in Figure 17.1.

A broad perspective on COBOL SQL program preprocessing helps

Let us take a step back from the preceding discussion to get a better perspective. A COBOL program has to be translated into machine code before it can execute. SQL expressions are not COBOL statements and therefore cannot be translated by the COBOL compiler. Consequently, each SQL expression must be removed and replaced with a suitable COBOL statement. So a precompiler needs to preprocess the program, extract the SQL expressions, and replace them with COBOL CALL statements. The COBOL program can then be compiled. (COBOL CALL statements are discussed in Chapter 19, in the context of subprograms you can write yourself. However, that discussion is not relevant here.)

An SQL expression in a COBOL program can be equivalent to a COBOL routine of many lines. So an SQL expression has to be translated to a named machine language routine. The bind system does this job. The bind system and the precompiler work in tandem. Thus, if the precompiler replaces an SQL expression with the equivalent of CALL XYZ, the bind system will translate the SQL expression into a subprogram called XYZ. When the program eventually executes, the CALL XYZ statement causes the XYZ subprogram to be executed. Thus each SQL expression is converted to a machine language routine, as are the COBOL statements.

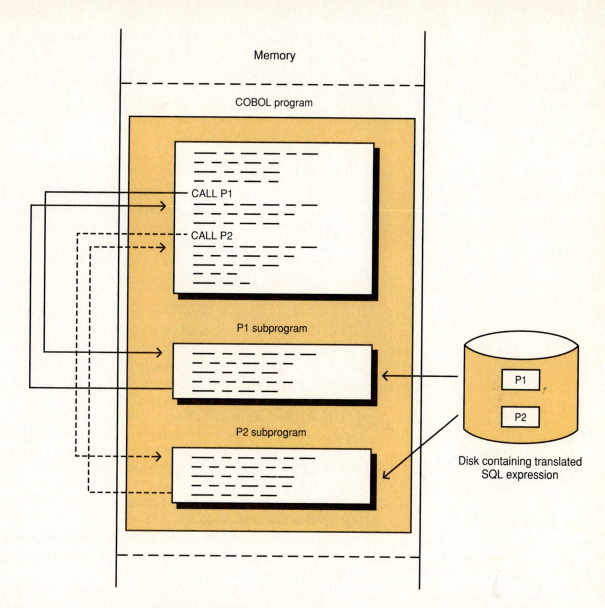

Figure 17.1 *When the object version of a COBOL SQL program executes, instructions are executed one by one. But when a CALL statement is executed, the data base system loads a subprogram of instructions that corresponds to an SQL expression. This subprogram is then executed, and following execution, control returns to the statement after the CALL in the COBOL object program.*

(You can find out more about this in books on relational data base systems. Some details have been glossed over here, but this description covers the essentials—all that is necessary for embedding SQL expressions in COBOL.)

A CALL statement calls up and executes a subprogram

A COBOL routine that is written, compiled, and stored separately from a main COBOL program, but which can nevertheless be executed as a paragraph of the main program, is called a *COBOL subprogram*. In the main, or calling, program, execution of a CALL statement will cause the subprogram to be executed. In Chapter 19 you will learn how to write your own subprograms.

The steps required to prepare a COBOL SQL program for execution are illustrated in Figure 17.2. First, the programmer uses an editor to enter the source COBOL SQL program at a terminal. The editor will store the program as an editor source file or source module.

Next, the programmer enters a command for precompilation of the COBOL program. This causes the source COBOL SQL program to be processed by the precompiler.

Two things happen here. First, the SQL expressions in the source COBOL program are replaced by COBOL CALL statements. The resulting modified source program (with CALLs) is stored on disk. Second, the precompiler extracts all the SQL statements from the source program, and stores them on disk. These SQL expressions on disk are not yet translated into subprograms.

Next, the programmer issues a command to have the extracted SQL expressions on disk translated to machine language. A translation component of the data base system, called *bind*, converts the extracted SQL expressions on disk into procedures in machine language – called translated SQL routines. Bind makes use of an optimizer component to ensure the procedure incorporated in a translated SQL routine is efficient. Each translated SQL routine is stored on disk.

Then the programmer issues a command to have the COBOL compiler translate the modified source program to machine language, giving the COBOL object program, which is placed on disk.

Finally, the COBOL object program is link-edited to form a load module, which can be executed. The load module is a composite program in which the COBOL object program is combined with the data base system. In the link-editing process, the addresses of memory locations within the machine code in the object program are adjusted so the program will link, in terms of memory addresses, with the data base system and thus with the translated SQL routines at execution time. Link-editing must be carried out before CALLs to the data base system, embedded earlier by the precompiler in the COBOL source program, can be executed correctly. With most data base systems, the programmer is not aware of the link-editing process. (In a similar manner, before execution, an ordinary COBOL object program is link-edited to the access method or input/output routine needed for ordinary file processing, to form a load module that is a composite of the object program and the input/output routine. The programmer is usually not aware of this step either.)

The application program will now execute, when the programmer gives the command.

Instead of issuing commands to have each of the preceding steps (precompilation, binding, compilation, link-editing, and execution) carried out, with some data base systems (notably IBM's DATABASE2 system),

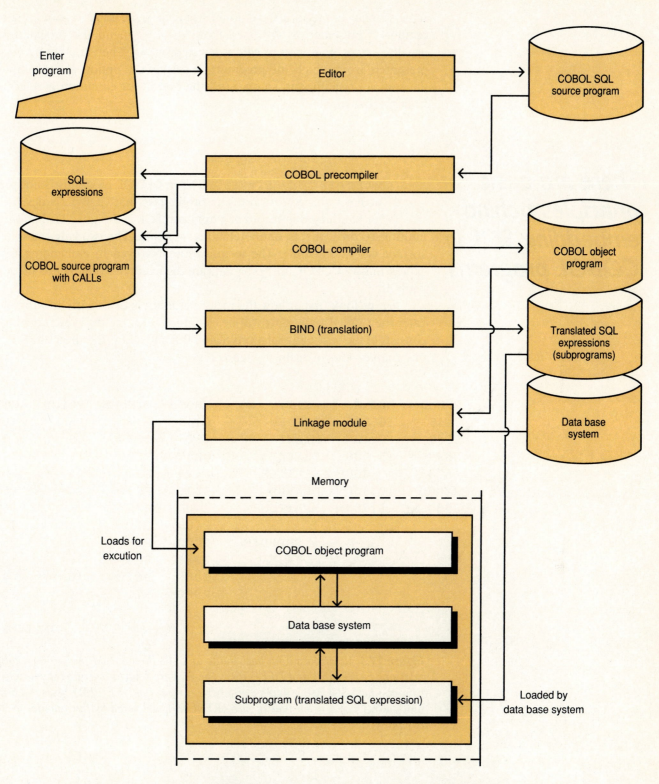

Figure 17.2 *System diagram showing how a COBOL SQL program is pre-processed and loaded into memory for execution.*

screen menus are used instead. Right from the start, a menu with a list of options is presented to the user. From the first menu the programmer usually selects the option to edit a source program. Then another menu is presented, from which the programmer selects the option to precompile the source program, and so on, until the option for execution is selected from the last menu.

17.2
There are basic principles behind embedding SQL in COBOL programs

E MBEDDING SQL EXPRESSIONS in COBOL programs is not particularly straightforward. The problem is that COBOL is designed for handling one record at a time and SQL is designed for handling multiple records (that is, entire relations) at a time. The two languages thus are not very compatible. The technicalities involved in embedding SQL expressions in COBOL host programs are the result of bridging this incompatibility.

Let us look first at how the incompatibility is dealt with in principle. Later the COBOL essentials will be examined. Assume that your data base consists of the base table relations SUPPLIER and DELIVERY from the previous chapter, shown again in Figure 17.3.

SNUMB	OWING	CITY		SNUMB	PTNUMB	PRICE	QTY
0445	10,500	DENVER		0045	P34	15	100
0589	5,400	MIAMI		0045	P67	9	50
0899	15,000	DENVER		0045	P88	12	100
1578	400	SEATTLE		0899	P34	14	200
2400	10,300	DENVER		0899	P55	20	50
2980	3,700	SEATTLE		2400	P55	21	100
				2400	P71	3	300
		SUPPLIER		2400	P88	11	250
				2980	P34	16	100
				2980	P67	10	40
				2980	P71	4	100

DELIVERY

Figure 17.3 *Relational data base made up of the two master files, or base table relations, SUPPLIER and DELIVERY. The files are related because they have the common field SNUMB (supplier number). A record of DELIVERY gives the price and quantity of a given type of part (PTNUMB) delivered by the supplier to the company.*

The data base system/COBOL interface must be understood

This discussion covers the interface between DATABASE2 and COBOL, as this interface is typical and by far the most commonly used. There are no standards here as yet, unfortunately.

Assume a retrieval SQL expression embedded within a COBOL host program. This expression could involve retrieval of all the fields of a SUPPLIER record, that is

```
SELECT SNUMB, OWING, CITY
FROM ...
```

There are two distinct possibilities here, from a record handling point of view.

- The SQL expression will have a WHERE condition specifying the primary key SNUMB field value, and will thus retrieve a single SUPPLIER record.
- The WHERE condition will not involve the SNUMB field, and will thus retrieve multiple records.

The programmer will know beforehand which of these two cases applies—the single-record or multiple-record—and will use different code in the COBOL program for each one.

In both cases, the retrieved records will be transferred to a data structure within the WORKING-STORAGE SECTION of the COBOL program. This data structure can be accessed by both COBOL program commands and the data base system. It is sometimes called a *host data structure*. This host data structure can hold only one retrieved record. (Any identifier, set of identifiers, or group identifier in a host COBOL program can be used as a host data structure.)

The host data structure will contain fields with names that correspond to the SQL-defined names SNUMB, OWING, and CITY. However, with DATABASE2 they must not be the same names. Let us use MS-SNUMB-IN, MS-OWING-IN, and MS-CITY-IN, with the prefix MS denoting "MASTER SUPPLIER."

In the case of a single-record retrieval, the SNUMB, OWING, and CITY field values will be transferred directly by the data base system to the host data structure identifiers MS-SNUMB-IN, MS-OWING-IN, and MS-CITY-IN. This is illustrated in Figure 17.4. The resulting data in these host data structure identifiers can then be manipulated as required by COBOL program commands.

The case of multiple-record retrieval is quite different. Obviously, the data base system cannot deliver the records resulting from an SQL expression execution to the host data structure identifiers all at once. Remember that the host data structure can hold only one record.

Some method is needed for delivering records to the host data structure one by one, at the command of the COBOL program. Figure 17.5 illustrates how this is done.

The data base system sets up a special structure called a *cursor structure*. It holds the multiple records retrieved by the SQL commands. This cursor structure is internal to the data base system. However, records can be delivered from this structure, one by one, to the host data structure. On execution of a special data base system command called FETCH, embedded within the COBOL program, the next record in the cursor structure can be moved to the host data structure. Thus, FETCH permits the records of the cursor structure to be scanned and delivered to the host data structure one

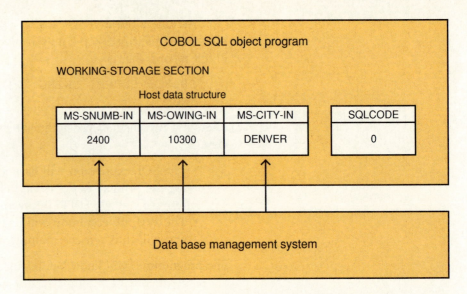

Figure 17.4 When an SQL retrieval expression in the COBOL SQL program retrieves a single record, the data base management system places the record in a host data structure defined in the WORKING-STORAGE SECTION. The field names must not be the same as those used to define the base table involved.

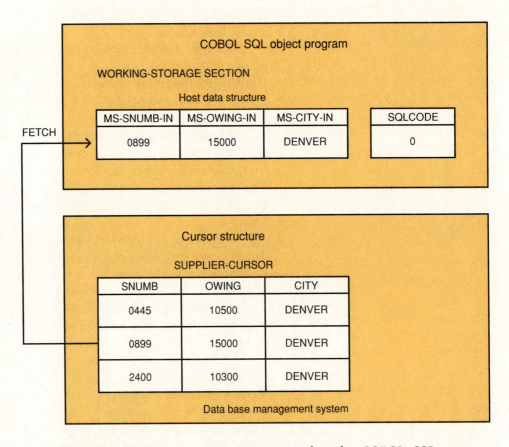

Figure 17.5 When an SQL expression within the COBOL SQL program retrieves multiple records, these records are placed in a cursor structure (like a one-dimensional array) that is internal to the data base management system. The COBOL program can transfer the records one by one to the host data structure by executing successive FETCH commands.

by one. The programmer places FETCH commands within the COBOL program.

Notice that Figures 17.4 and 17.5 show an additional host data structure identifier called SQLCODE. This *data base status identifier* corresponds to the file status identifier (F-STATUS in this book) in COBOL file processing. Following each execution of a data base system command, the data base system places a completion code in SQLCODE. Generally, a zero means the command was executed successfully; for example, a value of 100 means no data was retrieved, and so on.

17.3
One kind of COBOL SQL is used for single-record manipulation

Now let us look at the COBOL details for the case of embedding an SQL expression that manipulates a single record. No cursor structure is needed for such manipulation. Information retrieval, change updating, deletion, and record insertion will be examined.

Retrieval of a single record requires simple embedded expressions

Beginning with a COBOL program that retrieves the record for SUPPLIER '0240' and prints the fields of the retrieved record, the SQL expression required for use at a terminal is

```
SELECT SNUMB, OWING, CITY
FROM SUPPLIER
WHERE SNUMB = '0240';
```

However, as you will see, this is not quite what is embedded in the COBOL host program. Figure 17.4 can be assumed to apply to the COBOL program involved.

Every SQL statement that can be embedded in a COBOL program is always sandwiched between EXEC SQL and END-EXEC, as follows:

```
EXEC SQL
  SQL statement
END-EXEC
```

A host COBOL program has the usual IDENTIFICATION DIVISION, ENVIRONMENT DIVISION, and DATA DIVISION, except for some EXEC SQL . . . END-EXEC statements at the end of the WORKING-STORAGE SECTION of the DATA DIVISION.

First, the host data structure identifiers corresponding to a SUPPLIER record will be specified in the WORKING-STORAGE SECTION, as normal COBOL identifiers.

```
01 MS-SNUMB-IN    PIC X(04).
01 MS-OWING-IN    PIC 9(05).
01 MS-CITY-IN     PIC X(15).
```

Then the actual relation and field names of SUPPLIER, as specified when the data base was originally set up (in Chapter 16), must be specified again within the WORKING-STORAGE SECTION.

```
EXEC SQL
  DECLARE SUPPLIER TABLE
 (SNUMB   CHAR (4) NOT NULL,
  OWING   SMALLINTEGER,
  CITY    CHAR (15))
END-EXEC.
```

Finally, you specify

```
EXEC SQL
  INCLUDE SQLCA
END-EXEC.
```

to finish the WORKING-STORAGE SECTION. INCLUDE SQLCA causes the precompiler to insert another group identifier definition, which includes the identifier SQLCODE, for error checking, as described in the previous section (see Figure 17.4). For most purposes, the programmer only has to know about SQLCODE.

In the PROCEDURE DIVISION, you use normal COBOL code. In addition, you can use any SQL expression, in slightly modified form, sandwiched between EXEC SQL and END-EXEC. Such a sandwiched SQL expression can then be used in COBOL as a sentence or as a statement.

Continuing with this example, suppose that you simply use the COBOL ACCEPT command to read the number of the target supplier. This value is input by a user at a terminal keyboard into an arbitrary WORKING-STORAGE identifier WS-TARGET-IN. You can use SQL to retrieve the record, and then print out the retrieved data on the system printing device. The PROCEDURE DIVISION, in brief, could be

```
PROCEDURE DIVISION
...
    ACCEPT WS-TARGET-IN.
**********************************************************************
*   ASSUME VALUE 0240 READ FROM TERMINAL AND NOW IN WS-TARGET-IN.   *
**********************************************************************
    EXEC SQL
        SELECT SNUMB, OWING, CITY
        INTO :MS-SNUMB-IN, :MS-OWING-IN, :MS-CITY-IN
        FROM SUPPLIER
        WHERE SNUMB = :WS-TARGET-IN
    END-EXEC .
**********************************************************************
*   TARGET RECORD RETRIEVED AND FIELD VALUES PLACED IN HOST DATA    *
*   STRUCTURE IDENTIFIERS MS-SNUMB-IN, MS-OWING-IN, MS-CITY-IN. BUT  *
*   CHECK IN SQLCODE FIRST, TO ENSURE THAT THINGS WENT NORMALLY.    *
**********************************************************************
    IF SQLCODE = 0 THEN
        DISPLAY 'SUPPLIER DATA FOR: ', WS-TARGET-IN
        DISPLAY MS-SNUMB-IN, MS-OWING-IN, MS-CITY-IN
```

COMPREHENSIVE STRUCTURED COBOL

```
        ELSE
            PERFORM 600-ERROR-ROUTINE
        END-IF.
        STOP RUN.
    600-ERROR-ROUTINE.
        ...
```

Notice how the SQL expression differs from its counterpart used at a terminal (see Chapter 16).

- First, there has to be an INTO clause following SELECT, to specify the host data structure or fields that will receive the data retrieved. (Remember that you are dealing with SQL expressions that retrieve only a single record here.)
- Second, the host data structure identifiers used after INTO must each have a colon prefixed. Also, any other WORKING-STORAGE identifier, such as WS-TARGET-IN, used within the SQL expression (for example, after WHERE) must also have a colon prefixed. This is a basic rule for using WORKING-STORAGE identifiers within SQL expressions.

The preceding SQL expression spelled out the individual field identifiers that received the record. Had there been defined a WORKING-STORAGE group identifier, MS-SUPPLIER-REC-IN, earlier as follows:

```
01  MS-SUPPLIER-REC-IN.
    05  MS-SNUMB-IN PIC X(04).
    05  MS-OWING-IN PIC 9(05).
    05  MS-CITY-IN PIC X(15)
```

we could have simply used the SQL expression

```
EXEC SQL
    SELECT SNUMB, OWING, CITY
    INTO :MS-SUPPLIER-REC-IN
    FROM SUPPLIER
    WHERE SNUMB = :WS-TARGET-IN
END-EXEC.
```

But note that you still need to prefix the host data structure, MS-SUPPLIER-REC-IN, with a colon.

Remember that the SQL expression counts as a COBOL statement. Thus, you could place the expression within an IF sentence, for example

```
IF WS-TARGET-IN NOT EQUAL TO SPACES
    EXEC SQL
        SELECT *
        INTO :MS-SNUMB-IN, :MS-OWING-IN, :MS-CITY-IN
        FROM SUPPLIER
        WHERE SNUMB = :WS-TARGET-IN
    END-EXEC
ELSE
    NEXT SENTENCE
END-IF.
```

Change updating requires simple embedded expressions

Suppose that your COBOL program change updated the record for SUP-PLIER 0240 and 0240 is the value in WS-TARGET-IN. The value of OWING is being increased by $3000 and the value 3000 is in the numeric WORKING-STORAGE identifier WS-AMOUNT. The SQL expression in the PROCEDURE DIVISION would simply be

```
EXEC SQL
   UPDATE SUPPLIER
   SET OWING = OWING + :WS-AMOUNT
   WHERE SNUMB = :WS-TARGET-IN
END-EXEC.
```

Note that both the WORKING-STORAGE identifiers used in the expression—namely WS-AMOUNT and WS-TARGET-IN—must be prefixed with a colon. Otherwise the SQL expression is constructed as described in Chapter 8.

Deletion updating also requires simple embedded expressions

If you now wanted to embed an SQL expression to delete the record for supplier 0240, with the 0240 value in WS-TARGET-IN, you would code

```
EXEC SQL
   DELETE
   FROM SUPPLIER
   WHERE SNUMB = :WS-TARGET-IN
END-EXEC.
```

Notice the colon before WS-TARGET-IN.

Insertion updating requires simple embedded expressions, as well

Suppose that you read a new record from a tape file TAPE-SUPPLIER into the host data structure MS-SUPPLIER-REC-IN, made up of MS-SNUMB-IN, MS-OWING-IN, and MS-CITY-IN. The relevant code to insert this record into the base table SUPPLIER would be

```
READ TAPE-SUPPLIER RECORD INTO MS-SUPPLIER-REC-IN, AT END ...
EXEC SQL
   INSERT
   INTO SUPPLIER (SNUMB, OWING, CITY)
   VALUES (:MS-SNUMB-IN, :MS-OWING-IN, :MS-CITY-IN)
END-EXEC.
```

Complete COBOL program for populating a data base file

In the previous chapter it was shown that the data base with relations SUP-PLIER and DELIVERY also shown in Figure 17.3 could be defined outside of any program. The data base administrator could simply enter the following CREATE commands at a terminal:

```
CREATE TABLE SUPPLIER    (SNUMB      CHAR (4) NOT NULL,
                          OWING      SMALLINTEGER,
                          CITY       CHAR (15));
CREATE TABLE DELIVERY    (SNUMB      CHAR (4) NOT NULL,
                          PTNUMB     CHAR (3) NOT NULL,
                          PRICE      SMALLINTEGER,
                          QTY        SMALLINTEGER);
```

These commands simply define the data base. At this point there are no records in any of the relations. Records must be placed in the relations by means of the INSERT command, either one by one at a terminal or from a source file using a COBOL program. Figure 17.6 is an example of a complete COBOL program, with an embedded INSERT command, to place records in (load or populate) the SUPPLIER relation from the source file SOURCE-SUPPLIER. The points explained earlier about the host data structure and SQLCODE are illustrated in context in this program.

Remember that this program cannot be compiled directly by the COBOL compiler. It must first be submitted to the data base system precompiler, for replacement of SQL expressions with CALL statements, before being submitted to the COBOL compiler.

```
IDENTIFICATION DIVISION.
PROGRAM-ID. DBPOP1.
ENVIRONMENT DIVISION.
INPUT-OUTPUT SECTION.
FILE-CONTROL.
    SELECT SOURCE-SUPPLIER
                    ASSIGN TO UT-S-DBDATA.
    SELECT CONTROL-LISTING
                    ASSIGN TO UR-S-SYSPRINT.
DATA DIVISION.
FILE SECTION.
FD   SOURCE-SUPPLIER                 LABEL RECORDS ARE STANDARD
                                     RECORD CONTAINS 24 CHARACTERS.
01   SOURCE-RECORD-IN      PIC X(24).
FD   CONTROL-LISTING                 LABEL RECORDS ARE OMITTED
                                     RECORD CONTAINS 133 CHARACTERS.
01   PRINTER-RECORD-OUT    PIC X(133).
WORKING-STORAGE SECTION.
01   MORE-RECORDS          PIC X(03)      VALUE 'YES'.
01   HEADER-OUT.
     05  FILLER            PIC X(06)      VALUE SPACES.
     05  FILLER            PIC X(127)     VALUE 'CONTROL-LISTING'.
```

```cobol
01  DETAIL-LINE-OUT.
    05  FILLER                PIC X          VALUE SPACE.
    05  DL-ERROR-RECORD-OUT PIC X(24).
    05  FILLER                PIC X(108)     VALUE SPACES.
01  SC-SUPPLIER-REC-IN.                      host data structure
    05    SC-SNUMB-IN         PIC X(04).
    05    SC-OWING-IN         PIC 9(05).
    05    SC-CITY-IN          PIC X(15).
        EXEC SQL
          DECLARE SUPPLIER TABLE
             (SNUMB      CHAR (4) NOT NULL,
              OWING      SMALLINTEGER,
              CITY       CHAR (15))
        END-EXEC.
        EXEC SQL
          INCLUDE SQLCA
        END-EXEC.
 PROCEDURE DIVISION.
 100-MAIN-MODULE.
***************************************************************************
*   DIRECTS PROGRAM LOGIC.                                                *
***************************************************************************
      PERFORM 200-INITIALIZATION.
      PERFORM 300-PROCESS-RECORD
               UNTIL MORE-RECORDS = 'NO'.
      PERFORM 600-TERMINATION.
 200-INITIALIZATION.
***************************************************************************
*   PERFORMED FROM 100-MAIN-MODULE. OPENS FILES. PRINTS REPORT HEADER.   *
*   READS FIRST SOURCE RECORD.                                           *
***************************************************************************
      OPEN INPUT SOURCE-SUPPLIER
             OUTPUT CONTROL-LISTING.
      PERFORM 500-REPORT-HEADER.
      READ SOURCE-SUPPLIER INTO SC-SUPPLIER-REC-IN
             AT END MOVE 'NO' TO MORE-RECORDS.
 300-PROCESS-RECORD.
***************************************************************************
*   PERFORMED FROM 100-MAIN-MODULE. WRITES CURRENT RECORD TO DATA BASE   *
*   RELATION SUPPLIER. READS NEXT SOURCE RECORD. IF RECORD IS NOT        *
*   ACCEPTED FOR DATA BASE, IT IS PRINTED IN THE CONTROL LISTING FOR     *
*   SUPPLIER.                                                            *
***************************************************************************
      EXEC SQL
        INSERT
        INTO SUPPLIER (SNUMB, OWING, CITY)
        VALUES (:SC-SNUMB-IN, :SC-OWING-IN, :SC-CITY-IN)
      END-EXEC.
      IF SQLCODE > 0
        PERFORM 400-PRINT-SOURCE-RECORD
      END-IF.
      READ SOURCE-SUPPLIER INTO SC-SUPPLIER-REC-IN
             AT END MOVE 'NO' TO MORE-RECORDS.
```

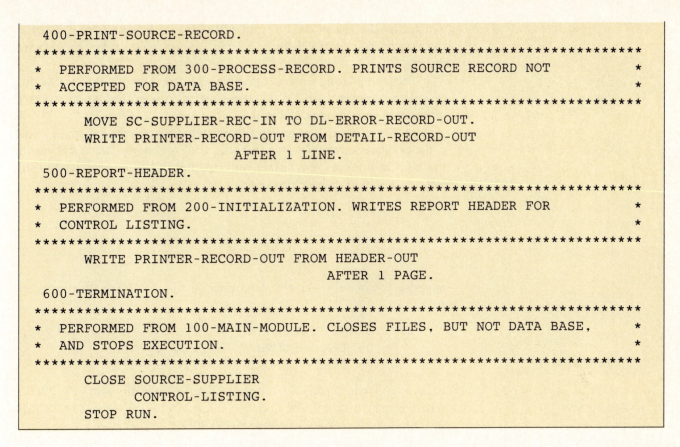

```
  400-PRINT-SOURCE-RECORD.
  ***************************************************************
  *   PERFORMED FROM 300-PROCESS-RECORD. PRINTS SOURCE RECORD NOT   *
  *   ACCEPTED FOR DATA BASE.                                       *
  ***************************************************************
        MOVE SC-SUPPLIER-REC-IN TO DL-ERROR-RECORD-OUT.
        WRITE PRINTER-RECORD-OUT FROM DETAIL-RECORD-OUT
                        AFTER 1 LINE.
  500-REPORT-HEADER.
  ***************************************************************
  *   PERFORMED FROM 200-INITIALIZATION. WRITES REPORT HEADER FOR   *
  *   CONTROL LISTING.                                              *
  ***************************************************************
        WRITE PRINTER-RECORD-OUT FROM HEADER-OUT
                                AFTER 1 PAGE.
  600-TERMINATION.
  ***************************************************************
  *   PERFORMED FROM 100-MAIN-MODULE. CLOSES FILES, BUT NOT DATA BASE,   *
  *   AND STOPS EXECUTION.                                          *
  ***************************************************************
        CLOSE SOURCE-SUPPLIER
              CONTROL-LISTING.
        STOP RUN.
```

Figure 17.6 Program for creating a data base file using the embedded SQL INSERT command. Code for printing the header on each new page is omitted.

Note the use of SQLCODE. A record being inserted may be rejected by the data base system, so that SQLCODE receives a value other than zero. A typical reason for rejection would be an attempt to insert a record with a primary key (SNUMB) value equal to one already in the relation. Since there would probably be a primary index for SNUMB (defined by the data base administrator with a CREATE UNIQUE INDEX command), a duplicate SNUMB value could not be accepted.

Data validation is necessary when loading a data base

A data base is a collection of master files that are related. Accordingly, only carefully validated data can be allowed into a data base. Typically the data in the source file used to load records into a data base will have been validated prior to use. It is assumed here that the data in SOURCE-SUPPLIER (in the loading program, Figure 17.6) have already been validated.

A control listing is needed when loading a data base

A control listing for a specific relation should be output during loading of records into the data base. The control listing can be comprehensive, in which case the fate of every record submitted to the data base is listed. A more restricted control listing, or error report, will simply list rejected records.

During updating from a transaction file, the fate of every transaction record can also be listed in a control listing. Alternatively, only rejected transaction records may be listed.

In this chapter, in order to enable you to focus on the essentials of the code for manipulating data base records, code for control listings is kept to the bare minimum or omitted. But remember that control listings are important with data base processing.

Complete program for change updating a data base

Suppose you have a sequential transaction file, TRANS, with the record structure

```
01    TRANS-RECORD-IN.
      05 TRANS-SNUMB        PIC X(04).
      05 TRANS-AMOUNT       PIC 9(05).
```

Each record has a supplier number value, to indicate which SUPPLIER record is to be updated. The update consists of adding the value in TRANS-AMOUNT to the OWING field of SUPPLIER.

The TRANS file is read by sequential access, but the order of the records does not matter, since the SUPPLIER record is directly accessed and updated with an embedded UPDATE command. The full program is illustrated in Figure 17.7.

```
IDENTIFICATION DIVISION.
PROGRAM-ID. DBUPD.
ENVIRONMENT DIVISION.
INPUT-OUTPUT SECTION.
FILE-CONTROL.
   SELECT CONTROL-LISTING
                ASSIGN TO UR-S-SYSPRINT.
   SELECT TRANS
                ASSIGN TO UT-S-TRINFO.
DATA DIVISION.
FILE SECTION.
FD   CONTROL-LISTING                LABEL RECORDS ARE OMITTED.
01   PRINTER-RECORD-OUT    PIC X(133).
FD   TRANS                          LABEL RECORDS ARE STANDARD
                                    RECORD CONTAINS 9 CHARACTERS.
01   TRANS-RECORD-IN.
     05 TRANS-SNUMB        PIC X(04).
     05 TRANS-AMOUNT       PIC 9(05).
```

```
WORKING-STORAGE SECTION.
01   WS-WORK-AREAS.
     05   MORE-RECORDS          PIC X(03)       VALUE 'YES'.
     05   RECORD-FOUND          PIC X(03).
01   HEADER-OUT.
     05   FILLER                PIC X(06)       VALUE SPACES.
     05   FILLER                PIC X(127)      VALUE 'CONTROL-LISTING'.
01   DETAIL-LINE-OUT.
     05   FILLER                PIC X           VALUE SPACE.
     05   DL-TRANS-RECORD-OUT PIC X(09).
     05   FILLER                PIC X(123)      VALUE SPACES.
01   MS-SUPPLIER-REC-IN.                        host data structure
     05   MS-SNUMB-IN           PIC X(04).
     05   MS-OWING-IN           PIC 9(05).
     05   MS-CITY-IN            PIC X(15).
          EXEC SQL
            DECLARE SUPPLIER TABLE
             (SNUMB        CHAR (4) NOT NULL,
              OWING        SMALLINTEGER,
              CITY         CHAR (15))
          END-EXEC.
          EXEC SQL
            INCLUDE SQLCA
          END-EXEC.
PROCEDURE DIVISION.
100-MAIN-MODULE.
***********************************************************************
*   DIRECTS PROGRAM LOGIC.                                          *
***********************************************************************
      PERFORM 200-INITIALIZATION.
      PERFORM 300-PROCESS-TRANSACTION
                  UNTIL MORE-RECORDS = 'NO'.
      PERFORM 600-TERMINATION.
200-INITIALIZATION.
***********************************************************************
*   PERFORMED FROM 100-MAIN-MODULE. OPENS FILES, PRINTS REPORT HEADER,  *
*   AND READS FIRST TRANS RECORD.                                   *
***********************************************************************
      OPEN INPUT TRANS
           OUTPUT CONTROL-LISTING.
      PERFORM 500-REPORT-HEADER.
      READ TRANS
           AT END MOVE ' NO FIRST TRANSACTION RECORD' TO
                                     PRINTER-RECORD-OUT
                 WRITE PRINTER-RECORD-OUT AFTER 1 LINE
                 STOP RUN.
```

```
300-PROCESS-TRANSACTION.
*******************************************************************
*   PERFORMED FROM 100-MAIN-MODULE. USES CURRENT TRANS RECORD TO   *
*   RETRIEVE MATCHING SUPPLIER RECORD FROM DATA BASE, CHANGE UPDATE IT,   *
*   AND REWRITE IT BACK TO THE DATA BASE. IF NO MATCHING SUPPLIER   *
*   RECORD IS FOUND, THE CURRENT TRANS RECORD IS PRINTED IN CONTROL   *
*   LISTING. READS NEXT TRANS RECORD.   *
*******************************************************************
        MOVE 'YES' TO RECORD-FOUND.
        EXEC SQL
            UPDATE SUPPLIER
            SET OWING = OWING + :TRANS-AMOUNT
            WHERE SNUMB = :TRANS-SNUMB
        END-EXEC.
        IF SQLCODE > 0
            MOVE 'NO' TO RECORD-FOUND.
        IF RECORD-FOUND = 'NO'
            PERFORM 400-PRINT-TRANS-RECORD
        END-IF.
        READ TRANS
            AT END MOVE 'NO' TO MORE-RECORDS.
400-PRINT-TRANS-RECORD.
*******************************************************************
*   PERFORMED FROM 300-PROCESS-RECORD. PRINTS TRANS RECORD NOT MATCHED   *
*   IN DATA BASE IN CONTROL LISTING.   *
*******************************************************************
        MOVE TRANS-RECORD-IN TO DL-TRANS-RECORD-OUT.
        WRITE PRINTER-RECORD-OUT FROM DETAIL-LINE-OUT
                        AFTER 1 LINE.
500-REPORT-HEADER.
*******************************************************************
*   PERFORMED FROM 200-INITIALIZATION. WRITES REPORT HEADER FOR CONTROL   *
*   LISTING.   *
*******************************************************************
        WRITE PRINTER-RECORD-OUT FROM HEADER-OUT
                            AFTER 1 PAGE.
600-TERMINATION.
*******************************************************************
*   PERFORMED FROM 100-MAIN-MODULE. CLOSES FILES, BUT NOT THE DATA   *
*   BASE, AND STOPS EXECUTION.   *
*******************************************************************
        CLOSE TRANS
            CONTROL-LISTING.
        STOP RUN.
```

Figure 17.7 *Change updating the relation SUPPLIER in a data base. Direct access to the relation is used.*

Note the use of SQLCODE. A TRANS-SNUMB value in a TRANS record may have no matching SNUMB value in any SUPPLIER record, so that the TRANS record is unmatched. In that case a non-zero value will be returned to SQLCODE. This permits the unmatched TRANS record to be listed in a control listing.

Information retrieval program

Let's look now at an information retrieval program, where a transaction file, TRANS, is used. There is to be a retrieval for each record in TRANS. A TRANS record holds a supplier number (TR-SNUMB) and part type number value (TR-PTNUMB), and thus identifies a delivery. The information retrieval request is

- For each delivery listed in TRANS, print the supplier number, part type number, quantity of parts delivered, and the city from which the parts are delivered.

If the delivery involved supplier 0899 and part type number P34, the SQL expression entered at a terminal would be

```
SELECT SNUMB, PTNUMB, QTY, CITY
FROM DELIVERY, SUPPLIER
WHERE SNUMB = '0899' AND PTNUMB = 'P34'
  AND SUPPLIER.SNUMB = DELIVERY.SNUMB;
```

Only one record would be retrieved, since SNUMB and PTNUMB together form a primary key in DELIVERY.

This retrieval expression is embedded in the program in Figure 17.9. If the TRANS file had the records shown in Figure 17.8a, then, using the data base in Figure 17.3, the data shown in Figure 17.8b would be output by the program.

```
0045      P88
2400      P55
4562      P55
2980      P67
```

Figure 17.8a TRANS records (spaces between data inserted for readability).

```
          RETRIEVAL REPORT

SNUMB     PTNUMB     QTY      CITY

0045      P88        100      DENVER
2400      P55        100      DENVER

UNMATCHED TRANS: 4562P55

2980      P67         10      SEATTLE
```

Figure 17.8b Retrieved data in retrieval report.

RETRIEVAL REPORT

SNUMB	PTNUMB	QTY	CITY
9999	XXX	ZZZZ9	XXXXXXXXXXXXXXX
9999	XXX	ZZZZ9	XXXXXXXXXXXXXXX
9999	XXX	ZZZZ9	XXXXXXXXXXXXXXX
9999	XXX	ZZZZ9	XXXXXXXXXXXXXXX

Figure 17.8c *Spacing chart for retrieval report.*

```
01  DETAIL-LINE-OUT.
    05  FILLER              PIC X           VALUE SPACE.
    05  DL-SNUMB-OUT        PIC X(04).
    05  FILLER              PIC X(05)       VALUE SPACES.
    05  DL-PTNUMB-OUT       PIC X(03).
    05  FILLER              PIC X(07)       VALUE SPACES.
    05  DL-QTY-OUT          PIC ZZZZ9.
    05  FILLER              PIC X(05)       VALUE SPACES.
    05  DL-CITY-OUT         PIC X(15).
    05  FILLER              PIC X(88)       VALUE SPACES.
```

Figure 17.8d *Record structure for a detail line of retrieval report.*

Note that the data output in Figure 17.8b has been edited, and thus is not exactly the data as retrieved from the data base. You should not attempt to use a COBOL-embedded SQL SELECT expression to place data in edited identifiers. Use numeric and alphanumeric identifiers, as appropriate, to receive data from execution of an SQL SELECT expression. Then move the data retrieved to edited identifiers (Figure 17.8d), as needed for printing.

The program in Figure 17.9 involves information retrieval from two relations—SUPPLIER and DELIVERY. For each TRANS-RECORD, data from the pair of relations are retrieved and placed in the host data structure RETRIEVAL-DATA, moved to the group identifier DATA-LINE-OUT (which contains the edited identifier DL-QTY-OUT, with PICTURE ZZZZ9), and printed in a report file.

If no record is found in the data base for a given TRANS record, the TRANS record is printed in the report file instead of the retrieved data.

```
IDENTIFICATION DIVISION.
PROGRAM-ID. DBINFO.
ENVIRONMENT DIVISION.
INPUT-OUTPUT SECTION.
FILE-CONTROL.
    SELECT RETRIEVAL-REPORT
                    ASSIGN TO UR-S-SYSPRINT.
    SELECT TRANS
                    ASSIGN TO UT-S-T12INFO.
DATA DIVISION.
FILE SECTION.
FD    RETRIEVAL-REPORT              LABEL RECORDS ARE OMITTED.
01    REPORT-RECORD-OUT     PIC X(133).
FD    TRANS                         LABEL RECORDS ARE STANDARD
                                    RECORD CONTAINS 7 CHARACTERS.

01    TRANS-RECORD-IN.
      05 TR-SNUMB            PIC X(04).
      05 TR-PTNUMB           PIC X(03).
WORKING-STORAGE SECTION.
01    WS-WORK-AREAS.
      05  MORE-RECORDS       PIC X(03)      VALUE 'YES'.
      05  RECORD-FOUND       PIC X(03).
01    REPORT-HEADER-OUT.
      05  FILLER             PIC X(06)      VALUE SPACES.
      05  FILLER             PIC X(16)      VALUE 'RETRIEVAL-REPORT'.
      05  FILLER             PIC X(111)     VALUE SPACES.
01    COL-HEADER-OUT.
      05  FILLER             PIC X          VALUE SPACE.
      05  FILLER             PIC X(31)      VALUE
                             'SNUMB    PTNUMB   QTY      CITY'.
      05  FILLER             PIC X(101)     VALUE SPACES.
01    ERROR-LINE-OUT.
      05  FILLER             PIC X          VALUE SPACE.
      05  FILLER             PIC X(16)      VALUE 'UNMATCHED TRANS:'.
      05  FILLER             PIC X(02)      VALUE SPACES.
      05  EL-TRANS-RECORD-OUT PIC X(09).
      05  FILLER             PIC X(105)     VALUE SPACES.
01 DETAIL-LINE-OUT.
      05  FILLER             PIC X          VALUE SPACE.
      05  DL-SNUMB-OUT       PIC X(04).
      05  FILLER             PIC X(07)      VALUE SPACES.
      05  DL-PTNUMB-OUT      PIC X(03).
      05  FILLER             PIC X(07)      VALUE SPACES.
      05  DL-QTY-OUT         PIC ZZZZ9.
      05  FILLER             PIC X(05)      VALUE SPACES.
      05  DL-CITY-OUT        PIC X(15).
      05  FILLER             PIC X(88)      VALUE SPACES.
```

```
01 RETRIEVAL-DATA.                                    host data structure
    05  FILLER              PIC X          VALUE SPACE.
    05  RTR-SNUMB           PIC X(04).
    05  FILLER              PIC X(05)      VALUE SPACES.
    05  RTR-PTNUMB          PIC X(03).
    05  FILLER              PIC X(07)      VALUE SPACES.
    05  RTR-QTY             PIC 9(05).
    05  FILLER              PIC X(05)      VALUE SPACES.
    05  RTR-CITY            PIC X(15).
    05  FILLER              PIC X(88)      VALUE SPACES.
      EXEC SQL
        DECLARE SUPPLIER TABLE
          (SNUMB       CHAR (4) NOT NULL,
           OWING       SMALLINTEGER,
           CITY        CHAR (15))
      END-EXEC.
      EXEC SQL
        DECLARE DELIVERY TABLE
          (SNUMB       CHAR (4) NOT NULL,
           PTNUMB      CHAR (3) NOT NULL,
           PRICE       SMALLINTEGER,
           QTY         SMALLINTEGER)
      END-EXEC.
      EXEC SQL
        INCLUDE SQLCA
      END-EXEC.
 PROCEDURE DIVISION.
 100-MAIN-MODULE.
****************************************************************************
*   DIRECTS PROGRAM LOGIC.                                               *
****************************************************************************
      PERFORM 200-INITIALIZATION.
      PERFORM 300-PROCESS-TRANSACTION
              UNTIL MORE-RECORDS = 'NO'.
      PERFORM 600-TERMINATION.
 200-INITIALIZATION.
****************************************************************************
*   PERFORMED FROM 100-MAIN-MODULE. OPENS FILES, WRITES REPORT HEADER,   *
*   AND READS CURRENT TRANS RECORD.                                      *
****************************************************************************
      OPEN INPUT TRANS
           OUTPUT RETRIEVAL-REPORT.
      PERFORM 500-REPORT-HEADER.
      READ TRANS
           AT END MOVE ' NO FIRST TRANSACTION RECORD' TO
                                    REPORT-RECORD-OUT
                WRITE REPORT-RECORD-OUT AFTER 1 LINE
                STOP RUN.
```

```
300-PROCESS-TRANSACTION.
*****************************************************************
*   PERFORMED FROM 100-MAIN-MODULE. USES COMPOSITE PRIMARY KEY IN       *
*   CURRENT TRANS RECORD TO RETRIEVE TWO RELATED RECORDS FROM SUPPLIER  *
*   AND DELIVERY DATA BASE RELATIONS. PRINTS DATA RETRIEVED. IF NO      *
*   MATCHING DATA, UNMATCHED TRANS RECORD IS PRINTED.                   *
*****************************************************************
        MOVE 'YES' TO RECORD-FOUND.
            EXEC SQL
              SELECT SNUMB, PTNUMB, QTY, CITY
              INTO :RTR-SNUMB, :RTR-PTNUMB, :RTR-QTY-OUT, :RTR-CITY
              FROM DELIVERY, SUPPLIER
              WHERE SNUMB = :TR-SNUMB AND PTNUMB = :TR-PTNUMB
              AND SUPPLIER.SNUMB = DELIVERY.SNUMB
            END-EXEC.
        IF SQLCODE > 0
            MOVE 'NO' TO RECORD-FOUND.
        IF RECORD-FOUND = 'YES'
            PERFORM 600-PRINT-DATA-RETRIEVED
        ELSE
            PERFORM 400-PRINT-UNMATCHED-TRANS
        END-IF.
        READ TRANS
            AT END MOVE 'NO' TO MORE-RECORDS.
 400-PRINT-UNMATCHED-TRANS.
*****************************************************************
*   PERFORMED FROM 300-PROCESS-TRANSACTION. PRINTS UNMATCHED TRANS      *
*   RECORD, IN RETRIEVAL REPORT.                                        *
*****************************************************************
        MOVE TRANS-RECORD-IN TO EL-TRANS-RECORD-OUT.
        WRITE REPORT-RECORD-OUT FROM ERROR-LINE-OUT
                                            AFTER 2 LINES.
        MOVE SPACES TO REPORT-RECORD-OUT.
        WRITE REPORT-RECORD-OUT
            AFTER ADVANCING 1 LINE.
 500-REPORT-HEADER.
*****************************************************************
*   PERFORMED FROM 200-INITIALIZATION. WRITES RETRIEVAL REPORT HEADERS. *
*****************************************************************
        WRITE REPORT-RECORD-OUT FROM REPORT-HEADER-OUT
                                AFTER 1 PAGE.
        WRITE REPORT-RECORD-OUT FROM COL-HEADER-OUT
                                AFTER 2 LINES.
        MOVE SPACES TO REPORT-RECORD-OUT.
        WRITE REPORT-RECORD-OUT
                                AFTER ADVANCING 1 LINE.
```

```
      600-PRINT-DATA-RETRIEVED.
  ******************************************************************
  *   PERFORMED FROM 300-PROCESS-TRANSACTION. PRINTS DATA RETRIEVED FROM   *
  *   DATA BASE IN EDITED FORMAT.                                          *
  ******************************************************************
          MOVE RETRIEVAL-DATA TO DETAIL-LINE-OUT.
          WRITE REPORT-RECORD-OUT FROM DETAIL-LINE-OUT
                  AFTER ADVANCING 1 LINE.
      700-TERMINATION.
  ******************************************************************
  *   PERFORMED FROM 100-MAIN-MODULE. CLOSES FILES AND STOPS PROGRAM.   *
  ******************************************************************
          CLOSE TRANS
                  RETRIEVAL-REPORT.
          STOP RUN.
```

Figure 17.9 *For each record in TRANS, information is retrieved as a single record from both SUPPLIER and DELIVERY records.*

17.4
A cursor structure is needed with multiple-record retrieval

REMEMBER, YOU NEED to use a cursor structure whenever you embed an SQL expression that can retrieve multiple records. You can also use SQL and a cursor when updating multiple records, but here you can sometimes also do without. Let us begin with the use of a cursor for multiple-record retrieval.

A cursor structure holds retrieved records

Consider a multiple-record retrieval from the SUPPLIER base table. If you wanted to retrieve the records for suppliers in Denver, the terminal SQL expression would be

```
SELECT *
FROM SUPPLIER
WHERE CITY = 'DENVER';
```

resulting in

```
SNUMB    OWING    CITY
0445     10500    DENVER
0899     15000    DENVER
2400     10300    DENVER
```

if the data in Figure 17.3 are used.

To embed this retrieval in a COBOL program, as far as the IDENTIFICATION, ENVIRONMENT, and DATA DIVISIONS are concerned, you would proceed initially exactly as if it were a case of single-record retrieval. In other words, you would probably specify host data structure identifiers

RTR-SNUMB, RTR-OWING, and RTR-CITY in the DATA DIVISION, as before, followed by the declarations

```
EXEC SQL
   DECLARE SUPPLIER TABLE
     (SNUMB      CHAR (4) NOT NULL,
      OWING      SMALLINTEGER,
      CITY       CHAR (15))
END-EXEC.
EXEC SQL
   INCLUDE SQLCA
END-EXEC.
```

Thus, there is no difference so far. But this time, instead of placing the necessary SQL retrieval expression in the PROCEDURE DIVISION, it goes at the end of the WORKING-STORAGE SECTION. A different format is used too, since you are specifying the contents of a data structure. This is the cursor structure that will hold the results of carrying out the retrieval expression. You thus code

```
EXEC SQL
   DECLARE SUPPLIER-CURSOR CURSOR FOR
                SELECT SNUMB, OWING, CITY
                FROM SUPPLIER
                WHERE CITY = :WS-TARGET-CITY
END-EXEC.
```

This is a WORKING-STORAGE specification of the cursor structure called SUPPLIER-CURSOR. As yet the structure is empty. It will be filled with data only after an OPEN SUPPLIER-CURSOR data base command is executed in the PROCEDURE DIVISION. The cursor structure can be regarded as a special kind of one-dimensional array that cannot be accessed by normal COBOL statements.

In the PROCEDURE DIVISION, you "open" the cursor structure. The SQL OPEN command causes the SQL retrieval expression to be executed, and the cursor structure SUPPLIER-CURSOR to be filled with records, three, in this case, as shown in Figure 17.5. The records can be taken from this structure one at a time (by means of a FETCH command), placed in host data structure identifiers RTR-SNUMB, RTR-OWING, and RTR-CITY, and then printed out.

In the following minimal PROCEDURE DIVISION example, it is assumed that the value of CITY for target records ('DENVER'), is read into the identifier WS-TARGET-CITY by a user at a terminal.

The records are transferred from the cursor structure to the host data structure identifiers by repeated execution of the paragraph 500-EXTRACT-RECORD. This repeated transfer will cease when no records are left in the cursor structure (SQLCODE value 100). If an SQLCODE value other than 0 is returned, it indicates an error. However, an SQLCODE of 100 means there are no further records in the cursor structure (end of cursor records). An SQLCODE value is returned after each execution of FETCH. The process of transferring the records is illustrated in Figure 17.5.

```
      PROCEDURE DIVISION.
          ...
          ACCEPT WS-TARGET-CITY.  WS-TARGET-CITY gets value 'DENVER'
          EXEC SQL
              OPEN SUPPLIER-CURSOR
          END-EXEC.
     ************************************************************************
     *   RECORDS NOW IN SUPPLIER-CURSOR STRUCTURE, INTERNAL TO THE DATA BASE  *
     *   SYSTEM (FIGURE 17.5).                                                *
     ************************************************************************
          EXEC SQL
              FETCH SUPPLIER-CURSOR
                  INTO :RTR-SNUMB, :RTR-OWING, :RTR-CITY
          END-EXEC.
     ************************************************************************
     *   THE FIRST RECORD IN SUPPLIER-CURSOR IS TRANSFERRED TO HOST DATA      *
     *   STRUCTURE IDENTIFIERS. NOTE THAT EACH HOST DATA STRUCTURE            *
     *   IDENTIFIER IS PREFIXED WITH A COLON. THIS STEP IS REPEATED UNTIL     *
     *   ALL RECORDS HAVE BEEN TRANSFERRED TO THE HOST DATA STRUCTURE         *
     *   IDENTIFIERS.                                                         *
     ************************************************************************
          PERFORM 500-EXTRACT-RECORD
              UNTIL SQLCODE = 100.
          EXEC SQL
              CLOSE SUPPLIER-CURSOR
          END-EXEC.
     ************************************************************************
     *   SUPPLIER-CURSOR STRUCTURE EMPTIED.                                   *
     ************************************************************************
          STOP RUN.
      500-EXTRACT-RECORD.
          IF SQLCODE = 0 THEN
              DISPLAY RTR-SNUMB, RTR-OWING, RTR-CITY
          ELSE
              DISPLAY 'ERROR.  ERROR-CODE IS: ', SQLCODE
              STOP RUN
          END-IF.
          EXEC-SQL
              FETCH SUPPLIER-CURSOR
                  INTO :RTR-SNUMB, :RTR-OWING, :RTR-CITY
          END-EXEC.
```

Cursor technicalities have to be learned

This section summarizes the technical points of cursor operation. Some of these points are not brought out by the example.

- The OPEN statement causes the SQL expression in the cursor declaration statement to be executed, resulting in the cursor structure being filled. It also sets a current position indicator to immediately before the first record in the cursor structure (that is, position 0).

- With each FETCH execution, the currency indicator or position advances by one (see Figure 17.5). The resulting record, now the current record, is transferred to the host data structure or host structure. Thus, after the first record of the cursor structure has been transferred, that record is still the current record and the cursor position is 1.
- The CLOSE statement empties the cursor structure.
- The only way to fill the cursor structure again is by opening it, at which point the SQL expression in the cursor declaration statement is executed again.
- Note that with a second or later execution of OPEN, an entirely different set of SUPPLIER records could be placed in SUPPLIER-CURSOR because of a different value being in the identifier WS-TARGET-CITY (declared in the WORKING-STORAGE SECTION).
- The current position, or currency indicator, within a cursor structure may be used with updating, as explained later.

Program for information retrieval with a cursor

Suppose you need a program to read in a part number value and output full details about all suppliers that have not delivered that type of part. For example, if the part type number in question was 'P71', then the SQL expression for terminal use would be

```
SELECT *
FROM SUPPLIER
WHERE SNUMB NOT IN (SELECT SNUMB
                    FROM DELIVERY
                    WHERE PTNUMB = 'P71');
```

Using the data base in Figure 17.3, this expression would retrieve multiple records.

```
SNUMB    OWING    CITY
0445     10500    DENVER
0589     05400    MIAMI
0899     15000    DENVER
1578     00400    SEATTLE
```

The COBOL program to carry out this retrieval with embedded SQL would require the use of a cursor structure, called SUPPLIER-CURSOR. The program is shown in Figure 17.10.

```
        IDENTIFICATION DIVISION.
        PROGRAM-ID. CURINFO.
        ENVIRONMENT DIVISION.
        INPUT-OUTPUT SECTION.
        FILE-CONTROL.
        DATA DIVISION.
        FILE SECTION.
        WORKING-STORAGE SECTION.
        01 MORE-RECORDS                PIC X(05)      VALUE 'YES'.
        01 RETR-SUPPLIER-RECORD.                    host data structure
            05  RTR-SNUMB              PIC X(04).
            05  RTR-OWING             PIC 9(05).
            05  RTR-CITY              PIC X(15)
        01    WS-TARGET-PTNUMB          PIC X(03).
                EXEC SQL
                  DECLARE SUPPLIER TABLE
                   (SNUMB       CHAR (4) NOT NULL,
                    OWING       SMALLINTEGER,
                    CITY        CHAR (15))
                END-EXEC.
                EXEC SQL
                  DECLARE DELIVERY TABLE
                     (SNUMB       CHAR (4) NOT NULL,
                      PTNUMB      CHAR (3) NOT NULL,
                      PRICE       SMALLINTEGER,
                      QTY         SMALLINTEGER)
                END-EXEC.
                EXEC SQL
                  INCLUDE SQLCA
                END-EXEC.
                EXEC SQL
                  DECLARE SUPPLIER-CURSOR CURSOR FOR
                      SELECT SNUMB, OWING, CITY
                      FROM SUPPLIER
                      WHERE SNUMB NOT IN (SELECT SNUMB
                                          FROM DELIVERY
                                          WHERE PTNUMB = :WS-TARGET-PTNUMB)
                END-EXEC.
        PROCEDURE DIVISION.
        100-MAIN-MODULE.
        ************************************************************************
        *   DIRECTS PROGRAM LOGIC.                                            *
        ************************************************************************
             PERFORM 200-INITIALIZATION.
             PERFORM 300-PROCESS-CURSOR-RECORD
                    UNTIL SQLCODE = 100.
             PERFORM 400-TERMINATION.
```

```
  200-INITIALIZATION.
  **************************************************************************
  *   PERFORMED FROM 100-MAIN-MODULE. READS TARGET PART NUMBER TERMINAL.   *
  *   OPENS AND FILLS CURSOR STRUCTURE. FETCHES FIRST RECORD FROM CURSOR    *
  *   INTO WORKING-STORAGE HOST DATA STRUCTURE.                             *
  **************************************************************************
        ACCEPT WS-TARGET-PTNUMB.
        EXEC SQL
            OPEN SUPPLIER-CURSOR
        END-EXEC.                   records now in cursor structure
        EXEC SQL
            FETCH SUPPLIER-CURSOR
            INTO :RTR-SNUMB, :RTR-OWING, :RTR-CITY
        END-EXEC.                   first record moved to host data structure
        IF SQLCODE = 100            no records in cursor
            DISPLAY 'NO SUPPLIERS MATCH CONDITION'
        END-IF.
  300-PROCESS-CURSOR-RECORD.
  **************************************************************************
  *  PERFORMED FROM 100-MAIN-MODULE. DISPLAYS RECORD RETRIEVED; DISPLAYS  *
  *  AN ERROR MESSAGE AND STOPS PROGRAM IF THERE IS AN ERROR IN           *
  *  TRANSFERRING THE RECORD FROM THE CURSOR STRUCTURE.                   *
  **************************************************************************
        IF SQLCODE = 0              no problems
            DISPLAY RTR-SNUMB, RTR-OWING, RTR-CITY
        ELSE IF SQLCODE NOT EQUAL TO 100        unidentified problem
                DISPLAY 'ERROR IN TRANSFER FROM CURSOR: ', SQLCODE
                STOP RUN
            END-IF
        END-IF.
        EXEC-SQL
            FETCH SUPPLIER-CURSOR
            INTO :RTR-SNUMB, :RTR-OWING, :RTR-CITY
        END-EXEC.
  400-TERMINATION.
  **************************************************************************
  *  PERFORMED FROM 100-MAIN-MODULE. CLOSES CURSOR, STOPS PROGRAM.        *
  **************************************************************************
        EXEC SQL
            CLOSE SUPPLIER-CURSOR
        END-EXEC.
        STOP RUN.
```

Figure 17.10 *This program uses a cursor structure to retrieve SUPPLIER records for suppliers that do not deliver the part type in the identifier WS-TARGET-PTNUMB. This value is input from a terminal. The results are also displayed on a terminal.*

You can change update a record in a cursor structure

Suppose once more that you want to retrieve the records for suppliers in Denver, so the terminal SQL expression would be

```
SELECT *
FROM SUPPLIER
WHERE CITY = 'DENVER';
```

resulting in

```
SNUMB____OWING____CITY
0445     10500    DENVER
0899     15000    DENVER
2400     10300    DENVER
```

Assume this retrieval will be carried out using a COBOL SQL program with a cursor structure, as illustrated earlier. Let us further suppose that in the retrieval example involving a cursor, you also want to change the city of any supplier owed more than $14,000 to Dallas. The value 'DALLAS' is in WS-NEW-CITY.

As before you define the cursor structure at the end of the WORKING-STORAGE SECTION. The identifier WS-TARGET-CITY will hold the value 'DENVER'.

```
EXEC SQL
   DECLARE SUPPLIER-CURSOR CURSOR FOR
               SELECT SNUMB, OWING, CITY
               FROM SUPPLIER
               WHERE CITY = :WS-TARGET-CITY
END-EXEC.
```

Once the cursor structure has been opened in the PROCEDURE DIVISION, you can change update any record previously retrieved (that is, the current record), as follows:

```
EXEC SQL
   FETCH SUPPLIER-CURSOR
   INTO :RTR-SNUMB, :RTR-OWING, :RTR-CITY
END-EXEC.
IF RTR-OWING > 14000  THEN
   EXEC SQL
      UPDATE SUPPLIER
      SET CITY = :WS-NEW-CITY
      WHERE CURRENT OF SUPPLIER-CURSOR
   END-EXEC
END-IF.
```

Suppose the record

```
0899     15,000    DENVER
```

is retrieved by the FETCH statement and placed in the host data structure. Then, since the RTR-OWING value can be tested as being > 14,000, the subsequent UPDATE statement will also be executed. This will cause the current record to be updated, both within the cursor structure and within the base table SUPPLIER.

You can delete a record in a cursor structure

Suppose that, in the previous example, instead of change updating records for suppliers who are owed more than $14,000, you want to delete them. In that case, a DELETE command will delete the record previously retrieved—that is, the current record of the cursor.

```
EXEC SQL
   FETCH SUPPLIER-CURSOR
   INTO :RTR-SNUMB, :RTR-OWING, :RTR-CITY
END-EXEC.
IF RTR-OWING > 14000 THEN
   EXEC SQL
      DELETE
      FROM SUPPLIER
      WHERE CURRENT OF SUPPLIER-CURSOR
END-EXEC.
```

Note that an INSERT statement cannot be used with a cursor.

You can delete multiple records with a single SQL expression

When you use a cursor structure to delete multiple records, you effectively delete the records one at a time. That is, you FETCH a record, then DELETE it, and so on, until the end of the records in the cursor structure.

But note that, in the case of deletion (and also change updating), if you have a selection condition that applies to multiple records, you can do without the cursor structure.

Suppose you are dealing with the SUPPLIER relation and want to delete all Denver SUPPLIER records. You proceed as in the case of single-record retrieval or update. In the WORKING-STORAGE SECTION, you specify the SUPPLIER relation with a DECLARE SUPPLIER command; you also specify SQLCODE with the INCLUDE command. Assume that the value 'DENVER' is in WS-TARGET-CITY. In the PROCEDURE DIVISION, you could simply code

```
EXEC SQL
   DELETE
   FROM SUPPLIER
   WHERE OWING = :WS-TARGET-CITY
END-EXEC.
```

This will delete all Denver records.

Each SQL command must be extensively tested before being embedded in a program. This testing will, of course, be particularly important in the case of a complex condition following WHERE in the SQL expressions. As you will have experienced, it is easy to get such conditions wrong. A wrong condition with a global delete command could cause a large part of a data base to be accidentally deleted.

You can change update multiple records with a single SQL expression

You can change update a large number of records in a relation without a cursor, if the same selection condition applies to all of them. Suppose you wanted to increase the amount owed to Denver suppliers by $5000, and that the value $5000 is in the identifier TRANS-AMOUNT. In the PROCEDURE DIVISION, you would simply code

```
EXEC SQL
   UPDATE SUPPLIER
   SET OWING = OWING  + :TRANS-AMOUNT
   WHERE OWING = :WS-TARGET-CITY
END-EXEC.
```

This will increase the OWING field value of all Denver SUPPLIER records by $5000, if DENVER is the value in WS-TARGET-CITY. The same considerations about global operations apply to UPDATE as to DELETE in the previous section.

You need to follow some rules when embedding SQL

It is worth remembering the following basic rules for embedded SQL statements in COBOL programs.

RULES   **Embedded SQL Syntax**

1. The PROCEDURE DIVISION data base commands are SELECT, UPDATE, DELETE, INSERT, OPEN, CLOSE, and FETCH.
2. Each of these commands is always sandwiched between EXEC SQL and END-EXEC.
3. Each of these commands counts as a COBOL statement and thus can be used within a nested IF-statement, for example.
4. Any WORKING-STORAGE identifier or group identifier can be used within a data base command, but it must be prefixed with a colon.

It is also worth remembering that the cursor declaration is placed at the end of the WORKING-STORAGE SECTION, not in the PROCEDURE DIVISION.

Summary

1. A data base processing program, written in COBOL or other higher language, may contain one or more embedded SQL expressions. This can result in a great saving in programming effort.

2. With the data base system, and most other relational systems, before such a processing program can be compiled, the SQL expressions are extracted in a precompilation step and replaced with CALLs to the data base system. The extracted SQL statements are translated in a separate step into low-level procedures, which are stored on disk. Then the COBOL program containing the CALLs is compiled in the normal way. When it executes, it calls up the data base system, which in turn executes the low-level procedures on disk as required.

3. How SQL expressions are embedded in COBOL depends on the number of records the expression will retrieve. If only one record will be retrieved, nothing special is needed and the retrieved record goes to a host data structure where it can be further processed by COBOL commands.

4. If an SQL expression will retrieve more than one record, the retrieved set of records must be directed to a special structure, called a cursor structure. The COBOL program cannot directly access the records in this structure. Instead, the records must be transferred one by one to the host data structure, which can hold only one record at a time. A FETCH command is executed to transfer a record to the host data structure from the cursor structure. Once a record is in the host data structure, it can be processed further by the COBOL program.

5. It is possible to update records that have been retrieved into the cursor structure, but generally records being updated are not retrieved, so the cursor structure is not needed.

6. A record being inserted into the data base must be made available in the host data structure.

Key Terms

host data structure
cursor structure
data base status identifier

Concept Review Questions

1. Why must a COBOL SQL program be precompiled before submission to the COBOL compiler?
2. What goes on during precompilation of a COBOL SQL program?
3. What does the bind system do?
4. What is an embedded SQL expression translated into?
5. List the steps in preparing a COBOL SQL program for execution.

6. What is the major difficulty in interfacing a COBOL program with an SQL retrieval expression.?
7. What is a host data structure?
8. What is a cursor structure?
9. What is a data base status identifier and what is it used for?
10. Why do you need control listings with data base processing?
11. If an SQL retrieval expression for a single relation has a condition involving equality with a primary key value, explain why you do not need to use a cursor structure.
12. What happens when the open-cursor command is executed?
13. What does the SQL FETCH command do?

COBOL/SQL Language Questions

1. What is wrong with the following?

```
EXEC SQL
   SELECT SNUMB, OWING
   INTO A, B
END-EXEC.
```

2. What is wrong with this?

```
EXEC SQL
   SELECT *
   INTO :MS-SUPPLIER-RECORD-IN
   WHERE CITY = TARGETCITY
END-EXEC.
```

3. What is wrong with the following?

```
EXEC SQL
 UPDATE SUPPLIER
 SET OWING = OWING * PERCENTAGE
END-EXEC.
```

4. Write the embedded SQL expression to insert the record 004312050NEW YORK into the SUPPLIER relation.

5. Write the embedded SQL expression to delete the record for supplier 0890 from the SUPPLIER relation.

6. Write the embedded SQL expression to increase the amount owing by all Denver suppliers by $1000.

7. Define the cursor structure for retrieving all SUPPLIER records for suppliers that are not in Seattle.

8. Write the routine for printing the records retrieved using the cursor structure from question 7.

Programming Assignments

1. **Data base loading**
   a. Write a program to load the SUPPLIER records in Figure 16.4 in a SUPPLIER relation. A comprehensive control listing should be printed.

b. Write a program to load the DELIVERY records in Figure 16.4 in a DELIVERY relation. A comprehensive control listing should be printed.

2. **Information retrieval (no cursor)**
    Write a program to accept a supplier number and part number at a terminal and display full details on the delivery so identified.

3. **Information retrieval (single relation, cursor needed)**
    Write a program to accept a city at a terminal and output full details on suppliers in that city.

4. **Information retrieval (single relation, cursor needed)**
    Write a program to accept a supplier number at a terminal and output full details on all deliveries made by that supplier.

5. **Information retrieval (two relations, cursor needed)**
    Write a program to accept a city at a terminal and display full details of suppliers in that city that have delivered part P34.

6. **Update (no cursor)**
    Write a program to use the following transaction file to update the relation SUPPLIER:

    ```
    089900400A
    044501500S
    568010000A
    157800600S
    298002500A
    ```

Columns 01–04	Supplier number
05–09	Amount
10	To be added to OWING if A, subtracted if S.

    The control listing will appear like this:

    ```
              CONTROL LISTING (TRANS RECORDS)
        DATA BASE RELATION SUPPLIER CHANGE UPDATE
    ```

SEQUENCE	SUPPLIER	AMOUNT	CODE	ACTION	PROBLEM
01	0899	00400	A	ACCEPTED	
02	0445	01500	S	ACCEPTED	
03	6599	10000	A	REJECTED	UNMATCHED KEY
04	1578	00600	S	REJECTED	AMOUNT TOO LARGE
05	2980	02500	A	ACCEPTED	

    a. Prepare the input record layout and printer spacing chart.
    b. Draw the flowchart and hierarchy diagram.
    c. Write and run the program.

7. **Update (no cursor)**
    Write a program to read a supplier number from a terminal and increase by $3 the price of all parts delivered by that supplier.

OBJECTIVES

- To explain basic on-line processing and CICS concepts
- To demonstrate the essentials of CICS COBOL statements
- To show how to write elementary CICS COBOL programs

OUTLINE

*T*HE CONCEPT OF on-line processing is best understood in comparison with batch processing. Most of the file processing programs in recent chapters can be classified as batch processing programs. The term *batch processing* is derived from batch updating.

With batch updating, a master file (or data base) is updated using a batch of updating records in a transaction file. Information about master records to be updated is collected in a transaction file over a period of time, perhaps days or weeks, and is then used to update the master. Thus, the master is only up-to-date immediately following batch updating. As time goes on, the master file becomes more and more out of date, until it is time for the next batch update, when it is up-to-date once more. Batch updating can involve either the classical method, as with sequential files, or the rewrite method, as with direct-access files.

In contrast to batch updating, with on-line updating an update is used to update a master file as soon as it becomes available. An operator at a terminal runs the updating program that accepts the update and uses it to update the master file. With on-line updating, the master file is always up to date.

At first glance, it might appear that there is nothing particularly sophisticated about *on-line processing*. After all, all you have to do is run the update program as soon as you have an update for a master file. There is a real problem, however. The problem is that in a large organization, the people receiving the data to update the master may be geographically dispersed—perhaps over the entire nation.

Consider a master file about products in a central warehouse, where the products can be sold by salespersons across the nation. Each salesperson has a terminal. As soon as a sale is made, the salesperson runs a specific update program. Suppose this update program accepts the quantity and type of products sold as input data. The program would use the input data to update the corresponding QUANTITY-REMAINING field in the master file. The situation is complicated, however, by the fact that at any instant hundreds of salespersons could be wanting to use the program to enter their updates into the master.

But the situation can be even more complex than that. In addition to salespersons wanting to make a specific type of update to the master, at any instant there may be many other widely dispersed persons, each wanting to execute other programs that use the master file. Some people may simply want to run a program to find out how many P45 parts are left in the warehouse. Others may want to run a program to cancel an order, and so on. For each of these activities there will be a file processing program. Thus at any instant, one group of people will want to use program 1, another group will want to use program 2, and so on. And all these people will be at different remote terminals.

An on-line system is a collection of programs and master files (or a data base) that can function in such a contentious environment. The situation is analogous to a very busy traffic intersection. Unless there is something to control the traffic, such as a police officer, a traffic jam will result. In the case of the on-line system, the equivalent of the police officer is a system software component called a *teleprocessing monitor*. The most widely used teleprocessing monitor is CICS (Customer Information Control System) from IBM. A program that is part of such a system is called an *on-line program*.

In this chapter you will learn some of the basic concepts of CICS and how to write basic on-line COBOL programs. In an on-line system, in order to avoid a traffic jam, CICS undertakes all reading and writing of records in the master files and all accepting and displaying of data at terminals. Thus, a COBOL program for use as an on-line program will not have conventional READ, WRITE, and REWRITE commands. Instead, special CICS commands are used. You will learn the essentials of how to write COBOL CICS commands in this chapter.

Before proceeding, here is a word of caution: The best this chapter can do is give you an overview that will let you run simple CICS programs. There are many more CICS details than can be covered in a single chapter. If you intend doing extensive programming with CICS and COBOL, you should acquire one of the many excellent CICS texts available.

18.1
CICS uses some unique concepts

*I*N A CICS ON-LINE system, there are communications hardware, many types of remote terminals, and a wide variety of on-line applications programs and associated files. Nevertheless, CICS handles most of the complexity, so that on-line COBOL programs can be written more easily than you might think.

CICS makes on-line programs independent of the hardware, especially with regard to different types of remote terminals. Thus, you can replace one terminal type with another without having to alter the on-line programs. CICS also provides very good response time to users at the remote terminals.

On-line programs are controlled by CICS

During normal business hours, CICS will be be executing continually. All on-line programs are considered to be subprograms of CICS. The on-line programs are stored in a special library, called the on-line program library. When a user at a remote terminal needs to execute a certain on-line program, he or she enters a code for that program, which is accepted by CICS. When there is space in memory, CICS reads that program from the on-line program library, places it in the memory and allows it to execute.

Like any program, CICS occupies a certain amount of space in memory (see Figure 18.1). But, in addition, there is associated memory space where the on-line programs execute after being loaded from the on-line program library by CICS. CICS does some clever things here. The memory space associated with CICS, called the CICS memory partition (or on-line partition), can be divided into subpartitions by CICS. Each subpartition can hold an on-line program.

At any instant, either CICS or an on-line program is executing. CICS decides which on-line program will execute next. It carries out all reading and writing of records in files and all sending of messages to and receiving of messages from remote terminals. When a program is waiting for a record from a file or a message from a terminal, CICS will allow some other on-line program to execute, if it does not have to execute itself. In this way, CICS functions as the traffic officer for the system.

On-line programs must correctly interface with CICS

CICS is connected via the telecommunications hardware to the remote on-line terminals. The applications programs are connected to the terminals via CICS. A user at a terminal interacts with CICS, and CICS in turn interacts with the on-line program serving the user. CICS thus acts as a kind of middleman.

Suppose there is an on-line file of inventory records containing a part type number field (PTNUMB) as primary key and a quantity (QTY) field. In any record, QTY gives the quantity of a part type in stock. Let the file be called INVENTORY.

Now suppose a remote user wants to know how many P77 part types are in stock. For such a specific type of CICS transaction, there has to be a transaction code stored earlier by a systems programmer in a CICS table. Suppose this transaction code is REQU, and that the corresponding on-line program is called PTPG. The user would then enter something resembling the following at a terminal:

```
REQU P77
```

This would be read by CICS. CICS would check in the appropriate table and determine that program PTPG was needed. If this program was not already in one of its subpartitions, CICS would take it from its on-line program library (see Figure 18.2) and load it into a subpartition. Shortly afterwards, CICS would let this program execute.

The value P77 entered at the terminal would first be passed by CICS to the on-line program PTPG. Actually, in the program PTPG, a CICS

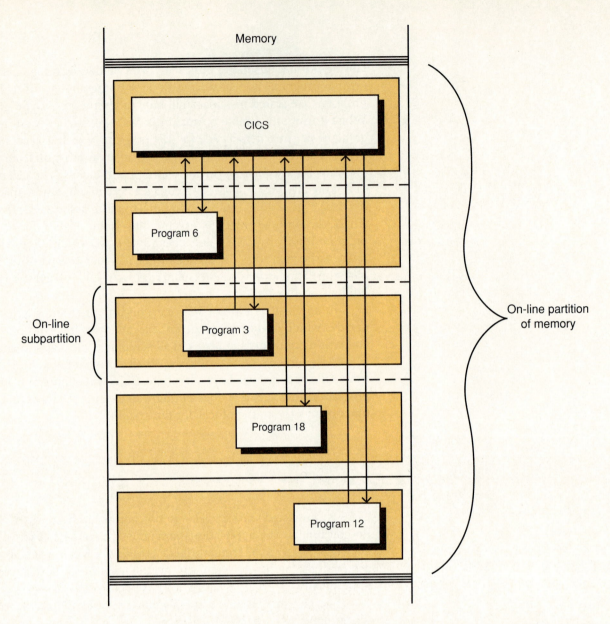

Figure 18.1 *CICS executes perpetually in a portion of memory called an on-line partition. Associated with CICS are subpartitions of memory. Each subpartition can hold an on-line program. CICS can stop any on-line program and start another one at any time.*

RECEIVE command would have to be included and executed for this to happen. The command would look like this:

```
EXEC CICS
    RECEIVE INTO (PART-TYPE-DATA) ...
END-EXEC.
```

This PTPG program instruction would cause CICS to place the value P77 into an identifier PTNUMB. This identifier would be part of a COBOL

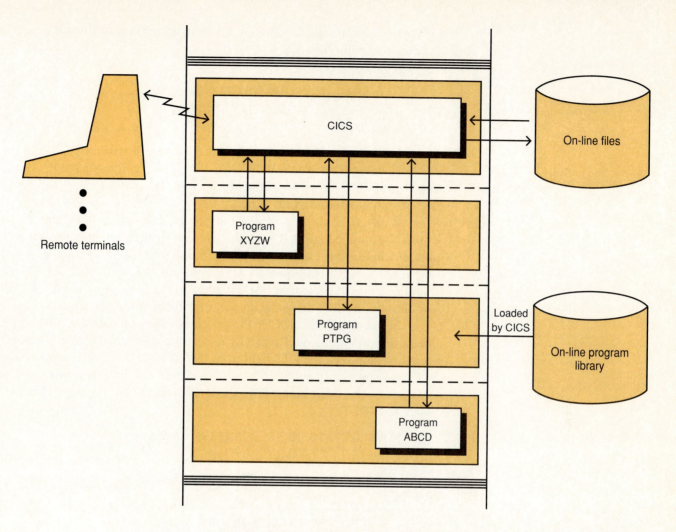

Figure 18.2 *An on-line system with CICS. When a message from a remote terminal asks for execution of a program such as PTPG, if that program is not already in a CICS subpartition in memory, CICS will load the program from a library of on-line programs into a vacant subpartition. CICS communicates with the remote terminals and on-line files—not the on-line programs. The on-line programs communicate only with CICS.*

group identifier PART-TYPE-DATA. PART-TYPE-DATA would be specified in the WORKING-STORAGE SECTION of the DATA DIVISION.

```
01 PART-TYPE-DATA.
   ...
   05 PTNUMB    X(03).
```

The program PTPG would then use the value P77 in PTNUMB to gain direct access to a file INVENTORY. This file would typically be a VSAM indexed-sequential file with the field PTNUMB as the primary key.

The program PTPG will not contain a COBOL READ to access the INVENTORY record for P77. CICS will ask VSAM to retrieve the required record. CICS controls all input and output operations. Instead, a request to CICS to read the P77 record from the INVENTORY file must be included within the on-line program. A special CICS READ command is used in place of the normal COBOL READ. The main portion of this CICS READ command would be

```
EXEC CICS
    READ INTO(INVENTORY-RECORD) ...
            RIDFLD(PTNUMB) ...
END-EXEC.
```

CICS would then get VSAM to read the record with key P77 into the COBOL group identifier INVENTORY-RECORD. CICS passes the P77 value in the RIDFLD record identifier field PTNUMB to the access method or input/output routine as the primary key.

While CICS is waiting for the record, the on-line program PTPG would be stopped and CICS would give some other on-line program permission to execute. Eventually, the record for part type P77 would be passed by VSAM to CICS and thus to the identifier INVENTORY-RECORD. This would enable CICS to give the program PTPG the status "active," which would indicate that the program was capable of running again.

Eventually, CICS will let the program PTPG execute again. When it does, the program would typically generate a reply to the user. The data required would be the QTY field from INVENTORY-RECORD. Suppose the QTY value is the quantity 150 and that within the program, this value is passed to the identifier MESS-QUANTITY-OUT in a group identifier MESSAGE-OUT.

```
MOVE QTY TO MESS-QUANTITY-OUT.
```

The program now asks CICS to send MESSAGE-OUT to the user. The program must include and execute the CICS SEND command, as follows:

```
CICS-EXEC
    SEND FROM MESSAGE-OUT ...
END-EXEC.
```

If the program sends no other data, the user would simply get the value 150 displayed on screen. But CICS can help the programmer display sophisticated messages. Systems programmers may have previously defined sophisticated screen maps for CICS to use. Such maps are stored on disk for use by CICS. A *map* is a detailed specification of the screen display for a specific terminal type. A map in this case might specify something resembling this:

```
PART TYPE INVENTORY REPORT
QUANTITY IN STOCK:.....
```

CICS could use this map to display on the user's screen the final message

```
PART TYPE INVENTORY REPORT
QUANTITY IN STOCK: 150
```

This means the programmer avoids having to write the details of the screen display in the application program PTPG.

Another advantage of CICS is brought out by this example. The screen formatting or panels could be different for each of the many types of terminal in use in the system. CICS will have a map stored for each type of terminal. This means that the applications program becomes independent of the terminals.

CICS allows for VSAM indexed-sequential file processing

O N - L I N E   P R O C E S S I N G normally uses direct-access files. Commonly, indexed-sequential files are used with on-line systems. Hash files can also be used, especially where speed of response is vital, but this is not common. This book is restricted to covering CICS commands for indexed-sequential files.

An inventory file for use in an on-line environment

Assume a VSAM indexed-sequential file called INVENTORY. A record of this file describes a type of part that is inventoried in a central warehouse by a parts supplier. A record of INVENTORY has the fields:

INV-PTNUMB	Primary key, identification number for a part type
INV-TYPE	Name of the type of part
INV-QTY	Quantity on hand of a part type
INV-PRICE	Price per unit

Some typical INVENTORY records are shown in Figure 18.3.

PTNUMB	TYPE	QTY	PRICE
P22	BOLT	4400	03
P29	CAM	1700	17
P31	CLAMP	6600	31
P44	RIM	4600	08
P57	NOZZLE	2700	10
P77	CAM	3400	35

INVENTORY

Figure 18.3 *Some records of the file INVENTORY used in an on-line system. (Blanks have been included to aid readability.)*

The file INVENTORY is used in illustrations of the CICS commands needed for indexed-sequential file processing. However, this file name is not specified in any on-line program. It will have been previously specified for CICS by systems programmers, and that is sufficient. The following sections give a summary of the CICS commands used for processing a VSAM indexed-sequential file.

A working-storage structure to hold an INVENTORY record must be defined in an on-line program that uses the INVENTORY file. The group identifier INVENTORY-RECORD will be used for this purpose.

```
01    INVENTORY-RECORD.
      05   INV-PTNUMB    PIC X(04).
      05   INV-TYPE      PIC X(15).
      05   INV-QTY       PIC 9(06).
      05   INV-PRICE     PIC 9(02).
```

A working-storage identifier WS-RECORD-KEY is also used.

```
01    WS-RECORD-KEY        PIC X(04).
```

This will hold the value of the key of a record being retrieved from INVENTORY. Let us now look at the essential CICS commands in some detail.

Opening Command

There is no CICS command for opening a file. An on-line file is always held open by CICS.

CICS Direct-Access READ Command

To read a record P31 from the file INVENTORY by direct access, the CICS command is

```
MOVE 'P31' TO WS-RECORD-KEY.
EXEC CICS
   READ INTO(INVENTORY-RECORD)
           DATASET('INVENTORY') RIDFLD(WS-RECORD-KEY)
END-EXEC.
```

The P31 record retrieved from INVENTORY will be placed in the WORKING-STORAGE identifier INVENTORY-RECORD. Note that the file name "INVENTORY" must be listed in an appropriate CICS table as an on-line file for manipulation by CICS. However, the file INVENTORY does not have to be specified anywhere in the COBOL program, as would be the case with an ordinary indexed-sequential file (see Chapter 14). The primary key of the record is placed in the identifier WS-RECORD-KEY after the word "RIDFLD" (record identifier field).

Exception Handling

But what if the preceding CICS READ command did not work, perhaps because no P31 record was in the file? In that case, what is called an exceptional (error) condition, or just an exception, occurs. A routine should be coded in the program to take care of an exception. However, if no such exception routine is coded, CICS will display a default message on the user's screen, and then terminate the on-line program. The user, who is unlikely to be a computer specialist, will probably not understand this default message. The program should therefore contain a routine to display more friendly messages, and perform recovery functions, when things go wrong.

Many different kinds of exception can occur, depending on both the CICS command and the circumstances. Each type of exception that can occur following execution of a CICS command has a standard name that is the same for all programs. The name for the "no record found" exception following a CICS direct-access READ command is NOTFND. The name for any general exception is ERROR.

Typically, you might use a COBOL paragraph with an arbitrary name, such as 700-RECORD-NOT-FOUND, to handle the case of the NOTFND exception. At the same time, you might use a different COBOL paragraph called 800-GENERAL-EXCEPTION to handle a general exception (ERROR) following that READ. To relate the exception NOTFND to the paragraph 700-RECORD-NOT-FOUND and the exception ERROR to the paragraph 800-GENERAL-EXCEPTION, you use a CICS HANDLE CONDITION command in the PROCEDURE DIVISION, as follows:

```
PROCEDURE DIVISION.
    ...
    EXEC CICS
        HANDLE CONDITION
            NOTFND(700-RECORD-NOT-FOUND)
            ERROR(800-GENERAL-EXCEPTION)
    END-EXEC.
    MOVE 'P31' TO WS-RECORD-KEY.
    EXEC CICS
        READ INTO(INVENTORY-RECORD)
            DATASET('INVENTORY') RIDFLD(WS-RECORD-KEY)
    END-EXEC.
    ...
700-RECORD-NOT-FOUND.
    instructions for no record matching target key
800-GENERAL-EXCEPTION.
    instructions for any general error
```

The CICS HANDLE CONDITION command is placed at the beginning of the PROCEDURE DIVISION. It simply lists each exception and the corresponding exception handling paragraph, in parentheses.

CICS READ for UPDATE Command

In addition to the normal direct-access CICS READ command, another direct-access read command is needed when the record read will be updated and written back to the file. This is the CICS READ for UPDATE command.

The problem with updating an on-line file with an on-line program is that there can be more than one program under CICS control updating the same record at about the same time. For example, both program A and program B could be executing in turn, under CICS control, and both updating record P44. Program A might retrieve record P44 first. Then CICS might give control to program B, which might next retrieve that record. Then CICS might give control back to program A, which would update the record and write it back to the file. Then CICS might give control to program B, which would carry out its update and write the record back to the file. The result could be that B will undo A's update.

For example, consider the following sequence:

1. **A executes**

   Record   P44 RIM 4600 08   in A's WORKING-STORAGE

2. **B executes**

   Record   P44 RIM 4600 08   in B's WORKING-STORAGE

3. A executes

Record	P44 RIM **7777** 08	INV-QTY updated in WORKING-STORAGE
Record	P44 RIM **7777** 08	rewritten to INVENTORY file

4. B executes

Record	P44 RIM 4600 13	INV-PRICE updated in WORKING-STORAGE
Record	P44 RIM 4600 13	rewritten to INVENTORY file

It is clear that program B has undone program A's update of the INV-QTY field to 7777.

This undoing of updates is called *update interference* and is a serious error. It is avoided if program A can prevent any other program from updating a record that A is currently updating. In practice, program A must ask CICS to maintain a "hands-off my record" policy until A is finished updating the record. This is the purpose of the READ for UPDATE command. A program that issues this command is telling CICS that it wants to read a record and have exclusive use of it until it tells CICS it is finished with it.

This exclusive use is known as *exclusive control*. The program will give up its exclusive control only when it either updates the record with a REWRITE or otherwise signals giving up control. Another program can update the record only after the first program has relinguished exclusive control.

To read a record from INVENTORY with primary key value P31, with the intention of updating it, you use the CICS READ for UPDATE command, as follows:

```
MOVE 'P31' TO WS-RECORD-KEY.
EXEC CICS
    READ INTO(INVENTORY-RECORD) DATASET('INVENTORY')
        RIDFLD(WS-RECORD-KEY) UPDATE
END-EXEC.
```

Record P31 is transferred by CICS to INVENTORY-RECORD, and the program is given exclusive control over that record. No other program can read that record from the INVENTORY file during the period of exclusive control. If the command is not carried out successfully, an exception condition will arise. An appropriate routine to handle the exception should be coded and referenced in the CICS HANDLE CONDITION command, at the beginning of the program. This was explained in the previous section.

The CICS REWRITE Command

The CICS REWRITE command will rewrite the WORKING-STORAGE record retrieved by an earlier CICS READ for UPDATE command. Thus, it could rewrite a record in INVENTORY-RECORD that has been updated. This rewriting operation would then update the corresponding record on disk in the file INVENTORY. Once the CICS REWRITE command has been executed, the exclusive control granted by CICS following the earlier READ for UPDATE command is relinquished by the program.

Suppose that you want to reduce the quantity on hand for part P31 by 700, as follows:

```
MOVE 'P31' TO WS-RECORD-KEY.
EXEC CICS
   READ INTO(INVENTORY-RECORD) DATASET('INVENTORY')
       RIDFLD(WS-RECORD-KEY) UPDATE
END-EXEC.
```
The P31 record is now in INVENTORY-RECORD
```
SUBTRACT 700 FROM INV-QTY IN INVENTORY-RECORD.
```
Record P31 has been updated in WORKING-STORAGE
```
EXEC CICS
   REWRITE FROM(INVENTORY-RECORD) DATASET('INVENTORY')
END-EXEC.
```

Notice that the REWRITE command does not use a primary key specification. CICS knows where to write the record, since it has kept the primary key of the record read by the earlier READ for UPDATE.

The CICS DELETE Command

There are two distinct versions of the CICS DELETE command, depending on whether the primary key of the record involved is used. One version is used after a CICS READ for UPDATE command. The other version simply deletes a record that has its key specified.

Let us first look at the version of the CICS DELETE used with the CICS READ for UPDATE command. As you have seen, the READ for UPDATE command gives the program exclusive control over the record read. On subsequent execution of the DELETE command, this record is deleted and the exclusive control is relinquished.

As an example of this first version of the command, suppose you wish to delete record P31, provided the INV-TYPE type of part is not a nozzle. You could code

```
MOVE 'P31' TO WS-RECORD-KEY.
EXEC CICS
    READ INTO(INVENTORY-RECORD) DATASET('INVENTORY')
       RIDFLD(WS-RECORD-KEY) UPDATE
END-EXEC.
IF INV-TYPE IN INVENTORY-RECORD NOT = 'NOZZLE'
     EXEC CICS
        DELETE DATASET('INVENTORY')
     END-EXEC
END-IF.
```

The READ command places record P31 in INVENTORY-RECORD and gives the on-line program exclusive control over the record. The DELETE causes the record previously read, that is, record P31, to be deleted. It also causes exclusive control over record P31 to be relinquished.

You may wonder what happens if the DELETE is not executed because the IF-condition is false. In that case, the program would not give up exclusive control. It would eventually have to do so, however, and a simple way to do this would be by execution of a special CICS command called UNLOCK. You will see the CICS UNLOCK command in a later section.

As mentioned, the other version of the CICS DELETE command simply deletes a record that has its key specified in the command. For example, to delete the record for key P31, you could code

```
MOVE 'P31' TO WS-RECORD-KEY.
EXEC CICS
    DELETE DATASET('INVENTORY') RIDFLD(WS-RECORD-KEY)
END-EXEC.
```

The CICS UNLOCK Command

A READ for UPDATE command reads a record and gives the on-line program involved exclusive control over that record. This exclusive control will be lost when the program executes either a REWRITE or a DELETE command. However, because of complex logic, it can happen that neither a REWRITE nor a DELETE is ever executed for an exclusively controlled record.

At any given time, it is most efficient if CICS has as few records as possible under the exclusive control of on-line programs. Too many records under exclusive control will slow down the traffic flow, as many programs are forced to wait for exclusive control of records held by other programs. It is clearly bad for a program to keep exclusive control if it is no longer needed. Therefore, as soon as exclusive control is not needed, an on-line program should give up its exclusive control. This is where the CICS UNLOCK command is used.

As an example, consider again the preceding processing excerpt, where a P31 record was deleted, provided the part INV-TYPE involved was not a nozzle. If the INV-TYPE was not 'NOZZLE', the DELETE command was not carried out, but the record remained under exclusive control because of the previous READ for UPDATE. An UNLOCK command should be executed where the IF-condition is false, in order to relinquish control.

```
MOVE 'P31' TO WS-RECORD-KEY.
EXEC CICS
    READ INTO(INVENTORY-RECORD) DATASET('INVENTORY')
        RIDFLD(WS-RECORD-KEY) UPDATE
END-EXEC.
IF INV-TYPE IN INVENTORY-RECORD NOT = 'NOZZLE'
    EXEC CICS
        DELETE DATASET(INVENTORY-RECORD)
    END-EXEC
ELSE EXEC CICS
        UNLOCK DATASET('INVENTORY')
    END-EXEC
END-IF.
```

The CICS WRITE Command

The CICS WRITE command is used for inserting a new record into a file by direct access. It may not replace REWRITE. To add the record 'P35 CAM 5500 17' to the file INVENTORY, you could code

```
MOVE 'P35' TO INV-PTNUMB.
MOVE 'CAM' TO INV-TYPE.
MOVE 5500 TO INV-QTY.
MOVE 17 TO INV-PRICE.
MOVE INV-PTNUMB TO WS-RECORD-KEY.
EXEC CICS
   WRITE FROM(INVENTORY-RECORD)
         DATASET('INVENTORY') RIDFLD(WS-RECORD-KEY)
END-EXEC.
```

CICS places the record in the INVENTORY file in ascending primary key order. The system uses the primary key in WS-RECORD-KEY to position the record in the file and will adjust the primary index for the file if necessary (see Chapter 14).

The CICS RECEIVE Command

The CICS RECEIVE command is used for accepting a message from a terminal and placing it in a program identifier. To identify which program should act on and process the message, the terminal user first inputs a CICS transaction code, or program code, for that program. This program code is followed by some input data that will be used by the on-line program.

Note that the message transmitted by RECEIVE is the program code plus the data to be used by the program. Remember that the terminal may be remote from the computer that is executing CICS and the on-line programs. Also, remember that the terminal "talks to" CICS—not to any on-line program. By having the entire message transmitted, CICS can use the program code part of the message to select the proper program for execution, and then the program can process the input data part of it.

Suppose a remote user wants the quantity of a given type of part. Also, suppose that the program PTPG can retrieve INV-QTY from a record, given the INV-PTNUMB value as input data. Thus, PTPG will retrieve the INV-QTY value in a record of the file INVENTORY in Figure 18.3. Suppose the transaction code that corresponds to the program PTPG is SEEK. To have PTPG retrieve the quantity of part INV-TYPE P31 for example, the remote user would then enter

```
SEEK P31
```

In the program, you could use the group identifier MESSAGE-IN for receiving the preceding message.

```
01 MESSAGE-IN.
   05 MI-PGM-CODE            PIC X(04).
   05 FILLER                 PIC X(01).
   05 MI-INPUT-DATA          PIC X(03).
```

Notice that this WORKING-STORAGE specification of the receiving identifier means that the maximum length of the input message is 4 + 1 + 3, or 8 characters.

The message is transmitted exactly as entered by the user, with no changes of any kind. Thus, you need the FILLER (or any PIC X identifier) for the blank character between the values SEEK and P31. The entire message is transmitted, blanks and all. The length of the message is also transmitted, so the program needs an identifier to receive this length value as well.

Suppose a remote user entered the following message:

```
SEEK P4
```

CICS would transmit length 7, which would be acceptable, since MI-INPUT-DATA can hold the value 'P4'. But if the user entered the message

```
SEEK P7786
```

CICS would transmit a message of length 10. This would not be acceptable, since MI-INPUT-DATA would not be able to hold the value P7786 and would lose the digits '86' on the right. The program could detect the nature of the problem by examining the message-length identifier. This problem would also cause an exception condition, and unless a suitable exception routine was included in the program, the user would get an incomprehensible default message from CICS. Let us look now at how to use the RECEIVE command and deal with exceptions caused by messages that are too long.

You need an identifier for the message length transmitted by CICS from the user to the program. Suppose you specify it in the WORKING-STORAGE SECTION as

```
01 MESSAGE-LEN  PIC S9(04) COMP.
```

(The S9(4) COMP is necessary. CICS runs on IBM computers, in which COMP means an integer value is to be stored as a binary value instead of as 1 byte per digit, which would be the case if COMP were omitted. COMP means faster arithmetic processing. See Chapter 19.)

The RECEIVE command needed will then be

```
EXEC CICS
    RECEIVE INTO(MESSAGE-IN) LENGTH(MESSAGE-LEN)
END-EXEC.
```

The RECEIVE command transmits the user's message from the remote terminal into MESSAGE-IN and the length of the message into MESSAGE-LEN.

The CICS standard name LENGERR is used for an exception caused by a message that is too long. The CICS HANDLE CONDITION command should have the routine 300-MESSAGE-TOO-LONG executed if the value of MESSAGE-LEN exceeds the length of MESSAGE-IN. When the previous RECEIVE command is executed, if MESSAGE-LEN receives a longer message than the length of MESSAGE-IN, the exception condition LENGERR occurs.

A COBOL program excerpt that ties all this together is as follows:

```
WORKING-STORAGE SECTION.
01 MESSAGE-LEN          PIC S9(04) COMP.
01  MESSAGE-IN.
    05 MI-PGM-CODE      PIC X(04).
    05 FILLER           PIC X.
    05 MI-INPUT-DATA    PIC X(03).
...
PROCEDURE DIVISION.
100-CONTROL-MODULE.
    EXEC CICS
       HANDLE CONDITION LENGERR(300-MESSAGE-TOO-LONG)
    END-EXEC.
    MOVE SPACES TO MESSAGE-IN.
    EXEC CICS
           RECEIVE INTO(MESSAGE-IN) LENGTH(MESSAGE-LEN)
    END-EXEC.
    PERFORM 500-PROCESS-MESSAGE.
    ...

300-MESSAGE-TOO-LONG.
```

This routine contains the instructions to handle the case where the message entered by the remote user is longer than MESSAGE-IN. This routine will probably send a message to the user (using the CICS SEND command) asking the user for a correctly formatted message.

```
500-PROCESS-MESSAGE.
```

This routine uses the primary key value P31 in MI-INPUT-DATA with a READ command to retrieve the P31 INVENTORY record. It then uses a SEND command to transmit the INV-QTY value to the user.

You should always put blanks in MESSAGE-IN before executing the RECEIVE command. This is because CICS always transmits the exact string of characters making up the message – neither more nor less. When the RECEIVE command is in a loop, this can cause problems if you do not blank the MESSAGE-IN identifier before using the RECEIVE command.

As an example, suppose that the RECEIVE command is in a loop and is executed many times, with a new message being received each time. The first message received by MESSAGE-IN could be

```
SEEK P57
```

This valid message will go to MESSAGE-IN, and the value P57 will go to MI-INPUT-DATA. Next time the RECEIVE command is executed, the message could be

```
SEEK P8
```

This too is a valid message, but only the first *seven* spaces of the *eight* character spaces in MESSAGE-IN will receive new characters. The message is transmitted character by character in left to right order. The last space will *not* be changed, so the new contents of MESSAGE-IN will be

```
SEEK P87
```

which is wrong.

Always remember to blank the message identifier before using a CICS RECEIVE command.

The CICS SEND Command

The CICS SEND command sends a message from working storage to a remote terminal. The message has a fixed length and is the contents of a WORKING-STORAGE identifier. As with a message received using the RECEIVE command, the message sent contains the program code and the output data. You could use the identifier MESSAGE-OUT to hold a message in working storage.

```
01 MESSAGE-OUT.
    05 MO-PGM-CODE       PIC X(04) VALUE 'LOOK'.
    05 FILLER            PIC X(01).
    05 MO-OUTPUT-DATA    PIC X(15).
```

Suppose that the transaction code involved is another one called LOOK, which corresponds to the new on-line program name TYPG. This new program, TYPG, returns the user the name of the type of part (INV-TYPE value) corresponding to the part type number entered (the primary key). Thus, if the user entered

```
LOOK P31
```

the response would be

```
CLAMP
```

The value 'CLAMP' would be placed in MO-OUTPUT-DATA and the value 'LOOK' in MO-PGM-CODE. The value 'LOOK' would be transmitted, but it would not be displayed on the user's screen.

A message-length identifier is also needed with the SEND command. You can use MESSAGE-LEN, as defined earlier in WORKING-STORAGE. The following is a typical CICS SEND command:

```
EXEC CICS
    SEND FROM(MESSAGE-OUT) LENGTH(MESSAGE-LEN)
END-EXEC.
```

A value must be placed in MESSAGE-LEN before SEND is executed. The value should be equal to the length of the data in MESSAGE-OUT starting from the left. Suppose that before execution of SEND you execute

```
MOVE 10 TO MESSAGE-LEN.
```

When SEND is executed, the first 10 characters (left to right) in MESSAGE-OUT will be transmitted to the remote terminal. This will be the string 'LOOK CLAMP' exactly. Only the 'CLAMP' value in MO-OUTPUT-DATA will be displayed on the user's screen, however.

There is a possibility of a severe error here, unfortunately. The value you place in MESSAGE-LEN should not exceed the length of MESSAGE-OUT (20 characters in this case). Suppose a value 30 was placed in MESSAGE-LEN before execution of SEND. CICS would transmit 30 characters from working storage, beginning where MESSAGE-OUT begins in memory. Thus, the 20 valid characters in MESSAGE-OUT would be transmitted, plus 10 unpredictable characters that just happened to be adjacent to MESSAGE-OUT in memory at the time. The message displayed might be something like

```
CLAMPbbbbbbbbbbW%#S(*&&!#
```

or some such nonsense. Such a message would not inspire confidence in the user. In addition, the nonsense characters may cause the terminal control system to perform some meaningful operation, such as emitting beeps or flashes. Therefore, care should be taken with the contents of MESSAGE-LEN.

You can include the optional word ERASE with a SEND command.

```
EXEC CICS
      SEND FROM(MESSAGE-OUT) LENGTH(MESSAGE-LEN)
      ERASE
END-EXEC.
```

ERASE will cause CICS to clear the screen of the terminal before the message is displayed.

The CICS RETURN Command

The CICS RETURN command

```
EXEC CICS
      RETURN
END-EXEC.
```

essentially corresponds to STOP RUN in a conventional COBOL program. An on-line COBOL program under CICS control is considered to be a subprogram of CICS. When an on-line program stops executing, execution control must return to CICS. The RETURN command is included to specify that control return to CICS.

A complete CICS retrieval program illustrates the use of CICS commands

This section gives an example of a complete retrieval program that uses CICS. This program returns quantity and INV-PRICE information from the INVENTORY file when a part number is entered at a remote terminal. Assume that the transaction code for the program is RETR. Thus, when a user enters

```
RETR P31
```

the on-line program in Figure 18.4 executes and finally displays

```
PART/INV-QTY/INV-PRICE DATA:  P31   6600 31
```

if the part P31 is in the file. If it is not, the program displays

```
RECORD NOT FOUND.
```

If the user enters a message that is too long, such as

```
RETRIEVE P31
```

it will display

```
MESSAGE TOO LONG.
```

You can see that the program is quite brief. That is how most CICS on-line programs are, since messages are being transmitted over long distances and users quickly get used to, and prefer, the brevity.

```
IDENTIFICATION DIVISION.
PROGRAM-ID. ONLIN1.
ENVIRONMENT DIVISION.
*******************************************************************
*   FILES ARE ON-LINE, DEFINED UNDER CICS.                       *
*******************************************************************
DATA DIVISION.
WORKING-STORAGE SECTION.
01 INVENTORY-RECORD.
     05 INV-PTNUMB              PIC X(04).
     05 INV-TYPE                PIC X(15).
     05 INV-QTY                 PIC 9(06).
     05 INV-PRICE               PIC 9(02).
01 MESSAGE-IN.
     05 MI-PGM-CODE             PIC X(04).
     05 FILLER                  PIC X.
     05 MI-INPUT-DATA           PIC X(03).
01 MESSAGE-OUT.
     05 MO-PGM-CODE             PIC X(04).
     05 FILLER                  PIC X           VALUE SPACE.
     05 MO-OUTPUT-DATA.
        10 MO-MESSAGE-TEXT      PIC X(28).
        10 FILLER               PIC X           VALUE SPACE.
        10 MO-PTNUMB            PIC X(04).
        10 FILLER               PIC X           VALUE SPACE.
        10 MO-QTY               PIC 9(06).
        10 FILLER               PIC X           VALUE SPACE.
        10 MO-PRICE             PIC 9(02).

01 EXCEPTION-MESSAGE.
     05 EXC-PGM-CODE            PIC X(04).
     05 FILLER                  PIC X           VALUE SPACES.
     05 EXC-TEXT                PIC X(20).
01 WS-WORK-AREAS.
     05  WS-RECORD-KEY          PIC X(04).
     05  MESSAGE-LEN            PIC S9(04) COMP.
PROCEDURE DIVISION.
100-CONTROL-MODULE.
*******************************************************************
*   DIRECTS PROGRAM LOGIC.                                       *
*******************************************************************
     PERFORM 200-INITIALIZATION.
     PERFORM 300-READ-FROM-TERMINAL.
     PERFORM 400-PROCESS-MESSAGE.
     PERFORM 500-RESPOND-TO-TERMINAL.
     PERFORM 600-TERMINATION.
```

```
 200-INITIALIZATION.
*************************************************************************
*   PERFORMED FROM 100-CONTROL-MODULE. DEFINES ERROR ROUTINES AND       *
*   CONDITIONS. BLANKS INPUT MESSAGE IDENTIFIER.                        *
*************************************************************************
     EXEC CICS
           HANDLE CONDITION NOTFND(700-RECORD-NOT-FOUND)
                            LENGERR(800-MESSAGE-TOO-LONG)
     END-EXEC.
     MOVE SPACES TO MESSAGE-IN.
 300-READ-FROM-TERMINAL.
*************************************************************************
*   PERFORMED FROM 100-CONTROL-MODULE. READS MESSAGE FROM REMOTE        *
*   TERMINAL. IF MESSAGE READ IS TOO LONG, AN ERROR PARAGRAPH IS        *
*   EXECUTED.                                                           *
*************************************************************************
     EXEC CICS
           RECEIVE INTO(MESSAGE-IN) LENGTH(MESSAGE-LEN)
     END-EXEC.
 400-PROCESS-MESSAGE.
*************************************************************************
*   PERFORMED FROM 100-CONTROL-MODULE. USES DATA IN MESSAGE FROM        *
*   TERMINAL TO RETRIEVE RECORD FROM MASTER FILE. USES DATA RETRIEVED   *
*   TO CONSTRUCT MESSAGE FOR RETURN TO REMOTE TERMINAL. IF NO RECORD    *
*   FOUND IN MASTER, ERROR PARAGRAPH IS EXECUTED.                       *
*************************************************************************
     MOVE MI-INPUT-DATA TO WS-RECORD-KEY.
     EXEC CICS
         READ INTO(INVENTORY-RECORD) DATASET('INVENTORY')
                 RIDFLD(WS-RECORD-KEY)
     END-EXEC.
     MOVE 48 TO MESSAGE-LEN.
     MOVE MI-INPUT-DATA TO MO-PTNUMB.
     MOVE INV-QTY TO MO-QTY.
     MOVE INV-PRICE TO MO-PRICE.
     MOVE MI-PGM-CODE TO MO-PGM-CODE.
         MOVE 'PART/INV-QTY/INV-PRICE DATA:' TO MO-MESSAGE-TEXT.
 500-RESPOND-TO-TERMINAL.
*************************************************************************
*   PERFORMED FROM 100-CONTROL-MODULE. RESPONSE, WITH RETRIEVE DATA,    *
*   IS SENT TO THE REMOTE TERMINAL.                                     *
*************************************************************************
     EXEC CICS
           SEND FROM(MESSAGE-OUT) LENGTH(MESSAGE-LEN)
     END-EXEC.
 600-TERMINATION.
*************************************************************************
*   PERFORMED FROM 100-CONTROL-MODULE. RETURNS CONTROL TO CICS.         *
*************************************************************************
     EXEC CICS
           RETURN
     END-EXEC.
```

```
 700-RECORD-NOT-FOUND.
 **************************************************************************
 *   PERFORMED FROM 200-INITIALIZATION. A 'NOT FOUND' MESSAGE IS SENT TO   *
 *   REMOTE TERMINAL IF THE RECORD SOUGHT IS NOT IN THE MASTER FILE.        *
 **************************************************************************
        MOVE MI-PGM-CODE TO EXC-PGM-CODE.
        MOVE 'RECORD NOT FOUND' TO EXC-TEXT.
        MOVE 25 TO MESSAGE-LEN.
        EXEC CICS
            SEND FROM(EXCEPTION-MESSAGE) LENGTH(MESSAGE-LEN)
        END-EXEC.
        EXEC CICS
             RETURN
        END-EXEC.
 800-MESSAGE-TOO-LONG.
 **************************************************************************
 *   PERFORMED FROM 200-INITIALIZATION. A 'TOO LONG' MESSAGE IS SENT TO    *
 *   REMOTE TERMINAL IF THE INPUT MESSAGE FROM THE USER IS TOO LONG.        *
 **************************************************************************
        MOVE MI-PGM-CODE TO EXC-PGM-CODE.
        MOVE 'MESSAGE TOO LONG' TO EXC-TEXT.
        MOVE 25 TO MESSAGE-LEN.
        EXEC CICS
            SEND FROM(EXCEPTION-MESSAGE) LENGTH(MESSAGE-LEN)
        END-EXEC.
        EXEC CICS
             RETURN
        END-EXEC.
```

Figure 18.4 *On-line retrieval program using CICS commands.*

Precompilation is necessary with CICS COBOL programs

COBOL programs containing CICS commands cannot be submitted directly to the COBOL compiler for translation to machine language. A CICS COBOL program must be submitted first to a CICS precompiler, known as the CICS *command translator*. The command translator precompiles the program, which essentially means that it converts CICS commands to COBOL CALL statements that call up CICS. The precompiled COBOL program can then be submitted to the COBOL compiler in the normal manner.

Care must be taken to prevent deadlock

Suppose a program needs exclusive control over records from two different files, F1 and F2. It can issue two READ for UPDATE commands in sequence, one for F1 and one for F2. When this is the case, the READ statements should be issued in ascending file name order.

```
EXEC CICS
    READ INTO(F1-RECORD) DATASET('F1')
        RIDFLD(WS-RECORD-KEY1) UPDATE
END-EXEC.
EXEC CICS
    READ INTO(F2-RECORD) DATASET('F2')
        RIDFLD(WS-RECORD-KEY2) UPDATE
END-EXEC.
```

If this is not done, there is a possibility of *deadlock*, which means that the program cannot proceed.

Suppose that both programs A and B need exclusive control over F1 and F2 records. And suppose that the two programs are executing at much the same time, that is, executing concurrently, and the order of execution of their READ for UPDATE statements is

Program A: READ . . . F2 . . .
Program B: READ . . . F1 . . .
Program A: READ . . . F1 . . . (Program A must wait for program
                  B to give up control of F1.)
Program B: READ . . . F2 . . . (Program B must wait for program
                  A to give up control of F2.)

Thus, A waits for B and B waits for A. Neither program can proceed, so they are said to be deadlocked. The problem is avoided if all programs request exclusive control of files in ascending file name order.

Complex screen panels can easily be sent to remote terminals

The preceding examples have shown how SEND can be used to send simple messages to a remote terminal. It is posssible to send many message lines to a terminal using multiple SEND commands. However, this is rarely done. Instead the program requests that CICS send and display one of many previously stored message formats or screen panels. This results in a great saving of programming effort, because the on-line program does not have to be concerned with the type of terminal. CICS looks after the details.

The stored screen panels are constructed by a systems programmer using a special CICS language that is much like assembly language. It has nothing to do with COBOL, so the COBOL techniques discussed in earlier chapters for writing complex reports (for a printer or a screen) do not apply.

The stored panels are called *maps*, which are stored in groups called *mapsets*. A mapset would be made up of all the screen panels or maps needed by a program for a particular type of terminal. In addition, a generic mapset is the collection of all mapsets, regardless of terminal, used by a program.

The following is an example of a CICS SEND command using maps:

```
CICS EXEC
    SEND MAP('Q1') MAPSET('QRST')
END-EXEC
```

Q1 is a specific map, and QRST is the generic mapset for the program. The details of defining mapsets are beyond the scope of this book. However, defining mapsets is a large part of the effort involved in developing on-line programs with CICS. Similar techniques are also used with other types of teleprocessing monitors.

Summary

1. On-line programs are executed concurrently when requested by users at diverse and geographically remote terminals. To avoid contention, a teleprocessing monitor is used to control execution of on-line programs and communications with remote terminals. CICS is a common teleprocessing monitor.
2. CICS has control over a relatively large region of memory, which it divides into subpartitions, each capable of holding an on-line program. An on-line program executes only when requested by CICS. On-line programs are held in an on-line program library and are loaded into memory for execution as requested by users. Users at terminals communicate only with CICS; output by an on-line program is first delivered to CICS, which forwards it to the correct terminal. Similarly, input from a terminal goes first to CICS and then to the on-line program. A request for input from a file by an on-line program must also go through CICS.
3. On-line programs can be written in COBOL, but input/output COBOL commands, such as ACCEPT, DISPLAY, READ, WRITE, REWRITE, and DELETE are replaced with special CICS commands.
4. Details of standard screen displays are normally not coded in on-line programs, but are stored instead in CICS maps. A CICS command to write data on a screen will refer to a particular map, thus causing the contents of that map to appear on the screen.

Key Terms

batch processing
on-line processing
teleprocessing monitor
maps
command translator
deadlock

Concept Review Questions

1. What is meant by on-line updating?
2. Explain what a teleprocessing monitor does.
3. What is a CICS transaction code?
4. What is a CICS transaction?
5. How does an on-line program access an on-line file?
6. What does the CICS precompiler do?
7. What is a CICS map?
8. Explain how update interference can occur with two concurrently executing on-line programs.
9. Explain how deadlock can occur and how it can be avoided.
10. Explain how a CICS/COBOL program is prepared for execution.
11. How does a CICS/COBOL program update a file?
12. How does CICS allow a program to be independent of the type of terminal?
13. Explain the idea behind the READ for UPDATE CICS command.
14. Explain exception handling with CICS.
15. What does a CICS record identifier field do?
16. In what language are CICS maps written?
17. Why is no OPEN command needed with a CICS on-line file?
18. What is a CICS HANDLE CONDITION clause used for?
19. Explain the two different CICS DELETE commands.
20. Why is the CICS UNLOCK command needed?
21. Why is the length of the message critical when using
    a. the CICS RECEIVE command
    b. the CICS SEND command?
22. Why is the STOP RUN statement not used with CICS programs? What is used instead?

CICS/COBOL Language Questions

1. What is wrong with the following?

```
EXEC CICS
    READ INTO(CUSTREC) DATASET('CUSTOMER') RIDFLD(CUSTNUMB)
    INVALID KEY DISPLAY 'RECORD NOT FOUND'
END-EXEC.
```

2. Code a correct version of the excerpt in question 1.

3. What is wrong with this?

```
MOVE 'C14' TO CUSTNUMB.
EXEC CICS
    READ INTO(CUSTREC) DATASET('CUSTOMER')
        RIDFLD(CUSTNUMB) UPDATE
END-EXEC.
IF CUSTSKILL = 'PROGRAMMER'
    ADD 1000 TO CUSTSALARY
    EXEC CICS
        REWRITE FROM(CUSTREC) DATASET('CUSTOMER')
    END-EXEC
END-IF.
```

4. Code a correct version of the excerpt in question 3.

Programming Assignments

1. **Program placing records in a file**
   Write a brief COBOL program to place some records in the INVENTORY file used in the chapter. Records are read from a terminal.

2. **Program that accepts and adds quantities**
   Write a brief COBOL program to accept a quantity of a given part type from a terminal and add that quantity to the INVENTORY file.

3. **Program that deletes records**
   Write a brief program to delete any INVENTORY record whose primary key is submitted by a user at a terminal.

4. **Program that displays quantities**
   Write a brief program to display the quantity listed in INVENTORY of the part type when its code is entered at a terminal.

IV

SUPPLEMENTARY COBOL FEATURES

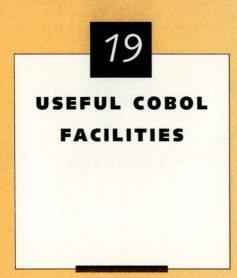

19

USEFUL COBOL FACILITIES

OBJECTIVES

- To show how to write sub-programs
- To demonstrate use of the COPY statement
- To explain the different kinds of numeric identifiers available
- To demonstrate the STRING and UNSTRING verbs for manipulating character strings

OUTLINE

*T*HIS CHAPTER COVERS some peripheral, yet important, features of COBOL. The major topics covered are

- CALL statements and subprograms
- The COPY statement
- The USAGE clause used with numeric identifiers
- The STRING and UNSTRING statements

19.1 The CALL statement is used with subprograms

*T*HE INDIVIDUAL PARAGRAPHS within a COBOL program can be regarded as separate routines under the control of the first, or main, paragraph of the program. Each paragraph is called up, then executed by a PERFORM statement. However, another kind of routine can be executed as part of a COBOL program. This type of routine is called a *subprogram* and is called up, or executed, by means of a CALL statement.

A subprogram functions as a paragraph

A subprogram is similar in function to a paragraph of an ordinary COBOL program. It has a name; it is made up of COBOL statements; and it can be executed anywhere within a COBOL program when the appropriate CALL (instead of PERFORM) statement is executed. However, there is a difference.

A subprogram is written (and can be compiled) separately from the calling program. The main idea is that the same subprogram can be used by many different main programs. For example, suppose many programs that process a particular hash file all use the same complex hashing routine. One way to handle this would be to have the hashing routine as a paragraph in each program, called up by a PERFORM. But since all the programs use the same paragraph, it will save coding effort if the hashing routine is written and compiled separately and stored on disk as an independent subprogram. Using a CALL statement, each program can call up the subprogram as needed.

Thus, a subprogram tends to be used for a function that will be needed by many programs. Examples of such functions are finding the roots of a quadratic equation, determining standard deviations, determining summaries, printing of totals, and so on.

The program that calls up a subprogram is called the calling program or *main program*.

The CALL statement executes a subprogram

The call statement has the simple format shown here:

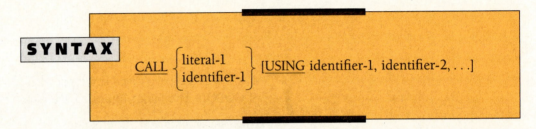

SYNTAX

$$\text{CALL} \left\{ \begin{array}{l} \text{literal-1} \\ \text{identifier-1} \end{array} \right\} \text{[USING identifier-1, identifier-2, . . .]}$$

Some examples of the statement might be

Example 1

```
MOVE 'P2345' TO PRIMARY-KEY.
CALL 'HASHPGM' USING PRIMARY-KEY, DISK-ADDRESS.
```

When the CALL statement is executed, the value 'P2345' in PRIMARY-KEY is passed to the subprogram HASHPGM, which executes. The subprogram HASHPGM could be a hashing routine. The subprogram processes the value 'P2345' and generates a relative disk address, which it places in DISK-ADDRESS. Then it ceases execution and the main routine continues execution, using the address in the identifier DISK-ADDRESS corresponding to a primary key.

Example 2

place 82 items in array ARRAY-1
```
MOVE 82 TO NUMBER-OF-ITEMS.
CALL 'STDEV'
        USING ARRAY-1, NUMBER-OF-ITEMS, STAND-DEV.
```

When the CALL statement is executed, the subprogram STDEV executes. It uses the 82 items in ARRAY-1 to compute the standard deviation for the data in ARRAY-1. It then places the resulting standard deviation in STAND-DEV and ceases to execute. The main program can then continue to execute, using this value.

The subprogram name is an external name, which means that it can be used in another (or external) program, such as the calling program. This name is treated as a literal and must have a maximum of eight characters, made up of only letters and digits. The subprogram name can be held in an identifier.

Subprograms and calling programs must interface correctly

Suppose you have a main program that first reads a record from a sequential file SEQUENTIAL-FILE. The record has the structure

```
01 SEQ-RECORD-IN.
   05 SQ-PART-NUMBER-IN    PIC 9(04).
   05 SQ-QTY-IN            PIC 9(05).
   05 SQ-DESCRIPTION-IN    PIC X(40).
```

The program then places the record in a hash file called HASH-FILE, in a disk address computed from the value of the primary key SQ-PART-NUMBER-IN in the record. This computation is carried out by a hashing routine called HASHPGM, which places, or returns, the computed disk address in the identifier REL-DISK-ADDRESS. The essentials of the calling program and the subprogram are shown in Figure 19.1.

A subprogram is structured exactly like a normal COBOL program except that

- A LINKAGE SECTION may be included. It must be placed after the WORKING-STORAGE SECTION and is like the WORKING-STORAGE SECTION in format. You may not define an identifier with a VALUE clause in the LINKAGE SECTION, however.
- If there is a LINKAGE SECTION, there will be a USING clause after the PROCEDURE DIVISION. This clause will list the identifiers in the order in which they appear in the LINKAGE SECTION.
- Instead of a STOP RUN statement to terminate execution, an EXIT PROGRAM statement is used.

The values, if any, in the identifiers in the CALL statement are passed to the identifiers in the LINKAGE SECTION when the subprogram begins execution. Thus, there is the following in Figure 19.1:

```
SQ-PART-NUMBER-IN ──────────────────→ INPUT-KEY
REL-DISK-ADDRESS ───────────────────→ RESULT
```

When the subprogram ceases execution, the opposite results, and the values in the LINKAGE SECTION are passed back to the identifiers in the CALL statement.

```
SQ-PART-NUMBER-IN ←────────────────── INPUT-KEY
REL-DISK-ADDRESS ←─────────────────── RESULT
```

Suppose that, before the CALL was executed, SQ-PART-NUMBER-IN had the value 3006 and no value had been assigned to REL-DISK-ADDRESS (value unassigned). At the beginning of execution of the subprogram,

```
IDENTIFIER DIVISION.
PROGRAM-ID. MAINPGM.
ENVIRONMENT DIVISION.
INPUT-OUTPUT SECTION.
FILE-CONTROL.
    SELECT SEQUENTIAL-FILE
                    ASSIGN TO UT-S-DATA.
    SELECT HASH-FILE
                ASSIGN TO MAST234
                ORGANIZATION IS RELATIVE
                ACCESS MODE IS RANDOM
                RELATIVE KEY IS REL-DISK-ADDRESS.
DATA DIVISION.
FILE SECTION.
FD   SEQUENTIAL-FILE               LABEL RECORDS ARE STANDARD
                                   RECORD CONTAINS 49 CHARACTERS.
01 SEQ-RECORD-IN.
    05 SQ-PART-NUMBER-IN     PIC 9(04).
    05 SQ-QTY-IN             PIC 9(05).
    05 SQ-DESCRIPTION-IN     PIC X(40).
FD HASH-FILE                       LABEL RECORDS ARE STANDARD
                                   RECORD CONTAINS 49 CHARACTERS.
01 HASH-RECORD-OUT          PIC X(49).

WORKING-STORAGE-SECTION.
01 REL-DISK-ADDRESS         PIC 9(03).
PROCEDURE DIVISION.
    ...
    READ SEQUENTIAL-FILE, AT END . . .
    CALL 'HASHPGM' USING SQ-PART-NUMBER-IN, REL-DISK-ADDRESS.
        disk address now in REL-DISK-ADDRESS identifier
    WRITE HASH-RECORD-OUT FROM SEQ-RECORD-IN,
        INVALID KEY ...
    ...
    STOP RUN.
```

```
IDENTIFIER DIVISION.
PROGRAM-ID. HASHPGM.
DATA DIVISION.
WORKING-STORAGE SECTION
01 QUOT             PIC 9(02)V99.
01 HASH-DIVISOR     PIC 9(04)          VALUE 100.
LINKAGE SECTION.
01  INPUT-KEY       PIC 9(04).
01  RESULT          PIC 9(03)
PROCEDURE DIVISION USING INPUT-KEY, RESULT.
100-MODULE-1.
    PERFORM 200-COMPUTE-ADDRESS.
    PERFORM 300-TERMINATION.
```

```
200-COMPUTE-ADDRESS.
    DIVIDE INPUT-KEY BY HASH-DIVISOR GIVING QUOT
                           REMAINDER RESULT.
300-TERMINATION.
    EXIT PROGRAM.
```

Figure 19.1 A calling program and the accompanying subprogram.

INPUT-KEY would get the value 3006 and RESULT would be unassigned. At the end of execution, the subprogram INPUT-KEY would have the value 3006 and RESULT the value 6. When control returned to the calling program, SQ-PART-NUMBER-IN would be sent 3006 and RESULT would be sent 6.

The match between identifiers used in the calling program and those used in the LINKAGE SECTION of the subprogram must be exact. Thus, if you have

```
CALL 'SUBPGM' USING A, B, C.
```

and in the subprogram you have

```
LINKAGE SECTION.
    01 X  ...
    01 Y  ...
    01 Z  ...
PROCEDURE DIVISION USING X, Y, Z.
```

then transfer of data will take place between A and X, between B and Y, and between C and Z. Matching takes place in the order in which the identifiers appear in the CALL USING statement and in the LINKAGE SECTION and USING clauses in the subprogram. This means that matching pairs of identifiers must have the same picture clauses. You can see that this is the case in Figure 19.1.

In rare cases, there will be no USING clause in the CALL statement, and thus no identifiers. In that case there will also be no LINKAGE SECTION in the subprogram. An example would be a subprogram that simply printed a standard message involving a complex format, such as a company logo.

A calling program can call a subprogram many times

There are a few points to note if a calling program calls a subprogram more than once.

The first time the subprogram is called, identifiers defined in the subprogram are "fresh," and will either have no values assigned, or the values specified in VALUE clauses. The next time the subprogram is called, the identifiers in the subprogram (apart from those in the LINKAGE SECTION) may have the values that prevailed when the subprogram ended execution last time. If you do not want that, but want a fresh set of subprogram identifiers each time, include the IS INITIAL PROGRAM clause after the subprogram name definition, as in

```
IDENTIFIER DIVISION.
PROGRAM-ID. HASHPGM IS INITIAL PROGRAM.
DATA DIVISION.
WORKING-STORAGE SECTION
01 QUOT            PIC 9(02)V99.
01 HASH-DIVISOR    PIC 9(04)        VALUE 100.
LINKAGE SECTION.
01  INPUT-KEY      PIC 9(04).
01  RESULT         PIC 9(03)

PROCEDURE DIVISION USING INPUT-KEY, RESULT.
100-MODULE-1.
...
```

Pairs of identifiers must match in specific ways

Suppose you have a calling program, C1, that calls a subprogram, SUB1. In the calling program you have

```
MOVE 2 TO B.
MOVE 6 TO C.
MOVE 5 TO D.
CALL 'SUB1' USING A, B, C, D.
```

The subprogram SUB1 has the following PROCEDURE DIVISION:

```
PROCEDURE DIVISION
        USING X, Y, Z, W.
COMPUTE X = (Y + Z) * W
EXIT PROGRAM.
```

Clearly, the values in B, C, and D are passed to Y, Z, and W in SUB1. When SUB1 has finished executing, X has the value (2 + 6) * 5, or 40, and the 40 in X is finally passed back to the identifier A in the calling program C1.

However, this is only what appears to be happening. What actually happens is that when the subprogram is executing, the identifiers X, Y, Z, and W denote the same memory locations as denoted by A, B, C, and D in the main program. To put this plainly, there are four memory locations. When the main program is executing, you can refer to them using the names A, B, C, and D. And when the subprogram is executing, you can refer to them as X, Y, Z, and W. This is the well-known call-by-reference.

This can have unexpected consequences at times. In the preceding excerpt, the values in B, C, and D were "passed" to Y, Z, and W, and a result expected to be "passed back" from X to A. There were no problems. But suppose the excerpt had been coded as follows:

```
PROCEDURE DIVISION
        USING X, Y, Z, W.
    ADD Y TO Z.
    MULTIPLY Z BY W GIVING X.
    EXIT PROGRAM.
```

This looks the same, and the value 40 would be returned to A from X as before, but there is a difference. During execution of the subprogram, the value in Z is changed to 8. Since identifier Z and identifier C are names for the same memory location, identifier C now has the value 8, as well. Thus, at the end of execution of the subprogram, A gets the result 40, and the value C is changed from 6 to 8. If C is used later in the calling program, and this change from 6 to 8 was not intended, a logical error will result.

As a result, when writing subprograms, care should be taken not to unintentionally change values in identifiers used for receiving data from a main program. Otherwise you will get unexpected changes appearing in the USING clause identifiers in the CALLING program.

19.2
The COPY statement copies text into a source program

THE ESSENTIAL format of the COPY statement is

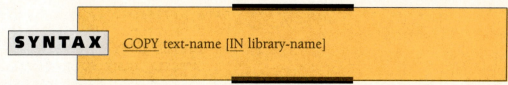

SYNTAX COPY text-name [IN library-name]

The identifier library-name is an external name and is limited to eight characters consisting of letters and digits.

The COPY statement is used with standard program text

A library can be set up by systems programmers. It consists of entries, each of which consists of one or more lines of COBOL program text and has a name. For example, there could be an entry in the library called ERROR-TEXT containing

```
MOVE A TO B.
MOVE C TO D.
MOVE ERROR-DATA TO PRINT-RECORD.
WRITE PRINT-RECORD AFTER 1 LINE.
```

This text could print a standard message. Suppose now that many programs written at an installation need to contain the code for printing this message. A programmer could include in a program either

```
800-ERROR-PARAGRAPH.
      MOVE A TO B.
      MOVE C TO
      MOVE ERROR-DATA TO PRINT-RECORD.
      WRITE PRINT-RECORD AFTER 1 LINE.
```

or, more simply

```
800-ERROR-PARAGRAPH. COPY ERROR-TEXT.
```

In the second case, when the program was compiled, the four lines of text from the library would be included after 800-ERROR-PARAGRAPH to replace the COPY statement.

The COPY statement thus saves the programmer having to write out standard statements or program file and identifier definitions that every program will use. They can simply be copied from a library.

The COPY statement can be used in the following:

- The INPUT-OUTPUT SECTION of the ENVIRONMENT DIVISION, for example:

```
ENVIRONMENT DIVISION.
INPUT-OUTPUT SECTION.
FILE-CONTROL. COPY SELECT-TEXT.
...
SELECT PRINT-FILE       ASSIGN TO...
```

- The FILE SECTION of the DATA DIVISION, for example:

  a.

```
DATA DIVISION.
FILE SECTION.
FD INFILE COPY FILE-TEXT1.
FD OUTFILE COPY FILE-TEXT2.
FD MASTERF    LABEL RECORDS ARE STANDARD
              RECORD CONTAINS ...
```

  b.

```
DATA DIVISION.
FILE SECTION.
FD OUTFILE     LABEL RECORDS ARE STANDARD
               RECORD CONTAINS 78 CHARACTERS
               BLOCK CONTAINS 40 RECORDS.
01 OUTFILE-RECORD COPY RECORD-TEXT.
```

- The PROCEDURE DIVISION, for example:

```
PROCEDURE DIVISION.
100-MAIN-PARAGRAPH. COPY MAIN-PAR-TEXT.
```

There is a big difference between CALL and COPY

Be clear about the difference between the use of CALL and COPY, especially where COPY is used in the PROCEDURE DIVISION to include a paragraph or routine. When you use COPY, you are simply using an abbreviation for a section of program text that is inserted in full before the program is compiled. When you use CALL, no text is inserted. Instead, when the program is executed, at the point where a CALL statement is executed, data are passed to another program, which then executes. When that other program or subprogram has executed, it passes data back to the original calling program.

19.3
The usage clause defines a numeric identifier

Following the picture specification in the definition of a numeric identifier, you can have any of the following:

[USAGE [IS]] DISPLAY
[USAGE [IS]] COMPUTATIONAL
[USAGE [IS]] COMP
[USAGE [IS]] PACKED-DECIMAL

The use of these can improve numerical computational efficiency.

DISPLAY is the default

The default specification is USAGE IS DISPLAY. This means that, if you have no USAGE CLAUSE, then 1 byte of storage is allocated for each digit specified. Thus, PIC 999 occupies three characters or bytes of memory storage, with 1 byte for each digit. The same is true of PIC S999, although there is a sign indicator stored in a bit of the last byte; the sign does not take up a byte of storage in memory. DISPLAY has been used, by default, throughout this book.

COMPUTATIONAL or COMP specifies binary format

Specification of COMPUTATIONAL or COMP means the number is not stored as one character per digit, but in binary format. Typically, binary format is used with integers. With many computers, integers PIC 9(05) and smaller are allocated 2 bytes (15 bits for the number with 1 bit for a sign), and integers between PIC 9(6) and 9(11) are allocated 4 bytes (31 bits for the number and 1 for the sign).

In most computers, binary arithmetic is carried out more efficiently than with DISPLAY-stored numbers. It is therefore a good idea to define integers that will be used as subscripts and counters as COMP. COMP is not useful for decimal quantities involving dollars and cents, since there is a small intrinsic error associated with storing binary fractions.

You cannot print COMP identifier values. They should first be moved to edit identifiers in DISPLAY format. However, you can conveniently store COMP identifer values on disk or tape, since they take up less space.

PACKED-DECIMAL usually specifies use of half a byte per digit

This format depends very much on the computer, but typically it means that each digit is allocated half a byte of storage, and half of the right-most byte holds the sign. Unlike COMP, PACKED-DECIMAL is useful for storing decimal quantities involving dollars and cents, since there is no intrinsic error associated with the storage. And many computers can do arithmetic with packed-decimal quantities more efficiently than with DISPLAY quantities.

You cannot print packed-decimal identifier values. They should first be moved to edit identifiers in DISPLAY format. You can conveniently store packed-decimal identifier values on disk or tape, since they take up less space.

PACKED-DECIMAL is equivalent to COMPUTATIONAL-3 or COMP-3 with IBM COBOL.

19.4
STRING and UNSTRING statements manipulate character strings

S TRING AND UNSTRING are commonly employed for creating character strings, for breaking up character strings, and for editing.

The STRING statement concatenates parts of strings

The format for the STRING statement is

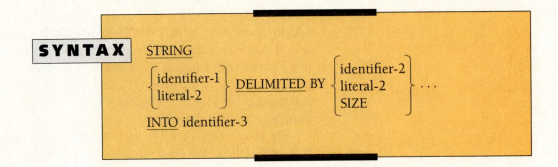

SYNTAX

STRING

$\left\{\begin{matrix} \text{identifier-1} \\ \text{literal-2} \end{matrix}\right\}$ DELIMITED BY $\left\{\begin{matrix} \text{identifier-2} \\ \text{literal-2} \\ \text{SIZE} \end{matrix}\right\}$ ...

INTO identifier-3

You can best understand the statement by examining examples of its use. For example, suppose you have the group identifier

```
01 PERSON-NAME.
    05 FIRST-NAME      PIC X(1Z).
    05 FILLER          PIC X     VALUE SPACE.
    05 MIDDLE-NAME     PIC X(12).
    05 FILLER          PIC X     VALUE SPACE.
    05 LAST-NAME       PIC X(12).
```

If FIRST-NAME, MIDDLE-NAME, and LAST-NAME have the values 'ARISTOPHANES', 'MICHELOVITCH', and 'HASSELBACHEN', then the statement DISPLAY PERSON-NAME would cause

```
ARISTOPHANES MICHELOVITCH HASSELBACHEN
```

to appear on the screen, which is fine. But if the values were 'JIM', 'FU', and 'LEE' then, DISPLAY PERSON-NAME would display

```
JIM          FU           LEE
```

which is often not acceptable—there are too many blanks. You can use the STRING statement to eliminate such unwanted blanks.

Suppose you always wanted just a single blank to appear between the values printed. If you use STRING, you will not need the FILLER entries in PERSON-NAME, so you could simply define the identifier as

```
01 PERSON-NAME.
    05 FIRST-NAME      PIC X(12).
    05 MIDDLE-NAME     PIC X(12).
    05 LAST-NAME       PIC X(12).
```

You do not print PERSON-NAME. Instead you use STRING to move the contents to any elementary non-numeric identifier large enough to hold the full 36 characters of PERSON-NAME, but with excess blanks, if any, in the values moved. The STRING statement will essentially concatenate the values in PERSON-NAME without the excess blanks. Suppose you want to move the concatenated contents of PERSON-NAME to an identifier CONCAT-NAME and display the result. You would write

```
STRING
        FIRST-NAME        DELIMITED BY ' '
        ' '               DELIMITED BY SIZE
        MIDDLE-NAME       DELIMITED BY ' '
        ' '               DELIMITED BY SIZE
        LAST-NAME         DELIMITED BY ' '
INTO CONCAT-NAME.
DISPLAY CONCAT-NAME.
```

If the two names used earlier were then printed by successive STRING and DISPLAY statements using this approach, you would get

```
ARISTOPHANES MICHELOVITCH HASSELBACHEN
JIM FU LEE
```

If you had coded

```
STRING
               FIRST-NAME             DELIMITED BY ' '
               '   '                  DELIMITED BY SIZE
               MIDDLE-NAME            DELIMITED BY
               '   '                  DELIMITED BY SIZE
               LAST-NAME              DELIMITED BY ' '
     INTO CONCAT-NAME.
     DISPLAY CONCAT-NAME.
```

repeated execution would give you

```
ARISTOPHANES   MICHELOVITCH   HASSELBACHEN
JIM   FU   LEE
```

with three spaces between values instead of one, as used previously.
      If you coded

```
STRING
               FIRST-NAME             DELIMITED BY ' '
               LAST-NAME              DELIMITED BY ' '
     INTO CONCAT-NAME.
     DISPLAY CONCAT-NAME.
```

you would get

```
ARISTOPHANESHASSELBACHEN
JIMLEE
```

If you coded

```
STRING
               FIRST-NAME             DELIMITED BY 'I'
               '   '                  DELIMITED BY SIZE
               MIDDLE-NAME            DELIMITED BY 'L'
               '   '                  DELIMITED BY SIZE
               LAST-NAME              DELIMITED BY 'E'
     INTO CONCAT-NAME.
     DISPLAY CONCAT-NAME.
```

you would get

```
AR   MICHE   HASS
J   FU   L
```

Each delimiter entry following STRING specifies a literal or the contents of an identifier (the sending field) to be moved to the concatenation (or receiving) identifier CONCAT-NAME. If you have a literal, such as 'I' after DELIMITED, the characters in the sending field that occur before 'I' are transferred, but not the 'I'. If you use ' ' after DELIMITED, the characters in the sending field before the first blank are transferred, but not the ' '.

If SIZE is specified, the entire length of the sending field is transferred to the receiving identifier. If an identifier is specified after DELIMITED (the delimiter identifier), the contents of the sending identifier or literal up to the contents of the delimiter identifier are transferred. The receiving identifier must be an elementary identifier with just a PIC X(n) or 9(n) specification.

The UNSTRING statement breaks up a string

Suppose you have an elementary identifier INPUT-NAME with the contents

```
'HARRY, PETER, SMITH'
```

And suppose you want to place these three names in each of FIRST-NAME, MIDDLE-NAME, and LAST-NAME in this group identifier:

```
01 PERSON-NAME.
   05 FIRST-NAME      PIC X(12).
   05 MIDDLE-NAME     PIC X(12).
   05 LAST-NAME       PIC X(12).
```

You clearly cannot just move INPUT-NAME to PERSON-NAME. You can, however, carry out the move using the UNSTRING statement.

```
UNSTRING INPUT-NAME
     DELIMITED BY ','
INTO FIRST-NAME MIDDLE-NAME LAST-NAME.
```

If you then executed DISPLAY PERSON-NAME, the following would appear:

```
HARRY        PETER        SMITH
```

The essential format for UNSTRING is

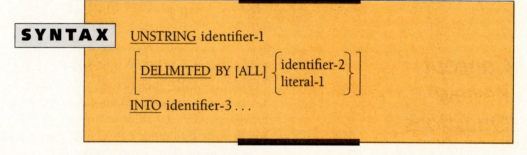

```
SYNTAX    UNSTRING identifier-1

          ⌈                     ⌠ identifier-2 ⌡ ⌉
          │ DELIMITED BY [ALL]  ⌡ literal-1    ⌠ │
          ⌊                                      ⌋

          INTO identifier-3 . . .
```

If ALL is used, any consecutive appearances of the delimiter value are treated as a single appearance. Thus, if the value of INPUT-DATA had been

```
'HARRY,,, PETER,, SMITH'
```

the statement

```
UNSTRING INPUT-NAME
     DELIMITED BY ALL ','
INTO FIRST-NAME MIDDLE-NAME LAST-NAME
```

would inhibit transmission of all of the commas. However, if you omitted the ALL with this sending data, the contents of PERSON-NAME would be

```
HARRY         ,, PETER     , SMITH
```

The contents of INPUT-NAME would probably have come from an entry at a terminal, when the statement

```
ACCEPT INPUT-NAME
```

is executed. Thus, it is often a good idea to use ALL, since a user might accidentally enter additional commas.

Summary

1. A subprogram carries out a function needed by many programs, and is written and compiled separately. It is called up by a calling program by means of a CALL statement. Identifiers with values that will match those used in the CALL statement are defined in a special LINKAGE SECTION of the DATA DIVISION of the subprogram.
2. A COPY statement can be included in the ENVIRONMENT, DATA, and PROCEDURE DIVISIONS. It causes named program text that is stored separately to be included in the program at compile time.
3. The USAGE clause with a picture clause permits selection of a data type that can improve numerical processing efficiency. You can have identifiers that hold numbers stored in display format, (DISPLAY), binary format, and packed-decimal format. DISPLAY is the default format, used throughout this book.
4. The STRING and UNSTRING verbs are used for creating, breaking up, and editing character strings.

Key Terms

subprogram   main program

Concept Review Questions

1. Distinguish between a subprogram and a calling program.
2. Explain the difference between COPY and CALL statements.
3. Explain how the value of an identifier passed to a subprogram can be changed by execution of the subprogram.
4. Explain the difference between display, packed-decimal, and binary format for numbers stored in memory in identifiers.

COBOL Language Questions

1. Code the shell of a main program that calls up a subprogram to compute the average value of numerical elements of an array.
2. Code the subprogram for question 1.
3. What would be output by

```
STRING
                FIRST-NAME            DELIMITED BY ' '
                '  '                  DELIMITED BY SIZE
                MIDDLE-NAME           DELIMITED BY ' '
                '  '                  DELIMITED BY SIZE
                LAST-NAME             DELIMITED BY ' '
INTO CONCAT-NAME.
DISPLAY CONCAT-NAME.
```

if the values in FIRST-NAME, MIDDLE-NAME, and LAST-NAME are as follows?

COMPREHENSIVE STRUCTURED COBOL

a. PETER, PAUL, SARTRE

b. TI TSE WONG

4. What are the values assigned to FIRST-NAME, MIDDLE-NAME, and LAST-NAME by

```
UNSTRING INPUT-NAME
     DELIMITED BY ALL ','
INTO FIRST-NAME MIDDLE-NAME LAST-NAME.
```

if INPUT-NAME receives these values?

a. JULIE,, JANE, DOE

b. MARY, MARY, QUITE CONTRARY

Programming Assignments

1. **A program to print scores, average, and standard deviation**
The input file contains the scores of students.

```
87ABOTT,J.P.
54ANDERSON,F.
...
```

Columns 01–02   Score, 0–99
        02–20   Name

The program outputs the file as a report.

```
              STUDENT SCORES

STUDENT NAME                    SCORE

ABOTT,J.P.                      87
ANDERSON,F.                     54
...
        AVERAGE SCORE:          67.3
        STANDARD DEVIATION:      9.5
```

The standard deviation is computed by a subprogram.

2. **A program to print scores, average, and range of scores**
The input data are the same as in Assignment 1, but the output data are

```
STUDENT NAME                    SCORE

ABOTT,J.P.                      87
ANDERSON,F                      54
...
        AVERAGE SCORE:          67.3
        RANGE OF SCORES:        62
```

The range is computed in the main program as the difference between the maximum and minimum scores. One subprogram is used to compute the maximum and another the minimum score.

20

THE REPORT WRITER FEATURE OF COBOL

OBJECTIVES

- To explain Report Writer concepts
- To show how to generate reports with programs that use the Report Writer feature

OUTLINE

*I*N CHAPTERS 7 and 10 you learned how to write programs that converted the records of a sequential file into a well-formatted report, complete with heading lines, detail lines, and the summary lines resulting from control breaks. The Report Writer feature of COBOL is an alternative method of generating such reports from an input file.

When the Report Writer is used, a COBOL program must still be written to do the processing. However, with the help of Report Writer definitions in the DATA DIVISION and Report Writer statements in the PROCEDURE DIVISION the task of writing the program is much simplified.

20.1 Report Writer concepts make sense of the details

*I*N A PROGRAM that uses the Report Writer feature, there is an additional section in the DATA DIVISION. This is called the REPORT SECTION and must follow the WORKING-STORAGE SECTION.

In the REPORT SECTION you specify the format of the overall report heading lines, page heading lines, detail lines, and each type of summary line. In addition, you specify the control-break identifier responsible for a particular summary line.

Report Writer follows a procedure for printing a report

In the PROCEDURE DIVISION, you first open the input file and output report file in the normal manner, using a COBOL OPEN statement. Then you use an INITIATE command to get the Report Writer to print the initial headings as specified in the REPORT SECTION.

After that, the input records are read one by one from the input file, using a normal COBOL READ statement. As each record is read, a GENER-

ATE command is used to get the Report Writer to take the record and print it in the format specified in the REPORT SECTION. When the Report Writer accepts a record in this way, it takes into account any necessary new page headings, page numbers, summary lines, and control breaks, before printing the record in the correct format.

When the last input record has been read and the Report Writer has been asked to print it, you use a TERMINATE statement. This statement gets the Report Writer to generate and print the final summary line. Then you close the files and stop.

The overall logic for generating a report with the Report Writer is as follows:

1. OPEN input and report files.
2. Use INITIATE to get the Report Writer to write the initial headings.
3. READ the first input record from input file.
4. PERFORM until no more input records in input file.
   a. Use GENERATE to get the Report Writer to look after printing the record and take end-of-page chores and control-break footings into proper consideration.
   b. READ the next input record.
   END-PERFORM.
5. Use TERMINATE to get Report Writer to print the final control footing.
6. CLOSE files and STOP RUN.

You can see that the Report Writer does all the work. It will handle multiple-level control breaks. For each control break, it will write the usual summary line or control footing. In addition, if required, for each control break it will write a control-break heading or control heading for the subsequent group of records. When the last record of a page has been written, before it writes the next record it will print any page footing required, plus the page headings for the next page.

However, the Report Writer cannot read your mind. It has to know the required format for each part of the report before it can deal with each record passed to it. The specifications for the format of the report, headings, control identifiers, and detail line formats must be specified in an additional section of the DATA DIVISION called the REPORT SECTION. Most of the effort in learning how to use the Report Writer involves learning how to put the proper entries in the REPORT SECTION.

An example illustrating use of Report Writer

Let us use the input file MONTHLY-SALES from Chapter 10. Recall that each record gives the monthly housing sales of a salesperson at a large real estate business that operates nationally, but each salesperson sells units in only one city. The input file is shown in Figure 20.1. In this file, the records are arranged or sorted in the order of the city field. Thus, all the records of salespeople in Albany come first, followed by Boston, and so on.

Suppose you need both detail records, as in Figure 20.2, and the total units and total volume for each city. You can see that there has to be a break

```
----------1---------2---------3---------4
         SMITH          EP0030410000ALBANY
         JONES          TY0010150000ALBANY
         GREEN          F 0152462000ALBANY
         PETERSON       PJ0000000000BOSTON
         HASSELBACH     RT0020350000BOSTON
         ...
```

Columns	
1–13	Last name of salesperson
14	First initial of salesperson
15	Second initial of salesperson
16–18	Number of units sold in month
19–25	Volume of sales for the salesperson for the month
26–40	City

Figure 20.1 Input file MONTHLY-SALES.

```
                    MONTHLY SALES REPORT
PAGE   1                                              02/09/91

         SALESPERSON        UNITS         VOLUME         CITY
                            SOLD          OF SALES

         E.P. SMITH           3        $   410,000      ALBANY
         T.Y. JONES           1        $   150,000      ALBANY
         F.   GREEN          15        $2,462,000       ALBANY

TOTALS FOR ALBANY            19        $3,022,000

         P.J. PETERSON        0        $         0      BOSTON
         R.T. HASSELBACH      2        $   350,000      BOSTON

TOTALS FOR BOSTON             2        $   350,000

         ...
         H.P. DEARING         1        $   125,000      DALLAS
         J.L. BUSH            2        $   290,000      DALLAS

PAGE   2                                              02/09/91

         SALESPERSON        UNITS         VOLUME         CITY
                            SOLD          OF SALES

         E.F. JONES           4        $   530,000      DALLAS
         T.J. JOHNSON         2        $   350,000      DALLAS
         G.H. BLACK           9        $1,246,000       DALLAS

TOTALS FOR DALLAS            18        $2,541,000

         R.U. HARDY           4        $   467,000      DENVER
         ...
```

Figure 20.2 Report generated from MONTHLY-SALES with the Report Writer, showing detail and summary lines.

in the detailed reporting, each time the city changes, to allow the printing of summary data.

The report in Figure 20.2 was generated in Chapter 10 using single-level control-break processing. The CITY-IN value from incoming records was used as a control identifier. Whenever the CITY-IN value changed, a break in the processing took place in order to print the summary line. In the program in Figure 20.3, this processing is carried out using the Report Writer.

```
IDENTIFICATION DIVISION.
PROGRAM-ID. MONTHLY2.
ENVIRONMENT DIVISION.
INPUT-OUTPUT SECTION.
FILE-CONTROL.   SELECT MONTHLY-SALES ASSIGN TO UT-S-DISK90.
                SELECT PRINTERFILE ASSIGN TO UR-S-SYSPRINT.
DATA DIVISION.
FILE SECTION.
FD   MONTHLY-SALES      LABEL RECORDS ARE STANDARD.
01   RECORD-IN.
     05 SURNAME-IN            PIC X(13).
     05 INITIAL1-IN           PIC X.
     05 INITIAL2-IN           PIC X.
     05 UNITS-IN              PIC X(03).
     05 VOLUME-IN             PIC 9(07).
     05 CITY-IN               PIC X(15).
FD   PRINTERFILE        LABEL RECORDS ARE OMITTED
                   REPORT IS SAMPLE-REPORT.
WORKING-STORAGE SECTION.
01   WS-WORK-AREAS.
     05 MORE-RECORDS          PIC X(03)       VALUE 'YES'.
     05 RUN-DATE              PIC X(08).
     05 POSSIBLE-PERIOD       PIC X(02).
REPORT SECTION.
RD   SAMPLE-REPORT
     CONTROLS ARE CITY-IN            control identifier is CITY-IN
     PAGE LIMIT IS 50 LINES          50 lines of page may be printed
     HEADING 2                       headings start on line 2
     FIRST DETAIL 8                  detail lines start on line 8
     FOOTING 50.                     no footing line beyond line 50
01   TYPE IS REPORT HEADING.
     05 LINE NUMBER IS 2.
        10 COLUMN 19          PIC X(20)       VALUE
                                              'MONTHLY SALES REPORT'.
01   TYPE IS PAGE HEADING.
     05 LINE NUMBER IS 3.
        10 COLUMN 1           PIC X(04)       VALUE 'PAGE'.
        10 COLUMN 6           PIC Z9          SOURCE PAGE-COUNTER.
        10 COLUMN 59          PIC X(08)       SOURCE RUN-DATE.
```

```cobol
        05 LINE NUMBER IS 5.
            10 COLUMN 13          PIC X(19)          VALUE 'SALESPERSON'.
            10 COLUMN 32          PIC X(13)          VALUE 'UNITS'.
            10 COLUMN 45          PIC X(14)          VALUE 'VOLUME'.
            10 COLUMN 59          PIC X(04)          VALUE 'CITY'.
        05 LINE NUMBER IS 6.
            10 COLUMN 32          PIC X(13)          VALUE 'SOLD'.
            10 COLUMN 45          PIC X(08)          VALUE 'OF SALES'.
        05 LINE NUMBER IS 7.
            10  COLUMN 1          PIC X(01)          VALUE ' '.
01 DETAIL-LINE TYPE IS DETAIL.
        05 LINE NUMBER IS PLUS 1.
            10 COLUMN 13          PIC X              SOURCE INITIAL1-IN.
            10 COLUMN 14          PIC X              VALUE '.'.
            10 COLUMN 15          PIC X              SOURCE INITIAL2-IN.
            10 COLUMN 16          PIC X(02)          SOURCE POSSIBLE-PERIOD.
            10 COLUMN 18          PIC X(14)          SOURCE SURNAME-IN.
            10 COLUMN 32          PIC Z9             SOURCE UNITS-IN.
            10 COLUMN 45          PIC $Z,ZZZ,999 SOURCE VOLUME-IN.
            10 COLUMN 59          PIC X(15)          SOURCE CITY-IN.
01 TYPE CONTROL FOOTING CITY-IN.
        05 LINE NUMBER IS PLUS 2.
            10  COLUMN 1          PIC X(11)          VALUE 'TOTALS FOR '.
            10  COLUMN 12         PIC X(15)          SOURCE CITY-IN.
            10  COLUMN 31         PIC ZZ9            SUM UNITS-IN.
            10  COLUMN 44         PIC $ZZ,ZZZ,999 SUM VOLUME-IN.
        05 LINE NUMBER IS PLUS 1.
            10  COLUMN 1          PIC X(1)           VALUE ' '.
PROCEDURE DIVISION.
100-MAIN-MODULE.
    OPEN INPUT MONTHLY-SALES,
         OUTPUT PRINTERFILE.
    MOVE CURRENT-DATE TO RUN-DATE.
    INITIATE SAMPLE-REPORT.    causes printing of initial headings
    READ MONTHLY-SALES,
            AT END MOVE 'NO' TO MORE-RECORDS.
    PERFORM 200-PROCESS-INPUT-RECORD
            UNTIL MORE-RECORDS = 'NO'.
    TERMINATE SAMPLE-REPORT.    printing of final footings
    CLOSE MONTHLY-SALES
          PRINTERFILE.
    STOP RUN.
200-PROCESS-INPUT-RECORD.
    IF INITIAL2-IN NOT EQUAL TO SPACES
        MOVE '. ' TO POSSIBLE-PERIOD
    ELSE
        MOVE SPACES TO POSSIBLE-PERIOD
    END-IF.
    GENERATE DETAIL-LINE.    printing of detail line, plus control footing and new page headings,
                            if needed
    READ MONTHLY-SALES,
        AT END MOVE 'NO' TO MORE-RECORDS.
```

Figure 20.3 *Use of the Report Writer feature to generate the report in Figure 20.2.*

This program is fairly typical. Entries and instructions relating to the Report Writer are shown in bold. The Report Writer can handle all details of constructing the report except for these two:

- A program instruction in the PROCEDURE DIVISION is used to generate the date in the identifier RUN-UNIT. The Report Writer takes the date from this identifier.
- In preparing initials for each salesperson, where there is no second initial you do not want a following period printed. The Report Writer uses the value of an identifier POSSIBLE-PERIOD to fill the space where the period should go. An IF-statement in the PROCEDURE DIVISION places a period in POSSIBLE-PERIOD if it is needed.

A more sophisticated program might, in addition

- Allow for two-level, or higher, control breaks
- Allow for a control-break heading following each control-break footing
- Suppress printing of the control field (CITY-IN) in each detail line of a group except the first
- Have an overall final summary line or lines at the end of the report

In the following sections, you will see the entries needed for the program in Figure 20.3 and for the additional, more sophisticated functions listed here.

FILE SECTION entries need an additional specification

In the INPUT-OUTPUT SECTION an output printer file, PRINTERFILE, was defined to hold the report. In the FILE SECTION, the FD entry must therefore specify that PRINTERFILE be used to hold a report generated by the Report Writer, as follows:

```
FD   PRINTERFILE    LABEL RECORDS ARE OMITTED.
                    REPORT IS SAMPLE-REPORT.
```

The name of the report is to be SAMPLE-REPORT, so as not to be confused with the name of the printer file (PRINTERFILE) that will contain it. The syntax for the entry is

SYNTAX   FD printer-file   LABEL RECORDS ARE OMITTED

$$\left\{ \begin{matrix} \underline{\text{REPORT IS}} \\ \underline{\text{REPORTS ARE}} \end{matrix} \right\} \text{report-name-1...}$$

More than one report can be generated (on the same printer file) by a single program.

20.2
Writing the REPORT SECTION definition is the major task

T HE REPORT SECTION follows the WORKING-STORAGE SEC-TION. In the REPORT SECTION each report is specified. The specification consists of a report definition entry plus a report group entry for each type of heading group, detail line, and footing group.

The RD (report definition) entry is an overall specification

The report is named in the report definition (RD) entry. To name the report SAMPLE-REPORT, you specify

```
REPORT SECTION.
RD  SAMPLE-REPORT
```

If you wanted to generate two distinct reports, REPORT-A and REPORT-B, on the printer file PRINTERFILE, you would specify

```
FILE SECTION.
...
FD  PRINTERFILE    LABEL RECORDS ARE OMITTED
                   REPORTS ARE REPORT-A, REPORT-B.
...
REPORT SECTION.
RD  REPORT-A
...
RD  REPORT-B
...
```

As part of an RD entry, you give a definition of the file in terms of

- Control fields
- Maximum size of a page
- Line number for the first heading line
- Line number for the first detail line
- Last possible line number for a footing line

For the program in Figure 20.3, these entries have been made as follows:

```
REPORT SECTION.
RD  SAMPLE-REPORT
    CONTROLS ARE CITY-IN        control-break identifier is CITY-IN
    PAGE LIMIT IS 50 LINES      50 lines of page may be printed
    HEADING 2                   headings start on line 2
    FIRST DETAIL 8              detail lines start on line 8
    FOOTING 50                  no footing line beyond line 50
```

The syntax for these entries is

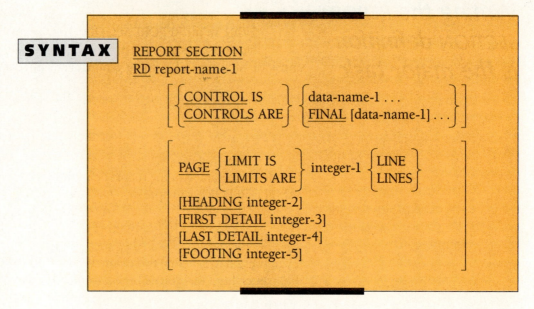

SYNTAX

REPORT SECTION
RD report-name-1

$$\left[\left\{ \begin{array}{l} \underline{\text{CONTROL IS}} \\ \underline{\text{CONTROLS ARE}} \end{array} \right\} \left\{ \begin{array}{l} \text{data-name-1} \ldots \\ \underline{\text{FINAL}} \text{ [data-name-1]} \ldots \end{array} \right\} \right]$$

$$\left[\begin{array}{l} \underline{\text{PAGE}} \left\{ \begin{array}{l} \underline{\text{LIMIT IS}} \\ \underline{\text{LIMITS ARE}} \end{array} \right\} \text{integer-1} \left\{ \begin{array}{l} \underline{\text{LINE}} \\ \underline{\text{LINES}} \end{array} \right\} \\ \text{[}\underline{\text{HEADING}}\text{ integer-2]} \\ \text{[}\underline{\text{FIRST DETAIL}}\text{ integer-3]} \\ \text{[}\underline{\text{LAST DETAIL}}\text{ integer-4]} \\ \text{[}\underline{\text{FOOTING}}\text{ integer-5]} \end{array} \right]$$

Let us look at these entries in turn.

The CONTROL entry specifies the control-break fields. The major control-break field comes first.

```
CONTROLS ARE MAJOR-FIELD, MINOR-FIELD
```

The entry CONTROL IS FIELD-A gives you a single control field, FIELD-A. The word FINAL counts as a special control field. If used, it comes first and is the major control-break field. Thus

```
CONTROLS ARE FINAL, CITY-IN
```

means that CITY-IN is the control-break field, but, in addition, FINAL means there will be a special control break when the last record has been printed, perhaps for printing a summary line for the entire file.

The other entries have the following meanings:

- PAGE LIMIT IS 50 means 50 lines can print on a page.
- HEADING 2 means the first heading line to be printed will be on line 2.
- FIRST DETAIL 8 means the first detail line of the entire file will print on line 8.
- LAST DETAIL 48 means no detail line may print beyond line 48 (not used much).
- FOOTING 50 means the last line on which a footing line can print is line 50. (There may be several lines in a single footing.)

Headings, detail lines, and footings are specified in report groups

Following the FD entries, you enter a sequence of report groups. The possible types of report group entries are listed here.

- A single report group that defines a report heading (one or more lines to be printed). It begins with the specification

01 [dataname-1] TYPE IS REPORT HEADING

- A single report group that defines a page heading (one or more lines to be printed). It begins with the specification

01 [dataname-1] TYPE IS PAGE HEADING

- A single report group that defines one or more detail lines that are printed from an input record. It begins with the specification.

01 [dataname-1] TYPE IS DETAIL

Dataname-1 is used here, since you have to refer to this report group in the PROCEDURE DIVISION to have it printed. Thus, in the program in Figure 20.3 there is

```
01 DETAIL-LINE TYPE IS DETAIL.
   ...
PROCEDURE DIVISION.
   ...
      GENERATE DETAIL-LINE.
```

- If needed, one or more report groups, each defining a control footing (one or more lines to be printed per control footing). It begins with the specification

01 [dataname-1] TYPE IS CONTROL FOOTING $\left\{ \begin{array}{l} \text{dataname-2} \\ \underline{\text{FINAL}} \end{array} \right\}$

Dataname-2 specifies the control-break field that triggers this control footing. FINAL means this footing comes only at the end of the file

- If needed, a report group that defines a control heading (one or more lines to be printed). It begins with the specification

01 [dataname-1] TYPE IS CONTROL HEADING $\left\{ \begin{array}{l} \text{dataname-2} \\ \underline{\text{FINAL}} \end{array} \right\}$

No control heading was used in the report in Figure 20.2. If one had been used, it would have followed each control footing, as in

```
   ...
   T.Y. JONES           1           $  150,000    ALBANY
   F.   GREEN          15           $2,462,000    ALBANY

TOTALS FOR ALBANY      19           $ 3,022,000

                 CITY OF BOSTON          control heading

   P.J. PETERSON        0           $        0    BOSTON
   R.T. HASSELBACH      2           $  350,000    BOSTON
```

- If needed, a report group that defines a footing for each new page (one or more lines to be printed). It begins with the specification

01 [dataname-1] TYPE IS PAGE FOOTING

- If needed, a report group that defines a footing for the end of the report (one or more lines to be printed). It begins with the specification

01 [dataname-1] TYPE IS REPORT FOOTING

Some of these types of entries are shown in bold in the following excerpt from the program in Figure 20.3.

```
REPORT SECTION.
RD   SAMPLE-REPORT
     CONTROLS ARE CITY-IN              control identifier is CITY-IN
     PAGE LIMIT IS 50 LINES            50 lines of page may be printed
     HEADING 2                         headings start on line 2
     FIRST DETAIL 8                    detail lines start on line 8
     FOOTING 50                        no footing line beyond line 50
01   TYPE IS REPORT HEADING.
     05 LINE NUMBER IS 2.
        10 COLUMN 19    PIC X(20)                VALUE IS
                                                 'MONTHLY SALES REPORT'.

01   TYPE IS PAGE HEADING.
     05 LINE NUMBER IS 3.
        10 COLUMN 1     PIC X(4)                 VALUE 'PAGE'.
        10 COLUMN 6     PIC Z9                    SOURCE PAGE-COUNTER.
        10 COLUMN 59    PIC X(8)                  SOURCE RUN-DATE.
     05 LINE NUMBER IS 5.
        10 COLUMN 13    PIC X(19)                 VALUE 'SALESPERSON'.
        10 COLUMN 32    PIC X(13)                 VALUE 'UNITS'.
        10 COLUMN 45    PIC X(14)                 VALUE 'VOLUME'.
        10 COLUMN 59    PIC X(4)                  VALUE 'CITY'.
     05 LINE NUMBER IS 6.
        10 COLUMN 32    PIC X(13)                 VALUE 'SOLD'.
        10 COLUMN 45    PIC X(8)                  VALUE 'OF SALES'.
     05 LINE NUMBER IS 7.
        10  COLUMN 1    PIC X(1)                  VALUE ' '.
01 DETAIL-LINE TYPE IS DETAIL.
     05 LINE NUMBER IS PLUS 1.
        10 COLUMN 13    PIC X                     SOURCE INITIAL1-IN.
        10 COLUMN 14    PIC X                     VALUE '.'.
        10 COLUMN 15    PIC X                     SOURCE INITIAL2-IN.
        10 COLUMN 16    PIC XX                    SOURCE POSSIBLE-PERIOD.
        10 COLUMN 18    PIC X(14)                 SOURCE SURNAME-IN.
        10 COLUMN 32    PIC Z9                    SOURCE UNITS-IN.
        10 COLUMN 45    PIC $9,999,999            SOURCE VOLUME-IN.
        10 COLUMN 59    PIC X(15)                 SOURCE CITY-IN.
01 TYPE CONTROL FOOTING CITY-IN.
     05 LINE NUMBER IS PLUS 2.
        10  COLUMN 1    PIC X(11)                 VALUE 'TOTALS FOR '.
        10  COLUMN 12   PIC X(15)                 SOURCE CITY-IN.
        10  COLUMN 31   PIC ZZ9                   SUM UNITS-IN.
        10  COLUMN 44   PIC $99,999,999           SUM VOLUME-IN.
     05 LINE NUMBER IS PLUS 1.
        10  COLUMN 1    PIC X(1)                  VALUE ' '.
```

You can only have one report group entry for a report heading, a page heading, a detail line (or group of detail lines), a page footing, and a report footing. However, each report group entry can specify more than one line to be printed.

LINE NUMBER entries specify where lines are to be printed on a page

With each report group entry for specifying heading lines, detail lines, or footing lines, there must be a specification of the line or lines to be printed for the group. Consider the preceding report group entry for page headings. This entry specifies that five lines be printed for the page heading group (with the last two as blank lines). The specification for each line to be printed in any group is a 05 entry containing the line number.

```
01    TYPE IS PAGE HEADING.
      05 LINE NUMBER IS 3.
         10 ..
         ...
      05 LINE NUMBER IS 5.
         10 ...
         ...
      05 LINE NUMBER IS 6.
         10 ...
      05 LINE NUMBER IS 7.
         10 ...
```

The line number is counted from the top of the page, so the first line of the page heading appears on line 3, and the third on line 6. In the program in Figure 20.3, the page heading being specified will print as

```
PAGE 01                                          02/09/91


SALESPERSON          UNITS          VOLUME          CITY
                     SOLD           OF SALES
```

blank

Actually, five lines are printed if you count the second blank line. It helps to know that a reserved identifier called LINE-COUNTER is used internally by the Report Writer to count lines. As the report is actually being printed, the LINE-NUMBER specification forces the Report Writer to set its LINE-COUNTER identifier to the value specified before printing the group. The essential syntax for the LINE NUMBER entry is

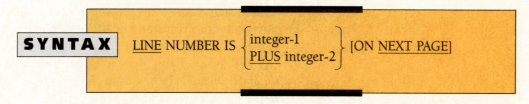

SYNTAX LINE NUMBER IS { integer-1 / PLUS integer-2 } [ON NEXT PAGE]

The LINE NUMBER clause is optional, but is normally included. There are essentially two options. If you use integer-1 you specify a specific line.

If you specify PLUS integer-2 you specify a relative line number. Thus, with the entry

```
01 TYPE CONTROL FOOTING CITY-IN.
   05 LINE NUMBER IS PLUS 2.
```

you have specified that the first line of the control-break footing is to be printed on the second line after the position contained by an internal REPORT-WRITER identifier, called LINE-COUNTER, when it has finished with any previous group.

The NEXT PAGE clause enables you to specify printing on a specific line of the next page.

The COLUMN entries specify the position of fields on a line to be printed

A column entry (level 10) is needed for each item to be printed. The column entries for the first line of the heading

```
01    TYPE IS PAGE HEADING.
      05 LINE NUMBER IS 3.
         10 COLUMN 1     PIC X(4)    VALUE 'PAGE'.
         10 COLUMN 6     PIC Z9      SOURCE PAGE-COUNTER.
         10 COLUMN 59    PIC X(8)    SOURCE RUN-DATE.
```

are specified by giving the column number where the first character of the field is to print. The 'PAGE' value is to print beginning at column 1 of the line. The page number is to print beginning at column 6 of the line, and so on. The length of each field to be printed is given by a PIC specification in the same manner as in the specification of a COBOL group identifier.

If the value to be printed is a literal, its value is specified by a VALUE clause. Thus the literal 'PAGE' is to be printed in the first five spaces of the line. If the value is that of an identifier from the program (specified in the WORKING-STORAGE SECTION or buffer record), instead of using a VALUE clause you specify SOURCE, followed by the identifier. Thus, the date to be printed at column 59 has its source in the identifier RUN-DATE. The program must put the date into RUN-DATE.

The page number value is looked after automatically by the Report Writer; it always maintains the current page number in a special reserved identifier called PAGE-COUNTER. Thus the value to be printed at column 6 has its source in this special identifier PAGE-COUNTER.

When specifying a detail line to be printed, the source identifiers are normally the fields from the input buffer record. Before the Report Writer is asked in the PROCEDURE DIVISION to print a detail record (with a GENERATE statement), a new record has to be read from the input file by the program (with a conventional READ statement), and placed in the input buffer record.

As well as specifying the source of values to be printed by means of VALUE and SOURCE clauses, as in the page heading entry, you can specify a value as a sum of record fields using the SUM clause. The SUM clause is used in specifying a CONTROL FOOTING.

```
01 TYPE CONTROL FOOTING CITY-IN.
     05 LINE NUMBER IS PLUS 2.
          10   COLUMN 1      PIC X(11)        VALUE 'TOTALS FOR '.
          10   COLUMN 12     PIC X(15)        SOURCE CITY-
          10   COLUMN 31     PIC ZZ9          SUM UNITS-IN.
          10   COLUMN 44     PIC $99,999,999  SUM VOLUME-IN.
```

This specifies that you want the value printed in column 31 of each control footing to be the sum of the UNITS-IN values for the records with the same current control identifier (CITY-IN) value. You also want the sum of the VOLUME-IN values to be printed at column 44.

The full syntax for the SUM clause is:

SYNTAX   SUM identifier-1 ... RESET ON $\left\{ \begin{array}{l} \text{data-name-2} \\ \underline{\text{FINAL}} \end{array} \right\}$

If there is no RESET clause, the SUM counter is set to zero as soon as a value is printed. However, if you had an entry

```
     10 COLUMN  30  PIC 9(6) SUM QTY-IN RESET ON STATE.
```

it would mean that even after the SUM counter was printed, it would not be reset to zero (and would continue to grow as each record was printed) until the identifier STATE value changed. STATE would normally be a higher-level control identifier. You would use this feature if you wanted the SUM-QTY-IN value to be printed for the higher-level control break as well.

Understand that if you use RESET (which really means "do not reset until") you will get ever-growing totals when printing the lower-level control footing for which RESET is specified. Thus, if you used RESET ON FINAL in the program in Figure 20.3, as follows

```
01 TYPE CONTROL FOOTING CITY-IN.
...
     10   COLUMN 32      PIC ZZ9 SUM UNITS-IN RESET ON FINAL.
     10   COLUMN 46      PIC $ZZ,ZZZ,999 SUM VOLUME-IN RESET ON FINAL.
```

then you would get ever-growing cumulative totals on each footing, so that the last footing would have the sums for the entire file.

The NEXT GROUP clause sets the line counter ahead

When control footings are to be printed, you normally cannot predict where they will be printed on the page. However, you can use a relative line spacing specification, such as

```
     05 LINE NUMBER IS PLUS 2.
```

which means that the first line of the footing will be two lines ahead of the previous line. In this way, you have specified that a line be skipped.

Now suppose you want to specify that a further line be skipped between the last line of this footing and the first following detail line. However, you may have specified for the detail line

```
01   DETAIL-LINE TYPE IS DETAIL.
     05 LINE NUMBER IS PLUS 1.
```

because you want detail lines to be printed on the next line after the page heading lines are printed and also immediately after each other. But this specification will also cause a detail line to be printed on the next line after the last line of the control-break group. You have two alternatives to avoid being trapped like this. One is to include a blank line in the control-break group, as was done in the program.

```
01 TYPE CONTROL FOOTING CITY-IN.
     05 LINE NUMBER IS PLUS 2.
        10   COLUMN 1      PIC X(11)      VALUE 'TOTALS FOR '.
        10   COLUMN 12     PIC X(15)      SOURCE CITY-IN.
        10   COLUMN 31     PIC ZZ9        SUM UNITS-IN.
        10   COLUMN 44     PIC $99,999,999 SUM VOLUME-IN.
     05 LINE NUMBER IS PLUS 1.
        10   COLUMN 1      PIC X(1) VALUE ' '.
```

This control-break footing consists of two lines, the second being blank. The alternative is to use the NEXT GROUP clause, as follows:

```
01 TYPE CONTROL FOOTING CITY-IN.
     05 LINE NUMBER IS PLUS 2 NEXT GROUP PLUS 1.
        10   COLUMN 1      PIC X(11)      VALUE 'TOTALS FOR '.
        10   COLUMN 12     PIC X(15)      SOURCE CITY-IN.
        10   COLUMN 31     PIC ZZ9        SUM UNITS-IN.
        10   COLUMN 44     PIC $99,999,999 SUM VOLUME-IN.
```

The NEXT GROUP clause will set the internal LINE-COUNTER of the Report Writer ahead by one when the last line of the group has been printed. Thus, if the next group to be printed is a DETAIL group with the specification

```
01   DETAIL-LINE TYPE IS DETAIL.
     05 LINE NUMBER IS PLUS 1.
```

the PLUS 1 specification for that group will also increment LINE-COUNTER, and so a line is skipped.

Recall that in the program it was specified that one line be blank at the end of each printing of the page headings. This was done by specifying a blank line. Alternatively, the NEXT GROUP clause could have been used as follows:

```
01   TYPE IS PAGE HEADING.
     05 LINE NUMBER IS 3.
     ...
     05 LINE NUMBER IS 5.
     ...
     05 LINE NUMBER IS 6 NEXT GROUP PLUS 1.
        10 COLUMN 32    PIC X(13)  VALUE 'SOLD'.
        10 COLUMN 45    PIC X(8)   VALUE 'OF SALES'.
```

This indicates that one line must be skipped before the next group (a detail line) can be printed.

The complete syntax for the NEXT GROUP clause is

SYNTAX

$$\text{NEXT GROUP IS} \left\{ \begin{array}{l} \text{integer-1} \\ \underline{\text{PLUS}}\ \text{integer-2} \\ \underline{\text{NEXT PAGE}} \end{array} \right\}$$

Thus, you can use NEXT GROUP to have LINE-COUNTER set to a specific value, increased by integer-2, or even set to a new page, *following* printing of a group. Note that if you use NEXT PAGE, the next group printed will automatically be the page heading group, and it will be printed at the top of the page.

Use GROUP INDICATE to suppress repeated printing of a control identifier

Often, you will want the value of the control identifier printed in only the first record of the group that shares the control identifier value. The GROUP INDICATE clause is used to specify such suppression of printing a field value.

For example, if you use the GROUP INDICATE clause with the specification for the detail line field equal to the CITY-IN value, this value will be printed only in the first line in which it occurs.

```
01 DETAIL-LINE TYPE IS DETAIL.
   05 LINE NUMBER IS PLUS 1.
      10 COLUMN 13    PIC X          SOURCE INITIAL1-IN.
      10 COLUMN 14    PIC X          VALUE '.'.
      10 COLUMN 15    PIC X          SOURCE INITIAL2-IN.
      10 COLUMN 16    PIC XX         SOURCE POSSIBLE-PERIOD.
      10 COLUMN 18    PIC X(14)      SOURCE SURNAME-IN.
      10 COLUMN 32    PIC Z9         SOURCE UNITS-IN.
      10 COLUMN 45    PIC $9,999,999 SOURCE VOLUME-IN.
      10 COLUMN 59    PIC X(15)      SOURCE CITY-IN GROUP INDICATE.
```

Thus, the detail lines printed would appear as

SALESPERSON	UNITS SOLD	VOLUME OF SALES	CITY
E.P. SMITH	3	$ 410,000	ALBANY
T.Y. JONES	1	$ 150,000	
F. GREEN	15	$2,462,000	
TOTALS FOR ALBANY	19	$ 3,022,000	
P.J. PETERSON	0	$ 0	BOSTON
R.T. HASSELBACH	2	$ 350,000	
TOTALS FOR BOSTON	2	$ 350,000	

The city values ALBANY and BOSTON each appear in only one detail line. GROUP INDICATOR can be used with any field, not just control identifiers.

20.3 PROCEDURE DIVISION statements are few with Report Writer

THERE ARE ONLY three simple statements to be used with the Report Writer. These are INITIATE, GENERATE, and TERMINATE.

The INITIATE statement gets headings printed

When you have opened the input file and extracted the date (if needed), execution of INITIATE causes initial headings to be printed. The syntax is

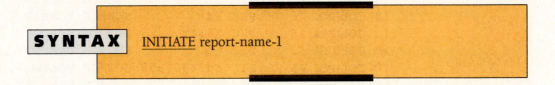

SYNTAX   INITIATE report-name-1

The GENERATE statement causes a detail line to be printed

Following reading of each record from the input file, the execution of a GENERATE statement typically causes a detail line to be printed. In addition to printing a detail line, if appropriate, the Report Writer will print control footings, control headings, and page footings. The statement in the program in Figure 20.3 was

```
GENERATE DETAIL-LINE.
```

where DETAIL-LINE is the name of the DETAIL group. GENERATE is typically placed in a paragraph that is executed repeatedly until there are no more input records.

An alternative is to specify the name of the report, as in

GENERATE SAMPLE-REPORT.

In that case, printing of detail lines is suppressed, but all other lines, including control-break lines, are printed. Thus, you get a pure summary report.

The syntax for GENERATE is

SYNTAX GENERATE $\begin{Bmatrix} \text{data-name-1} \\ \text{report-name-1} \end{Bmatrix}$

The TERMINATE statement prints final footings

The TERMINATE statement is executed after the last detail line has been generated. This causes the final footings to be printed. The syntax is

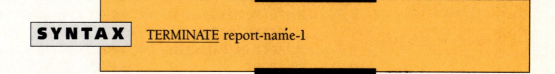

SYNTAX TERMINATE report-name-1

Summary

1. The Report Writer feature of COBOL simplifies the task of printing a report from an input file. In a program that uses the Report Writer feature, there is an additional section in the DATA DIVISION called the REPORT SECTION.

2. In the REPORT SECTION, you specify the format of the overall report heading lines, page heading lines, detail line, and each type of summary line. In addition, you specify the particular control-break identifier responsible for a particular summary line.

3. In the PROCEDURE DIVISION you first open the input file and
    output report file in the normal manner, using a COBOL OPEN
    statement. Then you use an INITIATE command to get the Report
    Writer to print the initial headings as specified in the REPORT SEC-
    TION. Then the input records are read using normal COBOL READ
    statements. A GENERATE command is used to get the Report Writer
    to take the current input record and print it in the format specified
    in the REPORT SECTION. When the last input record has printed,
    you finally use a TERMINATE statement to get the Report Writer to
    generate and print the final summary line.

Programming Assignments

1. **Single-level control-break processing (sorted input file)**
    The input file describes U.S. companies.

```
---------1---------2---------3---------4---------5
BOEING                47720+1734AEROSPACE
GENCORP               05134+0044AEROSPACE
GENERAL DYNAMICS      24872+1124AEROSPACE
LOCKHEED              30124+1043AEROSPACE
MARTIN MARIETTA       14557+0247AEROSPACE
MCDONNELL DOUGLAS     43440+1479AEROSPACE
NORTHROP              18236-0861AEROSPACE
CHRYSLER              84573+4325AUTOMOTIVE
FORD MOTOR            24915+1156AUTOMOTIVE
GENERAL MOTORS        27893+1396AUTOMOTIVE
AMERICAN CYNAMID      12046+0627CHEMICALS
DU PONT               84710+5000CHEMICALS
ENGELHARD             06951+0193CHEMICALS
FUQUA INDUSTRIES      02337-0148CONGLOMERATE
PENN CENTRAL          04686+0193CONGLOMERATE
TENNECO               35899-1684CONGLOMERATE
ADVANCED MICRO        02481-0341SEMICONDUCTORS
INTEL                 07864+0834SEMICONDUCTORS
NATIONAL SEMI         07067-0267SEMICONDUCTORS
```

    Columns 01–21   Company name
            22–26   Quarterly revenue ($ millions, last digit
                       fractional)
            27–31   Quarterly profits ($ millions, last digit
                       fractional)
            32–50   Industry sector

    The output data will look like this:

```
----------1---------2---------3---------4---------5---------6---------7
                    U.S. INDUSTRY QUARTERLY RESULTS
PAGE  01                                                    05/06/91


        COMPANY                REVENUE            PROFITS        SECTOR


        BOEING                $4,772.0           $173.4         AEROSPACE
        GENCORP               $  513.4           $  4.4         AEROSPACE
        GENERAL DYNAMICS      $2,487.2           $112.4         AEROSPACE
        ...
        NORTHROP              $1,823.6           $ 86.1(loss)   AEROSPACE
TOTALS FOR AEROSPACE    $?,???,???.?       $??,???.?(????)


        CHRYSLER              $8,457.3           $432.5         AUTOMOTIVE
        ...
```

Assume that the normal number of lines available for headers and detail lines is 14 (in order to have multiple pages with limited data).

a. Write a Report Writer program to generate the report.

2. **Single-level control-break processing (unsorted input file)**
The records of the input file describe ship cargoes:

```
----------1---------2---------3---------4---------5
        ARROWHEAD           OIL         050002040
        ASTONHEAD           WHEAT       143500322
        BULKFELLOW          IRON ORE    022603547
        CRANSTON            COPPER      045607289
        DEVONSHIRE          OIL         256002572
        DOVEBIRD            WHEAT       189700754
        DUSTY               IRON ORE    007563798
        EVERYMAN            WHEAT       089670321
        FORWARDBOUNTY       COPPER      007857382
        FUNNELHEAD          OIL         200002176
        GOODWILL            OIL         150002174
        GOVERNOR            WHEAT       045200376
        GULLLAKE            OIL         150002019
        HALIFAXGULL         OIL         010002260
        HEAVYSIDE           IRON ORE    006003422
        HOODDOWN            COPPER      067007598
        IVANHOE             IRON ORE    065003542
        KARLSTAD            COPPER      002407486
        KINGSTON            OIL         195002056
        KUNGHU              WHEAT       200540342
```

         Columns 01–20   Ship name
                 21–30   Cargo type
                 31–35   Units of cargo (tons, bushels, etc.)
                 36–39   Cost per unit (cents in last two digits)

The output shows the data sorted in ascending cargo order, with summaries for each type of cargo.

```
---------1---------2---------3---------4---------5---------6---------7
                    SHIPPING DATA BY CARGO
PAGE   1                                                06/05/92


          SHIPMENTS OF COPPER

     SHIP NAME              UNITS         COST PER      CARGO
                           ON BOARD       UNIT          VALUE

     CRANSTON              4,560          $72.89        $   332,378
     FORWARDBOUNTY           785          $73.82        $   ?
     HOODDOWN             6,700          $75.98        $   ?
     KARLSTAD               240          $74.86        $   ?

TOTAL SHIPMENT          ??,???,???                     $??,???,???

          SHIPMENTS OF IRON ORE


     SHIP NAME              UNITS         COST PER      CARGO
                           ON BOARD       UNIT          VALUE

     BULKFELLOW           2,260          $35.47        $   ?
     ...
```

a. Write a Report Writer program to generate the report.

3. **Printing a report**

Use the Report Writer and two-level control breaks to print the report in Figure 10.10b.

APPENDIX 1
COBOL
LANGUAGE
FORMATS
(COBOL 74
and COBOL 85)

The complete language formats of American National Standard COBOL are given here. Because the formats are complete, they have not all been covered in the text. The formats actually allow for commas, but these have been omitted here, since commas are generally regarded as a source of error. The shaded parts of the formats are for COBOL 85 only.

Note that in COBOL 74, the ENVIRONMENT DIVISION, the CONFIGURATION SECTION, and the INPUT-OUTPUT SECTION are required.

General Format for the IDENTIFICATION DIVISION

IDENTIFICATION DIVISION.

PROGRAM-ID.   program-name $\left[\text{IS} \left\{ \begin{array}{l} \underline{\text{COMMON}} \\ \underline{\text{INITIAL}} \end{array} \right\} \text{PROGRAM} \right]$.

[AUTHOR.   [comment-entry] . . .]

[INSTALLATION.   [comment-entry] . . .]

[DATE-WRITTEN.   [comment-entry] . . .]

[DATE-COMPILED.   [comment-entry] . . .]

[SECURITY.   [comment-entry] . . .]

General Format for the ENVIRONMENT DIVISION

[ENVIRONMENT DIVISION.

[CONFIGURATION SECTION.

[SOURCE-COMPUTER. [computer-name [WITH DEBUGGING MODE].]]

[OBJECT-COMPUTER. [computer-name [PROGRAM COLLATING SEQUENCE IS alphabet-name-1]

      [SEGMENT-LIMIT IS segment-number].]]

[SPECIAL-NAMES. [[implementor-name-1

$$
\left\{
\begin{array}{l}
\text{IS mnemonic-name-1 [\underline{ON} STATUS IS condition-name-1} \\
\qquad\qquad\qquad\text{[\underline{OFF} STATUS IS condition-name-2]]} \\
\text{IS mnemonic-name-2 [\underline{OFF} STATUS IS condition-name-2} \\
\qquad\qquad\qquad\text{[\underline{ON} STATUS IS condition-name-1]]} \\
\text{\underline{ON} STATUS IS condition-name-1 [\underline{OFF} STATUS IS condition-name-2]} \\
\text{\underline{OFF} STATUS IS condition-name-2 [\underline{ON} STATUS IS condition-name-1]}
\end{array}
\right\}
$$

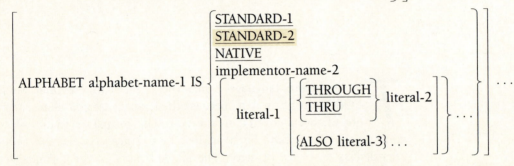

$$
\left[\text{ALPHABET alphabet-name-1 IS}
\left\{
\begin{array}{l}
\underline{\text{STANDARD-1}} \\
\underline{\text{STANDARD-2}} \\
\underline{\text{NATIVE}} \\
\text{implementor-name-2} \\
\left\{ \text{literal-1} \left[\left\{ \begin{array}{l} \underline{\text{THROUGH}} \\ \underline{\text{THRU}} \end{array} \right\} \text{literal-2} \right] \dots \right. \\
\qquad\qquad \{\underline{\text{ALSO}} \text{ literal-3}\} \dots
\end{array}
\right\} \dots
\right] \dots
$$

$$
\left[\underline{\text{SYMBOLIC}} \text{ CHARACTERS}
\left\{
\left\{ \text{symbolic character-1} \right\} \dots
\left\{ \begin{array}{l} \text{IS} \\ \text{ARE} \end{array} \right\}
\{\text{integer-1}\} \dots
\right. \right.
$$

$$
\left. \left. [\underline{\text{IN}} \text{ alphabet-name-2}] \right\} \dots \right]
$$

$$
\left[\underline{\text{CLASS}} \text{ class-name- IS}
\left\{ \text{literal-4} \left[\left\{ \begin{array}{l} \underline{\text{THROUGH}} \\ \underline{\text{THRU}} \end{array} \right\} \text{literal-5} \right] \right\} \dots \right] \dots
$$

[CURRENCY SIGN IS literal-6]

[DECIMAL-POINT IS COMMA].]]]

[INPUT-OUTPUT SECTION.

FILE-CONTROL.

    {file-control-entry} . . .

[I-O-CONTROL.

$$
\left[\left[\underline{\text{SAME}} \left[\begin{array}{l} \underline{\text{RECORD}} \\ \underline{\text{SORT}} \\ \underline{\text{SORT-MERGE}} \end{array} \right] \text{AREA FOR file-name-1 \{file-name-2\} . . .} \right] \dots \right.
$$

    [MULTIPLE FILE TAPE CONTAINS {file-name-3 [POSITION integer-1]} . . .] . . . .]]]]

Sequential File

SELECT [OPTIONAL] file-name-1

ASSIGN TO $\left\{ \begin{array}{l} \text{implementor-name-1} \\ \text{literal-1} \end{array} \right\}$ . . .

$\left[\text{RESERVE integer-1} \left[\begin{array}{l} \text{AREA} \\ \text{AREAS} \end{array} \right] \right]$

[[ORGANIZATION IS] SEQUENTIAL]

$\left[\text{PADDING CHARACTER IS} \left\{ \begin{array}{l} \text{data-name-1} \\ \text{literal-2} \end{array} \right\} \right] \left[\text{RECORD DELIMITER IS} \left\{ \begin{array}{l} \text{STANDARD-1} \\ \text{implementor-name-2} \end{array} \right\} \right]$

[ACCESS MODE IS SEQUENTIAL]

[FILE STATUS IS data-name-2].

Relative File

SELECT [OPTIONAL] file-name-1

ASSIGN TO $\left\{ \begin{array}{l} \text{implementor-name-1} \\ \text{literal-1} \end{array} \right\}$ . . .

$\left[\text{RESERVE integer-1} \left[\begin{array}{l} \text{AREA} \\ \text{AREAS} \end{array} \right] \right]$

[ORGANIZATION IS] RELATIVE

$\left[\text{ACCESS MODE IS} \left\{ \begin{array}{l} \text{SEQUENTIAL [RELATIVE KEY IS data-name-1]} \\ \left\{ \begin{array}{l} \text{RANDOM} \\ \text{DYNAMIC} \end{array} \right\} \text{RELATIVE KEY IS data-name-1} \end{array} \right\} \right]$

[FILE STATUS IS data-name-2].

Indexed File

SELECT [OPTIONAL] file-name-1

ASSIGN TO $\left\{ \begin{array}{l} \text{implementor-name-1} \\ \text{literal-1} \end{array} \right\}$ . . .

$\left[\text{RESERVE integer-1} \left[\begin{array}{l} \text{AREA} \\ \text{AREAS} \end{array} \right] \right]$

[ORGANIZATION IS] INDEXED

$$\left[\underline{ACCESS} \text{ MODE IS} \left\{ \begin{array}{l} \underline{SEQUENTIAL} \\ \underline{RANDOM} \\ \underline{DYNAMIC} \end{array} \right\} \right]$$

RECORD KEY IS data-name-1

[ALTERNATE RECORD KEY IS data-name-2 [WITH DUPLICATES]] . . .

[FILE STATUS IS data-name-3].

Sort or Merge File

SELECT file-name-1 ASSIGN TO $\left\{ \begin{array}{l} \text{implementor-name-1} \\ \text{literal-1} \end{array} \right\}$ . . .

Report File

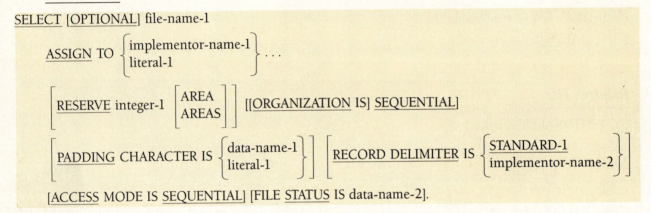

SELECT [OPTIONAL] file-name-1

ASSIGN TO $\left\{ \begin{array}{l} \text{implementor-name-1} \\ \text{literal-1} \end{array} \right\}$ . . .

$\left[\underline{RESERVE} \text{ integer-1} \left[\begin{array}{l} \text{AREA} \\ \text{AREAS} \end{array} \right] \right]$ [[ORGANIZATION IS] SEQUENTIAL]

$\left[\underline{PADDING} \text{ CHARACTER IS} \left\{ \begin{array}{l} \text{data-name-1} \\ \text{literal-1} \end{array} \right\} \right]$ $\left[\text{RECORD DELIMITER IS} \left\{ \begin{array}{l} \underline{STANDARD-1} \\ \text{implementor-name-2} \end{array} \right\} \right]$

[ACCESS MODE IS SEQUENTIAL] [FILE STATUS IS data-name-2].

General Format for the DATA DIVISION

[DATA DIVISION.

[FILE SECTION.

[file-description-entry

{file-description-entry} . . .] . . .

[sort-merge-file-description-entry

{record-description-entry} . . .] . . .

[report-file-description-entry] . . .]

[WORKING-STORAGE SECTION.

$\left[\begin{array}{l} \text{77-level-description-entry} \\ \text{record-description-entry} \end{array} \right]$ . . .

[LINKAGE SECTION.

$$\left[\begin{array}{l} \text{77-level-description-entry} \\ \text{record-description-entry} \end{array}\right] \ldots$$

[COMMUNICATION SECTION.

[communication-description-entry

[record-description-entry] ...] ...]

[REPORT SECTION.

report-description-entry

{report-group-description-entry} ...] ...]]

General Format for File Description Entry

Sequential File

FD file-name-1

    [IS <u>EXTERNAL</u>] [IS <u>GLOBAL</u>]

$$\left[\underline{\text{BLOCK}} \text{ CONTAINS [integer-1 }\underline{\text{TO}}\text{] integer-2} \left\{\begin{array}{l} \text{RECORDS} \\ \text{CHARACTERS} \end{array}\right\}\right]$$

$$\left[\underline{\text{RECORD}} \left\{\begin{array}{l} \text{CONTAINS integer-3 CHARACTERS} \\ \text{IS }\underline{\text{VARYING}}\text{ IN SIZE [[FROM integer-4] [}\underline{\text{TO}}\text{ integer-5] CHARACTERS]} \\ \quad\quad\text{[}\underline{\text{DEPENDING}}\text{ ON data-name-1]} \\ \text{CONTAINS integer-6 }\underline{\text{TO}}\text{ integer-7 CHARACTERS} \end{array}\right\}\right]$$

$$\left[\underline{\text{LABEL}} \left\{\begin{array}{l} \underline{\text{RECORD}}\text{ IS} \\ \underline{\text{RECORDS}}\text{ ARE} \end{array}\right\} \left\{\begin{array}{l} \underline{\text{STANDARD}} \\ \underline{\text{OMITTED}} \end{array}\right\}\right]$$

$$\left[\underline{\text{VALUE OF}} \left\{\text{implmentor-name-1 IS} \left\{\begin{array}{l} \text{data-name-2} \\ \text{literal-1} \end{array}\right\}\right\} \ldots\right]$$

$$\left[\underline{\text{DATA}} \left\{\begin{array}{l} \underline{\text{RECORD}}\text{ IS} \\ \underline{\text{RECORDS}}\text{ ARE} \end{array}\right\} \{\text{data-name-3}\} \ldots\right]$$

$$\left[\underline{\text{LINAGE}}\text{ IS} \left\{\begin{array}{l} \text{data-name-4} \\ \text{integer-8} \end{array}\right\} \text{LINES} \left[\text{WITH }\underline{\text{FOOTING}}\text{ AT} \left\{\begin{array}{l} \text{data-name-5} \\ \text{integer-11} \end{array}\right\}\right]\right.$$

$$\left.\left[\text{LINES AT }\underline{\text{TOP}} \left\{\begin{array}{l} \text{data-name-6} \\ \text{integer-10} \end{array}\right\}\right] \left[\text{LINES AT }\underline{\text{BOTTOM}} \left\{\begin{array}{l} \text{data-name-7} \\ \text{integer-11} \end{array}\right\}\right]\right]$$

    [<u>CODE-SET</u> IS alphabet-name-1].

Relative File

```
FD file-name-1
    [IS EXTERNAL] [IS GLOBAL]

    ┌                                    ┌ RECORDS    ┐ ┐
    │ BLOCK CONTAINS [integer-1 TO] integer-2 │          │ │
    └                                    └ CHARACTERS ┘ ┘

    ┌          ┌ CONTAINS integer-3 CHARACTERS                                      ┐ ┐
    │          │ IS VARYING IN SIZE [[FROM integer-4] [TO integer-5] CHARACTERS]    │ │
    │ RECORD   │     [DEPENDING ON data-name-1]                                     │ │
    │          └ CONTAINS integer-6 TO integer-7 CHARACTERS                         ┘ │
    └                                                                                 ┘

    ┌       ┌ RECORD IS   ┐ ┌ STANDARD ┐ ┐
    │ LABEL │             │ │          │ │
    │       └ RECORDS ARE ┘ └ OMITTED  ┘ │
    └                                     ┘

    ┌                                     ┌ data-name-2 ┐ ┐     ┐
    │ VALUE OF  implementor-name-1 IS     │             │ │ ... │
    │                                     └ literal-1   ┘ ┘     │
    └                                                           ┘

    ┌      ┌ RECORD IS   ┐                ┐
    │ DATA │             │ {data-name-3} ... │ .
    │      └ RECORDS ARE ┘                │
    └                                     ┘
```

Indexed File

```
FD file-name-1
    [IS EXTERNAL] [IS GLOBAL]

    ┌                                    ┌ RECORDS    ┐ ┐
    │ BLOCK CONTAINS [integer-1 TO] integer-2 │          │ │
    └                                    └ CHARACTERS ┘ ┘

    ┌          ┌ CONTAINS integer-3 CHARACTERS                                      ┐ ┐
    │          │ IS VARYING IN SIZE [[FROM integer-4] [TO integer-5] CHARACTERS]    │ │
    │ RECORD   │     [DEPENDING ON data-name-1]                                     │ │
    │          └ CONTAINS integer-6 TO integer-7 CHARACTERS                         ┘ │
    └                                                                                 ┘

    ┌       ┌ RECORD IS   ┐ ┌ STANDARD ┐ ┐
    │ LABEL │             │ │          │ │
    │       └ RECORDS ARE ┘ └ OMITTED  ┘ │
    └                                     ┘

    ┌                                     ┌ data-name-2 ┐ ┐     ┐
    │ VALUE OF  implementor-name-1 IS     │             │ │ ... │
    │                                     └ literal-1   ┘ ┘     │
    └                                                           ┘

    ┌      ┌ RECORD IS   ┐                ┐
    │ DATA │             │ (data-name-3) ... │ .
    │      └ RECORDS ARE ┘                │
    └                                     ┘
```

COMPREHENSIVE STRUCTURED COBOL

Sort-Merge File

SD file-name-1

$$\left[\underline{RECORD} \left\{ \begin{array}{l} CONTAINS\ integer\text{-}1\ CHARACTERS \\ IS\ \underline{VARYING}\ IN\ SIZE\ [[FROM\ integer\text{-}2]\ [\underline{TO}\ integer\text{-}3]\ CHARACTERS] \\ \quad [\underline{DEPENDING}\ ON\ data\text{-}name\text{-}1] \\ CONTAINS\ integer\text{-}4\ \underline{TO}\ integer\text{-}5\ CHARACTERS \end{array} \right\} \right]$$

$$\left[\underline{DATA} \left\{ \begin{array}{l} \underline{RECORD}\ IS \\ \underline{RECORDS}\ ARE \end{array} \right\} \{data\text{-}name\text{-}2\} \ldots \right]$$

Report File

FD file-name-1

   [IS \underline{EXTERNAL}] [IS \underline{GLOBAL}]

$$\left[\underline{BLOCK}\ CONTAINS\ [integer\text{-}1\ \underline{TO}]\ integer\text{-}2 \left\{ \begin{array}{l} \underline{RECORDS} \\ CHARACTERS \end{array} \right\} \right]$$

$$\left[\underline{RECORD} \left\{ \begin{array}{l} CONTAINS\ integer\text{-}3\ CHARACTERS \\ IS\ \underline{VARYING}\ IN\ SIZE\ [[FROM\ integer\text{-}4]\ [\underline{TO}\ integer\text{-}5]\ CHARACTERS] \\ \quad [\underline{DEPENDING}\ ON\ data\text{-}name\text{-}1] \\ CONTAINS\ integer\text{-}6\ \underline{TO}\ integer\text{-}7\ CHARACTERS \end{array} \right\} \right]$$

$$\left[\underline{LABEL} \left\{ \begin{array}{l} \underline{RECORD}\ IS \\ \underline{RECORDS}\ ARE \end{array} \right\} \left\{ \begin{array}{l} \underline{STANDARD} \\ \underline{OMITTED} \end{array} \right\} \right]$$

$$\left[\underline{VALUE\ OF} \left\{ implementor\text{-}name\text{-}1\ IS \left\{ \begin{array}{l} data\text{-}name\text{-}2 \\ literal\text{-}1 \end{array} \right\} \right\} \ldots \right]$$

   [\underline{CODE-SET}\ IS\ alphabet-name-1]

$$\left\{ \begin{array}{l} \underline{REPORT}\ IS \\ \underline{REPORTS}\ ARE \end{array} \right\} \{report\text{-}name\text{-}1\} \ldots$$

General Format for Data Description Entry

Format 1

$$level\text{-}number \left[\begin{array}{l} data\text{-}name\text{-}1 \\ FILLER \end{array} \right]$$

   [\underline{REDEFINES}\ data-name-2]

   [IS \underline{EXTERNAL}] [IS GLOBAL]

$$\left[\left\{ \begin{array}{l} \underline{PICTURE} \\ \underline{PIC} \end{array} \right\} IS\ character\text{-}string \right]$$

$$\left[\text{[USAGE IS]}\left\{\begin{array}{l}\underline{\text{BINARY}}\\ \underline{\text{COMPUTATIONAL}}\\ \underline{\text{COMP}}\\ \underline{\text{DISPLAY}}\\ \underline{\text{INDEX}}\\ \underline{\text{PACKED-DECIMAL}}\end{array}\right\}\right]$$

$$\left[\text{[SIGN IS]}\left\{\begin{array}{l}\underline{\text{LEADING}}\\ \underline{\text{TRAILING}}\end{array}\right\}\text{[\underline{SEPARATE} CHARACTER]}\right]$$

$$\left[\begin{array}{l}\text{OCCURS integer-2 TIMES }\left[\left\{\begin{array}{l}\underline{\text{ASCENDING}}\\ \underline{\text{DESCENDING}}\end{array}\right\}\text{KEY IS \{data-name-3\}} \ldots\right] \ldots \\ \qquad \text{[\underline{INDEXED} BY \{index-name-1\} \ldots]}\\ \text{OCCURS integer-1 \underline{TO} integer-2 TIMES \underline{DEPENDING} ON data-name-4}\\ \qquad \left[\left\{\begin{array}{l}\underline{\text{ASCENDING}}\\ \underline{\text{DESCENDING}}\end{array}\right\}\text{KEY IS \{data-name-3\}} \ldots\right] \ldots \text{[\underline{INDEXED} BY \{index-name-1\} \ldots]}\end{array}\right]$$

$$\left[\left\{\begin{array}{l}\underline{\text{SYNCHRONIZED}}\\ \underline{\text{SYNC}}\end{array}\right\}\left[\begin{array}{l}\underline{\text{LEFT}}\\ \underline{\text{RIGHT}}\end{array}\right]\right]$$

$$\left[\left\{\begin{array}{l}\underline{\text{JUSTIFIED}}\\ \underline{\text{JUST}}\end{array}\right\}\text{RIGHT}\right]$$

[\underline{BLANK} WHEN \underline{ZERO}]

[\underline{VALUE} IS literal-1].

Format 2

66   data-name-1 \underline{RENAMES} data-name-2 $\left[\left\{\begin{array}{l}\underline{\text{THROUGH}}\\ \underline{\text{THRU}}\end{array}\right\}\text{data-name-3}\right]$.

Format 3

88   condition-name-1 $\left\{\begin{array}{l}\underline{\text{VALUE}} \text{ IS}\\ \underline{\text{VALUES}} \text{ ARE}\end{array}\right\}\left\{\text{literal-1}\left[\left\{\begin{array}{l}\underline{\text{THROUGH}}\\ \underline{\text{THRU}}\end{array}\right\}\text{literal-2}\right]\right\} \ldots.$

General Format for Communication Description Entry

Format 1

CD cd-name-1 FOR [INITIAL] INPUT

[[SYMBOLIC QUEUE IS data-name-1]
    [SYMBOLIC SUB-QUEUE-1 IS data-name-2]
    [SYMBOLIC SUB-QUEUE-2 IS data-name-3]
    [SYMBOLIC SUB-QUEUE-3 IS data-name-4]
    [MESSAGE DATE IS data-name-5]
    [MESSAGE TIME IS data-name-6]
    [SYMBOLIC SOURCE IS data-name-7]
    [TEXT LENGTH IS data-name-8]
    [END KEY IS data-name-9]
    [STATUS KEY IS data-name-10]
    [MESSAGE COUNT IS data-name-11]]
[data-name-1, data-name-2, data-name-3, data-name-4, data-name-5, data-name-6, data-name-7, data-name-8, data-name-9, data-name-10, data-name-11]

Format 2

CD cd-name-1 FOR OUTPUT
    [DESTINATION COUNT IS data-name-1]
    [TEXT LENGTH IS data-name-2]
    [STATUS KEY IS data-name-3]
    [DESTINATION TABLE OCCURS integer-1 TIMES [INDEXED BY index-name-1 . . .]]
    [ERROR KEY IS data-name-4]
    [SYMBOLIC DESTINATION IS data-name-5].

Format 3

CD cd-name-1 FOR [INITIAL] I-O

[[MESSAGE DATE IS data-name-1]
    [MESSAGE TIME IS data-name-2]
    [SYMBOLIC TERMINAL IS data-name-3]
    [TEXT LENGTH IS data-name-4]
    [END KEY IS data-name-5]
    [STATUS KEY IS data-name-6]]
[data-name-1, data-name-2, data-name-3, data-name-4, data-name-5, data-name-6]

General Format for Report Description Entry

RD report-name-1
    [IS GLOBAL] [CODE literal-1]

$$\left[\left\{\begin{array}{l}\underline{\text{CONTROL}}\text{ IS}\\\underline{\text{CONTROLS}}\text{ ARE}\end{array}\right\}\left\{\begin{array}{l}\{\text{data-name-1}\}\dots\\\underline{\text{FINAL}}\text{ [data-name-1]}\dots\end{array}\right\}\right]$$

$$\left[\underline{\text{PAGE}}\left[\begin{array}{l}\text{LIMIT IS}\\\text{LIMITS ARE}\end{array}\right]\text{integer-1}\left[\begin{array}{l}\text{LINE}\\\text{LINES}\end{array}\right][\underline{\text{HEADING}}\text{ integer-2}]\ [\underline{\text{FIRST}}\ \underline{\text{DETAIL}}\text{ integer-3}]\right.$$

$$\left.[\underline{\text{LAST}}\ \underline{\text{DETAIL}}\text{ integer-4}]\ [\underline{\text{FOOTING}}\text{ integer-5}]\right] .$$

General Format for Report Group Description Entry

Format 1

01 [data-name-1]

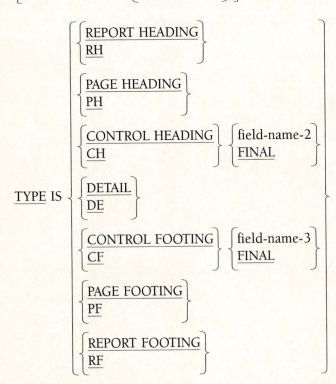

$$\left[\underline{\text{LINE}}\text{ NUMBER IS}\left\{\begin{array}{l}\text{integer-1 [ON }\underline{\text{NEXT PAGE}}\text{]}\\\underline{\text{PLUS}}\text{ integer-2}\end{array}\right\}\right]$$

$$\left[\underline{\text{NEXT GROUP}}\text{ IS}\left\{\begin{array}{l}\text{integer-3}\\\underline{\text{PLUS}}\text{ integer-4}\\\underline{\text{NEXT PAGE}}\end{array}\right\}\right]$$

$$\underline{\text{TYPE}}\text{ IS}\left\{\begin{array}{ll}\left\{\begin{array}{l}\underline{\text{REPORT HEADING}}\\\underline{\text{RH}}\end{array}\right\}&\\\left\{\begin{array}{l}\underline{\text{PAGE HEADING}}\\\underline{\text{PH}}\end{array}\right\}&\\\left\{\begin{array}{l}\underline{\text{CONTROL HEADING}}\\\underline{\text{CH}}\end{array}\right\}\left\{\begin{array}{l}\text{field-name-2}\\\underline{\text{FINAL}}\end{array}\right\}&\\\left\{\begin{array}{l}\underline{\text{DETAIL}}\\\underline{\text{DE}}\end{array}\right\}&\\\left\{\begin{array}{l}\underline{\text{CONTROL FOOTING}}\\\underline{\text{CF}}\end{array}\right\}\left\{\begin{array}{l}\text{field-name-3}\\\underline{\text{FINAL}}\end{array}\right\}&\\\left\{\begin{array}{l}\underline{\text{PAGE FOOTING}}\\\underline{\text{PF}}\end{array}\right\}&\\\left\{\begin{array}{l}\underline{\text{REPORT FOOTING}}\\\underline{\text{RF}}\end{array}\right\}&\end{array}\right\}$$

[[<u>USAGE</u> IS] <u>DISPLAY</u>].

Format 2

level-number [data-name-1]

$$\left[\text{\underline{LINE}\ NUMBER\ IS}\ \begin{Bmatrix} \text{integer-1 [ON \underline{NEXT PAGE}]} \\ \text{\underline{PLUS}\ integer-2} \end{Bmatrix}\right]$$

[\underline{USAGE} IS] \underline{DISPLAY}].

Format 3

level-number [data-name-1]

$$\begin{Bmatrix} \text{\underline{PICTURE}} \\ \text{\underline{PIC}} \end{Bmatrix}\text{IS character-string}$$

[[\underline{USAGE} IS] \underline{DISPLAY}]

$$\left[\text{[\underline{SIGN} IS]}\ \begin{Bmatrix} \text{\underline{LEADING}} \\ \text{\underline{TRAILING}} \end{Bmatrix}\text{\underline{SEPARATE} CHARACTER}\right]$$

$$\left[\begin{Bmatrix} \text{\underline{JUSTIFIED}} \\ \text{\underline{JUST}} \end{Bmatrix}\text{RIGHT}\right]$$

[\underline{BLANK} WHEN \underline{ZERO}]

$$\left[\text{\underline{LINE}\ NUMBER\ IS}\ \begin{Bmatrix} \text{integer-1 [ON \underline{NEXT PAGE}]} \\ \text{\underline{PLUS}\ integer-2} \end{Bmatrix}\right]$$

[\underline{COLUMN} NUMBER IS integer-3]

$$\begin{Bmatrix} \text{\underline{SOURCE} IS identifier-1} \\ \text{\underline{VALUE} IS literal-1} \\ \text{\{\underline{SUM}\{identifier-2\} \dots [\underline{UPON}\{data-name-2\} \dots]\} \dots \left[\underline{RESET}\ \text{ON}\ \begin{Bmatrix} \text{data-name-3} \\ \text{\underline{FINAL}} \end{Bmatrix}\right]} \end{Bmatrix}$$

[\underline{GROUP} INDICATE].

General Format for PROCEDURE DIVISION

Format 1

[PROCEDURE DIVISION [USING {data-name-1} ...].

[DECLARATIVES.

{section-name SECTION [segment-number].
    USE statement.
[paragraph-name.
    [sentence] ...] ... } ...
END DECLARATIVES.]
{section-name SECTION [segment-number].
[paragraph-name.
    [sentence] ...] ... } ...]

Format 2

[PROCEDURE DIVISION [USING {data-name-1} ...].
{paragraph-name.
    [sentence] ... } ...]

General Format for COBOL Verbs

ACCEPT identifier-1 [FROM mnemonic-name-1]

$$\text{ACCEPT identifier-2 } \underline{\text{FROM}} \begin{Bmatrix} \text{DATE} \\ \text{DAY} \\ \text{DAY-OF-WEEK} \\ \text{TIME} \end{Bmatrix}$$

ACCEPT cd-name-1 MESSAGE COUNT

$$\underline{\text{ADD}} \begin{Bmatrix} \text{identifier-1} \\ \text{literal-1} \end{Bmatrix} \dots \underline{\text{TO}} \{\text{identifier-2 } [\underline{\text{ROUNDED}}]\} \dots$$

    [ON SIZE ERROR imperative-statement-1]

    [NOT ON SIZE ERROR imperative-statement-2] [END-ADD]

$$\underline{\text{ADD}} \begin{Bmatrix} \text{identifier-1} \\ \text{literal-1} \end{Bmatrix} \dots \text{TO} \begin{Bmatrix} \text{identifier-2} \\ \text{literal-2} \end{Bmatrix}$$

    GIVING {identifier-3 [ROUNDED]} ...

    [ON SIZE ERROR imperative-statement-1]

    [NOT ON SIZE ERROR imperative-statement-2] [END-ADD]

ADD $\left\{\begin{array}{l}\underline{\text{CORRESPONDING}}\\ \underline{\text{CORR}}\end{array}\right\}$ identifier-1 $\underline{\text{TO}}$ identifier-2 [$\underline{\text{ROUNDED}}$]

    [ON $\underline{\text{SIZE ERROR}}$ imperative-statement-1]

    [$\underline{\text{NOT}}$ ON $\underline{\text{SIZE ERROR}}$ imperative-statement-2] [$\underline{\text{END-ADD}}$]

$\underline{\text{ALTER}}$ {procedure-name-1 $\underline{\text{TO}}$ [$\underline{\text{PROCEED TO}}$] prodecure-name-2} . . .

$\underline{\text{CALL}}$ $\left\{\begin{array}{l}\text{identifier-1}\\ \text{literal-1}\end{array}\right\}$ $\left[\underline{\text{USING}}\left\{\begin{array}{l}\text{[BY }\underline{\text{REFERENCE}}\text{] \{identifier-2\} . . .}\\ \text{BY }\underline{\text{CONTENT}}\quad\text{\{identifier-2\} . . .}\end{array}\right\}. . .\right]$

    [ON $\underline{\text{OVERFLOW}}$ imperative-statement-1 [$\underline{\text{END-CALL}}$]]

$\underline{\text{CALL}}$ $\left\{\begin{array}{l}\text{identifier-1}\\ \text{literal-1}\end{array}\right\}$ $\left[\underline{\text{USING}}\left\{\begin{array}{l}\text{[BY }\underline{\text{REFERENCE}}\text{] \{identifier-2\} . . .}\\ \text{BY }\underline{\text{CONTENT}}\quad\text{\{identifier-2\} . . .}\end{array}\right\}. . .\right]$

    [ON $\underline{\text{EXCEPTION}}$ imperative-statement-1]
    [[$\underline{\text{NOT}}$ ON $\underline{\text{EXCEPTION}}$ imperative-statement-2] [$\underline{\text{END-CALL}}$]

$\underline{\text{CANCEL}}$ $\left\{\begin{array}{l}\text{identifier-1}\\ \text{literal-1}\end{array}\right\}$ . . .

SW $\underline{\text{CLOSE}}$ $\left\{\text{file-name-1}\left[\begin{array}{l}\left\{\begin{array}{l}\underline{\text{REEL}}\\ \underline{\text{UNIT}}\end{array}\right\}\text{[FOR }\underline{\text{REMOVAL}}\text{]}\\ \text{WITH}\left\{\begin{array}{l}\underline{\text{NO REWIND}}\\ \underline{\text{LOCK}}\end{array}\right\}\end{array}\right]\right\}$ . . .

RI $\underline{\text{CLOSE}}$ {file-name-1 [WITH $\underline{\text{LOCK}}$]} . . .

    $\underline{\text{COMPUTE}}$ {identifier-1 [$\underline{\text{ROUNDED}}$]} . . . $\Leftarrow$ arithmetic-expression-1

        [ON $\underline{\text{SIZE ERROR}}$ imperative-statement-1]

        [$\underline{\text{NOT}}$ ON $\underline{\text{SIZE ERROR}}$ imperative-statement-2] [$\underline{\text{END-COMPUTE}}$]

$\underline{\text{CONTINUE}}$

$\underline{\text{DELETE}}$ file-name-1 RECORD

    [$\underline{\text{INVALID}}$ KEY imperative-statement-1]

    [$\underline{\text{NOT INVALID}}$ KEY imperative-statement-2] [$\underline{\text{END-DELETE}}$]

$\underline{\text{DISABLE}}$ $\left\{\begin{array}{l}\underline{\text{INPUT}}\text{ [}\underline{\text{TERMINAL}}\text{]}\\ \underline{\text{I-O TERMINAL}}\\ \underline{\text{OUTPUT}}\end{array}\right\}$ cd-name-1

$\underline{\text{DISPLAY}}$ $\left\{\begin{array}{l}\text{identifier-1}\\ \text{literal-1}\end{array}\right\}$ . . . [$\underline{\text{UPON}}$ mnemonic-name-1] [WITH $\underline{\text{NO ADVANCING}}$]

DIVIDE $\begin{Bmatrix} \text{identifier-1} \\ \text{literal-1} \end{Bmatrix}$ <u>INTO</u> {identifier-2 [<u>ROUNDED</u>]} . . .

    [ON <u>SIZE ERROR</u> imperative-statement-1]

    [<u>NOT</u> ON <u>SIZE ERROR</u> imperative-statement-2] [<u>END-DIVIDE</u>]

DIVIDE $\begin{Bmatrix} \text{identifier-1} \\ \text{literal-1} \end{Bmatrix}$ <u>INTO</u> $\begin{Bmatrix} \text{identifier-2} \\ \text{literal-2} \end{Bmatrix}$

    <u>GIVING</u> {identifier-3 [<u>ROUNDED</u>]} . . .

    [ON <u>SIZE ERROR</u> imperative-statement-1]

    [<u>NOT</u> ON <u>SIZE ERROR</u> imperative-statement-2] [<u>END-DIVIDE</u>]

DIVIDE $\begin{Bmatrix} \text{identifier-1} \\ \text{literal-1} \end{Bmatrix}$ <u>BY</u> $\begin{Bmatrix} \text{identifier-2} \\ \text{literal-2} \end{Bmatrix}$

    <u>GIVING</u> {identifier-3 [<u>ROUNDED</u>]} . . .

    [ON <u>SIZE ERROR</u> imperative-statement-1]

    [<u>NOT</u> ON <u>SIZE ERROR</u> imperative-statement-2] [<u>END-DIVIDE</u>]

DIVIDE $\begin{Bmatrix} \text{identifier-1} \\ \text{literal-1} \end{Bmatrix}$ <u>INTO</u> $\begin{Bmatrix} \text{identifier-2} \\ \text{literal-2} \end{Bmatrix}$ <u>GIVING</u> identifier-3 [<u>ROUNDED</u>]

    <u>REMAINDER</u> identifier-4

    [ON <u>SIZE ERROR</u> imperative-statement-1]

    [<u>NOT</u> ON <u>SIZE ERROR</u> imperative-statement-2] [<u>END-DIVIDE</u>]

DIVIDE $\begin{Bmatrix} \text{identifier-1} \\ \text{literal-1} \end{Bmatrix}$ <u>BY</u> $\begin{Bmatrix} \text{identifier-2} \\ \text{literal-2} \end{Bmatrix}$ <u>GIVING</u> identifier-3 [<u>ROUNDED</u>]

    <u>REMAINDER</u> identifier-4

    [ON <u>SIZE</u> <u>ERROR</u> imperative-statement-1]

    [<u>NOT</u> ON <u>SIZE ERROR</u> imperative-statement-2] [<u>END-DIVIDE</u>]

<u>ENABLE</u> $\begin{Bmatrix} \text{INPUT [\underline{TERMINAL}]} \\ \text{\underline{I-O} TERMINAL} \\ \text{\underline{OUTPUT}} \end{Bmatrix}$ cd-name-1

EVALUATE $\left\{\begin{array}{l}\text{identifier-1}\\\text{literal-1}\\\text{expression-1}\\\underline{\text{TRUE}}\\\underline{\text{FALSE}}\end{array}\right\}$ $\left[\underline{\text{ALSO}}\left\{\begin{array}{l}\text{identifier-2}\\\text{literal-2}\\\text{expression-2}\\\underline{\text{TRUE}}\\\underline{\text{FALSE}}\end{array}\right\}\right]$ . . .

$\Big\{\Big\{\underline{\text{WHEN}}$

$\left\{\begin{array}{l}\underline{\text{ANY}}\\\text{condition-1}\\\underline{\text{TRUE}}\\\underline{\text{FALSE}}\\\text{[\underline{NOT}]}\left\{\begin{array}{l}\text{identifier-3}\\\text{literal-3}\\\text{arithmetic-expression-1}\end{array}\right\}\left[\left\{\begin{array}{l}\underline{\text{THROUGH}}\\\underline{\text{THRU}}\end{array}\right\}\left\{\begin{array}{l}\text{identifier-4}\\\text{literal-4}\\\text{arithmetic-expression-2}\end{array}\right\}\right]\end{array}\right\}$

$\left[\underline{\text{ALSO}}\right.$

$\left.\left\{\begin{array}{l}\underline{\text{ANY}}\\\text{condition-2}\\\underline{\text{TRUE}}\\\underline{\text{FALSE}}\\\text{[\underline{NOT}]}\left\{\begin{array}{l}\text{identifier-5}\\\text{literal-5}\\\text{arithmetic-expression-3}\end{array}\right\}\left[\left\{\begin{array}{l}\underline{\text{THROUGH}}\\\underline{\text{THRU}}\end{array}\right\}\left\{\begin{array}{l}\text{identifier-6}\\\text{literal-6}\\\text{arithmetic-expression-4}\end{array}\right\}\right]\end{array}\right\}\right]$ . . . $\Big\}$ . . .

imperative-statement-1} . . .

[WHEN OTHER imperative-statement-2]

[END-EVALUATE]

<u>EXIT</u>

<u>EXIT-PROGRAM</u>

<u>GENERATE</u> $\left\{\begin{array}{l}\text{data-name-1}\\\text{report-name-1}\end{array}\right\}$

<u>GO</u> TO [procedure-name-1]

<u>GO</u> TO {procedure-name-1} . . . <u>DEPENDING</u> ON identifier-1

<u>IF</u> condition-1 <u>THEN</u> $\left\{\begin{array}{l}\text{\{statement-1\} . . .}\\\underline{\text{NEXT SENTENCE}}\end{array}\right\}$ $\left\{\begin{array}{l}\underline{\text{ELSE}}\text{ \{statement-2\} . . . [\underline{END-IF}]}\\\underline{\text{ELSE NEXT SENTENCE}}\\\underline{\text{END-IF}}\end{array}\right\}$

<u>INITIALIZE</u> {identifier-1} . . .

$\left[\underline{\text{REPLACING}}\left\{\begin{array}{l}\underline{\text{ALPHABETIC}}\\\underline{\text{ALPHANUMERIC}}\\\underline{\text{NUMERIC}}\\\underline{\text{ALPHANUMERIC-EDITED}}\\\underline{\text{NUMERIC-EDITED}}\end{array}\right\}\underline{\text{DATA}}\ \underline{\text{BY}}\left\{\begin{array}{l}\text{identifier-2}\\\text{literal-1}\end{array}\right\}\right]$ . . .

INITIATE {report-name-1} . . .

INSPECT identifier-1 TALLYING

$$\left[\left\{\text{identifier-2 } \underline{\text{FOR}} \left\{\begin{array}{l}\underline{\text{CHARACTERS}}\left[\left\{\begin{array}{l}\underline{\text{BEFORE}}\\\underline{\text{AFTER}}\end{array}\right\}\text{INITIAL}\left\{\begin{array}{l}\text{identifier-4}\\\text{literal-2}\end{array}\right\}\right]\ldots\\\left\{\begin{array}{l}\underline{\text{ALL}}\\\underline{\text{LEADING}}\end{array}\right\}\left\{\begin{array}{l}\text{identifier-3}\\\text{literal-1}\end{array}\right\}\left[\left\{\begin{array}{l}\underline{\text{BEFORE}}\\\underline{\text{AFTER}}\end{array}\right\}\text{INITIAL}\left\{\begin{array}{l}\text{identifier-4}\\\text{literal-2}\end{array}\right\}\right]\ldots\ldots\end{array}\right\}\right\}\ldots\right]\ldots$$

INSPECT identifier-1 REPLACING

$$\left[\begin{array}{l}\underline{\text{CHARACTERS}}\ \underline{\text{BY}}\left\{\begin{array}{l}\text{identifier-5}\\\text{literal-3}\end{array}\right\}\left[\left\{\begin{array}{l}\underline{\text{BEFORE}}\\\underline{\text{AFTER}}\end{array}\right\}\text{INITIAL}\left\{\begin{array}{l}\text{identifier-4}\\\text{literal-2}\end{array}\right\}\right]\ldots\\\left\{\begin{array}{l}\underline{\text{ALL}}\\\underline{\text{LEADING}}\\\underline{\text{FIRST}}\end{array}\right\}\left\{\left\{\begin{array}{l}\text{identifier-3}\\\text{literal-1}\end{array}\right\}\underline{\text{BY}}\left\{\begin{array}{l}\text{identifier-5}\\\text{literal-3}\end{array}\right\}\left[\left\{\begin{array}{l}\underline{\text{BEFORE}}\\\underline{\text{AFTER}}\end{array}\right\}\text{INITIAL}\left\{\begin{array}{l}\text{identifier-4}\\\text{literal-2}\end{array}\right\}\right]\ldots\right\}\ldots\end{array}\right]\ldots$$

INSPECT identifier-1 TALLYING

$$\left[\left\{\text{identifier-2 } \underline{\text{FOR}} \left\{\begin{array}{l}\underline{\text{CHARACTERS}}\left[\left\{\begin{array}{l}\underline{\text{BEFORE}}\\\underline{\text{AFTER}}\end{array}\right\}\text{INITIAL}\left\{\begin{array}{l}\text{identifier-4}\\\text{literal-2}\end{array}\right\}\right]\ldots\\\left\{\begin{array}{l}\underline{\text{ALL}}\\\underline{\text{LEADING}}\end{array}\right\}\left\{\begin{array}{l}\text{identifier-3}\\\text{literal-1}\end{array}\right\}\left[\left\{\begin{array}{l}\underline{\text{BEFORE}}\\\underline{\text{AFTER}}\end{array}\right\}\text{INITIAL}\left\{\begin{array}{l}\text{identifier-4}\\\text{literal-2}\end{array}\right\}\right]\ldots\ldots\end{array}\right\}\right\}\ldots\right]\ldots$$

REPLACING

$$\left[\begin{array}{l}\underline{\text{CHARACTERS}}\ \underline{\text{BY}}\left\{\begin{array}{l}\text{identifier-5}\\\text{literal-3}\end{array}\right\}\left[\left\{\begin{array}{l}\underline{\text{BEFORE}}\\\underline{\text{AFTER}}\end{array}\right\}\text{INITIAL}\left\{\begin{array}{l}\text{identifier-4}\\\text{literal-2}\end{array}\right\}\right]\ldots\\\left\{\begin{array}{l}\underline{\text{ALL}}\\\underline{\text{LEADING}}\\\underline{\text{FIRST}}\end{array}\right\}\left\{\left\{\begin{array}{l}\text{identifier-3}\\\text{literal-1}\end{array}\right\}\underline{\text{BY}}\left\{\begin{array}{l}\text{identifier-5}\\\text{literal-3}\end{array}\right\}\left[\left\{\begin{array}{l}\underline{\text{BEFORE}}\\\underline{\text{AFTER}}\end{array}\right\}\text{INITIAL}\left\{\begin{array}{l}\text{identifier-4}\\\text{literal-2}\end{array}\right\}\right]\ldots\right\}\ldots\end{array}\right]\ldots$$

INSPECT identifier-1 CONVERTING $\left\{\begin{array}{l}\text{identifier-6}\\\text{literal-4}\end{array}\right\}$ TO $\left\{\begin{array}{l}\text{identifier-7}\\\text{literal-5}\end{array}\right\}$

$$\left[\left\{\begin{array}{l}\underline{\text{BEFORE}}\\\underline{\text{AFTER}}\end{array}\right\}\text{INITIAL}\left\{\begin{array}{l}\text{identifier-4}\\\text{literal-2}\end{array}\right\}\right]\ldots$$

MERGE file-name-1 $\left\{\text{ON}\left\{\begin{array}{l}\underline{\text{ASCENDING}}\\\underline{\text{DESCENDING}}\end{array}\right\}\text{KEY \{data-name-1\}}\ldots\right\}\ldots$

[COLLATING SEQUENCE IS alphabet-name-1]

USING file-name-2 {file-name-3} . . .

$$\left\{\begin{array}{l}\underline{\text{OUTPUT PROCEDURE}}\text{ IS procedure-name-1}\left[\left\{\begin{array}{l}\underline{\text{THROUGH}}\\\underline{\text{THRU}}\end{array}\right\}\text{procedure-name-2}\right]\\\underline{\text{GIVING}}\text{ \{file-name-4\}}\ldots\end{array}\right\}$$

MOVE $\begin{Bmatrix} \text{identifier-1} \\ \text{literal-1} \end{Bmatrix}$ TO {identifier-2} ...

MOVE $\begin{Bmatrix} \underline{\text{CORRESPONDING}} \\ \underline{\text{CORR}} \end{Bmatrix}$ identifier-1 TO identifier-2

MULTIPLY $\begin{Bmatrix} \text{identifier-1} \\ \text{literal-1} \end{Bmatrix}$ BY {identifier-2 [ROUNDED]} ...

    [ON SIZE ERROR imperative-statement-1]

    [NOT ON SIZE ERROR imperative-statement-2] [END-MULTIPLY]

MULTIPLY $\begin{Bmatrix} \text{identifier-1} \\ \text{literal-1} \end{Bmatrix}$ BY $\begin{Bmatrix} \text{identifier-2} \\ \text{literal-1} \end{Bmatrix}$

    GIVING {identifier-3 [ROUNDED]} ...
    [ON SIZE ERROR imperative-statement-1]
    [NOT ON SIZE ERROR imperative-statement-2] [END-MULTIPLY]

S   OPEN $\begin{Bmatrix} \underline{\text{INPUT}} \text{ \{file-name-1\} [WITH } \underline{\text{NO REWIND}}]\} \ldots \\ \underline{\text{OUTPUT}} \text{ \{file-name-2 [WITH } \underline{\text{NO REWIND}}]\} \ldots \\ \underline{\text{I-O}} \text{ \{file-name-3\} } \ldots \\ \underline{\text{EXTEND}} \text{ \{file-name-4\} } \ldots \end{Bmatrix}$ ...

RI OPEN $\begin{Bmatrix} \underline{\text{INPUT}} \text{ \{file-name-1\} } \ldots \\ \underline{\text{OUTPUT}} \text{ \{file-name-2\} } \ldots \\ \underline{\text{I-O}} \text{ \{file-name-3\} } \ldots \\ \underline{\text{EXTEND}} \text{ \{file-name-4\} } \ldots \end{Bmatrix}$ ...

W OPEN $\begin{Bmatrix} \underline{\text{OUTPUT}} \text{ \{file-name-1 [WITH } \underline{\text{NO REWIND}}]\} \ldots \\ \underline{\text{EXTEND}} \text{ \{file-name-2\} } \ldots \end{Bmatrix}$ ...

PERFORM $\left[\text{procedure-name-1} \left[\begin{Bmatrix} \underline{\text{THROUGH}} \\ \underline{\text{THRU}} \end{Bmatrix} \text{procedure-name-2} \right] \right]$

    [imperative-statement-1 END-PERFORM

PERFORM $\left[\text{procedure-name-1} \left[\begin{Bmatrix} \underline{\text{THROUGH}} \\ \underline{\text{THRU}} \end{Bmatrix} \text{procedure-name-2} \right] \right]$

    $\begin{Bmatrix} \text{identifier-1} \\ \text{integer-1} \end{Bmatrix}$ TIMES [imperative-statement-1 END-PERFORM]

PERFORM $\left[\text{procedure-name-1} \left[\begin{Bmatrix} \underline{\text{THROUGH}} \\ \underline{\text{THRU}} \end{Bmatrix} \text{procedure-name-2} \right] \right]$

$$\left[\text{WITH } \underline{\text{TEST}} \left\{ \begin{array}{l} \underline{\text{BEFORE}} \\ \underline{\text{AFTER}} \end{array} \right\} \right] \underline{\text{UNTIL}} \text{ condition-1 [imperative-statement-1 } \underline{\text{END-PERFORM}}]$$

$$\underline{\text{PERFORM}} \left[\text{procedure-name-1} \left[\left\{ \begin{array}{l} \underline{\text{THROUGH}} \\ \underline{\text{THRU}} \end{array} \right\} \text{procedure-name-2} \right] \right]$$

$$\left[\text{WITH } \underline{\text{TEST}} \left\{ \begin{array}{l} \underline{\text{BEFORE}} \\ \underline{\text{AFTER}} \end{array} \right\} \right]$$

$$\underline{\text{VARYING}} \left\{ \begin{array}{l} \text{identifier-2} \\ \text{index-name-1} \end{array} \right\} \underline{\text{FROM}} \left\{ \begin{array}{l} \text{identifier-3} \\ \text{index-name-2} \\ \text{literal-1} \end{array} \right\} \underline{\text{BY}} \left\{ \begin{array}{l} \text{identifier-4} \\ \text{literal-2} \end{array} \right\} \underline{\text{UNTIL}} \text{ condition-1}$$

$$\left[\underline{\text{AFTER}} \left\{ \begin{array}{l} \text{identifier-5} \\ \text{index-name-3} \end{array} \right\} \underline{\text{FROM}} \left\{ \begin{array}{l} \text{identifier-6} \\ \text{index-name-4} \\ \text{literal-3} \end{array} \right\} \underline{\text{BY}} \left\{ \begin{array}{l} \text{identifier-7} \\ \text{literal-4} \end{array} \right\} \underline{\text{UNTIL}} \text{ condition-2} \right] \ldots$$

[imperative-statement-1 $\underline{\text{END-PERFORM}}$]

$\underline{\text{PURGE}}$ cd-name-1

SRI $\underline{\text{READ}}$ file-name-1 [$\underline{\text{NEXT}}$] RECORD [$\underline{\text{INTO}}$ identifier-1]
         [AT $\underline{\text{END}}$ imperative-statement-1]
         [$\underline{\text{NOT}}$ AT $\underline{\text{END}}$ imperative-statement-2] [$\underline{\text{END-READ}}$]

R $\underline{\text{READ}}$ file-name-1 RECORD [$\underline{\text{INTO}}$ identifier-1]
         [$\underline{\text{INVALID}}$ KEY imperative-statement-3]
         [$\underline{\text{NOT INVALID}}$ KEY imperative-statement-4] [$\underline{\text{END-READ}}$]

I $\underline{\text{READ}}$ file-name-1 RECORD [$\underline{\text{INTO}}$ identifier-1]
         [$\underline{\text{KEY}}$ IS data-name-1]
         [$\underline{\text{INVALID}}$ KEY imperative-statement-3]
         [$\underline{\text{NOT INVALID}}$ KEY imperative-statement-4] [$\underline{\text{END-READ}}$]

$\underline{\text{RECEIVE}}$ cd-name-1 $\left\{ \begin{array}{l} \underline{\text{MESSAGE}} \\ \underline{\text{SEGMENT}} \end{array} \right\}$ $\underline{\text{INTO}}$ identifier-1

[$\underline{\text{NO DATA}}$ imperative-statement-1]
[$\underline{\text{WITH DATA}}$ imperative-statement-2] [$\underline{\text{END-RECEIVE}}$]

$\underline{\text{RELEASE}}$ record-name-1 [$\underline{\text{FROM}}$ identifier-1]

$\underline{\text{RETURN}}$ file-name-1 RECORD [$\underline{\text{INTO}}$ identifier-1]
      AT $\underline{\text{END}}$ imperative-statement-1
      [$\underline{\text{NOT}}$ AT $\underline{\text{END}}$ imperative-statement-2] [$\underline{\text{END-RETURN}}$]

S $\underline{\text{REWRITE}}$ record-name-1 [$\underline{\text{FROM}}$ identifier-1]
RI $\underline{\text{REWRITE}}$ record-name-1 [$\underline{\text{FROM}}$ identifier-1]
         [$\underline{\text{INVALID}}$ KEY imperative-statement-1]
         [$\underline{\text{NOT INVALID}}$ KEY imperative-statement-2] [$\underline{\text{END-REWRITE}}$]

SEARCH identifier-1 $\left[\underline{\text{VARYING}} \left\{ \begin{array}{l} \text{identifier-2} \\ \text{index-name-1} \end{array} \right\} \right]$

    [AT <u>END</u> imperative-statement-1]

    $\left\{ \underline{\text{WHEN}} \text{ condition-1} \left\{ \begin{array}{l} \text{imperative-statement-2} \\ \underline{\text{NEXT SENTENCE}} \end{array} \right\} \right\}$ ... [END-SEARCH]

<u>SEARCH ALL</u> identifier-1 [AT <u>END</u> imperative-statement-1]

$\underline{\text{WHEN}} \left\{ \begin{array}{l} \text{data-name-1} \left\{ \begin{array}{l} \text{IS } \underline{\text{EQUAL}} \text{ TO} \\ \text{IS } = \end{array} \right\} \left\{ \begin{array}{l} \text{identifier-3} \\ \text{literal-1} \\ \text{arithmetic-expression-1} \end{array} \right\} \\ \text{condition-name-1} \end{array} \right\}$

$\left[\underline{\text{AND}} \left\{ \begin{array}{l} \text{data-name-2} \left\{ \begin{array}{l} \text{IS } \underline{\text{EQUAL}} \text{ TO} \\ \text{IS } = \end{array} \right\} \left\{ \begin{array}{l} \text{identifier-4} \\ \text{literal-2} \\ \text{arithmetic-expression-2} \end{array} \right\} \\ \text{condition-name-2} \end{array} \right\} \right]$ ...

$\left\{ \begin{array}{l} \text{imperative-statement-2} \\ \underline{\text{NEXT SENTENCE}} \end{array} \right\}$ [END-SEARCH]

<u>SEND</u> cd-name-1 <u>FROM</u> identifier-1

<u>SEND</u> cd-name-1 [<u>FROM</u> identifier-1] $\left\{ \begin{array}{l} \text{WITH identifier-2} \\ \text{WITH } \underline{\text{ESI}} \\ \text{WITH } \underline{\text{EMI}} \\ \text{WITH } \underline{\text{EGI}} \end{array} \right\}$

$\left[\left\{ \begin{array}{l} \underline{\text{BEFORE}} \\ \underline{\text{AFTER}} \end{array} \right\} \text{ADVANCING} \left\{ \begin{array}{l} \left\{ \begin{array}{l} \text{identifier-3} \\ \text{integer-1} \end{array} \right\} \left[\begin{array}{l} \text{LINE} \\ \text{LINES} \end{array} \right] \\ \left\{ \begin{array}{l} \text{mnemonic-name-1} \\ \underline{\text{PAGE}} \end{array} \right\} \end{array} \right\} \right]$

[<u>REPLACING</u> LINE]

<u>SET</u> $\left\{ \begin{array}{l} \text{index-name-1} \\ \text{identifier-1} \end{array} \right\}$ ... <u>TO</u> $\left\{ \begin{array}{l} \text{index-name-2} \\ \text{identifier-2} \\ \text{integer-1} \end{array} \right\}$

<u>SET</u> {index-name-3} ... $\left\{ \begin{array}{l} \underline{\text{UP BY}} \\ \underline{\text{DOWN BY}} \end{array} \right\}$ $\left\{ \begin{array}{l} \text{identifier-3} \\ \text{integer-2} \end{array} \right\}$

<u>SET</u> $\left\{ \text{\{mnemonic-name-1\}} ... \underline{\text{TO}} \left\{ \begin{array}{l} \underline{\text{ON}} \\ \underline{\text{OFF}} \end{array} \right\} \right\}$ ...

<u>SET</u> {condition-name-1} ... <u>TO TRUE</u>

<u>SORT</u> file-name-1 $\left\{ \text{ON} \left\{ \begin{array}{l} \underline{\text{ASCENDING}} \\ \underline{\text{DESCENDING}} \end{array} \right\} \text{KEY \{data-name-1\}} ... \right\}$ ... [WITH <u>DUPLICATES</u> IN ORDER]

[COLLATING SEQUENCE IS alphabet-name-1]

$$\left\{ \begin{array}{l} \text{INPUT PROCEDURE IS procedure-name-1} \left[\left\{ \begin{array}{l} \text{THROUGH} \\ \text{THRU} \end{array} \right\} \text{procedure-name-2} \right] \\ \text{USING \{file-name-2\} ...} \end{array} \right\}$$

$$\left\{ \begin{array}{l} \text{OUTPUT PROCEDURE IS procedure-name-3} \left[\left\{ \begin{array}{l} \text{THROUGH} \\ \text{THRU} \end{array} \right\} \text{procedure-name-4} \right] \\ \text{GIVING \{file-name-3\} ...} \end{array} \right\}$$

$$\text{START file-name-1} \left[\text{KEY} \left\{ \begin{array}{l} \text{IS EQUAL TO} \\ \text{IS =} \\ \text{IS GREATER THAN} \\ \text{IS >} \\ \text{IS NOT LESS THAN} \\ \text{IS NOT <} \\ \text{IS GREATER THAN OR EQUAL TO} \\ \text{IS >=} \end{array} \right\} \text{data-name-1} \right]$$

[INVALID KEY imperative-statement-1]

[NOT INVALID KEY imperative-statement-2] [END-START]

$$\text{STOP} \left\{ \begin{array}{l} \text{RUN} \\ \text{literal-1} \end{array} \right\}$$

$$\text{STRING} \left\{ \left\{ \begin{array}{l} \text{identifier-1} \\ \text{literal-1} \end{array} \right\} \text{... DELIMITED BY} \left\{ \begin{array}{l} \text{identifier-2} \\ \text{literal-2} \\ \text{SIZE} \end{array} \right\} \right\} \text{...}$$

INTO identifier-3

[WITH POINTER identifier-4]

[ON OVERFLOW imperative-statement-1]

[NOT ON OVERFLOW imperative-statement-2] [END-STRING]

$$\text{SUBTRACT} \left\{ \begin{array}{l} \text{identifier-1} \\ \text{literal-1} \end{array} \right\} \text{... FROM \{identifier-3 [ROUNDED]\} ...}$$

[ON SIZE ERROR imperative-statement-1]

[NOT ON SIZE ERROR imperative-statement-2] [END-SUBTRACT]

$$\text{SUBTRACT} \left\{ \begin{array}{l} \text{identifier-1} \\ \text{literal-1} \end{array} \right\} \text{... FROM} \left\{ \begin{array}{l} \text{identifier-2} \\ \text{literal-2} \end{array} \right\}$$

GIVING {identifier-3 [ROUNDED]} ...

[ON SIZE ERROR imperative-statement-1]

[NOT ON SIZE ERROR imperative-statement-2] [END-SUBTRACT]

SUBTRACT $\left\{ \begin{array}{l} \underline{\text{CORRESPONDING}} \\ \underline{\text{CORR}} \end{array} \right\}$ identifier-1 FROM identifier-2 [ROUNDED]

    [ON SIZE ERROR imperative-statement-1]
    [NOT ON SIZE ERROR imperative-statement-2] [END-SUBTRACT]

SUPPRESS PRINTING
TERMINATE {report-name-1} . . .
UNSTRING identifier-1

    $\left[\underline{\text{DELIMITED}} \text{ BY } [\underline{\text{ALL}}] \left\{ \begin{array}{l} \text{identifier-2} \\ \text{literal-1} \end{array} \right\} \left[\underline{\text{OR}} \; [\underline{\text{ALL}}] \left\{ \begin{array}{l} \text{identifier-3} \\ \text{literal-2} \end{array} \right\} \right] \; \cdots \right]$

    INTO {identifier-4 [DELIMITER IN identifier-5] [COUNT IN identifier-6]} . . .

    [WITH POINTER identifier-7]

    [TALLYING IN identifier-8]

    [ON OVERFLOW imperative-statement-1]

    [NOT ON OVERFLOW imperative-statement-2] [END-UNSTRING]

USE [GLOBAL] AFTER STANDARD $\left\{ \begin{array}{l} \underline{\text{EXCEPTION}} \\ \underline{\text{ERROR}} \end{array} \right\}$ PROCEDURE ON $\left\{ \begin{array}{l} \{\text{file-name-1}\} \; \cdots \\ \text{INPUT} \\ \text{OUTPUT} \\ \text{I-O} \\ \text{EXTEND} \end{array} \right\}$

USE GLOBAL BEFORE REPORTING identifier-1

USE FOR DEBUGGING ON $\left\{ \begin{array}{l} \text{cd-name-1} \\ [\underline{\text{ALL}} \text{ REFERENCES OF}] \text{ identifier-1} \\ \text{file-name-1} \\ \text{procedure-name-1} \\ \underline{\text{ALL PROCEDURES}} \end{array} \right\} \; \cdots$

S   WRITE record-name-1 [FROM identifier-1]

    $\left[\left\{ \begin{array}{l} \underline{\text{BEFORE}} \\ \underline{\text{AFTER}} \end{array} \right\} \text{ADVANCING} \left\{ \begin{array}{l} \left\{ \begin{array}{l} \text{identifier-2} \\ \text{integer-1} \end{array} \right\} \left\{ \begin{array}{l} \text{LINE} \\ \text{LINES} \end{array} \right\} \\ \left\{ \begin{array}{l} \text{mnemonic-name-1} \\ \underline{\text{PAGE}} \end{array} \right\} \end{array} \right\} \right]$

    $\left[\text{AT} \left\{ \begin{array}{l} \text{END-OF-PAGE} \\ \text{EOP} \end{array} \right\} \text{imperative-statement-1} \right]$

    $\left[\underline{\text{NOT}} \text{ AT} \left\{ \begin{array}{l} \text{END-OF-PAGE} \\ \text{EOP} \end{array} \right\} \text{imperative-statement-2} \right]$ [END-WRITE]

RI WRITE report-name-1 [FROM identifier-1]
    [INVALID KEY imperative-statement-1]
    [NOT INVALID KEY imperative-statement-2] [END-WRITE]

General Format for Copy and Replace Statements

COPY text-name-1 $\left[\left\{\begin{array}{c}\underline{OF}\\\underline{IN}\end{array}\right\}\text{ library-name-1}\right]$

$\left[\underline{REPLACING}\left\{\left\{\begin{array}{l}==\text{pseudo-text-1}==\\\text{identifier-1}\\\text{literal-1}\\\text{word-1}\end{array}\right\}\underline{BY}\left\{\begin{array}{l}==\text{pseudo-text-2}==\\\text{identifier-2}\\\text{literal-2}\\\text{word-2}\end{array}\right\}\right\}\ldots\right]$

$\underline{REPLACE}\ \{==\text{pseudo-text-1}==\ \underline{BY}\ ==\text{pseudo-text-2}==\}\ldots$
$\underline{REPLACE\ OFF}$

General Format for Conditions

Relational Condition

$\left\{\begin{array}{l}\text{identifier-1}\\\text{literal-1}\\\text{arithmetic-expression-1}\\\text{index-name-1}\end{array}\right\}\left\{\begin{array}{l}\text{IS [NOT] \underline{GREATER} \underline{THAN}}\\\text{IS [\underline{NOT}] >}\\\text{IS [NOT] \underline{LESS} THAN}\\\text{IS [\underline{NOT}] <}\\\text{IS [NOT] \underline{EQUAL} TO}\\\text{IS [\underline{NOT}] =}\\\text{IS \underline{GREATER} THAN \underline{OR EQUAL} TO}\\\text{IS >=}\\\text{IS \underline{LESS} THAN \underline{OR EQUAL} TO}\\\text{IS <=}\end{array}\right\}\left\{\begin{array}{l}\text{identifier-2}\\\text{literal-2}\\\text{arithmetic-expression-2}\\\text{index-name-2}\end{array}\right\}$

Class Condition

identifier-1 IS [NOT] $\left\{\begin{array}{l}\text{NUMERIC}\\\underline{ALPHABETIC}\\\underline{ALPHABETIC-LOWER}\\\underline{ALPHABETIC-UPPER}\\\text{class-name}\end{array}\right\}$

Condition-Name Condition

condition-name-1

Switch-Status Condition

condition-name-1

Sign Condition

arithmetic-expression-1 IS [NOT] $\left\{ \begin{array}{l} \underline{\text{POSITIVE}} \\ \underline{\text{NEGATIVE}} \\ \underline{\text{ZERO}} \end{array} \right\}$

Negated Condition

NOT condition-1

Combined Condition

condition-1 $\left\{ \left\{ \begin{array}{l} \underline{\text{AND}} \\ \underline{\text{OR}} \end{array} \right\} \text{condition-2} \right\}$ ...

Abbreviated Combined Relation Condition

relation-condition $\left\{ \left\{ \begin{array}{l} \underline{\text{AND}} \\ \underline{\text{OR}} \end{array} \right\} [\underline{\text{NOT}}] \text{[relational-operator] object} \right\}$ ...

Qualification

Format 1

$\left\{ \begin{array}{l} \text{data-name-1} \\ \text{condition-name} \end{array} \right\}$ $\left\{ \left\{ \begin{array}{l} \underline{\text{IN}} \\ \underline{\text{OF}} \end{array} \right\} \text{data-name-2} \right\} \ldots \left[\left\{ \begin{array}{l} \underline{\text{IN}} \\ \underline{\text{OF}} \end{array} \right\} \left\{ \begin{array}{l} \text{file-name} \\ \text{cd-name} \end{array} \right\} \right]$ $\left\{ \begin{array}{l} \underline{\text{IN}} \\ \underline{\text{OF}} \end{array} \right\} \left\{ \begin{array}{l} \text{file-name} \\ \text{cd-name} \end{array} \right\}$

Format 2

paragraph-name $\left\{ \begin{array}{l} \underline{\text{IN}} \\ \underline{\text{OF}} \end{array} \right\}$ section-name

Format 3

text-name $\left\{ \begin{array}{c} \underline{\text{IN}} \\ \underline{\text{OF}} \end{array} \right\}$ library-name

Format 4

<u>LINAGE-COUNTER</u> $\left\{ \begin{array}{c} \underline{\text{IN}} \\ \underline{\text{OF}} \end{array} \right\}$ report-name

Format 5

$\left\{ \begin{array}{l} \underline{\text{PAGE-COUNTER}} \\ \underline{\text{LINE-COUNTER}} \end{array} \right\}$ $\left\{ \begin{array}{c} \underline{\text{IN}} \\ \underline{\text{OF}} \end{array} \right\}$ report-name

Format 6

data-name-3 $\left\{ \begin{array}{l} \left\{ \begin{array}{c} \underline{\text{IN}} \\ \underline{\text{OF}} \end{array} \right\} \text{data-name-4} \left[\left\{ \begin{array}{c} \underline{\text{IN}} \\ \underline{\text{OF}} \end{array} \right\} \text{report-name} \right] \\ \left\{ \begin{array}{c} \underline{\text{IN}} \\ \underline{\text{OF}} \end{array} \right\} \text{report-name} \end{array} \right\}$

Miscellaneous Formats

Subscripting

$\left\{ \begin{array}{l} \text{condition-name-1} \\ \text{data-name-1} \end{array} \right\}$ ($\left\{ \begin{array}{l} \text{integer-1} \\ \text{data-name-2 } [\{\pm\} \text{ integer-2}] \\ \text{index-name-1 } [\{\pm \text{ integer-3}] \end{array} \right\}$ ...)

Reference Modification

data-name-1 (leftmost-character-position: [length])

Identifier

$$\text{data-name-1}\left[\left\{\begin{array}{c}\underline{\text{IN}}\\\underline{\text{OF}}\end{array}\right\}\text{data-name-2}\right]\ldots\left\{\left\{\begin{array}{c}\underline{\text{IN}}\\\underline{\text{OF}}\end{array}\right\}\left\{\begin{array}{l}\text{cd-name}\\\text{file-name}\\\text{report-name}\end{array}\right\}\right\}[(\{\text{subscript}\}\ldots)]$$

[(left-most-character-position: [length])]

General Format for Nested Source Programs

IDENTIFICATION DIVISION,
PROGRAM-ID, program-name-1 [IS INITIAL PROGRAM].
[ENVIRONMENT DIVISION, environment-division-content]
[DATA DIVISION, data-division-content]
[PROCEDURE DIVISION, procedure-division-content]
[nested-source-program] . . .
END PROGRAM program-name-1.]

General Format for Nested-Source-Program

IDENTIFICATION DIVISION,

$$\text{PROGRAM-ID, program-name-2}\left[\text{IS}\left\{\left\{\begin{array}{c}\underline{\text{COMMON}}\\\underline{\text{INITIAL}}\end{array}\right\}\right\}\text{PROGRAM}\right].$$

[ENVIRONMENT DIVISION, environment-division-content]
[DATA DIVISION, data-division-content]
[PROCEDURE DIVISION, procedure-division-content]
[nested-source-program] . . .
END PROGRAM program-name-2.

General Format for a Sequence of Source Programs

{IDENTIFICATION DIVISION,
PROGRAM-ID, program-name-3 [IS INITIAL PROGRAM].
[ENVIRONMENT DIVISION, environment-division-content]
[DATA DIVISION, data-division-content]
[PROCEDURE DIVISION, procedure-division-content]
[nested-source-program] . . .
END PROGRAM program-name-3.] . . .
IDENTIFICATION DIVISION,
PROGRAM-ID, program-name-4 [IS INITIAL PROGRAM].
[ENVIRONMENT DIVISION, environment-division-content]
[DATA DIVISION, data-division-content]
[PROCEDURE DIVISION, procedure-division-content]
[[nested-source-program] . . .
END PROGRAM program-name-4.]

APPENDIX 2 COBOL RESERVED WORDS

T HE FOLLOWING LIST is derived from both ANS COBOL 74 and ANS COBOL 85. New reserved words found in COBOL 85, but not in COBOL 74, are marked with a single asterisk (*). Reserved words found in COBOL 74, but not in COBOL 85, are marked with a double asterisk (**).

No list of reserve words will be complete. An individual compiler may use additional reserved words. The compiler will give you a message if you use a reserved word incorrectly.

ACCEPT	AREA	CLASS *
ACCESS	AREAS	CLOCK-UNITS **
ADD	ASCENDING	CLOSE
ADVANCING	ASSIGN	COBOL *
AFTER	AT	CODE
ALL	AUTHOR	CODE-SET
ALPHABET *		COLLATING
ALPHABETIC	BEFORE	COLUMN
ALPHABETIC-	BINARY *	COMMA
LOWER *	BLANK	COMMON
ALPHABETIC-	BLOCK	COMMUNICATION
UPPER *	BOTTOM	COMP
ALPHANUMERIC *	BY	COMPUTATIONAL
ALPHANUMERIC-		COMPUTE
EDITED *	CALL	CONFIGURATION
ALSO	CANCEL	CONTAINS
ALTER	CD	CONTENT *
ALTERNATE	CF	CONTINUE *
AND	CH	CONTROL
ANY	CHARACTER	CONTROLS
ARE	CHARACTERS	CONVERTING *

COPY	END-READ *	INITIAL
CORR	END-RECEIVE *	INITIALIZE *
CORRESPONDING	END-RETURN *	INITIATE
COUNT	END-REWRITE *	INPUT
CURRENCY	END-SEARCH *	INPUT-OUTPUT
	END-START *	INSPECT
DATA	END-STRING *	INSTALLATION
DATE	END-SUBTRACT *	INTO
DATE-COMPILED	END-UNSTRING *	INVALID
DATE-WRITTEN	END-WRITE *	IS
DAY	ENTER **	
DAY-OF-WEEK *	ENVIRONMENT	JUST
DE	EOP	JUSTIFIED
DEBUG-CONTENTS	EQUAL	
DEBUG-ITEM	ERROR	KEY
DEBUG-LINE	ESI	
DEBUG-NAME	EVALUATE *	LABEL
DEBUG-SUB-1	EVERY **	LAST
DEBUG-SUB-2	EXCEPTION	LEADING
DEBUG-SUB-3	EXIT	LEFT
DEBUGGING	EXTEND	LENGTH
DECIMAL-POINT	EXTERNAL *	LESS
DECLARATIVES		LIMIT
DELETE	FALSE *	LIMITS
DELIMITED	FD	LINAGE
DELIMITER	FILE	LINAGE-COUNTER
DEPENDING	FILE-CONTROL	LINE
DESCENDING	FILLER	LINE-COUNTER
DESTINATION	FINAL	LINES
DETAIL	FIRST	LINKAGE
DISABLE	FOOTING	LOCK
DISPLAY	FOR	LOW-VALUE
DIVIDE	FROM	LOW-VALUES
DIVISION		
DOWN	GENERATE	MEMORY **
DUPLICATES	GIVING	MERGE
DYNAMIC	GLOBAL *	MESSAGE
	GO	MODE
EGI	GREATER	MODULES **
ELSE	GROUP	MOVE
EMI		MULTIPLE
ENABLE	HEADING	MULTIPLY
END	HIGH-VALUE	
END-ADD *	HIGH-VALUES	NATIVE
END-CALL *		NEGATIVE
END-COMPUTE *	I-O	NEXT
END-DELETE *	I-O-CONTROL	NO
END-DIVIDE *	IDENTIFICATION	NOT
END-EVALUATE *	IF	NUMBER
END-IF *	IN	NUMERIC
END-MULTIPLY *	INDEX	NUMERIC-EDITED
END-OF-PAGE	INDEXED	
END-PERFORM *	INDICATE	OBJECT-COMPUTER

OCCURS
OF
OFF
OMITTED
ON
OPEN
OPTIONAL
OR
ORDER *
ORGANIZATION
OTHER *
OUTPUT
OVERFLOW

PACKED-
    DECIMAL *
PADDING *
PAGE
PAGE-COUNTER
PERFORM
PF
PH
PIC
PICTURE
PLUS
POINTER
POSITION
POSITIVE
PRINTING
PROCEDURE
PROCEDURES
PROCEED
PROGRAM
PROGRAM-ID
PURGE *

QUEUE
QUOTE
QUOTES

RANDOM
RD
READ
RECEIVE
RECORD
RECORDS
REDEFINES
REEL
REFERENCE
REFERENCES *
RELATIVE
RELEASE

REMAINDER
REMOVAL
RENAMES
REPLACE *
REPLACING
REPORT
REPORTING
REPORTS
RERUN **
RESERVE
RESET
RETURN
REWIND
REWRITE
RF
RH
RIGHT
ROUNDED
RUN

SAME
SD
SEARCH
SECTION
SECURITY
SEGMENT
SEGMENT-LIMIT
SELECT
SEND
SENTENCE
SEPARATE
SEQUENCE
SEQUENTIAL
SET
SIGN
SIZE
SORT
SORT-MERGE
SOURCE
SOURCE-
    COMPUTER
SPACE
SPACES
SPECIAL-NAMES
STANDARD
STANDARD-1
STANDARD-2 *
START
STATUS
STOP
STRING
SUB-QUEUE-1

SUB-QUEUE-2
SUB-QUEUE-3
SUBTRACT
SUM
SUPPRESS
SYMBOLIC
SYNC
SYNCHRONIZED

TABLE
TBLAYING
TAPE
TERMINAL
TERMINATE
TEST *
TEXT
THAN
THEN *
THROUGH
THRU
TIME
TIMES
TO
TOP
TRAILING
TRUE *
TYPE

UNIT
UNSTRING
UNTIL
UP
UPON
USAGE
USE
USING

VALUE
VALUES
VARYING

WHEN
WITH
WORDS **
WORKING-
    STORAGE
WRITE

ZERO
ZEROES
ZEROS

GLOSSARY

array   A named collection of elementary or group identifiers, each with the same format and name and distinguished by one or more subscripts; a one-dimensional array has a single subscript, a two-dimensional array requires two subscripts, and so on.

backup file   A safe copy of a frequently updated original file.

batch processing   The updating of computer files from transactions that are collected in batches over a period of time.

binary search   A search for a match in a collection of keys K(1), K(2), . . . , K(n), arranged in ascending or descending key order, where, if K(*Page 2i*) has been checked, followed by K(j), the next key checked will be K(j - (|i - j|)/2) if K(j) was too big, otherwise K(j + (|i - j|)/2).

bit   The smallest unit of data that can be stored, with a value of either 0 or 1.

block   A collection of records transmitted between a storage device and a buffer in memory.

blocking factor   The number of records in a block.

buffer record   The most recently read input record or most recently written output record in a buffer.

byte   A collection of eight bits, used for coding characters.

call-by-reference   A call to a subprogram in which the identifiers used in the CALL statement, although they may have different names, refer to the same memory locations as identifiers listed in the USING clause of the subprogram.

check digit   A digit used in identification numbers to ensure validity.

class condition   A condition used for testing the class of an identifier, such as numeric class.

classical update method Sequential updating of an old master file from a transaction file, so that a new updated master is generated without affecting the old master.

coherence An ideal property of a paragraph of a COBOL program in which the paragraph is restricted, as much as possible, to operations that constitute a single function.

collating sequence The order in which characters are represented in a computer, where, for example, A < B < ... Z and 0 < 1 < ... 9; the two common sequences are ASCII and EBCDIC, in which the orders for special characters and lowercase letters differ.

collision The phenomenon in which applying a hashing routine to two or more primary keys is the same result (relative disk address).

command translator A program, or precompiler, used to translate embedded CICS commands in a COBOL program into COBOL, so that the COBOL program can later be compiled.

compiler A program for converting a source program to a machine language object program.

condition A clause used in a conditional or PERFORM statement that can have the value true or false.

condition name An arbitrary name for a single value or group of values that an identifier can have.

condition table A table showing what should happen for each possible combination of condition values in a compound condition.

conditional statement An IF- or EVALUATE statement.

control field A field used in control break processing to partition a file into groups of records, so that a summary line can be computed for each value of the control field.

control listing Printed output from creating or updating a master file; used for checking purposes, it typically lists the fate of some or all of the master records or the transaction records, particularly where errors are detected.

control break processing Processing where the file is partitioned into groups of records, according to a control field value, so that a summary line can be computed for each partition.

cursor structure A collection of records retrieved from a relational data base, from which the next record can be released to working storage by execution of an embedded SQL FETCH command.

data validation Methods used for checking input records to minimize the risk of invalid data.

data base status identifier An identifier used for checking what has happened following execution of an embedded data base manipulation command, such as an embedded SQL expression.

deadlock The situation that occurs when a group of concurrent programs cannot proceed because each is waiting for resources, typically files, that are exclusively held by one or more of the other programs.

detail line A line of a printed report corresponding to an input record.

detail report A printed report consisting of detail lines.

direct access Access to a record in a disk file by going directly to the record's disk address, without having to access the prior records of the file in sequence.

direct file A file organization used with IBM operating systems in which there is direct access to a track of records and overflow records are managed automatically.

disk address The location of a record on disk as specified by cylinder, track, and either block or sector number.

edit symbol A symbol used to specify the value of a character space in an identifier where the contents are to be printed, for example, the $ symbol.

edited field A field that will be printed and that thus corresponds to an identifier specified with one or more edit symbols.

editor A program that is supplied as part of an operating system and that is used for inputting and editing source programs and data.

elementary identifier An identifier that does not include any other identifiers.

exception report A report that lists records that satisfy an exceptional condition.

field A part of a record that will be held in an elementary identifier when a copy of the record is in memory.

figurative constants Named constants, such as SPACES and ZEROS.

file navigation diagram A diagram used to show the sequence of accesses to records of a file during processing.

file A collection of records.

forcing a control break The generation of a summary line for the last record partition of a file during control break processing.

group identifier An identifier that contains a collection of identifiers.

group MOVE The assignment of values in a collection of identifiers to another identifier.

hash To convert a primary key to a relative disk address by means of a standard computation method.

hashing routine A routine for hashing primary keys.

header line A line in a printed report that explains the meaning of subsequent detail lines.

host data structure An identifier into which a record retrieved from a data base is placed, or from which a record inserted into a data base is taken.

identifier A named location in memory that may contain a value which may be changed by execution of a COBOL statement.

imperative statement A COBOL statement or sentence that is not, or does not contain, a conditional statement.

in-line PERFORM A PERFORM statement where the statements immediately following are executed, instead of a paragraph referenced in the PERFORM statement.

independence An ideal for a COBOL paragraph such that changes to the paragraph will not necessitate changes to another paragraph.

indexed-sequential file A file in which records are stored in ascending primary key order, so as to permit sequential processing; an accompanying index containing primary keys and disk addresses permits direct access to a record.

infinite loop A situation in which the condition that controls repetition of a group of instructions can never acquire the value needed to stop the iteration.

input area The part of an input buffer containing the input buffer record.

key of reference A secondary key value used in sequential access to the records with that value.

left justified Characters inserted into an identifier so that there are no blanks on the left.

linear search A search for a match in a collection of keys arranged in any order, where each record is checked in sequence.

literal The name for an alphanumeric or numeric constant in COBOL.

logical error An error in a program that causes an incorrect result to be computed from correct input data.

look-up table An array in which data about a target value is obtained from the array element that contains the target value, so that the array must be searched for a match.

machine language instruction An instruction in memory that can be executed.

main program A program that calls up a subprogram; also known as a calling program.

major control field A control field that partitions a file into major or large partitions, each of which will be further divided into minor partitions corresponding to the values of a minor control field.

map A specification of the fixed part of a screen display, stored for use by the teleprocessing monitor CICS.

matched-key file A relative file in which there is a relative address corresponding to each primary key value.

minor control field See **major control field**.

multiple-level index An index used with an indexed-sequential file, where each level permits direct access to an entry at the level below, and at the lowest level, to the actual records.

nested loop The repetition of a group of operations within a group of operations that are themselves repeated; a common example is seen in a clock, where the minute hand goes around the clock face 12 times for each time the hour hand goes around.

object program A program made up of machine language instructions that are the translation of a source program.

on-line processing A process in which a transaction record is entered, at any of a widely dispersed group of terminals and is used to update master files; records are not collected in a batch as in batch processing.

output area The part of an output buffer that contains an output buffer record.

paragraph A named collection of COBOL sentences within the PROCEDURE DIVISION.

printer spacing chart A grid used to lay out the output data as it will appear when printed.

pseudocode Instructions that correspond to computer language instructions (such as COBOL), but which are even more English-like.

record A collection of fields or items of data that describe some entity.

record layout The exact specification of the fields of a record.

record of reference The most recently retrieved record during sequential access to records with a given secondary key value (the key of reference).

relative file A file made up of numbered slots, each of which can hold a record; a slot number is a relative address.

repeating group A group of fields in a record that occurs more than once within the record.

rewrite method A method of change updating a disk file by changing fields within the old master to form the new master, destroying the old master in the process.

run error An error caused by an attempt to execute an instruction that is impossible for the data involved, such as an attempt to divide by zero; typically the program will end execution abnormally when a run error occurs.

scope terminator A word, such as END-IF or END-PERFORM, that is used to indicate the end of a lengthy COBOL statement.

search key An identifier within an array that holds a value being checked for a match.

secondary index An index that permits direct access to all the records with the same secondary key value.

secondary key A non-unique field value used for obtaining direct access to the records of a file.

section A collection of COBOL paragraphs.

sentence A COBOL statement, or sequence of statements, ending in a period.

sequential access Access to a file where the Nth record is accessed only by reading the prior N-1 records first.

sign condition A condition that is true or false according to whether the value of an identifier is positive or negative.

source program A program whose instructions cannot be executed and that is written in a language such as COBOL; a machine language translation of a correctly written source program can be executed, however.

start key A value used with the START command with an indexed-sequential file in order to begin processing at a specific record in the file.

statement A basic COBOL command that uses a COBOL verb such as MOVE or ADD. See also **imperative statement**.

subprogram A program that is subsidiary to a main program; it is written, compiled, and stored separately, and it will carry out some subsidiary processing task when called up by a CALL statement in the main program.

subscript The non-zero integer value used with an array element to distinguish it from other elements of the array.

summary line A line of a printed report containing a summary of data from a group of input records.

summary report A report that contains summary lines, but no detail lines.

syntax error An error in the syntax of a COBOL word, clause, or statement that causes it to be rejected by the compiler.

teleprocessing monitor A sophisticated program, comparable to an operating system, that controls on-line processing involving concurrently executing programs and many widely dispersed terminals. CICS is a common example.

transaction file A file containing records that will be used to update a master file.

working storage That part of memory encompassing the memory locations (identifiers) whose contained data is being worked on.

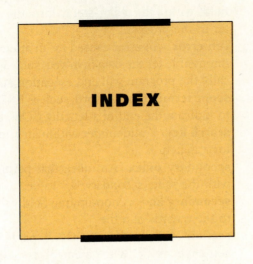

INDEX

ACCEPT, 142–143
Access method, 492, 538
ACCESS MODE DYNAMIC
    index, 542, 547–548
    relative, 613–615
ACCESS MODE RANDOM (index), 542, 545–547
ACCESS MODE SEQUENTIAL
    index, 542, 543–545
    relative, 612–613
Access speed, disks and tapes, 492
ADD, 61, 150–152
AFTER ADVANCING, 61, 133–134, 263–265
AFTER, PERFORM . . . VARYING, 467
ALPHABETIC
    identifiers 182
    -LOWER, 182
    -UPPER, 182
ALTER TABLE, 641
ALTERNATE KEY, 583–585
A-margin, 26–27
AND, 178
ANSI (American National Standards Institute), 11
Arithmetic operations, 83–84
Array
    defined, 400
    initialization, 415–417
    subscript, 402
    two-level, 461
ASCENDING KEY, 449–450
ASCII (American Standard Code for Information Interchange), 4, 180–181
ASSIGN TO, 28, 49–53
AT END, 131–132

Base table, 635, 638
Batch processing, 693
BEFORE ADVANCING, 133–134
Binary search, array, 438–439, 448
Bind system, SQL, 658
Bits, 4
Blank, edit symbol, 233

Block, 75–76
BLOCK CONTAINS, 75–76, 493
Block size, 493
Blocking, 493
Blocking factor, 76
B-margin, 26–27
Buffer record, 70–73, 495
Buffers
    input and output, 494
    double, 496
Bytes, 4

CALL, 720
CALL, SQL translation, 659
Call-by-reference, 724
CASE structure, 195–196
Central processing unit (CPU), 8
Chained progressive overflow management, 609
Check bit, 5
Check protection symbol, 251
Check-digit, 302
CICS
    concepts, 694
    commands
        CICS DELETE, 703–704
        CICS READ, 700
        CICS READ for UPDATE, 701–702
        CICS RECEIVE, 705–707
        CICS RETURN, 709
        CICS REWRITE, 702–703
        CICS SEND, 707–709
        CICS UNLOCK, 704
        CICS WRITE, 705
    CICS exception handling, 700–701
Class conditions, 182–184
Classical updating See Updating
CLOSE, 130–131
COBOL
    coding sheet, 21–23
    history, 10–11
    SQL programs, 657
CODASYL, 10–11

Collating sequences, 180–181
Collision, 609
Command translator, CICS, 712
Comment, 27
COMP, 727
COMP-3, 728
Compiler, 6
Compound conditions, 178–180
Compound interest, 221
COMPUTE
    uses, 38, 144–150
    evaluation, 148
    truncation errors, 149–150
Computer file, 4
Condition codes, 299–300
Condition names, 183–184
Condition table, 190–191
Condition, with PERFORM, 215–219
Conditional statement, 118
Conditions
    defined, 126, 177–184
    class, 182–184
    compound, 178–180
    sign, 182–183
    simple, 177
Continuation line, 88–89
Continuation of a literal, 27
Control break
    single-level, 355–372
    three-level, 388
    two-level, 372–387
Control field
    defined, 355
    major, 372
    minor, 372
Control listing, 498, 501, 554, 559, 612
Control listing, data base, 671
COPY, 725
CPU See Central processing unit
CREATE INDEX, 639
CREATE TABLE, 639
CREATE VIEW, 640
Cursor structure, 663, 680–687

Cursor technicalities, 682–683
Cylinder concept, 491

Data base, 633
Data base administrator, 636
Data base creation, 638
DATA DIVISION, 21
Data independence, 640
Data recording technology, 4–5
Data validation
    defined, 291
    data base, 671
DATABASE2, 660, 662
Dataset name, 53
Date extraction
    ANS, 256–260
    IBM, 260
DD statement, 53
De Morgan's Rules, 179
Deadlock, 713
Debugging techniques, 388–392
Decimal point marker, 55
DELETE, CICS See CICS
DELETE, SQL See SQL
DESCENDING KEY, 449–450
Desk check, 31–32
Detail report, 246, 248
Direct file, 610, 624
Direct-access file, 490
Disk address, 537
Disk file, 51
Disk storage mechanism, 490
Disks, 4–5, 8–9
DISPLAY (USAGE IS), 727
DISPLAY verb, 142–143, 390–392
DIVIDE, 61
DIVIDE . . . BY, . . . INTO, 154–155
Divisions, COBOL, 21
Double buffers, 496
Duplicates, with SORT, 339

EBCDIC, 6, 180–181
Edit item (symbol), 56–59, 92–96, 248–255
Edited identifiers, 92–96, 139–140, 156,
    248–255
Editor, 6, 8
END-COMPUTE, 144
END-IF, 170–172, 185–190
END-READ, 131–132
END-WRITE, 132–134
ENVIRONMENT DIVISION, 21, 48
Errors, 34
EVALUATE
    syntax, 195–199
    use, 195–201
Exception report, 246–248
EXEC SQL . . . END-EXEC, 665
EXHIBIT, 392
EXIT, 128
Exponentiation operator, 145

FD (File description), 73–75
FETCH, 663
Fibonacci sequence, 238, 241
Field, 12–13
Figurative constant, 89–90
File, 12–13
File navigation diagram, 30
FILE SECTION, 70
FILE STATUS, 554–555
FILLER, 90–92
Floating edit symbols, 254
Flowchart, 29–30

GENERATE, 751
Group identifier, 77, 80–83, 86
Group MOVE, 138–140, 255

HANDLE CONDITION, CICS, 701
Hash file, 608–611
Hashing routine, 608
Headers
    in output files, 59–60
    printing, 261–266
Hierarchical structure, 119–120
Hierarchy diagram, 120
HIGH VALUES, 505
Histogram, with array, 418–424
Home address, 609
Host data structure, 663

IBM disks, 493
IBM Job Control Language (JCL), 53
IDENTIFICATION DIVISION, 21, 47
Identifier
    defined, 28, 79
    edited, 92–96
    elementary, 77, 86
    group, 77, 80–83, 86
    name rules, 79–80
IF
    uses, 168–169
    nested, 171, 184–195
    pseudocode, 176
    semantics, 172
    syntax, 170
Imperative statement, 118
Implementor names, 51–54
Index
    defined, 536
    multiple-level, 539
Index identifier, 441, 444, 446, 447
Indexed file
    definition, 536
    file creation, 549–555
    information retrieval, 577–580
Infinite loop, 217–219
Information retrieval See Indexed file
Initialization, 89–90
INITIALIZE, 90
INITIATE, 750
In-line PERFORM, 233–234
Input area, buffer, 13–14, 78
In-line PERFORM . . . VARYING, 411–412
Input area record, 70–73

Input procedure (SORT), 326–333
Input/output routine, 492, 538
INSERT, SQL See SQL
INSPECT, 296, 299
Interblock gap, 493
Intermediate results, 102
INVALID KEY, 565
ISAM (Indexed-sequential access method),
    541
JCL (Job Control Language), 53, 76
Job Control Language See JCL, 76
JUSTIFIED RIGHT, 256

LABEL RECORDS, 73–75
Labels, 27, 74–75
Left justified, 84–85
Level numbers, 80
Linear search, array, 438, 440–444
LINKAGE SECTION, 721
Link-editing, COBOL SQL, 660
Literal, 87–90, 134–135

Logical errors, 34, 35
Look-up table, 433

Machine language, 6, 7
Map, CICS, 698, 713
Master file
    uses, 304, 497
    creation, 304–313, 497–499
    updating 500–528
Matched-key relative file, 605–608, 615–624
Memory, 8, 12
MERGE, 344–349
Merging
    with MERGE, 344–349
    with SORT, 339–344
Minus sign
    specifying, 94–96
    edit symbol, 252
Mobile buffer record, 495
Module coherence, independence, 370–371
MOVE, 37, 135–138
MOVE CORRESPONDING, 142–143, 260
MOVE, group, 138–140, 255
Multiple MOVE, 142
Multiple-level index See Index
MULTIPLY, 61, 153–154

Nested IF, 171, 184–195
Nested loop, 225–228
NEXT RECORD, 548
NEXT SENTENCE, 170–172, 188–189
NOMINAL KEY, 544, 606
NOT, 177–179
NOT INVALID KEY, 566
NUMERIC, 182

Object program, 8
OCCURS, 401
On-line partition, 695
On-line processing, 693
OPEN, 37, 129–130
OPEN I-O, 542
Optimizer, SQL translation, 660
OR, 178
Order, COMPUTE evaluation, 148
Output area, buffer, 13–14, 78
Output procedure (SORT), 333–338
Overprinting, 265

PACKED-DECIMAL, 728
PAGE, 265–266
paragraph (COBOL), 119
PERFORM, 122–124
PERFORM . . . TIMES, 219–221
PERFORM . . . TIMES (in-line), 233–234
PERFORM . . . UNTIL, 125–128, 211–219
PERFORM . . . UNTIL (in-line), 233–234
PERFORM . . . VARYING, 409–413
PICTURE symbols, 249
PICTUREs, 83–86
Plus sign
    specifying, 94–96
    edit symbol, 252
Precompilation
    of CICS, 712
    of SQL, 658
Primary key, 537, 554
Printer file, 51
Printer line length, 26, 78
Printer spacing chart, 21, 24–25
Printing headers, 261–266
PROCEDURE DIVISION, 21, 114
Processor, 9

COBOL Program Sheet

System		Sheet	of
Program		Date	
Programmer			

Sequence		Cont.	A	B	COBOL Statement
(Page) 1 3	(Serial) 4 6	7	8	12 16 20 24 28 32 36 40 44 48 52 56 60 64 68 72	

COBOL Program Sheet

System		Sheet	of
Program		Date	
Programmer			

Sequence		Cont.	A	B	COBOL Statement
(Page) 1 3	(Serial) 4 6	7	8	12 16 20 24 28 32 36 40 44 48 52 56 60 64 68 72	

Special offer on RM/COBOL–85!

See previous page for details.